IF FOUND, please notify and arrange return to owner. Th
the Certified Management Accountant Examination and/or th
Examination.

Name of CMA/CFM Candidate ____________________

Address ____________________

City, State, Zip ____________________

Telephone ( ) ____________ E-mail ____________

MW01714862

Additional Gleim *CMA/CFM Review* books, software, and other accounting study materials are available directly from

Gleim Publications, Inc.
P.O. Box 12848
University Station
Gainesville, Florida 32604

(352) 375-0772
(800) 87-GLEIM or (800) 874-5346
FAX: (352) 375-6940

E-mail: admin@gleim.com
Internet: www.gleim.com

CMA/CFM Review: Part 1, Economics, Finance, and Management	$24.95
CFM Review: Part 2CFM, Corporate Financial Management	24.95
CMA Review: Part 2CMA, Financial Accounting and Reporting	24.95
CMA/CFM Review: Part 3, Mgmt. Reporting, Analysis, and Behavioral Issues	24.95
CMA/CFM Review: Part 4, Decision Analysis and Information Systems	24.95

CMA/CFM Test Prep software ($39.95 per section) and *CMA/CFM Review* audiotapes ($64.95 per section) are also available to complement your study.

CIA Review: Part I, Internal Audit Process	$24.95
CIA Review: Part II, Internal Audit Skills	24.95
CIA Review: Part III, Management Control and Information Technology	24.95
CIA Review: Part IV, The Audit Environment	24.95

CIA Test Prep software ($39.95 per section) is also available to complement your study.

CPA Review: Financial	$29.95
CPA Review: Auditing	29.95
CPA Review: Business Law	29.95
CPA Review: TAX-MAN-GOV	29.95

CPA Test Prep software ($39.95 per section) and *CPA Review* audiotapes ($79.95 per section) are also available to complement your study.

Order forms for these and all of our other publications are provided at the back of this book.

All orders must be prepaid. Shipping and handling charges will be added to all orders. Library and company orders may be purchased on account. Add applicable sales tax to shipments within Florida. All payments must be in U.S. funds and payable on a U.S. bank. Please write or call for prices and availability of all foreign country shipments. Orders will usually be shipped the day after your request is received. Allow 10 days for delivery in the United States. Please contact us if you do not receive your shipment within 2 weeks.

Gleim Publications, Inc. guarantees the immediate refund of all resalable texts and unopened software and audiotapes purchased directly from Gleim Publications, Inc. if they are returned within 30 days. Shipping and handling charges are nonrefundable. Returns of books purchased from bookstores and other resellers should be made to the respective bookstore or reseller.

Groundwood Paper and Highlighters -- This book is printed on high quality groundwood paper. It is lightweight and easy-to-recycle. We recommend that you purchase a highlighter specifically designed to be non-bleed-through (e.g., Avery *Glidestick*™) at your local office supply store.

REVIEWERS AND CONTRIBUTORS

Karen Hom, B.A., University of Florida, is our book production coordinator. Ms. Hom coordinated the production staff and provided production assistance throughout the project.

Grady M. Irwin, J.D., University of Florida Levin College of Law, has taught in the University of Florida College of Business. Mr. Irwin provided many answer explanations and extensive editorial assistance throughout.

Travis Moore, M.B.A., University of Florida, provided technical and editorial assistance, reviewed the final manuscript, and prepared the page layout.

Jan Strickland is our production assistant. Ms. Strickland reviewed the final manuscript and prepared the page layout.

A PERSONAL THANKS

This manual would not have been possible without the extraordinary effort and dedication of Jim Collis and Terry Hall who typed the entire manuscript and all revisions as well as prepared the camera-ready pages.

The authors appreciate the proofreading and production assistance of Kim Blackburn, Jaime Gentile, Rob Gallardo, Melissa Guinand, Bonnie Johnston, Lynn Li, Jessica Medina, Shane Rapp, McKenzie Rogers, and Jenna Zirkel.

The authors also appreciate the editorial assistance of Jennifer Forrester, Nefertiti Griffin, Ryan Kroll, Walter Mansfield, and Jose Martinez.

Finally, we appreciate the encouragement and tolerance of our families throughout the project.

NONDISCLOSED EXAM

The CMA/CFM is a nondisclosed exam, and you will encounter questions which may be totally unfamiliar to you. That is the nature of nondisclosed exams. Please follow the study suggestions on pages 13 and 14. We have the best and most efficient CMA/CFM exam prep system for success.

TENTH EDITION

CMA REVIEW

for PART 2CMA
FINANCIAL ACCOUNTING & REPORTING

by Irvin N. Gleim, Ph.D., CPA, CIA, CMA, CFM
and
Dale L. Flesher, Ph.D., CPA, CIA, CMA, CFM

ABOUT THE AUTHORS

Irvin N. Gleim is Professor Emeritus in the Fisher School of Accounting at the University of Florida and is a member of the American Accounting Association, Academy of Legal Studies in Business, American Institute of Certified Public Accountants, Association of Government Accountants, Florida Institute of Certified Public Accountants, Institute of Internal Auditors, and the Institute of Management Accountants. He has had articles published in the *Journal of Accountancy, The Accounting Review,* and *The American Business Law Journal* and is author/coauthor of numerous accounting and aviation books and CPE courses.

Dale L. Flesher is the Arthur Andersen Alumni Professor in the School of Accountancy at the University of Mississippi and has written over 180 articles for business and professional journals, including *Management Accounting, Journal of Accountancy,* and *The Accounting Review,* as well as numerous books. He is a member of the Institute of Management Accountants, American Institute of Certified Public Accountants, Institute of Internal Auditors, American Accounting Association, and American Taxation Association. He is a past editor of *The Accounting Historians' Journal* and is a trustee and past president of the Academy of Accounting Historians.

Gleim Publications, Inc.
P.O. Box 12848
University Station
Gainesville, Florida 32604
(352) 375-0772
(800) 87-GLEIM or (800) 874-5346
FAX: (352) 375-6940
E-mail: admin@gleim.com
Internet: www.gleim.com

This is the first printing of the tenth edition of

CMA Review: Part 2CMA.

Please e-mail update@gleim.com with CMA Part 2CMA 10-1 included in the subject or text. You will receive our current update as a reply.

EXAMPLE:

To:	update@gleim.com
From:	your e-mail address
Subject:	CMA Part 2CMA 10-1

ISSN: 1093-2550

ISBN 1-58194-124-2

First Printing: February 2001

ACKNOWLEDGMENTS

The authors are indebted to the Institute of Certified Management Accountants for permission to use problem materials from past CMA examinations. Questions and unofficial answers from the Certified Management Accountant Examinations, copyright © 1976 through 1997 by the Institute of Certified Management Accountants, are reprinted and/or adapted with permission.

The authors are also indebted to The Institute of Internal Auditors, Inc. for permission to use Certified Internal Auditor Examination Questions and Suggested Solutions, copyright © 1980 through 1997 by The Institute of Internal Auditors, Inc.

The authors also appreciate and thank the American Institute of Certified Public Accountants, Inc. Material from Uniform Certified Public Accountant Examination questions and unofficial answers. Copyright © 1977-1999 by the American Institute of Certified Public Accountants, Inc. is reprinted and/or adapted with permission.

The authors would also like to thank the following professors for contributing questions to this book: J.O. Hall of Western Kentucky University, R. O'Keefe of Jacksonville University, A. Oddo of Niagara University, S. Rubin of Brooklyn College - CUNY, and C.J. Skender of North Carolina State University.

This publication was printed and bound by Corley Printing Company, St. Louis, MO, a registered ISO-9002 company. More information about Corley Printing Company is available at www.corleyprinting.com or by calling (314) 739-3777.

PREFACE FOR CMA CANDIDATES

The purpose of this book is to help YOU prepare YOURSELF to pass Part 2CMA of the CMA examination. The overriding consideration is an inexpensive, effective, and easy-to-use study program. This manual

1. Defines topics tested on Part 2CMA of the CMA exam.
2. Explains how to optimize your exam score by analyzing how the CMA exam is constructed, administered, and graded.
3. Outlines all of the subject matter tested on Part 2CMA in 10 easy-to-use study units.
4. Presents multiple-choice questions to prepare you to answer questions on Part 2CMA. The answer explanations are presented to the immediate right of the questions for your convenience. You MUST cover these answers until you commit to the correct answer. Use the bookmark provided at the back of this book.
5. Illustrates **individual question answering techniques** to minimize selecting incorrect answers and to maximize your exam score.
6. Suggests **exam-taking techniques** to help you maintain control and achieve success.

This is the Tenth Edition of *CMA Review* for Part 2CMA, which covers only Part 2CMA of the CMA exam. Recall that the only difference between the CFM exam and the CMA exam is Part 2. Part 2CFM is "Corporate Financial Management." Part 2CMA is "Financial Accounting and Reporting."

To maximize the efficiency of your review program, begin by **studying** (not reading) the introduction in this book. "Preparing for and Taking the CMA/CFM Exams" is very short but very important. It has been carefully organized and written to provide you with important information to assist you in successfully completing Part 2CMA of the CMA examination.

Thank you for your interest in our review materials. We very much appreciate the thousands of letters and suggestions received from CIA, CMA/CFM, and CPA candidates since 1974. Please give us feedback concerning this book. Do NOT disclose information about individual questions beyond subject matter not covered in our books. Tell us which part and which topics were NOT covered or were inadequately covered. The last page has been designed to help you note corrections and suggestions throughout your study process. Please tear it out and mail or fax it to us with your comments.

Good Luck on the Exam,

Irvin N. Gleim
Dale L. Flesher

February 2001

TABLE OF CONTENTS

PUBLISHER'S NOTE:

This is the first printing of the tenth edition of ***CMA Review: Part 2CMA***. Please help. Use the form on pages 519 and 520 to send us corrections and suggestions for improvement (please send after you take the exam). FAX the support form on page vii or e-mail irvin@gleim.com for inquiries about errors, omissions, etc.

For updates and information on this and other Gleim books, please see our web page (www.gleim.com/updates.html), or send e-mail to update@gleim.com with "CMA Part 2CMA 10-1" in the subject line.

Gleim's *CMA/CFM Review* Support via Fax

If you fax us inquiries about errors, omissions, etc., before 1:00 p.m. eastern time, we will respond by fax the following business day. If we have trouble faxing our response, it will be mailed. Technical support is also available via e-mail (support@gleim.com). Please include your e-mail address on the fax form below if you wish to receive a response to your request by e-mail (required if you are outside the United States).

Please photocopy this Support Request fax form. It must be completed as requested so we can address the issues and questions you have. All items should refer to a specific page number and outline letter/number or question number.

Wait until after you take the exam to send us the separate evaluation form provided on pages 519 and 520.

Gleim Publications, Inc. FAX (352) 375-6940

CMA/CFM REVIEW SUPPORT REQUEST

Complete this form and attach additional pages as necessary.

Your name ______________________ Your Fax # (   )   -

Address: ______________________________________

____

City: ______________________ State: ______ Zip: ________

E-mail: ______________________________________

Inquiry: ______________________________________

____

____

____

____

____

____

____

____

____

PREPARING FOR AND TAKING THE CMA/CFM EXAMS

ABOUT THE CMA/CFM EXAMS

INTRODUCTION

CMA is the acronym for Certified Management Accountant. CFM is an acronym for Certified in Financial Management. The CFM exam is an offshoot of the CMA. The two exams are identical except that the Part 2CFM exam is "Corporate Financial Management," while the Part 2CMA exam is "Financial Accounting and Reporting."

The CMA examination has been, and the CMA/CFM exams will continue to be, developed and offered by the Institute of Certified Management Accountants (ICMA) in approximately 200 locations in the U.S. and an additional 200 international locations.

CMA/CFM Review: Part 2CMA contains this 22-page Introduction and 10 study units of outlines and multiple-choice questions that cover all of the material tested on Part 2CMA of the CMA/CFM exams. This Introduction discusses exam content, pass rates, administration, organization, background information, preparing for the CMA/CFM exams, and taking the CMA/CFM exams. We urge you to read the next 20 pages carefully because they will help you dramatically improve your study and test-taking procedures.

CORPORATE MANAGEMENT ACCOUNTANTS AND FINANCIAL MANAGERS

1. Objective: Maximize the value of the firm by optimizing
   a. Long-term investment strategies
   b. The capital structure, i.e., how these long-term investments are funded
   c. Short-term cash flow management
2. Corporate financial management involves a financial manager, usually a vice-president/chief financial officer, who is assisted by the
   a. Treasurer -- cash, credit, capital outlay management
   b. Controller -- financial, cost, tax accounting
3. All accounting and finance personnel are beneficiaries of CFM and/or CMA participation.
4. The CMA/CFM tools are set forth in the ICMA's Content Specification Outlines for the CMA/CFM exams.
5. The diagram below illustrates an entity combining the factors of production into finished goods (arrows to the right) with money flowing to the left.

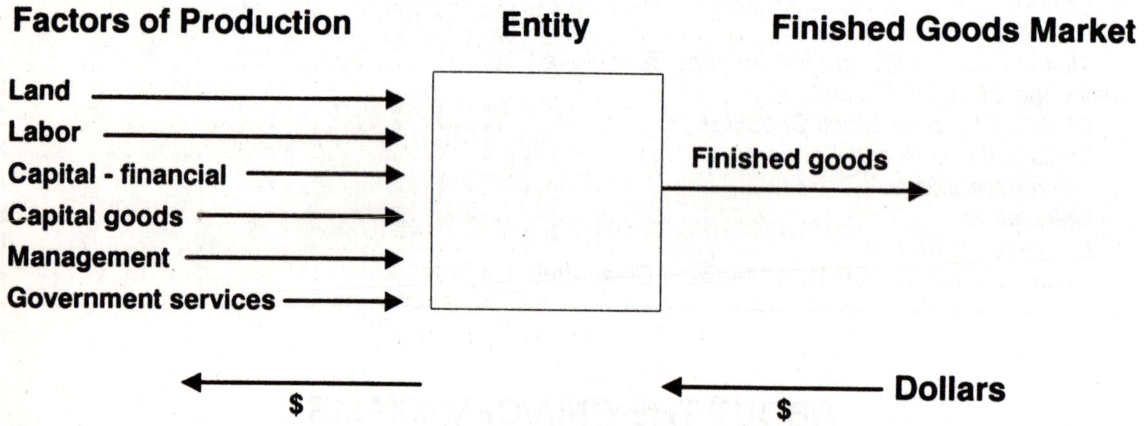

6. Put CMA and CFM in perspective of goods or services production in our capitalistic society. An entity combines the factors of production into finished goods.
   a. Note that the CMA/CFM programs focus on financial capital and the other factors of production as well as the finished goods market. The CEO (chief executive officer) has overall responsibility for the entity's operations.

OBJECTIVES AND CONTENT OF THE CMA/CFM EXAMINATIONS

The primary purpose of the CMA/CFM examination programs is "to establish an objective measure of an individual's knowledge and competence in the fields of management accounting and financial management." Three other objectives set forth by the ICMA are to

1. "Establish management accounting and financial management as recognized professions by identifying the role of the professional, the underlying body of knowledge, and a course of study by which such knowledge is acquired"
2. "Encourage higher educational standards in the management accounting and financial management fields"
3. "Encourage continued professional development"

The exams test the candidates' knowledge and ability with respect to the current state of the art in the fields of management accounting and financial management.

We have arranged the subject matter tested on the CMA/CFM examinations into 10 study units for each part. Each part is presented in a separate book. For CMA/CFM Parts 1, 3, and 4, study the corresponding *CMA/CFM Review* book. For Part 2CMA, study *CMA Review: Part 2CMA* and, for Part 2CFM, study *CFM Review: Part 2CFM*. All contain review outlines and prior CMA/CFM exam questions and answers. The 50 study units are organized as follows:

CMA/CFM Part 1: ECONOMICS, FINANCE, AND MANAGEMENT*

Study Unit 1: Microeconomics
Study Unit 2: Macroeconomics
Study Unit 3: International Business Environment
Study Unit 4: Domestic Institutional Environment of Business
Study Unit 5: Working Capital Finance
Study Unit 6: Capital Structure Finance
Study Unit 7: Risk
Study Unit 8: Organizational Theory
Study Unit 9: Motivation and the Directing Process
Study Unit 10: Communication

Part 2CMA: FINANCIAL ACCOUNTING AND REPORTING

Study Unit 1: Accounting Standards
Study Unit 2: Financial Statements
Study Unit 3: Conceptual Framework
Study Unit 4: Assets
Study Unit 5: Liabilities
Study Unit 6: Equity
Study Unit 7: Other Income Items
Study Unit 8: Other Reporting Issues
Study Unit 9: Financial Statement Analysis
Study Unit 10: External Auditing

***WARNING!!!**

About 25 to 30% of Part 1 test questions will require mathematical calculations. All other parts are approximately 35 to 40% computational questions. Practice computational questions to prepare for exam success!

Part 2CFM: CORPORATE FINANCIAL MANAGEMENT

Study Unit 1: Financial Statements and Annual Reports
Study Unit 2: Financial Statements: Special Topics
Study Unit 3: Long-Term Capital Financing
Study Unit 4: Financial Markets and Interest Rates
Study Unit 5: Investment Banking and Commercial Banking
Study Unit 6: Financial Statement Analysis
Study Unit 7: Business Combinations and Restructurings
Study Unit 8: Risk Management
Study Unit 9: External Financial Environment
Study Unit 10: Accounting Standard Setting

CMA/CFM Part 3: MANAGEMENT REPORTING, ANALYSIS, AND BEHAVIORAL ISSUES

Study Unit 1: Cost and Managerial Accounting Definitions
Study Unit 2: Product Costing and Related Topics
Study Unit 3: Cost Behavior
Study Unit 4: Statements on Management Accounting
Study Unit 5: Planning
Study Unit 6: Budgeting
Study Unit 7: The Controlling Process
Study Unit 8: Standard Costs and Variance Analysis
Study Unit 9: Responsibility Accounting
Study Unit 10: Behavioral Issues

CMA/CFM Part 4: DECISION ANALYSIS AND INFORMATION SYSTEMS

Study Unit 1: Decision Analysis
Study Unit 2: Cost-Volume-Profit Analysis
Study Unit 3: Capital Budgeting
Study Unit 4: Decision Making under Uncertainty
Study Unit 5: Quantitative Methods I
Study Unit 6: Quantitative Methods II
Study Unit 7: Information Systems I
Study Unit 8: Information Systems II
Study Unit 9: Internal Control
Study Unit 10: Internal Auditing

Recap: The only difference between the CFM exam and the CMA exam is Part 2. This book covers Part 2CMA of the CMA/CFM exam.

The *CMA/CFM Review* study unit titles and organization differ somewhat from the subtopic titles used by the ICMA in its content specification outlines for the CMA/CFM exams. The detailed ICMA Content Specification Outline for Part 2CMA is presented in Appendix D beginning on page 500. The selection of study units in *CMA/CFM Review: Part 2CMA* is based on the types and number of questions that have appeared on past CMA and CFM exams as well as the extensiveness of past and expected future exam coverage.

CONTENT SPECIFICATION OUTLINES

The ICMA has developed content specification outlines and has committed to follow them on each examination. A complete CSO is presented in Appendix D beginning on page 500. Thus, each examination will cover the major topics specified below; e.g., external auditing will constitute 10% to 15% of Part 2CMA on each examination.

Candidates for the CMA/CFM designations are expected to have a minimum level of business knowledge that transcends all examination parts. This minimum level includes knowledge of basic financial statements, time value of money concepts, and elementary statistics. Specific discussion of the ICMA's Levels of Performance (A, B, and C) is provided on the next page.

CMA/CFM Part 1: Economics, Finance, and Management

A. Microeconomics--10%-15% (Level B)
B. Macroeconomics--10%-15% (Level A)
C. International Business Environment--10%-15% (Level B)
D. Domestic Institutional Environment of Business--10%-15% (Level A)
E. Working Capital Policy and Management--10%-15% (Level C)
F. Long-term Finance and Capital Structure--10%-15% (Level B)
G. Organizational Structures, Management, and Communication--20%-30% (Level B)

Part 2CMA: Financial Accounting and Reporting

A. Development of Accounting Standards--10%-15% (Level A)
B. Advanced Topics on the Preparation of Financial Statements--50%-70% (Level C)
C. Interpretation and Analysis of Financial Statements--10%-15% (Level C)
D. External Auditing--10%-15% (Level A)

Part 2CFM: Corporate Financial Management

A. Use of Financial Statements--10%-20% (Level B)
B. Advanced Topics in Corporate Financial Management--50%-70% (Level C)
C. Risk Management--10%-15% (Level C)
D. External Financial Environment--10%-20% (Level A)
E. Accounting Standard Setting Environment--5%-10% (Level A)

CMA/CFM Part 3: Management Reporting, Analysis, and Behavioral Issues

A. Cost Measurement--20%-30% (Level C)
B. Planning--20%-30% (Level C)
C. Control and Performance Evaluation--20%-30% (Level C)
D. Behavioral Issues--20%-30% (Level B)

CMA/CFM Part 4: Decision Analysis and Information Systems

A. Decision Theory and Operational Decision Analysis--20%-30% (Level C)
B. Investment Decision Analysis--20%-30% (Level C)
C. Quantitative Methods for Decision Analysis--10%-15% (Level B)
D. Information Systems--20%-30% (Level B)
E. Management Controls--10%-15% (Level B)

LEVEL OF PERFORMANCE REQUIRED

All parts of the exams appear to be tested at the skill level of a final examination for the appropriate course at a good school of business. The ICMA has specified three levels of coverage as reproduced below and indicated in its content specification outlines. You will evaluate and compare the difficulty of each part of the CMA/CFM exams as you work the questions in this book.

Authors' Note: Rely on the questions at the back of each study unit in each *CMA/CFM Review* book and *CMA/CFM Test Prep* software.

Level A: Requiring an appreciation of the broad nature and fundamentals, the ability to recognize the existence of special features and problems in various business transactions, and the ability to apply this knowledge in new and concrete situations, i.e., requiring the skill levels of knowledge and comprehension.

Level B: Requiring a sound understanding of the broad aspects of practices and procedures and awareness of the problems relating to more detailed aspects, the ability to apply such broad knowledge in new and concrete situations, the ability to analyze the components of the material and their relationships, and the ability to reformulate the components into a new whole, i.e., requiring the skill levels of knowledge, comprehension, application and analysis.

Level C: Requiring a sound understanding of principles, practices, and procedures, the ability to analyze material so that its organizational structure can be understood, the proficiency to apply such knowledge to situations likely to be encountered, the ability to deal with all aspects of the situation without extensive recourse to technical research and assistance, and the ability to judge the value of material for a given purpose, i.e., requiring all six skill levels.

HOW ETHICS AND TAXES ARE TESTED

Ethics will be tested on every exam within the context of a specific subject area tested on that part. Appendix A beginning on page 472 covers ethics.

Federal income taxes are tested as (1) accounting for income taxes and (2) tax implications for decisions. Accounting for income taxes including the proper treatment of deferred income taxes is tested in Part 2CMA, Financial Accounting and Reporting, and Part 2CFM, Corporate Financial Management.

The tax code provisions that affect business decisions may be tested in (1) questions that require decision analysis regarding debt versus equity issues in CMA/CFM Part 1, Economics, Finance, and Management; (2) questions in Part 2CFM, Corporate Financial Management; and (3) the decision analysis questions in CMA/CFM Part 4, Decision Analysis and Information Systems.

REQUIREMENTS TO ATTAIN THE CMA/CFM DESIGNATIONS

The CMA and/or the CFM designations are granted only by the ICMA. Candidates must complete five steps to become a CMA and/or CFM:

1. Become a member of the Institute of Management Accountants.
2. File an application for admission with the ICMA and register for the CMA/CFM exams.

3. Pass all four parts of the CMA or CFM examination. To attain both designations, CMAs in good standing need only pass Part 2CFM; CFMs in good standing need only pass Part 2CMA. "Continuous candidacy" is required to retain credit after successful completion of one or more parts. "Continuous candidacy" includes IMA membership, 20 hours of CPE annually, and at least one examination part attempted every 2 years.
4. Meet the CMA/CFM experience requirement.
5. Comply with the Standards of Ethical Conduct.
6. Meet the CMA/CFM education requirements (see below).

Credit can be retained indefinitely as long as these requirements are fulfilled.

Once a designation is earned, the CMA and/or CFM is a member of the Institute of Certified Management Accountants and must comply with the program's CPE requirement and maintain IMA membership in good standing. The certificate of a CMA or CFM delinquent in these requirements will be subject to recall.

ADMISSION TO THE CMA/CFM PROGRAMS

In addition to the above requirements, candidates seeking admission to the CMA/CFM programs must also meet one of the following educational credentials:

1. Hold a baccalaureate degree, in any area, from an accredited college or university. Students may apply when they attain senior standing and will be permitted to take the examination pending receipt of a degree. Degrees from foreign institutions must be evaluated by an independent agency approved by the ICMA; or
2. Hold a CPA license to practice or other professional qualification issued in a foreign country that is comparable to the CPA, CMA, CFM, etc., or
3. Achieve a score in the 50th percentile or higher on either the Graduate Management Admissions Test (GMAT) or the Graduate Record Examination (GRE).

NOTE: Educational credentials may be submitted at a later date, i.e., a degree or senior standing is not required to sit for the exam but must be satisfied before you are certified.

Also, the applicant must

1. Be a member of the Institute of Management Accountants or submit an IMA application when applying to the ICMA
2. Fulfill or expect to fulfill the educational requirements
3. Be employed or expect to be employed in a position that meets the experience requirement
4. Submit the names of two character references (one from employer, one from a person who is neither employed by the same firm nor a family member)
5. Be of good moral character
6. Abide by the Standards of Ethical Conduct

CMA/CFM WORK EXPERIENCE REQUIRED

Two continuous years of professional experience in financial management and/or management accounting are required any time prior to, or within 7 years of, passing the examination.

1. Professional experience shall be defined as full-time continuous experience at a level where judgments are regularly made that employ the principles of financial management and/or management accounting, e.g.,
   a. Financial analysis
   b. Budget preparation
   c. Management information systems analysis
   d. Management accounting in government, finance, or industry
   e. Auditing in government, finance, or industry
   f. Management consulting
   g. Audit work in public accounting (3 years required)
   h. Research, teaching, or consulting related to management accounting (for teaching, a significant portion required to be above the principles level)
2. Employment in functions that require the occasional application of financial management or management accounting principles but are not essentially management accounting oriented will not satisfy the requirement, e.g.,
   a. Computer operations
   b. Sales and marketing
   c. Manufacturing
   d. Engineering
   e. Personnel
   f. Employment in internships, trainee, clerical, or nontechnical positions

If you have any questions about the acceptability of your work experience or baccalaureate degree, please write or call the ICMA. Include a complete description of your situation. You will receive a response from the ICMA as soon as your request is evaluated.

Institute of Certified Management Accountants
10 Paragon Drive
Montvale, NJ 07645-1759
(201) 573-9000
(800) 638-4427

NOTE: If you have passed the U.S. CPA exam, you can waive Part 2CMA. There is an $80 fee for the processing of this waiver. To receive a waiver, you must request that a letter from your state board be sent directly to the ICMA confirming your licensure or passing of the U.S. CPA exam; copies are not acceptable.

THE INSTITUTE OF MANAGEMENT ACCOUNTANTS (IMA)

Conceived as an educational organization to develop the individual management accountant professionally and to provide business management with the most advanced techniques and procedures, the IMA was founded as the National Association of Accountants in 1919 with 37 charter members. It grew rapidly, with 2,000 applications for membership in the first year, and today it is the largest management accounting association in the world, with approximately 75,000 members and more than 300 chapters in the U.S. and abroad.

The IMA has made major contributions to business management through its continuing education program, with courses and seminars conducted in numerous locations across the country; its two magazines, *Strategic Finance*, which is a new monthly publication, and *Management Accounting*, which is now a quarterly; other literature, including research reports, monographs, and books; a technical inquiry service; a library; the annual international conference; and frequent meetings at chapter levels.

Membership in the IMA is open to all persons interested in advancing their knowledge of accounting or financial management. It is required for CMA/CFM candidates and CMAs/CFMs.

IMA Dues in the USA and Canada

1. **Regular**: 1 year, $140
2. **Associate**: $47.00 (2nd year, $93.00); must apply within 2 years of completing fulltime studies
3. **Academic member**: $70; must be a full-time faculty member and reside in the U.S. or Canada
4. **Student**: $28.00; must have 6 or more equivalent hours per semester and reside in the U.S. or Canada

Membership application forms may be obtained by writing the Institute of Management Accountants, 10 Paragon Drive, Montvale, NJ 07645-1760, or calling (201) 573-9000 or (800) 638-4427. A sample of the two-page form appears in Appendix C on pages 495 and 496.

THE INSTITUTE OF CERTIFIED MANAGEMENT ACCOUNTANTS (ICMA)

The ICMA is located at the IMA headquarters in Montvale, New Jersey. The only function of the ICMA is to offer and administer the CFM and CMA designations. The staff consists of the senior director, the director of examinations, and three associates (all of whom are professional accountants), plus support personnel. The ICMA occupies about 4,000 square feet of office space in the IMA headquarters. This office is where the examinations are prepared and graded and where all records are kept.

ICMA BOARD OF REGENTS AND STAFF

The ICMA Board of Regents is a special committee of the IMA established to direct the CFM and CMA programs for financial managers and management accountants through the ICMA.

The Board of Regents consists of 16 regents, one of whom is designated as chair by the president of the IMA. The regents are appointed by the president of the IMA to serve 3-year terms. Membership on the Board of Regents rotates, with one-third of the regents being appointed each year. The regents usually meet two times a year for 1 or 2 days.

The managing director of the ICMA, the director of examinations, and the ICMA staff are located at the ICMA office in Montvale, NJ. They undertake all of the day-to-day work with respect to the CFM and CMA programs.

HOW TO (1) APPLY AND (2) REGISTER FOR THE CMA/CFM EXAMS

First, you are required to **apply** both for membership in the IMA (see sample application form in Appendix C on pages 495 and 496) and for admission into the ICMA (see sample application form in Appendix C on pages 497 and 498). Thus, currently two applications are required if you are not already an IMA member. The ICMA is also phasing in a single combined IMA and ICMA application. Contact the ICMA for more information.

Apply to join the IMA and the ICMA **today** -- it only takes a few minutes. Application to the ICMA requires education, employment, and reference data. The educational experience requirements are discussed on page 7. You must provide two references: one from your employer and the second from someone other than a family member or fellow employee. Character reference forms are sent by the ICMA with your application forms. An official transcript providing proof of graduation is also required. There is a $50 credentialing fee (waived for students). Once a person has become a candidate, there is no participant's fee other than IMA membership dues.

Second, it is necessary to **register** each time you wish to sit for the exams. The exam registration form (see page 499) is very simple (it takes about 2 minutes to complete). The registration fee for each part of the exam is $80. There is an additional $40 processing fee per part for candidates taking the examination at an international site making the fee $120 per part. Graduating seniors and full-time graduate students are charged a one-time special rate of $40 per part. Full-time faculty are permitted to take the exam one time at no cost and thereafter pay $40 per part.

A sample of the first page of the ICMA registration form available to candidates from the ICMA appears in Appendix C. Order a registration booklet and IMA membership application form from the ICMA at (800) 638-4427, extension 510. The IMA encourages candidates to view information and complete IMA and ICMA applications and exam registration forms online. Visit the IMA's web site at www.imanet.org for more information.

SPECIAL STUDENT EXAMINATION FEE

U.S. college students may take five examination parts at $40 per part (versus the normal $80). These discounts must be used within the year following application or they will be forfeited. To be eligible for this discount, students must

1. Provide the name of someone who can verify student status
2. Apply to the ICMA while enrolled in school
3. Be undergraduates who have attained senior status or graduate students who are enrolled for at least 6 credit hours in the current term, or undergraduate or graduate students who are taking less than 6 hours but have taken 6 credit hours for the prior two semesters or three quarters and can be expected to graduate at the end of the current term

FEES FOR FULL-TIME PROFESSORS

Full-time faculty members are permitted to take five examination parts once at no charge. The fee for any parts that must be retaken is 50% of the normal fee. The $50 credentialing fee is no longer waived. To qualify, a faculty member must submit a letter on school stationery affirming his/her full-time status. Faculty should sit for the CMA/CFM examinations because a professor's status as a CMA/CFM encourages students to enter the program. Full-time doctoral students who plan to pursue a teaching career are treated as faculty members for purposes of qualifying for the free examination.

ICMA REFUND POLICY

In general, the fees paid to the ICMA discussed above are nonrefundable. However, a candidate withdrawing from the examination within 30 days of registration may receive a credit for the examination fee less a $25 processing charge. Failure to take the examination within the assigned 120-day authorization period will result in the loss of examination fees; there will be no refund or credit available.

PASS/FAIL AND GRADE REPORTS

The passing score is approximately 60-70%. You will receive your test results immediately after completion of the computerized exam. In addition to pass or fail, you are told a "scaled score" between 200 and 700, with 500 being the passing mark. This provides information about how close, above or below, you were to passing. If you fail the exam, there is a 90-day waiting period before you may retake the part failed.

MAINTAINING YOUR CMA/CFM DESIGNATIONS

Membership in the IMA is required to maintain your CMA/CFM certificates. The general membership fee is $140. There is no additional participant fee.

Continuing professional education is required of CMAs/CFMs to maintain their proficiency in the fields of managerial accounting and financial management. Every year, 30 hours of CPE must be completed, which is about 4 days per year. Qualifying topics include management accounting, financial management, corporate taxation, statistics, computer science, systems analysis, management skills, marketing, business law, and insurance.

Credit for hours of study will be given for participation in programs sponsored by businesses, educational institutions, or professional and trade associations at either the national or local level. Programs conducted by an individual's employer must provide for an instructor or course leader. There must be formal instructional training material. On-the-job training does not qualify. An affidavit from the employer is required to attest to the hours of instruction. The programs may be seminars, workshops, technical meetings, or college courses under the direction of an instructor. The method of instruction may include lecture, discussion, case studies, and teaching aids such as training films and cassettes.

Credit for hours of study may be given for technical articles published in business, professional, or trade journals, and for major technical talks given for the first time before business, professional, or trade organizations. The specific hours of credit in each case will be determined by the Institute.

CMA/CFM TEST ADMINISTRATION AND GRADING

The ICMA will send you authorization to take the exam, which will have a 120-day window. The authorization will instruct you to call the Prometric registration office 1(800) 479-6370 and register for your test at a local Prometric testing center. Your test will be graded by the computer as soon as you complete the test.

COMPUTER TESTING PROCEDURES

When you arrive at the computer testing center, you will be required to check in. Be sure to bring your authorization letter and two forms of identification, one with a photograph, both with your signature. If you have any questions, please call the IMA at 1(800) 638-4427.

Next, you will be taken into the testing room and seated at a computer terminal. A person from the testing center will assist you in logging on the system, and you will be asked to confirm your personal data. Then you will be prompted and given an online introduction to the computer testing system and you will view a tutorial.

If you have used our ***CMA/CFM Test Prep*** software, you will be conversant with the computer testing methodology and environment, and you will probably want to skip the tutorial and begin the actual test immediately. Once you begin your test, you will be allowed 3 hrs. to complete the actual test. This is just over 1.6 minutes per question. You may take a break during the exam, BUT the clock continues to run during your break. Before you leave the testing center, you will be required to check out of the testing center.

CONCEPTUAL VS. CALCULATION QUESTIONS

About 35 to 40% of CMA/CFM Part 2CMA test questions will be calculations in contrast to conceptual questions. When you take the test, it will appear that more than 40% of the questions are calculation-type because they take longer and are "more difficult."

PREPARING FOR THE CMA/CFM EXAMS

HOW MANY PARTS TO TAKE

We suggest that you take one part at a time.

CMA/CFM Part 1:	Economics, Finance, and Management
Part 2CMA:	Financial Accounting and Reporting
Part 2CFM:	Corporate Financial Management
CMA/CFM Part 3:	Management Reporting, Analysis, and Behavioral Issues
CMA/CFM Part 4:	Decision Analysis and Information Systems

Parts 2CMA, 2CFM, and 3 cover many of the accounting and finance topics included in typical undergraduate accounting/finance programs. Part 1 covers the material found in management, microeconomics, macroeconomics, and corporate finance courses. Part 4 covers computer systems, quantitative methods, and statistics courses.

There is no time limit for taking and passing all of the parts. Candidates can maintain credit for passed parts as long as they maintain continuous candidacy. To maintain candidacy, individuals must continue their membership in the IMA, complete 20 hours of continuing education each year beginning the calendar year after they passed their first part, and take (not necessarily pass) an exam part every 2 years. Note that a candidate receives 12 hours of continuing professional education for each exam part passed.

HOW TO STUDY A STUDY UNIT (books only*)

1. Gain an overview of the study unit -- familiarity with the topic, number of pages of outline, number of multiple-choice questions -- and estimate the time you will invest.
2. Answer five to ten multiple-choice questions. Choose one or two questions from each subunit.

   The purpose of answering multiple-choice questions before working through the study outline is to understand the standards to which you will be held. This will motivate you to concentrate on the study outline. You will also practice answering questions for which you are unprepared. Become an educated guesser when you encounter questions in doubt; you will outperform the inexperienced exam candidate.
3. Work through the study outline. Learn and understand the concepts. Remember, you are aiming toward the analysis, synthesis, and evaluation levels of knowledge, not rote memorization. Study the outlines with the objective of being able to explain the subject matter to third parties.
4. After you are comfortable with the study outlines, apply your multiple-choice question answering technique (see page 18) to answer all of the multiple-choice questions by marking the correct answer before consulting the answer and answer explanation. It is essential to mark your answer choice before looking at the answer and answer explanation. Use the bookmark at the back of each Gleim ***CMA/CFM Review*** book.
5. Develop a 90% proficiency level within each study unit. You will achieve this proficiency level by studying the outlines and answering multiple-choice questions.

   Learning from questions you answer incorrectly is very important. Each question you answer incorrectly is an opportunity to avoid missing actual test questions on your CMA/CFM exam. Thus, you should carefully study the answer explanations provided until you understand why the original answer you chose is wrong, as well as why the correct answer indicated is correct. This study technique may prove to be the difference between passing and failing for many candidates.

* We recommend using *CMA/CFM Test Prep* software discussed on page 14. It will give you a definite advantage.

You **must** determine why you answered questions incorrectly and learn how to avoid the same error in the future. Reasons for missing questions include

a. Misreading the requirement (stem)
b. Failing to understand what is required
c. Making a math error
d. Applying the wrong rule or concept
e. Being distracted by one or more of the answers
f. Incorrectly eliminating answers from consideration
g. Lacking any knowledge of the topic tested
h. Employing bad intuition (Why?) when guessing

6. Gleim ***CMA/CFM Test Prep*** software will significantly benefit your study efforts, especially when using the 20-question test routine suggested below or the Prometric test emulation contained in the software.

ADDING CMA/CFM TEST PREP SOFTWARE

Using ***CMA/CFM Test Prep*** really works! The software forces you to commit to your answer choice before looking at answer explanations. It also keeps track of your time and the results of your effort. Each study session and each test session are kept in the performance history and are viewable in either a table or a graphical format. You can know exactly what to expect when you go to take your exam by using the Prometric test emulation contained within the software.

Each Test Prep disk covers a different part of the exam and includes over 1,000 questions. All questions have been updated to reflect the current subject matter.

Read and study the following six steps regarding how to use the software with the books. Using ***CMA/CFM Test Prep*** will greatly facilitate your study and success on the exam! DO NOT neglect diagnosing the reasons for answering questions incorrectly; i.e., learn from your mistakes while studying so you avoid making mistakes on the exam.

The best way to prepare to PASS:

1. In test mode, answer a 20-question test from each study unit before studying the study unit.
2. Study the knowledge transfer outline for the study unit in your Gleim book.
3. Take two or three 20-question tests in test mode after studying knowledge transfer outlines.
4. After EACH test session, immediately switch to study mode and select questions "missed on last session" so you can reanswer these questions AND analyze why you answered each question incorrectly.
5. Continue the process until you approach a 90% proficiency level.
6. Modify the process to suit your individual learning process.

Avoid studying Gleim questions to learn the correct answers. Use Gleim questions to help you learn how to answer CMA/CFM questions under exam conditions. Expect the unexpected and be prepared to deal with the unexpected. Always take one 20-question test in test mode *before* studying the material in each study unit. These test sessions will allow you to practice answering questions you have not seen before. Become an educated guesser when you encounter questions in doubt; you will outperform the inexperienced exam taker.

STUDY PLAN AND TIME BUDGET

Complete one study unit at a time. Initially, budget 3 to 4 hours per study unit (1 to 2 hours studying the outline and 1 to 2 minutes each on all the multiple-choice questions).

This Introduction	2
10 study units at 3.5 hours each	35
General review	3
Total Hours	40

Each week you should evaluate your progress and review your preparation plans for the time remaining prior to the exam. Review your commitments, e.g., out-of-town assignments, personal responsibilities, etc., and note them on your calendar. This precaution will assist you in keeping to your schedule.

CONTROL

You have to be in control to be successful during exam preparation and execution. Control can also contribute greatly to your personal and other professional goals. Control is a process whereby you

1. Develop expectations, standards, budgets, and plans.
2. Undertake activity, production, study, and learning.
3. Measure the activity, production, output, and knowledge.
4. Compare actual activity with expected, or budgeted.
5. Modify the activity, behavior, or production to better achieve the desired outcome.
6. Revise expectations and standards in light of actual experience.
7. Continue the process.

The objective is to be confident that the best possible performance is being generated. Most accountants study this process in relation to standard costs, i.e., establish cost standards and compute cost variances.

Every day you rely on control systems implicitly. When you groom your hair, you have expectations about the desired appearance of your hair and the time required to style it. You monitor your progress and make adjustments as appropriate, e.g., brush it a different way or speed up.

Develop and enforce standards in all of your endeavors. Exercise control, implicitly or explicitly. Most endeavors will improve with explicit control. This is particularly true with certification examinations and other academic tests.

1. Practice your question answering techniques (and develop control) as you prepare answers/solutions to practice questions/problems during your study program.
2. Develop explicit control over your study programs based on the control process discussed previously.
3. Think about using more explicit control systems over any and all of your endeavors.
4. Seek continuous improvement to meet your needs given a particular situation or constraint. Additional practice will result in further efficiencies.

PROMETRIC TESTING CENTERS (Domestic Only): Part of the Prometric Learning Center Network

ALABAMA
Birmingham
Decatur
Dothan
Mobile
Montgomery

ALASKA
Anchorage

ARIZONA
Chandler
Phoenix
Tucson

ARKANSAS
Ft. Smith
Little Rock

CALIFORNIA
Anaheim Hills
Atascadero
Brea
Culiver City
Diamond Bar
Fair Oaks
Fremont
Gardena
Irvine
La Jolla
Piedmont
Rancho Cuca
Redlands
Riverside
San Francisco
San Jose
Santa Rosa
Walnut Creek
Westlake

COLORADO
Boulder
Colorado Springs
Littleton
Pueblo

CONNECTICUT
Glastonbury
Hamden

FLORIDA
Davie
Ft. Myers
Gainesville
Jacksonville
Miami Lakes
Sarasota
Tallahassee
Temple Terr.
Winter Park

GEORGIA
Augusta
Jonesboro
Macon
Savannah
Smyrna
Valdosta

HAWAII
Kailua/Oahu

IDAHO
Boise

ILLINOIS
Carbondale
Carpentersville
Chicago
Homewood
Normal
Northbrook
Springfield
Westchester

INDIANA
Ft. Wayne
Indianapolis
Layfayette
Merrillville
Mishawaka

IOWA
Bettendorf
Cedar Rapids
W. Des Moines

KANSAS
Topeka
Wichita

KENTUCKY
Lexington
Louisville

LOUISIANA
Baton Rouge
Bossier City
New Orleans

MAINE
Pikesville
South Portland

MARYLAND
Bethesda
Columbia
Pikesville

MASSACHUSETTS
Boston
E. Longmeadow
Worcester

MICHIGAN
Ann Arbor
Grand Rapids
Lansing
Livonia
Troy
Utica

MINNESOTA
Bloomington
Duluth
Rochester
Woodbury

MISSISSIPPI
Jackson

MISSOURI
Ballwin
Creve Coeur
Gladstone
Springfield

MONTANA
Billings
Helena

NEBRASKA
Lincoln
Omaha

NEVADA
Las Vegas
Reno

NEW HAMPSHIRE
Concord

NEW JERSEY
East Brunswick
Fairlawn
Hamilton Town
Verona

NEW MEXICO
Albuquerque

NEW YORK
Albany
Amherst
East Syracuse
Forest Hills
Garden City
Ithaca
Penn Plaza
Rochester
Staten Island
Vestal
Wappingers Falls
White Plains

NORTH CAROLINA
Charlotte
Gastonia
Greensboro
Greenville
Raleigh

NORTH DAKOTA
Bismarck

OHIO
Akron
Centerville
Cincinnati-North
Columbus
Lima
Mentor
Niles
Reynoldsburg
Solon
Strongsville
Toledo

OKLAHOMA
Oklahoma City
Tulsa

OREGON
Eugene
Milwaukie
Portland
Salem

PENNSYLVANIA
Allentown
Center City
Erie
Harrisburg
Lancaster
North Hills
North Wales
Pittsburgh
Plymouth Meeting
Scranton
York

RHODE ISLAND
Cranston

SOUTH CAROLINA
Charleston
Greenville
Irmo

SOUTH DAKOTA
Sioux Falls

TENNESSEE
Chattanooga
Clarksville
Franklin
Knoxville
Madison

TEXAS
Abilene
Amarillo
Austin
Beaumont
Bedford
Corpus Christi
Dallas Metro/ Arlington
El Paso
Houston
Lubbock
Midland
San Antonio
Waco

UTAH
Orem
Salt Lake City

VERMONT
Williston

VIRGINIA
Arlington
Newport News
Richmond
Roanoke

WASHINGTON
Lynnwood
Puyallup
Spokane

WASHINGTON, DC

WEST VIRGINIA
Charleston
Morgantown

WISCONSIN
Brookfield

WYOMING
Casper

CAUTION: Since actual sites change often, you should contact the Prometric registration office [1(800) 479-6370] to verify the location of your local testing center or obtain international test sites.

After you register to take each part of the CMA/CFM exams and pay $80 ($120 internationally), the ICMA will send you a letter with an authorization number and instructions on contacting Prometric to schedule your test. Call your local Prometric testing center a day or two before your test to confirm your time and obtain directions to the testing center or visit the Prometric web site at www.prometric.com. A listing of Prometric testing centers is presented on page 16.

DOMESTIC INSTRUCTIONS TO CANDIDATES

The letter accompanying these instructions is your authorization to schedule the taking of your examination part(s) with Prometric Technologies. Please note that you have a separate authorization number for each part that you registered to take. Questions regarding your registration with IMA should be directed to 800-638-4427, ext. 301 or 303.

Scheduling with Prometric Technologies

The interval dates shown on your authorization letter represent the time/authorization period during which you are authorized to take CMA/CFM examination part(s).

- Before calling for your appointment, select two or three dates during your authorization period that are convenient for you to take the examination in case your first choice is not available. Please be aware that Saturdays fill quickly and you may not be able to get a Saturday appointment.
- Choose a Prometric Technology Center from the accompanying list of locations.
- Be sure you have your authorization number(s) from the accompanying letter handy when you call as you will be required to provide this information.
- To schedule your examination, please call Prometric Technologies National Registry at 800-479-6370 at your earliest convenience. You also have the option of calling directly to the Prometric Technology Center of your choice.

You must schedule your examination during the dates provided as your authorization will expire at the end of the period, and your fees will be forfeited.

Cancellation of a Scheduled Appointment

If you find that you are unable to keep a scheduled appointment at Prometric, you must cancel 48 business hours before the appointment. To cancel, call 800-479-6370 at any time; if you cannot speak to a Prometric representative, you may leave a voice mail message as these messages are marked with the date and time. Be sure to leave sufficient information for identification such as your name, your authorization number, and the site location where you are scheduled. If you cancel an appointment, you must wait 72 hours before calling to reschedule. If you do not comply with this 48-hour policy, you will be considered a "no-show" and you will need to reregister with ICMA and repay the examination fee.

General Instructions

- Be sure to arrive at the Prometric Technology Center on time. If you are more than 30 minutes late, you may lose your scheduled sitting and be required to reschedule at a later date at an additional cost.
- You will be required to sign the Prometric Log Book when you enter the center.
- Be sure to take your authorization letter with you as you will be asked to show this document. You may wish to make a copy of this letter if you are taking multiple parts.
- For admission to the examination, you will be required to present two forms of identification, one with a photograph, both with your signature. Approved IDs are a passport, driver's license, military ID, credit card with photo, or company ID. Student IDs are **not** acceptable. You will not be permitted into the examination without proper photo identification.
- Small lockers are available at the test centers for personal belongings. Items such as purses, briefcases, and jackets will not be allowed in the testing room.
- Small battery or solar powered electronic calculators restricted to a maximum of six functions - addition, subtraction, multiplication, division, square root, and percent - are allowed. The calculator must be non-programmable and must not use any type of tape. Memory must erase when the calculator is turned off. Candidates **will not** be allowed to use calculators that do not comply with these restrictions.
- On request, candidates will be provided with scrap paper which will be counted by the test center personnel when given to candidates and will also be counted when collected from candidates. Candidates should bring pencils or pens to the test center for use in making calculations, etc., on the provided scrap paper.
- The staff at the Prometric Technology Centers is not involved in the development of the examination or the procedures governing the evaluation of your performance. Questions or comments on the examination content or performance evaluation should be directed only to the ICMA as this is a nondisclosed examination. You may also include comments on the survey at the end of the exam.
- At the beginning of your test administration, you will be given the opportunity to take a tutorial that introduces the testing screens; the tutorial is not part of your testing time and may be repeated if the candidate wishes; however, total tutorial time is limited.
- You will have three hours to complete the examination; your time remaining will be displayed on the screen.
- Upon completion of each examination part, your performance results will be displayed on the screen, and you will also receive a printed copy of your results before leaving the testing center.
- If you pass your final part, you will receive further certification information from the ICMA. If you do not pass an examination, you will receive a new registration form from the ICMA; it should be noted that you may retake a part at any time, but you are limited to taking the part three times in a 12-month period.

MULTIPLE-CHOICE QUESTION ANSWERING TECHNIQUE

1. **Budget your time.**
   a. We make this point with emphasis. Just as you should fill up your gas tank prior to reaching empty, you should finish your exam before time expires.
   b. You have 180 minutes to answer 110 questions, i.e., 1.6 minutes per question. We suggest you attempt to answer eight questions every 10 minutes, which is 1.25 minutes per question. This would result in completing 110 questions in 137 minutes to give you almost 45 minutes to review questions that you have marked. (See 3.c.2) for a brief discussion of marking questions at Prometric.)
   c. On your Prometric computer screen, the time remaining (starting with 180 minutes) appears at the upper right of your screen.
2. **Answer the questions in chronological order.**
   a. Do **not** agonize over any one question. Stay within your time budget.
   b. It is not necessary to "mark" unanswered questions. Prometric provides options to review both unanswered questions and marked questions.
3. **For each question**
   a. **Read the question** stem carefully (the part of the question that precedes the answer choices) to determine the precise requirement.
      1) Focusing on what is required enables you to ignore extraneous information and to proceed directly to determining the correct answer.
         a) Be especially careful to note when the requirement is an **exception**; e.g., "All of the following statements regarding a company's internal rate of return are true **except**:."
   b. **Determine the correct answer** before reading the answer choices. The objective is to avoid allowing the answer choices to affect your reading of the question.
      1) When four answer choices are presented, three of them are incorrect. They are called **distractors** for a very good reason.
      2) **Read each answer choice** with close attention.
         a) Even if answer (A) appears to be the correct choice, do **not** skip the remaining answer choices. Answer (B), (C), or (D) may be better.
         b) Treat each answer choice as a true-false question.
   c. **Select the best answer**. The answer is selected by either pressing the answer letter on your keyboard or by using your mouse. Select the most likely or best answer choice. If you are uncertain, make an educated guess.
      1) The CMA/CFM does not penalize guessing because your score is determined by the number of correct responses. Thus, you should answer every question.
      2) As you answer a question, you can mark it by pressing "M" or unmark a marked question by pressing "M." After you have answered, marked, or looked at and not answered all 110 questions, you will be presented with a summary screen that shows how many questions you did not answer and how many you marked. You then have the option of revisiting all of the unanswered questions and "marked" questions.

4. Prometric Computer Screen Layout

Question 10 of 120	YOUR NAME	Time remaining: 02:51

The sky is ______________

O A. blue

O B. brown

O C. green

O D. silver

Directions: Select the best answer

← Previous   Next →   Mark   ? Help

NOTE: A menu offering a number of options is displayed at the bottom of the question screen. The options enable you to view the previous question or the next question, mark a question to be revisited, or request help. You may select an option by pressing the appropriate symbol key or highlighted letter on your keyboard or by clicking on the symbol or letter with your mouse.

1) View the previous question by indicating the letter **P** or the left arrow key.
2) View the next question by indicating the letter **N** or the right arrow key.
3) Mark a question by indicating the letter **M**.
4) Request help by indicating the question mark.

USE GLEIM *CMA/CFM TEST PREP* SOFTWARE. It emulates the Prometric testing procedures and environment including computer screen layout, software operation, etc.

TAKING THE CMA/CFM EXAMS

CMA/CFM EXAMINATIONS CHECKLIST

1. Acquire your study materials. Rely on this book and *CMA/CFM Test Prep* software. It's all you need!
2. **Apply** for membership in the IMA (see pages 495 and 496) and for admission to the ICMA (pages 497 and 498).
3. **Register** to take the desired part of the exam using the examination registration form (page 499) and send it with your applications to the ICMA. Take one part at a time. When you register and pay $80 for a part ($120 for exams at international sites), you have 120 days to take the part. Upon receipt of authorization to take the exam, call Prometric to schedule your test.
4. Plan your preparation process. It's easy. You have 10 study units to complete.
5. Orderly, controlled preparation builds confidence, reduces anxiety, and produces success!
6. PASS THE EXAMINATION (study this Introduction)!

LOGISTICAL AND HEALTH CONCERNS

As soon as the ICMA sends you a computer-based test authorization, call and schedule your test at a convenient time and convenient Prometric testing center. In almost all cases, you should be able to drive to your testing site, take the test, and return home in one day. If the exam is not being given within driving distance of your home, call Prometric Technology Centers to inquire about accommodations. Stay by yourself at a hotel to be assured of avoiding distractions. The hotel should be soundproof and have a comfortable bed and desk suitable for study. If possible, stay at a hotel with recreational facilities you normally use, e.g., a swimming pool.

Proper exercise, diet, and rest in the weeks before you take your exam are very important. High energy levels, reduced tension, and an improved attitude are among the benefits. A good aerobic fitness program, a nutritious and well-balanced diet, and a regular sleep pattern will promote your long-term emotional and physical well-being as well as contribute significantly to a favorable exam result. Of course, the use of health-undermining substances should be avoided.

EXAM PSYCHOLOGY

Plan ahead and systematically prepare. Then go to the exam and give it your best: neither you nor anyone else can expect more. Having undertaken a systematic preparation program, you will do fine.

Maintain a positive attitude and do not become depressed if you encounter difficulties either before or during the exam. An optimist will usually do better than an equally well-prepared pessimist. Remember, you have reason to be optimistic because you will be competing with many less qualified persons who have not prepared as well as you have.

CALCULATORS

Only simple six-function calculators are permitted (i.e., addition, subtraction, multiplication, division, square root, percent). Candidates are responsible for providing their own calculators. You should be thoroughly experienced in the operations of your calculator. Make sure it has fresh batteries just prior to the examination.

1. Consider bringing a backup calculator with you.
2. The calculator must be small, quiet, and battery- or solar-powered so it will not be distracting to other candidates.
3. The calculator may have a memory. However, the memory must be temporary and erase when the memory is cleared or the calculator is turned off.
4. The calculator must not use any type of tape.
5. The calculator must be nonprogrammable.
6. Nonconforming calculators and calculator instruction books are **not** permitted.

EXAMINATION TACTICS

1. Remember to bring your authorization and appropriate identification to the exam site. The photo ID requirement is **strictly** enforced.
2. Arrive at the test center at least 30 minutes prior to the scheduled exam time to allow for orientation and check-in procedures. Your appointment may be canceled if you are 30 minutes late.
3. Dressing for exam success means emphasizing comfort, not appearance. Be prepared to adjust for changes in temperature, e.g., to remove or put on a sweater.
4. Do not bring notes, this text, other books, etc., into the Prometric testing center. You will only make yourself nervous and confused by trying to cram the last 5 minutes before the exam. Books are not allowed in the testing room, anyway. You should, however, bring an appropriate calculator.
5. Adequate scratch paper and pencils are provided. You must turn in your scratch paper as you leave the exam site. Any breath mints, gum, etc., should be in your pocket as they may distract other persons taking the test.
6. As soon as you complete the exam, we would like you to e-mail, fax, or write to us with your comments on our books and software. We are particularly interested in which topics need to be added or expanded in our books and software. We are NOT asking about specific CMA/CFM questions; rather we are asking for feedback on our books and software.

RECAP OF PART 2CMA EXAM COVERAGE

ICMA Major Topics and Percent Coverage	Gleim/Flesher Study Units
A. Development of Accounting Standards--10%-15% (Level A)	1. Accounting Standards
B. Advanced Topics on the Preparation of Financial Statements--50%-70% (Level C)	2. Financial Statements 3. Conceptual Framework 4. Assets 5. Liabilities 6. Equity 7. Other Income Items 8. Other Reporting Issues
C. Interpretation and Analysis of Financial Statements--10%-15% (Level C)	9. Financial Statement Analysis
D. External Auditing--10%-15% (Level A)	10. External Auditing

GO FOR IT!
IT'S YOURS TO PASS!

***WARNING!!!**

About 25 to 30% of Part 1 test questions will require mathematical calculations. All other parts are approximately 35 to 40% computational questions. Practice computational questions to prepare for exam success!

STUDY UNIT 1: ACCOUNTING STANDARDS

22 pages of outline
48 multiple-choice questions

Financial accounting concerns reporting the results of operations (income statement) and financial position (balance sheet). Other primary financial statements are the statement of cash flows and the statement of retained earnings. A separate statement of changes in equity may also be presented if these changes are not disclosed in the other statements or in the notes. Moreover, comprehensive income must be presented in a financial statement given the same prominence as other statements, but no specific format is required. Although financial statements can be prepared for any entity, this study unit concerns the body of knowledge regarding financial statement preparation for business enterprises and the underlying accounting theory.

Generally accepted accounting principles (GAAP) for nongovernmental entities include those conventions, rules, and procedures that the Financial Accounting Standards Board (FASB) and its predecessors, the Accounting Principles Board and the Committee on Accounting Procedure (two now-defunct AICPA committees), have deemed preferable in their official pronouncements. In the absence of officially established accounting principles, GAAP are deemed to include such sources of established principles as FASB Technical Bulletins, AICPA Audit and Accounting Guides, and AICPA Statements of Position. If no sources of established principles exist, other accounting literature (e.g., Statements of Financial Accounting Concepts) may furnish guidance.

The subject matter of this study unit has been assigned a relative weight range of 10% to 15% of Part 2.

A. External Financial Reporting

1. Users of financial statements may directly or indirectly have an economic interest in a specific business. Users with direct interests usually invest in or manage the business, whereas users with indirect interests advise, influence, or represent users with direct interests.
   a. Users with direct interests include
      1) Investors or potential investors
      2) Suppliers and creditors
      3) Employees
      4) Management
   b. Users having indirect interests include
      1) Financial advisers and analysts
      2) Stock markets or exchanges
      3) Regulatory authorities

2. The users of financial statements can also be grouped by their relation to the business.
   a. Internal users use financial statements to make decisions affecting the internal operations of the business. These users include management, employees, and the board of directors.
      1) Internal users gather information so that they may more efficiently plan and control the business and its allocation of resources.
   b. External users of financial statements need to determine whether to create, continue, or terminate a relationship with a firm. Creditors, investors, and the general public use the statements to decide whether doing business with the firm will be beneficial.
3. The needs of users of financial statements are diverse.
   a. Investors need information to decide whether to increase, decrease, or obtain an investment in a firm.
   b. Creditors need information to determine whether to extend credit and under what terms.
   c. Employees want financial information to negotiate wages and fringe benefits based on the increased productivity and value they provide to a profitable firm.
   d. Management needs financial statements to assess financial strengths and deficiencies, to evaluate performance results and past decisions, and to plan for future financial goals and steps toward accomplishing them.
   e. Financial advisers and analysts need financial statements to help investors evaluate particular investments.
   f. Stock exchanges need financial statements to evaluate whether to accept a firm's stock for listing or whether to suspend the stock's trading.
   g. Regulatory agencies may need financial statements to evaluate the firm's conformity with regulations and to determine price levels in regulated industries.
4. Stop and review! You have completed the outline for this subunit. Study multiple-choice questions 1 through 3 on page 45.

B. Development of Accounting Standards

1. Prior to the Securities Act of 1933 and the Securities Exchange Act of 1934, little financial reporting was required. The securities acts assigned the power of accounting rule-making for publicly held companies to the Securities and Exchange Commission (SEC). They also required most publicly held companies to be audited by independent CPAs. The SEC in turn delegated the rule-making authority to the American Institute of Accountants (later the AICPA), which formed the Committee on Accounting Procedure (CAP) and later the Accounting Principles Board (APB). The APB was terminated after 15 years because the increasing number of financial reporting issues demanded full-time attention. Consequently, the Financial Accounting Standards Board (FASB) was established in the early 1970s.
2. The FASB has seven salaried members, all having extensive experience in financial accounting, with four required to be CPAs. Each member severs all other business affiliations during his/her term. Two related organizations assist the FASB. The Financial Accounting Foundation (FAF) selects the board members, appoints an advisory council, raises supporting funds, and reviews the whole plan and operation periodically. The Financial Accounting Standards Advisory Council (FASAC) advises on priorities and proposed standards and evaluates the FASB's performance.

3. The board members determine the FASB's agenda by a majority decision. The members decide which subjects require attention and the order of their importance. A separate task force is appointed to consider each subject on the agenda. The task force is responsible for considering all aspects of a problem (in a discussion memorandum) rather than selecting from among the possible solutions.
4. Due process for the FASB's development of accounting standards includes public hearings on each issue. A 60-day notice of the hearings is given so that anyone wishing to prepare presentations will have sufficient time. A written position or outline must be submitted by those who wish to participate in the hearing.
5. All proposed statements of the FASB must be exposed to public comments (by means of an exposure draft) for 30 days before being made official. Official pronouncements require five or more affirmative votes. All dissenting opinions of board members must be published along with the statement. Each pronouncement includes the opinion of the FASB, background on the research results and the various solutions considered, the effective date, and the date of implementation.
6. FASB procedures may be summarized as follows:
   a. A project is placed on the agenda.
   b. A task force of experts defines specific problems, issues, and alternatives.
   c. The FASB technical staff conducts research and analysis.
   d. A **discussion memorandum** is drafted and released.
   e. A public hearing is held (usually 60 days after the discussion memorandum is released).
   f. Public response is analyzed and evaluated by the FASB.
   g. The FASB deliberates on various issues and prepares an **exposure draft** of a proposed statement.
   h. The exposure draft is released.
   i. There is at least a 30-day waiting period for public comment.
   j. All letters and comments are evaluated.
   k. The FASB reevaluates its position and revises the draft if necessary.
   l. The entire FASB gives final consideration to the draft.
   m. The FASB votes on the issuance of a **Statement of Financial Accounting Standards**.
7. Subsequently, the FASB may issue formal interpretations of its own statements. Like the original pronouncement, interpretations require at least five affirmative votes. Unlike the AICPA's accounting interpretations, FASB interpretations are developed and voted upon by the board itself and have the same status as Statements of Financial Accounting Standards. Accounting Research Bulletins (ARBs) issued by the CAP and APB Opinions continue to be authoritative until they are amended or superseded by FASB pronouncements.

8. **The SEC and Its Relationship with the FASB**. As mentioned earlier, the SEC was granted the power to establish accounting practices and procedures. The SEC originally delegated this authority to the accounting profession. With the creation of the FASB, the SEC issued Accounting Series Release No. 150, which acknowledged that the SEC would continue to look to the private sector (through the FASB) for leadership in establishing and improving accounting principles. However, the release also stated that the SEC would identify areas for which additional information is needed and would determine the appropriate methods of disclosure to meet those needs. The SEC is a strong supporter of the FASB. The Commission provides the FASB with advice when requested and has declared "that financial statements conforming to standards set by the FASB will be presumed to have authoritative support."

9. Groups of users of accounting standards are very influential in the development of accounting principles. Each group may want transactions and events to be accounted for in a particular way. Accordingly, they seek to persuade the FASB during the process of standard setting. Each of the following user groups has an effect on the establishment of accounting principles by the FASB.

   a. **Emerging Issues Task Force (EITF)**. In 1984, the FASB created the Emerging Issues Task Force to develop principles of accounting for new and unusual accounting issues. Its purpose is to resolve new accounting issues quickly. Essentially, the EITF identifies controversial accounting issues as they arise and determines whether the FASB needs to become involved in solving them. The EITF addresses short-term issues so that the FASB can concentrate on long-term issues. The EITF has 13 voting members and three nonvoting members; 10 votes are needed to reach a consensus position. Consensus positions are on the third level of the GAAP hierarchy for nongovernmental entities.

   b. **Accounting Standards Executive Committee (AcSEC)**. Following the demise of the APB, the AICPA created the AcSEC to act as its official representative in regard to accounting and reporting issues. Initially, the AcSEC promulgated Statements of Position (SOPs) on questions not addressed by the FASB. However, so many SOPs were issued that the FASB feared the AICPA would become a competing standard-setting body. Accordingly, the AcSEC now focuses on releasing issues papers that identify current accounting issues and present alternative treatments. If the FASB does not choose to address a topic in an issues paper, the AcSEC may still decide to promulgate an SOP. The AcSEC also publishes Practice Bulletins and Audit and Accounting Guides.

   c. **International Accounting Standards Committee (IASC)**. The IASC was established to harmonize accounting standards used by its 153 members in 112 countries. Currently, representatives of private-sector professional accounting bodies in 13 countries (or groups of countries) and up to four other organizations serve on the Board. An affirmative vote by three-fourths of the Board is required to publish a standard, and 41 have been issued to date. However, IASC pronouncements are not binding. Its authority is restricted to the willingness of foreign governments to adopt its standards. No members of the IASC are from national standard-setting bodies. Thus, the IASC's members have no direct influence on governmental legislation.

d. **Cost Accounting Standards Board (CASB)**. The CASB was created by Congress in 1970 with the objective of establishing cost accounting principles for federal defense contractors and subcontractors. The creation of the CASB was a response to complaints about inconsistent accounting practices of companies that had cost-plus contracts with the government. Many state governments also require adherence to CASB standards in cost-plus contract situations.

1) The standards established by the CASB are not necessarily acceptable for financial statement reporting purposes. They are required only for price-setting. GASB pronouncements are designed to mandate the reporting of useful information for users of governmental financial statements and to educate the public with respect to governmental financial reports.

2) Once the CASB standards are approved, they are published twice in the *Federal Register*. The standards become law 60 days after the second publication if Congress does not enact a contrary resolution.

3) The original CASB had five members, including the Comptroller General of the United States. Although the CASB was only a part-time board, it had a large staff of full-time employees. With its objectives significantly accomplished, the CASB was abolished in 1980, but many standards that were promulgated by the original CASB are still law and must be followed by government contractors.

a) In 1988, Congress reestablished the CASB as an independent body in the Office of Federal Procurement Policy, U.S. Office of Management and Budget. It has "exclusive authority to make, promulgate, amend, and rescind cost accounting standards and interpretations thereof" for negotiated contracts and subcontracts over $500,000.

b) CASB standards are incorporated into Federal Acquisition Regulations (FARs).

Governmental Accounting Standards Board (GASB). The Governmental Accounting Standards Board establishes standards for state and local governmental entities with the oversight of the Financial [illegible]ccounting Foundation. The GASB was formed to address the problem of compa[illegible]bility of governmental financial statements with those of private enterprises. G[illegible] pronouncements have the status of GAAP. To date, the GASB has issued 3[illegible] Statements.

1) Until changed by a GASB pronouncement, all currently effective statements from the National Council on Governmental Accounting and the AICPA remain in force.

The GASB uses Technical Bulletins to clarify, explain, or elaborate an underlying statement or interpretation. Technical Bulletins apply to issues that are too specific to be addressed by a statement.

The GASB has also issued Concepts Statements and Interpretations of GASB Statements.

ederal Accounting Standards Advisory Board (FASAB) was established 90 by the Secretary of the Treasury, the Director of the Office of agement and Budget (OMB), and the Comptroller General. In 1999, the A designated it as the accounting standard setter for the federal nment. In March 2000, its statements and interpretations of federal ial accounting standards were recognized as officially established nting principles for federal governmental entities.

g. **Other groups**. Other groups that have some influence on the development of accounting principles include the American Accounting Association (AAA), Institute of Management Accountants (IMA, formerly the National Association of Accountants or NAA), Financial Executives Institute (FEI), Congress, and the Internal Revenue Service (IRS).

1) The AAA affects the development of accounting theory through the influen its members exert on future accountants. Many of the AAA's members accounting professors who shape future principles by their current teaching activity and by promoting and sponsoring accounting resea The AAA has had a pronounced effect on accounting principles, but years may elapse before those effects become obvious.

2) The IMA and FEI affect the development of accounting principles th the publication of monthly magazines and various research studi and FEI committees respond to exposure drafts of the FASB, GA AcSEC.

3) The U.S. Congress affects accounting principles through the Inte Revenue Code. The IRS is one of the groups having the most accounting practice because an effort to minimize taxable inc accounting procedures is often inconsistent with good financi accounting.

a) The IRS also has the power to influence accounting prir adopting regulations affecting various practices for ta purposes.

10. Stop and review! You have completed the outline for this subunit. St choice questions 4 through 6 on page 46.

C. Annual Report

1. The SEC has authority to regulate external financial reporting by publicly companies. Nevertheless, its traditional role has been to promote dis than to exe se its power to establish accounting standards. Thus, the accou g profession (through the FASB) to promulgate GAAP.

a. To pr e disclosure, the SEC has adopted a system that integra info required to be presented in annual reports to shareh SEC Form 10-K is the annual report to the SEC).

2. Certain information must be included in both Form 10-K (due 90 days company's fiscal year-end) and the annual report to the shareholder

a. Information about the market for the company's common stock is principally traded, high and low sales prices, frequency and dividends, and number of shares

b. Selected financial data summarized for the past 5 years, with financial trends, including net sales or operating revenues, i continuing operations, total assets, long-term obligations, re stock, and cash dividends per share

c. **Management's discussion and analysis** (MD&A) of financial condition and results of operations

   1) This discussion must address liquidity, capital resources, results of operations, and the effects of inflation and changing prices.

   2) Forward-looking information (a forecast) is encouraged but not required.

      a) The SEC's safe harbor rule protects a company that issues an erroneous forecast if it is prepared on a reasonable basis and in good faith.

   3) The MD&A need not be audited.

   4) SEC Regulation S-K provides guidelines for MD&A disclosures.

d. Financial statements and supplementary data

   1) Standardized consolidated financial statements are required. They must be audited and include

      a) Balance sheets for the two most recent fiscal year-ends

      b) Statements of income, cash flows, and changes in shareholders' equity for the three most recent fiscal years

   2) The accountant certifying the financial statements must be independent of the management of the filing company. The accountant is not required to be a CPA, but (s)he must be registered with a state.

e. Changes in accountants and disagreements about accounting and financial disclosures

3. Other matters are required to be included in Form 10-K but not in the annual report. However, companies often include these items in their annual reports.

   a. A history and description of the business encompassing important recent developments, such as reorganizations, bankruptcies, and major dispositions or acquisitions of assets; information on industry segments and foreign operations; and principal products and services

   b. Locations and descriptions of physical properties

   c. Pending litigation, e.g., principal parties, allegations, and relief sought

   d. Matters submitted to shareholders for approval

   e. Information about officers and directors, for example, transactions with the company and executive compensation

   f. Ownership of the company's securities

   g. Description of certain other business relationships, such as those with related parties

   h. Exhibits, supporting schedules, and other reports

4. Management has the responsibility to adopt sound accounting policies and to establish and maintain internal controls that will record, process, summarize, and report transactions, events, and conditions consistent with the assertions in the financial statements. The fairness of the representations made therein is the responsibility of management alone because the transactions and the related assets, liabilities, and equity reflected are within management's direct knowledge and control.

5. The financial statements of a publicly traded company are accompanied by the report of the independent external auditors. Their audit is conducted in accordance with generally accepted auditing standards and is intended to provide assurance to creditors, investors, and other users of financial statements.

   a. The auditors' report is issued in accordance with the following generally accepted auditing standards of reporting:

      1) *The report shall state whether the financial statements are presented in accordance with GAAP.*

      2) *The report shall identify circumstances in which GAAP have not been consistently observed in the current period in relation to the preceding period.*

      3) *Informative disclosures in the financial statements are to be regarded as reasonably adequate unless otherwise stated in the report.*

      4) *The report shall either contain an expression of opinion regarding the financial statements, taken as a whole, or an assertion to the effect that an opinion cannot be expressed. When an overall opinion cannot be expressed, the reasons therefor should be stated. In all cases in which an auditor's name is associated with financial statements, the report should contain a clear-cut indication of the character of the auditor's work, if any, and the degree of responsibility the auditor is taking.*

   b. The following types of reports may be issued:

      1) **Unqualified opinion**. An unqualified opinion states that the financial statements present fairly, in all material respects, the financial position, results of operations, and cash flows of the entity in conformity with GAAP. This is the most common type of opinion expressed.

      2) **Explanatory language added to the auditor's standard report**. Certain circumstances, although not affecting the auditor's unqualified opinion, may require explanatory language (with or without a separate paragraph).

      3) **Qualified opinion**. A qualified opinion states that, **except for** the effects of the matter(s) to which the qualification relates, the financial statements present fairly, in all material respects, the financial position, results of operations, and cash flows of the entity in conformity with GAAP.

      4) **Adverse opinion**. An adverse opinion states that the financial statements do not present fairly the financial position, results of operations, or cash flows of the entity in conformity with GAAP.

      5) **Disclaimer of opinion**. A disclaimer of opinion states that the auditor does not express an opinion on the financial statements. It is appropriate when the scope of the audit is not sufficient to permit formation of an opinion or when the auditor is not independent.

   c. Following is the auditor's standard report expressing an unqualified opinion.

      1) Financial statements prepared in conformity with U.S. GAAP and audited in conformity with U.S. GAAS may be distributed in other nations. Accordingly, the reference to GAAP in the opinion paragraph may be replaced by the words "accounting principles generally accepted in the United States." The reference to GAAS in the middle paragraph may be replaced by the words "auditing standards generally accepted in the United States."

<u>Independent Auditor's Report</u>

To: <------------ Addressed to the Board of Directors and/or Shareholders

We have audited the accompanying balance sheets of X Company as of December 31, 20x2 and 20x1, and the related statements of income, retained earnings, and cash flows for the years then ended. These financial statements are the responsibility of the Company's management. Our responsibility is to express an opinion on these financial statements based on our audits.

We conducted our audits in accordance with generally accepted auditing standards. Those standards require that we plan and perform the audit to obtain reasonable assurance about whether the financial statements are free of material misstatement. An audit includes examining, on a test basis, evidence supporting the amounts and disclosures in the financial statements. An audit also includes assessing the accounting principles used and significant estimates made by management, as well as evaluating the overall financial statement presentation. We believe that our audits provide a reasonable basis for our opinion.

In our opinion, the financial statements referred to above present fairly, in all material respects, the financial position of X Company as of [at] December 31, 20x2 and 20x1, and the results of its operations and its cash flows for the years then ended in conformity with generally accepted accounting principles.

Signature <------------ May be signed, typed, or printed

Date <------------ Date of completion of field work

6. Stop and review! You have completed the outline for this subunit. Study multiple-choice questions 7 through 13 beginning on page 47.

D. SEC and Its Reporting Standards

1. The SEC was created by the Securities Exchange Act of 1934 to regulate the trading of securities and otherwise to enforce securities legislation.
   a. The basic purposes of the securities laws are to
      1) Prevent fraud and misrepresentation
      2) Require full and fair disclosure so investors can evaluate investments on their own
   b. Under the **Securities Act of 1933**, disclosure is made before the initial issuance of securities by registering with the SEC (i.e., initial filing) and disseminating a prospectus to potential investors.
   c. Under the **Securities Exchange Act of 1934**, disclosures regarding subsequent trading of securities are made by filing periodic reports that are available to the public for review.
   d. The SEC requires registration statements and reports to comply with certain accounting standards and policies.
      1) **Regulation S-X** governs the reporting of financial statements, including footnotes and schedules.
      2) **Regulation S-K** provides disclosure standards, including many of a nonfinancial nature. Regulation S-K also covers certain aspects of corporate annual reports to shareholders.

3) **Financial Reporting Releases (FRRs)** announce accounting and auditing matters of general interest.
   a) They provide explanations and clarifications of changes in accounting or auditing procedures used in reports filed with the SEC.
   b) These and **Accounting and Auditing Enforcement Releases (AAERs)** replace what used to be called Accounting Series Releases.
4) AAERs disclose enforcement actions involving accountants.
5) **Staff Accounting Bulletins (SABs)** are promulgated as interpretations to be followed by the SEC staff in administering disclosure requirements.
   a) SABs are not requirements to be followed by registrants.

2. **Integrated Disclosure System**

a. In 1982, a revised disclosure system became effective.
   1) Previously, disclosures were duplicative, i.e., required similar information in different formats under the 1933 and 1934 acts.
   2) To alleviate this problem, the integrated disclosure system
      a) Standardizes the financial statements
      b) Uses a Basic Information Package (BIP) common to most of the filings
      c) Allows incorporation by reference from the annual shareholders' report to the annual SEC report (Form 10-K)

b. Standardized financial statements are required.
   1) They must be audited and include
      a) Balance sheets for the 2 most recent fiscal year-ends
      b) Statements of income, cash flows, and changes in equity for the 3 most recent fiscal years
   2) They are required in the annual shareholders' report as well as in forms filed with the SEC.
   3) The accountant certifying the financial statements must be independent of the management of the filing company. The accountant is not required to be a CPA, but (s)he must be registered with a state.

c. The **Basic Information Package (BIP)** includes the following:
   1) Standardized financial statements
   2) Selected financial information
      a) Columnar format for the preceding 5 fiscal years
      b) Presentation of financial trends through comparison of key information from year to year
   3) **Management's discussion and analysis** of financial condition and results of operations
      a) This information addresses such matters as liquidity, capital resources, results of operations, effects of tax legislation, and the impact of changing prices.
      b) Forward-looking information (a forecast) is encouraged but not required.

4) Market price of securities and dividends
   a) Principal market in which security is traded
   b) High and low sales prices for each quarter in the last 2 years
   c) Most recent number of shareholders
   d) Frequency and amount of dividends in the last 2 years
   e) Any restrictions on the payment of dividends

5) Description of business
   a) Fundamental developments for past 5 years, e.g., organization, reorganizations, bankruptcies, and major dispositions or acquisitions of assets
   b) Financial information of industry segments, and also foreign and domestic operations
   c) Narrative description including
      i) Principal products or services for each industry segment and principal markets for them
      ii) Total revenues of each class of products equaling 10% or more of consolidated revenue (15% if consolidated revenue is not in excess of $50,000,000)
      iii) Other information material to the business on the basis of industry segments

6) Locations and descriptions of physical properties

7) Pending litigation, e.g., principal parties, allegations, and relief sought

8) Management
   a) General data for each director and officer
   b) Financial transactions with the company involving amounts in excess of $60,000
   c) Remuneration for the five highest paid directors and officers whose compensation exceeds $50,000 (including personal benefits)

9) Security holdings of directors, officers, and those owning 5% or more of the security

10) Matters submitted to shareholders for approval

11) Description of certain business relationships, such as those with related parties

3. **Registration (Initial Filing)**

a. The issuer must register new issuances of securities with the SEC.

   1) **Form S-1** is used for the registration statement for companies that have never registered securities.
      a) Incorporation by reference is usually not allowed, and all material must be included.

2) **Form S-2** is a shorter form for companies that have been reporting to the SEC (Form 10-K, etc.) for at least 3 years and have done so on a timely basis.

   a) Form S-2 allows BIP to be incorporated by reference from the latest annual shareholders' report.

3) **Form S-3** is another short form for companies that meet the requirements for Form S-2 and have at least $50,000,000 of stock held by nonaffiliates (or at least $100,000,000 with an annual trading volume of 3,000,000 or more shares).

   a) Form S-3 allows most information to be incorporated by reference from other filings with the SEC.

4) Other forms

   a) **Form S-4** is a simplified form for business combinations.

      i) **Form F-4** is to be used by foreign registrants in business combinations.

      ii) **Form N-14** is to be used by investment companies to register securities in business combinations.

   b) **Form S-8** is for securities offered to employees under a stock option or other employee benefit plan.

   c) **Form S-11** is used by real estate investment trusts and real estate companies.

   d) **Form SB-1** is used by certain small business issuers to register up to $10 million of securities provided that no more than $10 million has been registered in the preceding 12 months. A small business issuer has revenues and public market float of less than $25 million.

   e) **Form SB-2** is also for small business issuers. It has no limit on the dollar amount of securities that may be sold.

5) Filings become public information.

6) Securities may not be offered for sale to the public until the registration is effective.

   a) The registration statement is examined by the Division of Corporation Finance.

   b) Registration becomes effective 20 days after filing unless an amendment is filed or the SEC issues a stop order.

   c) A preliminary prospectus is allowed that contains the same information as a regular prospectus (prices are omitted) but is clearly marked in red. Thus, it is called a **red herring prospectus**.

b. Registration forms requirements (especially Form S-1)

1) Basic information package
2) Plan of distribution, name of underwriter, use of broker, and commissions
3) Use of proceeds and details of offerings other than cash
4) Description of the capital structure of the registrant
5) Risk factors
6) Signatures of

a) Issuer
b) Principal executive, financial, and accounting officers
c) Majority of board of directors

c. The **prospectus** is part of the registration statement.

1) Its purpose is to provide investors with information to make an informed investment decision.

2) However, it usually may be presented in a more condensed or summarized form than Form S-1.

4. **Form 10** is used to register securities under the 1934 act.

a. Securities must be registered if they are traded in one of the ways listed below.

1) On a national securities exchange

2) Over the counter if the issuer has assets in excess of $5,000,000 and there are 500 or more shareholders

b. An issuer may voluntarily register its securities.

c. An issuer may deregister its securities if its shareholders decrease to fewer than 300 or if its shareholders are fewer than 500 and it had less than $10,000,000 in assets for each of the three most recent fiscal year-ends.

d. Banks must also register their securities, but they file with the appropriate banking authority, not with the SEC.

e. The required contents of Form 10 are

1) Basic information package
2) Other information required for Form S-1

5. **Form 10-K** is the annual report to the SEC. It must be

a. Filed within 90 days of corporation's year-end
b. Certified by an independent accountant
c. Signed by the following:

1) Principal executive, financial, and accounting officers
2) Majority of the board of directors

d. Presented with the basic information package

1) Information contained in the annual report to shareholders may be incorporated by reference.

2) Information contained in proxy statements may also be incorporated by reference into Form 10-K because the proxy statement is a published source readily available to the shareholders and investing public.

6. **Form 10-Q** is the quarterly report to the SEC.
   a. It must be filed for each of the first three quarters of the year within 45 days after the end of each quarter.
   b. Financial statements need not be audited by an independent accountant, but they must be prepared in accordance with APB 28, *Interim Financial Reporting*. However, an SEC registrant must obtain a review by an independent auditor of interim financial information that will be included in a quarterly report to the SEC.
   c. Also required are changes during the quarter, for example,
      1) Legal proceedings
      2) Increase, decrease, or change in securities or indebtedness
      3) Matters submitted to shareholders for a vote
      4) Exhibits and reports on Form 8-K
      5) Other material events not reported on Form 8-K
   d. SEC Staff Accounting Bulletin 74 requires a public company to disclose in its registration statement and in Form 10-Q the anticipated effect of recently issued accounting standards on financial statements when they are adopted in a future period.
7. **Form 8-K** is a current report to disclose material events.
   a. In certain cases, it must be filed within 15 calendar days after the material event occurs. However, a change in independent accountants or the resignation of a director must be reported within 5 business days.
   b. Material events
      1) Change in control (15 calendar days)
      2) Acquisition or disposition of a significant amount of assets not in the ordinary course of business (15 calendar days)
      3) Bankruptcy or receivership (15 calendar days)
      4) Resignation of directors (5 business days)
      5) A change in the registrant's certifying accountant (5 business days). The reporting requirements are
         a) Date
         b) Disclosure of any disagreements in the prior 2 years
         c) Disclosure of certain reportable events, e.g., the former accountants' concerns about internal control or the reliability of management's representations
         d) Disclosure of prior consultations with the new accountants
         e) Whether a disagreement or reportable event was discussed with the audit committee
         f) Whether the company authorized the former accountants to respond fully to the new accountants' inquiries about disagreements
         g) Whether the former accountants were dismissed, resigned, or refused to seek reemployment

h) Disclosure of any qualification of reports in the prior 2 years

i) Letter from the former accountant indicating agreement (or disagreement) with the above. The letter must be submitted within 10 business days.

j) Whether the decision to change was recommended or approved by the audit committee or the board of directors

6) Other events. Reporting of "other events" is optional, so no mandatory time for filing is established. Nevertheless, registrants are encouraged to file promptly and with due regard for the accuracy, completeness, and currency of the information.

8. **Shareholder Proposal Rules**

a. Minority shareholders are permitted to submit proposals in a proxy statement to be voted upon at meetings of shareholders.

b. However, the SEC has placed limitations on this right of shareholders because of abuses. For example, without these restrictions, an owner of one share of stock can submit a proposal supporting his/her favorite political cause. Although the proposal may be certain to be defeated, the shareholder may receive much free publicity.

c. To submit a proposal, a shareholder or group of shareholders must have owned at least 1% of the voting shares or $1,000 in market value of voting securities, whichever is less, for at least 1 year and must continue to own them through the date of the meeting.

d. A shareholder may submit only one proposal per meeting to an issuer.

e. Persons engaged in proxy contests (persons who deliver written proxy materials to holders of more than 25% of a class of voting securities) are ineligible to use the shareholder proposal process.

f. Proposals may be rejected if

1) They are not a proper subject for shareholder voting under state law.

2) They relate to operations that account for less than 5% of an issuer's total assets or less than 5% of its net earnings and gross sales for the current year, and are not otherwise significant to the business.

g. To be resubmitted to shareholders in a proxy statement, proposals that have been previously voted down must be approved by at least 5% of the shareholders if submitted once before, 8% if submitted twice before, and 10% if submitted three times before.

9. **Shelf Registration.** SEC Rule 415 (under the Securities Act of 1933) allows corporations to file registration statements covering a stipulated amount of securities that may be issued over the 2-year effective period of the statement. The securities are placed on the shelf and issued at an opportune moment without the necessity of filing a new registration statement, observing a 20-day waiting period, or preparing a new prospectus. The issuer is required only to provide updating amendments or to refer investors to quarterly and annual statements filed with the SEC. It is most advantageous to large corporations that frequently offer securities to the public.

10. **Proxy Solicitations**
    a. A proxy is a written grant of authority by a shareholder allowing the holder of the proxy to vote for the shareholder at a meeting. A proxy is revoked by signing a later proxy, by personally voting the shares, or upon death.
    b. A formal proxy statement must be sent before or with any proxy solicitation.
        1) A proxy solicitation is a request by any person (usually management or someone trying to take over the management) to a shareholder for that shareholder's proxy to vote at a corporate meeting.
    c. The proxy statement must
        1) Contain disclosure of all material facts of matters to be voted upon at the meeting
        2) Include an annual shareholders' report if the solicitation is on behalf of the current management at a meeting at which directors are to be elected
        3) Be filed with the SEC
        4) Contain representations by the audit committee about its oversight function, for example, whether the members discussed the financial statements with management and the outside auditors
    d. Management must mail proxy materials of insurgents, if so requested and the insurgents pay the expenses.
11. Stop and review! You have completed the outline for this subunit. Study multiple-choice questions 14 through 28 beginning on page 49.

E. Public Reporting Standards

1. According to the AICPA, **generally accepted accounting principles** (GAAP) are the "conventions, rules, and procedures necessary to define accepted accounting practice at a particular time." They include both the broad guidelines and the detailed practices and procedures promulgated by the profession that provide uniform standards to measure financial presentations (**AU 411**, *The Meaning of "Present Fairly in Conformity with Generally Accepted Accounting Principles" in the Independent Auditor's Report*).
2. AU 411 presents GAAP hierarchies for nongovernmental entities, state and local governments, and federal governmental entities. The nongovernmental hierarchy is given below. Conduct Rule 203 of the AICPA's *Code of Professional Conduct* provides that a member shall not express assurances about conformity with GAAP if the financial statements contain a material departure from a principle promulgated by bodies designated by the AICPA Council to establish such principles. However, in unusual circumstances, a departure may be permissible if literal application of a principle would be misleading. The FASB is the body designated by the AICPA Council to promulgate principles for nongovernmental entities, and the pronouncements in category 2.a. on the next page (officially established accounting principles) constitute principles as contemplated in Conduct Rule 203. **Established accounting principles** form the first four levels of the GAAP hierarchy for nongovernmental entities.

a. Category (a) includes the primary sources of nongovernmental GAAP: FASB Statements and Interpretations, APB Opinions, and AICPA Accounting Research Bulletins.

NOTE: SEC pronouncements have category (a) authority, but they apply only to SEC registrants.

b. Category (b) consists of FASB Technical Bulletins and, if cleared by the FASB, AICPA Audit and Accounting Guides and AICPA Statements of Position.

c. Category (c) includes consensus positions of the FASB Emerging Issues Task Force and, if cleared by the FASB, AICPA Accounting Standards Executive Committee (AcSEC) Practice Bulletins.

d. Category (d) consists of AICPA accounting interpretations, "Qs and As" published by the FASB staff, and practices widely recognized and prevalent generally or in the industry.

e. **Other accounting literature** may be considered in the absence of a source of established accounting principles. Other accounting literature includes FASB Concepts Statements (ordinarily the most influential source in this category); AICPA Issues Papers; International Accounting Standards Committee Statements; GASB Statements, Interpretations, and Technical Bulletins; FASAB Statements, Interpretations, and Technical Bulletins; pronouncements of other professional associations or regulatory agencies; AICPA Technical Practice Aids; and accounting textbooks, handbooks, and articles.

3. **Comprehensive Bases of Accounting Other than GAAP**. The applicable pronouncement is **AU 623** (SAS 62), *Special Reports*. A comprehensive basis of accounting other than GAAP may be

a. A basis of accounting that the reporting entity uses to comply with the requirements or financial reporting provisions of a regulatory agency

b. A basis of accounting used for tax purposes

c. The cash basis, and modifications of the cash basis having substantial support, such as recording depreciation on fixed assets or accruing income taxes

d. A definite set of criteria having substantial support that is applied to all material items, for example, the price-level basis

4. Financial statements prepared in conformity with a comprehensive basis of accounting other than GAAP should be suitably titled.

a. Terms such as "balance sheet," "statement of financial position," "statement of cash flows," and similar unmodified titles imply that the statements were prepared in conformity with GAAP.

1) AU 623 suggests that cash-basis financial statements might be appropriately titled "statement of assets and liabilities arising from cash transactions" or "statement of revenue collected and expenses paid."

2) A statement prepared in conformity with provisions of a statutory or regulatory agency might be titled "statement of income -- statutory basis."

b. Suitable titles avoid the misrepresentation that the financial statements were prepared in accordance with GAAP.

5. Financial statements prepared on a comprehensive basis of accounting other than GAAP should include a summary of significant accounting policies, including

a. Discussion of the comprehensive basis used to prepare the financial statements and how that basis differs from GAAP.

6. Stop and review! You have completed the outline for this subunit. Study multiple-choice questions 29 and 30 on page 54.

F. Selected Disclosures in Financial Statements

1. **APB 22**, *Disclosure of Accounting Policies*, requires that all significant accounting policies of a reporting entity be disclosed as an integral part of its financial statements.
   a. Disclosure of significant accounting policies is required when
      1) A selection has been made from existing acceptable alternatives.
      2) A policy is unique to the industry in which the entity operates, even if the policy is predominantly followed in that industry.
      3) GAAP have been applied in an unusual or innovative way.
   b. Certain items are explicitly listed in APB 22 as commonly required disclosures in a summary of significant accounting policies.
      1) These items include the basis of consolidation, depreciation methods, amortization of intangibles, inventory pricing, recognition of profit on long-term construction-type contracts, and recognition of revenue from franchising and leasing operations.
      2) APB 22 recognizes that financial statement disclosure of accounting policies should not duplicate details presented elsewhere in the financial statements. For example, the summary of significant policies should not contain the composition of plant assets or inventories or the maturity dates of long-term debt. Instead, the summary can refer to details about matters that are presented elsewhere in the financial statements.
   c. According to SFAS 95, an enterprise must disclose its policy for determining which items are cash equivalents.
2. **APB 28**, *Interim Financial Reporting*, requires certain minimum disclosures of interim data by public companies: sales; provisions for income taxes; extraordinary items; cumulative effect of accounting changes; net income; comprehensive income; basic and diluted EPS; seasonal revenues, costs, or expenses; significant changes in estimates or provisions for income taxes; disposal of a segment; unusual or infrequent items; contingent items; unusual or infrequently occurring items; changes in accounting principles or estimates; significant changes in financial information; and certain disclosures about reportable operating segments. Moreover, if condensed balance sheet or cash flow data are not presented, significant changes in liquid assets, net working capital, long-term liabilities, or equity should be disclosed. Interim financial statements are considered a part of the annual period. Only a few modifications to the criteria for the recognition of revenue and expense for annual reporting purposes are permitted.
   a. Revenue recognition criteria are the same as for annual statements.
   b. Modifications of expense recognition are inconsequential.
      1) Gross profit methods can be used to estimate inventory.
      2) Declines in inventory value may be ignored if they are temporary.
      3) Liquidation of LIFO base-period inventory may be accounted for at current prices if the inventory will be replaced prior to year-end.
   c. The main concern is to prorate nonrecurring annual charges equitably to interim periods, e.g., year-end bonuses, vacation pay, major repairs.
      1) Seasonal variations should be disclosed in notes or by use of 12-month, year-to-date statements. Extraordinary items are reported separately in the interim period in which they occur.

d. Taxes are based on the expected annual effective rate after all tax-planning tools are implemented and include the effect of credits, special deductions, etc. This rate also includes the effect of any expected year-end valuation allowance for deferred tax assets related to originating deductible temporary differences and carryforwards during the year (FASB Interpretation No. 18 and SFAS 109).

1) Each interim period's tax is the revised annual tax rate times year-to-date income, minus tax expense recognized in prior interim periods.

2) SFAS 109 amended APB 28 and FASB Interpretation No. 18. It provides that a tax benefit is recognized for a loss arising early in the year if the benefits are expected to be (a) realized during the year or (b) recognizable as a deferred tax asset at year-end. A tax benefit is recognized for a loss arising in an interim period if realization is more likely than not. A valuation allowance must be recognized if it is likely that some portion of a deferred tax asset will not be realized. These principles are applied in determining the estimated tax benefit of an ordinary loss for the fiscal year used to calculate the annual effective tax rate and year-to-date tax benefit of a loss.

3) Taxes on all items other than continuing operations are determined at incremental rates; i.e., their marginal effect on taxes is calculated.

e. Accounting changes in interim periods are governed by SFAS 3.

1) Cumulative-effect-type changes are reported as occurring in the first interim period, and all subsequent interim periods reflect the new principle. Interim periods are restated no matter when the change was made.

a) The cumulative effect on the beginning retained earnings of the first interim period is calculated.

2) Restatement-type accounting changes are the same as for changes in annual statements, i.e., per APB 20, *Accounting Changes*.

3) All disclosures required by APB 20 for accounting changes in annual statements are required in interim statements.

3. **SFAS 47**, *Disclosure of Long-Term Obligations*, requires that a company disclose commitments under unconditional purchase obligations that are associated with suppliers.

a. Unconditional purchase obligations are commitments to transfer funds in the future for fixed or minimum amounts of goods or services at fixed or minimum prices.

b. In addition to the disclosures required by other official pronouncements, SFAS 47 requires the disclosure of the following information for recorded obligations and redeemable stock for each of the 5 years following the date of the latest balance sheet presented:

1) The aggregate amount of payments for unconditional purchase obligations

2) The aggregate amount of maturities and sinking-fund requirements for all long-term borrowings

3) The amount at which all issues of stock are redeemable at fixed or determinable prices on fixed or determinable dates

c. If an unconditional purchase obligation is not presented in the balance sheet, certain disclosures are required, including

1) The nature and term of the obligation
2) The variable components of the obligation
3) The amounts purchased under the obligation for each period an income statement is presented
4) The amount of the fixed and determinable portion of the obligation at the latest balance sheet date and, if determinable, for each of the 5 succeeding fiscal years

4. **SFAS 57**, *Related Party Disclosures*, requires the disclosure of material related-party transactions other than compensation arrangements (officers' salaries and expenses), expense allowances, and other similar items in the ordinary course of business.

a. According to SFAS 57, related-party transactions include transactions between

1) A parent and its subsidiaries
2) Subsidiaries of a common parent
3) An enterprise and employee trusts managed by or under the trusteeship of the enterprise's management
4) An enterprise and its principal owners, management, or members of their immediate families
5) Affiliates
6) An enterprise and its equity-based investees
7) An enterprise and any other entity if one party can significantly influence the other to the extent that one party may be prevented from fully pursuing its own interests
8) Parties all of which can be significantly influenced by another party

b. SFAS 57 requires disclosure of

1) The nature of the relationship involved
2) A description of the transactions for each period an income statement is presented and such other information as is deemed necessary to an understanding of the effects of the transactions
3) The dollar amounts of transactions for each period an income statement is presented and the effects of any change in the method of establishing their terms
4) Amounts due from or to related parties as of the date of each balance sheet, including the terms of settlement
5) Certain tax information required by SFAS 109 if the enterprise is part of a group that files a consolidated tax return

5. **SFAS 107**, *Disclosures about Fair Value of Financial Instruments*, as amended by SFAS 133, requires certain entities to disclose the fair value of financial instruments, whether or not they are recognized in the balance sheet, if it is practicable to estimate such fair values.

   a. If estimating fair value is not practicable, disclosures include information pertinent to estimating the fair value of the financial instrument or class of financial instruments, such as the carrying amount, effective interest rate, and maturity. The reasons that estimating the fair value is not practicable should also be disclosed.

   b. Under **SFAS 126**, disclosures are optional if the entity is nonpublic, has total assets of less than $100 million, and has not held or issued any derivative financial instruments, other than loan commitments, during the reporting period.

   c. SFASs 107 and 133 define a **financial instrument** as cash, evidence of an ownership interest in an entity, or a contract that both

      1) Imposes on one entity a contractual obligation

         a) To deliver cash or another financial instrument to a second entity or

         b) To exchange other financial instruments on potentially unfavorable terms with the second entity, and

      2) Conveys to that second entity a contractual right

         a) To receive cash or another financial instrument from the first entity or

         b) To exchange other financial instruments on potentially favorable terms with the first entity.

   d. Disclosures about fair value are not required for the following: employers' and plans' obligations for pension, postemployment, and other postretirement benefits; employee stock option and stock purchase plans; and other deferred compensation arrangements. Also exempt are substantively extinguished debt, insurance contracts (but not financial guarantees and investment contracts), leases, warranties, unconditional purchase obligations, equity-based investments, minority interests in consolidated entities, and equities issued by the reporting entity and classified in shareholders' equity.

      1) Trade receivables and payables are also exempt if the carrying value approximates fair value.

   e. **Quoted market prices**, if available, are the best evidence of the fair value.

   f. Ordinarily, disclosures should not net the fair values of financial instruments even if they are of the same class or are related, e.g., by a risk management strategy. However, exceptions are made for **rights of setoff** and for **master netting arrangements** executed with the same counterparty (in regard to such items as forward contracts, interest-rate swaps, currency swaps, and options).

g. **Credit risk** is the risk of accounting loss from a financial instrument because of the possibility that a loss may occur from the failure of another party to perform according to the terms of a contract. In most instances, an entity must disclose all significant **concentrations of credit risk** arising from all financial instruments, whether from one counterparty or groups. Group concentrations arise when multiple counterparties have similar activities and economic characteristics that would cause their ability to meet obligations to be similarly affected by changes in conditions. Disclosures include

1) Information about the (shared) activity, region, or economic characteristic that identifies the concentration.

2) The maximum loss due to credit risk if parties failed completely to perform and the security, if any, proved to be of no value.

3) The policy of requiring security, information about access to that security, and the nature and a brief description of the security.

4) The policy of entering into master netting arrangements to mitigate the credit risk, information about them, and a description of the terms, including the extent to which they reduce the maximum amount of loss.

h. The requirements in 5.g. do not apply to financial instruments of pension plans, various deferred compensation arrangements, insurance contracts, warranties, and unconditional purchase obligations.

i. SFAS 107 (as amended) encourages, but does not require, disclosure of quantitative information about the **market risks** of financial instruments that is consistent with the way an entity manages those risks.

6. Stop and review! You have completed the outline for this subunit. Study multiple-choice questions 31 through 46 beginning on page 54.

G. Reporting Issues for Multinational Companies

1. A U.S. corporation that operates a business through a foreign branch or division must report the income from that foreign operation on the company's U.S. income tax return. This foreign income will be taxed the same way as domestic income.

2. A foreign subsidiary's income will not be taxed to the U.S. parent until it is distributed as a dividend to the parent.

3. All U.S. companies doing business in foreign countries will be taxed by the foreign countries on their foreign income.

   a. Taxes may be levied on dividend income, undistributed income, or the value added to goods and services.

   b. Many countries lower taxes on foreign companies to increase incentives to foreign investors.

   c. The U.S. has entered into tax treaties with many foreign governments to avoid international double taxation and prevent tax evasion.

4. **SFAS 52**, *Foreign Currency Translation*, requires a foreign subsidiary of a U.S. parent company to determine a functional currency for its operations, measure financial statement elements in terms of that currency, and translate those amounts into the reporting currency. For an outline, see Study Unit 7, subunit F.

5. Stop and review! You have completed the outline for this subunit. Study multiple-choice questions 47 and 48 on page 60.

MULTIPLE-CHOICE QUESTIONS

A. External Financial Reporting

1. Financial statement users with a direct economic interest in a specific business include

A. Financial advisers.

B. Regulatory bodies.

C. Stock markets.

D. Suppliers.

The correct answer is (D). *(Publisher)*

REQUIRED: The financial statement users with direct economic interests.

DISCUSSION: Users with direct interests include investors or potential investors, suppliers and creditors, employees, and management.

Answers (A), (B), and (C) are incorrect because financial advisers, regulatory bodies, and stock markets have indirect interests.

2. Which of the following is not a need of financial statement users?

A. Financial advisers and analysts need financial statements to help investors evaluate particular investments.

B. Stock exchanges need financial statements to set a firm's stock price.

C. Regulatory agencies need financial statements to evaluate price changes for regulated industries.

D. Employees need financial information to negotiate wages and fringe benefits.

The correct answer is (B). *(Publisher)*

REQUIRED: The item not a need of financial statement users.

DISCUSSION: Investors' purchases and sales set stock prices. Stock exchanges need financial statements to evaluate whether to accept a firm's stock for listing or whether to suspend trading in the stock.

Answer (A) is incorrect because financial advisers use financial statements for evaluating investments. Answer (C) is incorrect because regulatory agencies use financial statements for rate making. Answer (D) is incorrect because employees use financial statements for labor negotiations.

3. A primary objective of external financial reporting is

A. Direct measurement of the value of a business enterprise.

B. Provision of information that is useful to present and potential investors, creditors, and others in making rational financial decisions regarding the enterprise.

C. Establishment of rules for accruing liabilities.

D. Direct measurement of the enterprise's stock price.

The correct answer is (B). *(CMA, adapted)*

REQUIRED: The primary objective of external financial reporting.

DISCUSSION: According to the FASB's Statement of Financial Accounting Concepts (SFAC) 1, the objectives are to provide information that (1) is useful to present and potential investors, creditors, and others in making rational financial decisions regarding the enterprise; (2) helps those parties in assessing the amounts, timing, and uncertainty of prospective cash receipts from dividends or interest and the proceeds from sale, redemption, or maturity of securities or loans; and (3) concerns the economic resources of an enterprise, the claims thereto, and the effects of transactions, events, and circumstances that change its resources and claims thereto.

Answer (A) is incorrect because SFAC 1 states that financial reporting is not designed to measure directly the value of a business. Answer (C) is incorrect because, while rules for accruing liabilities are a practical concern, the establishment of such rules is not a primary objective of external reporting. Answer (D) is incorrect because the objectives of financial accounting are unrelated to the measurement of stock prices; stock prices are a product of stock market forces.

B. Development of Accounting Standards

4. Accounting standard setting in the U.S. is

A. Done primarily by the Securities and Exchange Commission.

B. Done primarily by the private sector.

C. The responsibility of the public sector.

D. Done primarily by the International Accounting Standards Committee.

The correct answer is (B). *(CMA, adapted)*

REQUIRED: The source of U.S. accounting standards.

DISCUSSION: Accounting standards for nongovernmental entities in the United States are set primarily by the private sector. The principal standard setters are the FASB and the AICPA's AcSEC. The SEC and the IRS have the authority to set accounting standards, but neither has exercised significant authority.

Answer (A) is incorrect because, although the SEC was granted the authority to establish accounting practices and procedures in 1934, it delegated this authority to the accounting profession. Accounting Series Release 150 acknowledged that the SEC would continue to look to the private sector for leadership in establishing and improving accounting principles. Answer (C) is incorrect because the public sector, through the SEC, has delegated accounting standard setting to the private sector. Answer (D) is incorrect because the IASC works to encourage uniform accounting principles worldwide, but it has no authority in a particular country.

5. When establishing financial accounting standards, the FASB

A. Issues an exposure draft as a final statement.

B. Holds a public hearing usually 60 days after the discussion memorandum is released.

C. Consults only with the SEC before the statement is released.

D. Delegates responsibility to the SEC.

The correct answer is (B). *(Publisher)*

REQUIRED: The true statement about standard setting by the FASB.

DISCUSSION: After a group of experts has defined specific problems and a range of solutions for an agenda item, the FASB's staff conducts research and analysis and drafts a discussion memorandum. The FASB then holds a public hearing usually 60 days after the discussion memorandum is released.

Answer (A) is incorrect because the exposure draft is usually amended following evaluation of public comment. Answer (C) is incorrect because all interested parties have an opportunity to comment. Answer (D) is incorrect because the SEC has effectively delegated standard-setting authority to the FASB.

6. The International Accounting Standards Committee (IASC)

A. Directly influences governmental legislation regarding accounting standards.

B. Develops binding pronouncements for its members.

C. Is composed of members from national standard-setting bodies.

D. Establishes uniform accounting standards to eliminate reporting differences among nations.

The correct answer is (D). *(Publisher)*

REQUIRED: The correct statement about the IASC.

DISCUSSION: The IASC was established to harmonize accounting standards used by member countries. Currently, representatives of professional accounting bodies in 13 nations (or groups of nations) and up to four other organizations are voting members of the IASC's Board, and 41 standards have been issued. An affirmative vote by three-fourths of the IASC's Board is required to publish a standard. However, IASC pronouncements are not binding.

Answer (A) is incorrect because the IASC has no direct influence on governmental legislation. Answer (B) is incorrect because the IASC's authority is restricted to the willingness of participating and other countries to adopt its standards. Answer (C) is incorrect because the IASC is composed of members from various national professional accounting organizations, such as the AICPA.

C. Annual Report

7. Regarding financial accounting for public companies, the role of the Securities and Exchange Commission (SEC) as currently practiced is to

A. Make rules and regulations regarding filings with the SEC but not to regulate annual or quarterly reports to shareholders.

B. Regulate financial disclosures for corporate, state, and municipal reporting.

C. Make rules and regulations pertaining more to disclosure of financial information than to the establishment of accounting recognition and measurement principles.

D. Develop and promulgate most generally accepted accounting principles.

The correct answer is (C). *(CMA, adapted)*

REQUIRED: The role of the SEC as it applies to financial accounting for public companies.

DISCUSSION: The SEC has the authority to regulate external financial reporting. Nevertheless, its traditional role has been to promote disclosure rather than to exercise its power to establish accounting recognition and measurement principles. Its objective is to allow the accounting profession (through the FASB) to establish principles and then to ensure that corporations abide by those principles. This approach allows investors to evaluate investments for themselves.

Answer (A) is incorrect because the SEC regulates both quarterly and annual reporting. Answer (B) is incorrect because the SEC has no jurisdiction over state and municipal reporting. Answer (D) is incorrect because the SEC has allowed the accounting profession to develop and promulgate GAAP.

8. Many firms include 5 or 10 years of financial data in their annual reports. This information

A. Is the forecast of future business.

B. Highlights trends in the financial statements.

C. Highlights inventory valuation methods used by the firm.

D. Is required by generally accepted accounting principles.

The correct answer is (B). *(CMA, adapted)*

REQUIRED: The true statement about financial data in annual reports.

DISCUSSION: The information required by the SEC to be reported in Part II of Form 10-K and in the annual report includes a 5-year summary of selected financial data. If trends are relevant, management's discussion and analysis should emphasize the summary. Favorable and unfavorable trends and significant events and uncertainties should be identified.

Answer (A) is incorrect because the required data are for prior periods. Answer (C) is incorrect because the required data include net sales or operating revenues, income from continuing operations, total assets, long-term obligations, redeemable preferred stock, and cash dividends per share. Answer (D) is incorrect because the data are required by the SEC.

9. The content of the Management's Discussion and Analysis (MD&A) section of an annual report is

A. Mandated by pronouncements of the Financial Accounting Standards Board.

B. Mandated by regulations of the Securities and Exchange Commission.

C. Reviewed by independent auditors.

D. Mandated by regulations of the Internal Revenue Service.

The correct answer is (B). *(CMA, adapted)*

REQUIRED: The true statement about the MD&A section of the annual financial report.

DISCUSSION: The content of the MD&A section is mandated by regulations of the SEC. The MD&A, standard financial statements, summarized financial data for at least 5 years, and other matters must be included in annual reports to shareholders and in Form 10-K filed with the SEC. Forward-looking information in the form of forecasts is encouraged in the MD&A but not required.

Answers (A) and (D) are incorrect because the MD&A is required by the SEC. Answer (C) is incorrect because auditors are expected to read (not review or audit) the contents of the MD&A to be certain it contains no material inconsistencies with the financial statements.

10. The Management's Discussion and Analysis (MD&A) section of an annual report

A. Includes the company president's letter.

B. Covers three financial aspects of a firm's business: liquidity, capital resources, and results of operations.

C. Is a technical analysis of past results and a defense of those results by management.

D. Covers marketing and product line issues.

The correct answer is (B). *(CMA, adapted)*

REQUIRED: The content of the MD&A section of the annual report.

DISCUSSION: The MD&A section is included in SEC filings. It addresses in a nonquantified manner the prospects of the company. The SEC examines it with care to determine that management has disclosed material information affecting the company's future results. Disclosures about commitments and events that may affect operations or liquidity are mandatory. Thus, the MD&A section pertains to liquidity, capital resources, and results of operations.

Answer (A) is incorrect because the MD&A section may be separate from the president's letter. Answer (C) is incorrect because a technical analysis and a defense are not required in the MD&A section; it is more forward looking. Answer (D) is incorrect because the MD&A section does not have to include marketing and product line issues.

11. The Securities and Exchange Commission continues to encourage management to provide forward-looking information to users of financial statements and has a safe harbor rule that

A. Protects a company that may present an erroneous forecast as long as the forecast is prepared on a reasonable basis and in good faith.

B. Allows injured users of the forecasted information to sue the company for damages but protects management from personal liability.

C. Delays disclosure of such forward-looking information until all major uncertainties have been resolved.

D. Bars competition from using the information to gain a competitive advantage.

The correct answer is (A). *(CMA, adapted)*

REQUIRED: The true statement about the SEC's safe harbor rule applicable to forward-looking information.

DISCUSSION: The SEC does not require forecasts but encourages companies to issue projections of future economic performance. To encourage the publication of such information in SEC filings, the safe harbor rule was established to protect a company that prepares a forecast on a reasonable basis and in good faith.

Answer (B) is incorrect because both the company and management are protected if the forecast is made in good faith. Answer (C) is incorrect because the objective is to encourage forecasts, not to delay them. Answer (D) is incorrect because anyone may use the forecast information.

12. An audit of the financial statements of Camden Corporation is being conducted by an external auditor. The external auditor is expected to

A. Express an opinion as to the fairness of Camden's financial statements.

B. Express an opinion as to the attractiveness of Camden for investment purposes.

C. Certify to the correctness of Camden's financial statements.

D. Critique the wisdom and legality of Camden's business decisions.

The correct answer is (A). *(CMA, adapted)*

REQUIRED: The responsibility of an external auditor for an audit of financial statements.

DISCUSSION: The fourth standard of reporting requires the auditor to express an opinion regarding the financial statements taken as a whole or to assert that an opinion cannot be expressed. The opinion concerns the fairness with which the statements have been presented in conformity with GAAP.

Answer (B) is incorrect because the external auditor does not interpret the financial statement data for investment purposes. Answer (C) is incorrect because the external audit normally cannot be so thorough as to permit a guarantee of correctness. Answer (D) is incorrect because the independent audit attests to the fair presentation of the data in the financial statements, not an evaluation of management decisions.

13. If the financial statements contain a departure from an official pronouncement of the Financial Accounting Standards Board that has a material effect on the financial statements, the auditor must express a(n)

A. Adverse opinion.

B. Qualified opinion.

C. Disclaimer of opinion.

D. An adverse opinion or a qualified opinion.

The correct answer is (D). *(CMA, adapted)*

REQUIRED: The opinion an auditor must express when financial statements contain a material departure from GAAP.

DISCUSSION: A qualified opinion states that the financial statements are fairly presented except for the effects of a certain matter. It is expressed when the statements contain a material, unjustified departure from GAAP, but only if an adverse opinion is not appropriate. An adverse opinion is expressed when the financial statements, taken as a whole, are not presented fairly in accordance with GAAP.

Answers (A) and (B) are incorrect because a departure from GAAP may justify either a qualified or an adverse opinion, depending on the circumstances. Answer (C) is incorrect because a disclaimer states that the auditor does not express an opinion. A disclaimer is not appropriate given a material departure from GAAP.

D. SEC and Its Reporting Standards

14. The act that gives the SEC the ultimate power to suspend trading of a security, delist a security, and prevent brokers and dealers from working in the securities market is the

A. Securities Investor Protection Act of 1970.

B. Securities Act of 1933.

C. Securities Exchange Act of 1934.

D. Investment Company Act of 1940.

The correct answer is (C). *(CMA, adapted)*

REQUIRED: The statute providing the SEC ultimate regulatory authority in the trading of securities.

DISCUSSION: The Securities Exchange Act of 1934 generally regulates the trading markets in securities. It requires the registration of brokers, dealers, and securities exchanges.

Answer (A) is incorrect because the Securities Investor Protection Act of 1970 created the Securities Investor Protection Corporation (SIPC) to intercede when brokers or dealers encounter financial difficulty endangering their customers. Answer (B) is incorrect because the Securities Act of 1933 requires registration of securities involved in initial public offerings but does not apply to subsequent trading. Answer (D) is incorrect because the Investment Company Act of 1940 deals narrowly with the registration of investment companies.

15. Requirements not imposed by the Securities Exchange Act of 1934 and its amendments are

A. Proxy solicitation requirements.

B. Prospectus requirements.

C. Insider trading requirements.

D. Tender offer requirements.

The correct answer is (B). *(CMA, adapted)*

REQUIRED: The requirements not imposed by the Securities Exchange Act of 1934.

DISCUSSION: Prospectus requirements are imposed by the Securities Act of 1933. Prospectuses are used to sell securities, and the Securities Act of 1933 regulates the initial sale of securities.

Answers (A), (C), and (D) are incorrect because each is imposed by the Securities Exchange Act of 1934.

16. The SEC has issued Regulation S-K to govern disclosures in filings with the SEC of nonfinancial statement matters. It concerns descriptions of the company's securities, business, properties, and legal proceedings; information about its directors and officers; management's discussion and analysis of financial condition and results of operations; and

A. The form and content of the required financial statements.

B. The requirements for filing interim financial statements.

C. Unofficial interpretations and practices regarding securities laws disclosure requirements.

D. Guidelines for voluntary financial projections.

The correct answer is (D). *(CMA, adapted)*

REQUIRED: The item included under the disclosure requirements of Regulation S-K.

DISCUSSION: In addition to those items mentioned in the body of the question, Regulation S-K also provides guidelines for the filing of projections of future economic performance (financial projections). The SEC encourages but does not require, the filing of management's projections as a supplement to the historical financial statements.

Answers (A) and (B) are incorrect because financial statement disclosures are specified in Regulation S-X, not S-K. Answer (C) is incorrect because unofficial interpretations and practices, if codified at all, are made public through the issuance of Staff Accounting Bulletins (SABs).

17. Regulation S-X disclosure requirements of the Securities and Exchange Commission (SEC) concern

A. Summary information, risk factors, and the ratio of earnings to fixed charges.

B. The requirements for filing interim financial statements and pro forma financial information.

C. Information concerning recent sales of unregistered securities.

D. Management's discussion and analysis of the financial condition and the results of operations.

The correct answer is (B). *(CMA, adapted)*

REQUIRED: The concern of Regulation S-X disclosure requirements.

DISCUSSION: Regulation S-X governs the reporting of financial statements, including footnotes and schedules. Both interim and annual statements are covered by Regulation S-X.

Answer (A) is incorrect because Regulation S-X requires more than summary information. Answer (C) is incorrect because Regulation S-X concerns financial statement reporting, not securities. Answer (D) is incorrect because the MD&A is part of the corporate annual report. Disclosure standards for annual reports are covered by Regulation S-K.

18. An external auditor's involvement with Form 10-Q that is being prepared for filing with the SEC most likely will consist of

A. An audit of the financial statements included in Form 10-Q.

B. A compilation report on the financial statements included in Form 10-Q.

C. A comfort letter that covers stub-period financial data.

D. A review of the interim financial statements included in Form 10-Q.

The correct answer is (D). *(CMA, adapted)*

REQUIRED: The external auditor's most likely involvement with Form 10-Q.

DISCUSSION: Form 10-Q is the quarterly report to the SEC. It must be filed for each of the first three quarters of the year within 45 days after the end of the quarter. It need not contain audited financial statements, but it should be prepared in accordance with APB 28, *Interim Financial Reporting*. A review by an accountant based on inquiries and analytical procedures permits an expression of limited assurance that no material modifications need to be made to interim information for it to be in conformity with GAAP. A review helps satisfy the SEC requirement of "accurate, representative, and meaningful" quarterly information. Thus, an SEC registrant must obtain a review by an independent auditor of its interim financial information that is to be included in a quarterly report to the SEC.

Answer (A) is incorrect because audited statements are not required in quarterly reports. Answer (B) is incorrect because a compilation provides no assurance and would thus not satisfy the SEC requirement stated above. Answer (C) is incorrect because comfort letters are addressed to underwriters, not the SEC.

19. Form 10-K is filed with the SEC to update the information a company supplied when filing a registration statement under the Securities Exchange Act of 1934. Form 10-K is a report that is filed

A. Annually within 90 days of the end of a company's fiscal year.

B. Semiannually within 30 days of the end of a company's second and fourth fiscal quarters.

C. Quarterly within 45 days of the end of each quarter.

D. Monthly within 2 weeks of the end of each month.

The correct answer is (A). *(CMA, adapted)*

REQUIRED: The true statement about filing Form 10-K.

DISCUSSION: Form 10-K is the annual report to the SEC. It must be filed within 90 days after the corporation's year-end. It must contain audited financial statements and be signed by the principal executive, financial, and accounting officers and by a majority of the board. The content is essentially that required in the Basic Information Package.

Answer (B) is incorrect because Form 10-K is an annual report. Answer (C) is incorrect because Form 10-Q is filed quarterly within 45 days of the end of each quarter except for the fourth quarter. Answer (D) is incorrect because no monthly reports are required.

20. SEC Form S-3 is an optional, short-form registration statement that relies on the incorporation by reference of periodic reports required by the Securities Exchange Act of 1934. Form S-3 offers substantial savings in filing costs over other forms since minimal disclosures are required in the prospectus. The SEC permits the use of Form S-3 only by those firms that have filed periodic reports with the SEC for at least 3 years and if the registrant

A. Has less than $150 million of voting stock held by nonaffiliates.

B. Is widely followed and actively traded.

C. Is seeking more than $150 million in funds.

D. Has not had to file Form 8-K during the most recent 2-year period.

The correct answer is (B). *(CMA, adapted)*

REQUIRED: The requirement for use of Form S-3.

DISCUSSION: Form S-1 is used for a first registration. Form S-2 is used by companies that have filed timely reports for 3 years. Incorporation by reference from the annual shareholders' report of Basic Information Package disclosures is allowed in Form S-2. If a company meets the requirements for use of Form S-2 and at least $50,000,000 in value of its stock is held by nonaffiliates (or at least $100,000,000 is outstanding and annual trading volume is at least 3,000,000 shares), Form S-3 may be used. It allows most information to be incorporated by reference to other SEC filings.

Answer (A) is incorrect because the language of the requirement is that a company may use Form S-3 if nonaffiliates hold "at least $50,000,000" of the company's stock (not "less than $150,000,000"). Answers (C) and (D) are incorrect because neither is a requirement for use of Form S-3.

21. In an effort to consolidate the registration process, the SEC has adopted a three-tier system of new security forms. However, these three forms do not cover all circumstances. Under which one of the following circumstances would a registrant use Form S-4?

A. Registering securities in connection with mergers and related business-combination transactions.

B. Registering securities in which the registrant does not qualify for Form S-1.

C. Registering securities when the registrant has not had to file Form 8-K during the most recent 2-year period.

D. Registering securities of real estate investment trusts.

The correct answer is (A). *(CMA, adapted)*

REQUIRED: The circumstance under which a registrant would use Form S-4.

DISCUSSION: Form S-4 is a simplified form for business combinations, such as mergers. It is part of the integrated disclosure system established to simplify reporting requirements under the Securities Act of 1933 and the Securities Exchange Act of 1934. Thus, Form S-4 may incorporate much information by reference to other reports already filed with the SEC. The integrated disclosure system permits many companies to use the required annual report to shareholders (if prepared in conformity with Regulations S-X and S-K) as the basis for the annual report to the SEC on Form 10-K. Some may even use this report as the basis for registration statements.

Answer (B) is incorrect because Form S-1 may be used by any registrant. Answer (C) is incorrect because the filing of Form 8-K to report certain material events has no effect on the subsequent filing of the S forms. Answer (D) is incorrect because Form S-11 is used by REITs and real estate companies.

22. The SEC has adopted a three-tier system of forms in an effort to consolidate the registration process. However, these three forms do not cover all circumstances. A registrant would use Form S-8 when registering securities

A. When the registrant does not qualify for Form S-1.

B. To be offered to employees under any stock option or other employee benefit plan.

C. Of real estate investment trusts.

D. When the registrant has not had to file Form 8-K during the most recent 2-year period.

The correct answer is (B). *(CMA, adapted)*

REQUIRED: The situation that would require a company to use Form S-8.

DISCUSSION: SEC Form S-8 is used when securities are to be offered to employees under any stock option or other employee benefit plan. It has become more commonly used in recent years because of the adoption of employee stock ownership plans (ESOPs).

Answer (A) is incorrect because Form S-1 is a long form than includes all possible required information. It can be used by any company. Forms S-2 and S-3 may be used as a substitute by companies that have been filing timely reports to the SEC for 3 years. Answer (C) is incorrect because Form S-11 is used by REITs and real estate companies. Answer (D) is incorrect because the filing of Form 8-K to report certain material events has no effect on the subsequent filing of the S forms.

23. Form 8-K ordinarily must be submitted to the SEC after the occurrence of a significant event. All of the following events would be reported by Form 8-K except

A. The acquisition of a major company.

B. The resignation of several directors.

C. A change in the registrant's certifying accountant.

D. A change from the percentage-of-completion method to the completed-contract method for a company in the construction business.

The correct answer is (D). *(CMA, adapted)*

REQUIRED: The event not reported on Form 8-K.

DISCUSSION: Form 8-K is a current report to disclose material events. It must be filed within 15 calendar days after the material event occurs. However, a change in independent accountants or the resignation of a director must be reported within 5 business days. Material events that must be reported include a change in control; acquisition or disposition of a significant amount of assets not in the ordinary course of business; bankruptcy or receivership; resignation of directors; and the resignation or dismissal of the firm's independent accountant. Reporting of other material events that are deemed by the registrant to be of importance to security holders is optional. A change in accounting principle does not require reporting on Form 8-K.

Answers (A), (B), and (C) are incorrect because a major acquisition, the resignation of several directors, and a change in the registrant's certifying accountant are events that must be reported on Form 8-K.

24. Shareholders may ask or allow others to enter their votes at a shareholders meeting that they are unable to attend. The document furnished to shareholders to provide background information for their vote is a

A. Registration statement.

B. Proxy statement.

C. 10-K report.

D. Prospectus.

The correct answer is (B). *(CMA, adapted)*

REQUIRED: The document furnished to shareholders on behalf of a person seeking to vote their shares.

DISCUSSION: Under the Securities Exchange Act of 1934, Section 14 seeks to ensure that proxy solicitations are accompanied by adequate disclosure of information about the agenda items for which authority to vote is being sought. One requirement is that the proxy statement be filed with the SEC at least 10 days prior to mailing proxy materials to shareholders. The proxy statement must identify the party making the solicitation and details about the matters to be voted on such as mergers, authorizations to issue new stock, or election of directors.

Answer (A) is incorrect because a registration statement is the document submitted to the SEC when a new issue of securities is being registered prior to sale. Answer (C) is incorrect because public companies must submit an annual 10-K report to the SEC. Answer (D) is incorrect because a prospectus is sent to potential investors to provide them with information about the investment potential of a new issue of securities. The prospectus is very similar to the registration statement.

25. Shelf registration is a registration with the Securities and Exchange Commission (SEC) in which the security issuer

A. Registers the issue price range for a specified period of time.

B. Registers a new issue with the SEC, then files an amendment to its initial filing, and then sells the security on a piecemeal basis.

C. Puts a new security out for bid to all of the underwriters associated with a particular market.

D. Announces its intention to issue a new security but delays its issuance until a detailed financial analysis is available.

The correct answer is (B). *(CMA, adapted)*

REQUIRED: The action of a security issuer pursuant to a shelf registration.

DISCUSSION: Shelf registration under SEC Rule 415 allows corporations to file registration statements covering a stipulated amount of securities that may be issued on a piecemeal basis over the two-year effective period of the statement. The securities are essentially placed on the shelf and issued at an opportune moment without the necessity of filing a new registration statement, observing a 20-day waiting period, or preparing a new prospectus. The issuer is only required to provide updating amendments or to refer investors to quarterly and annual statements filed with the SEC. Shelf registration is most advantageous to large corporations that frequently offer securities to the public.

Answer (A) is incorrect because shelf registration does not stipulate the price that will be charged for securities. Answer (C) is incorrect because shelf registration has nothing to do with the bidding by underwriters. Answer (D) is incorrect because the detailed financial analysis is required as a part of a shelf registration.

26. A red herring prospectus is a

A. Misleading or false prospectus.

B. Prospectus that has not been filed with the Securities and Exchange Commission.

C. Prospectus that has been disapproved by the Securities and Exchange Commission.

D. Preliminary prospectus filed with the Securities and Exchange Commission but not approved and, accordingly, subject to change.

The correct answer is (D). *(CMA, adapted)*

REQUIRED: The definition of a red herring prospectus.

DISCUSSION: A red herring prospectus is a preliminary prospectus filed with the SEC. The red herring prospectus contains the same information as a regular prospectus, but prices are omitted and the information is subject to change. The prospectus is clearly marked in red to indicate that it is preliminary.

Answer (A) is incorrect because a red herring prospectus is not misleading or false; it is simply subject to change. Answer (B) is incorrect because a red herring prospectus has been filed with the SEC. Answer (C) is incorrect because a red herring prospectus is filed with the SEC, but is neither approved or disapproved.

27. Form 8-K must be filed within

A. 90 days after the end of an employee stock purchase plan's fiscal year.

B. 15 calendar days or, in certain cases, 5 business days after the occurrence of a significant event.

C. 90 days after the end of the fiscal year covered by the report.

D. 45 days after the end of each of the first three quarters of each fiscal year.

The correct answer is (B). *(CMA, adapted)*

REQUIRED: The time when Form 8-K must be filed with the SEC.

DISCUSSION: Form 8-K is a current report to disclose material events. For specified events, it must be filed within 15 calendar days after the material event occurs. However, a change in independent accountants or the resignation of a director must be reported within 5 business days. Other material events that must be reported on Form 8-K are a change in control, bankruptcy or receivership, and the acquisition or disposition of a significant amount of assets not in the ordinary course of business.

Answer (A) is incorrect because Form S-8 must be filed within 90 days after the end of an employee stock purchase plan's fiscal year. Answer (C) is incorrect because Form 10-K must be filed within 90 days after the end of the fiscal year covered by the report. Answer (D) is incorrect because Form 10-Q must be filed within 45 days after the end of each of the first three quarters of each fiscal year.

28. Form 10-Q is filed with the SEC to keep both investors and experts appraised of a company's operations and financial position. Form 10-Q is a report that is filed within

A. 90 days after the end of an employee stock purchase plan's fiscal year.

B. 15 days after the occurrence of a significant event.

C. 90 days after the end of the fiscal year covered by the report.

D. 45 days after the end of each of the first three quarters of each fiscal year.

The correct answer is (D). *(CMA, adapted)*

REQUIRED: The time when Form 10-Q must be filed.

DISCUSSION: Form 10-Q is a quarterly report to the SEC. It must be filed for each of the first three quarters of the year within 45 days after the end of each quarter. Quarterly financial statements need not be audited, but they must be prepared in accordance with APB 28, *Interim Financial Reporting*. Moreover, an SEC registrant must obtain a review by an independent auditor of its interim financial information that is to be included in a quarterly report to the SEC.

Answer (A) is incorrect because Form 10-Q is the regular quarterly financial report; it is not a specific report for employee stock purchase plans. Answer (B) is incorrect because Form 10-Q is a quarterly financial report. It is not related to specific events. Answer (C) is incorrect because Form 10-Q is a quarterly report, not an annual report.

E. Public Reporting Standards

29. The auditor's opinion refers to generally accepted accounting principles (GAAP). Which of the following best describes GAAP?

A. The interpretations of accounting rules and procedures by certified public accountants on audit engagements.

B. The pronouncements of the Financial Accounting Standards Board and its predecessor, the Accounting Principles Board.

C. The guidelines set forth by various governmental agencies that derive their authority from Congress.

D. The conventions, rules, and procedures that are necessary to define accepted accounting practice at a particular time.

The correct answer is (D). *(CPA, adapted)*

REQUIRED: The statement that best describes GAAP.

DISCUSSION: GAAP are the "conventions, rules, and procedures necessary to define accepted accounting practice at a particular time." They include both the broad guidelines and the detailed practices and procedures promulgated by the profession that provide uniform standards to measure financial presentations (AU 411).

Answer (A) is incorrect because interpretations of GAAP made by CPAs on audit engagements are judgments about the application of GAAP to particular circumstances. Answer (B) is incorrect because GAAP include but are not limited to pronouncements of the APB and FASB. Answer (C) is incorrect because, although the federal government can require disclosures by public companies, for example, through regulations of the SEC, GAAP are much broader. They apply to all entities, whether public or private and regardless of size.

30. Which of the following is a source of officially established accounting principles for nongovernmental entities?

A. International Accounting Standards.

B. FASB Concepts Statements.

C. FASB Interpretations.

D. AICPA Issues Papers.

The correct answer is (C). *(Publisher)*

REQUIRED: The source of GAAP as designated by the AICPA for nongovernmental entities.

DISCUSSION: AU 411 presents GAAP hierarchies for nongovernmental entities, state and local governments, and federal governmental entities. The nongovernmental hierarchy has five tiers. The first tier [category (a)] consists of sources of officially established accounting principles (FASB Statements and Interpretations, APB Opinions, and AICPA Accounting Research Bulletins). The next three tiers [categories (b), (c), and (d)] contain other sources of established accounting principles. The fifth tier includes other accounting literature.

Answers (A), (B), and (D) are incorrect because International Accounting Standards, FASB Concepts Statements, and AICPA Issues Papers are considered other accounting literature rather than established accounting principles.

F. Selected Disclosures in Financial Statements

31. Which of the following should be disclosed in the summary of significant accounting policies?

A. Valuation method used for work-in-process inventory.

B. Interest capitalized for the period.

C. Adequacy of pension plan assets in relation to vested benefits.

D. Depreciation charges for the period.

The correct answer is (A). *(CIA, adapted)*

REQUIRED: The item that should be disclosed in the summary of significant accounting policies.

DISCUSSION: APB 22 requires that all significant accounting principles and methods that involve selection from among alternatives, are peculiar to a given industry, or are innovative or unusual applications be specifically identified and described in an initial note to the financial statements or in a separate summary. The disclosure should include accounting principles adopted and the method of applying them. This summary of significant accounting policies should not duplicate other facts to be disclosed elsewhere in the statements. The valuation method for inventory is one example of an accounting method (policy) that should be disclosed.

Answers (B), (C), and (D) are incorrect because the summary of significant accounting policies should not duplicate facts required to be disclosed elsewhere in the financial statements.

32. The accounting profession has adopted various standards to be followed when reporting inventory in the financial statements. All of the following are required to be reported in the financial statements or disclosed in notes to the financial statements except for

A. Inventory detail, such as raw materials, work-in-process, and finished goods.

B. Significant financing agreements, such as product financing arrangements and pledging of inventories.

C. The basis upon which inventory amounts are stated.

D. Unrealized profit on inventories.

The correct answer is (D). *(CMA, adapted)*

REQUIRED: The item not a required disclosure about inventory.

DISCUSSION: APB 22 requires disclosure of accounting policies in a separate summary of significant policies or as the first footnote to the financial statements. The disclosure should specify accounting principles adopted and the method of applying those principles. Examples include inventory valuation methods; inventory details, such as the mix of finished goods, work-in-progress, and raw materials; methods used in determining costs; and any significant financing agreements, such as leases, related party transactions, product financing arrangements, firm purchase commitments, pledging of inventories, and involuntary liquidation of LIFO layers. Unrealized profit on inventories is not reported because the company usually has no assurance that the inventories will be sold.

Answers (A), (B), and (C) are incorrect because inventory details, financing agreements, and valuation methods should be disclosed in the notes.

33. APB 22, *Disclosure of Accounting Policies*, recommends that when financial statements are issued, information identifying the accounting policies adopted by the reporting entity should be presented as part of the financial statements. All of the following are required to be disclosed with respect to accounting policies except the

A. Depreciation methods used for plant assets.

B. Inventory valuation and costing methods.

C. Accounting for long-term construction contracts.

D. Estimated lives of depreciable assets.

The correct answer is (D). *(CMA, adapted)*

REQUIRED: The item not a required disclosure by APB 22.

DISCUSSION: APB 22 requires disclosure of accounting policies in a separate summary of significant accounting policies or in the initial footnote to the financial statements. The disclosures should identify the principles followed and the methods of applying them that materially affect the statements. Moreover, the disclosures should encompass principles and methods involving a selection from acceptable alternatives, accounting principles peculiar to a particular industry, and innovative or unusual applications of GAAP. However, the disclosures should not repeat details presented elsewhere, e.g., the estimated lives of depreciable assets.

Answers (A), (B), and (C) are incorrect because examples of required disclosures include depreciation and amortization methods, inventory valuation methods, means of accounting for long-term construction contracts, basis of consolidation, and recognition of revenue from franchising and leasing activities.

34. A company is required to disclose in a note to the financial statements the

A. Names of the members of the board of directors.

B. Method of inventory valuation used.

C. Market value of fixed assets.

D. Five highest paid employees.

The correct answer is (B). *(CMA, adapted)*

REQUIRED: The information that must be disclosed in the footnotes to financial statements.

DISCUSSION: APB 22 requires disclosure of accounting policies in a separate summary of significant accounting policies or as the initial footnote to the financial statements. The disclosure should emphasize selection of alternative accounting principles, accounting principles peculiar to a particular situation or industry, and innovative or unusual applications. The disclosure should include accounting principles adopted and the method of applying them. Examples include depreciation and amortization methods, inventory valuation methods, consolidation method, and franchising and leasing activities.

Answer (A) is incorrect because the names of directors are not shown in the footnotes. Answer (C) is incorrect because there is no requirement to show the market value of fixed assets. Answer (D) is incorrect because the IRS requires not-for-profit organizations to identify the five highest paid employees.

35. Publicly traded companies must report all of the following interim financial data except

A. Basic and diluted earnings per share for each period presented.

B. Summarized information on sales, income taxes, extraordinary items, effect of change in accounting principles, net income, and comprehensive income.

C. A condensed balance sheet, income statement, and statement of cash flows for each interim period presented.

D. The disposal of a segment of a business, and extraordinary, unusual, or infrequently occurring items.

The correct answer is (C). *(CMA, adapted)*

REQUIRED: The item not a required disclosure by publicly traded companies in interim financial data.

DISCUSSION: APB 28 does not require presentation of interim income statements, statements of financial position, or statements of cash flows. Although interim financial statements may be presented, minimum disclosures required when a publicly held company does issue summarized financial information include

1) Sales or gross revenues, provision for income taxes, extraordinary items, cumulative effect of changes in accounting principles, net income, and comprehensive income
2) Basic and diluted EPS
3) Seasonal revenues, costs, or expenses
4) Significant changes in estimates or provisions for income taxes
5) Disposal of a segment and extraordinary, unusual, or infrequent items
6) Contingent items
7) Changes in accounting principles or estimates
8) Significant changes in financial position
9) Certain information about reportable operating segments

Answers (A), (B), and (D) are incorrect because BEPS and DEPS; sales; income taxes; extraordinary items; the effect of a change in accounting principles; net income; comprehensive income; disposal of a segment; and extraordinary, unusual, and infrequent items are disclosed.

36. When reporting on interim periods, APB 28, *Interim Financial Reporting*, as amended, specifies that

A. Basic and diluted earnings per share need not be disclosed each quarter.

B. Income tax expense must be determined by applying progressive tax rates to income on a quarterly basis.

C. The method used to determine the value of interim inventories must be the same as that used for annual inventory valuation.

D. The cumulative effect from an accounting change is always reported as occurring in the first quarter, and all subsequent interim periods reflect the change.

The correct answer is (D). *(CMA, adapted)*

REQUIRED: The true statement about the requirements for interim financial reporting.

DISCUSSION: SFAS 3, *Reporting Accounting Changes in Interim Financial Statements*, covers cumulative-effect-type accounting changes. If an accounting change occurs in other than the first quarter of the enterprise's fiscal year, the proper treatment is to calculate the cumulative effect on retained earnings at the beginning of the year and include it in restated net income presented in the first quarter financial statements. In addition, all previously issued interim financial statements of the current year must be restated to reflect the new accounting method.

Answer (A) is incorrect because interim and annual statements use the same principles for reporting EPS. Answer (B) is incorrect because taxes are based on the expected annual effective rate after all tax planning tools are implemented and include the effect of credits and special deductions. Each interim period's tax expense is the revised annual tax rate times year-to-date income, minus tax expense recognized in prior interim periods. Answer (C) is incorrect because APB 28 allows the gross profit method to be used for interim valuation of inventories.

37. APB 28, *Interim Financial Reporting*, provides guidelines for interim reporting that state firms

A. May use the gross profit method for interim inventory pricing although a different inventory method is used for annual reporting.

B. Must determine income tax expense by applying progressive tax rates to income on a quarterly basis.

C. May prorate extraordinary items over four quarters.

D. Need not disclose basic and diluted earnings per share each quarter.

The correct answer is (A). *(CMA, adapted)*

REQUIRED: The true statement about interim reporting.

DISCUSSION: APB 28 requires companies to use basically the same reporting methods for interim and annual financial statements. However, one exception is that the gross profit method may be used for interim inventory valuation even though it is not used for year-end statements.

Answer (B) is incorrect because tax expense is based on the expected annual effective rate after all credits and special deductions have been considered. Answer (C) is incorrect because an extraordinary item is to be reported in the interim period in which the gain or loss occurred. Answer (D) is incorrect because SFAS 128 requires that basic and diluted EPS be reported by an entity with a complex capital structure if it has publicly traded common stock or potential common stock.

38. When interim financial statements are prepared, they should be prepared

A. Employing the same accounting principles used for annual reports.

B. Without determining estimated income tax expense.

C. Quarterly only, not on a monthly basis.

D. Containing only operating income data.

The correct answer is (A). *(CMA, adapted)*

REQUIRED: The provisions to be followed in the preparation of interim financial statements.

DISCUSSION: With few exceptions, APB 28, *Interim Financial Reporting*, specifies that interim statements are to follow the same principles as those for annual reports. APB 28 views each interim period primarily as an integral part of an annual period. Certain principles and practices used for annual reporting, however, may require modification at interim dates so interim reports may relate more closely to the results of operations for the annual period.

Answer (B) is incorrect because tax expense is to be recorded based on the expected annual effective rate after all tax-planning tools are implemented (according to FASB Interpretation No. 18). Answer (C) is incorrect because interim periods of any length may be used. Answer (D) is incorrect because APB 28 requires interim statements to be similar to annual reports, including such items as extraordinary gains and losses and the effects of changes in accounting principle. The all-inclusive income statement approach is required by GAAP for both annual and interim statements.

39. SFAS 47, *Disclosure of Long-Term Obligations*, resulted in identifying disclosure requirements for long-term obligations as a group. The Financial Accounting Standards Board believed that a particular group of long-term obligations frequently was not disclosed adequately. Thus, this statement was specifically addressed to

A. Loss contingencies.

B. Noncancelable purchase obligations.

C. Severance pay.

D. Pension plans.

The correct answer is (B). *(CMA, adapted)*

REQUIRED: The type of obligation specifically addressed by SFAS 47.

DISCUSSION: SFAS 47 requires disclosure of unconditional purchase obligations associated with suppliers' financing arrangements and future payments required by long-term debt and redeemable stock agreements. Unconditional purchase obligations are commitments to transfer funds in the future for fixed or minimum amounts of goods or services at fixed or minimum prices. SFAS 47 provides the standards of accounting for an unconditional purchase obligation that was negotiated as part of the financing arrangement for facilities that will provide contracted goods or services or for costs related to those goods or services, has a remaining term of more than 1 year, and is either noncancelable or cancelable only under specific terms.

Answer (A) is incorrect because loss contingencies are liabilities covered by SFAS 5. Answer (C) is incorrect because severance pay is a form of deferred compensation, a topic not addressed by SFAS 47. Answer (D) is incorrect because pension liabilities are covered by SFASs 87 and 88.

40. SFAS 47, *Disclosure of Long-Term Obligations*, does not apply to an unconditional purchase obligation that is cancelable under which of the following conditions?

A. Upon the occurrence of a remote contingency.

B. With the permission of the other party.

C. If a replacement agreement is signed between the same parties.

D. Upon payment of a nominal penalty.

The correct answer is (D). *(Publisher)*

REQUIRED: The condition excluding unconditional purchase obligation coverage by SFAS 47.

DISCUSSION: SFAS 47 provides the standards of accounting for an unconditional purchase obligation that

1) Was negotiated as part of the financing arrangement for facilities that will provide contracted goods or services
2) Has a remaining term of more than 1 year
3) Is either noncancelable or cancelable only under specific terms

Excluded from these terms and from the provisions of SFAS 47 is a purchase obligation cancelable upon the payment of a nominal penalty.

Answers (A), (B), and (C) are incorrect because each is a condition indicating that the obligation is noncancelable.

41. If an unconditional purchase obligation is not presented in the balance sheet, certain disclosures are required. A disclosure that is not required is

A. The nature and term of the obligation.

B. The variable components of the obligation.

C. The imputed interest necessary to reduce the unconditional purchase obligation to its present value.

D. The amounts purchased under the obligation for each period an income statement is presented.

The correct answer is (C). *(Publisher)*

REQUIRED: The item not required to be disclosed if an unconditional purchase obligation is not recognized in the balance sheet.

DISCUSSION: When an unconditional purchase obligation is not recorded in the balance sheet, SFAS 47 encourages, but does not require, the disclosure of the amount of imputed interest necessary to reduce the unconditional purchase obligation to its present value.

Answers (A), (B), and (D) are incorrect because each disclosure is explicitly required by SFAS 47 when an unconditional purchase obligation is not recorded in the balance sheet. SFAS 47 also requires disclosure of the amount of the fixed and determinable portion of the obligation in the aggregate as of the latest balance sheet date and the amounts due in each of the next 5 years.

42. In accordance with SFAS No. 47, *Disclosure of Long-Term Obligations*, for unconditional purchase obligations not recorded on the purchaser's statement of financial position, all of the following disclosures are required except for the

A. Nature and term of the obligations.

B. Total amount of the fixed and determinable portion of the obligations at the financial statement date and for each of the next 5 years.

C. Nature of any variable portions of the obligations.

D. Sources of funds used for payments.

The correct answer is (D). *(CMA, adapted)*

REQUIRED: The item not a required disclosure regarding unconditional purchase obligations not recorded on the purchaser's balance sheet.

DISCUSSION: SFAS 47 requires disclosure of unconditional purchase obligations associated with suppliers' financing arrangements (e.g., in the form of take-or-pay and throughput contracts) and future payments required by long-term debt and redeemable stock agreements. Unrecorded unconditional purchase obligations are those requiring payment for future goods or services and are not cancelable or, if so, provide for a substantial penalty. Disclosures required for unrecorded obligations include the nature and term of the item, fixed and determinable payments in total and for each of the next 5 years, the nature of any variable payments, and amounts purchased in the periods for which an income statement is being prepared. Sources of funds to be used for payments need not be disclosed.

Answers (A), (B), and (C) are incorrect because they are required disclosures for undisclosed obligations under SFAS 47.

43. The Financial Accounting Standards Board has provided guidance on disclosures of transactions between related parties, for example, transactions between subsidiaries of a common parent. SFAS 57, *Related Party Disclosures*, requires all of the following disclosures except

A. The nature of the relationship involved.

B. A description of the transactions for each period an income statement is presented.

C. The dollar amounts of transactions for each period an income statement is presented.

D. The effect on the cash flow statement for each period a cash flow statement is presented.

The correct answer is (D). *(CMA, adapted)*

REQUIRED: The related-party transaction disclosure not required by SFAS 57.

DISCUSSION: SFAS 57 requires disclosure of related-party transactions except for compensation agreements, expense allowances, and transactions eliminated in consolidated working papers. Required disclosures include the relationship(s) of the related parties; a description and dollar amounts of transactions for each period presented and the effects of any change in the method of establishing their terms; and amounts due to or from the related parties and, if not apparent, the terms and manner of settlement. The effect on the cash flow statement need not be disclosed.

Answer (A) is incorrect because disclosure of the nature of the relationship involved is required. Answer (B) is incorrect because disclosure of a description of the transactions for each period an income statement is presented is required. Answer (C) is incorrect because disclosure of the dollar amounts of transactions for each period an income statement is presented is required.

44. SFAS 107, *Disclosures about Fair Value of Financial Instruments*, requires all entities to disclose the fair value of all financial instruments for which it is practicable to estimate fair value. Which of the following is a financial instrument?

A. Merchandise inventory.

B. Deferred subscription revenue.

C. A note payable in U.S. Treasury bonds.

D. A warranty payable.

The correct answer is (C). *(Publisher)*

REQUIRED: The definition of a financial instrument.

DISCUSSION: SFAS 107 defines a financial instrument as cash, evidence of an ownership interest in an entity, or a contract that both (1) imposes on one entity a contractual obligation (A) to deliver cash or another financial instrument to a second entity or (B) to exchange other financial instruments on potentially unfavorable terms with the second entity, and (2) conveys to that second entity a contractual right (A) to receive cash or another financial instrument from the first entity or (B) to exchange other financial instruments on potentially favorable terms with the first entity. A note payable in U.S. Treasury bonds gives the holder the contractual right to receive, and imposes on the issuer the contractual obligation to deliver, bonds that are themselves financial instruments. Thus, given that one entity has a contractual obligation to deliver another financial instrument and the second entity has a contractual right to receive another financial instrument, the note payable in U.S. Treasury bonds meets the definition of a financial instrument.

Answer (A) is incorrect because, although the sale of inventory could result in the receipt of cash, the holder of the inventory has no current contractual right to receive cash. Answers (B) and (D) are incorrect because these obligations will result in the delivery of goods or services.

45. Whether recognized or unrecognized in an entity's financial statements, disclosure of the fair values of the entity's financial instruments is required when

A. Estimating those values is practicable.

B. The entity maintains accurate cost records.

C. Aggregated fair values are material to the entity.

D. Individual fair values are material to the entity.

The correct answer is (A). *(CPA, adapted)*

REQUIRED: The circumstances in which disclosure of the fair values of the entity's financial instruments is required.

DISCUSSION: SFAS 107, *Disclosures about Fair Value of Financial Instruments*, as amended by SFAS 133, requires certain entities to disclose the fair value of financial instruments, whether or not they are recognized in the balance sheet, if it is practicable to estimate such fair values. If estimating fair value is not practicable, disclosures include information pertinent to estimating the fair value of the financial instrument or class of financial instruments, such as the carrying amount, effective interest rate, and maturity. The reasons that estimating the fair value is not practicable should also be disclosed.

Answers (B), (C), and (D) are incorrect because the disclosure requirement is based on a practicability standard, not record keeping or materiality.

46. Disclosure of information about significant concentrations of credit risk is required for

A. Most financial instruments.

B. Financial instruments with off-balance-sheet credit risk only.

C. Financial instruments with off-balance-sheet market risk only.

D. Financial instruments with off-balance-sheet risk of accounting loss only.

The correct answer is (A). *(CPA, adapted)*

REQUIRED: The financial instruments for which disclosure of significant concentrations of credit risk is required.

DISCUSSION: SFAS 107 requires the disclosure of information about the fair value of financial instruments, whether recognized or not (certain nonpublic entities and certain instruments, such as leases and insurance contracts, are exempt from the disclosure requirements). SFAS 107 also requires disclosure of all significant concentrations of credit risk for most financial instruments (except for obligations for deferred compensation, certain instruments of a pension plan, insurance contracts, warranty obligations and rights, and unconditional purchase obligations).

Answers (B), (C), and (D) are incorrect because disclosure of significant concentrations of credit risk is required for most financial instruments.

G. Reporting Issues for Multinational Companies

47. The economic effects of a change in foreign exchange rates on a relatively self-contained and integrated operation within a foreign country relate to the net investment by the reporting enterprise in that operation. Consequently, translation adjustments that arise from the consolidation of that operation

A. Directly affect cash flows but should not be reflected in income.

B. Directly affect cash flows and should be reflected in income.

C. Do not directly affect cash flows and should not be reflected in income.

D. Do not directly affect cash flows but should be reflected in income.

The correct answer is (C). *(Publisher)*

REQUIRED: The true statement about translation adjustments arising from consolidation of a self-contained foreign operation with its U.S. parent/investor.

DISCUSSION: SFAS 52, *Foreign Currency Translation*, concludes that foreign currency translation adjustments for a foreign operation that is relatively self-contained and integrated within its environment do not affect cash flows of the reporting enterprise and should be excluded from net income. When an operation is relatively self-contained, the cash generated and expended by the entity is normally in the currency of the foreign country, and that currency is deemed to be the operation's functional currency.

Answers (A) and (B) are incorrect because, when an operation is relatively self-contained, the assumption is that translation adjustments do not affect cash flows.

Answers (B) and (D) are incorrect because translation adjustments should be included in other comprehensive income, not recognized in income.

48. Certain balance sheet accounts of a foreign subsidiary of Rowan, Inc., on December 31 have been translated into U.S. dollars as follows:

	Translated at	
	Current Rates	Historical Rates
Note receivable, long-term	$240,000	$200,000
Prepaid rent	85,000	80,000
Patent	150,000	170,000
	$475,000	$450,000

The subsidiary's functional currency is the currency of the country in which it is located. What total amount should be included in Rowan's December 31 consolidated balance sheet for the above accounts?

A. $450,000

B. $455,000

C. $475,000

D. $495,000

The correct answer is (C). *(CPA, adapted)*

REQUIRED: The total translated amount to be included in the consolidated balance sheet.

DISCUSSION: When the currency used to prepare a foreign entity's financial statements is its functional currency, SFAS 52 specifies that the current rate method be used to translate the foreign entity's financial statements into the reporting currency. The translation gains and losses arising from applying this method are included in other comprehensive income in the owners' equity section of the consolidated balance sheet. Thus, Rowan's listed assets translated at current rates should be included in the consolidated balance sheet at $475,000.

Answer (A) is incorrect because $450,000 reflects translation at historical rates. Answer (B) is incorrect because the note and patent are translated at historical rates. Answer (D) is incorrect because the patent is translated at historical rates.

STUDY UNIT 2: FINANCIAL STATEMENTS

17 pages of outline
66 multiple-choice questions

A. *Balance Sheet*
B. *Income Statement*
C. *Statement of Cash Flows*

This study unit covers the basic financial statements. It is the first of seven concerning the preparation of financial statements, a major topic that has been assigned a relative weight range of 50% to 70% of Part 2. Subsequent study units cover the conceptual framework, the elements of financial statements, other reporting issues, and statement analysis.

A. Balance Sheet

1. **Basic Financial Statements**. The balance sheet is a basic financial statement. The others are the statements of income, retained earnings, and cash flows.
   a. Disclosures of **changes in equity** and in the number of shares of equity securities are necessary whenever financial position and results of operations are presented.
      1) These disclosures may occur in the basic statements, in the notes thereto, or in separate statements (**APB 12**, *Omnibus Opinion -- 1967*).
   b. **Comprehensive income** must be displayed in a financial statement given the same prominence as the other statements, but no specific format is required.
   c. **Purposes**. The basic financial statements and notes, including the balance sheet, are vehicles for achieving the objectives of financial reporting. Supplementary information (e.g., on changing prices) and various other means of financial reporting (such as management's discussion and analysis) are also useful.
      1) The basic financial statements complement each other because they describe different aspects of the same transactions and because more than one statement will be necessary to provide information for a specific economic decision. Moreover, the elements of one statement articulate with those of other statements.
      2) The notes are considered part of the basic financial statements. They amplify or explain information recognized in the statements and are an integral part of statements prepared in accordance with GAAP. Notes should not be used to correct improper presentations.
2. **Definition**. The balance sheet (statement of financial position) "provides information about an entity's assets, liabilities, and equity and their relationships to each other at a moment in time." It helps users to assess "the entity's liquidity, financial flexibility, profitability, and risk" (SFAC 5).

3. **Conceptual Elements and Classifications**

   a. **Elements.** The balance sheet is a detailed presentation of the basic accounting equation: ***Assets = Liabilities + Equity***. The equation is based on the proprietary theory. The owners' interest in an enterprise (residual equity) is what remains after the economic obligations of the enterprise are deducted from its economic resources.

   b. **Classifications.** Some variation of the following classifications is used by most enterprises:

Assets	Liabilities
Current assets	Current liabilities
Noncurrent assets	Noncurrent liabilities
Long-term investments and funds	
Property, plant, and equipment	**Equity**
Intangible assets	Contributed capital
Other noncurrent assets	Retained earnings
Deferred charges	Accumulated other comprehensive income

      1) In the classification scheme, assets are usually presented in descending order of liquidity; for example, inventory (a current asset) is more liquid than property, plant, and equipment.

      2) Liabilities are shown in ascending order of time to maturity. Thus, trade payables (a current liability) will appear before bonds payable (a long-term liability).

      3) Items in the equity section are presented in descending order of permanence, e.g., common stock before retained earnings.

   c. **Presentation formats.** The format of the balance sheet is not standardized, and any method that promotes full disclosure and understandability is acceptable.

      1) The account (or horizontal) form presents assets on the left and liabilities and equity on the right.

      2) The report (or vertical) form is also commonly used. It differs from the account form only in that liabilities and equity are presented below rather than beside assets.

4. **The Resource Structure**

   a. **Current assets.** Current assets consist of "cash and other assets or resources commonly identified as reasonably expected to be realized in cash or sold or consumed during the normal operating cycle of the business" (ARB 43, Ch. 3A).

      1) The **operating cycle** is the average time between the acquisition of resources and the final receipt of cash from their sale as the culmination of the entity's revenue-generating activities. If the operating cycle is less than a year, 1 year is the basis for defining current and noncurrent assets.

      2) Current assets include cash and cash equivalents; inventories; receivables; certain trading, available-for-sale, and held-to-maturity securities; and prepaid expenses.

b. **Noncurrent assets**. Assets not qualifying as current are classified as noncurrent.

1) **Long-term investments and funds**. These assets include a variety of nonoperating investments and funds intended to be held beyond the longer of 1 year or the operating cycle. The following assets are typically included:

   a) Advances or investments in securities made to control or influence another entity and other securities not classified as current

   b) Restricted funds, for example, funds earmarked to retire long-term debt, satisfy pension obligations, or pay for the acquisition or construction of noncurrent assets

   c) Cash surrender value of life insurance policies

   d) Capital assets not used in current operations, such as idle facilities or land held for a future plant site or for speculative purposes

2) **Property, plant, and equipment (PP&E)**. These assets are tangible items used in operations. They are recorded at cost and are shown net of accumulated depreciation if depreciable. They include

   a) Land and depletable natural resources, e.g., oil and gas reserves

   b) Buildings, machinery, equipment, furniture, fixtures, leasehold improvements, land improvements, leased assets held under capital leases, and other depreciable assets

3) **Intangible assets**. Intangibles are long-term assets ordinarily used in operations. Intangible assets lack physical substance, and there is usually great uncertainty about their future benefits. They may be acquired externally or developed internally, and may be identifiable or unidentifiable. Intangibles are recorded at cost and shown net of accumulated amortization. Examples are patents, copyrights, trademarks, trade names, franchises, and purchased goodwill.

   a) The value of an intangible asset must be established in an arm's-length transaction; thus, research and development costs and internally generated goodwill are not capitalized.

4) **Other noncurrent assets**. This category includes noncurrent assets not readily classifiable elsewhere. Accordingly, there is little uniformity of treatment. Among the items typically shown as other assets are

   a) Long-term receivables arising from unusual transactions, e.g., loans to officers or employees and sales of capital assets

   b) Bond issue costs

   c) Machinery rearrangement costs (also classifiable as PP&E)

   d) Long-term prepayments

   e) Deferred tax assets arising from interperiod tax allocation

5) **Deferred charges**. Some balance sheets contain a category for deferred charges (long-term prepayments). Many of these items, for example, bond issue costs and rearrangement costs, which involve long-term prepayments, are frequently classified as other assets.

5. **The Financing Structure**

a. **Current liabilities**. Current liabilities are "obligations whose liquidation is reasonably expected to require the use of existing resources properly classifiable as current assets, or the creation of other current liabilities" (ARB 43, Ch. 3A).

1) This classification includes the following:

a) Payables for items entering into the operating cycle, for example, those incurred to obtain materials and supplies to be used in producing goods or services for sale

b) Payables arising from operations directly related to the operating cycle, such as accrued wages, salaries, rentals, royalties, and taxes

c) Collections made in advance of delivering goods or performing services, e.g., ticket sales revenue or magazine subscription revenue

d) Other obligations expected to be liquidated in the ordinary course of business during the longer of 1 year or the operating cycle

i) These include short-term notes given to acquire capital assets, payments required under sinking-fund provisions, payments on the current portion of serial bonds, and agency obligations incurred by the collection of assets on behalf of third parties.

e) Estimated amounts expected to be required within a relatively short time to pay known obligations even though

i) The amount can only be approximated, e.g., accrual of bonus payments, or

ii) The specific payee has not been designated, for example, in the case of warranties for repair of products already sold.

f) Obligations that, by their terms, are due on demand within the longer of 1 year or the operating cycle. Liquidation need not be expected.

g) Long-term obligations callable at the balance sheet date because of the debtor's violation of the debt agreement or long-term obligations that will become callable if the violation is not cured within a specified grace period

2) Current liabilities require the use of current assets or the creation of other current liabilities and therefore do not include

a) Short-term obligations intended to be refinanced on a long-term basis when the ability to consummate the refinancing has been demonstrated

i) This ability is demonstrated by a post-balance-sheet-date issuance of long-term debt or by entering into a financing agreement that meets certain criteria.

b) Debts to be paid from funds accumulated in accounts classified as noncurrent assets

i) Hence, a liability for bonds payable in the next period will not be classified as current if payment is to be from a noncurrent fund.

b. **Noncurrent liabilities**. Liabilities not qualifying as current are noncurrent. The non-current portions of the following are shown in this section of the balance sheet:

1) Long-term notes and bonds payable (Any unamortized premium or discount should be separately disclosed in the presentation of bonds payable.)
2) Liabilities under capital leases
3) Pension obligations
4) Deferred tax liability arising from interperiod tax allocation
5) Obligations under product or service warranty agreements
6) Advances for long-term commitments to provide goods or services
7) Advances from affiliated companies
8) Deferred revenue

c. **Equity**. Equity of a business enterprise is the residual after total liabilities are deducted from total assets.

1) Equity is divided into capital contributed by owners, retained earnings, and accumulated other comprehensive income (all comprehensive income items not included in net income). Treasury stock recorded at cost is a deduction from total equity, not an asset. Treasury stock recorded at par is a direct reduction of common stock.

6. A bankrupt entity about to be liquidated is not a going concern. A **statement of affairs** prepared as of a specific date presents assets and liabilities of the debtor at liquidation values, with carrying amounts shown on a memorandum basis.

7. Stop and review! You have completed the outline for this subunit. Study multiple-choice questions 1 through 14 beginning on page 78.

B. Income Statement

1. The results of operations are reported in the income statement (statement of earnings) on the accrual basis using an approach oriented to historical transactions.

a. The traditional income statement reports revenues from and expenses of the entity's major activities and gains and losses from other activities incurred over a period of time.

Revenues – Expenses + Gains – Losses = Income or Loss

1) Revenue and expense (nominal) accounts are temporary holding accounts that are periodically closed to permanent (real) accounts. The accountant need not close each revenue and expense transaction directly to capital.
2) Income/loss is closed to retained earnings at the end of the period.
3) Revenue is a part of continuing operations; therefore, discontinued operations, extraordinary items, and the cumulative effect of changes in accounting principle are listed separately.

2. **Transactions Included in Income**

a. **APB 9**, *Reporting the Results of Operations*, prescribes the **all-inclusive approach** with some modifications. Thus, all transactions affecting the net change in proprietorship equity during the period are included except transactions with owners and the rare transaction treated as a prior-period adjustment.

1) The net income reported in this way over the life of the entity reflects the sum of the periodic net incomes, including the nonrecurring items that are an appropriate part of the earnings history.
   a) An additional advantage of the all-inclusive approach is that manipulation is less likely; that is, the income statement will be less subject to variation caused by differences in judgment.
   b) The utility of the statement as a predictor of future income is not impaired if full disclosure of unusual, irregular, or nonrecurring items is made and an appropriate format is used.

b. The current operating performance concept emphasizes the ordinary, normal, recurring operations of the entity during the current period. Inclusion of extraordinary items or prior-period adjustments is believed to impair the significance of net income.

3. **Income Statement Format**

a. **APB 30**, *Reporting the Results of Operations*, requires the following items to be reported separately and in the indicated order on the face of the income statement:

1) Pretax income from continuing operations
2) The provision for income taxes on income from continuing operations
3) Income from continuing operations
4) Discontinued operations
   a) The income or loss from operations of the discontinued segment up to the measurement date and the gain or loss on disposal should both be reported net of tax. The gain or loss on disposal includes estimated operating income or loss of the segment from the measurement date to the disposal date, any direct disposal costs incurred during the phase-out period, and the estimated gain or loss on the actual disposal. Taxes applicable to these components should be disclosed in the notes or on the face of the statement.
   b) The gain or loss on disposal is estimated on the measurement date, which is the date on which management commits itself to a plan to dispose of a segment either by sale or abandonment. An estimated loss is recognized and treated as realized in the period that includes the measurement date. An estimated gain is not recognized until it is actually realized, which is usually the disposal date.
   c) In addition to reporting gains or losses on disposals, there are several required footnote disclosures, including
      i) The identity of the segment being discontinued.
      ii) The expected disposal date.
      iii) The expected manner of disposition.
      iv) A description of the remaining assets and liabilities of the segment at the balance sheet date.
5) Income before extraordinary items and the cumulative effect of accounting changes (if any)

6) Extraordinary items

a) These are material items that are both unusual in nature and infrequent in the environment in which the entity operates. They also include items designated as extraordinary by a pronouncement, e.g., debt extinguishments. This component is also presented net of tax (the tax is reported on the face of the statement or in a note).

b) Individual items should be reported on the face of the statement, but note disclosure is acceptable.

c) If an item is unusual or infrequent but not both, it is reported, not net of tax, as a separate component of income from continuing operations.

d) Certain items are not to be treated as extraordinary: write-downs of receivables and inventories, translation of foreign currency amounts, disposal of a segment, sale of productive assets, effects of strikes, and accruals on long-term contracts.

7) Cumulative effect of a change in accounting principle

a) This amount is reported net of tax (with disclosure of the related tax on the face of the statement or in a note).

8) Net income

9) EPS data are not given in the example below, but SFAS 128 requires that basic and diluted EPS for each period presented be reported for each of the following, if they exist. However, if an entity has a simple capital structure, it reports only basic EPS. EPS amounts for items a) and e) are reported on the face of the income statement. EPS amounts for items b), c), and d) are reported there or in the notes. Whether the amounts are pretax or net of tax should be stated.

a) Income from continuing operations
b) Discontinued operations
c) Extraordinary items
d) Cumulative effect of accounting changes
e) Net income

10) EXAMPLE:

Amy Corp.
Income Statement
For the Year Ended December 31

Income from continuing operations before income tax		$400,000
Income taxes		(100,000)
Income from continuing operations		$300,000
Discontinued operations		
Income from Bird Foods, minus applicable tax of $10,000	$30,000	
Loss on disposal of Bird Foods, net of tax benefit of $3,000	(4,000)	26,000
Income before extraordinary items and the effects of cumulative accounting changes		$326,000
Extraordinary items -- loss from hurricane in North Dakota plant minus applicable tax of $9,000		(45,000)
Cumulative effect of change in depreciation method, minus applicable tax of $14,000		(90,000)
Net income		$191,000

b. Presentation of income from continuing operations

1) The **single-step income statement** provides one grouping for revenue items and one for expense items. The single step is the one subtraction necessary to arrive at net income from continuing operations.

Revenues		
Net sales	$XXX	
Other revenues	XXX	
Gains	XXX	
Total revenues		$ XXX
Expenses		
Cost of goods sold	$XXX	
Selling and administrative expenses	XXX	
Interest expense	XXX	
Losses	XXX	
Income tax expense	XXX	
Total expenses		$(XXX)
Net income from continuing operations		$ XXX

2) The **multiple-step income statement** matches operating revenues and expenses in a section separate from nonoperating items, enhancing disclosure by presenting intermediary totals rather than one net income figure.

Net sales	$XXX
Cost of goods sold	(XXX)
Gross profit	$XXX
Selling and administrative expenses	(XXX)
Operating profit	$XXX
Other revenues and gains	XXX
	$XXX
Other expenses and losses	(XXX)
Pretax income from continuing operations	$XXX
Income taxes	(XXX)
Net income from continuing operations	$XXX

c. **Cost of goods sold** equals cost of goods manufactured (or purchases for a retailer) adjusted for the change in finished goods inventory.

1) **Cost of goods manufactured** is equivalent to a retailer's purchases. It equals all manufacturing costs incurred during the period, plus beginning work-in-process, minus ending work-in-process.

d. Other expenses

1) **General and administrative expenses** are incurred for the direction of the enterprise as a whole and are not related wholly to a specific function, e.g., selling or manufacturing. They include accounting, legal, and other fees for professional services; officers' salaries; insurance; wages of office staff; miscellaneous supplies; and office occupancy costs.

2) **Selling expenses** are those incurred in selling or marketing. Examples include sales representatives' salaries, rent for sales department, commissions, and traveling expense; advertising; selling department salaries and expenses; samples; and credit and collection costs. Shipping costs are also often classified as selling costs.

3) **Interest expense** is recognized based on the passage of time. In the case of bonds, notes, and capital leases, the effective interest method is used.

4. **Statement of retained earnings** reconciles the beginning balance of retained earnings with the ending balance.

   a. Net income is added to the beginning balance and dividends are subtracted.

   b. Prior-period adjustments are corrections of errors from prior-period financial statements. They are reported net of applicable taxes.

   c. Format of retained earnings statement

Statement of Retained Earnings	
Beginning balance	$ XXX
± Prior periods' adjustments	XXX
Adj. beginning balance	$ XXX
± N.I. (loss)	XXX
− Dividends	XXX
Ending balance	$ XXX

   d. **Changes in equity** (in addition to retained earnings) are reported in a separate statement, the basic statements, or the notes.

5. **Comprehensive Income.**

   a. **SFAS 130**, *Reporting Comprehensive Income*, applies to enterprises issuing a full set of financial statements if they have items of **other comprehensive income (OCI)**, but it does not apply to not-for-profit organizations. However, the terms "comprehensive income" and "OCI" are not required to be used. SFAS 130 divides comprehensive income into net income and OCI. Under existing accounting standards, OCI is classified separately into

      1) Foreign currency items (translation adjustments; gains and losses on a hedge of a net investment in a foreign operation, which are accounted for as if they were translation adjustments; and gains and losses on derivatives designated, qualifying, and effective as hedging instruments in foreign currency cash flow hedges)

         a) See Study Unit 7 for a treatment of foreign currency translation. See Study Unit 8 for a treatment of derivatives and hedging.

      2) Minimum pension liability adjustments (see Study Unit 5)

      3) Unrealized gains and losses on available-for-sale securities, except those that are hedged items in a fair value hedge (see Study Unit 4)

      4) The effective portions (minus amounts reclassified into earnings) of gains or losses on derivatives designated and qualifying as hedges of the exposure to variability in the cash flows of a recognized asset or liability or of a forecasted transaction (see Study Unit 8)

   b. SFAS 130 requires that comprehensive income and its components be displayed in a financial statement given the same prominence as other statements. No specific format is specified, but SFAS 130 encourages an enterprise to display the components of OCI and comprehensive income below net income. Regardless of the format, net income must be presented as a component of comprehensive income in the statement.

1) Among the possible formats for reporting comprehensive income are
    a) A separate statement of comprehensive income
    b) A combined statement of income and comprehensive income
    c) A statement of changes in equity
2) Each component of OCI is displayed net of tax, or one amount is shown for the aggregate tax effect on OCI, but the tax effect on each component must be disclosed.

c. The total of OCI for a period is transferred to a component of equity separate from retained earnings and additional paid-in capital. The accumulated balance for each classification in that component must be disclosed in the balance sheet, a statement of changes in equity, or the notes.

d. **Reclassification adjustments** are made for each component of OCI except minimum pension liability adjustments. Their purpose is to avoid double counting when an item included in net income was also included in OCI for the same or a prior period. For example, if a gain or loss on available-for-sale securities is realized in the current period, the prior recognition of an unrealized holding gain or loss must be eliminated from OCI.

e. A total for comprehensive income is reported in interim-period condensed statements.

6. Stop and review! You have completed the outline for this subunit. Study multiple-choice questions 15 through 31 beginning on page 82.

C. Statement of Cash Flows

1. **SFAS 95**, *Statement of Cash Flows*, requires a statement of cash flows as part of a full set of financial statements of all business entities (both publicly and privately held) and not-for-profit organizations.
    a. If a business enterprise or not-for-profit organization reports financial position and results of operations, it must present a statement of cash flows for any period for which results of operations are presented.
        1) However, defined benefit pension plans, certain other employee benefit plans, and certain highly liquid investment companies are exempt.
    b. SFAS 95 states, "Financial statements shall not report an amount of cash flow per share." The per-share amount may improperly imply that the cash flow is an alternative to net income as a performance measure.
2. The **primary purpose** of a statement of cash flows is to provide relevant information about the cash receipts and payments of an entity during a period. A secondary purpose is to provide information about investing and financing activities.
    a. If used with information in the other financial statements, the statement of cash flows should help investors, creditors, donors, and others to assess the entity's ability to generate positive future net cash flows, meet its obligations, and pay dividends. Cash flow information also helps users to assess
        1) The entity's needs for external financing
        2) The reasons for differences between income and associated cash receipts and payments

3) The cash and noncash aspects of investing and financing activities

a) Information about transactions that do not directly affect cash flow for the period must be disclosed. These transactions are excluded from the body of the statement to avoid undue complexity and detraction from the objective of providing information about cash flows.

i) Examples of **noncash investing and financing activities** to be reported in related disclosures but not in the statement include converting debt to equity, obtaining assets by assuming liabilities or entering into a capital lease, obtaining a building or investment asset by receiving a gift, and exchanging a noncash asset or liability for another.

3. The changes in cash and in cash equivalents during the period are to be explained in a statement of cash flows.

a. If an entity invests its cash in excess of immediate needs in short-term, highly liquid investments (cash equivalents), it should use the descriptive term "cash and cash equivalents." Otherwise, the term "cash" is acceptable. Terms such as "funds" or "quick assets" may not be used.

1) **Cash equivalents** are readily convertible to known amounts of cash and are so near their maturity that they present insignificant risk of changes in value because of changes in interest rates. Thus, an exchange of cash for cash equivalents has no effect on the statement of cash flows.

2) Usually, only investments with original maturities of 3 months or less qualify as cash equivalents. Money market funds, commercial paper, and treasury bills are examples.

3) However, not all qualifying investments must be classified as cash equivalents. An entity should establish and consistently apply a policy concerning which qualifying investments are to be treated as cash equivalents.

4. A statement of cash flows reports the cash effects of operating activities, investing activities, and financing activities during the period.

a. **Operating activities** include all transactions and other events not classified as investing and financing activities. In general, the cash effects of transactions and other events that enter into the determination of income are to be classified as operating activities.

1) Cash flows from operating activities include cash receipts from interest on loans and dividends on equity securities. They also include cash payments to employees and suppliers; to governments for taxes, duties, and fees; and to lenders for interest.

2) **SFAS 102** classifies as operating items cash flows from certain securities and other assets acquired for resale and carried at market value in a trading account (e.g., by banks, brokers, and dealers in securities), or from loans acquired for resale and carried at lower of cost or market.

3) Moreover, **SFAS 115** states that cash flows from purchases, sales, and maturities of trading securities are cash flows from operating activities.

b. **Investing activities** include making and collecting loans and acquiring and disposing of debt or equity instruments and property, plant, and equipment and other productive assets, that is, assets held for or used in the production of goods or services (other than the materials held in inventory).

1) Investing activities exclude transactions in cash equivalents and in certain loans or other debt or equity instruments acquired specifically for resale.

2) Cash flows from purchases, sales, and maturities of available-for-sale and held-to-maturity securities are cash flows from investing activities and are reported gross for each classification of security in the cash flows statement (SFAS 115).

c. **Financing activities** include the issuance of stock, the payment of dividends, treasury stock transactions, the issuance of debt, and the repayment or other settlement of debt obligations. It also includes receiving restricted resources that by donor stipulation must be used for long-term purposes.

d. **Hedging transactions**. Cash flows from derivative instruments accounted for as fair value or cash flow hedges may be classified in the same category as the flows from the hedged item, provided that this policy is disclosed. However, if hedge accounting is discontinued, subsequent cash flows are classified in accordance with the nature of the instrument (SFAS 104 and SFAS 133).

5. **Netting**. In general, cash inflows and outflows should be reported separately at gross amounts in a statement of cash flows. In certain instances, however, the net amount of related cash receipts and payments may provide sufficient information for certain classes of cash flows.

a. If the turnover of an item is quick, amounts are large, and the maturity is short, or if the entity is essentially holding or disbursing cash for customers, net reporting is proper.

1) Examples are demand deposits of a bank and customer accounts payable of a broker-dealer.

2) SFAS 104 permits banks, savings institutions, and credit unions to report net cash receipts and payments for deposits, time deposits, and loans.

6. SFAS 95 also requires translation of **foreign currency cash flows**.

a. A weighted-average exchange rate may be used if the result is substantially the same as would be obtained by using the rates in effect when the flows occurred.

b. The effect of exchange rate fluctuations must be separately reported as part of the reconciliation of cash and cash equivalents.

7. The statement of cash flows may report operating activities in the form of either an indirect or a direct presentation, although the direct method is encouraged.

a. The **direct presentation** reports major classes of gross operating cash receipts and payments and their sum (net operating cash flow). At a minimum, the following classes are included in a direct presentation:

1) Cash collected from customers, including lessees, licensees, and the like

2) Interest and dividends received (excluding those donor-restricted for long-term purposes)

3) Other operating cash receipts, if any

4) Cash paid to employees and other suppliers of goods or services, including suppliers of insurance, advertising and the like

5) Interest paid
6) Income taxes paid
7) Other operating cash payments, if any

b. The **indirect presentation** reconciles net income of a business enterprise or the change in net assets of a not-for-profit organization to net operating cash flow. It removes from net income or the change in net assets the effects of

1) All past deferrals of operating cash receipts and payments
   a) Examples are changes in inventory, deferred income, and prepaid expenses.
2) All accruals of expected future operating cash receipts and payments
   a) Examples are changes in receivables and payables.
3) Items whose cash effects are investing or financing cash flows
   a) Examples are bad debt expense; depreciation; goodwill amortization; and gains or losses on sales of property, plant, and equipment, on discontinued operations, or on debt extinguishment.

c. The same net operating cash flow will be reported under both methods. The reconciliation of net income or the change in net assets to net operating cash flow must be disclosed in a separate schedule under the direct method. The reconciliation may be reported in the statement of cash flows or in the related disclosures if the indirect method is used.

d. **EXAMPLE: Indirect presentation**

Dice Corp's balance sheet accounts as of December 31, year 2 and year 1 are presented in the next column. Information relating to year 2 activities is presented below.

Information Relating to year 2 Activities

- Net income for year 2 was $690,000.
- Cash dividends of $240,000 were declared and paid in year 2.
- Equipment costing $400,000 and having a carrying amount of $150,000 was sold on January 1, year 2 for $150,000 in cash.
- A long-term investment was sold in year 2 for $135,000 in cash.
- 10,000 common shares were issued in year 2 for $22 a share.
- Short-term investments consist of Treasury bills maturing on 6/30/year 3. They are not cash equivalents because their maturities are not 3 months or less.
- The provision for year 2 income taxes was $210,000.
- The accounts receivable balances at the beginning and end of year 2 were net of allowances for bad debts of $50,000 and $60,000, respectively. Dice wrote off $40,000 of bad debts during year 2. The only transactions affecting accounts receivable and the allowance were credit sales, collections, write-offs, and recognition of bad debt expense.
- During year 2, Dice constructed a plant asset. The accumulated expenditures during the year included $11,000 of capitalized interest.
- Dice accounts for its interest in Thrice Corp. under the equity method. Its equity in Thrice's year 2 earnings was $25,000. At the end of year 2, Dice received a $10,000 cash dividend from Thrice.

	December 31,	
Assets	**Year 2**	**Year 1**
Cash	$ 195,000	$ 100,000
Short-term investments	300,000	0
Accounts receivable (net)	480,000	510,000
Inventory	680,000	600,000
Prepaid expenses	15,000	20,000
Long-term investments	215,000	300,000
Plant assets	1,700,000	1,000,000
Accumulated depreciation	(450,000)	(450,000)
Goodwill	90,000	100,000
Total assets	$3,225,000	$2,180,000
Liabilities and Equity		
Accounts payable	$ 825,000	$ 720,000
Interest payable	15,000	10,000
Income tax payable	20,000	30,000
Short-term debt	325,000	0
Deferred taxes	250,000	300,000
Common stock, $10 par	800,000	700,000
Additional paid-in capital	370,000	250,000
Retained earnings	620,000	170,000
Total assets and equity	$3,225,000	$2,180,000

1) The following computations are required to determine **net cash provided by operations** ($905,000 as shown in the reconciliation on page 75):

   a) **Depreciation**. In year 2, Dice must have recognized $250,000 of depreciation [$450,000 accumulated depreciation at 12/31/year 2 – ($450,000 accumulated depreciation at 12/31/year 1 – $250,000 accumulated depreciation on equipment sold on 1/1/year 2)]. The depreciation and the $10,000 ($100,000 at 12/31/year 1 – $90,000 at 12/31/year 2) amortization of goodwill should be added to net income because both are noncash items included in net income.

   b) **Cost of goods sold**. The adjustment from cost of goods sold (an accrual accounting amount) to cash paid to suppliers requires two steps: from CGS to purchases and from purchases to cash paid to suppliers. The $80,000 ($680,000 – $600,000) increase in inventory is a deduction from net income because it indicates that purchases were $80,000 greater than the cost of goods sold amount used to compute net income.

   c) **Accounts payable**. The $105,000 ($825,000 – $720,000) increase in accounts payable is an addition to net income. It indicates that cash disbursements to suppliers were $105,000 less than purchases. The net effect of the changes in inventory and accounts payable is that cash paid to suppliers was $25,000 less than CGS.

   d) **Accounts receivable.** The net accounts receivable balance declined by $30,000 ($510,000 – $480,000), implying that cash collections exceeded net income. Given that sales, collections, write-offs, and recognition of bad debt expense were the only relevant transactions, $30,000 should be added to net income. Use of the change in net accounts receivable as a reconciliation adjustment is a short-cut method. It yields the same net adjustment to net income as separately including the effects of the change in gross accounts receivable [($510,000 + $50,000 bad debt allowance) – ($480,000 + $60,000 bad debt allowance) = an addition of $20,000], bad debt expense (a noncash item resulting in an addition of $50,000), and bad debt write-offs (a deduction of $40,000 to reflect that write-offs did not result in collections).

   e) **Prepaid expenses**. The $5,000 decrease in prepaid expenses signifies that noncash expenses were recognized and should be added back to net income.

   f) **Dividends received**. Earnings of an affiliate accounted for under the equity method are debited to the investment account and credited to net income. A cash dividend from the affiliate is debited to cash and credited to the investment account. Thus, an adjustment reducing net income by $15,000 ($25,000 earnings – $10,000 cash dividend) for undistributed earnings is necessary.

   g) **Long-term investments**. A $100,000 ($300,000 + $25,000 equity in affiliate's earnings – $10,000 cash dividend – $215,000) decrease in the long-term investments account occurred when these investments were sold for $135,000. The resulting $35,000 gain was included in the determination of net income. The cash effect is properly classified as an investing activity, and the $35,000 should be subtracted from net income to remove it from the operating section. SFAS 115 is not applicable because the Thrice investment is accounted for under the equity method.

h) **Interest payable**. Interest payable increased by $5,000, which represents a noncash expense and a reconciling addition to net income. The interest capitalized is ignored for reconciliation purposes because it is not reported as interest expense in the income statement or as interest paid in the statement of cash flows or in related disclosures. The $11,000 of capitalized interest is included in the capitalized cost of the plant asset.

i) **Income tax payable**. Income tax payable decreased by $10,000, giving rise to a reconciling deduction from net income because tax expense was less than cash paid for taxes.

j) **Deferred taxes**. Deferred taxes decreased by $50,000. This reconciling deduction from net income resulted when temporary differences reversed and cash payments for taxes exceeded tax expense.

Reconciliation of Net Income to Net Operating Cash Flow		
Net income for year 2	$690,000	
Depreciation	250,000	a)
Amortization	10,000	a)
Inventory	(80,000)	b)
Accounts payable	105,000	c)
Accounts receivable (net)	30,000	d)
Prepaid expenses	5,000	e)
Undistributed earnings of an affiliate	(15,000)	f)
Gain on sale of investments	(35,000)	g)
Interest payable	5,000	h)
Income tax payable	(10,000)	i)
Deferred taxes	(50,000)	j)
Net operating cash flow	$905,000	

2) **Net investing cash flow**

a) The $300,000 increase in short-term investments indicates that a purchase occurred.

b) The balance sheet further indicates that plant assets increased by $700,000 ($1,700,000 – $1,000,000). Moreover, plant assets (equipment) costing $400,000 were sold. Thus, the cost of constructing the plant asset must have equaled $1,100,000 [$1,700,000 ending plant assets balance – ($1,000,000 beginning balance – $400,000 cost of equipment sold)].

c) The cash flows from investing activities include the cash effects of the sale of equipment and the long-term investments, the purchases of short-term investments (assuming they are held-to-maturity or available-for-sale securities), and the construction of a plant asset. The equipment was sold for $150,000 and the long-term investments for $135,000. Thus, the net cash used in investing activities was $1,115,000.

Purchases:		
Short-term investments	$ (300,000)	a)
Plant assets	(1,100,000)	b)
Sales:		
Equipment	150,000	c)
Long-term investments	135,000	c)
Net investing cash flow	$(1,115,000)	

3) **Net financing cash flow**

   a) Dice Corp.'s year 2 financing activities included the issuance of short-term debt ($325,000 – $0 = $325,000), the issuance of common stock and the recording of additional paid-in capital [($800,000 – $700,000) + ($370,000 – $250,000) = $220,000], and the payment of cash dividends ($240,000). The net cash provided by these financing activities was $305,000.

Short-term debt	$325,000	a)
Common stock	220,000	a)
Cash dividends	(240,000)	a)
Net financing cash flow	$305,000	

4) **Net change in cash**. According to Dice Corp.'s balance sheets, the net change in cash was an increase of $95,000 ($195,000 – $100,000).

   a) This amount reconciles with the net cash provided by (used in) operating, investing, and financing activities ($905,000 – $1,115,000 + $305,000 = $95,000).

5) **Noncash financing and investing activities**. Dice Corp. had no such transactions in year 2 to be reported in supplemental disclosures.

6) **Supplemental cash flow disclosures**. If Dice Corp. uses the indirect method to present its statement of cash flows, the interest paid (excluding amounts capitalized) and income taxes paid must be reported in related disclosures. Interest paid cannot be calculated here because interest expense is not given in the example.

7) Income taxes paid were $270,000 ($210,000 provision for income taxes + $50,000 decrease in deferred taxes + $10,000 decrease in taxes payable).

Dice Corp.
Statement of Cash Flows -- Indirect Method
for the Year Ended December 31, Year 2
Increase (Decrease) in Cash and Cash Equivalents

Operating cash flows:		
Net income for year 2	$ 690,000	
Depreciation	250,000	
Amortization	10,000	
Inventory	(80,000)	
Accounts payable	105,000	
Accounts receivable (net)	30,000	
Prepaid expenses	5,000	
Undistributed earnings of an affiliate	(15,000)	
Gain on sale of investments	(35,000)	
Interest payable	5,000	
Income tax payable	(10,000)	
Deferred taxes	(50,000)	
Net cash provided by operating activities		$ 905,000
Investing cash flows:		
Proceeds from sale of equipment	$ 150,000	
Proceeds from sale of long-term investments	135,000	
Payments for short-term investments	(300,000)	
Payments for plant assets	(1,100,000)	
Net cash used in investing activities		(1,115,000)
Financing cash flows:		
Proceeds from short-term debt	$ 325,000	
Proceeds from issuing common stock	220,000	
Dividends paid	(240,000)	
Net cash provided by financing activities		305,000
Net increase		$ 95,000
Beginning balance		100,000
Ending balance		$ 195,000

e. **Direct presentation**. The difference between the direct and indirect methods lies in the way in which the net cash provided by operations is determined. Compare the direct method format presented below with the indirect method format on page 75. Calculations for deriving the amounts of the major classes of gross cash flows have been omitted.

Operating cash flows:		
Cash collected from customers	$ 7,790,000	
Cash paid to employees and suppliers	(6,520,000)	
Dividend from affiliate	10,000	
Interest received	30,000	
Interest paid	(135,000)	
Income taxes paid	(270,000)	
Net cash provided by operating activities		$905,000

1) **Cash collected from customers** may be determined by adjusting sales for the changes in customer receivables. This calculation requires information similar to that used in an indirect presentation to reconcile net income to net operating cash flow: total operating receivables (which are usually separate from those for interest and dividends), bad debt write-offs, and any other noncash entries in customer accounts.

2) **Cash paid to employees and suppliers** of goods and services may be determined by adjusting cost of goods sold and expenses (excluding interest, income tax, and depreciation) for the changes in inventory, prepaid expenses, and operating payables. This calculation is also similar to the process used in reconciling net income to net operating cash flow. It requires that operating payables and expenses be separated from interest and income tax payable.

3) Dividends received, not the amount of equity-based earnings recognized in net income, is included.

4) Interest income is adjusted for changes in interest receivable.

5) Interest expense is adjusted for changes in interest payable. Interest capitalized is not considered in determining interest paid because it is included in payments for plant assets, not in interest expense.

6) Income taxes paid equaled tax expense adjusted for the changes in deferred taxes and in taxes payable.

8. Stop and review! You have completed the outline for this subunit. Study multiple-choice questions 32 through 66 beginning on page 88.

MULTIPLE-CHOICE QUESTIONS

A. Balance Sheet

1. The basic financial statements include a

A. Balance sheet, income statement, statement of retained earnings, and statement of changes in retained earnings.

B. Statement of financial position, income statement, statement of retained earnings, and statement of changes in retained earnings.

C. Balance sheet, statement of financial position, income statement, and statement of changes in retained earnings.

D. Statement of financial position, income statement, statement of cash flows, and statement of retained earnings.

The correct answer is (D). *(CMA, adapted)*

REQUIRED: The statements included in the basic financial statements.

DISCUSSION: Under GAAP, the basic required statements are the statements of financial position, income, cash flows, and retained earnings. Changes in equity must be disclosed in the basic statements, the notes thereto, or a separate statement. A statement of cash flows is now a required part of a full set of financial statements of all business entities (both publicly held and privately held) (SFAS 95). The statement of cash flows has replaced the statement of changes in financial position. Moreover, comprehensive income must be displayed in a financial statement given the same prominence as other statements, but no specific format is required as long as net income is displayed as a component of comprehensive income in the statement.

Answers (A), (B), and (C) are incorrect because the basic statements include the statements of financial position, income, cash flows, and retained earnings.

2. What are the disclosure requirements with respect to changes in capital accounts other than retained earnings and changes in other owners' equity data?

A. When the income statement and balance sheet are presented, all changes in the capital accounts and changes in the number of shares of equity securities must be disclosed.

B. When the balance sheet is presented, all changes in the capital accounts must be disclosed.

C. When the income statement is presented, all changes in the capital accounts and changes in the number of shares of equity securities must be disclosed.

D. Changes in the number of shares of equity securities must be disclosed when a balance sheet is presented, but there is no specific disclosure requirement with respect to the capital accounts other than retained earnings.

The correct answer is (A). *(Publisher)*

REQUIRED: The disclosure requirements with respect to changes in capital accounts other than retained earnings and changes in other owners' equity data.

DISCUSSION: APB 12, *Omnibus Opinion-1967*, requires disclosure both of changes in the separate accounts appearing in equity (in addition to retained earnings) and of changes in the number of shares of equity securities when both the balance sheet and the income statement are presented. This disclosure may be in separate statements, the basic financial statements, or the notes.

Answers (B) and (C) are incorrect because the requirement applies only when both the balance sheet and the income statement are presented. Answer (D) is incorrect because there is a specific disclosure requirement with respect to the changes in the capital accounts.

3. The primary purpose of the statement of financial position is to reflect

A. The fair value of the firm's assets at some moment in time.

B. The status of the firm's assets in case of forced liquidation of the firm.

C. The success of a company's operations for a given amount of time.

D. Items of value, debt, and net worth.

The correct answer is (D). *(CMA, adapted)*

REQUIRED: The primary purpose of the statement of financial position.

DISCUSSION: The balance sheet presents three major financial accounting elements: assets (items of value), liabilities (debts), and equity (net worth). According to SFAC 6, *Elements of Financial Statements*, assets are probable future economic benefits resulting from past transactions or events. Liabilities are probable future sacrifices of economic benefits arising from present obligations as a result of past transactions or events. Equity is the residual interest in the assets after deduction of liabilities.

Answer (A) is incorrect because the measurement attributes of assets include but are not limited to fair value. Answer (B) is incorrect because financial statements reflect the going concern assumption. Hence, they usually do not report forced liquidation values. Answer (C) is incorrect because the income statement provides this type of information.

4. A statement of financial position allows investors to assess all of the following except

A. The efficiency with which enterprise assets are used.

B. The liquidity and financial flexibility of the enterprise.

C. The capital structure of the enterprise.

D. The net realizable value of enterprise assets.

The correct answer is (D). *(CMA, adapted)*

REQUIRED: The attribute not assessable.

DISCUSSION: Assets are usually valued at original historical cost in a statement of financial position, although some exceptions exist. For example, some short-term receivables are reported at their net realizable value. Thus, the statement of financial position cannot be relied upon to assess NRV.

Answers (A) and (B) are incorrect because efficiency of asset use, liquidity, and financial flexibility are assessed by calculating liquidity, leverage, and asset management ratios. These ratios require balance sheet data. Answer (C) is incorrect because the capital structure of the enterprise is reported in the equity section of the statement of financial position.

5. Notes to financial statements are beneficial in meeting the disclosure requirements of financial reporting. The notes should not be used to

A. Describe significant accounting policies.

B. Describe depreciation methods employed by the company.

C. Describe principles and methods peculiar to the industry in which the company operates, when these principles and methods are predominantly followed in that industry.

D. Correct an improper presentation in the financial statements.

The correct answer is (D). *(CMA, adapted)*

REQUIRED: The improper use of notes in financial statements.

DISCUSSION: Financial statement notes should not be used to correct improper presentations. The financial statements should be presented correctly on their own. Notes should be used to explain the methods used to prepare the financial statements and the amounts shown.

Answers (A), (B), and (C) are incorrect because each describes an appropriate and required disclosure that should appear in the notes to the financial statements (APB 22, *Disclosure of Accounting Policies*).

6. The accounting equation (assets – liabilities = equity) reflects the

A. Entity point of view.

B. Fund theory.

C. Proprietary point of view.

D. Enterprise theory.

The correct answer is (C). *(CMA, adapted)*

REQUIRED: The concept on which the basic accounting equation is based.

DISCUSSION: The equation is based on the proprietary theory. Equity in an enterprise is what remains after the economic obligations of the enterprise are deducted from its economic resources.

Answer (A) is incorrect because the entity concept limits accounting information to that related to a specific entity (possibly not the same as the legal entity). Answer (B) is incorrect because fund theory stresses that assets equal obligations (equity and liabilities are sources of assets). Answer (D) is incorrect because the enterprise concept stresses ownership of the assets; that is, the emphasis is on the credit side of the balance sheet.

7. Karen's Crafts, Inc. has the following accounts included in its December 31 trial balance:

Accounts payable	$250,000
Discount on bonds payable	34,000
Wages payable	29,000
Interest payable	14,000
Bonds payable (Issued 1/1/96; due 1/1/06)	500,000
Income taxes payable	26,000

What amount of current liabilities will be reported on Karen's December 31 statement of financial position?

A. $285,000

B. $319,000

C. $353,000

D. $819,000

The correct answer is (B). *(Publisher)*

REQUIRED: The total of current liabilities.

DISCUSSION: Current liabilities consist of those debts that will have to be paid in the coming year or the normal operating cycle, whichever period is longer. Examples include accounts payable, wages payable, interest payable, and income taxes payable. Bonds payable and its contra account, discount on bonds payable, would both be shown under the long-term liability classification. The total current liabilities would be $319,000 ($250,000 + $29,000 + $14,000 + $26,000).

Answer (A) is incorrect because the discount on bonds payable is erroneously deducted from the total. Answer (C) is incorrect because $353,000 includes discount on bonds payable. Answer (D) is incorrect because $819,000 includes bonds payable.

8. Perry Mansfield Corporation has the following accounts included in its December 31 trial balance:

Accounts receivable	$110,000
Inventories	250,000
Patents	90,000
Prepaid insurance	19,500
Accounts payable	72,000
Cash	28,000

What amount of current assets should Perry Mansfield include in its statement of financial position at December 31?

A. $335,500

B. $388,000

C. $407,500

D. $479,500

The correct answer is (C). *(Publisher)*

REQUIRED: The amount of current assets.

DISCUSSION: Current assets consist of cash, certain marketable securities, receivables, inventories, and prepaid expenses. Adding these elements together produces a total of $407,500 ($28,000 cash + $110,000 receivables + $250,000 inventories + $19,500 prepaid insurance).

Answer (A) is incorrect because deducting accounts payable from the current assets results in the amount of working capital, rather than the total of current assets. Answer (B) is incorrect because it fails to include prepaid insurance in the total. Answer (D) is incorrect because it erroneously includes accounts payable.

9. According to SFAS 78, *Classification of Obligations That Are Callable by the Creditor*, long-term obligations that are or will become callable by the creditor because of the debtor's violation of a provision of the debt agreement at the balance sheet date should be classified as

A. Long-term liabilities.

B. Current liabilities unless the debtor goes bankrupt.

C. Current liabilities unless the creditor has waived the right to demand repayment for more than 1 year from the balance sheet date.

D. Contingent liabilities until the violation is corrected.

The correct answer is (C). *(CMA, adapted)*

REQUIRED: The classification of long-term debt callable because of the debtor's violation of a loan agreement.

DISCUSSION: In these circumstances, the obligation should be classified as current. However, the debt need not be reclassified if the violation will be cured within a specified grace period or if the creditor formally waives or subsequently loses the right to demand repayment for a period of more than a year from the balance sheet date. Also, reclassification is not required if the debtor expects and has the ability to refinance the obligation on a long-term basis.

Answer (A) is incorrect because SFAS 78 requires classification as a current liability. Answer (B) is incorrect because bankruptcy is not an exception. Answer (D) is incorrect because SFAS 78 concerns callable, not contingent, liabilities.

10. Abernathy Corporation uses a calendar year for financial and tax reporting purposes and has $100 million of mortgage bonds due on January 15, year 2. By January 10, year 2, Abernathy intends to refinance this debt with new long-term mortgage bonds and has entered into a financing agreement that clearly demonstrates its ability to consummate the refinancing. This debt is to be

A. Classified as a current liability on the statement of financial position at December 31, year 1.

B. Classified as a long-term liability on the statement of financial position at December 31, year 1.

C. Retired as of December 31, year 1.

D. Considered off-balance-sheet debt.

The correct answer is (B). *(CMA, adapted)*

REQUIRED: The balance sheet treatment of maturing long-term debt that is to be refinanced on a long-term basis.

DISCUSSION: SFAS 6 states that short-term obligations expected to be refinanced should be reported as current liabilities unless the firm both plans to refinance and has the ability to refinance the debt on a long-term basis. The ability to refinance on a long-term basis is evidenced by a post-balance-sheet date issuance of long-term debt or a financing arrangement that will clearly permit long-term refinancing.

Answer (A) is incorrect because the company intends to refinance the debt on a long-term basis. Answer (C) is incorrect because the debt has not been retired. Answer (D) is incorrect because the debt is on the balance sheet.

11. Lister Company intends to refinance a portion of its short-term debt in year 2 and is negotiating a long-term financing agreement with a local bank. This agreement would be noncancellable and would extend for a period of 2 years. The amount of short-term debt that Lister Company can exclude from its statement of financial position at December 31, year 1

A. May exceed the amount available for refinancing under the agreement.

B. Depends on the demonstrated ability to consummate the refinancing.

C. Is reduced by the proportionate change in the working capital ratio.

D. Is zero unless the refinancing has occurred by year-end.

The correct answer is (B). *(CMA, adapted)*

REQUIRED: The amount of short-term debt excluded from the current section of the balance sheet.

DISCUSSION: If an enterprise intends to refinance short-term obligations on a long-term basis and demonstrates an ability to consummate the refinancing, the obligations should be excluded from current liabilities and classified as noncurrent (SFAS 6, *Classification of Short-Term Obligations Expected to Be Refinanced*). The ability to consummate the refinancing may be demonstrated by a post-balance-sheet-date issuance of a long-term obligation or equity securities, or by entering into a financing agreement that meets certain criteria. These criteria are that the agreement does not expire within 1 year, it is noncancelable by the lender, no violation of the agreement exists at the balance sheet date, and the lender is financially capable of honoring the agreement.

Answer (A) is incorrect because the amount excluded cannot exceed the amount available for refinancing. Answer (C) is incorrect because SFAS 6 has no provision for adjustments or reductions. Answer (D) is incorrect because the refinancing need not have occurred if the firm intends and demonstrates an ability to consummate such refinancing.

12. When treasury stock is accounted for at cost, the cost is reported on the balance sheet as a(n)

A. Asset.

B. Reduction of retained earnings.

C. Reduction of additional paid-in-capital.

D. Unallocated reduction of equity.

The correct answer is (D). *(CMA, adapted)*

REQUIRED: The reporting of treasury stock.

DISCUSSION: Treasury stock is a corporation's own stock that has been reacquired but not retired. The entry to record the acquisition of treasury stock accounted for at cost is to debit a contra equity account and to credit cash. In the balance sheet, treasury stock recorded at cost is subtracted from the total of the capital stock balances, additional paid-in capital, retained earnings, and accumulated other comprehensive income. It is not allocated. If treasury stock is recorded at par, it is a direct reduction of common stock, not total equity.

Answer (A) is incorrect because treasury stock is not an asset. A corporation cannot own itself. Answers (B) and (C) are incorrect because treasury stock accounted for at cost is subtracted from the total of the other equity accounts.

13. When a company was in the process of closing its original store, no accounting notice of the liquidation values of the discontinued store's assets were considered in the accounting records. The accountant did not make any entries until the assets were disposed of because the company was still a going concern. However, when liquidation of a business is foreseen but not yet accomplished, a different financial statement is prepared. This statement is known as the

A. Statement of liquidation.

B. Charge and discharge statement.

C. Statement of realization.

D. Statement of affairs.

The correct answer is (D). *(CMA, adapted)*

REQUIRED: The additional financial statement that is prepared when a company is in the process of liquidation.

DISCUSSION: A statement of affairs is prepared for a company in the process of liquidation. It reflects the financial condition of the company on a going-out-of-business rather than a going-concern basis. Liquidation value instead of historical cost is used to value assets. Moreover, assets are not classified as current or noncurrent but according to the extent to which they are subject to secured claims. Liabilities are shown based on categories of creditors, and shareholders' equity may become shareholders' deficiency because a liquidating company may have a negative net worth.

Answers (A) and (C) are incorrect because the statement prepared by the trustee in bankruptcy to reconcile the book amounts to his/her administration of the estate is the statement of realization and liquidation. Answer (B) is incorrect because a charge and discharge statement is prepared by the personal representative of a decedent's estate.

14. Felicity Company has the following accounts included in its December 31 trial balance:

Treasury stock	$ 48,000
Retained earnings	141,000
Trademarks	32,000
Preferred stock	175,000
Common stock	50,000
Deferred income taxes	85,000
Additional paid-in capital	196,000
Accumulated depreciation	16,000

What amount of shareholders' equity will be reported on Felicity's December 31 statement of financial position?

A. $373,000

B. $514,000

C. $562,000

D. $610,000

The correct answer is (B). *(Publisher)*

REQUIRED: The total shareholders' equity.

DISCUSSION: Shareholders' equity consists of paid-in capital, retained earnings, and other comprehensive income. Shareholders' equity accounts may therefore include retained earnings, preferred stock, common stock, and additional paid-in capital. Moreover, treasury stock is a contra account in the shareholders' equity section of the balance sheet. The total would be $514,000 ($141,000 + $175,000 + $50,000 + $196,000 – $48,000 of treasury stock).

Answer (A) is incorrect because retained earnings should be included in shareholders' equity. Answer (C) is incorrect because $562,000 results from a failure to deduct treasury stock. Answer (D) is incorrect because treasury stock should be deducted from, not added to, shareholders' equity.

B. Income Statement

15. An income statement for a business prepared under the current operating performance concept would include only the recurring earnings from its normal operations and

A. No other items.

B. Any extraordinary items.

C. Any prior-period adjustments.

D. Any gains or losses from extinguishment of debt.

The correct answer is (A). *(CMA, adapted)*

REQUIRED: The items included in a current operating performance income statement.

DISCUSSION: The current operating performance concept emphasizes the ordinary, normal, recurring operations of the entity during the current period. Inclusion of extraordinary items or prior-period adjustments is believed to impair the significance of net income. The current operating performance concept is not consistent with GAAP.

Answers (B) and (C) are incorrect because extraordinary items and prior-period adjustments are excluded under the current operating performance concept. Answer (D) is incorrect because gains and losses from extinguishment of debt are extraordinary.

16. In Hopkins Co.'s Year 3 single-step income statement, the section titled *Revenues* consisted of the following:

Net sales revenue		$187,000
Results from discontinued operations:		
Loss from operations of segment (net of $1,200 tax effect)	$(2,400)	
Gain on disposal of segment (net of $7,200 tax effect)	14,400	12,000
Interest revenue		10,200
Gain on sale of equipment		4,700
Cumulative change in Year 1 and Year 2 income due to change in depreciation method (net of $750 tax effect)		1,500
Total revenues		$215,400

In the revenues section of the Year 3 income statement, Hopkins should have reported total revenues of

A. $217,800

B. $215,400

C. $203,700

D. $201,900

The correct answer is (D). *(Publisher)*

REQUIRED: The total revenues under GAAP.

DISCUSSION: Revenue is a component of income from continuing operations. Results of discontinued operations and the cumulative effect of a change in accounting principle are classifications in the income statement separate from continuing operations. Hence, total revenues were $201,900 ($215,400 – $12,000 results from discontinued operations – $1,500 cumulative-effect type change). Alternatively, total revenues consist of net sales of $187,000, plus interest revenue of $10,200, plus gain on sale of equipment (which is not an extraordinary item) of $4,700.

Answer (A) is incorrect because $217,800 equals $215,400 reported total revenues, plus the $2,400 loss from operations of the segment. Answer (B) is incorrect because $215,400 reflects no adjustment for results from discontinued operations and the cumulative-effect type change. Answer (C) is incorrect because $203,700 improperly subtracts interest revenue and does not adjust for the results from discontinued operations.

17. A company decided to sell a line of its business. The assets were sold for $100,000 and had a net book value of $70,000. The applicable tax rate was 20%. The result of this transaction will appear on the

A. Balance sheet as a prior-period adjustment.

B. Income statement as an extraordinary item.

C. Income statement as discontinued operations.

D. Income statement as an accounting change.

The correct answer is (C). *(CIA, adapted)*

REQUIRED: The reporting of a sale of a line of business.

DISCUSSION: The results of operations of a segment that has been or will be discontinued, together with any gain or loss on disposal, should be reported separately as a component of income before extraordinary items and the cumulative effect of accounting changes. Income from discontinued operations and the gain or loss on disposal should each be disclosed net of tax.

Answer (A) is incorrect because gain or loss from discontinued operations appears on the income statement. Answer (B) is incorrect because discontinued operations is a separate caption in the income statement just before extraordinary items. Answer (D) is incorrect because disposal of a segment is not a change in accounting principle.

18. The gain or loss from disposal of a segment

A. Includes the operating gain or loss realized by the segment from the beginning of the fiscal year to the disposal date.

B. Is reported as an addition to or subtraction from the beginning balance of retained earnings on the statement of retained earnings.

C. Is reported as an extraordinary item on the income statement.

D. Is reported as a component of net income and distinguished from the operating gain or loss realized by the segment prior to the measurement date.

The correct answer is (D). *(CMA, adapted)*

REQUIRED: The true statement about the gain or loss from disposal of a segment.

DISCUSSION: Discontinued operations should be presented as two subcategories. The first is operating income or loss of the segment prior to the measurement date. The second is the gain or loss on disposal. The gain or loss on disposal includes estimated operating income or loss of the segment from the measurement date to the disposal date, any direct disposal costs incurred during the phase-out period, and the estimated gain or loss on the actual disposal.

Answer (A) is incorrect because the operating gain or loss for the partial period is not combined with the gain or loss on disposal. Answer (B) is incorrect because a prior-period adjustment is an adjustment to beginning retained earnings. Answer (C) is incorrect because gain or loss on disposal is reported in a discontinued operations section prior to extraordinary items.

19. When reporting the discontinuance of a business segment, APB 30, *Reporting the Results of Operations*, specifies that

A. The results of the segment operations during the phase-out period be reported as part of the gain or loss from continuing operations.

B. The gain or loss on discontinued operations be reported net of tax as a separate item before extraordinary items.

C. The costs directly associated with discontinuance be included as an expense of continuing operations.

D. All gains or losses expected from discontinuance be reported at the measurement date even though the disposal date is in a subsequent period.

The correct answer is (B). *(CMA, adapted)*

REQUIRED: The true statement about discontinued operations reporting requirements.

DISCUSSION: The results of operations of a segment that has been or will be discontinued, together with any gain or loss on disposal, should be reported separately as a component of income before extraordinary items and the cumulative effect of accounting changes. Income from discontinued operations and the gain or loss on disposal should each be disclosed net of tax.

Answer (A) is incorrect because operating results during the phase-out period are part of the gain (loss) on disposal. Answer (C) is incorrect because the direct costs of discontinuance are included in the gain (loss) on the actual disposal. Answer (D) is incorrect because losses are to be reported at the measurement date even if the disposal date is in a subsequent period. Gains are not to be recognized until realized.

20. Brett Corporation had retained earnings of $529,000 at January 1 of the current year. Net income for the year was $2,496,000, and cash dividends of $750,000 were declared and paid. Another $50,000 of dividends were declared late in December, but were unpaid at year-end. Brett's ending balance of its statement of retained earnings is

A. $1,696,000

B. $2,225,000

C. $2,275,000

D. $3,025,000

The correct answer is (B). *(Publisher)*

REQUIRED: The year-end balance of retained earnings.

DISCUSSION: Dividends declared but not paid reduce retained earnings. Thus, the year-end balance of retained earnings is calculated as follows:

January 1 balance		$ 529,000
Net income		2,496,000
Retained earnings available		$3,025,000
Dividends	$750,000	
	50,000	(800,000)
		$2,225,000

Answer (A) is incorrect because $1,696,000 does not include the beginning balance. Answer (C) is incorrect because $2,275,000 results from a failure to deduct the dividend that was unpaid; such a dividend would be a liability of the corporation. Answer (D) is incorrect because $3,025,000 results from a failure to deduct dividends.

21. Which one of the following material events would be classified as an extraordinary item on an income statement?

A. A loss due to the effects of a strike against a major supplier.

B. A gain or loss on the disposal of a portion of the business.

C. A gain or loss from the extinguishment of debt.

D. A gain or loss from the translation of foreign currency due to a major devaluation.

The correct answer is (C). *(CMA, adapted)*

REQUIRED: The event classified as an extraordinary item on the income statement.

DISCUSSION: APB 30 gives examples of certain transactions that are not to be considered extraordinary items. These include write-downs of receivables and inventories, translation of foreign currency amounts, disposal of a business segment, disposal of productive assets, the effects of strikes, and the adjustments of accruals on long-term contracts. A gain or loss on the early extinguishment of debt is to be shown as an extraordinary item under the provisions of SFAS 4.

Answers (A), (B), and (D) are incorrect because APB 30 specifically excludes a loss due to the effects of a strike against a major supplier, a gain or loss on the disposal of a portion of the business, and a gain or loss from the translation of foreign currency due to a major devaluation from the definition of extraordinary items.

22. SFAS 128, *Earnings per Share*, requires which of the following policies regarding presentation of extraordinary items?

A. Earnings-per-share amounts should be presented in a separate schedule.

B. Extraordinary items should be presented as an aggregate amount.

C. Income taxes applicable to extraordinary items should be presented in a separate schedule.

D. Earnings-per-share amounts should be presented on the face of the income statement or in the notes.

The correct answer is (D). *(Publisher)*

REQUIRED: The presentation required by SFAS 128 regarding extraordinary items.

DISCUSSION: Basic and diluted per-share amounts for extraordinary items are presented either on the face of the income statement or in the related notes. Prior to the issuance of SFAS 128, APB 15 required presentation of EPS amounts for income before extraordinary items and net income on the face of the income statement.

Answer (A) is incorrect because EPS amounts may be presented either on the face of the income statement or in the notes. Answer (B) is incorrect because extraordinary items should be presented individually, rather than in the aggregate, and on the face of the income statement, if practicable; otherwise, disclosure in related notes is acceptable (APB 30). Answer (C) is incorrect because income taxes applicable to extraordinary items should be presented on the face of the income statement or in a related note.

23. When reporting extraordinary items,

A. Each item (net of tax) is presented on the face of the income statement separately as a component of net income for the period.

B. Each item is presented exclusive of any related income tax.

C. Each item is presented as an unusual item within income from continuing operations.

D. All extraordinary gains or losses that occur in a period are summarized as total gains and total losses, then offset to present the net extraordinary gain or loss.

The correct answer is (A). *(CMA, adapted)*

REQUIRED: The true statement about the reporting of extraordinary items.

DISCUSSION: Extraordinary items should be presented net of tax after income from operations. APB 30 states, "Descriptive captions and the amounts for individual extraordinary events or transactions should be presented, preferably on the face of the income statement, if practicable; otherwise, disclosure in related notes is acceptable."

Answer (B) is incorrect because extraordinary items are to be reported net of the related tax effect. Answer (C) is incorrect because extraordinary items are not reported in the continuing operations section of the income statement. Answer (D) is incorrect because each extraordinary item is to be reported separately.

24. Which one of the following items is included in the determination of income from continuing operations?

A. Discontinued operations.

B. Extraordinary loss.

C. Cumulative effect of a change in an accounting principle.

D. Unusual loss from a write-down of inventory.

The correct answer is (D). *(CMA, adapted)*

REQUIRED: The item included in the computation of income from continuing operations.

DISCUSSION: APB 30 specifies certain items that are not to be treated as extraordinary gains and losses. Rather, they are included in the determination of income from continuing operations. These gains and losses include those from write-downs of receivables and inventories, translation of foreign currency amounts, disposal of a business segment, sale of productive assets, strikes, and accruals on long-term contracts. A write-down of inventory is therefore included in the computation of income from continuing operations.

Answers (A), (B), and (C) are incorrect because discontinued operations, extraordinary loss, and cumulative effect of a change in an accounting principle are reported separately from income from continuing operations.

25. The major distinction between the multiple-step and single-step income statement formats is the separation of

A. Operating and nonoperating data.

B. Income tax expense and administrative expenses.

C. Cost of goods sold expense and administrative expenses.

D. The effect on income taxes due to extraordinary items and the effect on income taxes due to income before extraordinary items.

The correct answer is (A). *(CIA, adapted)*

REQUIRED: The major distinction between the multiple-step and single-step income statement formats.

DISCUSSION: Within the income from continuing operations classification, the single-step income statement provides one grouping for revenue items and one for expense items. The single-step is the one subtraction necessary to arrive at income from continuing operations prior to the effect of income taxes. In contrast, the multiple-step income statement matches operating revenues and expenses separately from nonoperating items. This format emphasizes subtotals such as gross margin, operating income, and nonoperating income within presentation of income from continuing operations.

Answers (B), (C), and (D) are incorrect because the major distinction is the separation of operating and nonoperating data.

26. In a multiple-step income statement for a retail company, all of the following are included in the operating section except

A. Sales.

B. Cost of goods sold.

C. Dividend revenue.

D. Administrative and selling expenses.

The correct answer is (C). *(CMA, adapted)*

REQUIRED: The item excluded from the operating section of a multiple-step income statement of a retailer.

DISCUSSION: The operating section of a retailer's income statement includes all revenues and costs necessary for the operation of the retail establishment, e.g., sales, cost of goods sold, administrative expenses, and selling expenses. Dividend revenue, however, is classified under other revenues. In a statement of cash flows, cash dividends received are considered an operating cash flow.

Answers (A), (B), and (D) are incorrect because sales, cost of goods sold, and administrative and selling expenses are all part of the normal operations of a retailer.

27. Earnings-per-share disclosures are required

A. Only if the entity has a complex capital structure.

B. For an entity that changes its capital structure.

C. If an entity has issued publicly traded potential common stock.

D. In statements of wholly owned subsidiaries.

The correct answer is (C). *(Publisher)*

REQUIRED: The true statement about EPS disclosures.

DISCUSSION: SFAS 128, *Earnings per Share*, applies to all entities that have issued publicly traded common stock or potential common stock (e.g., options, warrants, convertible securities, or contingent stock agreements). SFAS 128 also applies if an entity has made, or is in the process of making, a filing with a regulatory body to prepare for the public sale of such securities. It does not apply to investment companies or to statements of wholly owned subsidiaries.

Answer (A) is incorrect because an entity with a simple capital structure (one with only common stock outstanding) must also make EPS disclosures if it is within the scope of SFAS 128. Answer (B) is incorrect because whether an entity's capital structure has changed does not determine the need for EPS disclosures. Answer (D) is incorrect because SFAS 128 does not apply to statements of wholly owned subsidiaries.

28. The changes in account balances of the Samson Corporation during the year are presented below:

	Increase
Assets	$356,000
Liabilities	108,000
Capital stock	240,000
Additional paid-in capital	24,000

Assuming there are no charges to retained earnings other than for a dividend payment of $52,000, the net income for the year should be

A. $16,000

B. $36,000

C. $52,000

D. $68,000

The correct answer is (B). *(Publisher)*

REQUIRED: The net income for the year given the increase in assets, liabilities, and paid-in capital.

DISCUSSION: To calculate net income, the dividend payment ($52,000) should be added to the increase in assets ($356,000). The excess of this sum ($408,000) over the increase in liabilities ($108,000) gives the total increase in owners' equity ($300,000). The excess of this amount over the combined increases in the capital accounts ($264,000) equals the increase in retained earnings ($36,000) arising from net income.

Answer (A) is incorrect because $16,000 is the excess of the sum of the increases in the capital accounts other than retained earnings over the increase in net assets. Answer (C) is incorrect because $52,000 is the dividend. Answer (D) is incorrect because $68,000 equals the sum of the dividend and the excess of the sum of the increases in the capital accounts other than retained earnings over the increase in net assets.

Questions 29 through 31 are based on the following information. The Horatio Company's beginning and ending inventories for the fiscal year ended September 30, year 2 are

	Oct. 1, Year 1	Sept. 30, Year 2
Materials	$30,000	$44,000
Work-in-process (WIP)	80,000	70,000
Finished goods	16,000	24,000

Production data for the fiscal year ended September 30, year 2 are

Materials purchased	$160,000
Purchase discounts taken	2,000
Direct labor	200,000
Manufacturing overhead	150,000

29. The cost of goods manufactured (CGM) for the year ended September 30, year 2 is

A. $484,000

B. $494,000

C. $504,000

D. $518,000

The correct answer is (C). *(Publisher)*

REQUIRED: The CGM.

DISCUSSION: CGM equals all manufacturing costs incurred during the period, plus BWIP, minus EWIP. Materials used equals $144,000 ($30,000 BI + $160,000 purchased – $2,000 discounts – $44,000 EI). Thus, manufacturing costs incurred during the period equal $494,000 ($144,000 materials used + $200,000 DL + $150,000 OH), and CGM equals $504,000 ($494,000 + $80,000 BWIP – $70,000 EWIP).

Answer (A) is incorrect because $484,000 results from reversing the effect of the change in WIP. Answer (B) is incorrect because $494,000 does not consider the change in WIP. Answer (D) is incorrect because $518,000 does not consider the change in materials inventory.

30. The cost of goods sold (CGS) for the year ended September 30, year 2 is

A. $500,000

B. $504,000

C. $508,000

D. $496,000

The correct answer is (D). *(Publisher)*

REQUIRED: The CGS.

DISCUSSION: CGS equals CGM adjusted for the change in finished goods inventory. CGM equals all manufacturing costs incurred during the period, plus BWIP, minus EWIP. Materials used equals $144,000 ($30,000 BI + $160,000 purchased – $2,000 discounts – $44,000 EI). Thus, manufacturing costs incurred during the period equal $494,000 ($144,000 materials used + $200,000 DL + $150,000 OH), and CGM equals $504,000 ($494,000 + $80,000 BWIP – $70,000 EWIP). Accordingly, CGS equals $496,000 ($504,000 CGM + $16,000 BFG – $24,000 EFG).

Answer (A) is incorrect because $500,000 results from reversing the treatment of purchase discounts. Answer (B) is incorrect because $504,000 is the CGM. Answer (C) is incorrect because $508,000 results from assuming that no beginning or ending inventories of materials, WIP, or finished goods existed.

31. The total value of inventory to be reported on the balance sheet at September 30, year 2 is

A. $44,000

B. $70,000

C. $24,000

D. $138,000

The correct answer is (D). *(Publisher)*

REQUIRED: The total year-end inventory.

DISCUSSION: The ending inventory consists of three elements: materials of $44,000, WIP of $70,000, and finished goods of $24,000, a total of $138,000.

Answer (A) is incorrect because $44,000 is the ending materials inventory. Answer (B) is incorrect because $70,000 is the EWIP. Answer (C) is incorrect because $24,000 is the finished goods inventory.

C. Statement of Cash Flows

32. A statement of cash flows is to be presented in general purpose external financial statements by which of the following?

A. Publicly held business enterprises only.

B. Privately held business enterprises only.

C. All business enterprises.

D. All business enterprises and not-for-profit organizations.

The correct answer is (D). *(Publisher)*

REQUIRED: The entities required to present a statement of cash flows.

DISCUSSION: SFAS 95 as amended by SFAS 117 requires a statement of cash flows as part of a full set of financial statements of all business entities (both publicly held and privately held) and not-for-profit organizations. Defined benefit pension plans, certain other employee benefit plans, and certain highly liquid investment companies, however, are exempted from this requirement by SFAS 102.

Answers (A), (B), and (C) are incorrect because all business entities and not-for-profit organizations are required to present a statement of cash flows.

33. When preparing the statement of cash flows, companies are required to report separately as operating cash flows all of the following except

A. Interest received on investments in bonds.

B. Interest paid on the company's bonds.

C. Cash collected from customers.

D. Cash dividends paid on the company's stock.

The correct answer is (D). *(CMA, adapted)*

REQUIRED: The item not reported separately as an operating cash flow on a statement of cash flows.

DISCUSSION: Under SFAS 95, a statement of cash flows should report as operating activities all transactions and other events not classified as investing or financing activities. In general, the cash flows from transactions and other events that enter into the determination of income are to be classified as operating. Cash receipts from sales of goods and services, from interest on loans, and from dividends on equity securities are from operating activities. Cash payments to suppliers for inventory; to employees for wages; to other suppliers and employees for other goods and services; to governments for taxes, duties, fines, and fees; and to lenders for interest are also from operating activities. However, distributions to owners (cash dividends on a company's own stock) are cash flows from financing, not operating, activities.

Answers (A), (B), and (C) are incorrect because interest received from investments, interest paid on bonds, and customer collections are operating cash flows.

34. A statement of cash flows is intended to help users of financial statements

A. Evaluate a firm's liquidity, solvency, and financial flexibility.

B. Evaluate a firm's economic resources and obligations.

C. Determine a firm's components of income from operations.

D. Determine whether insiders have sold or purchased the firm's stock.

The correct answer is (A). *(CMA, adapted)*

REQUIRED: The reason companies are required to prepare a statement of cash flows.

DISCUSSION: The primary purpose of a statement of cash flows is to provide information about the cash receipts and payments of an entity during a period. If used with information in the other financial statements, the statement of cash flows should help users to assess the entity's ability to generate positive future net cash flows (liquidity), its ability to meet obligations (solvency) and pay dividends, the need for external financing, the reasons for differences between income and cash receipts and payments, and the cash and noncash aspects of the investing and financing activities.

Answer (B) is incorrect because the statement of cash flows deals with only one resource--cash. Answer (C) is incorrect because the income statement shows the components of income from operations. Answer (D) is incorrect because the identity of stock buyers and sellers is not shown.

35. Which of the following items is specifically included in the body of a statement of cash flows?

A. Operating and nonoperating cash flow information.

B. Conversion of debt to equity.

C. Acquiring an asset through a capital lease.

D. Purchasing a building by giving a mortgage to the seller.

The correct answer is (A). *(CMA, adapted)*

REQUIRED: The information specifically included within the body of a statement of cash flows.

DISCUSSION: SFAS 95 excludes all noncash transactions from the body of the statement of cash flows to avoid undue complexity and detraction from the objective of providing information about cash flows. Information about all noncash financing and investing activities affecting recognized assets and liabilities shall be reported in related disclosures.

Answers (B), (C), and (D) are incorrect because SFAS 95 specifically excludes noncash transactions from the body of the statement of cash flows.

36. A financial statement includes all of the following items: net income, depreciation, operating activities, and financing activities. What financial statement is this?

A. Balance sheet.

B. Income statement.

C. Statement of cash flows.

D. Statement of changes in equity.

The correct answer is (C). *(CIA, adapted)*

REQUIRED: The financial statement that includes net income, depreciation, operating activities, and financing activities.

DISCUSSION: A statement of cash flows is a required financial statement. Its primary purpose is to provide information about cash receipts and payments by reporting the cash effects of an enterprise's operating, investing, and financing activities. Related disclosures report the effects of noncash investing and financing activities. Because the statement or a separate schedule reconciles net income and net operating cash flow, depreciation, a noncash expense, is included in the presentation.

Answer (A) is incorrect because the balance sheet does not include periodic net income or depreciation expense. Answer (B) is incorrect because the income statement does not have captions for operating and financing activities. Answer (D) is incorrect because equity does not include captions for operating and investing activities, depreciation, and net income.

37. Select the combination below that explains the impact of credit card interest incurred and paid during the period on (1) equity on the balance sheet and (2) the statement of cash flows.

	(1) Effect on Equity on Balance Sheet	(2) Reflected on Statement of Cash Flows as a(n)
A.	Decrease	Financing outflow
B.	Decrease	Operating outflow
C.	No effect	Financing outflow
D.	No effect	Operating outflow

The correct answer is (B). *(CIA, adapted)*

REQUIRED: The effect of interest expense on the balance sheet and cash flow statement.

DISCUSSION: Credit card interest incurred is classified as interest expense on the income statement, which in turn reduces equity on the balance sheet by reducing retained earnings. Cash payments to lenders and other creditors for interest, e.g., credit card interest payments, are to be classified on the statement of cash flows as an outflow of cash from operating activities.

Answers (A), (C), and (D) are incorrect because credit card interest charges reduce equity, and interest payments are classified as an operating outflow on the statement of cash flows.

38. In the statement of cash flows, the payment of common share dividends appears in the <List A> activities section as a <List B> of cash.

	List A	List B
A.	Operating	Source
B.	Financing	Use
C.	Investing	Use
D.	Investing	Source

The correct answer is (B). *(CIA, adapted)*

REQUIRED: The treatment of cash dividends in a statement of cash flows.

DISCUSSION: Financing activities include, among other things, obtaining resources from owners and providing them with a return on, and a return of, their investment. Consequently, the payment of cash dividends to providers of common equity financing is a use of cash that appears in the financing section of the statement of cash flows.

Answers (A), (C), and (D) are incorrect because payment of cash dividends is a use of cash for a financing activity.

39. Which of the following related cash transactions should be disclosed as gross amounts of cash receipts and cash payments rather than as net amounts?

A. The purchase and sale of fixed assets.

B. Changes in cash and cash equivalents.

C. The purchase and sale of federal funds.

D. The receipts and payments from demand deposits.

The correct answer is (A). *(Publisher)*

REQUIRED: The related receipts and payments that should be classified as gross amounts.

DISCUSSION: In general, cash inflows and cash outflows from operating, investing, and financing activities should be reported separately at gross amounts in a statement of cash flows. In certain instances, however, the net amount of related cash receipts and cash payments may provide sufficient information about particular classes of cash flows. For example, SFAS 104 permits banks, saving institutions, and credit unions to report net amounts for (1) the placement and withdrawal of deposits with other financial institutions, (2) the acceptance and repayment of time deposits, and (3) the making of loans to customers and the collection of principal.

Answers (B), (C), and (D) are incorrect because changes in cash and cash equivalents, the purchase and sale of federal funds, and the receipts and payments from demand deposits are classes of related cash flows that may be presented as net amounts.

40. The following information was taken from the accounting records of Oak Corporation for the year ended December 31:

Proceeds from issuance of preferred stock	$4,000,000
Dividends paid on preferred stock	400,000
Bonds payable converted to common stock	2,000,000
Payment for purchase of machinery	500,000
Proceeds from sale of plant building	1,200,000
2% stock dividend on common stock	300,000
Gain on sale of plant building	200,000

The net cash flows from investing and financing activities that should be presented on Oak's statement of cash flows for the year December 31 are, respectively

A. $700,000 and $3,600,000

B. $700,000 and $3,900,000

C. $900,000 and $3,900,000

D. $900,000 and $3,600,000

The correct answer is (A). *(CMA, adapted)*

REQUIRED: The respective net cash flows from investing and financing activities.

DISCUSSION: Investing activities include the lending of money and the collecting of those loans, and the acquisition, sale, or other disposal of securities that are not cash equivalents and of productive assets that are expected to generate revenue over a long period of time. Financing activities include the issuance of stock, the payment of dividends, treasury stock transactions, the issuance of debt, the receipt of donor-restricted resources to be used for long-term purposes, and the repayment or other settlement of debt obligations. Investing activities include the purchase of machinery and the sale of a building. The net inflow from these activities is $700,000 ($1,200,000 – $500,000). Financing activities include the issuance of preferred stock and the payment of dividends. The net inflow is $3,600,000 ($4,000,000 – $400,000). The conversion of bonds into common stock and the stock dividend do not affect cash.

Answer (B) is incorrect because the stock dividend is a noncash transaction. Answers (C) and (D) are incorrect because the gain on the sale of the building is double counted in determining the net cash flow from investing activities.

41. Frazier Company reported current net income of $161,000. During the year, accounts receivable increased by $14,000 and accounts payable increased by $10,500. Inventories declined by $8,000. Depreciation expense was $40,000. Net cash provided by operating activities is

A. $165,000

B. $189,500

C. $205,500

D. $212,500

The correct answer is (C). *(Publisher)*

REQUIRED: The net cash provided by operating activities.

DISCUSSION: The net income of $161,000 must be adjusted by noncash expenses (such as depreciation) and the amount of changes in current assets. The calculation would be:

Net income	$161,000
Depreciation expense	40,000
Increase in receivables	(14,000)
Increase in payables	10,500
Decrease in inventories	8,000
	$205,500

Answer (A) is incorrect because $165,000 results from a failure to add back depreciation--a noncash expense. Answer (B) is incorrect because $189,500 results from deducting the inventory change rather than adding it. Answer (D) is incorrect because $212,500 results from reversing the treatment of receivables and payables.

Questions 42 through 44 are based on the following information. Royce Company had the following transactions during the fiscal year ended December 31, year 2:

- Accounts receivable decreased from $115,000 on December 31, year 1 to $100,000 on December 31, year 2.
- Royce's board of directors declared dividends on December 31, year 2 of $.05 per share on the 2.8 million shares outstanding, payable to shareholders of record on January 31, year 3. The company did not declare or pay dividends for fiscal year year 1.
- Sold a truck with a net book value of $7,000 for $5,000 cash, reporting a loss of $2,000.
- Paid interest to bondholders of $780,000.
- The cash balance was $106,000 on December 31, year 1 and $284,000 on December 31, year 2.

42. Royce Company uses the direct method to prepare its statement of cash flows at December 31, year 2. The interest paid to bondholders is reported in the

A. Financing section, as a use or outflow of cash.

B. Operating section, as a use or outflow of cash.

C. Investing section, as a use or outflow of cash.

D. Debt section, as a use or outflow of cash.

The correct answer is (B). *(CMA, adapted)*

REQUIRED: The proper reporting of interest paid.

DISCUSSION: Payment of interest on debt is considered an operating activity, although repayment of debt principal is a financing activity.

Answer (A) is incorrect because interest paid on bonds is an operating cash flow. Answer (C) is incorrect because investing activities include the lending of money and the acquisition, sale, or other disposal of securities that are not cash equivalents and the acquisition, sale, or other disposal of long-lived productive assets. Answer (D) is incorrect because SFAS 95 does not provide for a debt section.

43. Royce Company uses the indirect method to prepare its year 2 statement of cash flows. It reports a(n)

A. Source or inflow of funds of $5,000 from the sale of the truck in the financing section.

B. Use or outflow of funds of $140,000 in the financing section, representing dividends.

C. Deduction of $15,000 in the operating section, representing the decrease in year-end accounts receivable.

D. Addition of $2,000 in the operating section for the $2,000 loss on the sale of the truck.

The correct answer is (D). *(CMA, adapted)*

REQUIRED: The correct presentation of an item on a statement of cash flows prepared under the indirect method.

DISCUSSION: The indirect method determines net operating cash flow by adjusting net income. Under the indirect method, the $5,000 cash inflow from the sale of the truck is shown in the investing section. A $2,000 loss was recognized and properly deducted to determine net income. This loss, however, did not require the use of cash and should be added to net income in the operating section.

Answer (A) is incorrect because, under the provisions of SFAS 95, the $5,000 inflow would be shown in the investing section. Answer (B) is incorrect because no outflow of cash dividends occurred in year 2. Answer (C) is incorrect because the decrease in receivables should be added to net income.

44. The total of cash provided (used) by operating activities plus cash provided (used) by investing activities plus cash provided (used) by financing activities is

A. Cash provided of $284,000.

B. Cash provided of $178,000.

C. Cash used of $582,000.

D. Equal to net income reported for fiscal year ended December 31, year 2.

The correct answer is (B). *(CMA, adapted)*

REQUIRED: The net total of cash provided and used.

DISCUSSION: The total of cash provided (used) by the three activities (operating, investing, and financing) should equal the increase or decrease in cash for the year. During year 2, the cash balance increased from $106,000 to $284,000. Thus, the sources of cash must have exceeded the uses by $178,000.

Answer (A) is incorrect because $284,000 is the ending cash balance, not the change in the cash balance; it ignores the beginning balance. Answer (C) is incorrect because the cash balance increased during the year. Answer (D) is incorrect because net income must be adjusted for noncash expenses and other accruals and deferrals.

45. With respect to the content and form of the statement of cash flows,

A. The pronouncements covering the cash flow statement encourage the use of the indirect method.

B. The indirect method adjusts ending retained earnings to reconcile it to net cash flows from operations.

C. The direct method of reporting cash flows from operating activities includes disclosing the major classes of gross cash receipts and gross cash payments.

D. The reconciliation of the net income to net operating cash flow need not be presented when using the direct method.

The correct answer is (C). *(CMA, adapted)*

REQUIRED: The true statement about the content and form of the statement of cash flows.

DISCUSSION: SFAS 95 encourages use of the direct method of reporting major classes of operating cash receipts and payments, but the indirect method may be used. The minimum disclosures of operating cash flows under the direct method are cash collected from customers, interest and dividends received, other operating cash receipts, cash paid to employees and other suppliers of goods or services, interest paid, income taxes paid, and other operating cash payments.

Answer (A) is incorrect because SFAS 95 encourages use of the direct method. Answer (B) is incorrect because the indirect method reconciles net income with the net cash flow from operations. Answer (D) is incorrect because the reconciliation is required regardless of the method used.

46. The statement of cash flows may be presented in either a direct or an indirect (reconciliation) format. In which of these formats would cash collected from customers be presented as a gross amount?

	Direct	Indirect
A.	No	No
B.	No	Yes
C.	Yes	Yes
D.	Yes	No

The correct answer is (D). *(R. O'Keefe)*

REQUIRED: The format in which cash collected from customers would be presented as a gross amount.

DISCUSSION: The statement of cash flows may report cash flows from operating activities in either an indirect (reconciliation) or a direct format. The direct format reports the major classes of operating cash receipts and cash payments as gross amounts. The indirect presentation reconciles net income to the same amount of net cash flow from operations that would be determined in accordance with the direct method. To arrive at net operating cash flow, the indirect method adjusts net income by removing the effects of (1) all deferrals of past operating cash receipts and payments, (2) all accruals of expected future operating cash receipts and payments, (3) all financing and investing activities, and (4) all noncash operating transactions.

Answers (A), (B), and (C) are incorrect because only the direct method format for the statement of cash flows presents cash collected from customers as a gross amount.

47. When using the indirect method to prepare the statement of cash flows, the amortization of goodwill should be presented as a(n)

A. Cash flow from investing activities.

B. Deduction from net income.

C. Addition to net income.

D. Investing and financing activity not affecting cash.

The correct answer is (C). *(CMA, adapted)*

REQUIRED: The treatment of goodwill amortization in a statement of cash flows based on the indirect method.

DISCUSSION: The statement of cash flows may report operating activities in the form of either an indirect or a direct presentation. The indirect presentation removes from net income the effects of past deferrals of past operating cash flows, all accruals of expected future operating cash flows, and net income items not affecting operating cash flows. The result is net operating cash flow. Goodwill amortization is a noncash expense and should be added to net income.

Answer (A) is incorrect because goodwill amortization is not a cash flow. Answer (B) is incorrect because goodwill amortization is added to net income. Answer (D) is incorrect because goodwill amortization must be included in the reconciliation of net income to net operating cash flow.

Questions 48 through 50 are based on the following information. Heniser Corporation engaged in the following cash transactions during the current year:

Sale of land and building	$280,000
Purchase of treasury stock	140,000
Purchase of land	137,000
Payment of cash dividend	185,000
Purchase of equipment	153,000
Issuance of common stock	247,000
Retirement of bonds	200,000

48. Heniser's net cash provided (used) by investing activities is

A. $280,000

B. ($10,000)

C. ($210,000)

D. ($350,000)

The correct answer is (B). *(Publisher)*

REQUIRED: The net cash provided (used) by investing activities.

DISCUSSION: Investing activities include making and collecting loans and acquiring and disposing of debt or equity instruments; property, plant, and equipment; and other productive assets. The calculation is

Sale of land and building	$ 280,000
Purchase of land	(137,000)
Purchase of equipment	(153,000)
Net cash provided (used)	$ (10,000)

Answer (A) is incorrect because $280,000 results from a failure to deduct the uses of cash. Answer (C) is incorrect because ($210,000) results from deducting the retirement of bonds. Answer (D) is incorrect because ($350,000) results from deducting the purchase of treasury stock, which would be a financing activity, not an investing activity.

49. Heniser's net cash provided (used) by financing activities is

A. $247,000

B. ($78,000)

C. ($138,000)

D. ($278,000)

The correct answer is (D). *(Publisher)*

REQUIRED: The net cash provided (used) by financing activities.

DISCUSSION: Financing activities include the issuance of stock, the payment of dividends, treasury stock transactions, and the issuance and repayment of debt. They also include receiving restricted resources that are donor-stipulated to be used for long-term purposes. The calculation is

Issuance of common stock	$ 247,000
Purchase of treasury stock	(140,000)
Payment of cash dividend	(185,000)
Retirement of bonds	(200,000)
Cash provided (used)	$(278,000)

Answer (A) is incorrect because $247,000 results from a failure to deduct the uses of cash. Answer (B) is incorrect because ($78,000) results from a failure to deduct the retirement of bonds. Answer (C) is incorrect because ($138,000) results from a failure to deduct for the purchase of treasury stock.

50. Heniser's net cash flow, assuming that it reported net cash provided by operating activities of $400,000, is

A. $112,000

B. $252,000

C. $392,000

D. $688,000

The correct answer is (A). *(Publisher)*

REQUIRED: The overall net cash flow.

DISCUSSION: A statement of cash flows reports cash flows from operating activities, investing activities, and financing activities. Combining the $400,000 of cash provided by operating activities with the $10,000 use for investing activities and $278,000 use for financing activities (see solutions to two preceding questions) results in a net source of cash of $112,000 ($400,000 – $10,000 – $278,000).

Answer (B) is incorrect because $252,000 results from a failure to deduct the purchase of treasury stock. Answer (C) is incorrect because $392,000 results from adding rather than deducting the treasury stock purchase. Answer (D) is incorrect because $688,000 results from adding the uses of cash rather than deducting them.

51. Depreciation expense is added to net income under the indirect method of preparing a statement of cash flows in order to

A. Report all assets at gross book value.

B. Ensure depreciation has been properly reported.

C. Reverse noncash charges deducted from net income.

D. Calculate net book value.

The correct answer is (C). *(CMA, adapted)*

REQUIRED: The reason depreciation expense is added to net income under the indirect method.

DISCUSSION: The indirect method begins with net income and then removes the effects of past deferrals of operating cash receipts and payments, accruals of expected future operating cash receipts and payments, and net income items not affecting operating cash flows (e.g., depreciation).

Answer (A) is incorrect because assets other than cash are not shown on the statement of cash flows. Answer (B) is incorrect because depreciation is recorded on the income statement. On the statement of cash flows, depreciation is added back to net income because it was previously deducted on the income statement. Answer (D) is incorrect because net book value of assets is shown on the balance sheet, not the statement of cash flows.

52. In reconciling net income on an accrual basis to net cash provided by operating activities, what adjustment is needed to net income because of (1) an increase during the period in prepaid expenses and (2) the periodic amortization of premium on bonds payable?

	(1) Increase in Prepaid Expenses	(2) Amortization of Premium on Bonds Payable
A.	Add	Add
B.	Add	Deduct
C.	Deduct	Add
D.	Deduct	Deduct

The correct answer is (D). *(CIA, adapted)*

REQUIRED: The adjustments to reconcile accrual-basis net income to cash provided by operating activities.

DISCUSSION: An increase in prepaid expenses indicates that cash outlays for expenses exceeded the related expense incurred; thus, net income exceeded net cash provided by operations and a deduction is needed in the reconciliation. Also, the amortization of premium on bonds payable causes a reduction of interest expense but does not increase cash; therefore, net income exceeds net cash from operating activities, and a deduction is needed in the reconciliation.

Answers (A), (B), and (C) are incorrect because both the increase in prepaid expenses and amortization of premium on bonds payable require a deduction from net income in the reconciliation.

Questions 53 through 55 are based on the following information. Northern Exposure, Inc. had the following transactions during the year just ended:

Proceeds from sale of land and building	$450,000
Purchase of common stock	60,000
Purchase of land for cash	45,000
Payment of cash dividend	90,000
Purchase of equipment for cash	120,000
Issuance of preferred stock	66,000
Cash repurchase of bonds	100,000
Issuance of a 5% common stock dividend	50,000
Recording of an asset and a liability for a capital lease	100,000

Northern Exposure, Inc. reported current net income of $290,000. During the year, accounts receivable increased by $22,000 and accounts payable decreased by $5,500. Depreciation expense was $20,000. Inventories increased by $11,000.

53. Northern Exposure's net cash provided by operating activities is

A. $271,500

B. $293,500

C. $310,000

D. $348,500

The correct answer is (A). *(Publisher)*

REQUIRED: The net cash provided by operating activities.

DISCUSSION: The net income of $290,000 must be adjusted for depreciation expense and changes in current assets. The calculation is

Net income	$290,000
Depreciation expense	20,000
Increase in receivables	(22,000)
Decrease in payables	(5,500)
Increase in inventories	(11,000)
	$271,500

Answer (B) is incorrect because $293,500 is the result of adding the inventory increase rather than deducting it. Answer (C) is incorrect because $310,000 occurs by failing to adjust for the changes in current assets. Answer (D) is incorrect because $348,500 is the result of reversing the treatment of all of the current asset changes.

54. Northern Exposure's net cash provided (used) by investing activities is

A. $185,000

B. $225,000

C. $285,000

D. $351,000

The correct answer is (C). *(Publisher)*

REQUIRED: The net cash provided by investing activities.

DISCUSSION: Investing activities include buying and selling investments and property, plant, and equipment. However, entering into a capital lease is a noncash investing activity. The calculation is

Sale of land and building	$ 450,000
Purchase of land	(45,000)
Purchase of equipment	(120,000)
	$ 285,000

Answer (A) is incorrect because $185,000 results from deducting the retirement of bonds, which is a financing activity. Answer (B) is incorrect because $225,0000 results from deducting the purchase of common stock, which is a financing activity. Answer (D) is incorrect because $351,000 results from adding in the issuance of preferred stock, which is a financing activity.

55. Northern Exposure's net cash provided (used) by financing activities is

A. $66,000

B. ($24,000)

C. ($84,000)

D. ($184,000)

The correct answer is (D). *(Publisher)*

REQUIRED: The net cash provided (used) by financing activities.

DISCUSSION: Financing activities include the issuance of stock, payment of dividends, treasury stock transactions, and the issuance and retirement of debt. They also include receiving restricted resources that are donor-stipulated to be used for long-term purposes. However, the stock dividend is a noncash financing activity. The calculation is

Issuance of preferred stock	$ 66,000
Purchase of common stock	(60,000)
Payment of cash dividend	(90,000)
Repurchase of bonds	(100,000)
Cash provided (used)	($184,000)

Answer (A) is incorrect because $66,000 results from a failure to deduct the uses of cash. Answer (B) is incorrect because ($24,000) results from a failure to deduct the purchase of common stock and the retirement of bonds. Answer (C) is incorrect because ($84,000) results from a failure to deduct the retirement of bonds.

56. In its statement of cash flows issued for the year ending June 30, Prince Company reported a net cash inflow from operating activities of $123,000. The following adjustments were included in the supplementary schedule reconciling cash flow from operating activities with net income:

Depreciation	$38,000
Increase in net accounts receivable	31,000
Decrease in inventory	27,000
Increase in accounts payable	48,000
Increase in interest payable	12,000

Net income is

A. $29,000

B. $41,000

C. $79,000

D. $217,000

The correct answer is (A). *(Publisher)*

REQUIRED: The net income given cash flow from operating activities and reconciling adjustments.

DISCUSSION: To derive net income from net cash inflow from operating activities, various adjustments are necessary. The depreciation of $38,000 should be subtracted because it is a noncash item included in the determination of net income. The increase in net accounts receivable of $31,000 should be added because it signifies that sales revenue was greater than the cash collections from customers. The increase in accounts payable should be subtracted because it indicates that purchases were $48,000 greater than cash disbursements to suppliers. The second step of the transformation from cash paid to suppliers to cost of goods sold is to subtract the decrease in inventory. This change means that cost of goods sold was $27,000 greater than purchases. The $12,000 increase in interest payable should also be subtracted because it indicates that interest expense was greater than the cash paid to the lenders. Thus, the net adjustment to net cash inflow from operating activities is –$94,000 (–$38,000 + $31,000 – $27,000 – $48,000 – $12,000). Net income is $29,000 ($123,000 net cash inflow – $94,000 net adjustment).

Answer (B) is incorrect because the increase in interest payable is not subtracted. Answer (C) is incorrect because depreciation and the increase in interest payable are not subtracted. Answer (D) is incorrect because depreciation, the increase in accounts payable, the decrease in inventory, and the increase in interest payable should be subtracted, and the increase in net accounts receivable should be added.

57. The following data were extracted from the financial statements of a company for the year ended December 31:

Net income	$70,000
Depreciation expense	14,000
Amortization of intangibles	1,000
Decrease in accounts receivable	2,000
Increase in inventories	9,000
Increase in accounts payable	4,000
Increase in plant assets	47,000
Increase in contributed capital	31,000
Decrease in short-term notes payable	55,000

There were no disposals of plant assets during the year. Based on the above, a statement of cash flows will report a net increase in cash of

A. $11,000

B. $17,000

C. $54,000

D. $69,000

The correct answer is (A). *(CIA, adapted)*

REQUIRED: The net increase in cash as reported on the statement of cash flows.

DISCUSSION: Depreciation and amortization are noncash expenses and are added to net income. A decrease in receivables indicates that cash collections exceed sales on an accrual basis, so it is added to net income. To account for the difference between cost of goods sold (a deduction from income) and cash paid to suppliers, a two-step adjustment of net income is necessary. The difference between cost of goods sold and purchases is the change in inventory. The difference between purchases and the amount paid to suppliers is the change in accounts payable. Accordingly, the conversion of cost of goods sold to cash paid to suppliers requires deducting the inventory increase and adding the accounts payable increase. An increase in plant assets indicates an acquisition of plant assets, causing a decrease in cash, so it is deducted. An increase in contributed capital represents a cash inflow and is added to net income. A decrease in short-term notes payable is deducted from net income because it reflects a cash outflow. Thus, cash increased by $11,000 ($70,000 NI + $14,000 + $1,000 + $2,000 – $9,000 + $4,000 – $47,000 + $31,000 – $55,000).

Answer (B) is incorrect because $17,000 results from subtracting the amortization and the decrease in receivables and adding the increase in inventories. Answer (C) is incorrect because $54,000 results from adjusting net income for the increase in plant assets and the increase in contributed capital only. Answer (D) is incorrect because $69,000 results from not making the adjustments for receivables, inventories, notes payable, and accounts payable.

58. The net income for Cypress Inc. was $3,000,000 for the year ended December 31. Additional information is as follows:

Depreciation on fixed assets	$1,500,000
Gain from cash sale of land	200,000
Increase in accounts payable	300,000
Dividends paid on preferred stock	400,000

The net cash provided by operating activities in the statement of cash flows for the year ended December 31 should be

A. $4,200,000

B. $4,500,000

C. $4,600,000

D. $4,800,000

The correct answer is (C). *(CMA, adapted)*

REQUIRED: The net cash provided by operations.

DISCUSSION: Net operating cash flow may be determined by adjusting net income. Depreciation is an expense not directly affecting cash flows that should be added back to net income. The increase in accounts payable is added to net income because it indicates that an expense has been recorded but not paid. The gain on the sale of land is an inflow from an investing, not an operating, activity and should be subtracted from net income. The dividends paid on preferred stock are cash outflows from financing, not operating, activities and do not require an adjustment. Thus, net cash flow from operations is $4,600,000 ($3,000,000 + $1,500,000 – $200,000 + $300,000).

Answer (A) is incorrect because $4,200,000 equals net cash provided by operating activities minus the $400,000 financing activity. Answer (B) is incorrect because $4,500,000 equals net income, plus depreciation. Answer (D) is incorrect because $4,800,000 equals net income, plus depreciation, plus the increase in accounts payable.

59. Appalachian Outfitters Inc., a mail order supplier of camping gear, is putting together its current year statement of cash flow. A comparison of the company's year-end balance sheet with the prior year's balance sheet shows the following changes from a year ago.

Assets	
Cash & Marketable Securities	$ (600)
Accounts Receivable	200
Inventories	(100)
Gross Fixed Assets	4,600
Accumulated Depreciation	(500)
Total	$3,600

Liabilities & Net Worth	
Accounts Payable	$ 250
Accruals	50
Long-term Note	(300)
Long-term Debt	1,400
Common Stock	0
Retained Earnings	2,200
Total	$3,600

The firm's payout ratio is 20%. During the current year, net cash provided by operations amounted to

A. $2,900

B. $3,050

C. $3,450

D. $4,050

The correct answer is (C). *(CMA, adapted)*

REQUIRED: The net cash provided by operations.

DISCUSSION: The net profit after taxes equals the change in retained earnings divided by 1 minus the dividend payout ratio, or $2,750 [$2,200 ÷ (1 – .2)]. Adjusting this amount for noncash items yields the net cash provided by operations. Depreciation is a noncash expense that should be added. To adjust for the difference between cost of goods sold and purchases, the inventory decrease is added (CGS exceeded purchases). To adjust for the difference between purchases and cash paid to suppliers, the increase in accounts payable is also added (purchases exceeded cash paid to suppliers). The increase in accounts receivable is subtracted because it indicates that accrued revenues were greater than cash collections. Finally, the increase in accrued liabilities is added. Thus, the net cash provided by operations is $3,450 ($2,750 + $500 + $100 + $250 – $200 + $50).

Answer (A) is incorrect because $2,900 excludes the adjustments for depreciation and accruals of liabilities other than accounts payable. Answer (B) is incorrect because $3,050 excludes the adjustments for inventory, accounts payable, and accruals. Answer (D) is incorrect because $4,050 results from adding the $600 decrease in cash and marketable securities.

60. In the indirect presentation of cash flows from operating activities in a statement of cash flows, net income of a business enterprise is adjusted for noncash revenues, gains, expenses, and losses to determine the cash flows from operating activities. A reconciliation of net cash flows from operating activities to net income

A. Must be reported in the statement of cash flows.

B. Must be presented separately in a related disclosure.

C. May be either reported in the statement of cash flows or presented separately in a related disclosure.

D. Need not be presented.

The correct answer is (C). *(Publisher)*

REQUIRED: The proper reporting of a reconciliation of net cash flows from operating activities to net income.

DISCUSSION: When an indirect presentation of net cash flows from operating activities is made, a reconciliation with net income must be provided for all noncash revenues, gains, expenses, and losses. This reconciliation may be either reported in the statement of cash flows or provided separately in related disclosures, with the statement of cash flows presenting only the net cash flows from operating activities.

Answer (A) is incorrect because the reconciliation may be presented in a related disclosure. Answer (B) is incorrect because the reconciliation may be reported in the statement of cash flows. Answer (D) is incorrect because a reconciliation must be reported in an indirect presentation of the statement of cash flows.

61. All of the following should be classified under the operating section in a statement of cash flows except a

A. Decrease in inventory.

B. Depreciation expense.

C. Decrease in prepaid insurance.

D. Purchase of land and building in exchange for a long-term note.

The correct answer is (D). *(CMA, adapted)*

REQUIRED: The item not classified as an operating item in a statement of cash flows.

DISCUSSION: Operating activities include all transactions and other events not classified as investing and financing activities. Operating activities include producing and delivering goods and providing services. Cash flows from such activities are usually included in the determination of net income. However, the purchase of land and a building in exchange for a long-term note is an investing activity. Because this transaction does not affect cash, it is reported in related disclosures of noncash investing and financing activities.

Answers (A), (B), and (C) are incorrect because a decrease in inventory, a depreciation expense, and a decrease in prepaid insurance are operating items.

62. Which one of the following transactions should be classified as a financing activity in a statement of cash flows?

A. Purchase of equipment.

B. Purchase of treasury stock.

C. Sale of trademarks.

D. Payment of interest on a mortgage note.

The correct answer is (B). *(CMA, adapted)*

REQUIRED: The transaction classified as a financing activity.

DISCUSSION: Under SFAS 95, financing activities are defined to include the issuance of stock, the payment of dividends, the receipt of donor-restricted resources to be used for long-term purposes, treasury stock transactions (purchases or sales), the issuance of debt, the repayment of amounts borrowed, and obtaining and paying for other resources obtained from creditors on long-term credit.

Answer (A) is incorrect because the purchase of equipment is an investing activity. Answer (C) is incorrect because the sale of trademarks, like the sale of any long-lived asset, is an investing activity. Answer (D) is incorrect because the payment of interest on a mortgage note is an operating activity.

63. All of the following should be classified as investing activities except

A. Cash outflows to purchase manufacturing equipment.

B. Cash inflows from the sale of bonds of other entities.

C. Cash outflows to creditors for interest.

D. Cash inflows from the sale of a manufacturing plant.

The correct answer is (C). *(CMA, adapted)*

REQUIRED: The item not an investing activity.

DISCUSSION: Under SFAS 95, investing activities are defined to include the lending of money and the collecting of those loans. They also include the acquisition, sale, or other disposal of securities that are not cash equivalents and of productive assets that are expected to generate revenue over a long period of time. However, interest payments to creditors are cash flows from operating activities.

Answers (A), (B), and (D) are incorrect because the purchase or sale of long-lived equipment or intangibles is an investing activity. Cash flows from purchases, sales, or maturities of available-for-sale and held-to-maturity securities are also considered to be from investing activities.

64. When using the indirect method to prepare a statement of cash flows, which one of the following should be deducted from net income when determining net cash flows from operating activities?

A. An increase in accrued liabilities.

B. Amortization of premiums on bonds payable.

C. A loss on the sale of plant assets.

D. Depreciation expense.

The correct answer is (B). *(CMA, adapted)*

REQUIRED: The item deducted from net income to determine net cash flows from operating activities.

DISCUSSION: The indirect method reconciles the net income of a business with the net operating cash flow. The indirect method removes the effects of all past deferrals of operating cash receipts and payments, all accruals of expected future operating cash receipts and payments, and all items not affecting operating cash flows to arrive at the net cash flow from operating activities. Hence, the amortization of the premium on bonds payable is deducted from net income in the reconciliation because it represents a noncash decrease in interest expense (an increase in net income).

Answer (A) is incorrect because an increase in accrued liabilities reflects an increase in noncash expenses and is added to net income. Answer (C) is incorrect because a loss on the sale of plant assets is from an investing activity. Thus, it should be added to net income to determine net operating cash flow. Answer (D) is incorrect because depreciation is a noncash expense that should be added to net income.

65. Metro, Inc. reported current net income of $150,000. Changes occurred in several balance sheet accounts during the year as follows:

Investment in Videogold, Inc. stock, carried on the equity basis	$5,500 increase
Accumulated depreciation, caused by major repair to projection equipment	2,100 decrease
Premium on bonds payable	1,400 decrease
Deferred income tax liability (long-term)	1,800 increase

In Metro's current cash flow statement, the reported net cash provided by operating activities should be

A. $150,400

B. $148,300

C. $144,900

D. $142,800

The correct answer is (C). *(CPA, adapted)*

REQUIRED: The reported net cash provided by operating activities.

DISCUSSION: The increase in the equity-based investment reflects the investor's share of the investee's net income after adjustment for dividends received. Hence, this increase is a noncash revenue and should be subtracted in the reconciliation of net income to net operating cash inflow. A major repair provides benefits to more than one period and therefore should not be expensed. One method of accounting for a major repair is to charge accumulated depreciation if the useful life of the asset has been extended, with the offsetting credit to cash, a payable, etc. However, the cash outflow, if any, is from an investing activity. The item has no effect on net income and no adjustment is necessary. Amortization of bond premium means that interest expense is less than cash paid out for interest, and should be subtracted in the reconciliation. The increase in the deferred tax liability is a noncash item that reduces net income and should be added in the reconciliation. Accordingly, net cash provided by operations is $144,900 ($150,000 – $5,500 – $1,400 + $1,800).

Answer (A) is incorrect because $150,400 results from omitting the adjustment for the equity-based investment. Answer (B) is incorrect because $148,300 results from omitting the adjustment for the equity-based investment and improperly subtracting the decrease in accumulated depreciation. Answer (D) is incorrect because $142,800 results from improperly subtracting the decrease in accumulated depreciation.

66. During the current year, Beck Co. purchased equipment for cash of $47,000, and sold equipment with a $10,000 carrying value for a gain of $5,000. How should these transactions be reported in Beck's statement of cash flows?

A. Cash outflow of $32,000.

B. Cash outflow of $42,000.

C. Cash inflow of $5,000 and cash outflow of $47,000.

D. Cash inflow of $15,000 and cash outflow of $47,000.

The correct answer is (D). *(CPA, adapted)*

REQUIRED: The reporting of a purchase and a sale of equipment in a statement of cash flows.

DISCUSSION: Investing activities include making and collecting loans and acquiring and disposing of debt or equity instruments and property, plant, and equipment and other productive assets, that is, assets held for or used in the production of goods or services (other than the materials held in inventory). Thus, the cash effects of purchases and sales of equipment should be reported in the investing cash flows section of the statement of cash flows. Moreover, cash inflows and outflows ordinarily are not netted. They should be reported separately at gross amounts. Accordingly, Beck should report a cash inflow of $15,000 ($10,000 carrying value + $5,000 gain) for the sale of equipment and a $47,000 outflow for the purchase. In adjusting accrual-based net income to net operating cash flow, the $5,000 gain on the sale of equipment should be subtracted to prevent double counting.

Answer (A) is incorrect because cash inflows and outflows ordinarily are not netted. Answer (B) is incorrect because an outflow of $42,000 assumes netting and a $5,000 inflow. Answer (C) is incorrect because the cash inflow was $15,000. Beck received the $10,000 carrying value and a $5,000 gain.

STUDY UNIT 3: CONCEPTUAL FRAMEWORK

22 pages of outline
71 multiple-choice questions

A. Conceptual Framework Underlying Financial Accounting
B. Revenue
C. Limitations of Financial Statement Information

This study unit is one of seven that address the preparation of financial statements, a major topic that has been assigned a relative weight range of 50% to 70% of Part 2. Study Unit 3 primarily addresses the conceptual framework, which consists of a set of fundamental principles on which the further development of accounting and reporting standards is based. Study Unit 3 also covers such related subjects as revenue recognition issues and limits on financial information.

A. **Conceptual Framework Underlying Financial Accounting**. The conceptual framework is described in the Statements of Financial Accounting Concepts (SFACs) issued by the FASB. It is a coherent set of interrelated objectives and fundamental concepts promulgated by the FASB.

1. **Objectives of Financial Reporting by Business Enterprises (SFAC 1)**

a. **Scope of financial reporting**. The objectives extend to all means of general purpose external financial reporting by business enterprises (financial reporting). They are a response to the needs of external users who lack the authority to prescribe the information they need.

1) Financial statements, including the notes and parenthetical disclosures, are crucial to financial reporting because they communicate accounting information to external parties, but the scope of financial reporting is much broader. It also embraces "other means of communicating information that relates, directly or indirectly, to the information provided by the accounting system."

a) Examples are disclosures required by authoritative pronouncements as supplementary information, annual reports, prospectuses, other filings with the SEC, news releases, and letters to shareholders.

2) Financial statements are often audited by independent accountants, but the information included in financial reporting is often not subject to outside scrutiny that would enhance its reliability or credibility.

b. **Characteristics and limitations of information**

1) Most information provided by financial reporting is financial in nature and quantified in nominal units of money, but as the general purchasing power of the unit of measure changes, financial statements expressed in nominal monetary units become less comparable and useful.

2) Financial reporting is ordinarily focused on individual entities.

3) Information supplied by financial reporting involves estimation, classification, summarization, judgment, and allocation.

4) Most forms of financial reporting reflect historical transactions, events, and circumstances (forecasts and projections are examples to the contrary).

5) Financial reporting requires the incurrence of costs, and the cost-benefit criterion must be considered in weighing the extent of financial reporting.

6) Financial reporting is not the only source of information required by economic decision makers.

c. **Objectives -- General considerations**

1) Although focused on investment and credit decisions, the objectives are intended to apply to information that is useful to anyone interested in the related enterprise's ability to meet its obligations or reward its investors.

2) Financial reporting should provide "evenhanded, neutral, or unbiased information" to facilitate business and economic decisions but not to determine what those decisions should be.

d. **Objective -- Information useful in investment and credit decisions**

1) Financial reporting should provide information that is useful to current and potential investors and creditors and other users in making rational investment, credit, and other similar decisions.

2) The information should be comprehensible to those who have a reasonable understanding of business and economic activities and who are willing to study the information with reasonable diligence.

e. **Objective -- Information useful in assessing cash flow prospects**

1) Financial reporting should provide information to help current and potential investors and creditors and other users in assessing the amounts, timing, and uncertainty of prospective cash receipts from dividends or interest and the proceeds from the sale, redemption, or maturity of securities or loans.

2) Financial reporting should also provide information to help investors, creditors, and others assess the amounts, timing, and uncertainty of prospective net cash inflows to the related enterprise.

3) Investing, lending, and similar activities are undertaken to obtain not merely a return of cash expended but also a return proportionate to the risk. Thus, information should be useful in assessing risk.

f. **Objective -- Information about enterprise resources, claims to those resources, and changes in them**

1) Financial reporting furnishes information that helps to identify the financial strengths and weaknesses of an enterprise, to assess its liquidity and solvency, and to evaluate its performance during a period. However, financial accounting does not directly measure the value of an enterprise, although it may provide information to those who wish to do so.

2) According to SFAC 1, "The primary focus of financial reporting is information about an enterprise's performance provided by measures of earnings and its components."

a) Although such information concerns the past, investors and creditors commonly use it to evaluate an enterprise's prospects. Information about past performance is most valuable when the going-concern assumption is appropriate, that is, when an enterprise is expected to continue in operation for an indefinite time.

b) Measures of earnings and its components are of special interest to those concerned with an enterprise's cash flow potential. However, cash-basis financial statements for a short period, such as a year, are less valuable for this purpose than accrual-basis statements.

3) Although the primary focus is on earnings, information about cash flows is useful for understanding operations, evaluating financing activities, assessing liquidity and solvency, and interpreting earnings information.

4) Financial reporting should provide information about management's stewardship of resources, including their efficient and profitable use.

a) However, it does not separate management performance from enterprise performance. The latter is affected by many factors other than management's activities. Thus, financial reporting does not directly provide information about management performance.

5) Financial reporting should include management's explanations and interpretations.

2. **Qualitative Characteristics of Accounting Information (SFAC 2)**

a. SFAC 2 describes the qualities or characteristics of accounting information that make it useful for decision making. These qualities apply to information of both business enterprises and not-for-profit organizations.

1) SFAC 2 presents the hierarchy of accounting qualities in the following table:

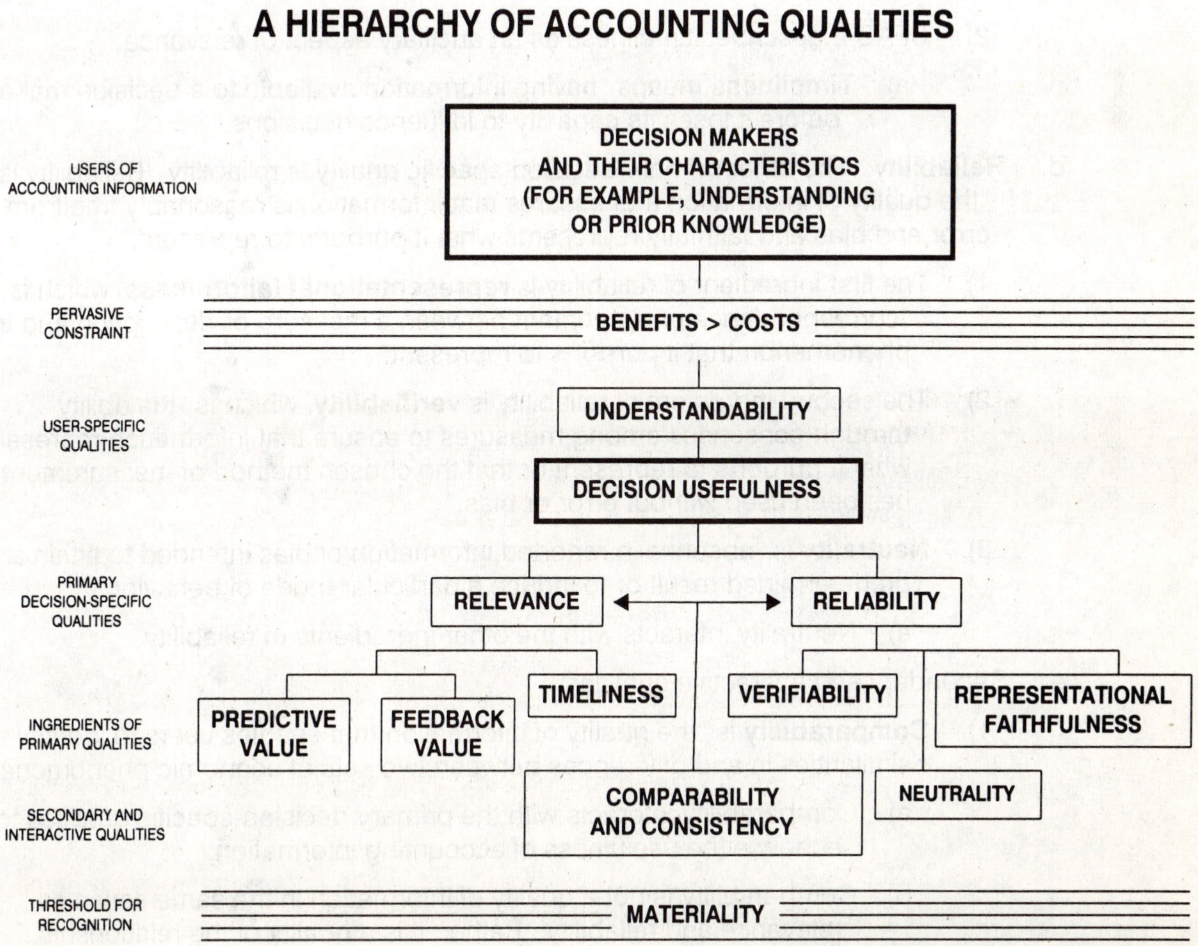

b. **Decision makers**. Decision making has a central role in financial reporting, and decision makers must ultimately determine what information is useful.

1) Information becomes more beneficial as it is understood by a greater number of users.

2) **Understandability** (a user-specific quality) depends on both the characteristics of users (such as prior training and knowledge) and those of the information (reliability, relevance, etc.).

c. **Relevance**. The primary decision-specific qualities are relevance and reliability. Relevance is "the capacity of information to make a difference in a decision by helping users to form predictions about the outcomes of past, present, and future events or to confirm or correct prior expectations."

1) The two principal ingredients of relevance are feedback value and predictive value.

a) **Feedback value** is defined as "the quality of information that enables users to confirm or correct prior expectations."

b) **Predictive value** is "the quality of information that helps users to increase the likelihood of correctly forecasting the outcome of past or current events."

2) SFAC 2 describes timeliness as an ancillary aspect of relevance.

a) **Timeliness** means "having information available to a decision maker before it loses its capacity to influence decisions."

d. **Reliability**. The other primary decision-specific quality is reliability. Reliability is "the quality of information that assures that information is reasonably free from error and bias and faithfully represents what it purports to represent."

1) The first ingredient of reliability is **representational faithfulness**, which is "correspondence or agreement between a measure or description and the phenomenon that it purports to represent."

2) The second ingredient of reliability is **verifiability**, which is "the ability through consensus among measures to ensure that information represents what it purports to represent or that the chosen method of measurement has been used without error or bias."

3) **Neutrality** is "absence in reported information of bias intended to attain a predetermined result or to induce a particular mode of behavior."

a) Neutrality interacts with the other ingredients of reliability.

e. Secondary and interactive qualities

1) **Comparability** is "the quality of information that enables users to identify similarities in and differences between two sets of economic phenomena."

a) Comparability interacts with the primary decision-specific qualities to enhance the usefulness of accounting information.

b) Comparability is not a quality of information in the same sense as relevance and reliability. Rather, it is a quality of the relationship among items of information.

2) **Consistency** is "conformity from period to period with unchanging policies and procedures."

a) Consistency restricts companies from changing accounting methods, unless they can demonstrate that the newly adopted method is preferable to the old method. Then the nature and effect of the accounting change, as well as the justification for it, must be disclosed in the financial statements for the period in which the change is made.

f. **Materiality** is the threshold for recognition. Materiality is "the magnitude of an omission or misstatement of accounting information that, in the light of surrounding circumstances, makes it probable that the judgment of a reasonable person relying on the information would have been changed or influenced by the omission or misstatement."

1) The importance of materiality is emphasized by the exemption of immaterial items from the application of GAAP.

2) Judgments about materiality are primarily quantitative but are affected by qualitative concerns about the nature of particular items and the circumstances in which the judgments are made.

a) Because the unique circumstances affecting materiality judgments differ substantially, general standards of materiality ordinarily have not been promulgated.

g. **Costs and benefits** is the pervasive constraint. Like other goods, financial information will not often be sought unless its benefits exceed its costs. However, these costs and benefits cannot be objectively quantified.

3. **Elements of Financial Statements (SFAC 6)**

a. SFAC 6 applies to business enterprises and not-for-profit entities. The elements defined are those that relate to measuring the performance and status of an entity based on information provided by accrual accounting.

b. The following elements reflect resources and claims thereto at a moment in time:

1) **Assets** are "probable future economic benefits obtained or controlled by a particular entity as a result of past transactions or events."

a) A valuation allowance changes the carrying amount of an asset. It is not a separate asset or a liability.

2) **Liabilities** are "probable future sacrifices of economic benefits arising from present obligations of a particular entity to transfer assets or provide services to other entities in the future as a result of past transactions or events."

a) A valuation account, e.g., bond premium or discount, changes the carrying amount of a liability.

3) **Equity or net assets** is "the residual interest in the assets of an entity that remains after deducting its liabilities."

a) Equity of a business enterprise, in contrast with the net assets of a nonprofit entity, is changed by investments by, and distributions to, owners.

c. The following elements describe transactions, events, and circumstances during intervals of time (the first three apply only to business enterprises):

1) **Investments by owners** are "increases in equity of a particular business enterprise resulting from transfers to it from other entities of something valuable to obtain or increase ownership interests (or equity) in it."

2) **Distributions to owners** are "decreases in equity of a particular business enterprise resulting from transferring assets, rendering services, or incurring liabilities by the enterprise to owners."

   a) A distribution to owners decreases equity (the ownership interest).

3) **Comprehensive income** is "the change in equity of a business enterprise during a period from transactions and other events and circumstances from nonowner sources." It excludes changes in equity resulting from investments by and distributions to owners.

   a) Comprehensive income and the financial statements are based on the financial capital maintenance concept; comprehensive income is a return on, not a return of, financial capital.

   b) Comprehensive income differs from measures of net income in current practice because it encompasses certain changes in equity recognized in the equity section of the balance sheet but not in the income statement, e.g., changes in the fair values of available-for-sale securities, foreign currency translation adjustments, and the excess of an additional minimum pension liability over any unrecognized prior service cost.

   c) Comprehensive income also differs from earnings as defined in SFAC 5. Moreover, adding to the terminological confusion, earnings is sometimes used in current practice as a synonym for net income. Earnings is similar to net income except that it excludes the cumulative effects of certain accounting adjustments of prior periods, e.g., the cumulative effect of a change in accounting principle.

   d) **SFAS 130**, *Reporting Comprehensive Income*, requires that all items recognized under current standards as components of comprehensive income be reported in a financial statement displayed with the same prominence as the other statements.

4) **Revenues** are "inflows or other enhancements of assets of an entity or settlements of its liabilities (or a combination of both) from delivering or producing goods, rendering services, or other activities that constitute the entity's ongoing major or central operations."

5) **Expenses** are "outflows or other using up of assets or incurrences of liabilities (or a combination of both) from delivering or producing goods, rendering services, or carrying out other activities that constitute the entity's ongoing major or central operations."

6) **Gains (losses)** are increases (decreases) in equity "from peripheral or incidental transactions of an entity and from all other transactions and other events and circumstances affecting the entity except those that result from revenues (expenses) or investments by (distributions to) owners."

4. **Recognition and Measurement Concepts (SFAC 5)**

a. Recognition criteria determine whether and when items should be incorporated into the financial statements, either initially or as changes in existing items.

1) Four fundamental recognition criteria apply to all recognition issues. However, each is subject to the pervasive cost-benefit constraint and the materiality threshold.

a) The item must meet the definition of an element of financial statements.

b) It must have a relevant attribute measurable with sufficient reliability (measurability).

c) The information about it must be capable of making a difference in user decisions (relevance).

d) The information must be representationally faithful, verifiable, and neutral (reliability).

2) According to the revenue recognition principle, revenue should be recognized when (1) realized or realizable and (2) earned.

a) Revenues are **realized** when goods or services have been exchanged for cash or claims to cash.

b) Revenues are **realizable** when goods or services have been exchanged for assets that are readily convertible into cash or claims to cash.

c) Revenues are **earned** when the earning process has been substantially completed and the entity is entitled to the resulting benefits or revenues.

d) The two conditions are usually met when goods are delivered or services are rendered, that is, at the time of sale, which is customarily the time of delivery.

e) As a reflection of the profession's conservatism, expenses and losses have historically been subject to less stringent recognition criteria than revenues and gains.

i) Expenses and losses are not subject to the realization criterion.

ii) Rather, expenses and losses are recognized when a consumption of economic benefits occurs during the entity's primary activities or when the ability of existing assets to provide future benefits has been impaired.

- An expense or loss may also be recognized when a liability has been incurred or increased without the receipt of corresponding benefits; a probable and reasonably estimable contingent loss is an example.

iii) Long-lived assets, such as equipment, buildings, and intangibles, are depreciated or amortized over their useful lives. Natural resources are depleted--usually on a units-of-production basis.

3) The following are exceptions to the basic revenue recognition rules:

a) Revenues from long-term contracts may be recognized using the **percentage-of-completion method**.

i) This method allows for revenue to be recognized at various stages of the contract although the entire job is not complete.

b) The **completion-of-production method** is an appropriate basis for recognition if products or other assets are readily realizable, e.g., precious metals and some agricultural products.

c) Although not an allowable exception under GAAP, some theorists believe the **accretion** method should be used to recognize revenue for growing assets such as timber.

d) If the collectibility of assets is relatively uncertain, revenues and gains may be recognized as cash is received using the **installment sales method**.

b. Different **measurement attributes** of assets and liabilities are used in current practice.

1) **Historical cost** is the acquisition price of an asset and is ordinarily adjusted subsequently for amortization (which includes depreciation) or other allocations. It is the relevant attribute for plant assets and most inventories.

2) **Historical proceeds** is the cash or equivalent that is actually received when an obligation was created and may be subsequently amortized. It is the relevant attribute for liabilities incurred to provide goods or services to customers. An example is a magazine subscription.

3) **Current (replacement) cost** is the cash or equivalent that would have to be paid for a current acquisition of the same or an equivalent asset. Inventory valued at the lower of cost or market may reflect current cost.

4) **Current market value (exit value)** is the cash or equivalent realizable by selling an asset in an orderly liquidation (not in a forced sale). It is used to measure some marketable securities, e.g., those held by investment companies, or assets expected to be sold at below their carrying amount. Certain liabilities, such as those incurred by writers of options who do not own the underlying assets, are also measured at current market value. More commonly, current market value is used when the **lower-of-cost-or-market** rule is applied to inventories and marketable securities.

5) **Net realizable value** is the cash or equivalent expected to be received for an asset in the due course of business, minus the costs of completion and sale. It is used to measure short-term receivables and some inventories, for example, damaged inventories. Net realizable value is distinct from liquidation value, which is the appropriate valuation of assets and liabilities when the going-concern assumption no longer holds.

6) **Net settlement value** is the cash or equivalent that the entity expects to pay to satisfy an obligation in the due course of business. It is used to measure such items as trade payables and warranty obligations. Net settlement value ignores present value considerations. The amounts that will be realized in a liquidation are usually less than those that would have been received in the due course of business.

7) **Present value** is in theory the most relevant method of measurement because it incorporates time value of money concepts. Determination of the present value of an asset or liability requires discounting at an appropriate interest rate the related future cash flows expected to occur in the due course of business. In practice, it is currently used only for long-term receivables and payables (but see SFAC 7).

c. **Nominal units of money** are expected to continue as the measurement scale in current practice.

1) The use of monetary units unadjusted for changes in purchasing power is not ideal, but it has the virtue of simplicity and does not result in excessive distortion if inflation or deflation is relatively low.

5. **Using Cash Flow Information and Present Value in Accounting Measurements (SFAC 7)**

a. Accounting measurements ordinarily use an observable amount determined by market forces, but, absent such a measurement, estimated cash flows often serve as a measure of an asset or a liability. Thus, SFAC 7 establishes a framework that uses cash flows for measurements at initial recognition, for fresh-start measurements, and for applications of the interest method of allocation.

1) An **estimated cash flow** is a future amount, whether paid or received.

2) A **fresh-start measurement** occurs in a period subsequent to initial recognition. It results in a carrying amount not based on prior amounts or accounting treatments. An example is the reporting of trading securities at fair value at each balance sheet date.

3) An **interest method of allocation** uses present value in the absence of a fresh-start measurement to calculate the periodic change in the carrying amount of an asset or liability.

b. SFAC 7 also states principles for the use of present value, especially when the amounts of future cash flows or their timing are uncertain, and describes the objective of present value.

1) **Present value** is a current measure of an estimated cash flow after discounting. Hence, the present value of \$1 due or payable in n periods and discounted at interest rate i is $\$1 \div (1 + i)^n$.

c. The scope of SFAC 7 is limited to measurement matters. It does not concern recognition issues or determine when fresh-start measurements should be used.

d. The objective of present value measurement is to distinguish the economic differences between sets of future cash flows that may vary in amount, timing, and uncertainty.

e. For initial recognition and fresh-start purposes, present value is based on an observable measurement attribute. Absent observed transaction prices, the present value measurement should encompass the elements of a market price if one existed (fair value).

1) **Fair value** is the amount at which an "asset (or liability) could be bought (or incurred) or sold (or settled) in a current transaction between willing parties, that is, other than in a forced or liquidation sale."

f. The market finally determines asset and liability values. However, if management's estimates are the sole source of information, the objective is still to estimate the likely market price if a market existed.

g. A measurement based on present value should reflect uncertainty so that variations in risks are incorporated. Accordingly, the following are the necessary elements of a present value measurement:
   1) Estimates of future cash flows
   2) Expected variability of their amount and timing
   3) The time value of money (risk-free interest rate)
   4) The price of uncertainty inherent in an asset or liability
   5) Other factors, such as lack of liquidity or market imperfections.

h. The traditional approach to calculating present value employs one set of estimated cash flows and one interest rate. This approach is expected to continue to be used in many cases, for example, when contractual cash flows are involved. However, SFAC 7 describes the **expected cash flow** approach, which is applicable in more complex circumstances, such as when no market or no comparable item exists for an asset or liability.

   1) The **expected cash flow** results from multiplying each possible estimated amount by its probability and adding the products.

   2) The expected cash flow approach emphasizes explicit assumptions about the possible estimated cash flows and their probabilities. The traditional method merely includes those uncertainties in the choice of interest rate. Moreover, by allowing for a range of possibilities, the expected cash flow method permits the use of present value when the timing of cash flows is uncertain.

   3) The FASB recognizes that the cost-benefit constraint applies to the use of the expected cash flow approach.

   4) Many pricing tools, for example, the Black-Scholes option-pricing model, have been developed to estimate fair value. If such a model includes the elements of present value with an objective of fair value (see 5.g. above), it is consistent with SFAC 7.

   5) Fair value should include an adjustment for risk (the price of the uncertainty of cash flows) if it is identifiable, measurable, and significant. But, if a reliable estimate of a market risk premium cannot be obtained, discounting expected cash flows at the risk-free rate may provide the best estimate of fair value.

      a) Measurements of present value occur under conditions of **uncertainty**; the cash flows are estimates rather than known amounts. Thus, as long as the uncertainty persists, the accounting entity is at **risk**, and it will require a risk premium to accept uncertainty.

      b) The inclusion of uncertainty and risk in a measurement is intended to reflect the market's treatment of assets and liabilities with uncertain cash flows. If a market price is not observable, a present value measurement may be the best available means of estimating a price.

      c) Finance theory provides various methods for estimating the risk premium. For example, portfolio theory states that the risk of a given asset depends on its effect on the total risk of a portfolio of assets.

d) Measurement using estimates is inherently imprecise, but reliability of accounting information should be weighted against its relevance. Use of expected cash flow techniques may result in sufficient reliability and greater relevance than the use of undiscounted measurements.

i. The purpose of a present value measurement of the **fair value of a liability** "is to estimate the value of the assets required currently to (a) settle the liability with the holder or (b) transfer the liability to an entity of comparable credit standing."

1) Measurement of certain liabilities, for example, bonds payable, involves the same process as that used for assets. The measure of such a liability is the price at which another entity is willing to hold it as an asset.

a) Some liabilities, however, are not typically held as salable assets by the obligee, for example, liabilities for warranties or environmental cleanup. But liabilities of this kind are sometimes assumed by a third person. In this case, the estimate of the liability would be the estimate of the price a third person would have to be paid to assume the liability.

2) The entity's **credit standing** is always incorporated into initial and fresh-start measurements of liabilities. Credit standing affects the price an entity is willing to pay to hold another entity's liability as an asset. The effect of credit standing on liability measures is ordinarily reflected in interest rate adjustments; improved credit-worthiness allows an entity to borrow at a lower rate.

j. Present value is a feature of **interest methods of allocation**. A typical example is amortization of the discount or premium on bonds. Unlike a fresh-start measurement, an accounting allocation does not attempt to reflect all factors that cause change in an asset or liability. It represents merely the consumption of assets or the reduction of liabilities, that is, the change in a reported amount corresponding to the change in the present value of a set of future cash flows.

1) Because no allocation method, whether or not interest-based, is preferable in every situation, the FASB will choose whether to require an interest method of allocation on a project-by-project basis.

2) An interest method is most likely relevant when

a) The transaction is a borrowing and a lending
b) Similar assets or liabilities are allocated using an interest method
c) The asset or liability has closely related estimated cash flows
d) The initial measurement was at present value

3) Application of an interest method requires careful definition of the cash flows (e.g., promised cash flows, expected cash flows, or another definition), the interest rate, the application of the interest rate, and the reporting of changes in the amount or timing of estimated cash flows.

4) Changes in estimated cash flows may result in a fresh-start measurement or in a change in the plan of amortization. If remeasurement is not done, a change in the scheme may be effected by

a) Prospectively determining a new effective rate given the carrying amount and the remaining cash flows.

b) Retrospectively determining a new effective rate given the original carrying amount, actual cash flows, and the newly estimated cash flows and using it to adjust the current carrying amount.

c) Adjusting the carrying amount to the present value of the remaining cash flows discounted at the original rate.

i) The FASB prefers this catch-up approach.

6. Stop and review! You have completed the outline for this subunit. Study multiple-choice questions 1 through 35 beginning on page 123.

B. Revenue

1. **Recognition at the Point of Sale**

a. Revenues are normally recognized when they are realized or realizable and earned. The revenue recognition criteria are ordinarily met at the point of sale. At this time, title and risk of loss usually pass to the buyer.

1) For example, if goods are shipped FOB shipping point, the point of sale is the shipping point. Thus, shipment is the event that causes title and risk of loss to pass to the buyer. However, if the shipping term is FOB destination, title and risk of loss do not pass to the buyer until a tender of delivery is made at the destination. Accordingly, the place of delivery is the point of sale.

b. Exceptions exist to this principle. For example, revenue may be recognized at the point of production if an established market exists for fungible goods, such as precious metals or agricultural products.

1) Revenue and profit may be recognized after the point of sale if considerable uncertainty exists about collection of the sales price. The installment method or cost-recovery method may be used in this case.

2) Certain multiperiod transactions, e.g., construction contracts, are accounted for by the percentage-of-completion or completed-contract method.

c. If the recognition criteria are not met, amounts received in advance are treated as liabilities (deferred revenues). Recognition is deferred until the obligation underlying the liability is partly or wholly satisfied.

1) Cash received in advance may initially be credited to a deferred revenue (liability) account. At the end of the accounting period, earned revenue is recognized with the following adjusting entry:

Deferred revenue	$XXX	
Revenue		$XXX

a) A reversing entry is not appropriate if advance receipts are initially credited to a deferred revenue account (a permanent or real account).

2) If cash received in advance is initially credited to a revenue account, an adjusting entry is needed to debit revenue and credit a deferred revenue (liability) account for unearned amounts.

Revenue	$XXX	
Deferred revenue		$XXX

a) If this entry is reversed at the beginning of the next period, no entry will be needed to recognize revenue. This procedure keeps unearned revenue in the revenue account (a temporary or nominal account) except at the end of the period when financial statements are prepared.

2. **Recognition at Completion of Production**. If products or other assets are readily realizable because they are salable at reliably determinable prices without significant effort (for example, certain agricultural products, precious metals, and marketable securities), revenues and some gains or losses may be recognized at completion of production or when prices of the assets change.

3. **Cash vs. Accrual Basis**

a. Accrual-basis accounting records revenues and expenses in the periods when they are earned or incurred. Cash-basis accounting records revenues when cash is received, and expenses when cash is paid.

b. Accrual-basis accounting uses deferrals to postpone recognition of revenues and expenses to subsequent periods if the related cash amounts are received or paid in a period prior to when they are earned or incurred. Accruals are used to recognize revenues and expenses as earned or incurred in a period prior to when the related cash amounts are received or paid. Use "T" accounts and journal entries to analyze cash-accrual questions.

4. **Installment Method**

a. The installment method recognizes income on a sale as the related receivable is collected. This method is normally used when the collection of the receivable is not reasonably assured (when collection problems, i.e., bad debts, are subject to reasonable estimate, profit is usually recognized at the point of sale).

b. The amount recognized each period is the gross profit percentage (gross profit ÷ selling price) on the sale multiplied by the cash collected. In addition, interest income must be accounted for separately from the gross profit on the sale.

c. If the goods sold are repossessed due to nonpayment, the goods' net realizable value, remaining deferred gross profit, and any loss are debited, and the remaining installment receivable credited.

d. EXAMPLE: Assume that a TV costing $600 is sold on the installment basis for a price of $1,000 on November 1, Year 1. A down payment of $100 was received and the remainder is due in nine monthly payments of $100 each. The entry for the sale is

Cash	$100	
Installment receivable (Year 1)	900	
Inventory		$600
Deferred gross profit (Year 1)		400

1) In December when the first installment is received, the entry is

Cash	$100	
Installment receivable (Year 1)		$100

2) At December 31, the deferred gross profit must be adjusted to report the portion that has been earned. Given that 20% of the total price has been received, 20% of the gross profit has been earned. The entry is

Deferred gross profit (Year 1)	$80	
Realized gross profit		$80

3) Net income should include only the $80 realized gross profit for the period. The balance sheet should report a receivable of $800 minus the deferred gross profit of $320. Thus, the net receivable is $480.

4) In Year 2, the remaining $800 is received, and the $320 balance of deferred gross profit is recognized. If only $400 were received in Year 2 (if payments were extended), the December Year 2 statements would report a $400 installment receivable and $160 of deferred gross profit.

5) If the TV in the example had to be repossessed because no payments after the down payment were made by the buyer, the used TV would be recorded at its net realizable value minus a resale profit. Assume that fair value at the time of repossession was only $500 because the TV had been damaged and that repair costs and sales commissions will amount to $100.

Inventory of used merchandise	$400	
Deferred gross profit	360	
Loss on repossession	140	
Installment receivable		$900

a) The loss on repossession represents the difference between the $400 net realizable value ($500 fair value – $100 repair and sales costs) and the $540 book value ($900 remaining on the contract – $360 deferred gross profit) of the receivable.

6) Installment receivables are shown as current assets regardless of the due date. Even though the receivable may be due in more than 1 year, the stipulation that a current receivable is one that will be collected within the normal operating cycle makes installment receivables current assets.

7) Normally, there is also an interest component, and APB 21, *Interest on Receivables and Payables*, applies. The recognition of deferred gross profit is based on receipt of principal. The interest is imputed at the time of issuance and remains constant for the life of the installment.

5. **Cost-Recovery Method**. The cost-recovery method may be used when receivables are collected over an extended period, there is considerable doubt as to collectibility, and a reasonable estimate of the loss cannot be made. Under the cost-recovery method, profit is recognized only after collections exceed the cost of the item sold. Subsequent amounts are treated entirely as revenues. This method is more conservative than the installment method.

a. EXAMPLE: In year 1, Creditor Co. made a $100,000 sale accounted for using the cost-recovery method. The cost of the item sold was $70,000, and year 1 collections equaled $50,000. In year 2, collections equaled $25,000, and $10,000 of the receivable was determined to be uncollectible. As a result of these transactions, the net receivable (receivable – deferred profit) was $0 at the end of year 2. The following entries were made in year 1 and year 2:

Year 1:	Receivable	$100,000	
	Inventory		$70,000
	Deferred gross profit		30,000
	Cash	$50,000	
	Receivable		$50,000
Year 2:	Cash	$25,000	
	Deferred gross profit	5,000	
	Receivable		$25,000
	Realized gross profit		5,000
	Deferred gross profit	$10,000	
	Receivable		$10,000

6. **Long-Term Construction Contracts**

a. The **completed-contract method** is used when the percentage-of-completion method is inappropriate. It defers all contract costs until the project is completed and then matches the costs of completing the contract with the revenues from the project. Hence, profit is recognized only in the year of completion.

1) All costs are deferred in a **construction-in-progress** account until the project is completed and revenue is recognized. Then construction-in-progress is closed to cost of sales.

b. According to SOP 81-1, the **percentage-of-completion method** is used to recognize revenue on long-term construction-type contracts when

1) The extent of progress toward completion, contract revenue, and contract costs are reasonably estimable.

2) The enforceable rights regarding goods or services to be provided, the consideration to be exchanged, and the manner and terms of settlement are clearly specified.

3) The contractual obligations of both the buyer and the contractor are expected to be fulfilled.

c. The **percentage-of-completion method** recognizes profit based upon the estimated total profit, the percentage completed based on the relationship of costs incurred to estimated total costs, and the profit recognized to date. The estimated total profit equals the contract price minus the total estimated costs. The percentage completed is multiplied times the total expected profit to determine the total profit to be recognized to date. The profit recognized in prior periods is then subtracted from the total profit to date to determine the profit to be recognized in the current period.

1) Under both the percentage-of-completion and the completed-contract methods, the full estimated loss on any project is recognized as soon as it becomes apparent.

d. EXAMPLE: A contractor has a contract to build a bridge that will take 3 years to complete. The contract price is $2,000,000. The contractor expects total costs to be $1,200,000. The following information applies to the costs incurred and expected to be incurred during the 3 years:

	Year 1	Year 2	Year 3
Costs incurred during each year	$300,000	$600,000	$550,000
Costs expected in future	900,000	600,000	0

1) By the end of the first year, the contractor has incurred 25% ($300,000 ÷ $1,200,000) of all costs expected to be incurred on the project. Thus, if the percentage-of-completion method is being used, the contractor will recognize 25% of the profit that will be earned on the project. The total profit is expected to be $800,000 ($2,000,000 – $1,200,000), and $200,000 (25% x $800,000) of profit should be recognized in the first year.

2) At the end of the second year, the company has incurred total costs of $900,000 ($300,000 in the first year and $600,000 in the second year). Given that an additional $600,000 of cost is expected to be incurred in the future, the total cost of the project is expected to be $1,500,000 ($900,000 + $600,000), and the new estimate of total profit is $500,000 ($2,000,000 contract price – $1,500,000 of costs). If the project is 60% complete after year 2 ($900,000 ÷ $1,500,000), 60% of all profit should be recognized by the end of year 2 or $300,000 (60% x $500,000). Because $200,000 was recognized in the first year, $100,000 remains to be recognized in year 2.

3) At the end of the third year, total costs are $1,450,000. Thus, the total profit is known to be $550,000. Because a total of $300,000 was recognized in the first 2 years, $250,000 should be recognized in year 3.

4) Journal entries:

		%-of-Completion		Completed-Contract	
Year 1:	Construction in progress	$300,000		$300,000	
	Cash or accounts payable		$300,000		$300,000
	Construction in progress	$200,000			
	Construction revenue		$200,000		No entry
Year 2:	Construction in progress	$600,000		$600,000	
	Cash or accounts payable		$600,000		$600,000
	Construction in progress	$100,000			
	Construction revenue		$100,000		No entry
Year 3:	Construction in progress	$550,000		$550,000	
	Cash or accounts payable		$550,000		$550,000
	Cash	$2,000,000		$2,000,000	
	Construction in progress		$1,750,000		$1,450,000
	Construction revenue		250,000		550,000

5) The preceding entries assume payment was made at the end of the contract.

a) Ordinarily, **progress billings** are made and payments are received during the term of the contract. Accounts receivable is debited and progress billings is credited. As cash is received, cash is debited and accounts receivable is credited. Neither billing nor the receipt of cash affects net income.

b) Progress billings is an offset to construction in progress (or vice versa) on the balance sheet.

i) The difference between construction in progress (costs and recognized income) and progress billings to date is reported as a current asset if construction in progress exceeds total billings, and as a current liability if billings exceed construction in progress.

ii) The closing entry is to debit progress billings and to credit construction in progress.

c) Another variation on the foregoing entries is to credit periodic revenue for the gross rather than net amount. This practice requires a debit to a cost of revenue earned account (similar to cost of goods sold) for the costs incurred in the present period.

7. **Consignment Accounting**

a. A **consignment sale** is an arrangement between the owner of goods and a sales agent. Goods on consignment are not sold to the sales agent but rather consigned for possible sale.

1) Title remains with the consignor (owner), and risk of loss does not transfer to the consignee (sales agent).

2) Sales are recorded on the books of the consignor only when the goods are sold to third parties by the consignee.

3) Inventory shipped on consignment should therefore not be reported as a sale by a consignor but rather be included in inventory. Costs of transporting the goods to the consignee are inventoriable costs, not selling costs.

4) The consignee records sales commissions when the goods are sold and at no time records the inventory as an asset.

b. **Accounting by the consignee**

1) The initial acquisition of inventory is not recorded in the ledger accounts, although a supplementary memorandum entry may be made.

2) Sales are recorded with a debit to cash (or accounts receivable) and credits to commission income and accounts payable to the consignor.

3) Any expenses incurred by the consignee on behalf of the consignor (such as freight-in or service costs) are reductions of the payable to the consignor.

4) Periodic remittances to the consignor result in a debit to accounts payable and a credit to cash.

c. **Accounting by the consignor**

1) The initial shipment is recorded with a debit to consigned goods out and a credit to inventory for the cost of the merchandise.

2) Periodic remittances and notification of expenses incurred by the consignee are recorded by debits to cash, commission expense, consigned goods out, and cost of goods sold. Credits are to sales and consigned goods out.

d. **Example entries on the books of the consignor and consignee**

1) 100 units, costing $50 each, are shipped to a consignee:

CONSIGNOR'S BOOKS			CONSIGNEE'S BOOKS		
Consigned goods out	$5,000		Only memorandum entry		
Inventory		$5,000			

2) Consignee pays $120 for freight-in:

CONSIGNOR'S BOOKS			CONSIGNEE'S BOOKS		
No entry at this time			Payable to consignor	$120	
			Cash		$120

3) 80 units are sold at $80 each. Consignee is to receive a 20% commission on all sales:

CONSIGNOR'S BOOKS			CONSIGNEE'S BOOKS		
No entry at this time			Cash	$6,400	
			Payable to consignor		$5,120
			Commission income		1,280

4) Consignee sends monthly statement to consignor along with balance owed:

CONSIGNOR'S BOOKS			CONSIGNEE'S BOOKS		
Cash	$5,000		Payable to consignor	$5,000	
Commission expense	1,280		Cash		$5,000
Consigned goods out	120				
Cost of goods sold	4,096				
Sales		$6,400			
Consigned goods out		4,096			

5) The consignee may use consignment in rather than payable to consignor. Consignment in is a receivable/payable account.

6) Consigned goods out is an account used in a perpetual inventory system. If the consignor uses a physical inventory system, the credit on shipment would be to consignment shipments, a contra cost of sales account. The balance in the account is closed at the end of the period when the inventory adjustments are made.

8. **Interest**

a. The basic **compound interest** concept is that a quantity of money to be received or paid in the future is worth less than the same amount of money today. The difference is interest calculated using the appropriate discount rate. Interest is the payment received by holders of money to forgo current consumption. The current consumer of money pays interest for its use.

1) Standard tables have been developed to facilitate the calculation of present and future values. Each entry in one of these tables represents the result of substituting in the pertinent present value or future value equation a payment of $1, the number of periods, and an interest rate.

2) The **present value (PV) of an amount** is the value today of some future payment.

a) It equals the future payment times the present value of $1 (a factor found in a standard table) for the given number of periods and interest rate.

b) EXAMPLE:

	Present Value		
No. of Periods	10%	12%	16%
1	0.909	0.893	0.862
2	0.826	0.797	0.743
3	0.751	0.712	0.641
4	0.683	0.636	0.552
5	0.621	0.567	0.476

The present value of $1,000, to be received in 3 years and discounted at 12%, is $712 ($1,000 x 0.712).

3) The **future value (FV) of an amount** is the amount available at a specified time in the future based on a single investment (deposit) today. The FV is the amount to be computed if one knows the present value and the appropriate discount rate.

a) It equals the current payment times the future value of $1 (a factor found in a standard table) for the given number of periods and interest rate.

b) EXAMPLE:

No. of Periods	Future Value 10%	12%	16%
1	1.1000	1.1200	1.1600
2	1.2100	1.2544	1.3456
3	1.3310	1.4049	1.5609
4	1.4641	1.5735	1.8106
5	1.6105	1.7623	2.1003

The future value of $1,000 invested today for 4 years at 10% interest will be $1,464 ($1,000 x 1.464).

4) **Annuities.** An annuity is usually a series of equal payments at equal intervals of time, e.g., $1,000 at the end of every year for 10 years.

a) An **ordinary annuity (annuity in arrears)** is a series of payments occurring at the end of each period. An **annuity due (annuity in advance)** is an annuity in which the payments are made (or received) at the beginning of each period.

i) In a present value calculation, the first payment of an ordinary annuity is discounted. The first payment of an annuity due is not.

ii) In a future value calculation, interest is not earned for the first period of an ordinary annuity or on the final payment. The future value is calculated as of the date of the last payment. Interest is earned on each payment of an annuity due.

b) The **PV of an annuity.** The same present value tables may be used for both kinds of annuities. Most tables are for ordinary annuities. The factor for an ordinary annuity of one less period (n – 1), increased by 1.0 to include the initial payment (which is not discounted), is the factor for an annuity due.

i) EXAMPLE: The following is part of a standard table for the present value of an ordinary annuity:

No. of Periods	Present Value 10%	12%	16%
1	0.909	0.893	0.862
2	1.736	1.690	1.605
3	2.487	2.402	2.246
4	3.170	3.037	2.798
5	3.791	3.605	3.274

To calculate the present value of an ordinary annuity of four payments of $1,000 each discounted at 16%, multiply $1,000 by the appropriate factor ($1,000 x 2.798 = $2,798).

Using the same table, the present value of an annuity due of four payments of $1,000 each may also be calculated. This value equals $1,000 times the factor for one less period (4 – 1 = 3), increased by 1.0. Thus, the present value of the annuity due for four periods at 16% is $3,246 [$1,000 x (2.246 + 1.0)].

The present value of the annuity due ($3,246) is greater than the present value of the ordinary annuity ($2,798) because the payments occur 1 year sooner.

c) The **FV of an annuity** is the value that a series of equal payments will have at a certain moment in the future if interest is earned at a given rate.

i) EXAMPLE: Future value for an ordinary annuity:

	Future Value		
No. of Periods	10%	12%	16%
1	1.0000	1.0000	1.0000
2	2.1000	2.1200	2.1600
3	3.3100	3.3744	3.5056
4	4.6410	4.7793	5.0665
5	6.1051	6.3528	6.8771

To calculate the FV of a 3-year ordinary annuity with payments of $1,000 each at 12% interest, multiply $1,000 by the appropriate factor ($1,000 x 3.374 = $3,374).

The FV of an annuity due can also be determined from the same table. Multiply the $1,000 payment by the factor for one additional period (3 + 1 = 4) decreased by 1.0 (4.779 – 1.0 = 3.779) to arrive at a FV of $3,779 ($1,000 x 3.779).

The future value of the annuity due ($3,779) is greater than the future value of an annuity ($3,374) because the deposits are made earlier.

b. **The interest method of amortizing discount or premium**

1) Whereas the straight-line method amortizes a constant amount each period, the **effective-interest method** results in a constant rate of return on a receivable or payable.

a) Under this method, the effective rate of interest is applied to the net book value of the receivable or payable to determine the **interest revenue** or **interest expense** for the period.

b) The amount of discount or premium amortized is the difference between interest revenue or interest expense and the actual amount of cash received or paid based on the nominal or contract rate of interest.

i) The amount of amortization increases or decreases from period to period, depending on whether a discount or premium, respectively, is being amortized. The reason is that net book value increases or decreases from period to period as discount or premium, respectively, is amortized.

c) The journal entry is

*Interest expense	$(Effective rate × Net book value)	
**Discount or premium	(Forced debit or credit)	
Cash or interest payable		$(Contract rate × Face value)

* Assumes a payable; a receivable requires a debit to cash and a credit to interest revenue.

** May be debited or credited directly to the payable if it is carried net of the discount or premium.

2) EXAMPLE: Assume a 10%, 10-year, $10,000 note receivable (interest paid annually), with a present value of $5,813 and a 20% effective rate.

a) Year 1. Interest income is $1,163 (20% x $5,813).

i) Cash received is $1,000 (10% x $10,000).
ii) Discount amortization is $163 ($1,163 – $1,000).

Cash	$1,000	
Notes receivable	163	
Interest revenue		$1,163

b) Year 2. Interest income is $1,195 [20% x ($5,813 + $163)].

i) Cash received is $1,000.
ii) Discount amortization is $195.

c) The amortization increases because 20% is applied to an increasing book value.

9. Stop and review! You have completed the outline for this subunit. Study multiple-choice questions 36 through 68 beginning on page 135.

C. Limitations of Financial Statement Information

1. The measurements made in financial statements do not necessarily represent the true worth of a firm or its segments. The following are common limitations of financial statements:

   a. The measurements are made in terms of money; therefore, qualitative aspects of a firm are not expressed.

   b. Information supplied by financial reporting involves estimation, classification, summarization, judgment, and allocation.

   c. Financial statements primarily reflect transactions that have already occurred; consequently, they are usually based on historical cost.

   d. Only transactions involving an entity being reported upon are reflected in that entity's financial reports. However, transactions of other entities, e.g., competitors, may be very important.

   e. Financial statements are based on the going-concern assumption. If that assumption is invalid, the appropriate attribute for measuring financial statement items is liquidation value, not historical cost, fair value, net realizable value, etc.

2. **Historical Cost Limitations**. As previously mentioned, most transactions on financial statements are recorded at their value on the date of the transaction. Many assets previously acquired are recorded on the balance sheet at their historical cost. When the values of these assets significantly change after the acquisition date, the balance sheet presentation of the assets becomes significantly less relevant in determining the company's worth.

   a. Over time, discrepancies develop between the current and the historical values of a transaction or an asset. For example, the replacement cost and the book value of assets will diverge. Moreover, the value of the unit of measure (the dollar for U.S. firms) will also change. Accordingly, comparisons between prior years and between competing firms become less meaningful.

3. Three major limitations exist in the reporting of a firm's segments.
   a. The definition of what constitutes a segment is a subjective determination in some respects. What represents a segment is inconsistently applied among firms and industries.
   b. Common cost allocations between related entities are subject to management manipulation. Many different allocation bases exist, allowing management to choose the one with the most benefits to a particular segment. Comparability of firms is again impaired.
   c. Transfer pricing exhibits the same limitations as cost allocation. Transfer prices tend to be set to benefit particular segments and are also subject to management manipulation.
4. **Constraints** (doctrines). There are certain constraints on the amount and type of information that is reported in the financial statements. The cost-benefit and materiality constraints were mentioned earlier in the discussion of qualitative characteristics. Two additional doctrines are discussed below.
   a. **Conservatism** constraint. Conservatism is "a prudent reaction to uncertainty to try to ensure that uncertainties and risks inherent in business situations are adequately considered" (SFAC 2).
      1) The conservatism doctrine originally directed accountants, when faced with two or more acceptable choices, to show the lowest amount for an asset or income. However, conservatism does not condone introducing bias into the financial statements through a deliberate understatement of net assets and net income.
         a) Thus, if estimates of future amounts to be paid or received differ but are equally likely, conservatism requires using the least optimistic estimate. However, if the estimates are not equally likely, conservatism does not necessarily require use of the estimate that results in understatement rather than the estimate that is the most likely.
      2) The application of the lower-of-cost-or-market rule to inventories is an example of the use of the conservatism constraint.
   b. **Industry practices** constraint. Occasionally, GAAP are not followed in an industry because adherence to them would generate misleading or unnecessary information. For instance, banks and insurance companies typically value marketable equity securities at market value, regardless of cost. Market value and liquidity are most important to these industries.
5. Stop and review! You have completed the outline for this subunit. Study multiple-choice questions 69 through 71 on page 147.

MULTIPLE-CHOICE QUESTIONS

A. Conceptual Framework Underlying Financial Accounting

1. A publicly held corporation is required to have its financial statements audited by an independent external auditor. The three purposes of these financial statements are to provide useful information (1) for credit and investment decisions, (2) about the firm's resources, and (3) for

A. Determining the impact of inflation.

B. Long-lived asset replacements.

C. Assessing market values of assets.

D. Evaluating prospective cash flows.

The correct answer is (D). *(CMA, adapted)*

REQUIRED: The third purpose of financial statements.

DISCUSSION: According to SFAC 1, *Objectives of Financial Reporting by Business Enterprises*, "Financial reporting should provide information to help present and potential investors and creditors and other users in assessing the amounts, timing, and uncertainty of prospective cash receipts from dividends or interest and the proceeds from the sale, redemption, or maturity of securities or loans. Since investors' and creditors' cash flows are related to enterprise cash flows, financial reporting should provide information to help investors, creditors, and others assess the amounts, timing, and uncertainty of prospective net cash inflows to the related enterprise."

Answer (A) is incorrect because the company is not required to present information about the effects of price level changes. Answer (B) is incorrect because such information will be communicated if the three broad purposes stated in SFAC 1 are satisfied. Answer (C) is incorrect because required financial statements for the most part reflect historical costs.

2. The information reported in the statement of cash flows should help investors, creditors, and others to assess all of the following except the

A. Amount, timing, and uncertainty of prospective net cash inflows of a firm.

B. Company's ability to pay dividends and meet obligations.

C. Company's ability to generate future cash flows.

D. Management of the firm with respect to the efficient and profitable use of its resources.

The correct answer is (D). *(CMA, adapted)*

REQUIRED: The item not an objective of a statement of cash flows.

DISCUSSION: The statement of cash flows is not designed to provide information with respect to the efficient and profitable use of the firm's resources. Financial reporting provides information about an enterprise's performance during a period when it was under the direction of a particular management but does not directly provide information about that management's performance. Financial reporting does not try to separate the impact of a particular management's performance from the effects of prior management actions, general economic conditions, the supply and demand for an enterprise's inputs and outputs, price changes, and other events.

Answers (A), (B), and (C) are incorrect because the primary purpose of a statement of cash flows is to provide information about the cash receipts and payments of an entity during a period. A secondary purpose is to provide information about investing and financing activities. The statement should help users to assess the entity's ability to generate positive future net cash flows, the ability to meet its obligations and pay dividends, the need for external financing, the reasons for differences between income and associated cash receipts and payments, and the cash and noncash aspects of the entity's investing and financing activities.

3. A statement of financial position is intended to help investors and creditors

A. Assess the amount, timing, and uncertainty of prospective net cash inflows of a firm.

B. Evaluate economic resources and obligations of a firm.

C. Evaluate economic performance of a firm.

D. Evaluate changes in the ownership equity of a firm.

The correct answer is (B). *(CMA, adapted)*

REQUIRED: The purpose of a statement of financial position.

DISCUSSION: The statement of financial position, or balance sheet, provides information about an entity's resource structure (assets) and financing structure (liabilities and equity) at a moment in time. The statement of financial position does not purport to show the value of a business, but it enables investors, creditors, and other users to make their own estimates of value. It helps users to assess liquidity, financial flexibility, profitability, and risk (SFAC 5).

Answer (A) is incorrect because providing information to help assess the amount, timing, and uncertainty of cash flows is an objective of the statement of cash flows. Answer (C) is incorrect because the primary focus of financial reporting is information about an enterprise's performance provided by measures of earnings and its components. Hence, an income statement is more directly useful to investors and creditors for evaluating economic performance. Answer (D) is incorrect because disclosures of changes in shareholders' equity, in either the basic statements, the notes thereto, or a separate statement, help users to evaluate changes in the ownership equity of a firm.

4. According to SFAC 1, *Objectives of Financial Reporting by Business Enterprises*,

A. External users have the ability to prescribe information they want.

B. Information is always based on exact measures.

C. Financial reporting is usually based on industries or the economy as a whole.

D. Financial accounting does not directly measure the value of a business enterprise.

The correct answer is (D). *(Publisher)*

REQUIRED: The true statement about the objectives of financial reporting.

DISCUSSION: Financial reporting furnishes information that helps to identify the financial strengths and weaknesses of an enterprise, to assess its liquidity and solvency, and to evaluate its performance during a period of time. However, financial accounting does not directly measure the value of an enterprise, although it may provide information to those who wish to do so.

Answer (A) is incorrect because some external users (e.g., taxing authorities) have the authority to obtain desired information, but most do not. The objectives are based on the needs of the latter class of users. Answer (B) is incorrect because financial information involves estimation and judgment. Answer (C) is incorrect because financial reporting is usually based on individual entities.

5. The accounting system should be designed

A. To meet external reporting requirements.

B. To balance management information needs with the cost of obtaining that information.

C. To eliminate fraud by accounting personnel.

D. By persons not directly involved with the system, such as consultants.

The correct answer is (B). *(CMA, adapted)*

REQUIRED: The true statement about the design of an internal accounting and reporting system.

DISCUSSION: One of the characteristics and limitations of the kind of information that financial reporting can provide is that the information is provided and used at a cost (see SFAC 1). All accounting information is subject to two quantitative constraints: materiality and cost-benefit. If a reasonable person relying on the information would not have changed his/her judgment as a result of an omission or misstatement, it is not considered material. The cost-benefit constraint states that the benefits of information must exceed the cost of obtaining it.

Answer (A) is incorrect because the first objective of the internal accounting and reporting system must be to provide relevant and reliable information for management decision making. Answer (C) is incorrect because the control of fraud is only an objective to the extent that the system is cost beneficial. Answer (D) is incorrect because those who best know the information needs should design the system.

6. If the going-concern assumption is no longer valid for a company,

A. Land held as an investment would be valued at its liquidation value.

B. All prepaid assets would be completely written off immediately.

C. Total contributed capital and retained earnings would remain unchanged.

D. The allowance for uncollectible accounts would be eliminated.

The correct answer is (A). *(CMA, adapted)*

REQUIRED: The true statement about a situation in which the going-concern assumption is not valid.

DISCUSSION: Under the going-concern, or business continuity, assumption, a financial statement user is to presume that a company will continue operating indefinitely in the absence of indications to the contrary. The essence of this assumption is that liquidation values are not used in the financial statements because the firm is unlikely to liquidate in the near future. When the going-concern assumption is not valid, it is necessary to make appropriate disclosures and to report assets at their liquidation values. For instance, land would no longer be reported at cost but at its liquidation value.

Answer (B) is incorrect because some prepaid assets may have a liquidation value. For example, supplies can be sold and prepaid insurance can be redeemed. Answer (C) is incorrect because capital would change to equalize the write-downs and write-ups on the asset side of the balance sheet. Answer (D) is incorrect because the allowance would still exist because many of the accounts may never be paid.

7. A company with total assets of $100,000,000 and net income of $9,000,000 purchases staplers with an estimated life of 10 years for $1,000. In connection with the purchase, the company debits miscellaneous expense. This scenario is most closely associated with which of the following concepts or principles?

A. Materiality and going concern.

B. Relevance and neutrality.

C. Reliability and comparability/consistency.

D. Materiality and cost-benefit.

The correct answer is (D). *(CIA, adapted)*

REQUIRED: The concepts or principles most closely associated with the choice of an accounting method.

DISCUSSION: In principle, wasting assets should be capitalized and depreciated. However, the effect on the financial statements of expensing rather than capitalizing and depreciating the staplers is clearly not material given that they cost $1,000 and the company has total assets of $100,000,000. The cost-benefit concept is tied to materiality and relates to the cost of information. Specifically, the cost of producing the information about depreciation expense over 10 years for the staplers probably is higher than the benefits of the information for decision making. Thus, the expedient procedure of expensing the $1,000 should be followed.

Answer (A) is incorrect because the going-concern principle relates to circumstances in which there is doubt as to the viability of the enterprise. Answer (B) is incorrect because SFAC 2 identifies relevance and reliability as the two primary qualities that make accounting information useful for decision making. Relevance is the capacity of information to make a difference in the user's decision. Reliability provides assurance that the information is reasonably free from error and bias, and that it represents what it purports to represent. Neutrality is an ingredient of reliability. Answer (C) is incorrect because reliability relates to using reproducible accounting numbers, such as historical cost to record assets. Comparability/consistency relates to using the same accounting principles from period to period. Comparability (including consistency) is an interactive quality that relates to both primary qualities of relevance and reliability.

8. One of the ingredients of the primary quality of relevance is

A. Verifiability.

B. Predictive value.

C. Neutrality.

D. Due process.

The correct answer is (B). *(CMA, adapted)*

REQUIRED: The ingredient of the primary quality of relevance.

DISCUSSION: Relevance and reliability are the two decision-specific primary qualities of accounting information. Relevant information is capable of making a difference in a decision. The ingredients of relevance are predictive value, timeliness, and feedback value. Predictive value is the quality "that helps users to increase the likelihood of correctly forecasting the outcome of past and present events" (SFAC 2).

Answers (A) and (C) are incorrect because verifiability and neutrality are the ingredients of reliability. Answer (D) is incorrect because due process is a nonsense answer.

9. Accounting information that enables decision makers to confirm or correct prior expectations is said to have

A. Predictive value.

B. Materiality.

C. Representational faithfulness.

D. Feedback value.

The correct answer is (D). *(CMA, adapted)*

REQUIRED: The characteristic of accounting information enabling confirmation or correction of prior expectations.

DISCUSSION: One of the qualitative characteristics of accounting information is relevance. Relevant information is capable of making a difference in a decision. Relevance has three elements: predictive value, feedback value, and timeliness. Feedback value permits users to confirm or correct prior expectations (SFAC 2).

Answer (A) is incorrect because predictive value enables users to predict the outcome of future events. Answer (B) is incorrect because materiality is a constraint on the reporting of accounting information. Answer (C) is incorrect because representational faithfulness is the agreement between a measure or description and the phenomenon that it purports to represent.

10. The historical cost of assets and liabilities is generally retained in accounting records because this information has the qualitative characteristics of

A. Neutrality, verifiability, and representational faithfulness.

B. Reliability and relevance.

C. Decision usefulness, reliability, and neutrality.

D. Timeliness, verifiability, and relevance.

The correct answer is (A). *(CMA, adapted)*

REQUIRED: The qualitative characteristics possessed by historical cost information.

DISCUSSION: The qualitative characteristics of accounting information include reliability. Reliable information is reasonably free from error and bias and faithfully represents what it purports to represent. According to SFAC 2, the three elements of reliability are verifiability, neutrality, and representational faithfulness. Verifiability means that the information can be verified by independent measurers using the same methods. Historical cost is a fixed amount arising from a past transaction and therefore is an objective measure. Neutrality means that information should be neutral; it cannot favor one statement user over another. Historical cost is neutral because it was determined by two individuals--a buyer and a seller--in an arm's-length transaction. Representational faithfulness means that financial statements accurately represent the events reported. Using historical cost results in an accurate depiction of the transaction that occurred.

Answers (B) and (D) are incorrect because some would argue that historical costs are not always relevant. Answer (C) is incorrect because historical costs may not possess decision usefulness.

11. Reliability as used in accounting includes

A. Determining the revenue first, then determining the costs incurred in earning that revenue.

B. The entity's giving the same treatment to comparable transactions from period to period.

C. Similar results being obtained by both the accountant and an independent party using the same measurement methods.

D. The disclosure of all facts that may influence the judgment of an informed reader.

The correct answer is (C). *(CMA, adapted)*

REQUIRED: The meaning of reliability as the term is used in accounting.

DISCUSSION: Accounting information is reliable if it is verifiable, is a faithful representation, and is reasonably free of error or bias. Verifiability is demonstrated when independent measurers use the same methods and obtain similar results. So, when the auditor verifies the accountant's results, (s)he is showing that part of the definition of reliability is met.

Answer (A) is incorrect because it concerns the matching principle. Answer (B) is incorrect because it refers to the consistency principle. Answer (D) is incorrect because it refers to the full disclosure principle.

Question 12 is based on the following information. Randolf Castell opened a small general store in 1946. A cousin, Alfred Bedford, served as bookkeeper and office manager while Castell concentrated on operations. The business prospered and each of Castell's three sons joined their father in the business. In fact, as each son finished school, Castell opened a new store and put the son in charge. In time, each son began to specialize: one in hardware, another in dry goods, and the third in furniture. Further expansion took place, and the business was incorporated as Four Castles Inc. with all of the stock being held by the family. Castell closed his original store to serve as president and concentrate on administration.

As Four Castles prospered and more stores opened, the company needed additional capital. Bedford suggested "going public" but pointed out that this required accounting and reporting procedures with which he was unfamiliar. Therefore, a trained and qualified accountant was hired as controller. The new controller has had to provide explanations to Castell and Bedford on the accounting and reporting requirements of public companies.

---

12. Four Castles' records have been kept on the tax basis of accounting to eliminate the need to maintain a second set of records. When the tax basis allowed for a choice between cash and accrual bases of accounting, the firm employed the cash basis. Neither the tax basis nor the cash basis of accounting is generally acceptable for the financial statements of a publicly held corporation such as Four Castles. The accrual basis of accounting must be used so that

A. Specific expenses are related to specific revenues.

B. Expenses of a time period are related to revenues of the same time period.

C. Expenses and related revenues are expressed in terms of economic reality.

D. Necessary time-period allocations of long-lived costs are made on a systematic or rational basis.

The correct answer is (B). *(CMA, adapted)*

REQUIRED: The reason the accrual basis of accounting must be used.

DISCUSSION: According to SFAC 1, "Accrual accounting attempts to record the financial effects on an enterprise of transactions and other events and circumstances that have cash consequences for an enterprise in the periods in which those transactions, events, and circumstances occur rather than only in the periods in which cash is received or paid by the enterprise."

Answer (A) is incorrect because perfect matching of expenses with revenues is often impossible. Answer (C) is incorrect because the accrual basis is principally used to match the occurrence and the effects of transactions. Economic reality is more difficult to express in historical cost/nominal dollar financial statements. Answer (D) is incorrect because it is a function of matching (depreciation is an allocation).

13. Accounting information that users can depend on to represent the economic conditions or events that it purports to represent best defines

A. Relevance.

B. Timeliness.

C. Feedback value.

D. Reliability.

The correct answer is (D). *(CMA, adapted)*

REQUIRED: The term meaning that accounting information represents the economic conditions or events that it purports to represent.

DISCUSSION: Reliability and relevance are the two primary decision-specific accounting qualities. Reliability is defined as the quality of information that provides assurance that the information is reasonably free from error and bias and faithfully represents what it purports to represent. The ingredients of reliability are verifiability, neutrality, and representational faithfulness (SFAC 2).

Answer (A) is incorrect because relevant accounting information must be capable of making a difference in a decision. Answers (B) and (C) are incorrect because timeliness and feedback value are elements of relevance.

Questions 14 and 15 are based on Statement of Financial Accounting Concepts No. 5, *Recognition and Measurement in Financial Statements of Business Enterprises*.

14. The concepts of earnings and comprehensive income have the same broad components, but they are not the same because certain classes of gains and losses are included in comprehensive income but are excluded from earnings. One of the items included in comprehensive income but excluded from earnings is

A. A gain on discontinued operations.

B. The cumulative effect of a change in accounting principle.

C. A loss from the obsolescence of a material amount of inventory.

D. An extraordinary gain.

The correct answer is (B). *(CMA, adapted)*

REQUIRED: The item included in comprehensive income but not earnings.

DISCUSSION: SFAC 5 defines earnings as a measure of entity performance during a period similar to, but distinct from, present net income. It excludes certain accounting adjustments of prior periods that are currently recognized, such as the cumulative effect of a change in principle. Comprehensive income is "a broad measure of the effects of transactions and other events on an entity, including all recognized changes in equity (net assets) of the entity during a period from transactions and other events and circumstances except those resulting from investments by owners and distribution to owners." Certain gains and losses included in comprehensive income (referred to as "cumulative accounting adjustments" and "other nonowner changes in equity") are excluded from earnings.

Answers (A), (C), and (D) are incorrect because a gain on discontinued operations, a loss from the obsolescence of a material amount of inventory, and an extraordinary gain, are all included in both earnings and comprehensive income.

15. Revenues of an entity are normally measured by the exchange values of the assets or liabilities involved. Recognition of revenue does not occur until

A. The revenue is realized and assured of collection.

B. The revenue is realized or realizable and earned.

C. Products or services are exchanged for cash or claims to cash.

D. The entity has substantially accomplished what it agreed to do.

The correct answer is (B). *(CMA, adapted)*

REQUIRED: The timing of the recognition of revenue.

DISCUSSION: Recognition is the process of recording an item in the financial records. Revenue should not be recognized until it is (1) realized or realizable and (2) earned. Revenues are realized in an exchange for cash or claims to cash. Revenues are realizable when "related assets received or held are readily convertible to known amounts of cash or claims to cash." Revenues are earned "when the entity has substantially accomplished what it must do to be entitled to the benefits represented by the revenues" (SFAC 5).

Answer (A) is incorrect because absolute assurance of collectibility is not required. Answer (C) is incorrect because some exchange may occur before the earning process is substantially complete. Answer (D) is incorrect because recognition also requires that revenue be realized or realizable as well as earned.

16. In December year 1, catalogues were printed for use in a special promotion in January year 2. The catalogues were delivered by the printer on December 13, year 1, with an invoice for $70,000 attached. Payment was made in January year 2. The $70,000 should be reported as a deferred cost at the December 31, year 1 balance sheet date because of the

A. Matching principle.

B. Revenue recognition principle.

C. Objectivity principle.

D. Cost principle.

The correct answer is (A). *(CIA, adapted)*

REQUIRED: The principle dictating that costs be deferred.

DISCUSSION: Matching is the simultaneous or combined recognition of revenues and expenses resulting directly and jointly from the same transactions or other events. Expenses should be associated with the revenues that they help to create. Because the catalogues are still on hand at the balance sheet date, they will not contribute to the earning process until the next period. Hence, the cost should be deferred and matched with the revenues of the following period.

Answer (B) is incorrect because the revenue recognition principle determines the period in which revenue is recognized. Answer (C) is incorrect because the objectivity principle indicates that, to the extent possible, accounting data should be unbiased and verifiable. Answer (D) is incorrect because the cost principle states that cost is the usual basis for recording most assets and liabilities.

17. The practice of recording advanced payments from customers as a liability is an example of applying the

A. Going-concern assumption.

B. Monetary-unit assumption.

C. Historical cost principle.

D. Revenue recognition principle.

The correct answer is (D). *(CIA, adapted)*

REQUIRED: The assumption or principle justifying recording advance receipts as liabilities.

DISCUSSION: Revenue should not be recognized until it is realized or realizable and earned. Thus, if the amounts received in cash have not yet been earned, they should be recorded as liabilities of the company.

Answer (A) is incorrect because the going-concern assumption is that the business will have an indefinite life. Answer (B) is incorrect because the monetary-unit assumption is that money is the common denominator by which economic activity is conducted and that the monetary unit provides an appropriate basis for accounting measurement and analysis. Answer (C) is incorrect because the historical cost principle is the requirement that most assets and liabilities be accounted for and reported on the basis of acquisition price.

18. On February 1, year 1, a computer software firm agrees to program a software package. Twelve payments of $10,000 on the first of each month are to be made, with the first payment March 1, year 1. The software is accepted by the client June 1, year 2. How much year 1 revenue should be recognized?

A. $0

B. $100,000

C. $110,000

D. $120,000

The correct answer is (A). *(CIA, adapted)*

REQUIRED: The revenue recognized in the year in which payments begin if delivery occurs in the next period.

DISCUSSION: Revenue is recognized when it is realized or realizable and the earning process is substantially complete. Delivery is the usual time at which recognition is appropriate. Because delivery occurred in year 2, no revenue should be recognized in year 1.

Answers (B), (C), and (D) are incorrect because no revenue should be recognized until realized or realizable.

19. A company provides fertilization, insect control, and disease control services for a variety of trees, plants, and shrubs on a contract basis. For $50 per month, the company will visit the subscriber's premises and apply appropriate mixtures. If the subscriber has any problems between the regularly scheduled application dates, the company's personnel will promptly make additional service calls to correct the situation. Some subscribers elect to pay for an entire year because the company offers an annual price of $540 if paid in advance. For a subscriber who pays the annual fee in advance, the company should recognize the related revenue

A. When the cash is collected.

B. Evenly over the year as the services are performed.

C. At the end of the contract year after all of the services have been performed.

D. At the end of the fiscal year.

The correct answer is (B). *(CIA, adapted)*

REQUIRED: The appropriate timing of revenue recognition.

DISCUSSION: In accordance with SFAC 5, revenues should be recognized when they are realized or realizable and earned. Revenues are realized when products, merchandise, or other assets are exchanged for cash or claims to cash. Revenues are realizable when related assets received or held are readily convertible to known amounts of cash or claims to cash. Revenues are earned when the entity has substantially accomplished what it must do to be entitled to the benefits represented by the revenues. The most common time at which these two conditions are met is when the product or merchandise is delivered or services are rendered to customers. In the situation presented, the performance of the service (monthly spraying) is so significant to completing the earning process that revenue should not be recognized until delivery occurs. At the time of performing the service (monthly spraying and any special visits), the revenue has been realized and earned and should be recognized.

Answer (A) is incorrect because the revenue has not been earned when the cash is collected. Answers (C) and (D) are incorrect because revenue from services rendered is recognized when the services have been performed. A portion of the services is performed monthly. Thus, a portion of the related revenue should be recognized monthly rather than when the contract year or the fiscal year is complete.

20. Although a transfer of ownership has not occurred, the percentage-of-completion method is acceptable under the revenue recognition principle because

A. The assets are readily convertible into cash.

B. The production process can be readily divided into definite stages.

C. Cash has been received from the customer.

D. The earning process is completed at various stages.

The correct answer is (D). *(CMA, adapted)*

REQUIRED: The reason percentage-of-completion is acceptable as a means of revenue recognition.

DISCUSSION: SFAC 5 states that revenue should be recognized when it is both realized or realizable and earned. If a project is contracted for before production and covers a long time period in relation to reporting periods, revenues may be recognized by a percentage-of-completion method as they are earned (as production occurs), provided reasonable estimates of results at completion and reliable measures of progress are available. Thus, contractors traditionally use the percentage-of-completion method because some revenue can be recognized during each period of the production process. In a sense, the earning process is completed in various stages; thus, revenues should be recorded in each stage.

Answer (A) is incorrect because, depending upon the terms of the contract, the assets may not be readily convertible into cash. Answer (B) is incorrect because, on a large construction project, the production process often cannot be easily divided into definite stages. Answer (C) is incorrect because cash is sometimes not received until the project is completed.

21. The mining industry frequently recognizes revenue using the completion-of-production method. This method is acceptable under the revenue recognition principle for all of the following reasons except that

A. Production costs can be readily determined.

B. Sales prices are reasonably assured.

C. Assets are readily realizable.

D. Units are interchangeable.

The correct answer is (A). *(CMA, adapted)*

REQUIRED: The reason that does not justify recognizing mining revenue at the completion of the production process.

DISCUSSION: Recognizing revenue at the time goods are produced is appropriate when the assets are readily realizable (convertible) because they are salable at reliably determinable prices without significant effort. Readily realizable assets are fungible, and quoted prices are available in an active market that can rapidly absorb the quantity produced (SFAC 5). Examples include some agricultural products and rare minerals. That production costs can be readily determined is not a justification for immediate recognition. Production costs can be readily determined for almost any product manufactured.

Answers (B) and (C) are incorrect because recognition at the time of production is appropriate if assets are readily realizable, i.e., if they are salable at reliably determinable prices without significant effort. Answer (D) is incorrect because interchangeability (fungibility) is a requirement for recognition at the time of production.

22. In SFAC 5, *Recognition and Measurement in Financial Statements of Business Enterprises*, several alternatives have been identified for measuring items on the statement of financial position. Which of the following alternatives may be used?

	Present Value	Current Cost	Net Realizable Value
A.	No	No	No
B.	No	Yes	Yes
C.	Yes	Yes	No
D.	Yes	Yes	Yes

The correct answer is (D). *(CMA, adapted)*

REQUIRED: The acceptable attribute(s) for measuring items in the balance sheet.

DISCUSSION: According to SFAC 5, items appearing in financial statements may, under certain circumstances, be measured by different attributes. The attributes used in current practice are historical cost (historical proceeds), current cost, current market value, net realizable (settlement) value, and the present value of future cash flows. For example, the present value of future cash flows is used to value long-term payables; current cost is the method used to measure and report some inventories; and net realizable value is used to measure short-term receivables.

Answers (A), (B), and (C) are incorrect because present value, current cost, and net realizable value are measurement attributes that may be used in appropriate circumstances.

23. Recognition is the process of formally recording and reporting an item in the financial statements. In order for a revenue item to be recognized, it must be all of the following except

A. Measurable.

B. Relevant.

C. Material.

D. Realized or realizable.

The correct answer is (C). *(CMA, adapted)*

REQUIRED: The characteristic not required for recognition of revenue.

DISCUSSION: Recognition means incorporating transactions into the accounting system so as to report them in the financial statements as assets, liabilities, revenues, expenses, gains, or losses. When items meet the criteria for recognition, disclosure by other means is not a substitute for recognition in the financial statements. The four fundamental recognition criteria are (1) the item meets the definition of an element of financial statements, (2) the item has an attribute measurable with sufficient reliability, (3) the information is relevant, and (4) the information is reliable (SFAC 5). In addition, revenue should be recognized when it is realized or realizable and earned. Materiality is not a recognition criterion. An immaterial item that meets the criteria for recognition may be recognized.

Answers (A), (B), and (D) are incorrect because revenue is recognized when the item meets the definition of revenue, the item is measurable, the information is relevant and reliable, and the item is realized or realizable.

Questions 24 through 27 are based on the following information. According to SFAC 5, *Recognition and Measurement in Financial Statements of Business Enterprises*, items reported in financial statements must meet certain criteria and are measured by different attributes, depending on the nature of the item.

---

24. In order for an event to be recognized in the financial statements, it must be

A. Relevant, reliable, and measurable.

B. Relevant, reliable, and useful.

C. Relevant, reliable, and timely.

D. Reliable, useful, and measurable.

The correct answer is (A). *(CMA, adapted)*

REQUIRED: The criteria for recognition in the financial statements.

DISCUSSION: SFAC 5 states that an item and information about the item should be recognized when the following four fundamental recognition criteria are met: (1) the item meets the definition of an element of financial statements; (2) it has a relevant attribute measurable with sufficient reliability (measurability); (3) the information about the item is capable of making a difference in user decisions (relevance); and (4) the information is representationally faithful, verifiable, and neutral (reliability).

Answers (B) and (D) are incorrect because usefulness is not one of the criteria for recognition stated in SFAC 5. Answer (C) is incorrect because timeliness is not a criterion for recognition under SFAC 5.

25. Long-term payables are measured using

A. Historical cost.

B. Current market value.

C. Net realizable value.

D. Present value of future cash flows.

The correct answer is (D). *(CMA, adapted)*

REQUIRED: The measurement attribute for long-term payables.

DISCUSSION: Under SFAC 5, long-term payables and receivables are measured and reported at the present, or discounted, value of future cash flows. For payables, this amount is the present value of future cash outflows expected to be required to satisfy the liability in due course of business.

Answer (A) is incorrect because historical cost, although used for many types of assets and liabilities, is not permitted for valuation of long-term payables under SFAC 5. Answer (B) is incorrect because current market value measures liabilities for certain marketable commodities and securities, e.g., obligations of writers of options or sellers of shares who do not own the underlying assets. Answer (C) is incorrect because net realizable value is the undiscounted amount of cash into which an asset is expected to be converted in due course of business minus direct costs necessary to make that conversion. Net settlement value is the equivalent term for liabilities but is applicable only to short-term payables.

26. Refer to information preceding question 24 on page 131. Damaged inventory is measured using

A. Historical cost.

B. Current cost.

C. Net realizable value.

D. Present value of future cash flows.

The correct answer is (C). *(CMA, adapted)*

REQUIRED: The measurement attribute for damaged inventory.

DISCUSSION: Net realizable value is the undiscounted amount of cash into which an asset is expected to be converted in due course of business, minus the direct costs necessary to make that conversion. Short-term receivables and damaged inventories are examples of assets commonly valued at net realizable value.

Answer (A) is incorrect because historical cost is not appropriate for damaged inventories. They are likely to be worth less than their original cost. Answer (B) is incorrect because current or replacement cost is the cash equivalent that would have to be paid if the same assets were acquired currently. The company is unlikely to purchase damaged goods, so current cost is irrelevant. Answer (D) is incorrect because the present value of future cash flows is not appropriate. The company presumably will sell the goods soon.

27. Refer to information preceding question 24 on page 131. Land currently used in the business is measured at

A. Historical cost.

B. Current cost.

C. Current market value.

D. Net realizable value.

The correct answer is (A). *(CMA, adapted)*

REQUIRED: The measurement attribute for land.

DISCUSSION: Land is normally carried in the accounting records at historical cost. According to SFAC 5, historical cost is the amount of cash or its equivalent paid to acquire an asset. Historical cost is the attribute at which assets such as property, plant, and equipment are measured.

Answer (B) is incorrect because current or replacement cost is difficult to measure for an asset such as land. Some inventories are carried at current cost. Answer (C) is incorrect because current market value is used to measure certain investments, such as trading securities. Answer (D) is incorrect because net realizable value is applicable only to assets that are to be disposed of in the near future. Land does not meet that criterion.

28. All of the following are acceptable methods for recognizing revenue from service transactions except the

A. Collection method.

B. Specific-performance method.

C. Completed-performance method.

D. Accretion method.

The correct answer is (D). *(CMA, adapted)*

REQUIRED: The method of revenue recognition that is not acceptable for service transactions.

DISCUSSION: The accretion method records revenue as the product grows. For example, it is theoretically feasible to record a timber company's revenue as the trees grow because the product is increasing in value each year. This kind of phenomenon does not occur in the service industries. Hence, the accretion method is not applicable.

Answer (A) is incorrect because, although the cash basis is theoretically acceptable only when the collection is not assured, the method has traditionally been used in many service industries. Answer (B) is incorrect because revenue may meet the criteria of being realized or realizable and earned when specific performance of a service has occurred. Answer (C) is incorrect because it is valid to record service revenue at the completion of performance.

29. Based on SFAC 5, *Recognition and Measurement in Financial Statements of Business Enterprises*, a complete set of financial statements for a period should show all of the following except the

A. Financial position at the end of the period.

B. Earnings for the period.

C. Comprehensive income for the period.

D. Management discussion and analysis.

The correct answer is (D). *(CMA, adapted)*

REQUIRED: The item that is not a part of a complete set of financial statements.

DISCUSSION: According to SFAC 5, a complete set of financial statements includes a balance sheet, an earnings (net income) statement, a cash flow statement, a statement of comprehensive income, and an explanation of investments by, and distributions to, owners during the period. Management's discussion and analysis of financial condition and results of operations is included in the Basic Information Package (BIP) required as part of the Integrated Disclosure System used in filings with the Securities and Exchange Commission.

Answers (A), (B), and (C) are incorrect because reporting of financial position at the end of the period, earnings for the period, and comprehensive income for the period are all required by SFAC 5.

30. Amortization of intangible assets, such as copyrights or patents, is the accounting process of

A. Determining the cash flow from operations for the current period.

B. Systematically allocating the cost of the intangible asset to the periods of use.

C. Accumulating a fund for the replacement of the asset at the end of its useful life.

D. Systematically reflecting the change in general price levels over the current period.

The correct answer is (B). *(CMA, adapted)*

REQUIRED: The meaning of amortization.

DISCUSSION: SFAC 6 defines amortization as "the accounting process of reducing an amount by periodic payments or write-downs. Specifically, amortization is the process of reducing a liability recorded as a result of a cash receipt by recognizing revenues or reducing an asset recorded as a result of a cash payment by recognizing expenses or costs of production." Amortization is a means of allocating an initial cost to the periods that benefit from that cost. It is similar to depreciation, a term associated with long-lived tangible assets, and depletion, which is associated with natural resources.

Answer (A) is incorrect because amortization is an allocation process that is not cash-based. Answer (C) is incorrect because no funding is associated with amortization. Answer (D) is incorrect because amortization has nothing to do with changes in price levels.

31. Inventory valued at the lower-of-cost-or-market is never valued at less than which measurement attribute?

A. Historical cost.

B. Current cost.

C. Present value.

D. Net realizable value.

The correct answer is (C). *(Publisher)*

REQUIRED: The measurement attribute never used with the lower-of-cost-or-market method.

DISCUSSION: Present value is not used for valuing assets under the lower-of-cost-or-market method. Present value incorporates time-value-of-money concepts into an asset valuation by discounting future cash flows at the appropriate interest rate. The lower-of-cost-or-market method values an asset at historical cost unless the market value of the asset is less than original cost. The value used for market is subject to ceiling and floor amounts.

Answer (A) is incorrect because historical cost is used unless the asset's market value is lower. Answer (B) is incorrect because current (replacement) cost is used to measure market value. Answer (D) is incorrect because the market valuation is subject to ceiling and floor values. The ceiling is NRV, and the floor is NRV minus a normal profit.

32. The appropriate attribute to use when selling assets in an orderly liquidation is

A. Historical cost.

B. Current cost.

C. Net realizable value.

D. Current market value.

The correct answer is (D). *(CMA, adapted)*

REQUIRED: The attribute to use when selling assets in an orderly liquidation.

DISCUSSION: According to SFAC 5, current market value (exit value) is used to measure the cash or equivalent that is realizable when selling assets in an orderly liquidation.

Answers (A), (B), and (C) are incorrect because exit value is used to measure proceeds from an orderly liquidation.

33. The assets of a company forced into liquidation should be shown on the balance sheet at their

A. Undepreciated historical cost.

B. Current market value.

C. Net realizable value.

D. Current cost.

The correct answer is (C). *(CIA, adapted)*

REQUIRED: The valuation of the assets of a liquidating company.

DISCUSSION: When forced liquidation of a company is imminent, and the going-concern assumption is no longer valid, the most appropriate valuation method for assets is net realizable value, which is the estimated selling price upon disposal minus costs of disposal.

Answer (A) is incorrect because a going concern should report assets at their undepreciated historical cost. When liquidation appears imminent, historical cost is inappropriate for balance sheet reporting. Answer (B) is incorrect because a company facing liquidation is expected to dispose of its assets in a "forced" or "distressed" sale. Current market value (exit value) may occur if the liquidation is orderly. Answer (D) is incorrect because current cost is appropriate only when the going-concern assumption is applicable and the effects of changing prices are to be measured and reported in the financial statements.

34. According to SFAC 7, *Using Cash Flow Information and Present Value in Accounting Measurements*, the objective of present value is to estimate fair value when used to determine accounting measurements for

	Initial-Recognition Purposes	Fresh-Start Purposes
A.	No	No
B.	Yes	Yes
C.	Yes	No
D.	No	Yes

The correct answer is (B). *(Publisher)*

REQUIRED: The objective of present value in initial-recognition and fresh-start measurements.

DISCUSSION: SFAC 7 states that the objective of present value in initial-recognition or fresh-start measurements is to estimate fair value. "Present value should attempt to capture the elements that taken together would comprise a market price if one existed, that is, fair value." A present value measurement includes five elements: estimates of cash flows, expectations about their variability, the time value of money (the risk-free interest rate), the price of uncertainty inherent in an asset or liability, and other factors (e.g., illiquidity or market imperfections). Fair value encompasses all these elements using the estimates and expectations of participants in the market.

Answers (A), (C), and (D) are incorrect because the objective of present value in both initial-recognition and fresh-start measurements is to estimate fair value.

35. The expected cash flow approach to measuring present value promulgated by SFAC 7

A. Uses a single set of estimated cash flows.

B. Is limited to assets and liabilities with contractual cash flows.

C. Focuses on explicit assumptions about the range of expected cash flows and their respective probabilities.

D. Focuses on the single most likely amount or best estimate.

The correct answer is (C). *(Publisher)*

REQUIRED: The nature of the expected cash flow approach.

DISCUSSION: The traditional approach to calculating present value employs one set of estimated cash flows and one interest rate. This approach is expected to continue to be used in many cases, for example, when contractual cash flows are involved. However, SFAC 7 describes the expected cash flow approach, which is applicable in more complex circumstances, such as when no market or no comparable item exists for an asset or liability. The expected cash flow results from multiplying each possible estimated amount by its probability and adding the products. The expected cash flow approach emphasizes explicit assumptions about the possible estimated cash flows and their probabilities. The traditional method merely includes those uncertainties in the choice of interest rate. Moreover, by allowing for a range of possibilities, the expected cash flow method permits the use of present value when the timing of cash flows is uncertain.

Answer (A) is incorrect because the traditional present value measurement approach uses a single set of estimated cash flows and a single interest rate. Answer (B) is incorrect because the expected cash flow approach may also apply when the timing of cash flows is uncertain or when nonfinancial assets and liabilities are to be measured and no market or comparable item exists for them. Answer (D) is incorrect because some current accounting applications use the estimated mode (single most likely amount or best estimate), but the expected cash flow approach arrives at an estimated mean by probabilistically weighting a range of possible estimated amounts.

B. Revenue

36. A company that sprays chemicals in residences to eliminate or prevent infestation of insects requires that customers prepay for 3 months' service at the beginning of each new quarter. Select the term that appropriately describes this situation from the viewpoint of the exterminating company.

A. Deferred revenue.

B. Earned revenue.

C. Accrued revenue.

D. Prepaid expense.

The correct answer is (A). *(CIA, adapted)*

REQUIRED: The classification of the collected fees.

DISCUSSION: Under the revenue recognition principle, revenue is recognized in the period in which it is earned; therefore, when it is received in advance of its being earned, the amount applicable to future periods is deferred. The amount received in advance is considered a liability because it represents an obligation to perform a service in the future arising from a past transaction. Unearned revenue is revenue that has been received but not earned.

Answer (B) is incorrect because the revenue is not earned. The exterminator has not performed the related services for the customer. Answer (C) is incorrect because accrued revenue is revenue that has been earned but not received. Answer (D) is incorrect because the customer has a prepaid expense (expense paid but not incurred); the exterminator has unearned revenue (revenue received but not earned).

Questions 37 through 39 are based on the following information. On May 28, Markal Company purchased a tooling machine from Arens and Associates for $1,000,000, payable as follows: 50 percent at the transaction closing date and 50 percent due June 28. The cost of the machine to Arens is $800,000. Markal paid Arens $500,000 at the transaction closing date and took possession of the machine. On June 10, Arens determined that a change in the business environment has created a great deal of uncertainty regarding the collection of the balance due from Markal, and the amount is probably uncollectible. Arens and Markal have a fiscal year end of May 31.

37. The revenue recognized by Arens and Associates on May 28 is

A. $200,000

B. $800,000

C. $1,000,000

D. $0

The correct answer is (C). *(CMA, adapted)*

REQUIRED: The revenue to be recognized on May 28.

DISCUSSION: Revenue is recognized when (1) realized or realizable and (2) earned. On May 28, $500,000 of the sales price was realized while the remaining $500,000 was realizable in the form of a receivable. The revenue was earned on May 28 since the title of the goods passed to the purchaser. The cost-recovery method is not used because the receivable was not deemed uncollectible until June 10.

Answer (A) is incorrect because $200,000 is the apparent gross profit on the sale, not the revenue. Answer (B) is incorrect because $800,000 was the original cost of the machine to Arens. Answer (D) is incorrect because at May 28 a sale appeared to have been consummated in the amount of $1,000,000.

38. The gross profit recognized by Arens and Associates on its financial statements dated and issued June 15 is

A. $1,000,000

B. $200,000

C. $0

D. $500,000

The correct answer is (C). *(CMA, adapted)*

REQUIRED: The gross profit recognized by Arens on its financial statements issued on June 15.

DISCUSSION: Gross profit is defined as the difference between selling price and the cost of goods sold. The balance sheet presentation should be based on the net realizable value of the receivable. Because that amount is assumed to be zero, the machine was actually sold for $500,000, not for $1,000,000. Therefore, no gross profit is shown on the financial statements.

Answer (A) is incorrect because the last $500,000 is not considered collectible; thus the sale was not for $1,000,000. Answer (B) is incorrect because $200,000 would have been the gross profit if the last $500,000 had been collectible. Answer (D) is incorrect because $500,000 was the amount of cash collected, not the amount of gross profit.

39. The effect of the purchase on Markal Company's financial reporting on May 28 is a(n)

A. Increase in fixed assets of $500,000 and a decrease in cash of $500,000.

B. Increase in fixed assets of $1,000,000, a decrease in cash of $500,000, and an increase in liabilities of $500,000.

C. Increase in fixed assets of $500,000 and an increase in liabilities of $500,000.

D. Decrease in fixed assets of $1,000,000, a decrease in cash of $500,000, and an increase in liabilities of $500,000.

The correct answer is (B). *(CMA, adapted)*

REQUIRED: The effect of the May 28 machine purchase on Markal Company's financial reporting.

DISCUSSION: The purchase of the machine involves a debit to fixed assets of $1,000,000, a credit to cash of $500,000, and a credit to a current liability of $500,000.

Answer (A) is incorrect because the contract price of the machine was $1,000,000, and that amount should be recorded as a fixed asset; Markal is liable for the remaining $500,000 unless it declares bankruptcy. Answer (C) is incorrect because the machine is valued at $1,000,000, and that amount should be debited to a fixed asset account. Answer (D) is incorrect because there is an increase in fixed assets.

40. A plot of land is acquired in exchange for $250,000 cash and a noninterest-bearing note with a face amount of $1,000,000 on January 1, 2001. The $1,000,000 is payable in installments of $250,000 each, with the first installment due December 31, 2001. With regard to imputing interest on this note, (1) what market rate should be used to account for interest for 2001, and (2) what should be done in future years when there is a change in prevailing interest rates?

	(1) Market Rate to Use to Compute Interest Expense for 2001	(2) Impact of Change in Prevailing Interest Rates in Future Periods on Rate Used to Account for This Note
A.	Rate prevailing at January 2, 2001	Ignore change in rate
B.	Rate prevailing at January 2, 2001	Use new market rate
C.	Rate prevailing at December 31, 2001	Ignore change in rate
D.	Rate prevailing at December 31, 2001	Use new market rate

The correct answer is (A). *(CIA, adapted)*

REQUIRED: The market rate used to impute interest on the note.

DISCUSSION: Determination of the imputed interest rate is made at the time the debt instrument is issued, assumed, or acquired. Any subsequent changes in prevailing interest rates are ignored (APB 21).

Answer (B) is incorrect because any subsequent changes in prevailing interest rates are ignored. Answer (C) is incorrect because determination of the imputed interest rate is made at the time the debt instrument is issued. Answer (D) is incorrect because determination of the imputed interest rate is made at the time the debt instrument is issued, and any subsequent changes in prevailing interest rates are ignored.

41. If sales are accounted for using the installment method, which of the following is (are) recognized only in proportion to the cash collected on the sales during the period?

A. Sales.

B. Sales and cost of sales.

C. Sales and cost of sales and selling expenses.

D. Sales and cost of sales and administrative expenses.

The correct answer is (B). *(CIA, adapted)*

REQUIRED: The item(s) recognized only in proportion to cash collected under the installment method.

DISCUSSION: Under the installment method, the gross profit on sales (sales – cost of sales) is not recognized until cash is collected. The proportion of cash collected on the sales during the accounting period determines the proportion of the gross profit on those sales that is recognized during the period. Hence, both sales and cost of sales are deferred.

Answer (A) is incorrect because sales and cost of sales are recognized in proportion to cash collections. Answers (C) and (D) are incorrect because only the gross profit (sales – cost of sales) is deferred on sales for which cash has not yet been collected.

42. On January 1, 2000, Dell, Inc. contracted with the City of Little to provide custom-built desks for the city schools. The contract made Dell the city's sole supplier, and required Dell to supply no less than 4,000 desks and no more than 5,500 desks per year for 2 years. In turn, Little agreed to pay a fixed price of $110 per desk. During 2000, Dell produced 5,000 desks for Little. At December 31, 2000, 500 of these desks were segregated from the regular inventory and were accepted and awaiting pickup by Little. Little paid Dell $450,000 during 2000. What amount should Dell recognize as contract revenue in 2000?

A. $450,000

B. $495,000

C. $550,000

D. $605,000

The correct answer is (C). *(CPA, adapted)*

REQUIRED: The contract revenue for the year.

DISCUSSION: Dell has done what it was required to do under the contract, that is, produce desks for Little. Thus, it has substantially accomplished what it must do to be entitled to the benefits represented by the revenues. Dell should therefore recognize as earned an amount equaling $550,000 (5,000 desks produced for Little x $110 fixed price per desk).

Answer (A) is incorrect because $450,000 is the amount received. Answer (B) is incorrect because $495,000 is based on production of 4,500 desks. Answer (D) is incorrect because $605,000 is based on production of 5,500 desks.

43. On October 1, 2000, Acme Fuel Co. sold 100,000 gallons of heating oil to Karn Co. at $3 per gallon. Fifty thousand gallons were delivered on December 15, 2000, and the remaining 50,000 gallons were delivered on January 15, 2001. Payment terms were 50% due on October 1, 2000, 25% due on first delivery, and the remaining 25% due on second delivery. What amount of revenue should Acme recognize from this sale during 2000?

A. $75,000

B. $150,000

C. $225,000

D. $300,000

The correct answer is (B). *(CPA, adapted)*

REQUIRED: The revenue to be recognized.

DISCUSSION: Revenue is recognized when it is realized or realizable and earned. Revenue is ordinarily earned upon delivery. Given that 50% of the heating oil was delivered in 2000, 50% of the price was earned in 2000. Thus, Acme should recognize $150,000 (50% x $300,000) of revenue from the sale.

Answer (A) is incorrect because $75,000 was the amount due on first delivery. Answer (C) is incorrect because $225,000 was the amount due in 2000. Answer (D) is incorrect because $300,000 is the total price, but this amount has not been earned because the last 50,000 gallons were not delivered in 2000.

44. Amar Farms produced 300,000 pounds of cotton during the 2000 season. Amar sells all of its cotton to Brye Co., which has agreed to purchase Amar's entire production at the prevailing market price. Recent legislation assures that the market price will not fall below $.70 per pound during the next 2 years. Amar's costs of selling and distributing the cotton are immaterial and can be reasonably estimated. Amar reports its inventory at expected exit value. During 2000, Amar sold and delivered 200,000 pounds to Brye at the market price of $.70. Amar sold the remaining 100,000 pounds during 2001 at the market price of $.72. What amount of revenue should Amar recognize in 2000?

A. $140,000

B. $144,000

C. $210,000

D. $216,000

The correct answer is (C). *(CPA, adapted)*

REQUIRED: The revenue recognized by an enterprise that reports its inventory at expected exit value.

DISCUSSION: According to SFAC 5, "If products or other assets are readily realizable because they are salable at reliably determinable prices without significant effort (for example, certain agricultural products, precious metals, and marketable securities), revenues and some gains or losses may be recognized at completion of production or when prices of the assets change." The cotton is readily realizable (convertible) because it consists of interchangeable (fungible) units and can be sold at a guaranteed price. Thus, Amar should recognize revenue at the completion of production in 2000 based on the guaranteed price (300,000 lbs. x $.70 = $210,000).

Answer (A) is incorrect because $140,000 is the revenue on 2000 sales. Answer (B) is incorrect because $144,000 equals 200,000 pounds times $.72 per pound. Answer (D) is incorrect because $216,000 is based on the 2001 price. However, in 2000, the price had not yet changed.

45. The following information pertains to Eagle Co.'s 2000 sales:

Cash sales	
Gross	$ 80,000
Returns and allowances	4,000
Credit sales	
Gross	120,000
Discounts	6,000

On January 1, 2000, customers owed Eagle $40,000. On December 31, 2000, customers owed Eagle $30,000. Under the cash basis of accounting, what amount of net revenue should Eagle report for 2000?

A. $76,000

B. $170,000

C. $190,000

D. $200,000

The correct answer is (D). *(CPA, adapted)*

REQUIRED: The revenue under the cash basis of accounting.

DISCUSSION: Under the cash-basis of accounting, revenue is recognized when cash is received. Eagle had $76,000 ($80,000 – $4,000) in net cash sales and $114,000 ($120,000 – $6,000) in net credit sales. Given that accounts receivable decreased, cash collections thereon must have exceeded net credit sales by $10,000 ($40,000 – $30,000). Accordingly, net revenue is $200,000 ($76,000 + $114,000 + $10,000).

Answer (A) is incorrect because $76,000 equals net cash sales. Answer (B) is incorrect because $170,000 equals total gross sales minus ending accounts receivable. Answer (C) is incorrect because $190,000 does not reflect an adjustment for the change in receivables.

Questions 46 through 48 are based on the following information. A company sells goods on an installment basis. The table below includes information about the level of installment sales, the cost of the goods sold on installment, and the cash receipts on installment sales for year 1 through year 3. All cash receipt amounts shown are net of any interest charges.

	year 1	year 2	year 3
Installment sales	$10,000	$5,000	$20,000
Cost of installment sales	6,000	4,000	10,000
Cash receipts on year 1 sales	$ 2,000	$4,000	$ 4,000
Cash receipts on year 2 sales		1,000	2,000
Cash receipts on year 3 sales			4,000

46. The company has a rate of gross profit on year 2 installment sales of

A. 20%

B. 40%

C. 50%

D. 80%

The correct answer is (A). *(CIA, adapted)*

REQUIRED: The rate of gross profit on year 2 installment sales.

DISCUSSION: The rate of gross profit on year 2 installment sales is 20% [($5,000 of year 2 installment sales – $4,000 cost of year 2 installment sales) ÷ $5,000 of year 2 installment sales].

Answer (B) is incorrect because 40% is the gross profit on year 1 installment sales. Answer (C) is incorrect because 50% is the gross profit on year 3 installment sales. Answer (D) is incorrect because 80% is the ratio of the cost of year 2 installment sales to year 2 installment sales.

47. The amount of gross profit the company will recognize in year 1 on year 1 installment sales is

A. $800

B. $2,000

C. $3,200

D. $4,000

The correct answer is (A). *(CIA, adapted)*

REQUIRED: The amount of gross profit the company will recognize in year 1 on year 1 installment sales.

DISCUSSION: In year 1, the company had cash receipts of $2,000 from its year 1 installment sales. The gross profit realized is the gross profit on the portion of sales for which payment has been received. This amount equals the year 1 gross profit percentage multiplied by the cash receipts, or $800 {[($10,000 – $6,000) ÷ $10,000] x $2,000}.

Answer (B) is incorrect because $2,000 is the amount of cash receipts during year 1 on year 1 installment sales. Answer (C) is incorrect because $3,200 is the amount of the total gross profit on year 1 installment sales that is deferred to future periods. Answer (D) is incorrect because $4,000 is the total gross profit on year 1 installment sales.

48. The company's gross profit amount from year 3 sales to be deferred to future years would be

A. $2,000

B. $3,000

C. $8,000

D. $10,000

The correct answer is (C). *(CIA, adapted)*

REQUIRED: The gross profit amount from year 3 sales to be deferred to future years.

DISCUSSION: The total gross profit on year 3 sales is $10,000 ($20,000 sales – $10,000 cost), and the amount realized is $2,000 {[($20,000 – $10,000) ÷ $20,000] x $4,000 of year 3 cash receipts}. Accordingly, the amount deferred is $8,000 ($10,000 – $2,000).

Answer (A) is incorrect because $2,000 is the realized gross profit on year 3 sales. Answer (B) is incorrect because $3,000 equals total receipts for year 2 and year 3 on year 2 sales. Answer (D) is incorrect because $10,000 is the total gross profit on year 3 sales.

49. A company sells inventory for $80,000 that had an inventory cost of $40,000. The terms of the sale involve payments receivable of $10,000 in the first year, $45,000 in the second year, and $25,000 in the third year. The buyer of the inventory is a new firm with no credit history. If the cost-recovery method of revenue recognition is used, then the amount of gross profit the company will recognize in the second year is

A. $0

B. $5,000

C. $15,000

D. $45,000

The correct answer is (C). *(CIA, adapted)*

REQUIRED: The gross profit in the second year under the cost-recovery method.

DISCUSSION: The profit recognized in the second year equals the cumulative payments received minus the seller's cost, or $15,000 [($10,000 + $45,000) – $40,000].

Answer (A) is incorrect because, under the cost-recovery method, profit is recognized in the second year when cash payments by the buyer exceed the seller's cost of merchandise. Answer (B) is incorrect because $5,000 is the profit to be recognized without consideration of the payment received in the first year. Answer (D) is incorrect because $45,000 is the payment received in the second year.

50. The percentage-of-completion method of accounting for long-term construction contracts is an exception to the

A. Matching principle.

B. Going-concern assumption.

C. Economic-entity assumption.

D. Revenue recognition principle.

The correct answer is (D). *(CMA, adapted)*

REQUIRED: The principle or assumption to which percentage-of-completion method is an exception.

DISCUSSION: The revenue recognition principle states that revenue should be recognized (recorded) when realized or realizable and earned. Revenue is earned when the earning process is essentially complete. In effect, revenue is recorded when the most important event in the earning of that revenue has occurred. Thus, revenue is normally recorded at the time of the sale or, occasionally, at the time cash is collected. However, sometimes neither the sales basis nor the cash basis is appropriate, such as when a construction contract extends over several accounting periods. As a result, contractors ordinarily recognize revenue using the percentage-of-completion method so that some revenue is recognized each year over the life of the contract. Hence, this method is an exception to the general principle of revenue recognition, primarily because it better matches revenues and expenses.

Answer (A) is incorrect because the percentage-of-completion method attempts to match revenues and expenses with the appropriate periods. Answers (B) and (C) are incorrect because the going-concern assumption and the economic-entity assumption are as appropriate for a contractor using the percentage-of-completion method as for any other type of company.

51. An organization has a long-term construction contract in process. During the current period, the estimated total contract cost has increased sufficiently so that there is a current-period loss, even though the contract is still estimated to be profitable overall. Under these circumstances, the <List A> method of revenue recognition would require a <List B> period adjustment of expected gross profit recognized on the contract.

	List A	List B
A.	Percentage-of-completion	Prior
B.	Percentage-of-completion	Current
C.	Completed-contract	Prior
D.	Completed-contract	Current

The correct answer is (B). *(CIA, adapted)*

REQUIRED: The adjustment needed for a current-period loss if the contract is expected to be profitable overall.

DISCUSSION: Under the percentage-of-completion method, a current-period loss on a profitable contract is treated as a change in accounting estimate. Thus, a current-period adjustment is required. Prior-period adjustments are made to correct errors, not to reflect changes in estimates.

Answer (A) is incorrect because, under the percentage-of-completion method, a current-period loss on a profitable contract requires a current-period adjustment. Answers (C) and (D) are incorrect because, under the completed-contract method, no profit is recognized until the contract is completed. Cost estimate adjustments while construction is in progress do not result in profit or loss recognition prior to completion unless an overall loss is expected on the contract.

52. Jessica, a consultant, keeps her accounting records on a cash basis. During 2000, Jessica collected $200,000 in fees from clients. At December 31, 1999, Jessica had accounts receivable of $40,000. At December 31, 2000, Jessica had accounts receivable of $60,000, and unearned fees of $5,000. On an accrual basis, what was Jessica's service revenue for 2000?

A. $175,000

B. $180,000

C. $215,000

D. $225,000

The correct answer is (C). *(CPA, adapted)*

REQUIRED: The accrual-basis service revenue.

DISCUSSION: Of the $200,000 in fees collected during 2000, $5,000 was unearned; therefore, $195,000 reflected collections of earned fees. Given that the ending balance in accounts receivable was $20,000 higher than the beginning balance ($60,000 – $40,000), and that $195,000 in fees were collected, service revenue on the accrual basis was $215,000 ($20,000 + $195,000).

Answer (A) is incorrect because $175,000 equals $200,000 collections, minus $20,000 change in accounts receivable, minus $5,000 unearned fees. Answer (B) is incorrect because $180,000 equals $200,000 collections, minus $20,000 change in accounts receivable. Answer (D) is incorrect because $225,000 is the result of assuming that the unearned fees were added to the $200,000 of fees collected.

53. Dolce Co., which began operations on January 1, 1999, appropriately uses the installment method of accounting to record revenues. The following information is available for the years ended December 31, 1999 and 2000:

	1999	2000
Sales	$1,000,000	$2,000,000
Gross profit realized on sales made in		
1999	150,000	90,000
2000	--	200,000
Gross profit percentages	30%	40%

What amount of installment accounts receivable should Dolce report in its December 31, 2000 balance sheet?

A. $1,100,000

B. $1,300,000

C. $1,700,000

D. $1,900,000

The correct answer is (C). *(CPA, adapted)*

REQUIRED: The amount of installment accounts receivable.

DISCUSSION: Gross profit realized equals the gross profit percentage times cash collected. Hence, cash collected on 1999 sales was $800,000 [($150,000 + $90,000) ÷ 30%], and cash collected on 2000 sales was $500,000 ($200,000 ÷ 40%). The remaining balance of installment receivables is therefore $1,700,000 ($1,000,000 + $2,000,000 – $800,000 – $500,000).

Answer (A) is incorrect because $1,100,000 equals the total gross profit (both realized and unrealized) for 1999 and 2000. Answer (B) is incorrect because $1,300,000 is the total cash collected. Answer (D) is incorrect because $1,900,000 equals total sales minus total gross profit for 1999 and 2000.

54. Leon Co., which began operations on January 2, 2000, appropriately uses the installment sales method of accounting. The following information is available for 2000:

Installment sales	$1,800,000
Realized gross profit on installment sales	240,000
Gross profit percentage on sales	40%

What amounts should Leon report as accounts receivable and deferred gross profit for the year ended December 31, 2000?

	Accounts Receivable	Deferred Gross Profit
A.	$600,000	$480,000
B.	$600,000	$360,000
C.	$1,200,000	$480,000
D.	$1,200,000	$720,000

The correct answer is (C). *(CPA, adapted)*

REQUIRED: The accounts receivable balance and deferred gross profit under the installment sales method.

DISCUSSION: The installment method recognizes income on a sale when the related receivable is collected. The amount recognized each period is the gross profit percentage (gross profit ÷ selling price) on the sale multiplied by the cash collected. Given realized gross profit on installment sales of $240,000 and a gross profit percentage on sales of 40%, cash collections must have been $600,000 ($240,000 ÷ 40%). The accounts receivable at year-end is the difference between total installment sales and cash collected; therefore, accounts receivable must be $1,200,000 ($1,800,000 – $600,000) on December 31, 2000. Deferred gross profit on the year-end accounts receivable is $480,000 ($1,200,000 x 40%).

Answer (A) is incorrect because $600,000 equals cash collections for the year. Answer (B) is incorrect because $600,000 equals cash collections for the year, and $360,000 is the difference between cash collections and realized gross profit. Answer (D) is incorrect because $720,000 is the total of realized and unrealized gross profit.

Questions 55 and 56 are based on the following information. A company began work on a long-term construction contract in year 1. The contract price was $3,000,000. Year-end information related to the contract is as follows:

	year 1	year 2	year 3
Estimated total cost	$2,000,000	$2,000,000	$2,000,000
Cost incurred	700,000	900,000	400,000
Billings	800,000	1,200,000	1,000,000
Collections	600,000	1,200,000	1,200,000

55. If the company uses the percentage-of-completion method of accounting for this contract, the gross profit to be recognized in year 1 is

A. ($100,000)

B. $100,000

C. $200,000

D. $350,000

The correct answer is (D). *(CIA, adapted)*

REQUIRED: The gross profit to be recognized.

DISCUSSION: The percentage-of-completion method recognizes income based on the ratio of the costs incurred to date to the estimated total costs. Billings and collections are irrelevant information when using the percentage-of-completion method. The percentage-of-completion at year-end is 35% ($700,000 ÷ $2,000,000). The gross profit for year 1 is the anticipated gross profit on the contract times the completion percentage. Thus, gross profit for year 1 is $350,000 [($3,000,000 – $2,000,000) x 35%].

Answer (A) is incorrect because ($100,000) is the difference between costs incurred and collections. Answer (B) is incorrect because $100,000 is the difference between billings and costs incurred. Answer (C) is incorrect because $200,000 is the difference between billings and collections.

56. If the company uses the completed-contract method of accounting for this contract, the gross profit to be recognized in year 3 is

A. $200,000

B. $600,000

C. $800,000

D. $1,000,000

The correct answer is (D). *(CIA, adapted)*

REQUIRED: The gross profit to be recognized.

DISCUSSION: Under the completed-contract method, profit is recognized as being realized or realizable and earned only when the contract is complete. The total contract price and total contract costs are recognized as revenue and cost of goods sold, respectively, in the year of completion of the contract. The gross profit in year 3 is $1,000,000 ($3,000,000 revenue – $2,000,000 COGS).

Answer (A) is incorrect because $200,000 is the difference between collections and billings in year 3. Answer (B) is incorrect because $600,000 is the difference between billings and costs incurred in year 3. Answer (C) is incorrect because $800,000 is the difference between estimated total cost and collections.

Questions 57 and 58 are based on the following information. Diamond Clover Construction Inc. uses the percentage-of-completion method of accounting. In year 1, the company began work on job #4115, with a contract price of $5,000,000.

Other data are

	Year 1	Year 2
Costs incurred during the year	$ 900,000	$2,350,000
Estimated costs to complete	2,700,000	0
Billings during the year	1,000,000	4,000,000
Collections during the year	700,000	4,300,000

57. The amount of total gross profit to be recognized in year 1 is

A. $350,000

B. $700,000

C. $1,400,000

D. $766,667

The correct answer is (A). *(CMA, adapted)*

REQUIRED: The amount of gross profit to be recognized in year 1 under the percentage-of-completion method of accounting.

DISCUSSION: By the end of year 1, the company had incurred costs of $900,000 and expected to incur additional costs of $2,700,000. Therefore, the total cost of completing the job was estimated to be the total of the two amounts, or $3,600,000. The $900,000 incurred in year 1 represents 25% of the total costs expected to be incurred. If 25% of the work has been completed, then the company should recognize 25% of the expected revenue. Because the total contract price is $5,000,000, the revenue associated with the 25% point is $1,250,000. Subtracting the $900,000 of costs incurred from the $1,250,000 of revenue produces a gross profit for year 1 of $350,000.

Answer (B) is incorrect because the $700,000 represents the cash collected for the year, which is irrelevant to the gross profit to be recognized. Answer (C) is incorrect because the $1,400,000 is the amount of gross profit that is expected over the life of the project. Answer (D) is incorrect because $766,667 is based on a percentage of completion greater than 25%.

58. If Diamond Clover Construction Inc. were to use the completed-contract method of accounting, the total amount to be recognized as income in year 2 would be

A. $1,400,000

B. $1,750,000

C. $2,650,000

D. $700,000

The correct answer is (B). *(CMA, adapted)*

REQUIRED: The total income to be recognized in year 2 if the company uses the completed-contract method of accounting.

DISCUSSION: Under the completed-contract method, no income is recognized until the year the project is completed. In this case, the costs incurred over 2 years ($900,000 + $2,350,000), or $3,250,000, are subtracted from the total contract price of $5,000,000 to arrive at income of $1,750,000. There would have been zero income in year 1 since the contract had not been completed during that year.

Answer (A) is incorrect because $1,400,000 was the estimated profit based on the costs incurred in year 1; ultimately those expectations proved erroneous since actual costs in year 2 were less than those estimated to complete the project at the end of year 1. Answer (C) is incorrect because the $2,650,000 overlooks the $900,000 of costs incurred during year 1. Answer (D) is incorrect because $700,000 was the cash collected during year 1, not the profit for any year.

59. A vendor sells specialty inks on consignment to a manufacturer of colored paper at a price of $200 per barrel. Payment is made to the vendor in the month the manufacturer uses the barrels in production. The vendor records revenues when the barrels are shipped and makes no adjusting entries to record unearned revenues until the December 31st closing of the books. At the end of July, the manufacturer had 40 barrels of ink on consignment. During August, the vendor consigned 50 barrels and received payment for 30 barrels. Another five barrels were returned to the vendor by the manufacturer for credit. At the end of August, what is the amount of unearned revenue contained in the vendor's accounts receivable from the manufacturer?

A. $3,000

B. $4,000

C. $11,000

D. $12,000

The correct answer is (C). *(CIA, adapted)*

REQUIRED: The amount of unearned revenue in the accounts receivable of a consignor.

DISCUSSION: Consignment does not meet the criteria for recognition of revenue. The barrels have not been sold, so revenue has not been realized or earned. However, 30 barrels have been paid for. Thus, the revenue is recognized for these barrels. The five barrels returned are not included in unearned revenue because they constitute a return of consigned goods. Accordingly, the amount of inappropriately recognized revenue is $11,000 [(40 consigned + 50 consigned – 30 paid for – 5 returns) x $200].

Answer (A) is incorrect because $3,000 does not include the 40 barrels consigned in July. Answer (B) is incorrect because $4,000 does not include the 40 barrels consigned in July or deduct the five barrels returned. Answer (D) is incorrect because $12,000 does not reflect the five barrels returned.

60. ABC Manufacturing Company ships merchandise costing $40,000 on consignment to XYZ Stores. ABC pays $3,000 of freight costs to a transport company, and XYZ pays $2,000 for local advertising costs that are reimbursable from ABC. By the end of the period, three-fourths of the consigned merchandise has been sold for $50,000 cash. XYZ notifies ABC of the sales, retains a 10% commission and the paid advertising costs, and remits the cash due ABC. Select the journal entry that appropriately records the notification of sale and the receipt of cash by ABC.

A.

Cash	$40,000	
Advertising expense	2,000	
Commission expense	5,000	
Freight expense	3,000	
Revenue from consignment sales		$50,000

B.

Cash	$43,000	
Advertising expense	2,000	
Commission expense	5,000	
Revenue from consignment sales		$50,000

C.

Cash	$50,000	
Revenue from consignment sales		$50,000

D.

Cash	$45,000	
Commission expense	5,000	
Revenue from consignment sales		$50,000

The correct answer is (B). *(CIA, adapted)*

REQUIRED: The journal entry to record the consignor's notification of sale and receipt of cash.

DISCUSSION: ABC debits the cash received $43,000 [$50,000 sales – $2,000 advertising – (.10 x $50,000) sales commission]. The advertising and commission expenses are debited for $2,000 and $5,000, respectively. Finally, $50,000 of gross revenue is credited.

Answer (A) is incorrect because the freight was paid earlier in the period and would have been recorded then by a credit to cash and a debit to inventory. Thus, the freight costs will be released to income via cost of goods sold. Answer (C) is incorrect because the 10% commission and the advertising costs are ignored in this answer. Answer (D) is incorrect because the reimbursable advertising costs are ignored in this answer.

61. How will net income be affected by the amortization of a premium on bonds payable?

A. Interest expense is decreased, so net income is increased.

B. Interest expense is increased, so net income is decreased.

C. Interest revenue is increased, so net income is increased.

D. Interest revenue is decreased, so net income is decreased.

The correct answer is (A). *(CIA, adapted)*

REQUIRED: The effect on net income of the amortization of a premium on bonds payable.

DISCUSSION: The entry is to debit interest expense, debit bond premium, and credit cash paid. Thus, the amortization of a premium on bonds payable reduces the interest expense, thereby increasing net income.

Answer (B) is incorrect because the amortization of a premium on bonds payable reduces interest expense. Answers (C) and (D) are incorrect because interest revenue is not affected by the amortization of a premium on bonds payable.

62. The effective-interest method and the straight-line method of amortizing a bond discount differ in that the effective-interest method results in

A. Higher total interest expense over the term of the bonds.

B. Escalating annual interest expense over the term of the bonds.

C. Shrinking annual interest expense over the term of the bonds.

D. Constant annual interest expense over the term of the bonds.

The correct answer is (B). *(CIA, adapted)*

REQUIRED: The difference between the effective-interest method and the straight-line method of amortizing a bond discount.

DISCUSSION: Under the effective-interest method, interest expense for each period equals the effective interest rate times the carrying value of the bond issue. As the discount is amortized, the carrying value rises and interest expense increases.

Answer (A) is incorrect because the two methods of amortization result in the same total interest expense over the term of the bonds. Answer (C) is incorrect because annual interest expense would decrease if a premium were being amortized. Answer (D) is incorrect because the straight-line method results in constant annual interest expense.

63. Several of Fox, Inc.'s customers are having cash flow problems. Information pertaining to these customers for the years ended March 31, 1999 and 2000 follows:

	3/31/99	3/31/00
Sales	$10,000	$15,000
Cost of sales	8,000	9,000
Cash collections		
on 1999 sales	7,000	3,000
on 2000 sales	--	12,000

If the cost-recovery method is used, what amount would Fox report as gross profit from sales to these customers for the year ended March 31, 2000?

A. $2,000

B. $3,000

C. $5,000

D. $15,000

The correct answer is (C). *(CPA, adapted)*

REQUIRED: The gross profit from sales if the cost-recovery method is used.

DISCUSSION: The cost-recovery method recognizes profit only after collections exceed the cost of the item sold, that is, when the full cost has been recovered. Subsequent amounts collected are treated entirely as revenue (debit cash and deferred gross profit, credit the receivable and realized gross profit). The sum of collections in excess of costs to be recognized as gross profit is $5,000 {[$3,000 for 2000 collections on 1999 sales – ($8,000 cost – $7,000 in 1999 collections on 1999 sales)] + ($12,000 collections on 2000 sales – $9,000 cost)}.

Answer (A) is incorrect because $2,000 excludes the profit on 2000 sales. Answer (B) is incorrect because $3,000 excludes the profit on 1999 sales. Answer (D) is incorrect because $15,000 equals 2000 sales.

64. During 2000, Kam Co. began offering its goods to selected retailers on a consignment basis. The following information was derived from Kam's 2000 accounting records:

Beginning inventory	$122,000
Purchases	540,000
Freight-in	10,000
Transportation to consignees	5,000
Freight-out	35,000
Ending inventory -- held by Kam	145,000
held by consignees	20,000

In its 2000 income statement, what amount should Kam report as cost of goods sold?

A. $507,000

B. $512,000

C. $527,000

D. $547,000

The correct answer is (B). *(CPA, adapted)*

REQUIRED: The total cost of goods sold.

DISCUSSION: Cost of goods sold is equal to the cost of goods available for sale minus the ending inventory. Cost of goods available for sale is equal to beginning inventory, plus purchases, plus additional costs (such as freight-in and transportation to consignees) that are necessary to prepare the inventory for sale. The cost of goods sold for Kam Co. is $512,000 [($122,000 beginning inventory + $540,000 purchases + $10,000 freight-in + $5,000 transportation to consignees) – ($145,000 Kam's ending inventory + $20,000 consignee ending inventory)]. Freight-out is a selling cost and is not included in cost of goods sold.

Answer (A) is incorrect because $507,000 does not include $5,000 for transportation to consignees. Answer (C) is incorrect because $527,000 does not include $5,000 for transportation to consignees or reflect the $20,000 of inventory held by consignees. Answer (D) is incorrect because $547,000 includes $35,000 of freight-out.

65. On December 31, year 1, Melanie Company sold on account and shipped merchandise with a list price of $150,000 to Desoto Company. The terms of the sale were n/30, FOB shipping point. The merchandise arrived at Desoto on January 5, year 2. Due to confusion about the shipping terms, the sale was not recorded until January year 2, and the merchandise, sold at a markup of 25% of cost, was included in Melanie's inventory on December 31, year 1. Melanie uses a periodic inventory system. As a result of the error, Melanie's income before income taxes for the year ended December 31, year 1 was

A. Understated by $30,000.

B. Understated by $150,000.

C. Understated by $37,500.

D. Overstated by $120,000.

The correct answer is (A). *(Publisher)*

REQUIRED: The effect on income for year 1 because a sale was not recorded in the proper year.

DISCUSSION: The freight term was FOB shipping point, so title to the goods passed to the buyer in December. Thus, the $150,000 sale should have been recorded in December. At December 31, the inventory included the merchandise at its cost of $120,000 ($150,000 price ÷ 1.25). Because of the failure to record the sale, the seller reported inventory of $120,000 instead of an account receivable of $150,000. Assets were therefore understated by $30,000. Moreover, income was understated by $30,000 because of the failure to report the $150,000 sale and the $120,000 of cost of goods sold.

Answer (B) is incorrect because revenue, not net income, is understated by $150,000. The net effect of the revenue and cost errors misstates income. Answer (C) is incorrect because $37,500 is the markup on selling price, not cost. Answer (D) is incorrect because the omission of $150,000 of revenue and $120,000 of cost of goods sold understated income.

Questions 66 through 68 are based on the following information. The Katie Howell Construction Company uses the percentage-of-completion method of accounting. In year 1, the company began work on Job 21, which had a contract price of $10 million. Other data are

	Year 1	Year 2
Costs incurred during the year	$1,800,000	$4,700,000
Estimated costs to complete	5,400,000	0
Billings during the year	2,000,000	8,000,000
Collections during the year	1,400,000	8,600,000

66. Using the percentage-of-completion method, the total gross profit to be recognized in year 1 is

A. $700,000

B. $1,400,000

C. $2,800,000

D. $2,500,000

The correct answer is (A). *(Publisher)*

REQUIRED: The gross profit to be recognized.

DISCUSSION: By the end of year 1, the company had incurred costs of $1.8 million and expected to incur additional costs of $5.4 million. Thus, the total cost of the job was estimated to be $7.2 million. The $1.8 million incurred in year 1 represents 25% of the total costs expected to be incurred. If 25% of the work has been completed, the company should recognize 25% of the expected revenue. Hence, gross profit for year 1 is $700,000 [25% x ($10,000,000 contract price – $7,200,000 total estimated costs)].

Answer (B) is incorrect because the $1,400,000 equals the cash collected for the year. Answer (C) is incorrect because $2,800,000 is the total estimated gross profit for the project. Answer (D) is incorrect because $2,500,000 is the total revenue to be recognized during year 1.

67. Using the percentage-of-completion method, the total gross profit to be recognized in year 2 is

A. $2,100,000

B. $2,800,000

C. $3,500,000

D. $3,900,000

The correct answer is (B). *(Publisher)*

REQUIRED: The gross profit to be recognized.

DISCUSSION: By the end of year 2, the company had incurred costs of $1.8 million in year 1 and $4.7 million in year 2. Consequently, the total cost of completing the job was $6.5 million. Given a total contract price of $10 million, the total gross profit over the life of the contract is $3.5 million. The gross profit recognized in year 1 was $700,000 {[$1,800,000 year 1 costs ÷ ($1,800,000 + $5,400,000 estimated costs to complete)] x [$10,000,000 contract price – ($1,800,000 + $5,400,000)]}. The gross profit recognized in year 2 is therefore $2,800,000 ($3,500,000 total – $700,000 recognized in year 1).

Answer (A) is incorrect because $2,100,000 is based on the total estimated gross profit at the end of year 1. Answer (C) is incorrect because $3,500,000 is the total gross profit over 2 years. Answer (D) is incorrect because $3,900,000 is the difference between collections and costs in year 2.

68. If Katie Howell Construction Company uses the completed-contract method, the income recognized in year 2 will be

A. $2,800,000

B. $3,500,000

C. $5,300,000

D. $1,400,000

The correct answer is (B). *(Publisher)*

REQUIRED: The income recognized.

DISCUSSION: Under the completed-contract method, no income is recognized until the project is completed. In this case, the costs incurred over 2 years ($1,800,000 + $4,700,000), or $6.5 million, are subtracted from the total contract price of $10 million to arrive at income of $3.5 million. No income would have been reported in year 1 because the contract had not been completed by the end of that year.

Answer (A) is incorrect because $2,800,000 was the estimated gross profit at the end of year 1. Answer (C) is incorrect because $5,300,000 does not consider the $1,800,000 of costs incurred during year 1. Answer (D) is incorrect because $1,400,000 was the cash collected during year 1.

C. Limitations of Financial Statement Information

69. Limitations of the statement of financial position include all of the following except

A. The use of historical cost for valuing assets and liabilities.

B. Inclusion of information on capital maintenance.

C. Exclusion of some economic resources and obligations.

D. The use of estimates in the determination of certain items.

The correct answer is (B). *(CMA, adapted)*

REQUIRED: The item not a limitation of the statement of financial position (balance sheet).

DISCUSSION: The basic financial statements are prepared using the concept of financial capital maintenance. A return on financial capital results only if the financial (money) amount of net assets at the end of the period exceeds the amount at the beginning. Hence, inclusion of information on capital maintenance is a fundamental approach to financial reporting, not a limitation (SFAC 5).

Answer (A) is incorrect because historical cost may not be an accurate valuation of a balance sheet item. Changing prices and other factors are not recognized in the basic financial statements. Answer (C) is incorrect because not all assets and liabilities are included in the balance sheet; for example, certain contingencies and pension obligations are not included. Answer (D) is incorrect because measurement in financial statements tends to be approximate rather than exact. Estimates are commonly used to determine reported amounts, e.g., depreciation and present value.

70. In accounting for inventories, generally accepted accounting principles require departure from the historical cost principle when the utility of inventory has fallen below cost. This rule is known as the "lower of cost or market" rule. "Market" as defined here means

A. Original cost minus allowance for obsolescence.

B. Original cost plus normal profit margin.

C. Replacement cost of the inventory.

D. Original cost minus cost to dispose.

The correct answer is (C). *(CMA, adapted)*

REQUIRED: The meaning of the term "market."

DISCUSSION: In the phrase "lower of cost or market," the term "market" means the replacement cost of the inventory as determined in the market in which the company buys its inventory, not the market in which it sells to customers. Market is limited to a ceiling amount equal to net realizable value and a floor amount equal to net realizable value minus a normal profit margin.

Answer (A) is incorrect because the market value is not a cost. Answer (B) is incorrect because the floor amount is net realizable value minus a normal profit margin. Answer (D) is incorrect because original cost minus cost to dispose equals net realizable value.

71. A Midwestern public utility reports noncurrent assets as the first item on its statement of financial position. This practice is an example of the

A. Going-concern assumption.

B. Conservatism.

C. Economic-entity assumption.

D. Industry practice constraint.

The correct answer is (D). *(CMA, adapted)*

REQUIRED: The reason a public utility reports noncurrent assets as the first item on the balance sheet.

DISCUSSION: Assets are normally listed in the order of their importance, with current assets typically being the most important. For a public utility, the physical plant is the most important asset. Thus, public utilities often report their noncurrent assets as the first item on the balance sheet. This departure from the customary presentation in accordance with GAAP is justified by the peculiarities of the industry.

Answer (A) is incorrect because the assumed continuity of the business is the basis for reporting financial statement items at other than liquidation value. Answer (B) is incorrect because conservatism is a prudent reaction to uncertainty. For example, if different estimates are available and none is more likely than another, the least optimistic should be used. However, conservatism is not a bias toward understatement. Answer (C) is incorrect because the affairs of an economic entity are distinct from those of its owners.

STUDY UNIT 4: ASSETS

26 pages of outline
84 multiple-choice questions

Study Unit 4 is one of seven devoted to preparation of financial statements, a major topic that has been assigned a relative weight range of 50% to 70% of Part 2. This study unit concerns the resource structure of the reporting entity.

A. Cash, Cash Equivalents, and Marketable Securities

1. **Nature of Cash**. Cash is ready money, the most liquid of assets. As the customary medium of exchange, it also provides the standard of value (the unit of measurement) of the transactions that are reported in the financial statements.

   a. According to SFAC 6, "Money (cash, including deposits in banks) is valuable because of what it can buy. It can be exchanged for virtually any good or service or it can be saved and exchanged for them in the future. Money's 'command over resources' -- its purchasing power -- is the basis of its value and future economic benefits."

   b. For the sake of simplicity, the changes in purchasing power over time are not recognized in standard financial statements; that is, nominal units of money provide the measurement scale.

   c. Because cash is the standard medium of exchange, its effective management is vital. Economic entities must plan to hold sufficient cash (have adequate liquidity) to execute transactions. The amount held should be limited, however, because cash usually does not increase in value (appreciate) unless invested.

   d. Assets are current if they are "reasonably expected to be realized in cash or sold or consumed during the normal operating cycle of the business" (ARB 43, Chapter 3A). Thus, cash itself is ordinarily a current asset.

      1) However, even though not actually set aside in special accounts, cash that is "clearly to be used in the near future for the liquidation of long-term debts, payments to sinking funds, or for other similar purposes should be excluded from current assets."

2. **Items of Cash**. To be classified as cash, an asset must be readily available for use by the business; its use should not be restricted.

   a. The cash account on the balance sheet should consist of

      1) Coin and currency on hand, including petty cash and change funds
      2) Demand deposits (checking accounts)
      3) Time deposits (savings accounts)

         a) Although technically subject to a bank's right to demand notice before withdrawal, savings accounts are treated as cash because the right is seldom exercised.

      4) Near-cash assets such as undeposited checks

         a) They are usually in the process of being deposited and are called "deposits in transit."

         b) They include many negotiable instruments, such as money orders, bank drafts, certified checks, cashiers' checks, and personal checks.

         c) They must be depositable and thus do not include unsigned or postdated checks.

d) Checks written to creditors but not mailed or delivered at the balance sheet date should be included in the payor's cash account (not considered cash payments at year-end).

b. Companies have either a general ledger cash control account with a subsidiary ledger of accounts for each bank account or a series of general ledger accounts to represent the various cash accounts.

1) On the balance sheet, only one cash account is presented. It reflects all unrestricted cash.

2) Each transfer of cash from one account to another requires an entry.

3) At the end of each period, a schedule of interaccount transfers should be prepared and reviewed to make certain all cash transfers are counted once and only once.

3. **Cash Equivalents**. These are short-term, highly liquid investments. According to SFAS 95,

a. They are readily convertible into known amounts of cash.

b. They are so near maturity that interest rate risk is insignificant.

c. Generally, only investments with an original maturity to the holder of 3 months or less qualify.

d. Common examples are Treasury bills, money market funds, and commercial paper.

4. **Noncash Short-Term Investments**. Because these investments are usually substantially restricted and thus not readily available for use by the entity, they should be classified as short-term investments, not cash. However, in some cases, they may qualify as cash equivalents (see A.3. above).

a. Certificates of deposit are formal debt instruments issued by a bank or another financial institution and are subject to penalties for withdrawal before maturity.

b. Money market funds are essentially mutual funds that have portfolios of commercial paper and T-bills.

1) However, a money market fund with a usable checking feature might be better classified as cash.

2) Commercial paper consists of short-term (no more than 270 days) corporate obligations.

3) Treasury bills are short-term guaranteed U.S. government obligations.

a) In contrast, an obligation of a federal agency is guaranteed only by the agency, not by the U.S. government.

c. Money market savings certificates are debt instruments with rates tied to the T-bill rate.

5. **Other Noncash Items**

a. Nonsufficient fund (NSF) checks, postdated checks, and IOUs should be treated as receivables. Advances for expenses to employees may be classified as receivables (if expected to be paid by employees) or as prepaid expenses.

1) Restricted cash in foreign banks should be reported as a receivable (current or noncurrent), but unrestricted deposits in foreign banks are classified as cash.

b. Postage stamps are accounted for as prepaid expenses or office supplies.

c. An overdraft is a current liability unless the entity has sufficient funds in another account in the same bank to cover it.

1) If a company has separate accounts in one bank, an overdraft will usually be subject to a right of offset: The funds in another account may be legally transferred by the bank to cover the shortage.

a) This right does not exist when the accounts are in different institutions. Thus, the overdraft must be reported as a liability, not netted against the other cash accounts.

6. **Restricted Cash**. Cash amounts designated for special uses should be separately presented.

a. Examples are bond sinking funds and new building funds.

b. The nature of the use will determine whether such an amount will be classified as current or noncurrent.

1) A bond sinking fund to redeem noncurrent bond debt would be noncurrent, whereas funds to be used to redeem bonds currently redeemable would be a current asset.

7. **Compensating Balances**. As part of an agreement regarding either an existing loan or the provision of future credit, a borrower may keep an average or minimum amount on deposit with the lender. This compensating balance not only increases the effective rate of interest paid by the borrower but also creates a disclosure issue because the full amount reported in the cash account might not be available to meet general obligations. The SEC's recommended solution depends on the duration of the lending arrangement and the nature of the restriction.

a. If the balance relates to a short-term agreement and is legally restricted, it is separately reported among the cash and cash equivalent items as a current asset.

1) If the agreement is long-term, the legally restricted balance is noncurrent and should be separately classified in either the investment or other asset section.

b. When the entity has a compensating balance agreement but the use of the balance is not restricted, full footnote disclosure but not separate classification is required.

8. **Petty Cash**. In an **imprest petty cash system**, a specific amount of money, e.g., $100, is set aside in the care of a petty cash custodian to pay office expenses that are too small to pay by check or to record in the accounting system as they occur. The entry is to debit petty cash and to credit cash.

a. Periodically, the fund is reimbursed for all expenditures based on expense receipts, and journal entries are made to reflect the transactions. However, entries are made to the petty cash account only to establish the fund, to change its amount, or to adjust the balance if it has not been reimbursed at year-end.

b. The **cash over and short account** is a nominal account for errors in petty cash. It is used when the total of the expense receipts and the cash remaining does not equal the amount that should be in the petty cash fund, i.e., the imprest amount. The over and short account is treated on the income statement as a miscellaneous revenue or expense.

9. **Bank Reconciliations**. A bank reconciliation is a schedule comparing the entity's cash balance per books with the balance shown on the bank statement (usually received monthly). The most common approach is to reconcile from the bank balance to the unadjusted book balance.

a. Because the two balances usually vary, this schedule permits the entity to determine whether the difference is attributable to normal conditions, errors, or fraud. It also serves as a basis for accounting entries to adjust the entity's books to reflect unrecorded items.

b. Common reasons for differences. The bank and the entity inevitably record many transactions at different times, and both may make errors.

1) Outstanding checks. The books may reflect checks drawn by the entity that have not yet cleared the bank. These amounts should be subtracted from the bank balance to arrive at the balance per books.

2) Deposits in transit. A time lag may occur between deposit of receipts and the bank's recording of the transaction. Thus, receipts placed in a night depository on the last day of the month would be reflected only in the next month's bank statement. These receipts should be added to the bank balance to arrive at the book balance.

3) Amounts added by the bank. Interest income added to an account may not be included in the book balance. Banks may act as collection agents, for example, for notes on which the depositor is the payee. If the depositor has not learned of a collection, it will not be reflected in the entity's records.

a) These amounts are subtracted from the bank balance to reconcile to the unadjusted book balance. They should be recorded on the entity's books, after which they are no longer reconciling items.

4) Amounts deducted by the bank. These amounts generally include service charges and customer checks returned for nonsufficient funds (NSF checks). Service charges cannot be recorded in the books until the bank statement is received. Also, customer checks returned for nonsufficient funds may have been deducted by the bank but still included in the book balance.

a) These amounts are added to the bank balance to reconcile to the unadjusted book balance. Once the amounts are recorded on the books, they are no longer reconciling items.

5) Errors. If the bank has wrongly charged or credited the entity's account (or failed to record a transaction at all), the error may be detected in the process of preparing the reconciliation. Book errors may likewise be discovered.

c. Bank reconciliation example. Raughley Company's bank statement on March 31 indicated a balance of $6,420. The book balance on that date was $7,920. The bank balance did not include $3,229 of receipts for March 31 that were deposited on that day but were not recorded until April 1 by the bank. It also did not include $450 of checks written in March that cleared in April. The March bank statement revealed that the bank had collected $1,500 in March on a note owed to Raughley, a $160 customer check had been returned for insufficient funds, and service charges totaled $7. Finally, the company had written a $60 check and recorded it as $6 (it cleared the bank).

Bank-to-Book Reconciliation

Bank balance -- March 31			$6,420
Add:	Deposits in transit	$3,229	
	Service charges	7	
	NSF check	160	
	$60 check recorded as $6	54	
			$3,450
			$9,870
Deduct:	Outstanding checks	$ 450	
	Note proceeds	1,500	
			(1,950)
Book balance -- March 31			$7,920

d. A **proof of cash**, also known as a four-column bank reconciliation, is a reconciliation of beginning balances, deposits-receipts, checks-disbursements, and ending balances. The proof of cash adds a time dimension to a bank reconciliation (horizontal). Instead of reconciling a balance per bank and a balance per depositor at a given date, the proof of cash reconciles the beginning balance, receipts, disbursements, and the ending balance for a period according to the bank statement with the respective amounts according to the books. The proof of cash actually includes four reconciliations, as shown below.

	Beginning	Receipts	Disbursements	Ending
Per Bank	$XXXX	$XXXX	$XXXX	$XXXX
Deposits in Transit				
Beginning	+ $____	– $____		
Ending		+ $____		+ $____
Outstanding Checks				
Beginning	– $____		– $____	
Ending			+ $____	– $____
Bank Charges			– $____	+ $____
Per Books	$____	$____	$____	$____

The beginning and ending columns are bank reconciliations. The two middle columns reconcile receipts and disbursements. If the book balance was properly adjusted at the end of the last period, only deposits in transit and outstanding checks should be reconciling items that also affect the reconciliation of that period's receipts and disbursements.

e. The reconciliation may also be done in a two-column format in which the bank balance and the book balance are reconciled to the adjusted (correct) balance.

10. Short-term marketable securities (e.g., T-bills and CDs) are sometimes held as a substitute for cash but are usually acquired as temporary investments.
    a. Most companies avoid large cash balances and prefer borrowing to meet short-term needs.
    b. As temporary investments, marketable securities may be purchased so that maturities are timed to meet seasonal fluctuations, to pay off a bond issue, to make tax payments, or to satisfy other anticipated needs.
11. Marketable securities should be chosen with a view to the risk of default (**financial risk**).
    a. U.S. government securities are the least risky.
12. **Interest rate risk** should be minimized given the reasons for holding marketable securities.
    a. Short-term securities are less likely to fluctuate in value because of changes in the general level of interest rates.
13. Changes in the general price level, which ordinarily are inflationary, determine the purchasing power of payments on investments (principal and interest) and thus the types of securities chosen and the rates charged.

14. The security's degree of marketability determines its **liquidity**, that is, the ability to resell the security at its quoted market price.
15. The firm's tax position will influence its choice of securities; for example, a firm with net loss carryforwards may prefer a higher-yielding taxable security to a tax-exempt municipal bond.
16. Short-term marketable securities are usually chosen for reasons that make high-yield, high-risk investments unattractive. Hence, a higher return may be forgone in exchange for greater safety.
    a. Thus, speculative tactics, such as selling short (borrowing and selling securities in the expectation that their price will decline by the time they must be replaced) and margin trading (borrowing from a broker to buy securities) are avoided.
17. Stop and review! You have completed the outline for this subunit. Study multiple-choice questions 1 through 8 beginning on page 175.

B. Receivables

1. Accounts receivable are recorded when title passes in a sale of goods or when services are performed. The balance sheet presentation is based on the net realizable value of the receivables.
    a. The net method records receivables net of the applicable discount. If the payment is not received during the discount period, an interest revenue account, such as sales discounts forfeited, is credited at the end of the discount period or when the payment is received.
    b. The gross method accounts for receivables at their face value. If a discount is taken, a sales discount is recorded and classified as an offset to sales in the income statement to yield net sales.
    c. Receivables from officers and owners are assets and should be presented in the balance sheet as assets, not as offsets to owners' equity.
2. **Bad Debts**. There are two approaches to bad debts: the direct write-off method and the allowance method.
    a. The **direct write-off method** expenses bad debts as uncollectible when they are determined to be uncollectible. The direct write-off method is subject to manipulation because the timing is at the discretion of management.
    b. The **allowance method** records bad debt expense systematically as a percentage of either sales or the level of accounts receivable on an annual basis.
        1) The credit is to an allowance account (an account contra to accounts receivable).
        2) As accounts receivable are written off, they are charged to the allowance account. The write-off of a bad debt has no effect on working capital or total assets because the asset account (accounts receivable) and the contra account are reduced by equal amounts.
        3) If bad debt expense is computed as a percentage of sales (e.g., 1% of sales), bad debts are considered a function of sales on account. This is an income-statement-oriented approach.

4) If the allowance is adjusted to reflect a percentage of accounts receivable (e.g., 10% at year-end), bad debt expense is a function of both sales and collections. This is a balance-sheet-oriented approach.

a) A common method of estimating bad debt expense is to develop an analysis of accounts receivable known as an **aging schedule**. Stratifying the receivables according to the time they have been outstanding permits the use of different percentages for each category. The result should be a more accurate estimate than if a single rate is used.

3. The **installment method** recognizes profit on a sale when cash is collected rather than when the sale occurs.

   a. The method can be used only when collection of the sales price is not reasonably assured.

   b. Both revenues and cost of sales are recognized in the period of sale, but the gross profit is deferred to the periods in which cash is collected.

   c. Special deferred gross profit and installment receivable accounts must be established for each year because the gross profit rate usually changes yearly.

4. The **cost-recovery method** may be used when receivables are collected over an extended period, considerable doubt exists as to collectibility, and a reasonable estimate of the loss cannot be made.

   a. Profit is recognized only after collections exceed cost. Subsequent receipts are treated entirely as revenues.

5. **Discounting Notes Receivable.** When a note receivable is discounted (usually at a bank), the holder is borrowing the maturity value (principal + interest at maturity) of the note. The bank usually collects the maturity value from the maker of the note.

   a. Thus, the steps are to

      1) Compute the maturity value.

      2) Compute the interest on the loan from the bank (the bank's interest rate times the maturity value of the note).

      3) Subtract the bank's interest charges from the maturity value to determine the loan proceeds.

   b. The entries to record the transaction are

Cash	$(amount received from the bank)	
Interest expense or revenue	(the difference dr or cr)	
Notes receivable		$(carrying value)

   c. The discounted note receivable must be disclosed as a contingent liability. If the maker dishonors the note, the bank will collect from the person or entity that discounted the note. Alternatively, the credit in the above entry is sometimes made to notes receivable discounted, a contra-asset account, and would be shown on the balance sheet as a deduction from notes receivable.

   d. When computing yearly interest, the day the note is received, made, etc., is not included, but the last day of the note is counted.

      1) EXAMPLE: A 30-day note dated January 17 matures on February 16. There are 14 days (31–17) left in January, and 16 days must be counted in February for a 30-day note. Accordingly, the maturity date is February 16.

6. Long-term notes receivable should be recorded at their present value. Thus, interest-bearing notes are recorded at the sum of the present values of the future payments discounted at the effective (usually the market) rate. The result may require recognition and amortization of discount or premium.

7. **Noninterest-Bearing Notes**. A note may bear no explicit interest because interest is included in its maturity value. The discount is amortized to interest revenue.

   a. Under **APB 21**, *Interest on Receivables and Payables*, when the note arises in the ordinary course of business and is "due in customary trade terms not exceeding approximately 1 year, " the interest element need not be recognized. However, the APB 21 rules regarding presentation of discount and premium still apply.

   b. Under APB 21, when a **note is exchanged solely for cash**, and no other right or privilege is exchanged, the proceeds are assumed to reflect the present value of the note, and the effective interest rate is therefore the interest rate implicit in that present value. Periodic interest will equal the nominal interest adjusted for amortization of any premium or discount.

8. **Unreasonable Interest**. The term "noninterest-bearing" is confusing because it is used not only when a note bears implicit interest but also when no actual interest is charged (the cash proceeds equal the face value). When a note is noninterest-bearing in the latter sense, or when it bears interest at a rate that is unreasonable in the circumstances, APB 21 requires imputation (estimation) of an interest rate.

   a. When a **note is exchanged for property, goods, or services**, the interest rate determined by the parties in an arm's-length transaction is presumed to be fair, but that presumption is overcome when no interest is stated, the stated rate is unreasonable, or the nominal amount of the note materially differs from the cash price of the item or the market value of the note.

      1) In these circumstances, the transaction should be recorded at the more clearly determinable of the fair value of the property, goods, or services; market value of the note; or discounted value of future payments based on an imputed rate.

      2) If the present value of a note with no stated rate or an unreasonable rate must be determined by discounting future payments using an imputed rate, the prevailing rate for similar instruments of issuers with similar credit ratings normally helps determine the appropriate rate.

   b. The stated rate may be less than the effective rate because the lender has received **other stated (or unstated) rights and privileges** as part of the bargain. The difference between the respective present values of the note computed at the stated rate and at the effective rate should be accounted for as the cost of the rights or privileges obtained.

9. An **assignment** of receivables (a specific assignment) is a secured borrowing. An entry should be made to debit the "receivables assigned" account and credit the "receivables" account, or the arrangement should be fully disclosed in the notes.

10. **SFAS 48**, *Revenue Recognition When Right of Return Exists*, requires sales revenue and cost of sales to be reduced by expected returns when goods are sold with a right of return (all related expected costs should be accrued in accordance with SFAS 5).

    a. This pronouncement states that revenue may be recognized at the time of sale only if all of the following conditions are met:

       1) The seller's price is substantially fixed or determinable.

       2) The buyer has paid the seller, or the buyer is obligated to pay, and the obligation is not contingent on resale of the product.

3) The buyer's obligation to the seller is unchanged by damage to, or theft or destruction of, the product.

4) The buyer has economic substance apart from the seller.

5) The seller does not have any significant obligations regarding resale of the product by the buyer.

6) The amount of future returns can be reasonably estimated.

b. If these conditions are not met, revenue recognition is deferred until they are met or the return privilege expires.

11. **SFAS 140**, *Accounting for Transfers and Servicing of Financial Assets and Extinguishments of Liabilities*, adopts a **financial-components approach** based on control. After a transfer, an entity recognizes the assets it controls and the liabilities it has incurred, derecognizes the assets it no longer controls, and derecognizes extinguished liabilities.

a. A transfer of financial assets (or a portion of an asset) over which the transferor surrenders control is a sale to the extent that the consideration does not consist of a beneficial interest in the transferred assets. The transferor surrenders **control** when three conditions are met:

1) The transferred assets are isolated from the transferor and are therefore presumed to be beyond the reach of the transferor and its creditors, even in bankruptcy.

2) Neither a regular transferee nor a holder of a beneficial interest in a qualifying special-purpose entity (e.g., certain trusts) is subject to a condition that both constrains its right to pledge or exchange the transferred interests and provides more than a trivial benefit to the transferor.

3) The transferor does not maintain effective control over the transferred assets through

a) An agreement entered into concurrently with the transfer that both entitles and obligates the transferor to repurchase or redeem substantially the same assets on substantially the agreed terms before their maturity and at a fixed or determinable price, or

b) The ability unilaterally to cause the holder to return specific assets, except through a cleanup call (e.g., an option held by a servicer to repurchase the transferred assets if they fall to a level at which servicing costs are burdensome relative to benefits).

b. After completing a transfer of financial assets, the transferor carries any retained interests in its balance sheet. It allocates the previous carrying amount between the assets sold and the retained interests based on their fair values at the transfer date.

c. If a transfer of financial assets qualifies as a sale, the transferor (seller) shall

1) Derecognize all assets sold.

2) Recognize all assets obtained and liabilities incurred in consideration as proceeds.

3) Initially measure the assets obtained and liabilities incurred at fair value, if practicable.

4) Recognize any gain or loss in earnings.

d. If a transfer of financial assets qualifies as a sale, the transferee initially recognizes assets obtained and liabilities incurred at fair value.

e. **Transfers of receivables with recourse**. When the conditions for surrender of control are met, which may depend on the law in a given jurisdiction with regard to the effect of the recourse provision, a transfer of receivables with recourse is accounted for as a sale, with the proceeds of the sale reduced by the fair value of the recourse obligation. Otherwise, the transfer is accounted for as a secured borrowing.

f. If the transfer does not meet the criteria for a sale, the parties account for the transfer as a **secured borrowing with a pledge** of noncash collateral. If the secured party (the transferee) **may sell or repledge** the collateral, the debtor (the transferor) reclassifies and separately reports that asset. If the transferee **sells** the collateral, it recognizes the proceeds and a liability to return the collateral. If the transferor **defaults**, it derecognizes the pledged asset, and the transferee initially recognizes an asset at fair value or derecognizes the liability to return the collateral. Thus, absent default, the collateral is an asset of the transferor, not the transferee.

12. **Factoring arrangements** discount receivables on a nonrecourse, notification basis. The receivables are sold outright, usually to a transferee (the factor) that assumes the full risk of collection, even in the event of a loss. When the three conditions in 11.a. above are met, a factoring arrangement is accounted for as a sale of financial assets because the transferor surrenders all control over the receivables.

a. The company involved receives money that can be immediately reinvested into new inventories. The company can offset the fee charged by the factor by eliminating their bad debts, credit department, and accounts receivable staff.

b. The factor usually receives a high financing fee (at least two points above prime), plus a fee for doing the collection. Furthermore, the factor can often operate more efficiently than its clients because of the specialized nature of its services.

c. EXAMPLE: A factor charges a 2% fee plus an interest rate of 18% on all monies advanced to the company. Monthly sales are $100,000, and the factor advances 90% of the receivables submitted after deducting the 2% fee and the interest. Credit terms are net 60 days. What is the cost to the company of this arrangement?

Amount of receivables submitted	$100,000
Minus: 10% reserve	(10,000)
Minus: 2% factor's fee	(2,000)
Amount accruing to the company	$ 88,000
Minus: 18% interest for 60 days (on $88,000)	(2,640)
Amount to be received immediately	$ 85,360

The company will also receive the $10,000 reserve at the end of the 60-day period if it has not been absorbed by sales returns and allowances. Thus, the total cost to the company to factor the sales for the month is $4,640 ($2,000 factor fee + interest of $2,640). Assuming that the factor has approved the customers' credit in advance, the seller will not absorb any bad debts.

d. The journal entry to record the preceding transaction is

Cash	$85,360	
Equity in factored receivables	10,000	
Factor fee expense	2,000	
Prepaid interest	2,640	
Accounts receivable		$100,000

13. Stop and review! You have completed the outline for this subunit. Study multiple-choice questions 9 through 25 beginning on page 178.

C. Inventories

1. Inventory quantities are usually determined by either physical counts at the end of reporting periods (known as the periodic system) or perpetual records, which keep running totals of the number of items on hand.
   a. In **perpetual systems**, purchases are recorded directly in the inventory account. Cost of goods sold is debited and inventory credited as goods are sold.
      1) Dollar values of inventory may be included in the perpetual records.
   b. Goods not physically on hand may properly be included in inventory, for example, goods on consignment.
      1) Moreover, whether goods recently purchased or sold and currently in transit are properly included in inventory may be a function of the shipping terms in the relevant contract.
         a) The term **FOB shipping point** means that title passes to the buyer at the time and place of shipment.
         b) The term **FOB destination** means that title passes when the goods arrive at their destination.
2. In a **periodic system**, a purchases account is used, and the beginning inventory balance is unchanged during the period.
   a. Cost of goods sold for the period equals purchases adjusted for the change in inventory.
   b. The entry to record cost of goods sold under a periodic inventory system:

Inventory	$(ending amount)	
Cost of goods sold	(residual amount)	
Purchases		$(for the period)
Inventory		(beginning amount)

   c. If perpetual records include dollar amounts (rather than just units), the entries to record purchases and sales are

Inventory	$XXX	
Cash, accounts payable		$XXX
Cost of goods sold	$XXX	
Inventory		$XXX

3. The following are methods used to cost ending inventory and determine CGS:
   a. **Weighted average** divides the total cost of beginning inventory and all purchases by the sum of the number of units in beginning inventory plus those purchased to obtain a weighted-average cost of goods in ending inventory (and the weighted average of goods sold).
      1) EXAMPLE:

	Units	Price per Unit	Amount
BI	20	$5	$100
PUR	10	6	60
PUR	20	8	160
	50		$320

      2) Ending inventory (and CGS) are priced at $6.40 per unit ($320 ÷ 50 units).

b. **First-in, first-out (FIFO)** considers the first goods purchased to be the first goods sold. Accordingly, ending inventory consists of the latest purchases. Cost of goods sold consists of goods purchased at the beginning of the current period and in prior periods.

1) Ending inventory is considered to be priced at the cost of the latest purchase if the number of units in ending inventory is equal to or less than the number of units in the latest purchase.

2) The valuation will be the same regardless of whether the inventory is valued at the end of the period (a periodic system) or on a perpetual basis.

3) EXAMPLE: In the example on the previous page, an ending inventory of 15 units would be priced at $8 per unit. 25 units would be priced at two levels: 20 at $8, and 5 at $6.

c. **Last-in, first-out (LIFO)** considers the most recent purchases to be sold first. Accordingly, ending inventory is priced at the cost of beginning inventory and the earliest purchases if inventory increases.

1) EXAMPLE: In the example on the previous page, a LIFO ending inventory of 20 units or less would be priced at $5 per unit. Inventory in excess of 20 units but less than 30 units would be priced at $6 per unit.

2) Physical and perpetual systems will yield different results under a LIFO assumption. If perpetual records include cost data, the results of the examples for LIFO would probably be different depending on when sales were made; i.e., if a sale were made on the first day of the period, it would be made out of beginning inventory.

3) Variations in LIFO valuation include **dollar-value LIFO** and **retail dollar-value LIFO**.

4) The dollar-value LIFO method eliminates some of the clerical problems of the unit LIFO method by using pooled quantities as its measurement basis. Increases or decreases in inventory levels are based upon comparison of dollar values adjusted by price indexes rather than by changes in the number of units.

a) EXAMPLE: A company began using dollar-value LIFO when the price index was 100%. The beginning inventory was $10,000 consisting of many different items valued at numerous prices. At the end of year 1, the ending inventory was $14,400 valued at year-end prices. The year-end price index had risen to 120%. The first step is to convert the value of the ending inventory to base-year prices. This is done by dividing the current dollar figures by the price index.

$$\$14{,}400 \div 1.20 = \$12{,}000 \text{ inventory at base-year prices}$$

The second step is to determine the increment in inventory for the period: $12,000 – $10,000 = $2,000 increment. Because LIFO is being used, the objective is to report the inventory at its original costs. The oldest costs are the $10,000 from beginning inventory. The incremental layer of $2,000 at base-year costs is converted into year-end dollars by multiplying the base-year dollars times the ratio of year-end price level over the base-year price level. $2,000 x 120% = $2,400. The ending inventory consists of two layers.

$10,000	×	100%	=	$10,000
2,000	×	120%	=	2,400
				$12,400

At the end of year 2, the inventory at year-end prices was $24,000 when the price index had risen to 150%. The calculations are

$24,000 ÷ 1.50 = $16,000
Increment = $4,000 ($16,000 – $12,000)

Ending inventory at dollar-value LIFO consists of the following three LIFO layers:

$10,000	× 100%	=	$10,000
2,000	× 120%	=	2,400
4,000	× 150%	=	6,000
			$18,400

5) The dollar-value LIFO method requires the following steps:
   a) Determine inventory value at year-end prices.
   b) Convert year-end value to base-year prices.
   c) Determine incremental layer (positive or negative).
   d) Convert increment (if inventory increases) to year-end prices.
   e) Add value of inventory layers.

6) Some companies use LIFO for external reporting but another method for internal reporting. In this case, a **LIFO reserve** may be established. It is an account contra to inventory stated using the other valuation method. At year-end, it should reflect the difference between LIFO and that method.

d. The **lower of cost or market (LCM)** rule requires that inventory be written down to market subsequent to acquisition if its utility is no longer as great as its cost.

1) The difference should be recognized as a loss of the current period. Thus, a loss should be recognized whenever the utility of goods is impaired by damage, deterioration, obsolescence, changes in price levels, changes in demand, style changes, or other causes. But the LCM rule is applicable only to goods that will be sold in the ordinary course of business. Damaged, obsolete, or deteriorated goods are usually carried at net realizable value in a separate account.

2) **Market** is the current cost to replace inventory (an input or entry value), subject to certain limitations. Market should not exceed a ceiling equal to **net realizable value (NRV)**. This amount is the estimated selling price in the ordinary course of business minus reasonably predictable costs of completion and disposal.
   a) Replacement cost does not accurately measure utility if the estimated sales value, reduced by the costs of completion and disposal, is lower, in which case the NRV more appropriately measures utility. Reporting inventory above NRV overstates its utility and will result in a loss at the time of sale.

3) Market should not be less than a floor equal to net realizable value reduced by an allowance for an approximately normal profit margin.
   a) If the inventory were written down to a replacement cost below this value, an abnormal profit element (net realizable value – normal profit – replacement cost) would be included in revenue at the time of sale.
   b) If cost will be recovered with an approximately normal profit upon sale in the ordinary course of business, no loss should be recognized even though replacement or production costs are lower.

4) Accordingly, the LCM rule results in valuation at original cost or current replacement cost. The latter cost is not to be greater than NRV or less than NRV minus a normal profit.

5) **Applying LCM**. Depending on the character and composition of the inventory, the LCM rule may properly be applied either directly to each item or to the aggregate total of the inventory (or, in some cases, to the total of the components of each major category).

   a) The method should be the one that most clearly reflects periodic income. Once inventory is written down, the reduced value is the new cost basis, and a write-up will ordinarily not be permitted if prices increase.

   b) LCM by item will always be equal to or less than the other LCM valuations, and LCM in total will always be equal to or greater than the other LCM valuations.

   c) Most companies use LCM by item, and this method is required for tax purposes.

      i) If dollar-value LIFO is employed, LCM should be applied to pools of items.

      ii) A company may not use LCM with LIFO for tax purposes.

6) EXAMPLE:

Replacement cost	$22
Cost	23
Selling price	38
Disposal (selling) costs	4
Normal profit	15

   a) Market is the replacement cost of $22 subject to a ceiling of NRV ($38 selling price – $4 disposal costs = $34) and a floor of NRV minus normal profit ($34 – $15 = $19). Because replacement cost of $22 is within this range ($19-$34), it is the market value. Market is therefore lower than the $23 cost, and LCM is $22.

7) **Recording LCM**. If inventory is written down to market, the unrealized inventory holding loss can be directly credited to the inventory and debited to cost of goods sold. This method has the theoretical drawback of charging a holding loss to an account that includes the costs of selling goods. Also, inventory will be presented at LCM rather than at cost net of write-downs.

   a) **Allowance method**. Charging a holding loss account and crediting an allowance (contra asset) account is the preferred technique. The unit costs in the subsidiary records need not be changed to agree with the control account.

8) **LCM at Interim Dates**. Nontemporary market declines should be recognized in the interim periods in which they occur.

   a) Recoveries of these losses on the same inventory later in the fiscal year should be recognized as gains (but only to the extent of the previously recognized losses).

   b) If market declines can reasonably be expected to be restored by year-end, they should not be recognized.

e. **Moving average** is a weighted average to date that can be used only with perpetual inventory records in which inventory values are also included.

   1) After each purchase, a new weighted average is computed for the cost of merchandise then on hand.

   2) Sales prior to the next purchase are then removed from credited inventory at the previously computed weighted average.

f. **Simple average** is an average of the beginning inventory unit cost and the unit cost of each purchase with no regard for the number of items in beginning inventory or any purchase. It is appropriate when beginning inventory and all purchases have approximately the same number of units.

g. **Specific identification** requires determining which specific items are sold. It can be used for various blocks of investment securities or special inventory items such as electric motors, automobiles, heavy equipment, etc. It allows manipulation because more costly inventory items could be considered sold if profit is to be lowered, and less costly inventory items could be considered sold if profit is to be increased.

h. **Retail method** is a method of converting ending inventory at retail to cost. The advantage is that a physical inventory can be taken at retail and then converted to cost. The cost ratio used to convert retail to cost depends upon the flow assumption used. If a **weighted-average** flow is assumed, the cost ratio should be goods available at cost over goods available at retail. If a **FIFO** assumption is used, the cost ratio should be cost of purchases over purchases at retail. If a **LIFO** flow assumption is used, the cost of ending inventory depends on the cost of beginning inventory. If ending inventory is less than beginning inventory, the cost ratio should be cost of beginning inventory over beginning inventory at retail. Any increase (stated at retail) should be valued at the ratio of cost of purchases over purchases at retail.

Also, the **lower-of-cost-or-market** concept may be applied to the retail method. In this approach, markups are added to beginning inventory and purchases at retail to obtain goods available at retail. Markdowns are not subtracted. This results in a higher denominator in the cost-retail ratio, which results in a lower ending inventory figure.

   1) EXAMPLE:

	At Cost	At Retail
Beginning inventory	$ 90,000	$130,000
Purchases	330,000	460,000
Markups		10,000
Markdowns		40,000
Sales		480,000

   2) Ending inventory at retail is thus $80,000 ($130,000 + $460,000 + $10,000 – $40,000 – $480,000).

   3) The cost-retail ratio for retail method weighted average is 420 ÷ 560. Include both markups and markdowns in goods available at retail.

   4) The cost-retail ratio for the retail method FIFO is 330 ÷ 430, assuming all markups and markdowns applied to goods purchased this period. Under FIFO, all inventory would come from current-period purchases.

5) The cost-retail ratio for the retail method LIFO is 90 ÷ 130 because ending inventory of $80,000 retail is less than beginning inventory of $130,000. If there had been an increase in inventory, the increment would be valued using a cost-retail ratio of 330 ÷ 430.

6) The cost-retail ratio for the retail method LCM, assuming weighted average, is 420 ÷ 600 because markups, not markdowns, are included in the calculation of the percentage. This method is typically used if LIFO is not used. The exclusion of markdowns from the ratio results in a valuation that approximates the lower of cost or market.

7) The dollar-value LIFO method can also be used in conjunction with the retail inventory method.

a) EXAMPLE:

	Cost	Retail
Beginning inventory	$12,000	$ 16,800
Purchases	70,000	100,000
Sales		90,000
Ending inventory at retail		$ 26,800

The beginning price index was 100%; the year-end index is 134%. The first step is to convert the year-end inventory to base-year prices: $26,800 ÷ 1.34 = $20,000. Determine the increment: $20,000 – $16,800 = $3,200. Convert the increment back to year-end prices: $3,200 × 134% = $4,288. The next step is to convert the retail prices to cost and then add the layers:

$16,800 × 100% (price index) × 71.43% (cost ratio) =	$12,000.24
3,200 × 134% (price index) × 70.00% (cost ratio) =	3,001.60
	$15,001.84

8) In summary, the retail dollar-value LIFO method requires the following steps:

a) Determine inventory value at year-end retail prices.
b) Convert year-end values to base-year prices.
c) Determine incremental layer (positive or negative).
d) Convert increment (if inventory increases) to year-end prices.
e) Convert retail prices to cost.
f) Add cost of inventory layers.

i. **Gross profit method** is a method of computing ending inventory given sales figures. The gross profit is subtracted from sales to determine cost of sales. The gross profit method is not acceptable for tax purposes. It can, however, be used when the inventory has been destroyed or stolen. It is also often used in the preparation of interim statements.

1) EXAMPLE: Assume beginning inventory of $10,000, purchases of $20,000, and sales of $50,000, given a 100% markup on cost. Because the cost of goods sold was $25,000 (50% of sales), ending inventory was $5,000 ($30,000 goods available – $25,000 CGS). The easy way to work this type of problem is to prepare the cost of goods sold section of an income statement and solve algebraically for those amounts that are not known.

j. **Market costing** values ending inventory at its current market rate, e.g., the current price of wheat or gold.

k. **Cost apportionment by relative sales value** is a means of allocating cost of common products or a group of items purchased together by their relative sales values. Thus, the lots in a real estate subdivision would be valued at a percentage of the total cost, that is, the ratio of the market value of an individual lot to the total estimated market value of all the lots.

l. **Variable costing** (direct costing) is a method of costing inventory arising from production processes that does not include fixed overhead. It is not acceptable for financial reporting purposes. It is a responsibility accounting approach.

m. **Standard costing** is a means of pricing inventory at budgeted, predetermined costs. Standard costing is an acceptable means of pricing inventory if, for financial reporting purposes, the standard costs approximate the actual costs. If actual costs are significantly different from standard costs, the ending inventory and cost of goods sold must be adjusted to actual cost.

n. **Completed contract** and **percentage of completion** are methods of accounting for long-term contracts (see Study Unit 3).

o. **Net realizable value** is an appropriate valuation method for damaged inventories.

4. Stop and review! You have completed the outline for this subunit. Study multiple-choice questions 26 through 53 beginning on page 184.

D. Investments (Current and Long-Term)

1. Short-term investments are current assets. They must be readily marketable and be intended to be converted into cash within the next year or operating cycle, whichever is longer. Bonds, other debt instruments, and stocks are typical investments.

   a. The accounting value of debt securities includes brokerage fees paid, but not accrued interest. Discounts or premiums on debt securities (e.g., bonds) are not amortized because the securities are expected to be sold within 1 year.

2. **SFAS 115**, *Accounting for Certain Investments in Debt and Equity Securities*, applies to investments in equity securities with readily determinable fair values (for example, if quoted market prices are currently available) and all investments in debt securities. It does not apply to investments in equity securities accounted for under the equity method, investments in consolidated subsidiaries, most derivative instruments, enterprises with specialized accounting practices that include accounting for all investments at fair or market value, and not-for-profit organizations.

   a. When acquired, debt and equity securities should be classified as held-to-maturity, trading, or available-for-sale.

      1) **Held-to-maturity securities** include debt securities, but only if the reporting enterprise has the positive intent and ability to hold the securities to maturity.

         a) Held-to-maturity securities are reported at amortized cost.

         b) Changes in circumstances may cause a change in the above-mentioned intent "without calling into question the intent to hold other debt securities to maturity in the future."

         c) Classifying securities as held-to-maturity is inappropriate if their sale may result from such factors as need for liquidity, changes in market rates, changes in foreign currency risk, changes in the yield of alternative investments, or changes in funding sources and terms.

d) Securities are deemed to be held to maturity in the following circumstances:

i) Sale near enough to the maturity or call date (e.g., within 3 months) so that interest rate risk (change in the market rate) does not have a significant effect on fair value

ii) Sale after collection of 85% or more of the principal

e) If a security can contractually be prepaid or otherwise settled in such a way that the holder would not recover substantially all of the recorded investment, it may not be classified as held-to-maturity.

2) **Trading securities** include debt securities that are not classified as held-to-maturity or available-for-sale and certain equity securities with readily determinable fair values.

a) Trading securities are bought and held primarily for sale in the near term. They are frequently purchased and sold.

b) Each trading security is measured at fair value at each balance sheet date. **Unrealized holding gains and losses** on trading securities are included in earnings. A holding gain or loss is the net change in fair value during the period, not including recognized dividends or interest not yet received.

c) To retain historical cost in the accounts, a valuation allowance may be established for each security or at the portfolio level (if records for individual securities are maintained).

3) **Available-for-sale securities** include equity securities with readily determinable fair values that are not classified as trading securities, and debt securities not classified as held-to-maturity or trading securities.

a) The accounting is similar to that for trading securities. However, unless an available-for-sale security is the hedged item in a fair value hedge, unrealized holding gains and losses, including those classified as current assets, are excluded from earnings and reported in other comprehensive income (OCI).

4) Income from dividends and interest for these types of securities, including amortization of premium or discount, continues to be included in earnings. SFAS 115 does not affect the methods of accounting for dividends and interest, and realized gains and losses on held-to-maturity and available-for-sale securities also continue to be included in earnings.

5) Transfers between categories are at fair value.

6) **Impairment**. If a decline in fair value of an individual held-to-maturity or available-for-sale security below the amortized cost basis is other than temporary, the cost basis is written down to fair value as a new cost basis.

a) The write-down is a realized loss and is included in earnings.

b) The new cost basis is not affected by subsequent recoveries in fair value.

c) Subsequent increases in fair value of available-for-sale securities are included in OCI. Subsequent decreases, except for other-than-temporary declines, are also included in OCI.

7) According to SFAS 115, as amended by SFAS 135, individual trading, held-to-maturity, and available-for-sale securities may be classified as current or noncurrent.

3. **Stock dividends** and **stock splits** are not considered income when received by the investors. They decrease the unit cost of the securities; more securities are owned, and their total cost is not affected.

   a. No journal entries are made to record the receipt of stock dividends or splits; however, a memorandum entry should be made in the investment account to record the additional shares owned.

   b. A **reverse stock split** reduces the number of shares outstanding.

4. When **stock rights** (options to purchase additional shares) are received, the cost of the stock on which the rights were issued is allocated between the rights and the stock.

   a. The journal entry is

Investment in stock rights	$XXX	
Investment in stock		$XXX

   b. Allocation is based on the relative market values of the rights and stock.
   c. The rights are either sold or exercised, or they expire on their expiration date.

5. Long-term debt securities (e.g., bonds) are carried at their historical cost (including brokerage fees but excluding accrued interest at purchase), and any discount or premium (difference between the purchase price and maturity value) is amortized over the remaining life of the debt instrument.

   a. If the amounts are not material, the straight-line method may be used.
   b. In all other cases, the effective-rate-of-interest method must be used.

      1) The effective-rate-of-interest method requires that the effective interest rate at the time of the instrument's purchase be multiplied by the book value of the security to determine the interest revenue for that period. The difference between the interest revenue and the amount of cash debited on the receipt of the contracted for amount of interest is amortization of discount or premium.

6. **The Equity Method of Accounting for Investments in Common Stock**

   a. The equity method recognizes both distributed and undistributed income arising from an investment in an investee.
   b. If the fair value method is applicable, only the dividends from investees are recognized as income.
   c. Under the equity method, the investor's share of investee income is recorded as the investee reports income.

Investment in investee	$XXX	
Income from investee		$XXX

Then, as dividends are received, the entry is

Cash	$XXX	
Investment in investee		$XXX

The net effect is

Cash	$(distributed income)	
Investment in investee	(undistributed income)	
Income from investee		$(total income)

d. Under **APB 18**, *The Equity Method of Accounting for Investments in Common Stock*, the excess of the cost of the investment over the equity in the book value of the investee's net assets should be amortized. This difference may be attributable wholly or partly to goodwill (excess of cost over the investor's interest in the fair value of the identifiable net assets). However, if the excess is attributable to specific undervalued assets, it should be amortized as appropriate for those assets, for example, over the remaining life of equipment. Also, intercompany profit items should be eliminated as in consolidations. See Consolidations in Study Unit 8.

e. The equity method is required by APB 18 whenever an investor exercises significant influence over the investee. Significant influence is assumed in the absence of contrary evidence when 20% or more of the voting stock of the investee is held. If more than 50% of the stock is held, however, consolidated statements are usually prepared (see SFAS 94).

7. The **cash surrender value** of life insurance policies on key executives is shown in the investment section of the balance sheet.

a. The annual premium for life insurance typically involves an allocation between expense and the cash surrender value (CSV), which is an asset. For the payment of a $1,000 premium, which results in an $800 increase in CSV, the entry is

Life insurance expense	$200	
Cash surrender value	800	
Cash		$1,000

b. If the key executive died shortly after the above entry was made and the company collected $50,000, the entry would be

Cash	$50,000	
Cash surrender value		$ 800
Gain from insurance		49,200

8. Stop and review! You have completed the outline for this subunit. Study multiple-choice questions 54 through 59 beginning on page 195.

E. Property, Plant, and Equipment

1. The costs of fixed assets (plant and equipment) are all costs necessary to acquire these assets and to bring them to the condition and location required for their intended use. These costs include shipping, installation, pre-use testing, sales taxes, interest, etc.

a. All costs of internally constructed assets are usually capitalized. The asset costs should not exceed what the asset could be purchased for; i.e., the cost of the asset is not recorded in excess of fair value.

1) An issue arises as to whether fixed overhead costs should be considered part of the asset cost.

a) Given idle capacity, fixed costs probably should not be included in asset costs.

b) If the construction of the asset displaced other production, the fixed overhead costs should be capitalized.

i) However, the cost of the asset should not exceed fair value.

ii) Any excess cost would be written off in the period of construction as a loss.

b. Criteria must be established to differentiate between capitalizable costs and expense-type costs. If costs are going to benefit more than one period, they should theoretically be capitalized and expensed in the periods they will benefit.

1) Ordinarily, if expenditures are for recurring maintenance, they are expensed.

2) Also, costs below a certain amount, e.g., for wastebaskets, are expensed by most companies.

3) Major asset improvements are usually capitalized.

a) If a major existing section of an asset is rebuilt, replaced, etc., the cost of the improvement is most often capitalized as the full cost of the section, and the remaining book value (original cost minus accumulated depreciation) is expensed as a loss on removal.

c. Under SFAS 116, **contributions received** ordinarily are recognized as assets at fair value and as revenues or gains in the period received.

1) This rule does not apply to tax exemptions, tax incentives, or tax abatements, or to transfers of assets from governmental units to business enterprises. Thus, debiting the donated asset at fair value and crediting donated capital is not contrary to GAAP if the donor is a governmental entity.

2. **APB 29**, *Accounting for Nonmonetary Transactions*, provides that the exchange of similar inventory items or of similar productive assets is not a culmination of an earning process; thus, the exchange of such assets should be recorded at book value.

a. **Monetary assets and liabilities** are assets and liabilities whose amounts are fixed in terms of units of currency by contract or otherwise, e.g., cash, payables. **Nonmonetary items** are all other items.

b. APB 29 **does** apply to nonreciprocal transfers to or from owners and other parties and to nonmonetary exchanges. APB 29 does **not** apply to business combinations, companies under common control, acquisition of assets with stock, and stock dividends or stock splits.

c. Nonmonetary transfers should be accounted for at their fair value.

1) An exception exists when fair value cannot be determined or when the exchange is not the culmination of an earning process, such as the exchange of similar inventory or productive assets.

2) In these cases, no gain is recognized, and the asset received is recorded at the cost or book value of the asset given up. Nevertheless, if a loss is indicated on an exchange of similar nonmonetary items, the entire amount should be recognized. Gain should not be recognized on liquidating distributions to owners.

d. When **boot** (cash) is received in a transaction that is not the culmination of an earning process, a gain may be recognized in the ratio of the cash received to the total consideration received.

1) This ratio multiplied times the total gain (total consideration received minus total book value given up) is the recognized gain.

2) Nevertheless, according to Emerging Issues Task Force Issue 86-29, the foregoing treatment of boot does not apply if it is at least 25% of the fair value of the exchange. In such a transaction, both parties should record a monetary exchange at fair value, with gains and losses recognized in full.

e. Fair value is based on quoted market prices, appraisals, similar transactions, etc.

3. **Depreciation** is the method of allocating costs of fixed assets to subsequent accounting periods that are benefited by the fixed assets. Usually, the cost of a fixed asset minus salvage value (the **depreciation base**) is expensed over the asset's useful life.
   a. In theory, costs of removing the asset should be included in the depreciation base.
   b. The useful life of assets is determined by normal physical usage, normal time of obsolescence, and rapid technological change.
   c. **Amortization** is defined broadly in SFAC 6 as the process of reducing a liability recorded as a result of a cash receipt by recognizing revenues or of reducing an asset recorded as a result of a cash payment by recognizing expenses or costs of production.
      1) Thus, amortization includes depreciation and depletion. Other examples of amortization include expenses for insurance and intangible assets and the recognition of subscriptions revenue.
   d. **Depletion** is amortization of the costs of natural resources.
      1) It is most often based on the number of recoverable units, e.g., tons of coal. Thus, the depletion base (capitalized costs of acquisition, exploration, and development, minus residual value adjusted for restoration costs) is divided by the number of economically recoverable units to determine the depletion rate.
4. **Depreciation Methods**
   a. **Straight-line** depreciation (S-L) allocates the depreciation base evenly over the estimated useful life of an asset.
      1) EXAMPLE: S-L depreciation is calculated by dividing the useful life, e.g., 5 years, into the asset cost, e.g., $9,000, resulting in an annual depreciation charge of $1,800. This calculation assumes that the asset cost $10,000 and had a $1,000 salvage value.
   b. **Declining-balance** depreciation allocates a series of decreasing depreciation charges over the asset's life.
      1) It is an accelerated method because larger amounts are charged in early years of the asset's life.
      2) A percentage (usually 200%, which is called double-declining-balance or DDB) of the straight-line rate is multiplied by the asset's book value each year.
         a) The asset is depreciated until the book value (cost minus accumulated depreciation) is equal to the salvage value.
         b) DDB EXAMPLE: Using the data in the S-L example, twice the straight-line ratio is 40%, which is multiplied times the book value.

Year	Book Value	Depreciation
1	$10,000	$4,000
2	6,000	2,400
3	3,600	1,440
4	2,160	864
5	1,296	296

(Not below salvage value)

c. **Sum-of-the-years'-digits** (SYD) is another accelerated depreciation method that gives results similar to those of the declining-balance method. The depreciation base is allocated based on a fraction.

1) The numerator is the years remaining in the asset's life.

2) The denominator is the sum of all the years in an asset's life.

3) EXAMPLE: Using the S-L example in 4.a. on the previous page, the sum of years 1 through 5 is 15 (1 + 2 + 3 + 4 + 5), and the depreciation base is $9,000.

Year	Fraction	Depreciation
1	5 ÷ 15	$3,000
2	4 ÷ 15	2,400
3	3 ÷ 15	1,800
4	2 ÷ 15	1,200
5	1 ÷ 15	600

4) For larger numbers, the denominator can be determined by the formula

$$n\left(\frac{n + 1}{2}\right)$$

For n = 7,

$$7\left(\frac{7 + 1}{2}\right) = 28$$

d. **Physical usage** depreciation is an allocation based on a fraction each year.

1) The numerator is the amount used, e.g., hours, miles, etc.

2) The denominator is the total expected usage, e.g., hours, miles, etc.

3) EXAMPLE: If total expected usage is 100,000 miles, 10% of the asset's cost would be expensed in a year when 10,000 miles were driven.

4) This approach is taken for most depletion computations.

e. Other depreciation methods

1) **Replacement**. Original asset cost is kept on the books and the cost of replacing the asset is expensed. It is sometimes used for assets such as utility poles and railroad ties, which are numerous and have long lives and low unit cost. The replacement method is a LIFO concept applied to the accounting for long-lived assets.

2) **Retirement**. Asset cost is expensed when the asset is retired. It is also sometimes used for utility poles and railroad ties. The retirement method is essentially a FIFO approach to accounting for long-lived assets.

3) **Composite and group**. The composite method relates to groups of dissimilar assets with varying useful lives. The group method concerns similar assets. Both methods depreciate a group of assets as if they were a single asset based on a weighted average of their useful lives.

a) Because depreciation applies to the entire group of assets, there are no fully depreciated assets, regardless of their age.

b) When a component asset of the group is disposed of, no gain or loss is recorded regardless of the amount received for the asset. The amount received is a debit, and the original cost of the asset is a credit, with the difference recorded in accumulated depreciation.

c) EXAMPLE: A company bought four similar trucks with an average service life of 5 years at a total cost of $100,000. The four trucks are carried in one asset account, and only one accumulated depreciation account is used for the group. Assuming zero salvage value, the depreciation recorded at the end of the first year is $20,000 ($100,000 ÷ 5). The entry for years 1 and 2 is

Depreciation expense	$20,000	
Accumulated depreciation		$20,000

i) On the first day of year 3, one of the trucks was destroyed. It was uninsured. No loss is recorded.

Accumulated depreciation	$25,000	
Trucks ($100,000 ÷ 4 trucks)		$25,000

ii) At the end of year 3, the balance of the trucks account is only $75,000. The 20% per year depreciation rate is applied, and the depreciation expense on the remaining three trucks is $15,000 (20% x $75,000).

iii) The balance in accumulated depreciation at the end of year 3 is $30,000 ($20,000 + $20,000 – $25,000 + $15,000).

5. **SFAS 121**, *Accounting for the Impairment of Long-Lived Assets and for Long-Lived Assets to Be Disposed Of*, establishes the accounting for the impairment of long-lived assets, certain identifiable intangibles, and goodwill related to assets to be held and used and for long-lived assets and certain identifiable intangibles to be disposed of.

   a. Long-lived assets and certain identifiable intangibles to be held and used should be reviewed for impairment whenever events or changes in circumstances indicate that the carrying amount may not be recoverable. The review for recoverability entails estimating the future cash flows expected from the use and disposal of the asset. If the undiscounted sum of those flows is less than the carrying amount, an impairment loss is recognized. The impairment loss is based on the fair value of the asset.

   b. Long-lived assets and certain identifiable intangibles to be disposed of should be reported at the lower of carrying amount or fair value minus cost to sell, except for assets involved in the disposal of a business segment, which continue to be reported at the lower of carrying amount or net realizable value.

6. **SFAS 34**, *Capitalization of Interest Cost*, requires capitalization of material interest costs for certain assets constructed for internal use and those constructed as discrete units (e.g., real estate projects and ships).

   a. It does not apply to products routinely produced for inventory, assets in use or ready for use, assets not being used or being prepared for use, and idle land.

   b. Because interest cost is an integral part of the total cost of acquiring a qualifying asset, its disposition should be the same as that of other components of asset cost.

c. Interest costs that could have been avoided if the asset had not been constructed should be capitalized.

    1) The capitalization rate is applied to the average accumulated expenditures for the asset during the period to determine the amount capitalized.
    2) An enterprise may use the interest rate on new borrowings for the asset. To the extent average accumulated expenditures exceed new borrowings associated with the asset, a weighted average of the rates on other borrowings must be used.
    3) The interest cost capitalized cannot exceed the amount incurred.

d. The capitalization period begins when the following three conditions are present:

    1) The company has made expenditures for the asset.
    2) Work on the asset is in progress.
    3) Interest cost is incurred.

e. The capitalization period ends when the asset is substantially complete.

7. Stop and review! You have completed the outline for this subunit. Study multiple-choice questions 60 through 79 beginning on page 198.

F. Intangible Assets

1. Intangibles are noncurrent assets that are differentiated from fixed assets because they are nonphysical. However, certain nonphysical assets are not classified as intangibles, e.g., stocks, bonds, prepayments, and accounts receivable. Intangibles often convey a right to do something that gives its holder some form of economic benefit.

    a. Acquired goodwill
    b. Licenses
    c. Patents
    d. Leases and leasehold improvements that cannot be removed
    e. Copyrights
    f. Franchises
    g. Trademarks and trade names
    h. Future advertising benefits
    i. Water rights
    j. Human resources
    k. Mortgage servicing rights

2. Costs of internally developed intangibles that are not specifically identifiable (such as goodwill) are to be expensed when incurred.

3. The costs of intangibles are **amortized** (rather than depreciated or depleted).

    a. The credit is usually directly into the asset account; no accumulated amortization account is used.

4. Acquired goodwill arises from the purchase of another business. It is the excess of cost over the fair value of the net identifiable assets acquired.

5. Under **APB 17**, *Intangible Assets*, all intangibles must be amortized over a period of 40 years or less. The straight-line method should be used unless another method is more appropriate.

    a. For example, the legal duration of a patent is now 20 years, but its amortization period may be much less as a result of obsolescence, contractual agreements, or other factors. Furthermore, the amount amortized includes the initial costs of obtaining the patent and legal fees incurred in a successful defense of the patent.

6. **SFAS 2**, *Accounting for Research and Development Costs*, prescribes accounting for research and development (R&D).
   a. Research is "planned search or critical investigation aimed at discovery of new knowledge with the hope that such knowledge will be useful in developing a new product or service or a new process or technique or in bringing about a significant improvement to an existing product or process."
   b. Development is "the translation of research findings or other knowledge into a plan or design for a new product or process or for a significant improvement to an existing product or process whether intended for sale or use."
   c. All R&D costs should be expensed as incurred, not capitalized as an intangible asset.
      1) Only expenditures for a tangible asset that has an alternative future use may be capitalized (and then must be depreciated to R&D expense as it is used).
   d. The following are examples of activities typically included in R&D unless conducted for others under a contract (reimbursable costs are not expensed):
      1) Laboratory research aimed at discovery of new knowledge
      2) Searching for applications of new research findings or using new technology
      3) Conceptual formulation and design of possible product or process alternatives
      4) Design, construction, and testing of preproduction prototypes and models
   e. The following are examples of activities that typically are not classified as R&D:
      1) Engineering follow-through in an early phase of commercial production
      2) Routine, ongoing efforts to refine, enrich, or otherwise improve upon the qualities of an existing product
      3) Adaptation of an existing capability to a particular requirement or customer's need as part of a continuing commercial activity
      4) Seasonal or routine design changes to existing products
      5) Legal work in connection with patent applications or litigation and the sale or licensing of patents
   f. The statement does not cover R&D costs incurred under a contract for the benefit of others.
      1) If R&D is performed for others, revenues and expenses should be recorded in the traditional manner. This assumes the risk has been transferred to others. If the risk is retained, i.e., if payment for R&D depends on the results, R&D expenditures performed for others should be expensed.
7. Stop and review! You have completed the outline for this subunit. Study multiple-choice questions 80 through 84 beginning on page 205.

MULTIPLE-CHOICE QUESTIONS

A. Cash, Cash Equivalents, and Marketable Securities

1. On a company's December 31, year 1 balance sheet, which of the following items should be included in the amount reported as cash?

I. A check payable to the company, dated January 2, year 2, in payment of a sale made in December year 1.
II. A check drawn on the company's account, payable to a vendor, dated and recorded in the company's books on December 31, year 1 but not mailed until January 10, year 2.

A. I only.

B. II only.

C. I and II only.

D. Neither I nor II.

The correct answer is (B). *(CIA, adapted)*

REQUIRED: The item(s) to be included in the amount reported as cash at year-end.

DISCUSSION: The check payable to the company is dated after the balance sheet date, so the amount of the check should be reported as a receivable in the December 31, year 1 balance sheet. The check drawn on the company's account was dated and recorded in the company books in year 1 but not mailed until after the financial statement date. Thus, the amount of the check should be included in both the amount reported as cash and the amount reported as accounts payable in the company's December 31, year 1 balance sheet. Control of cash requires a proper cutoff of cash receipts and cash disbursements.

Answers (A) and (C) are incorrect because the check payable to the company is a receivable. Answer (D) is incorrect because the check drawn on the company's account was dated and recorded in the company's books in year 1, so it should be included in both the amount reported as cash and the amount reported as accounts payable.

2. The following information pertains to a checking account of a company at July 31:

Balance per bank statement	$40,000
Interest earned for July	100
Outstanding checks	3,000
Customers' checks returned for insufficient funds	1,000
Deposit in transit	5,000

At July 31, the company's correct cash balance is

A. $41,100

B. $41,000

C. $42,100

D. $42,000

The correct answer is (D). *(CIA, adapted)*

REQUIRED: The correct cash balance.

DISCUSSION: The correct cash balance is $42,000 ($40,000 cash balance per bank statement + $5,000 deposit in transit – $3,000 checks outstanding). The $100 interest earned and the $1,000 NSF checks are reflected in the $40,000 bank balance.

Answer (A) is incorrect because $41,100 mistakenly includes the $100 interest and subtracts the $1,000 of NSF checks, amounts already reflected in the bank statement balance. Answer (B) is incorrect because $41,000 is computed by subtracting the $1,000 of NSF checks, an amount already reflected in the bank statement balance. Answer (C) is incorrect because $42,100 includes the $100 interest, an amount already reflected in the bank statement balance.

3. The following information pertains to Grey Co. at December 31, 2000:

Checkbook balance	$12,000
Bank statement balance	16,000
Check drawn on Grey's account, payable to a vendor, dated and recorded 12/31/00 but not mailed until 1/10/01	1,800

On Grey's December 31, 2000 balance sheet, what amount should be reported as cash?

A. $12,000

B. $13,800

C. $14,200

D. $16,000

The correct answer is (B). *(CPA, adapted)*

REQUIRED: The amount of cash that should be reported on the balance sheet.

DISCUSSION: The cash account on the balance sheet should consist of (1) coin and currency on hand, (2) demand deposits (checking accounts), (3) time deposits (savings accounts), and (4) near-cash assets (e.g., deposits in transit or checks written to creditors but not yet mailed). Thus, the cash balance should be $13,800 ($12,000 checkbook balance + $1,800 check drawn but not mailed). The checkbook balance should be used because it more closely reflects the amount of cash that is unrestricted as of the balance sheet date.

Answer (A) is incorrect because $12,000 excludes the check that was recorded but not mailed. Answer (C) is incorrect because $14,200 equals the bank statement balance minus the check not mailed. Answer (D) is incorrect because $16,000 is the bank statement balance.

4. Castillo Co. had the following balances at December 31, 2000:

Cash in checking account	$ 35,000
Cash in money market account	75,000
U.S. Treasury bill, purchased 11/1/2000, maturing 1/31/2001	350,000
U.S. Treasury bill, purchased 12/1/2000, maturing 3/31/2001	400,000

Castillo treats all highly liquid investments with a maturity of three months or less when purchased as cash equivalents. What amount should Castillo report as cash and cash equivalents in its December 31, 2000, balance sheet?

A. $110,000

B. $385,000

C. $460,000

D. $860,000

The correct answer is (C). *(CPA, adapted)*

REQUIRED: The balance of cash and cash equivalents.

DISCUSSION: Cash is an asset that must be readily available for use by the business. It normally consists of (1) coin and currency on hand, (2) demand deposits (checking accounts), (3) time deposits (savings accounts), and (4) near-cash assets (e.g., money market accounts). In this case, cash equivalents include investments with original maturities of 3 months or less. The original maturity is the date on which the obligation becomes due. Accordingly, the amount to be reported as cash and cash equivalents is $460,000 ($35,000 + $75,000 + $350,000).

Answer (A) is incorrect because $110,000 excludes the T-bill maturing on 1/31/2000. Answer (B) is incorrect because $385,000 excludes the cash in the money market account. Answer (D) is incorrect because $860,000 includes the T-bill maturing on 3/31/2000.

Questions 5 through 7 are based on the following information. On January 1, a company establishes a petty cash account and designates one employee as petty cash custodian. The original amount included in the petty cash fund is $500, and it will be used to make small cash disbursements. The fund will be replenished on the first of each month, after the petty cash custodian presents receipts for disbursements to the general cashier. The following disbursements are made in January. The balance in the petty cash box at the end of January is $163.

Office supplies	$173
Postage	112
Entertainment	42

---

5. Who is responsible, at all times, for the amount of the petty cash fund?

A. The president of the company.

B. The general office manager.

C. The general cashier.

D. The petty cash custodian.

The correct answer is (D). *(CIA, adapted)*

REQUIRED: The person responsible for petty cash.

DISCUSSION: The duties of the petty cash custodian include obtaining signed receipts for cash disbursements and requesting reimbursement from the general cashier. Consequently, the petty cash custodian is responsible for the petty cash fund (both cash and signed receipts) at all times.

Answers (A), (B), and (C) are incorrect because the company's president, general office manager, and general cashier are not directly responsible for the amount of the petty cash fund.

6. Which of the following is not an appropriate procedure for controlling the petty cash fund?

A. The petty cash custodian files receipts by category of expenditure after their presentation to the general cashier so that variations in different types of expenditures can be monitored.

B. Surprise counts of the fund are made from time to time by a superior of the petty cash custodian to determine that the fund is being accounted for satisfactorily.

C. The petty cash custodian obtains signed receipts from each individual to whom petty cash is paid.

D. Upon receiving petty cash receipts as evidence of disbursements, the general cashier issues a company check to the petty cash custodian, rather than cash, to replenish the fund.

The correct answer is (A). *(CIA, adapted)*

REQUIRED: The inappropriate procedure for controlling the petty cash fund.

DISCUSSION: It would be inappropriate for the petty cash custodian to retain the petty cash receipts because the receipts could be used for a second reimbursement. The receipts should be canceled or mutilated after submission for reimbursement.

Answer (B) is incorrect because surprise counts may deter fraudulent activity. Answer (C) is incorrect because requiring signed receipts is an appropriate control procedure. The signed receipts provide documentation of cash transactions. Answer (D) is incorrect because reimbursement by company check is an appropriate control procedure. It is unwise to have excessive amounts of cash readily available.

7. The entry required at the end of January is

A. Office supplies expense $173
Postage expense 112
Entertainment expense 42
Cash $327

B. Office supplies expense $173
Postage expense 112
Entertainment expense 42
Petty cash $327

C. Office supplies expense $173
Postage expense 112
Entertainment expense 42
Cash over and short 10
Cash $337

D. Office supplies expense $173
Postage expense 112
Entertainment expense 42
Cash $317
Cash over and short 10

The correct answer is (C). *(CIA, adapted)*

REQUIRED: The entry for petty cash fund disbursements.

DISCUSSION: Each expense item is recognized, cash is credited for the total expenditures plus the cash shortage ($173 + $112 + $42 + $10 = $337), and the discrepancy is debited to the cash over and short account. The discrepancy is the original balance of the fund, minus total documented expenditures, minus the ending balance of the fund ($500 – $327 – $163 = $10).

Answer (A) is incorrect because this entry does not recognize that $10 is missing from the petty cash fund. Answer (B) is incorrect because this entry credits petty cash rather than cash and does not recognize that $10 is missing from the petty cash fund. Answer (D) is incorrect because this entry credits the cash account for the wrong amount ($317 rather than $337) and credits the cash over and short account rather than debiting it.

8. Ral Corp.'s checkbook balance on December 31, 2000 was $5,000. In addition, Ral held the following items in its safe on that date:

Check payable to Ral Corp., dated January 2, 2001, in payment of a sale made in December 2000, not included in December 31 checkbook balance	$2,000
Check payable to Ral Corp., deposited December 15 and included in December 31 checkbook balance, but returned by Bank on December 30 stamped "NSF." The check was redeposited on January 2, 2001 and cleared on January 9.	500
Check drawn on Ral Corp.'s account, payable to a vendor, dated and recorded in Ral's books on December 31, but not mailed until January 10, 2001	300

The proper amount to be shown as cash on Ral's balance sheet at December 31, 2000 is

A. $4,800

B. $5,300

C. $6,500

D. $6,800

The correct answer is (A). *(CPA, adapted)*

REQUIRED: The amount to be recorded as cash on the year-end balance sheet.

DISCUSSION: The December 31 checkbook balance is $5,000. The $2,000 check dated January 2, 2001 is properly not included in this balance because it is not negotiable at year-end. The $500 NSF check should not be included in cash because it is a receivable. The $300 check that was not mailed until January 10 should be added to the balance. This predated check is still within the control of the company and should not decrease the cash account. Consequently, the cash balance to be reported on the December 31, 2000 balance sheet is $4,800.

Balance per checkbook	$5,000
Add: Predated check	300
Deduct: NSF check	(500)
Cash balance 12/31/00	$4,800

Answer (B) is incorrect because $5,300 does not include deduction of the NSF check. Answer (C) is incorrect because $6,500 includes the postdated check but not the predated check. Answer (D) is incorrect because $6,800 includes the postdated check.

B. Receivables

9. Bad debt expense must be estimated in order to satisfy the matching principle when expenses are recorded in the same periods as the related revenues. In estimating the provision for doubtful accounts for a period, companies generally accrue

A. Either an amount based on a percentage of total sales or an amount based on a percentage of accounts receivable after adjusting for any balance in the allowance for doubtful accounts.

B. A percentage of total sales.

C. Either an amount based on a percentage of credit sales or an amount based on a percentage of accounts receivable after adjusting for any balance in the allowance for doubtful accounts.

D. An amount equal to last year's bad debt expense.

The correct answer is (C). *(CMA, adapted)*

REQUIRED: The true statement about the accrual entry for bad debts.

DISCUSSION: The allowance method records bad debt expense systematically as a percentage of either sales or the level of accounts receivable. The latter calculation considers the amount already existing in the allowance account. The credit is to a contra asset (allowance) account. As accounts receivable are written off, they are charged to the allowance account.

Answer (A) is incorrect because credit sales should be used instead of total sales. Answer (B) is incorrect because credit sales are preferred to total sales, and the ending balance in receivables can also be used as the basis for estimating bad debts. Answer (D) is incorrect because each year's bad debt expense should be matched with its revenues.

10. Oxford Company sold $300,000 of its accounts receivables without recourse to a factoring agency. The purchaser assessed a finance charge of 5%. It also retained 5% to cover adjustments (sales returns, discounts, etc.). Oxford should record

A. A debit to cash of $300,000.

B. A credit to accounts receivable of $300,000.

C. A credit to liability on transferred accounts receivable of $300,000.

D. Interest expense of $15,000.

The correct answer is (B). *(Publisher)*

REQUIRED: The journal entry to record a sale of accounts receivable on a nonrecourse basis.

DISCUSSION: The entry to record a nonrecourse sale of receivables is to debit cash for the proceeds of the sale [(100% – 5% – 5%) x $300,000 = $270,000], debit a receivable from the factor for the proceeds retained to cover probable adjustments (5% x $300,000 = $15,000), and credit accounts receivable for the face value of the receivables transferred ($300,000). The difference of $15,000 (the finance charge) is debited to a loss on sale of receivables.

Answer (A) is incorrect because cash is debited for $270,000. Answer (C) is incorrect because the company will have no contingent liability. The accounts were transferred without recourse. Answer (D) is incorrect because the company did not borrow money; it sold an asset. Thus, "interest expense" is not an appropriate term.

Questions 11 through 13 are based on the following information. Madison Corporation uses the allowance method to value its accounts receivable and is making the annual adjustments at fiscal year-end, November 30. The proportion of uncollectible accounts is estimated based on past experience, which indicates 1.5% of net credit sales will be uncollectible. Total sales for the year were $2,000,000 of which $200,000 were cash transactions. Madison has determined that the Norris Corporation accounts receivable balance of $10,000 is uncollectible and will write off this account before year-end adjustments are made. Listed below are Madison's account balances at November 30 prior to any adjustments and the $10,000 write-off.

Sales	$2,000,000
Accounts receivable	750,000
Sales discounts	125,000
Allowance for doubtful accounts	16,500
Sales returns and allowances	175,000
Bad debt expense	0

11. The entry to write off Norris Corporation's accounts receivable balance of $10,000 will

A. Increase total assets and decrease net income.

B. Decrease total assets and net income.

C. Have no effect on total assets and decrease net income.

D. Have no effect on total assets and net income.

The correct answer is (D). *(CMA, adapted)*

REQUIRED: The effect of an entry to write off accounts receivable.

DISCUSSION: If a company uses the allowance method, the write-off of a receivable has no effect on total assets. The journal entry involves a debit to the allowance account (a contra asset) and a credit to accounts receivable (an asset). The net effect is that the asset section is both debited and credited for the same amount. Thus, there will be no effect on either total assets or net income.

Answers (A) and (B) are incorrect because assets and income will be unchanged. Answer (C) is incorrect because income will be unchanged.

12. As a result of the November 30 adjusting entry to provide for bad debts, the allowance for doubtful accounts will

A. Increase by $30,000.

B. Increase by $25,500.

C. Increase by $22,500.

D. Decrease by $22,500.

The correct answer is (C). *(CMA, adapted)*

REQUIRED: The effect on the allowance account of the year-end adjusting entry for bad debt expense.

DISCUSSION: The entry is to debit bad debt expense and credit the allowance account. Net credit sales were $1,500,000 ($1,800,000 – $125,000 of discounts – $175,000 of returns). Thus, the expected bad debt expense is $22,500 (1.5% x $1,500,000). This amount is recorded regardless of the balance remaining in the allowance account from previous periods. The net effect is that the allowance account is increased by $22,500.

Answers (A), (B), and (D) are incorrect because the allowance account is increased by $22,500.

13. After a suggestion from the company's external auditors, Madison wishes to value its accounts receivable using the balance sheet approach. The chart below presents the aging of the accounts receivable subsidiary ledger accounts at November 30.

Account	Total Balance	Less than 60 days	61-90 days	91-120 days	Greater than 120 days
Arcadia	$ 50,000	$ 50,000			
Dawson	128,000	90,000	$ 38,000		
Gracelon	327,000	250,000	77,000		
Prentiss	25,000				$25,000
Strauss	210,000			$210,000	
Total	$740,000	$390,000	$115,000	$210,000	$25,000
% uncollectible		1%	5%	15%	40%

After the entries in questions 11 and 12, the final entry to the related accounts is

A. Debit allowance for doubtful accounts for $22,150, and credit bad debt expense for $22,150.

B. Debit allowance for doubtful accounts for $12,150, and credit sales for $12,150.

C. Credit accounts receivable for $12,150, and debit bad debt expense for $12,150.

D. Credit allowance for doubtful accounts for $22,150, and debit bad debt expense for $22,150.

The correct answer is (D). *(CMA, adapted)*

REQUIRED: The entry needed to change to the balance sheet approach to recording bad debts.

DISCUSSION: The balance sheet approach emphasizes asset valuation. Hence, it determines the amount that should be in the allowance (valuation) account to absorb future bad debts. This process may be accomplished by preparing an aging schedule and multiplying each column by the expected uncollectibility rate.

Receivables	Rate	Expected Bad Debt
$390,000	1%	$ 3,900
115,000	5%	5,750
210,000	15%	31,500
25,000	40%	10,000
		$51,150

Accordingly, the allowance account should have a credit balance of $51,150. After recording the entries in the two preceding questions, the account balance was $29,000 ($16,500 beginning balance – $10,000 written off + $22,500 adjustment). The allowance account should have a $51,150 credit balance. Hence, the necessary correction is to debit bad debt expense and credit (increase) the allowance for $22,150 ($51,150 – $29,000).

Answers (A), (B), and (C) are incorrect because the entry is to debit bad debt expense and credit (increase) the allowance for $22,150.

14. At January 1, 2000, Jamin Co. had a credit balance of $260,000 in its allowance for uncollectible accounts. Based on past experience, 2% of Jamin's credit sales have been uncollectible. During 2000, Jamin wrote off $325,000 of uncollectible accounts. Credit sales for 2000 were $9 million. In its December 31, 2000 balance sheet, what amount should Jamin report as allowance for uncollectible accounts?

A. $115,000

B. $180,000

C. $245,000

D. $440,000

The correct answer is (A). *(CPA, adapted)*

REQUIRED: The allowance for uncollectible accounts.

DISCUSSION: The beginning balance in the allowance account is $260,000, write-offs equal $325,000, and bad debt expense is $180,000 ($9,000,000 x .02). Thus, the ending balance in the allowance account is $115,000.

Allowance		
Write-offs $325,000	$260,000	1/1/00
	180,000	Bad debt expense
	$115,000	12/31/00

Answer (B) is incorrect because $180,000 equals the bad debt expense ($9,000,000 x .02). Answer (C) is incorrect because $245,000 results from debiting $180,000 instead of crediting the allowance account for that amount. Answer (D) is incorrect because $440,000 ignores the write-offs.

15. Ward Co. estimates its uncollectible accounts expense to be 2% of credit sales. Ward's credit sales for 2000 were $1 million. During 2000, Ward wrote off $18,000 of uncollectible accounts. Ward's allowance for uncollectible accounts had a $15,000 balance on January 1, 2000. In its December 31, 2000 income statement, what amount should Ward report as uncollectible accounts expense?

A. $23,000

B. $20,000

C. $18,000

D. $17,000

The correct answer is (B). *(CPA, adapted)*

REQUIRED: The uncollectible accounts expense as a percentage of sales.

DISCUSSION: When bad debt expense is estimated on the basis of net credit sales, a cost (bad debt expense) is being directly associated with a revenue of the period (net credit sales). Thus, uncollectible accounts expense is $20,000 (2% x $1,000,000 credit sales).

Answer (A) is incorrect because $23,000 assumes that $20,000 is the required ending balance in the allowance account (expense = write-offs + the change in the allowance). Answer (C) is incorrect because $18,000 equals the write-offs for 2000. Answer (D) is incorrect because $17,000 is the ending balance in the allowance account.

16. An internal auditor is deriving cash flow data based on an incomplete set of facts. Bad debt expense was $2,000. Additional data for this period follow:

Net income	$100,000
Accounts receivable beginning balance	5,000
Allowance for bad debts beginning balance	(500)
Accounts receivable written off	1,000
Increase in net accounts receivable (after subtraction of allowance for bad debts)	30,000

How much cash was collected this period?

A. $67,000

B. $68,500

C. $68,000

D. $70,000

The correct answer is (D). *(CIA, adapted)*

REQUIRED: The cash collected on accounts receivable.

DISCUSSION: The cash collected equals net income adjusted for the change in net accounts receivable (gross A/R – allowance for bad debts). An increase in net accounts receivable implies that cash collected was less than net income. Hence, cash collected was $70,000 ($100,000 – $30,000 increase in net A/R). Write-offs (debit the allowance, credit A/R) do not affect the computation of cash collected because the allowance and gross accounts receivable are reduced by the same amount. Moreover, recognition of bad debt expense (debit bad debt expense, credit the allowance) is not included in this calculation because it is already reflected in the net accounts receivable balance.

Answer (A) is incorrect because $67,000 results from subtracting the write-offs and the bad debt expense from the sum of net income and beginning net accounts receivable. Answer (B) is incorrect because $68,500 assumes a zero balance in the beginning allowance account and deducts bad debt expense from the sum of net income and beginning net accounts receivable. Answer (C) is incorrect because $68,000 deducts bad debt expense from the sum of net income and beginning net accounts receivable.

17. An analysis of a company's $150,000 accounts receivable at year-end resulted in a $5,000 ending balance for its allowance for uncollectible accounts and a bad debt expense of $2,000. During the past year, recoveries on bad debts previously written off were correctly recorded at $500. If the beginning balance in the allowance for uncollectible accounts was $4,700, what was the amount of accounts receivable written off as uncollectible during the year?

A. $1,200

B. $1,800

C. $2,200

D. $2,800

The correct answer is (C). *(CIA, adapted)*

REQUIRED: The amount of accounts receivable written off during the year.

DISCUSSION: Under the allowance method, uncollectible accounts are written off by a debit to the allowance account and a credit to accounts receivable. The $500 of recovered bad debts is accounted for by a debit to accounts receivable and a credit to the allowance account. The $2,000 bad debt expense is also credited to the allowance account. The amount of accounts receivable written off as uncollectible is $2,200 [$5,000 ending allowance – ($4,700 beginning allowance + $500 recoveries + $2,000 bad debt expense)].

Answer (A) is incorrect because $1,200 results from subtracting the recoveries instead of adding them. Answer (B) is incorrect because $1,800 results from subtracting bad debt expense from the allowance account. Answer (D) is incorrect because $2,800 results from subtracting the recoveries and bad debt expense from the allowance account.

18. A government has just levied $140,000 in taxes and estimates that $14,000 of the taxes will never be collected. The journal entry of the government at the time the taxes are levied is

A.	Tax revenue	$140,000	
	Tax receivable		$140,000
B.	Tax receivable	$140,000	
	Tax revenue		$140,000
C.	Tax revenue	$126,000	
	Allowance for uncollectible taxes	$14,000	
	Tax receivable		$140,000
D.	Tax receivable	$140,000	
	Tax revenue		$126,000
	Allowance for uncollectible taxes		$14,000

The correct answer is (D). *(CIA, adapted)*

REQUIRED: The journal entry required at the time the taxes are levied.

DISCUSSION: Tax receivable is debited for the full amount of the taxes levied. Only the portion of the taxes levied that is expected to be collected is credited to tax revenue. The uncollectible portion is credited to an allowance for uncollectible taxes.

Answer (A) is incorrect because tax receivable should be debited and tax revenue credited. Also, only the portion of the taxes levied that is expected to be collected should be credited to tax revenue, with the remainder credited to an allowance for uncollectible taxes. Answer (B) is incorrect because only the portion of the taxes levied that is expected to be collected should be credited to tax revenue, with the remainder credited to an allowance for uncollectible taxes. Answer (C) is incorrect because tax revenue and allowance for uncollectible taxes are credited and tax receivable is debited.

19. Wren Company had the following account balances at December 31, 2000:

Accounts receivable	$ 900,000
Allowance for doubtful accounts (before any provision for 2000 doubtful accounts expense)	16,000
Credit sales for 2000	1,750,000

Wren is considering the following methods of estimating doubtful accounts expense for 2000:

- Based on credit sales at 2%
- Based on accounts receivable at 5%

What amount should Wren charge to doubtful accounts expense under each method?

	Percentage of Credit Sales	Percentage of Accounts Receivable
A.	$51,000	$45,000
B.	$51,000	$29,000
C.	$35,000	$45,000
D.	$35,000	$29,000

The correct answer is (D). *(CPA, adapted)*

REQUIRED: The amount charged to doubtful accounts expense under each method.

DISCUSSION: Doubtful accounts expense is estimated in two ways. The first, which emphasizes asset valuation, is based on an aging of the receivables to determine the balance in the allowance for uncollectible accounts. Bad debt expense is the amount necessary to adjust the allowance account to this estimated balance. The second, which emphasizes income measurement, recognizes bad debt expense as a percentage of sales. The corresponding credit is to the allowance for uncollectible accounts. Under the first method, if doubtful accounts are estimated to be 5% of gross accounts receivable, the allowance account should have a balance of $45,000 (5% x $900,000), and the entry is to debit doubtful accounts expense and credit the allowance for $29,000 ($45,000 – $16,000 existing balance). Under the second method, bad debt expense is $35,000 (2% x $1,750,000).

Answer (A) is incorrect because $51,000 equals 2% of credit sales plus the balance of the allowance account, and $45,000 equals 5% of gross accounts receivable. Answer (B) is incorrect because $51,000 equals 2% of credit sales plus the balance of the allowance account. Answer (C) is incorrect because $45,000 equals 5% of gross accounts receivable.

20. According to SFAS 48, *Revenue Recognition When Right of Return Exists*, if a company sells its product but gives the buyer the right to return the product, the revenue from the sale will be recognized at the time of the sale only when all of the following conditions have been met except when the

A. Seller's price to the buyer is determinable at the date of the sale.

B. Seller has significant obligations for future performance to help the buyer resell the product.

C. Buyer is obligated to pay the seller and the obligation is not contingent on resale of the product.

D. Buyer's obligation would not be changed in the event of theft of the product.

The correct answer is (B). *(CMA, adapted)*

REQUIRED: The item not a condition allowing a seller to record a sale when a right of return exists.

DISCUSSION: SFAS 48 requires sales revenue and cost of sales to be reduced by expected returns when goods are sold with a right of return. The pronouncement states that the sale may be recognized at the time of sale if all of the following conditions are met: (1) The seller's price is substantially fixed or determinable; (2) the buyer has paid the seller, or the buyer is obligated to pay, and the obligation is not contingent on resale; (3) the buyer's obligation to the seller is unchanged by damage to, or theft or destruction of, the product; (4) the buyer has economic substance apart from the seller; (5) the seller does not have any significant obligations regarding resale of the product by the buyer; and (6) the amount of future returns can be reasonably estimated. Hence, if the seller has significant obligations for future performance to help the buyer resell the product, revenue should not be recorded.

Answers (A), (C), and (D) are incorrect because they are conditions for recognition of a sale.

21. One of the conditions necessary to recognize a transfer of receivables with recourse as a sale is that the

A. Transferee surrenders control of the receivables but retains a beneficial interest.

B. Transferor has the unconstrained right to pledge or exchange the receivables.

C. The transferor is not both entitled and obligated to repurchase the receivables.

D. Transferred assets are isolated from the transferee.

The correct answer is (C). *(CMA, adapted)*

REQUIRED: The condition for recognizing a transfer of receivables with recourse as a sale.

DISCUSSION: The transferor of a financial asset surrenders control and the transaction is treated as a sale only if three conditions are met: (1) The assets have been isolated from the transferor (i.e., they are beyond the reach of the transferor and its creditors); (2) neither a regular transferee nor a holder of a beneficial interest in a qualifying special-purpose entity (e.g., certain trusts) is subject to a condition that both constrains its right to pledge or exchange those interests and provides more than a trivial benefit to the transferor; and (3) the transferor does not maintain effective control over the transferred assets through certain repurchase or redemption agreements or the ability unilaterally to cause the holder to return specific assets (SFAS 140).

Answer (A) is incorrect because the transferor must surrender control. Answer (B) is incorrect because the transferee must have the unconstrained right to pledge or exchange the receivables. Answer (D) is incorrect because the transferred assets must be isolated from the transferor.

22. On March 31, 2000, Vale Co. had an unadjusted credit balance of $1,000 in its allowance for uncollectible accounts. An analysis of Vale's trade accounts receivable at that date revealed the following:

Age	Amount	Estimated Uncollectible
0 - 30 days	$60,000	5%
31 - 60 days	4,000	10%
Over 60 days	2,000	$1,400

What amount should Vale report as allowance for uncollectible accounts in its March 31, 2000 balance sheet?

A. $4,800

B. $4,000

C. $3,800

D. $3,000

The correct answer is (A). *(CPA, adapted)*

REQUIRED: The amount in the allowance for uncollectible accounts based on an aging schedule.

DISCUSSION: The aging schedule determines the balance in the allowance for uncollectible accounts. Of the accounts that are no more than 30 days old, the amount uncollectible is $3,000 ($60,000 x 5%). Accounts that are 31-60 days old and over 60 days old have estimated uncollectible balances of $400 ($4,000 x 10%) and $1,400, respectively. Hence, the amount that should be in the allowance for uncollectible accounts is $4,800 ($3,000 + $400 + $1,400). The $1,000 balance already in the account is disregarded because the aging schedule determines the balance that should be in the account.

Answer (B) is incorrect because $4,000 equals the existing balance plus the estimated uncollectible amount for the newest receivables. Answer (C) is incorrect because $3,800 is the credit to the allowance account. Answer (D) is incorrect because $3,000 is the estimated uncollectible amount for the newest receivables.

23. If a transfer of receivables with recourse qualifies to be recognized as a sale, the proceeds from the sale are

A. Accounted for as a secured borrowing.

B. Recorded at fair value for the assets obtained and liabilities incurred.

C. Recorded at the historical cost of the assets obtained.

D. Reduced by the fair value of the recourse obligation.

The correct answer is (D). *(CMA, adapted)*

REQUIRED: The interest rate used in estimating the selling price of receivables.

DISCUSSION: When a transfer of receivables with recourse meets the criteria to be accounted for as a sale, the proceeds of the sale are reduced by the fair value of the recourse obligation. When the transfer does not meet these criteria, the transfer is accounted for as a secured borrowing.

Answers (A), (B), and (C) are incorrect because the proceeds of the sale are reduced by the fair value of the recourse obligation.

24. A transfer of financial assets should be reported as a sale if certain conditions are met. Which of the following is one of the conditions?

A. Transferees may pledge or exchange the assets.

B. The assets are within the reach of the transferor's creditors.

C. The transferor has an option to repurchase the asset.

D. The transferor receives beneficial interests in the asset as consideration.

The correct answer is (A). *(Publisher)*

REQUIRED: The condition for treating a transfer of financial assets as a sale.

DISCUSSION: The transferor of a financial asset surrenders control and the transaction is treated as a sale only if three conditions are met: (1) The assets have been isolated from the transferor (i.e., they are beyond the reach of the transferor and its creditors); (2) neither a regular transferee nor a holder of a beneficial interest in a qualifying special-purpose entity (e.g., certain trusts) is subject to a condition that both constrains its right to pledge or exchange those interests and provides more than a trivial benefit to the transferor; and (3) the transferor does not maintain effective control over the transferred assets through certain repurchase or redemption agreements or the ability unilaterally to cause the holder to return specific assets (SFAS 140).

Answer (B) is incorrect because the assets should be isolated from the transferor and its creditors. Answer (C) is incorrect because the transferor should not have effective control through repurchase or redemption agreements. Answer (D) is incorrect because the transfer is a sale only to the extent the transferor receives consideration other than beneficial interests.

25. A company offers its customers credit terms of a 2% discount if paid within 10 days, or the full balance is due within 30 days (2/10, n/30). If some customers take advantage of the cash discount and others do not, which of the following accounts will appear on the income statement if the net method of recording receivables is employed?

	Sales Discounts	Sales Discounts Forfeited
A.	Yes	Yes
B.	Yes	No
C.	No	No
D.	No	Yes

The correct answer is (D). *(CIA, adapted)*

REQUIRED: The account(s) appearing on the income statement if the net method is used.

DISCUSSION: The gross method accounts for receivables at their face value. If a discount is taken, a sales discount is recorded and classified as an offset to sales in the income statement to yield net sales. The net method records receivables net of the applicable discount. If the payment is not received during the discount period, an interest revenue account, such as sales discounts forfeited, is credited at the end of the discount period or when the payment is received. Accordingly, the application of the net method requires a sales discount forfeited but not a sales discount account.

Answers (A), (B), and (C) are incorrect because the net method requires a sales discount forfeited but not a sales discount account.

C. Inventories

26. The following inventory valuation errors have been discovered for Knox Corporation:

- The year 1 year-end inventory was overstated by $23,000.
- The year 2 year-end inventory was understated by $61,000.
- The year 3 year-end inventory was understated by $17,000.

The reported income before taxes for Knox was

Year	Income before Taxes
Year 1	$138,000
Year 2	254,000
Year 3	168,000

Reported income before taxes for year 1, year 2, and year 3, respectively, should have been

A. $161,000, $170,000, and $212,000.

B. $115,000, $338,000, and $124,000.

C. $161,000, $338,000, and $90,000.

D. $115,000, $338,000, and $212,000.

The correct answer is (B). *(CMA, adapted)*

REQUIRED: The reported income after correction of inventory errors.

DISCUSSION: Cost of sales equals beginning inventory, plus purchases or cost of goods manufactured, minus ending inventory. Hence, over (under) statement of inventory affects cost of sales and income. The year 1 pretax income was affected by the $23,000 year 1 overstatement of year-end inventory. This error understated year 1 cost of sales and overstated pretax income. The corrected income is $115,000 ($138,000 – $23,000). The same $23,000 error caused year 2 income to be understated by overstating beginning inventory. In addition, the $61,000 understatement of year 2 year-end inventory also caused year 2 income to be understated. Thus, the corrected year 2 pretax income is $338,000 ($254,000 + $23,000 + $61,000). The $61,000 understatement at the end of year 2 caused year 3 income to be overstated by understating beginning inventory. Income for year 3 is understated by the $17,000 of year-end inventory understatement. Accordingly, the corrected income is $124,000 ($168,000 – $61,000 + $17,000).

Answer (A) is incorrect because year 1 income of $161,000 results from adding, not subtracting, the $23,000 overstatement of ending inventory. Similarly, year 2 income of $170,000 results from subtracting, not adding, the $23,000 overstatement of beginning inventory and the $61,000 understatement of ending inventory. Finally, year 3 income of $212,000 results from adding, not subtracting, the $61,000 understatement of beginning inventory and subtracting, not adding, the understatement of ending inventory. Answer (C) is incorrect because year 3 income of $90,000 results from subtracting, not adding, the $17,000 understatement of ending inventory. Answer (D) is incorrect because year 3 pre-tax income should be $124,000.

27. All sales and purchases for the year at Ross Corporation are credit transactions. Ross uses a perpetual inventory system. During the year, it shipped certain goods that were correctly excluded from ending inventory although the sale was not recorded. Which one of the following statements is correct?

A. Accounts receivable was not affected, inventory was not affected, sales were understated, and cost of goods sold was understated.

B. Accounts receivable was understated, inventory was not affected, sales were understated, and cost of goods sold was understated.

C. Accounts receivable was understated, inventory was overstated, sales were understated, and cost of goods sold was overstated.

D. Accounts receivable was understated, inventory was not affected, sales were understated, and cost of goods sold was not affected.

The correct answer is (D). *(CMA, adapted)*

REQUIRED: The effect on various related accounts resulting from a failure to record a sale when goods are shipped.

DISCUSSION: The failure to record a sale means that both accounts receivable and sales will be understated. However, inventory was correctly counted, so that account and cost of goods sold were unaffected.

Answer (A) is incorrect because accounts receivable was understated and cost of goods sold was unaffected. Answer (B) is incorrect because cost of goods sold was unaffected. Answer (C) is incorrect because inventory and cost of goods sold were unaffected.

28. During the year 1 year-end physical inventory count at Tequesta Corporation, $40,000 worth of inventory was counted twice. Assuming that the year 2 year-end inventory was correct, the result of the year 1 error was that

A. Year 1 retained earnings was understated, and year 2 ending inventory was correct.

B. Year 1 cost of goods sold was overstated, and year 2 income was understated.

C. Year 1 income was overstated, and year 2 ending inventory was overstated.

D. Year 1 cost of goods sold was understated, and year 2 retained earnings was correct.

The correct answer is (D). *(CMA, adapted)*

REQUIRED: The effect on year 1 and year 2 financial statements of a year 1 overstatement of inventory.

DISCUSSION: The overstatement (double counting) of inventory at the end of year 1 caused year 1 cost of goods sold (BI + Purchases – EI) to be understated and both inventory and income to be overstated. The year 1 ending inventory equals year 2 beginning inventory. Thus, the same overstatement caused year 2 beginning inventory and cost of goods sold to be overstated and income to be understated. This is an example of a self-correcting error; by the end of year 2, the balance sheet is correct.

Answer (A) is incorrect because the year 1 overstatement in inventory caused income and retained earnings to be overstated. Answer (B) is incorrect because year 1 costs were understated given that inventory was overstated. Answer (C) is incorrect because the year 2 ending inventory was given as correct.

29. An item of inventory purchased in year 1 for $25.00 has been incorrectly written down to a current replacement cost of $17.50. The item is currently selling in year 2 for $50.00, its normal selling price. Which one of the following statements is correct?

A. The income for year 1 is overstated.

B. The cost of sales for year 2 will be overstated.

C. The income for year 2 will be overstated.

D. The closing inventory of year 1 is overstated.

The correct answer is (C). *(CMA, adapted)*

REQUIRED: The effect of an inventory understatement.

DISCUSSION: Because the inventory was written down incorrectly, the ending inventory value will be understated at the end of year 1. The understatement in ending inventory causes cost of goods sold to be overstated. The overstatement in cost of goods sold causes year 1 income to be understated. Conversely, the understatement in year 2 beginning inventory causes cost of goods sold for year 2 to be understated and income to be overstated.

Answer (A) is incorrect because the year 1 income will be understated as a result of the understatement in ending inventory. Answer (B) is incorrect because the cost of goods sold for year 1 will be overstated, therefore causing the year 2 cost of goods sold to be understated. Answer (D) is incorrect because the closing inventory for year 1 will be understated since the inventory will be valued at $17.50 instead of the $25 correct figure.

30. All sales and purchases for the year at Ross Corporation are credit transactions. Ross shipped goods via FOB shipping point. In error, the goods were not recorded as a sale and were included in ending inventory. Which one of the following statements is correct?

A. Accounts receivable was not affected, inventory was overstated, sales were understated, and cost of goods sold was understated.

B. Accounts receivable was understated, inventory was not affected, sales were understated, and cost of goods sold was understated.

C. Accounts receivable was understated, inventory was overstated, sales were understated, and cost of goods sold was overstated.

D. Accounts receivable was understated, inventory was overstated, sales were understated, and cost of goods sold was understated.

The correct answer is (D). *(CMA, adapted)*

REQUIRED: The impact on various related accounts resulting from a failure to record a sale shipped FOB shipping point.

DISCUSSION: The term "FOB shipping point" means that title passes to the buyer at the time and place of shipment. Thus, a sale should have been recorded at the time the goods were shipped. The result is that accounts receivable and sales will be understated since no entry was recorded. At the same time, inventory will be overstated since the goods that have been sold are still included in inventory. The overstatement in ending inventory will cause the cost of goods sold to be understated on the income statement.

Answer (A) is incorrect because accounts receivable will be understated. Answer (B) is incorrect because inventory will be overstated. Answer (C) is incorrect because cost of goods sold will be understated due to the overstatement in inventory.

Questions 31 through 35 are based on the following information. Thomas Engine Company is a wholesaler of marine engine parts. The activity of carburetor 2642J during the month of March is presented below.

Date	Balance or Transaction	Units	Unit Cost	Unit Sales Price
March 1	Inventory	3,200	$64.30	$86.50
4	Purchase	3,400	64.75	87.00
14	Sales	3,600		87.25
25	Purchase	3,500	66.00	87.25
28	Sales	3,450		88.00

31. If Thomas uses a first-in, first-out perpetual inventory system, the total cost of the inventory for carburetor 2642J at March 31 is

A. $196,115

B. $197,488

C. $201,300

D. $263,825

The correct answer is (C). *(CMA, adapted)*

REQUIRED: The total cost of inventory at March 31 under the FIFO perpetual method.

DISCUSSION: The company began March with 3,200 units in inventory at $64.30 each. The March 4 purchase added 3,400 additional units at $64.75 each. Under the FIFO assumption, the 3,600 units sold on March 14 were the oldest units. That sale eliminated all of the 3,200 units priced at $64.30 and 400 of the units priced at $64.75, leaving an inventory of 3,000 units at $64.75 prior to the March 25 purchase. On March 25, 3,500 units were acquired at $66. The 3,450 units sold on March 28 were the 3,000 remaining units priced at $64.75 and 450 units priced at $66. Therefore, the ending inventory consists of 3,050 units at $66 each, or $201,300. Note that the answer would have been the same under the periodic FIFO method.

Answer (A) is incorrect because $196,115 is the answer under the periodic LIFO method. Answer (B) is incorrect because $197,488 is the answer under the LIFO method using the $64.75 cost of the March 4 purchase (instead of the beginning inventory cost). Answer (D) is incorrect because $263,825 is based on the $86.50 selling price at March 1, not the cost of the items.

32. If Thomas uses a last-in, first-out periodic inventory system, the total cost of the inventory for carburetor 2642J at March 31 is

A. $196,115

B. $197,488

C. $201,300

D. $268,400

The correct answer is (A). *(CMA, adapted)*

REQUIRED: The total cost of inventory at March 31 under the LIFO periodic method.

DISCUSSION: The ending inventory consists of 3,050 units (beginning inventory plus purchases, minus sales). Under the periodic LIFO method, those units are valued at the oldest prices for the period, which is $64.30 of the beginning inventory. Multiplying $64.30 times 3,050 units produces a total inventory value of $196,115.

Answer (B) is incorrect because $197,488 is the answer under the LIFO method but is based on the $64.75 cost of the March 4 purchase, instead of the beginning inventory cost. Answer (C) is incorrect because $201,300 is based on the FIFO method. Answer (D) is incorrect because $268,400 is based on the $88 selling price at the end of the month, not the cost.

33. If Thomas uses a last-in, first-out perpetual inventory system, the total cost of the inventory for carburetor 2642J at March 31 is

A. $196,200

B. $197,488

C. $263,863

D. $268,400

The correct answer is (A). *(CMA, adapted)*

REQUIRED: The value of the ending inventory using the perpetual LIFO method.

DISCUSSION: Under the perpetual LIFO method, the company begins with 3,200 units at $64.30. To this is added the March 4 purchase of 3,400 units at $64.75. The March 14 sale uses all of the March 4 purchase and 200 of the original inventory units. Thus, the firm is left with 3,000 units at $64.30. The March 25 purchase of 3,500 at $66 is added to the previous 3,000 units. The March 28 sale of 3,450 units comes entirely from the March 25 purchase, leaving just 50 of those units at $66 each. Thus, at the end of the month, the inventory consists of two layers: 3,000 units at $64.30, or $192,900, and 50 units at $66, or $3,300. Adding the two layers together produces a total ending inventory of $196,200.

Answer (B) is incorrect because $197,488 is the answer under the periodic LIFO method but is based on the $64.75 cost of the March 4 purchase. Answer (C) is incorrect because $263,863 is based on the $86.50 selling price at March 1, not the cost of the items. Answer (D) is incorrect because $268,400 is based on the $88 selling price at the end of the month, not the cost.

34. If Thomas uses a weighted-average periodic inventory system, the total cost of the inventory for carburetor 2642J at March 31 is

A. $194,200

B. $198,301

C. $198,374

D. $199,233

The correct answer is (C). *(CMA, adapted)*

REQUIRED: The value of the March 31 inventory under the weighted-average method of calculation.

DISCUSSION: Under the weighted-average method, all inventory available for sale during the period is weighted, as follows, to determine the average cost per unit:

3,200 @ $64.30	=	$205,760
3,400 @ $64.75	=	220,150
3,500 @ $66.00	=	231,000
Total 10,100	=	$656,910

Dividing the $656,910 total cost by the 10,100 available units produces an average unit cost of $65.04059. Multiplying the unit cost times the 3,050 units in ending inventory produces a total value at March 31 of $198,374.

Answer (A) is incorrect because $194,200 ignores the March 25 purchase. Answer (B) is incorrect because $198,301 is based on the unweighted average of the three unit purchase prices. Answer (D) is incorrect because $199,233 is based on a perpetual moving average, not a periodic weighted average.

35. Refer to the information preceding question 31 on page 186. If Thomas uses a moving-average perpetual inventory system, the total cost of the inventory for carburetor 2642J at March 31 is

A. $194,200

B. $198,301

C. $199,233

D. $265,960

The correct answer is (C). *(CMA, adapted)*

REQUIRED: The March 31 inventory valuation using the perpetual moving-average basis.

DISCUSSION: Under the perpetual moving-average method, the inventory is revalued after every purchase and sale. The unit cost will change after every purchase. The calculations for the first purchase are as follows:

	3,200 @ $64.30	=	$205,760
	3,400 @ $64.75	=	220,150
Total	6,600	=	$425,910

The unit cost of $64.531818 was calculated by dividing the total inventory value of $425,910 by the 6,600 units. After selling 3,600 units on March 14, the company would be left with 3,000 units at $64.531818, or $193,595.45. This amount is added to the next purchase on March 25:

	3,000 @ $64.531818	=	$193,595.45
	3,500 @ $66.00	=	231,000.00
Total	6,500	=	$424,595.45

The unit cost of $65.322376 was calculated by dividing the $424,595.45 of total cost by the 6,500 available units. Deducting the 3,450 units sold on March 28 leaves 3,050 ending units at $65.322376 each, for a total cost of $199,233.

Answer (A) is incorrect because $194,200 ignores the March 25 purchase. Answer (B) is incorrect because $198,301 is based on the unweighted average of the three unit purchase prices. Answer (D) is incorrect because $265,960 is based on selling prices, not cost.

Questions 36 and 37 are based on the following information. Jensen Company uses a perpetual inventory system. The following purchases and sales were made during the month of May:

Date	Activity	Description
May 1	Balance	100 units at $10 per unit
May 9	Purchase	200 units at $10 per unit
May 16	Sale	190 units
May 21	Purchase	150 units at $12 per unit
May 29	Sale	120 units

36. If Jensen Company uses the first-in, first-out (FIFO) method of inventory valuation, the May 31 inventory would be

A. $1,400

B. $1,460

C. $1,493

D. $1,680

The correct answer is (D). *(CMA, adapted)*

REQUIRED: The inventory under the FIFO method.

DISCUSSION: The FIFO assumption is that the first units purchased are the first sold, so the ending inventory consists of the most recent units purchased. Thus, ending inventory consists of 140 units (100 beginning balance + 200 purchased – 190 sold + 150 purchased – 120 sold) from the May 21 purchase of 150 units. Its value is $1,680 ($12 x 140). Under FIFO, the inventory value is the same regardless of whether the inventory system is perpetual or periodic.

Answer (A) is incorrect because $1,400 is the value under periodic LIFO. Answer (B) is incorrect because $1,460 is the value under perpetual LIFO. Answer (C) is incorrect because $1,493 is the value under the weighted-average method.

37. If Jensen Company uses the last-in, first-out (LIFO) method of inventory valuation, the May 31 inventory would be

A. $1,400

B. $1,460

C. $1,493

D. $1,562

The correct answer is (B). *(CMA, adapted)*

REQUIRED: The inventory under perpetual LIFO.

DISCUSSION: The LIFO assumption is that the last items purchased are the first sold. Moreover, the inventory value must be recalculated after each purchase and sale of merchandise when the perpetual LIFO method is used. After the May 16 sale, the company held 110 units (100 beginning balance + 200 May 9 purchase – 190 May 16 sale) at a unit cost of $10. The May 21 purchase created a layer of 150 units at $12 per unit. Because the May 29 sale of 120 units is deemed to have come entirely from the layer created on May 21, the ending inventory of 140 units has two layers: 110 units at $10 and 30 units at $12. Ending inventory is therefore $1,460 [(110 x $10) + (30 x $12)].

Answer (A) is incorrect because $1,400 is the value under periodic LIFO. Answer (C) is incorrect because $1,493 is the value under the weighted-average method. Answer (D) is incorrect because $1,562 is the value under the moving-average method.

38. The following FCL Corporation inventory information is available for the year ended December 31:

	Cost	Retail
Beginning inventory at 1/1	$35,000	$100,000
Net purchases	55,000	110,000
Net markups		15,000
Net markdowns		25,000
Net sales		150,000

The December 31 ending inventory at cost using the conventional (lower of average cost or market) retail inventory method equals

A. $17,500

B. $20,000

C. $27,500

D. $50,000

The correct answer is (B). *(CMA, adapted)*

REQUIRED: The ending inventory using the conventional retail inventory method.

DISCUSSION: The conventional retail inventory method adds beginning inventory, net purchases, and markups (but not markdowns) to calculate a cost percentage. The purpose of excluding markdowns is to approximate a lower-of-average-cost-or-market valuation. The cost percentage is then used to reduce the retail value of the ending inventory to cost. FCL's cost-retail ratio is 40% ($90,000 ÷ $225,000), and ending inventory at cost is therefore $20,000 (40% x $50,000 ending inventory at retail).

	Cost	Retail
Beginning inventory	$35,000	$ 100,000
Purchases	55,000	110,000
Markups		15,000
Total goods available	$90,000	$ 225,000
Sales		(150,000)
Markdowns		(25,000)
Calculated retail value of ending inventory		$ 50,000

Answer (A) is incorrect because $17,500 is the ending inventory based on LIFO retail. Answer (C) is incorrect because $27,500 is based on FIFO retail. Answer (D) is incorrect because $50,000 is the ending inventory at retail.

39. Walt Co. adopted the dollar-value LIFO inventory method as of January 1, 2000, when its inventory was valued at $500,000. Walt's entire inventory constitutes a single pool. Using a relevant price index of 1.10, Walt determined that its December 31, 2000 inventory was $577,500 at current-year cost, and $525,000 at base-year cost. What was Walt's dollar-value LIFO inventory at December 31, 2000?

A. $525,000

B. $527,500

C. $552,500

D. $577,500

The correct answer is (B). *(CPA, adapted)*

REQUIRED: The dollar-value LIFO inventory cost reported in the balance sheet.

DISCUSSION: A price index for the current year may be calculated by dividing the ending inventory at current-year cost by the ending inventory at base-year cost. This index is then applied to the current-year inventory layer stated at base-year cost. Consequently, the index for 2000 is 1.1 ($577,500 ÷ $525,000), and the dollar-value LIFO cost at December 31, 2000 is $527,500 [$500,000 base layer + 1.1($525,000 – $500,000)].

Answer (A) is incorrect because $525,000 is the base-year cost. Answer (C) is incorrect because $552,500 results from using $525,000 as the base layer. Answer (D) is incorrect because $577,500 is the year-end inventory at current cost.

Questions 40 through 45 are based on the following information. Farmers' Supply Company is a wholesaler of tractor parts. The activity of a particular type of mower blade during the month of May is presented below:

Date	Activity	Units	Unit Cost	Unit Sales Price
May 1	Beginning inventory	6,400	$64.30	$86.50
May 4	Purchase	6,800	$64.75	87.00
May 13	Sales	7,200		87.25
May 24	Purchase	7,000	$66.00	87.25
May 27	Sales	6,900		88.00

40. If Farmers' uses a first-in, first-out (FIFO) perpetual inventory system, the total cost of the inventory for mower blades at May 31 is

A. $392,230

B. $394,975

C. $402,600

D. $536,800

The correct answer is (C). *(Publisher)*

REQUIRED: The total cost of inventory at May 31 under the FIFO perpetual method.

DISCUSSION: The available inventory consisted of 20,200 units (6,400 BI + 6,800 May 4 purchase + 7,000 May 24 purchase), and 14,100 units (7,200 May 13 sale + 6,900 May 27 sale) were sold. Hence, ending inventory consists of 6,100 units. Under a FIFO assumption, these units are deemed to be from the last purchase. The value of the ending inventory is therefore $402,600 (6,100 units x $66 unit cost of the May 24 purchase). The answer would have been the same in a periodic system, a statement that cannot be made for other inventory flow assumptions.

Answer (A) is incorrect because $392,230 is the inventory under the periodic LIFO method. Answer (B) is incorrect because $394,975 is the inventory under the periodic LIFO method using the $64.75 cost of the May 4 purchase. Answer (D) is incorrect because $536,800 is based on the $88 selling price at the end of the month.

41. If Farmers' uses a first-in, first-out (FIFO) periodic inventory system, the total cost of the inventory for mower blades at May 31 is

A. $392,230

B. $394,975

C. $402,600

D. $536,800

The correct answer is (C). *(Publisher)*

REQUIRED: The total cost of inventory at May 31 under the FIFO periodic method.

DISCUSSION: The available inventory consisted of 20,200 units (6,400 BI + 6,800 May 4 purchase + 7,000 May 24 purchase), and 14,100 units (7,200 May 13 sale + 6,900 May 27 sale) were sold. Hence, ending inventory consists of 6,100 units. Under a FIFO assumption, these units are deemed to be from the last purchase. The value of the ending inventory is therefore $402,600 (6,100 units x $66 unit cost of the May 24 purchase). The answer would have been the same in a perpetual system, a statement that cannot be made for other inventory flow assumptions.

Answer (A) is incorrect because $392,230 is the inventory under the periodic LIFO method. Answer (B) is incorrect because $394,975 is the inventory under the periodic LIFO method using the $64.75 cost of the May 4 purchase. Answer (D) is incorrect because $536,800 is based on the $88 selling price at the end of the month.

42. If Farmers' uses a last-in, first-out (LIFO) periodic inventory system, the total cost of the inventory for mower blades at May 31 is

A. $392,230

B. $394,975

C. $402,600

D. $536,800

The correct answer is (A). *(Publisher)*

REQUIRED: The total cost of inventory at May 31 under the LIFO periodic method.

DISCUSSION: The ending inventory consists of 6,100 units (beginning inventory + purchases – sales). Under the periodic LIFO method, ending inventory is deemed to come from the beginning 6,400-unit inventory priced at $64.30 per unit. Thus, the inventory value is $392,230 (6,100 x $64.30).

Answer (B) is incorrect because $394,975 is based on the $64.75 cost of the March 4 purchase. Answer (C) is incorrect because $402,600 is based on the FIFO method. Answer (D) is incorrect because $536,800 is based on the $88 selling price at the end of the month.

43. If Farmers' uses a last-in, first out (LIFO) perpetual inventory system, the total cost of the inventory for mower blades at May 31 is

A. $392,230

B. $392,400

C. $394,975

D. $402,600

The correct answer is (B). *(Publisher)*

REQUIRED: The value of the ending inventory using the perpetual LIFO method.

DISCUSSION: Under perpetual LIFO, the 7,200-unit sale on May 13 is deemed to have eliminated the 6,800-unit layer acquired on May 4 and to have reduced the 6,400-unit May 1 layer to 6,000 units. The 6,900-unit sale on May 27 reduced the 7,000-unit May 24 layer to 100 units. The ending inventory therefore has two layers under LIFO periodic: 6,000 units at $64.30 per unit and 100 units at $66.00 per unit, a total of $392,400.

Answer (A) is incorrect because $392,230 is the inventory under the LIFO periodic method. Answer (C) is incorrect because $394,975 is based on the $64.75 cost of the May 4 purchase. Answer (D) is incorrect because $402,600 is based on the FIFO method.

44. At May 31, if Farmers' uses a weighted-average periodic inventory system, the total cost of the inventory for mower blades (assuming all calculations are rounded to two decimal places) is

A. $393,633

B. $396,622

C. $396,744

D. $398,467

The correct answer is (C). *(Publisher)*

REQUIRED: The May 31 inventory under the weighted-average method.

DISCUSSION: Under the weighted-average periodic method, all inventory available for sale during the period is weighted to determine the average cost per unit.

6,400	×	$64.30	=	$ 411,520
6,800	×	$64.75	=	440,300
7,000	×	$66.00	=	462,000
20,200				$1,313,820

Thus, the weighted-average unit cost (rounded) is $65.04 ($1,313,820 ÷ 20,200 units). The total value at March 31 is therefore $396,744 ($65.04 x 6,100 units).

Answer (A) is incorrect because $393,633 is based on the amount of the weighted-average unit cost immediately after the May 4 purchase. Answer (B) is incorrect because $396,622 is based on the unweighted average of the three unit purchase prices. Answer (D) is incorrect because $398,467 is based on a perpetual moving average.

45. At May 31, if Farmers' uses a moving-average perpetual inventory system, the total cost of the inventory for mower blades (assuming all calculations are rounded to two decimal places) is

A. $393,633

B. $396,622

C. $396,744

D. $398,452

The correct answer is (D). *(Publisher)*

REQUIRED: The May 31 inventory valuation using the perpetual moving-average method.

DISCUSSION: Under the perpetual moving-average method, the inventory is revalued after every purchase and sale. The calculations for the first purchase are as follows:

Units		Unit Cost		
6,400	×	$64.30	=	$411,520
6,800	×	$64.75	=	440,300
13,200			=	$851,820

The unit cost is $64.53 (rounded) ($851,820 ÷ 13,200 units). After selling 7,200 units on May 13, the company had 6,000 units at $64.53, or $387,180. This amount is added to the next purchase on May 25:

6,000	×	$64.53	=	$387,180
7,000	×	$66.00	=	462,000
13,000			=	$849,180

The unit cost is $65.32 (rounded) ($849,180 ÷ 13,000 units). Subtracting the 6,900 units sold on May 27 leaves 6,100 units at $65.32 each, or $398,452.

Answer (A) is incorrect because $393,633 is based on the amount of the weighted-average unit cost immediately after the May 4 purchase. Answer (B) is incorrect because $396,622 is based on the unweighted average of the three unit purchase prices. Answer (C) is incorrect because $396,744 is based on a periodic weighted average.

Questions 46 and 47 are based on the following information. Price's Food Market adopted the dollar-value LIFO method of inventory valuation at December 31, year 1. Inventory balances and price indices are shown below:

December 31	Ending Inventory at End-of-Year Prices	Price Index at December 31
Year 1	$480,000	1.00
Year 2	550,000	1.10
Year 3	600,000	1.20

46. Price's Food Market's ending inventory as of December 31, year 2, computed by the dollar-value LIFO method, was

A. $480,000

B. $500,000

C. $502,000

D. $550,000

The correct answer is (C). *(Publisher)*

REQUIRED: The inventory under the dollar-value LIFO method for year 2.

DISCUSSION: The year 2 ending inventory must be converted into base-year prices by dividing it by the year 2 price index of 1.10, resulting in an inventory value of $500,000 ($550,000 ÷ 1.10) at base-year prices. This amount consists of two layers: $480,000 purchased during the base year and $20,000 acquired in year 2. The latter amount must be converted back into year-end prices because the merchandise was not purchased during the base year. Accordingly, this $20,000 increment is multiplied by the price index for the current year. The result is an increment of $22,000 ($20,000 x 1.10). The total inventory is $502,000 ($480,000 + $22,000).

Answer (A) is incorrect because $480,000 is the inventory at the end of year 1. Answer (B) is incorrect because $500,000 is the year 2 inventory at base-year prices. Answer (D) is incorrect because $550,000 is the value at year-end prices.

47. Price's Food Market's ending inventory as of December 31, year 3, computed by the dollar-value LIFO method, is

A. $480,000

B. $500,000

C. $502,000

D. $600,000

The correct answer is (C). *(Publisher)*

REQUIRED: The inventory under the dollar-value LIFO method for year 3.

DISCUSSION: The ending inventory at year-end prices must be converted into base-year prices by dividing it by the year 3 price index of 1.20, resulting in an inventory value of $500,000 ($600,000 ÷ 1.20) at base-year prices. This amount is the same as the inventory for year 2 at base-year prices (see the solution to the previous question). Thus, no increment was added during year 3. Consequently, the ending inventory for year 3 is the same as at the end of year 2, or $502,000. This amount consists of $480,000 of inventory purchased in year 1 and $22,000 purchased in year 2. Under LIFO, the assumption is that nothing is still on hand from year 3 purchases because the inventory is the same as at the end of the preceding year.

Answer (A) is incorrect because $480,000 was the inventory at the end of year 1. Answer (B) is incorrect because $500,000 is the year 3 inventory at base-year prices. Answer (D) is incorrect because $600,000 is the year 3 inventory at year-end prices.

Questions 48 and 49 are based on the following information. During January 2000, Metro Co., which maintains a perpetual inventory system, recorded the following information pertaining to its inventory:

	Units	Unit Cost	Total Cost	Units On Hand
Balance on 1/1/00	1,000	$1	$1,000	1,000
Purchased on 1/7/00	600	3	1,800	1,600
Sold on 1/20/00	900			700
Purchased on 1/25/00	400	5	2,000	1,100

48. Under the moving-average method, what amount should Metro report as inventory at January 31, 2000?

A. $1,300

B. $2,640

C. $3,225

D. $3,900

The correct answer is (C). *(CPA, adapted)*

REQUIRED: The ending inventory using the moving-average method.

DISCUSSION: The moving-average system is only applicable to perpetual inventories. It requires that a new weighted average be computed after every purchase. This moving average is based on remaining inventory held and the new inventory purchased. Based on the calculations below, the moving-average cost per unit for the 1/20/00 sale is $1.75, and the cost of goods sold (CGS) for January is $1,575 ($1.75 x 900 units sold). Thus, ending inventory is $3,225 ($1,000 beginning balance + $1,800 purchase on 1/7/00 – $1,575 CGS on 1/20/00 + $2,000 purchase on 1/25/00).

	Units	Moving-Average Cost/Unit	Total Cost
Balance 1/1	1,000	$1.00	$1,000
Purchase 1/7	600	3.00	1,800
	1,600	$1.75	$2,800

Answer (A) is incorrect because $1,300 is based on the periodic LIFO method. Answer (B) is incorrect because $2,640 is based on the weighted-average method. Answer (D) is incorrect because $3,900 is based on the FIFO method.

49. Under the LIFO method, what amount should Metro report as inventory at January 31, 2000?

A. $3,225

B. $1,300

C. $2,700

D. $3,900

The correct answer is (C). *(CPA, adapted)*

REQUIRED: The value of ending inventory using a perpetual LIFO system.

DISCUSSION: In a perpetual inventory system, purchases are directly recorded in the inventory account, and cost of goods sold (CGS) is determined as the goods are sold. Under LIFO, the latest goods purchased are assumed to be the first to be sold. Using LIFO perpetual, 600 of the 900 units sold on 1/20/00 are assumed to have come from the last purchase. Their cost was $1,800 ($3 x 600). The remaining 300 came from the beginning balance at a cost of $300 ($1 x 300). Hence, the total CGS for January was $2,100, and ending inventory must equal $2,700 ($1,000 beginning inventory + $1,800 purchase on 1/7/00 + $2,000 purchase on 1/25/00 – $2,100 CGS).

Answer (A) is incorrect because $3,225 is based on the moving-average method. Answer (B) is incorrect because $1,300 is based on the periodic LIFO method. Answer (D) is incorrect because $3,900 is based on the periodic FIFO method.

50. Brock Co. adopted the dollar-value LIFO inventory method as of January 1, 1999. A single inventory pool and an internally computed price index are used to compute Brock's LIFO inventory layers. Information about Brock's inventory follows:

	Inventory		
Date	At Base-Year Cost	At Current-Year Cost	At Dollar-Value LIFO
1/1/99	$40,000	$40,000	$40,000
1999 layer	5,000	14,000	6,000
12/31/99	45,000	54,000	46,000
2000 layer	15,000	26,000	?
12/31/00	$60,000	$80,000	?

What was Brock's dollar-value LIFO inventory at December 31, 2000?

A. $80,000

B. $74,000

C. $66,000

D. $60,000

The correct answer is (C). *(CPA, adapted)*

REQUIRED: The year-end dollar-value LIFO inventory.

DISCUSSION: To compute the ending inventory under dollar-value LIFO, the ending inventory stated in year-end or current-year cost must be restated at base-year cost. The layers at base-year cost are computed using a LIFO flow assumption and then weighted (multiplied) by the relevant indexes to price the ending inventory. The relevant price index for the 2000 layer is 1.331/3 ($80,000 current-year cost ÷ $60,000 base-year cost). The 2000 layer at base-year cost is multiplied by this index to translate it to the price in effect when the layer was added. Accordingly, the 2000 layer at dollar-value LIFO is $20,000 (1.331/3 x $15,000), and ending inventory is $66,000 ($46,000 at 12/31/99 + $20,000).

Answer (A) is incorrect because $80,000 is the current-year cost at year-end. Answer (B) is incorrect because $74,000 is the beginning inventory at current-year cost plus the 2000 layer at dollar-value LIFO. Answer (D) is incorrect because $60,000 is the base-year cost at year-end.

51. Based on a physical inventory taken on December 31, 2000, Chewy Co. determined its chocolate inventory on a FIFO basis at $26,000 with a replacement cost of $20,000. Chewy estimated that, after further processing costs of $12,000, the chocolate could be sold as finished candy bars for $40,000. Chewy's normal profit margin is 10% of sales. Under the lower-of-cost-or-market rule, what amount should Chewy report as chocolate inventory in its December 31, 2000 balance sheet?

A. $28,000

B. $26,000

C. $24,000

D. $20,000

The correct answer is (C). *(CPA, adapted)*

REQUIRED: The LCM value of inventory.

DISCUSSION: Market equals current replacement cost subject to maximum and minimum values. The maximum is net realizable value (NRV), and the minimum is NRV minus normal profit. When replacement cost is within this range, it is used as the market value. Cost is given as $26,000. NRV is $28,000 ($40,000 selling price – $12,000 additional processing costs), and NRV minus a normal profit equals $24,000 [$28,000 – (10% x $40,000)]. Because the lowest value in the range ($24,000) exceeds replacement cost ($20,000), it is used as the market value. Because market value ($24,000) is less than cost ($26,000), it is also the inventory valuation.

Answer (A) is incorrect because $28,000 is the NRV. Answer (B) is incorrect because $26,000 is the cost. Answer (D) is incorrect because $20,000 is the replacement cost.

52. The following information is available for the Silver Company for the 3 months ended March 31 of this year:

Merchandise inventory, January 1 of this year	$ 900,000
Purchases	3,400,000
Freight-in	200,000
Sales	4,800,000

The gross margin recorded was 25% of sales. What should be the merchandise inventory at March 31?

A. $700,000

B. $900,000

C. $1,125,000

D. $1,200,000

The correct answer is (B). *(CPA, adapted)*

REQUIRED: The estimated ending inventory using the gross profit method.

DISCUSSION: If the gross profit margin is 25% of sales, cost of goods sold equals 75% of sales. Ending inventory is equal to goods available for sale minus cost of goods sold.

Beginning inventory	$ 900,000
Purchases	3,400,000
Freight-in	200,000
Goods available for sale	$4,500,000
CGS (1 – .25) × ($4,800,000)	(3,600,000)
Ending inventory	$ 900,000

Answer (A) is incorrect because $700,000 does not include freight-in from the calculation. Answer (C) is incorrect because $1,125,000 is 25% of goods available for sale. Answer (D) is incorrect because $1,200,000 is the gross margin.

53. On December 31, 1999, Jason Company adopted the dollar-value LIFO retail inventory method. Inventory data for 2000 are as follows:

	LIFO Cost	Retail
Inventory, 12/31/99	$360,000	$500,000
Inventory, 12/31/00	?	660,000
Increase in price level for 2000		10%
Cost-retail ratio for 2000		70%

Under the dollar-value LIFO retail method, Jason's inventory at December 31, 2000 should be

A. $437,000

B. $462,000

C. $472,000

D. $483,200

The correct answer is (A). *(CPA, adapted)*

REQUIRED: The ending inventory under the dollar-value LIFO retail inventory method.

DISCUSSION: The ending inventory at retail end-of-year prices must first be transformed to ending inventory at retail base year prices to determine whether a liquidation has occurred or a layer has been added. The layers are then restated by multiplying each by its specific price index. Finally, these amounts are transformed from retail prices to estimated cost prices by multiplying the layers by the appropriate cost-retail ratios. The 12/31/00 inventory in base year (1999) prices is $600,000 ($660,000 ÷ 1.10). Thus, a $100,000 layer was added in 2000.

Layers at Retail		Specific Price Index		Cost-Retail Ratio		Layers at Cost
$500,000	×	1.0	×	($360 ÷ $500)	=	$360,000
$100,000	×	1.1	×	70%	=	77,000
Ending inventory						$437,000

Answer (B) is incorrect because $462,000 equals 70% of inventory on 12/31/00. Answer (C) is incorrect because $472,000 assumes the 2000 layer is $160,000 and that no price-index adjustment is made. Answer (D) is incorrect because $483,200 assumes the 2000 layer is $160,000.

D. Investments (Current and Long-Term)

54. An investment in trading securities is valued on the statement of financial position at the

A. Cost to acquire the asset.

B. Accumulated income minus accumulated dividends since acquisition.

C. Lower of cost or market.

D. Fair value.

The correct answer is (D). *(CMA, adapted)*

REQUIRED: The means of valuing trading securities on the balance sheet.

DISCUSSION: Under SFAS 115, trading securities are those held principally for sale in the near term. They consist of debt securities and equity securities with readily determinable fair values. Unrealized holding gains and losses on trading securities are reported in earnings. Hence, these securities are reported at fair value, which is "the amount at which a financial instrument could be exchanged in a current transaction between willing parties, other than in a forced or liquidation sale."

Answer (A) is incorrect because cost is adjusted for changes in fair value. Answer (B) is incorrect because an equity-based investment is adjusted for the investor's share of the investee's earnings, minus dividends received. However, SFAS 115 does not apply to investments accounted for using the equity method. Answer (C) is incorrect because lower of cost or market was the measurement basis prescribed by SFAS 12, a pronouncement superseded by SFAS 115.

55. An investment in available-for-sale securities is valued on the statement of financial position at

A. The cost to acquire the asset.

B. Accumulated income minus accumulated dividends since acquisition.

C. Fair value.

D. The par or stated value of the securities.

The correct answer is (C). *(CMA, adapted)*

REQUIRED: The means of valuing available-for-sale securities on the balance sheet.

DISCUSSION: According to SFAS 115, available-for-sale securities are investments in debt securities that are not classified as held-to-maturity or trading securities and in equity securities with readily determinable fair values that are not classified as trading securities. They are measured at fair value in the balance sheet.

Answer (A) is incorrect because cost is adjusted for changes in fair value. Answer (B) is incorrect because an equity-based investment is adjusted for the investor's share of the investee's earnings, minus dividends received. However, SFAS 115 does not apply to investments accounted for using the equity method. Answer (D) is incorrect because the par or stated value is an arbitrary amount.

Questions 56 and 57 are based on the following information. Information concerning Monahan Company's portfolio of debt securities at May 31, year 2 and May 31, year 3 is presented in the next column. All of the debt securities were purchased by Monahan during June, year 1. Prior to June, year 1, Monahan had no investments in debt or equity securities.

As of May 31, Year 2	Amortized Cost	Fair Value
Cleary Company bonds	$164,526	$168,300
Beauchamp Industry bonds	204,964	205,200
Morrow Inc. bonds	305,785	285,200
Total	$675,275	$658,700

As of May 31, Year 3	Amortized Cost	Fair Value
Cleary Company bonds	$152,565	$147,600
Beauchamp Industry bonds	193,800	204,500
Morrow Inc. bonds	289,130	291,400
Total	$635,495	$643,500

56. Assuming that the above securities are properly classified as available-for-sale securities under SFAS 115, *Accounting for Certain Investments in Debt and Equity Securities*, the unrealized holding gain or loss as of May 31, year 3 would be

A. Recognized as an $8,005 unrealized holding gain on the income statement.

B. Recognized in other comprehensive income by a year-end credit of $8,005.

C. Recognized in other comprehensive income by a year-end debit of $8,005.

D. Not recognized.

The correct answer is (B). *(CMA, adapted)*

REQUIRED: The unrealized holding gain or loss on available-for-sale securities.

DISCUSSION: Available-for-sale securities include (1) equity securities with readily determinable fair values that are not classified as trading securities and (2) debt securities that are not classified as held-to-maturity or trading securities. Unrealized holding gains and losses are measured by the difference between the amortized cost and fair value at year-end. These holding gains and losses are excluded from earnings and reported in other comprehensive income (unless the securities are designated as being hedged in a fair value hedge). The balance is reported net of the tax effect (ignored in this question). Thus, the difference at May 31, year 3 is $8,005 ($643,500 fair value – $635,495 amortized cost). This unrealized gain is reported as a credit to accumulated other comprehensive income.

Answer (A) is incorrect because unrealized gains and losses on available-for-sale securities do not appear on the income statement. Answer (C) is incorrect because gains are credits (increases in equity) and losses are debits (decreases in equity). Answer (D) is incorrect because SFAS 115 requires unrealized gains and losses on available-for-sale securities to be recorded in other comprehensive income.

57. Assuming that the above securities are properly classified as held-to-maturity securities under SFAS 115, *Accounting for Certain Investments in Debt and Equity Securities*, the unrealized holding gain or loss as of May 31, year 2 would be

A. Recognized as an $8,005 unrealized holding gain on the income statement.

B. Recognized in other comprehensive income by a year-end credit of $8,005.

C. Recognized in other comprehensive income by a year-end debit of $8,005.

D. Not recognized.

The correct answer is (D). *(CMA, adapted)*

REQUIRED: The proper financial statement treatment of held-to-maturity securities.

DISCUSSION: Debt securities that the reporting enterprise has the positive intent and ability to hold to maturity are classified as held-to-maturity. Held-to-maturity securities are reported at amortized cost. Under the provisions of SFAS 115, any unrealized gains or losses are not recognized.

Answers (A), (B), and (C) are incorrect because unrealized gains and losses on held-to-maturity securities are not recorded.

Questions 58 and 59 are based on the following information. On January 1, Boggs, Inc. paid $700,000 for 100,000 shares of Mattly Corporation representing 30% of Mattly's outstanding common stock. The following computation was made by Boggs:

Purchase price	$700,000
30% equity in book value of Mattly's net assets	500,000
Excess cost over book value	$200,000

The excess cost over book value was attributed to goodwill and will be amortized over 20 years. Mattly reported net income for the year ended December 31 of $300,000. Mattly Corporation had paid cash dividends of $100,000 on July 1.

58. If Boggs, Inc. exercised significant influence over Mattly Corporation and properly accounted for the long-term investment under the equity method, the amount of net investment revenue Boggs should report from its investment in Mattly would be

A. $30,000

B. $60,000

C. $80,000

D. $90,000

The correct answer is (C). *(CMA, adapted)*

REQUIRED: The net investment revenue reported using the equity method.

DISCUSSION: Under the equity method, Boggs should recognize 30% of Mattly's reported income of $300,000, or $90,000. However, the annual goodwill amortization ($200,000 ÷ 20 years = $10,000) reduces that amount. Thus, net investment income is $80,000 ($90,000 – $10,000). Dividends received from an investee must be recorded in the books of the investor as a decrease in the carrying value of the investment and an increase in assets (cash).

Answer (A) is incorrect because $30,000 is the net investment revenue reported using the cost method. Answer (B) is incorrect because $60,000 equals 30% of the investee's net income minus 30% of the dividends paid. Answer (D) is incorrect because $90,000 equals 30% of the investee's net income.

59. If Boggs, Inc. did not exercise significant influence over Mattly Corporation and properly accounted for the long-term investment under the cost method, the amount of net investment revenue Boggs should report from its investment in Mattly would be

A. $20,000

B. $30,000

C. $60,000

D. $80,000

The correct answer is (B). *(CMA, adapted)*

REQUIRED: The net investment revenue reported using the cost method.

DISCUSSION: Under the fair value method or the cost method (the latter is appropriate if the equity method is not applicable, and the equity securities do not have readily determinable fair values), the investor records as revenue only the amount actually received as dividends. Boggs receives 30% of the $100,000 total dividend and records $30,000 of investment revenue. The cost method involves no write-off of goodwill.

Answer (A) is incorrect because $20,000 results from subtracting $10,000 of goodwill. Answer (C) is incorrect because $60,000 equals 30% of the investee's net income minus 30% of the dividends paid. Answer (D) is incorrect because $80,000 is the net investment revenue reported using the equity method.

E. Property, Plant, and Equipment

60. Pearl Corporation acquired manufacturing machinery on January 1 for $9,000. During the year, the machine produced 1,000 units, of which 600 were sold. There was no work-in-process inventory at the beginning or at the end of the year. Installation charges of $300 and delivery charges of $200 were also incurred. The machine is expected to have a useful life of five years with an estimated salvage value of $1,500. Pearl uses the straight-line depreciation method. The original cost of the machinery to be recorded in Pearl's books is

A. $9,500

B. $9,300

C. $9,200

D. $9,000

The correct answer is (A). *(CMA, adapted)*

REQUIRED: The original cost of the machinery to be recorded in the books.

DISCUSSION: The costs of fixed assets (plant and equipment) are all costs necessary to acquire these assets and to bring them to the condition and location required for their intended use. These costs include shipping, installation, pre-use testing, sales taxes, interest capitalization, etc. Thus, the original cost of the machinery to be recorded in the books is the sum of the purchase price, installation, and delivery charges, or $9,500 ($9,000 + $300 + $200).

Answer (B) is incorrect because $9,300 does not include the delivery charges. Answer (C) is incorrect because $9,200 omits the installation charges. Answer (D) is incorrect because $9,000 does not include the delivery and installation charges.

61. Lambert Company acquired a machine on October 1 that was placed in service on November 30. The cost of the machine was $63,000, of which $20,000 was given as a down payment. The remainder was borrowed at 12% annual interest. Additional costs included $2,500 for shipping, $4,000 for installation, $3,000 for testing, and $1,290 of interest on the borrowed funds. How much should be reported for this acquisition in the machine account on Lambert Company's statement of financial position as of November 30?

A. $63,000

B. $65,500

C. $69,500

D. $72,500

The correct answer is (D). *(CMA, adapted)*

REQUIRED: The cost of the machine reported on the balance sheet.

DISCUSSION: The initial cost of a machine consists of all costs necessary to prepare it for operation. These include the purchase price minus any discounts ($63,000), shipping costs ($2,500), installation costs ($4,000), and pre-use testing ($3,000). Interest is capitalized only in the case of construction of assets for an enterprise's own use, and then only for the interest incurred during construction. Total acquisition cost is therefore $72,500.

Answer (A) is incorrect because $63,000 equals the price. Answer (B) is incorrect because $65,500 equals the price plus shipping. Answer (C) is incorrect because $69,500 equals the price plus shipping and installation.

62. A steel press machine is purchased for $50,000 cash and a $100,000 interest-bearing note payable. The cost to be recorded as an asset (in addition to the $150,000 purchase price) should include all of the following except

A. Freight and handling charges.

B. Insurance while in transit.

C. Interest on the note payable.

D. Assembly and installation costs.

The correct answer is (C). *(CMA, adapted)*

REQUIRED: The expenditure not capitalized as part of the cost of a new fixed asset.

DISCUSSION: The capitalized cost of fixed assets includes all costs necessary to acquire them and to bring them to the condition and location required for their intended use. Costs of acquisition include shipping, assembly and installation, insurance while in transit, pre-use testing, trial runs, and sales taxes. Interest can also be a cost when assets are self constructed. However, capitalized interest is not a cost of acquisition when long-lived assets are purchased from outside vendors.

Answers (A), (B), and (D) are incorrect because freight and handling charges, insurance while in transit, and assembly and installation costs are elements included in the cost of a fixed asset.

63. The value of property, plant, and equipment that is included in total assets on the statement of financial position is

A. Appraisal or market value.

B. Replacement cost.

C. Acquisition cost.

D. Cost minus accumulated depreciation.

The correct answer is (D). *(CMA, adapted)*

REQUIRED: The value of PPE included in total assets.

DISCUSSION: Fixed assets are reported at their cost minus accumulated depreciation. The capitalized cost of fixed assets includes all costs necessary to acquire them and to bring them to the condition and location required for their intended use.

Answer (A) is incorrect because appraisal values are specifically excluded under ARB 43. Answer (B) is incorrect because replacement cost (current cost) is not acceptable for external financial reporting purposes. However, GAAP formerly required presentation of supplementary current cost information. Answer (C) is incorrect because acquisition cost should be reduced by periodic depreciation.

Questions 64 and 65 are based on the following information. Harper is contemplating exchanging a machine used in its operations for a similar machine on May 31. Harper will exchange machines with either Austin Corporation or Lubin Company. The data relating to the machines are presented below.

	Harper	Austin	Lubin
Original cost of the machine	$162,500	$180,000	$150,000
Accumulated depreciation through May 31	98,500	70,000	65,000
Fair value at May 31	80,000	95,000	60,000

---

64. If Harper exchanges its used machine and $15,000 cash for Austin's used machine, the gain that Harper should recognize from this transaction for financial reporting purposes would be

A. $0

B. $2,526

C. $15,000

D. $16,000

The correct answer is (A). *(CMA, adapted)*

REQUIRED: The gain recognized by Harper from a like-kind exchange if boot is given.

DISCUSSION: APB 29, *Accounting for Nonmonetary Transactions*, requires that an enterprise recognize losses but not gains on like-kind exchanges unless boot (cash) is received. The justification for this conservative view is that the exchange of nonmonetary assets is not the culmination of an earnings process. Harper's used machine has a book value of $64,000 ($162,500 cost – $98,500 accumulated depreciation). The book value surrendered is thus $79,000 ($64,000 + $15,000 cash). The transaction is valued at the fair value of the consideration given ($80,000 + $15,000 = $95,000), a gain of $16,000 ($95,000 – $79,000). But gains may not be recognized on a like-kind exchange under APB 29 if boot is not received. The result for financial reporting purposes is a zero gain.

Answers (B), (C), and (D) are incorrect because no gain is recognized.

65. If Harper exchanges its used machine for Lubin's used machine and also receives $20,000 cash, the gain that Harper should recognize from this transaction for financial reporting purposes would be

A. $0

B. $4,000

C. $16,000

D. $25,000

The correct answer is (B). *(CMA, adapted)*

REQUIRED: The gain recognized by Harper from a like-kind exchange with Lubin if boot is received.

DISCUSSION: In these circumstances, a portion of gains is recorded when boot (monetary assets) is received in the transaction, but the gain recognized cannot exceed the amount of boot received. The gain is recognized in the same proportion that the cash received bears to the total consideration received.

Harper's used machine has a book value of $64,000, and the fair value of the consideration received is $80,000 ($60,000 machine + $20,000 cash). Consequently, there is a gain of $16,000 ($80,000 – $64,000). Of the total consideration, cash is 25% ($20,000 ÷ $80,000). The recognizable gain is $4,000 (25% x $16,000 total gain).

Answers (A), (C), and (D) are incorrect because the gain is $4,000.

66. WD Mining Company purchased a section of land for $600,000 in 1985 to develop a zinc mine. The mine began operating in 1993. At that time, management estimated that the mine would produce 200,000 tons of quality ore. A total of 100,000 tons of ore was mined and processed from 1993 through December 31, 2000. During January 2001, a very promising vein was discovered. The revised estimate of ore still to be mined was 250,000 tons. Estimated salvage value for the mine land was $100,000 in both 1993 and 2001. Assuming that 10,000 tons of ore was mined in 2001, the computation WD Mining company should use to determine the amount of depletion to record in 2001 would be

A. $\dfrac{\$600{,}000 - \$100{,}000}{450{,}000 \text{ tons}} \times 10{,}000 \text{ tons}$

B. $\dfrac{\$600{,}000 - \$100{,}000}{350{,}000 \text{ tons}} \times 10{,}000 \text{ tons}$

C. $\dfrac{\$600{,}000 - \$100{,}000 - \$250{,}000}{350{,}000 \text{ tons}} \times 10{,}000 \text{ tons}$

D. $\dfrac{\$600{,}000 - \$100{,}000 - \$250{,}000}{250{,}000 \text{ tons}} \times 10{,}000 \text{ tons}$

The correct answer is (D). *(CMA, adapted)*

REQUIRED: The computation for determining the annual depletion.

DISCUSSION: Because 50% of the original estimate of quality ore was recovered during the years 1993 through 2000, recorded depletion must have been $250,000 [50% x ($600,000 – $100,000 salvage value)]. In 2001, the earlier depletion of $250,000 is deducted from the $600,000 cost along with the $100,000 salvage value. The remaining depletable cost of $250,000 will be allocated over the 250,000 tons believed to remain in the mine. The $1 per ton depletion is then multiplied times the tons mined each year.

Answers (A), (B), and (C) are incorrect because the denominator should include only 250,000 tons. Also, (A) and (B) fail to deduct prior depletion.

Questions 67 through 69 are based on the following information. In year 1, Ace Industries made the strategic decision to upgrade its manufacturing facility and has since purchased the equipment listed below. The company uses a calendar year as its fiscal year and uses the half-year convention when determining depreciation expense.

- An extruding machine purchased on April 1, year 2 for $200,000. Installation costs were $40,000, and the machine has an estimated 8-year life with no expected salvage value.
- High-speed molding equipment placed in service July 1, year 2. This equipment cost $500,000, has an estimated 10-year life, and is reasonably expected to have a $50,000 salvage value.
- Computer-controlled assembly equipment purchased on August 1, year 3 for $800,000. This equipment has an estimated 8-year life with a salvage value of $60,000.

---

67. Using the straight-line depreciation method, Ace Industries' year 3 depreciation expense is

A. $121,250

B. $233,750

C. $242,500

D. $246,400

The correct answer is (A). *(CMA, adapted)*

REQUIRED: The annual depreciation expense using the straight-line method.

DISCUSSION: The extruding machine's depreciable base is $240,000 ($200,000 + $40,000 installation costs – $0 salvage), so the annual charge is $30,000 ($240,000 ÷ 8). The molding equipment's depreciable base is $450,000 ($500,000 – $50,000 salvage). Hence, annual depreciation is $45,000 ($450,000 ÷ 10). The assembly equipment's depreciable base is $740,000 ($800,000 – $60,000 salvage), resulting in an annual charge of $92,500 ($740,000 ÷ 8). However, given that year 3 is the first year of use, the half-year convention is applied. Under this income tax convention, half a year's depreciation is recorded in the year of acquisition and in the year of disposal. Accordingly, year 3 depreciation is $46,250 ($92,500 ÷ 2). Total depreciation for the three types of equipment is $121,250 ($30,000 + $45,000 + $46,250).

Answer (B) is incorrect because $233,750 is based on the double-declining-balance method and fails to consider installation costs. Answer (C) is incorrect because $242,500 is based on the double-declining-balance method. Answer (D) is incorrect because $246,400 is based on the composite method.

68. Using the double-declining-balance depreciation method, Ace Industries' year 3 depreciation expense is

A. $121,250

B. $233,750

C. $242,500

D. $246,400

The correct answer is (C). *(CMA, adapted)*

REQUIRED: The annual depreciation expense using the double-declining-balance method.

DISCUSSION: Under the double-declining-balance method, the depreciation rate is twice the straight-line rate, and salvage value is ignored initially. The extruding machine is depreciated at a 25% rate because it has an 8-year life. For year 2, depreciation based on the half-year convention is $30,000 {[25% x ($200,000 + $40,000 installation cost)] ÷ 2}. The depreciation for year 3 is therefore $52,500 [25% x ($240,000 – $30,000). The molding equipment is depreciated at a 20% rate given its 10-year life, so year 2 depreciation based on the half-year convention is $50,000 [(20% x $500,000) ÷ 2]. Accordingly, year 3 depreciation is $90,000 [20% x ($500,000 – $50,000)]. The assembly equipment is depreciated at a 25% rate based on an 8-year life. Under the half-year convention, year 3 depreciation is $100,000 [(25% x $800,000) ÷ 2]. Total depreciation expense is $242,500 ($52,500 + $90,000 + $100,000).

Answer (A) is incorrect because $121,250 is the depreciation under the straight-line method. Answer (B) is incorrect because $233,750 fails to consider installation costs. Answer (D) is incorrect because $246,400 is based on the composite method.

69. Ace Industries has decided to simplify its recordkeeping in year 4 by changing to composite depreciation for its manufacturing equipment. The appropriate composite rate has been determined to be 16%. If no additional equipment is purchased in year 4, Ace Industries' year 4 depreciation expense will be

A. $121,250

B. $233,750

C. $242,500

D. $246,400

The correct answer is (D). *(CMA, adapted)*

REQUIRED: The depreciation expense for year 4 under the composite method of depreciation.

DISCUSSION: The composite method of depreciation relates to groups of dissimilar assets with varying useful lives. The depreciation rate applied is an average found by dividing the sum of the straight-line amounts (after allowance for salvage value) by the total cost. The rate is applied to the total cost, and the group is depreciated to the salvage value (if no changes occur in the group). Accordingly, year 4 composite depreciation is $246,400 [16% given composite rate x ($240,000 + $500,000 + $800,000)].

Answer (A) is incorrect because $121,250 is the year 3 straight-line depreciation. Answer (B) is incorrect because $233,750 is the year 3 DDB depreciation without regard to installation costs. Answer (C) is incorrect because $242,500 is the DDB depreciation for year 3.

70. The factors primarily relied upon to determine the economic life of an asset are

A. Passage of time, asset usage, and obsolescence.

B. Tax regulations and SEC guidelines.

C. Tax regulations and asset usage.

D. SEC guidelines and asset usage.

The correct answer is (A). *(CMA, adapted)*

REQUIRED: The factors primarily relied upon to determine the economic life of an asset.

DISCUSSION: Under the straight-line method, depreciation expense is a constant amount for each period of the estimated useful life of the asset. The straight-line method ignores fluctuations in the use of an asset and in maintenance and service charges. The book value is dependent upon the length of time the asset has been held rather than the amount of use. Physical wear and tear is a justification for an activity method of depreciation, e.g., depreciation based on hours of machine use. If technological developments are a primary factor in determining the period of use of an asset, a write-down method of depreciation based on market values may be appropriate.

Answers (B) and (C) are incorrect because the lives that are acceptable for tax purposes may not always be used for financial accounting purposes. Answers (B) and (D) are incorrect because the SEC has not issued depreciation life guidelines.

Questions 71 through 73 are based on the following information. Kruse Company acquired a company airplane on June 3, 1997. The following information relates to this purchase:

Airplane cost	$123,750
Estimated useful life in years	6
Estimated useful life in operating hours	15,000
Estimated residual value	$11,250

Actual hours flown in the year ended May 31,

1998	1,984
1999	2,800
2000	1,690
2001	1,824

71. The depreciation expense for the fiscal year ended May 31, 2001 using the units-of-output method for all years would be

A. $13,680

B. $14,880

C. $15,048

D. $18,750

The correct answer is (A). *(CMA, adapted)*

REQUIRED: The depreciation for the year ending May 31, 2001 based on units of output.

DISCUSSION: The depreciable cost of the plane is $112,500 ($123,750 cost – $11,250 residual value). Hence, the per-hour depreciation charge is $7.50 ($112,500 ÷ 15,000-hour useful life), and the total 2001 depreciation expense is $13,680 ($7.50 x 1,824 hours).

Answer (B) is incorrect because $14,880 is based on 1998 operations. Answer (C) is incorrect because $15,048 ignores the residual value of the airplane. Answer (D) is incorrect because $18,750 is based on the straight-line method.

72. The depreciation expense for the fiscal year ended May 31, 1999 using the double-declining-balance (DDB) method for all years would be

A. $17,188

B. $25,000

C. $27,500

D. $41,250

The correct answer is (C). *(CMA, adapted)*

REQUIRED: The depreciation for the year ending May 31, 1999 under the DDB method.

DISCUSSION: Under the DDB method, the depreciation percentage used is double the straight-line rate. For the airplane, the DDB rate is 33⅓% [2 x (100% ÷ 6 years)]. In the first year, the DDB rate is applied to the initial cost of the asset (residual value is ignored). Thus, depreciation is $41,250 (33⅓% x $123,750). This amount is subtracted from the initial cost to determine the new depreciable base. Accordingly, depreciation for the second year is $27,500 [33⅓% x ($123,750 – $41,250)].

Answer (A) is incorrect because $17,188 is based on the straight-line percentage of 16⅔%. Answer (B) is incorrect because $25,000 subtracted residual value from initial cost. Answer (D) is incorrect because $41,250 is the depreciation expense for the first year.

73. The depreciation expense for the fiscal year ended May 31, 2000 using the sum-of-the-years'-digits (SYD) method for all years would be

A. $17,679

B. $18,750

C. $21,429

D. $23,571

The correct answer is (C). *(CMA, adapted)*

REQUIRED: The depreciation for the year ending May 31, 2000 under the SYD method.

DISCUSSION: Under the SYD method, the depreciable base is $112,500 ($123,750 cost – $11,250 residual value). The annual depreciation rate equals the years remaining divided by the sum of the digits in the years of the asset's life. For a 6-year life, the denominator is 21 (1 + 2 + 3 + 4 + 5 + 6). Thus, third-year depreciation is $21,429 [$112,500 x (4 ÷ 21)].

Answer (A) is incorrect because $17,679 is based on the fourth-year rate and ignores residual value. Answer (B) is incorrect because $18,750 is based on the straight-line method. Answer (D) is incorrect because $23,571 ignores residual value.

Questions 74 through 79 are based on the following information. Felicity Company has the information in the next column on one of its trucks purchased on January 1, 1997. No estimates were changed during the life of the truck.

Truck cost		$100,000
Useful life-years (estimated)		5 years
Useful life-miles (estimated)		100,000
Estimated salvage value		$ 20,000
Actual miles driven:	1997	30,000
	1998	20,000
	1999	15,000
	2000	25,000
	2001	12,000

74. The 1999 depreciation expense for the truck using the sum-of-the-years'-digits (SYD) method was

A. $12,000

B. $16,000

C. $20,000

D. $26,667

The correct answer is (B). *(Publisher)*

REQUIRED: The 1999 depreciation expense.

DISCUSSION: Under SYD, the amount depreciated is the original cost ($100,000) minus salvage value ($20,000), or $80,000. The portion expensed each year is based on a fraction, the denominator of which is the sum of the years of life of the asset. For an asset with a 5-year life, the denominator is 15 (5 + 4 + 3 + 2 + 1). The numerator is 5 in the first year, 4 in the second year, etc. The year 1999 was the third year of the vehicle's life; thus, the fraction is 3 ÷ 15, and annual expense was $16,000 [(3 ÷ 15) x $80,000].

Answer (A) is incorrect because $12,000 is based on the units-of-production method. Answer (C) is incorrect because $20,000 results from not deducting salvage value from the cost. Answer (D) is incorrect because $26,667 was the depreciation for the first year.

75. Assuming the company uses the double-declining-balance (DDB) method, the fiscal 1998 year-end accumulated depreciation was

A. $16,000

B. $24,000

C. $32,000

D. $64,000

The correct answer is (D). *(Publisher)*

REQUIRED: The accumulated depreciation.

DISCUSSION: For an asset with a 5-year life, the straight-line rate is 20%. Under DDB, the applicable percentage is double the straight-line rate, or 40%. This rate is multiplied times the book value of the asset, which for the first year is the original cost. Hence, DDB depreciation was $40,000 (40% x $100,000) for 1997 and $24,000 [40% x ($100,000 – $40,000)] for 1998. Accumulated depreciation at the end of 1998 was therefore $64,000 ($40,000 + $24,000).

Answer (A) is incorrect because $16,000 is the difference between 1997 and 1998 depreciation expense. Answer (B) is incorrect because $24,000 is the depreciation expense for 1998. Answer (C) is incorrect because $32,000 is the first year's depreciation if salvage value were deducted to determine the depreciable amount.

76. Using the units-of-production method, what is the 2001 depreciation expense?

A. $8,000

B. $9,600

C. $10,000

D. $12,000

The correct answer is (A). *(Publisher)*

REQUIRED: The depreciation expense for 2001.

DISCUSSION: Unit depreciation is calculated and then multiplied by the units produced in a given year. Unit depreciation is $.80 per mile [($100,000 cost – $20,000 salvage value) ÷ 100,000 miles]. For 1997 through 2000, the annual depreciation equaled the unit depreciation times the miles driven. For 2001, this must be modified because 90,000 (30,000 + 20,000 + 15,000 + 25,000) of the 100,000 miles of the estimated useful life have already been driven. Because only 10,000 miles of the useful life remain after 2000, 2001 depreciation is $8,000 ($.80 x 10,000 miles).

Answer (B) is incorrect because $9,600 assumes the full 12,000 miles driven in 2001 are eligible for depreciation. Answer (C) is incorrect because $10,000 assumes that depreciation is based on original cost without regard to salvage value. Answer (D) is incorrect because $12,000 is based on 12,000 miles and ignores salvage value.

77. If the company uses the half-year convention in recording depreciation, how much depreciation was recorded in 1997 under the sum-of-the-years'-digits (SYD) method?

A. $13,333

B. $16,667

C. $26,667

D. $33,333

The correct answer is (A). *(Publisher)*

REQUIRED: The 1997 depreciation expense under the SYD method and the half-year convention.

DISCUSSION: Under SYD, the amount depreciated is the original cost ($100,000) minus salvage value ($20,000), or $80,000. The portion expensed each year equals the depreciable base times the SYD fraction (remaining years of useful life ÷ sum of the years' digits). The fraction for 1997 was 5 ÷ 15 [5 years remaining ÷ (5 + 4 + 3 + 2 + 1)], so annual expense was $26,667. However, the half-year convention reduced this amount to $13,333 (50% x $26,667).

Answer (B) is incorrect because $16,667 results from not subtracting salvage value. Answer (C) is incorrect because $26,667 does not consider the half-year convention. Answer (D) is incorrect because $33,333 does not consider either salvage value or the half-year convention.

78. If the company uses the half-year convention in recording depreciation, how much depreciation was recorded in 1998 under the sum-of-the-years'-digits (SYD) method?

A. $8,000

B. $10,667

C. $21,333

D. $24,000

The correct answer is (D). *(Publisher)*

REQUIRED: The 1998 depreciation expense under the SYD method and the half-year convention.

DISCUSSION: Under SYD, the amount depreciated is the original cost ($100,000) minus salvage value ($20,000), or $80,000. The portion expensed each year equals the depreciable base times the SYD fraction. For 1997, this fraction was 5 ÷ 15 [5 years remaining ÷ (5 + 4 + 3 + 2 + 1)], and annual depreciation was $26,667 [(5 ÷ 15) x 80,000]. Under the half-year convention, $13,333 (50% x $26,667) of this amount was expensed in 1997. The remaining $13,333 was expensed during the first 6 months of 1998. The expense for the last 6 months of 1998 was half of the second year's depreciation, or $10,667 [(4 ÷ 15) x 50% x $80,000]. Thus, total depreciation for 1998 was $24,000 ($13,333 + $10,667).

Answer (A) is incorrect because $8,000 is the units-of-production depreciation for 2001. Answer (B) is incorrect because $10,667 is the depreciation for the last half of 1998. Answer (C) is incorrect because $21,333 is the charge for the full second year of the asset's life.

79. Assuming the half-year convention was not used, the fiscal 2000 depreciation expense under the double-declining-balance (DDB) method was

A. $1,600

B. $6,912

C. $8,640

D. $14,400

The correct answer is (A). *(Publisher)*

REQUIRED: The depreciation expense for 2000 under the DDB method.

DISCUSSION: For an asset with a 5-year life, the straight-line rate is 20%. Under DDB, the applicable percentage is double the straight-line rate, or 40%. This rate is multiplied by the book value of the asset, which for the first year is the original cost. Consequently, DDB depreciation was $40,000 (40% x $100,000) for 1997, $24,000 for 1998 [40% x ($100,000 – $40,000)], and $14,400 for 1999 [40% x ($100,000 – $40,000 – $24,000)]. Because accumulated depreciation through 1999 was $78,400 ($40,000 + $24,000 + $14,400), book value was $21,600 ($100,000 – $78,400), and 2000 depreciation (before considering salvage value) was $8,640 (40% x $21,600). However, the asset cannot be depreciated below its salvage value. Thus, the company cannot recognize more than $1,600 of depreciation expense ($21,600 – $20,000 salvage value) in 2000.

Answer (B) is incorrect because $6,912 is the amount that would be expensed if the depreciable base was net of the salvage value and the asset was depreciated below this salvage value. Answer (C) is incorrect because $8,640 assumes no salvage value. Answer (D) is incorrect because $14,400 is the expense for 1999.

F. Intangible Assets

80. Costs that are capitalized with regard to a patent include

A. Legal fees of obtaining the patent, incidental costs of obtaining the patent, and costs of successful patent infringement suits.

B. Legal fees of obtaining the patent, incidental costs of obtaining the patent, and research and development costs incurred on the invention that is patented.

C. Legal fees of obtaining the patent, costs of successful patent infringement suits, and research and development costs incurred on the invention that is patented.

D. Incidental costs of obtaining the patent, costs of successful and unsuccessful patent infringement suits, and the value of any signed patent licensing agreement.

The correct answer is (A). *(CMA, adapted)*

REQUIRED: The proper items to be capitalized as part of the cost of a patent.

DISCUSSION: The cost should be amortized over the remaining legal life or useful life, whichever is shorter. In addition to the initial costs of obtaining a patent, legal fees incurred in the successful defense of a patent should be capitalized as part of the cost, whether it was internally developed or purchased from an inventor. The legal fees capitalized then should be amortized over the remaining useful life of the patent.

Answers (B) and (C) are incorrect because R&D costs must be expensed as incurred. Answer (D) is incorrect because unsuccessful patent infringement suit costs should not be capitalized.

81. APB 17, *Intangible Assets*, provides guidelines for the accounting and reporting of specifically identifiable intangible assets. All of the following are specifically identifiable intangible assets except

A. Patents and trademarks.

B. Copyrights.

C. Goodwill.

D. Leaseholds.

The correct answer is (C). *(CMA, adapted)*

REQUIRED: The item not a specifically identifiable intangible asset.

DISCUSSION: Intangible assets are noncurrent, nonphysical assets. APB 17 requires intangible assets to be capitalized if purchased from outsiders. Specifically identifiable intangible assets, such as patents, trademarks, and copyrights, may be capitalized even when developed internally. Intangibles that are not specifically identifiable, such as goodwill, may be capitalized only when acquired externally. Goodwill is the difference between the cost and the fair value of the net identifiable assets acquired in a business combination.

Answers (A), (B), and (D) are incorrect because patents and trademarks, copyrights, and leaseholds are all identifiable intangible assets.

82. On September 1, year 1, for $4,000,000 cash and $2,000,000 notes payable, Norbend Corporation acquired the net assets of Crisholm Company, which had a fair value of $5,496,000 on that date. Norbend's management is of the opinion that the goodwill generated has an indefinite life and should be amortized over the longest allowable period. During the December 31, year 3 year-end audit after all adjusting entries have been made, the goodwill is determined to be worthless. The amount of the write-off as of December 31, year 3 should be

A. $504,000

B. $478,800

C. $466,200

D. $474,600

The correct answer is (D). *(CMA, adapted)*

REQUIRED: The goodwill write-off.

DISCUSSION: APB 17 requires that goodwill be amortized over a period of 40 years or less. Given that the company paid $6,000,000 for net identifiable assets with a fair value of $5,496,000, goodwill was $504,000. Annual amortization was $12,600 ($504,000 ÷ 40). For the year of purchase, the amortization period was only 4 months; thus, year 1 amortization was $4,200 [$12,600 x (4 ÷ 12)]. Amortization was $12,600 per year for year 2 and year 3, bringing the total amortization to $29,400 [$4,200 + (2 x $12,600)]. Hence, the book value to be written off is $474,600 ($504,000 – $29,400).

Answer (A) is incorrect because $504,000 does not reflect amortization in previous years. Answer (B) is incorrect because $4,200 would have been amortized in year 1. Answer (C) is incorrect because year 1 amortization would have been only $4,200, not the full year's $12,600.

83. During 2000, Orr Co. incurred the following costs:

Research and development services performed by Key Corp. for Orr	$150,000
Design, construction, and testing of preproduction prototypes and models	200,000
Testing in search for new products of process alternatives	175,000

In its 2000 income statement, what should Orr report as research and development expense?

A. $150,000

B. $200,000

C. $350,000

D. $525,000

The correct answer is (D). *(CPA, adapted)*

REQUIRED: The R&D expense.

DISCUSSION: Research is planned search or critical investigation aimed at discovery of new knowledge useful in developing a new product, service, process, or technique, or in bringing about a significant improvement to an existing product, etc. Development is translation of research findings or other knowledge into a plan or design for a new or improved product or process. R&D expenses include R&D performed under contract by others; design, construction, and testing of prototypes; and testing in search for new products (SFAS 2). Thus, all $525,000 should be expensed.

Answer (A) is incorrect because $150,000 does not include design, construction, and testing of preproduction prototypes or testing in search of new products. Answer (B) is incorrect because $200,000 does not include R&D performed under contract by others or testing in search for new products. Answer (C) is incorrect because $350,000 does not include testing in search for new products.

84. West, Inc. made the following expenditures relating to Product Y:

- Legal costs to file a patent on Product Y -- $10,000. Production of the finished product would not have been undertaken without the patent.
- Special equipment to be used solely for development of Product Y -- $60,000. The equipment has no other use and has an estimated useful life of 4 years.
- Labor and material costs incurred in producing a prototype model -- $200,000
- Cost of testing the prototype -- $80,000

What is the total amount of costs that will be expensed when incurred?

A. $280,000

B. $295,000

C. $340,000

D. $350,000

The correct answer is (C). *(CPA, adapted)*

REQUIRED: The total amount of costs that will be expensed when incurred.

DISCUSSION: R&D costs are expensed as incurred. However, SFAS 2 specifically excludes legal work in connection with patent applications or litigation and the sale or licensing of patents from the definition of R&D. The legal costs of filing a patent should be capitalized. West's R&D costs include those incurred for the design, construction, and testing of preproduction prototypes. Moreover, the cost of equipment used solely for a specific project is also expensed immediately. Thus, the total amount of costs that will be expensed when incurred is $340,000.

Answer (A) is incorrect because $280,000 does not include the cost of the special equipment. Answer (B) is incorrect because $295,000 includes 1 year's straight-line depreciation on the special equipment instead of the full cost. Answer (D) is incorrect because $350,000 includes the legal costs of filing a patent.

Study Unit 5: Liabilities

30 pages of outline
87 multiple-choice questions

Study Unit 5 is one of seven covering preparation of financial statements, a major topic that has been assigned a relative weight range of 50% to 70% of Part 2. This study unit and the next concern the financing structure of the reporting entity.

A. Current Liabilities, Accruals, and Deferred Revenues

1. **Accounts payable**, commonly termed trade accounts payable, are liabilities; that is, they are probable future sacrifices of economic benefits arising from current obligations to transfer assets or to provide services in the future as a result of past transactions and events. Accounts payable reflect the obligations to sellers that are incurred when an entity purchases inventory, supplies, or services on credit.
   a. Accounts payable should be recorded at their settlement value.
   b. Short-term liabilities, such as accounts payable, do not usually provide for a periodic payment of interest unless the accounts are not settled when due or payable.
      1) They also are usually not secured by collateral.
   c. Accounts payable are **current liabilities.**
      1) **ARB 43, Chapter 3A**, *Current Assets and Current Liabilities*, defines a current liability as an obligation that will be either liquidated using current assets or replaced by another current liability.
         a) **SFAS 78**, *Classification of Obligations That Are Callable by the Creditor*, amends ARB 43 to include the following as current liabilities: (1) obligations that, by their terms, are or will be due on demand within 1 year (or the operating cycle if longer), and (2) obligations that are or will be callable by the creditor within 1 year because of a violation of a debt covenant.
         b) "The current liability classification is not intended to include debts to be liquidated by funds that have been accumulated in accounts of a type not properly classified as current assets" (ARB 43).
   d. Checks written before the end of the period, but not mailed to creditors, should not be accounted for as cash payments for the period; the amounts remain current liabilities until control of the checks has been surrendered.

e. Purchases and related accounts payable may be recorded using the gross method or the net method.

1) The **gross method** records purchases and accounts payable without regard to purchase discounts available, for example, cash discounts for early payment.

a) In a periodic system, purchase discounts taken are credited to a contra purchases account and closed to cost of goods sold. In a perpetual system, they are credited to inventory.

2) The **net method** records purchases and accounts payable at the cash (discounted) price.

a) The advantage of the net method is that it isolates purchase discounts lost, which are treated as financing charges.

f. The timing of recognition of accounts payable may depend on the **shipping terms**.

1) When goods are shipped **FOB shipping point**, title and risk of loss pass to the buyer at the time and place of shipment. Thus, the buyer records inventory and a payable at the time of shipment.

2) When goods are shipped **FOB destination**, title and risk of loss do not pass until they are duly tendered to the buyer at the destination. Hence, the buyer does not record inventory and a payable until that time.

2. **Accrued Expenses**. Ordinarily, accrued expenses meet recognition criteria in the current period but have not been paid as of year-end. They are accounted for using basic accrual entries.

a. **Reversing entries** may be used to facilitate accounting for accrued expenses in the next period. For example, if wages payable are accrued at year-end (the adjusting entry is to debit wages expense and credit wages payable), the reversing entry at the beginning of the next period is to debit the liability and credit wages expense. If the reversing entry is made, no allocation between the liability and wages expense is needed when wages are paid in the subsequent period (the entry will simply be to debit wages expense and to credit cash).

1) If accrual entries are reversed, all expenses paid in the next period can be charged to expense.

2) If reversing entries are not made, either of the following methods is used in the next period:

a) The liability is debited when the accrued expense is actually paid. For example, the first wages payment of the year will be accounted for by debiting wages expense and wages payable and crediting cash. Thus, this entry will differ from subsequent entries recording the payment of wages.

b) Payments are recorded by debiting expense for the full amounts paid. At year-end, the liability is adjusted to the balance owed at that date. For example, if the liability for accrued wages has decreased, the adjusting entry will be to debit wages payable and credit wages expense.

b. If an entity fails to accrue expenses at year-end, income is overstated in that period and understated in the next period (when they are paid and presumably expensed).

1) Moreover, expenses incurred but unpaid and not recorded result in understated accrued liabilities and possibly understated assets (for example, if the amounts should be inventoried). In addition, working capital (current assets – current liabilities) will be overstated, but cash flows will not be affected.

3. **Taxes Payable**

a. Accounting for deferred income taxes is explained in subunit F. of this study unit.

b. Federal unemployment tax and the employer's share of FICA taxes are expenses incurred as employees earn wages, but they are paid only on a periodic basis to the federal government. Accordingly, liabilities should also be accrued for both expenses, as well as for wages earned but not paid.

1) Income taxes withheld and the employee's share of FICA taxes are accrued as withholding taxes (employee payroll deductions) and not as employer payroll taxes.

c. Property taxes are usually expensed by monthly accrual over the fiscal period of the taxing authority.

d. Sales taxes are levied on certain types of merchandise by most states. Ordinarily, the tax is paid by the customer purchasing the merchandise but is collected and remitted by the seller. Most states require quarterly or monthly filing of sales tax returns and remittance of taxes collected.

4. **Deposits and Other Advances**

a. A deposit or other advance is a liability because it involves a probable future sacrifice of economic benefits arising from a current obligation of a particular entity to transfer assets or provide services to another entity in the future as a result of a past transaction (SFAC 6).

b. An issue is whether deposits/advances are classified as current or noncurrent liabilities. They are current liabilities if they will be liquidated using current assets or be replaced by another current liability.

5. **Coupons and Premiums**

a. Many sellers include boxtops, stamps, rebates, coupons, special labels, etc., with merchandise that can be redeemed for premiums (cash or goods). The purpose is to increase sales.

b. In accordance with the principle of associating cause and effect (matching as defined in SFAC 6), the expense involved in making premium offers should be recognized in the same period as the related revenue. Moreover, the premiums must be purchased and recorded as inventory, the expense of redemptions must be debited, and a liability for estimated redemptions must be credited at the end of the accounting period.

6. **Warranties**
   a. A warranty is a written guarantee of the integrity of a product or service and an undertaking by the seller to repair or replace a product, refund all or part of the price, or provide additional service. It is customarily offered for a limited time, such as 90 days.
   b. If incurrence of warranty expense is probable, the amount can be reasonably estimated, and the amount is material, accrual accounting methods should be used. Under the accrual method, the total estimated warranty cost is debited to operating expense and credited to a liability in the year of sale. When the accrual method is inapplicable, warranty expense should be recorded as incurred, that is, on the cash basis.
7. **SFAS 43**, *Accounting for Compensated Absences*, applies to employees' rights to receive compensation for future absences, such as vacations, sick leave, and holidays. It requires an accrual when four criteria are met:
   a. The payment of compensation is probable.
   b. The amount can be reasonably estimated.
      1) Otherwise, disclosure but not recognition is necessary.
   c. The benefits either vest or accumulate.
      1) Benefits vest if they are not contingent on future service.
      2) Sick pay benefits are accrued only if they vest.
      3) Benefits accumulate if earned, but unused rights may be carried forward to subsequent periods.
   d. The compensation relates to employees' services already rendered.
8. **SFAS 112**, *Employers' Accounting for Postemployment Benefits*, applies the criteria in SFAS 43 to all postemployment benefits except those provided by pensions, postretirement benefit plans, certain deferred compensation arrangements, special or contractual termination agreements, and stock compensation plans. These benefits include, but are not limited to, salary continuation, supplemental unemployment benefits, severance benefits, disability-related benefits (including workers' compensation), job training and counseling, and continuation of benefits such as health care and life insurance coverage.
   a. If postemployment (and preretirement) benefits within the scope of SFAS 112 do not meet the criteria in SFAS 43, they are accounted for as contingencies.
9. Under **SFAS 49**, *Accounting for Product Financing Arrangements*, these arrangements (to finance inventory) should be accounted for by the sponsor (the party seeking financing) as borrowings, not sales. The following are examples:
   a. A buyer purchases a product that the sponsor agrees to repurchase.
   b. The buyer is a separate entity established for the above purpose or is an existing credit grantor, trust, or nonbusiness entity.
   c. The sponsor guarantees the debt of the buyer.
   d. The financed product is to be used or sold by the sponsor.

10. **Deferred Revenues**

    a. If the recognition criteria are not met, amounts received in advance are treated as liabilities (deferred revenues). Recognition is deferred until the obligation underlying the liability is partly or wholly satisfied.

    1) Cash received in advance may initially be credited to a deferred revenue (liability) account. At the end of the accounting period, earned revenue is recognized with the following adjusting entry:

Deferred revenue	$XXX	
Revenue		$XXX

    a) A reversing entry is not appropriate if advance receipts are initially credited to deferred revenue (a permanent or real account).

    2) If cash received in advance is initially credited to a revenue account, an adjusting entry is needed to credit a deferred revenue (liability) account for unearned amounts.

Revenue	$XXX	
Deferred revenue		$XXX

    a) If this entry is reversed at the beginning of the next period, no entry will be needed to recognize revenue. This procedure keeps unearned revenue in the revenue account (a temporary or nominal account) except at the end of the period when statements are prepared.

11. Stop and review! You have completed the outline for this subunit. Study multiple-choice questions 1 through 13 beginning on page 237.

B. Contingent Liabilities and Commitments

1. A **contingency** is "an existing condition, situation, or set of circumstances involving uncertainty as to possible gain (hereinafter a **gain contingency**) or loss (hereinafter a **loss contingency**) to an enterprise that will ultimately be resolved when one or more future events occur or fail to occur" (**SFAS 5**, *Accounting for Contingencies*).

    a. An estimate should not be confused with a contingency; thus, the estimated depreciation for the period is not consistent with the foregoing definition of a contingency because it is certain that the utility of a depreciable asset will expire.

2. SFAS 5 requires that a contingent loss be accrued (debit loss, credit liability or asset valuation allowance) when, based on information available prior to the issuance of the financial statements, two conditions are met: (1) It is **probable** that at a balance sheet date an asset has been impaired or a liability has been incurred, and (2) the amount of the loss can be **reasonably estimated**.

    a. If the loss is probable and can be reasonably estimated, it should be accrued if the amount is material. If the estimate is stated within a given range, and no amount within that range appears to be a better estimate than any other, the minimum of the range should be accrued. In these circumstances, disclosure of the nature of the contingency, any additional loss exposure (if reasonably possible), and possibly the amount accrued is required.

3. If both conditions are not met, but the probability of the loss is at least **reasonably possible**, an estimate of the loss or the range of loss must be disclosed or a statement should be included indicating that an estimate cannot be made. An accrued loss and a loss that is disclosed but not accrued may arise from the same situation.
   a. The financial statements should disclose the nature of the contingency and the amount or range of the possible loss. If an estimate cannot be made, the footnote should so state.
4. Normally, loss contingencies are not disclosed if the probability of occurrence is remote.
   a. For debt guarantees, however, SFAS 5 requires that disclosure be made of the loss contingency, even though the possibility of loss is considered remote.
      1) This disclosure is required whether the guarantee is direct or indirect and should include the nature and amount of the guarantee.
   b. Other remote loss contingencies that should be disclosed are obligations of commercial banks under standby letters of credit and guarantees to repurchase receivables (or the related property) that were sold or assigned.
   c. General or unspecified business risks, for example, those related to national and international economic conditions, require neither accrual nor disclosure.
5. SFAS 5 also mentions the following possible loss contingencies:
   a. Collectibility of receivables
   b. Obligations related to product warranties or defects
   c. Risk of loss from catastrophes
   d. Threats of expropriation by a foreign government
   e. Pending or threatened litigation
   f. Actual or possible claims and assessments
6. Gain contingencies should not be recognized until they are realized. For example, an award of damages in a lawsuit is not deemed to be realized if it is being appealed.
   a. A gain contingency should be disclosed, but care should be taken to avoid misleading implications as to the likelihood of realization.
7. **Off-balance-sheet risk** arises when the ultimate obligation from a liability exceeds that recognized in the balance sheet. It also arises when a recorded asset involves conditional rights and obligations that expose the entity to a risk of accounting loss that may exceed the amount recognized. Thus, many of the new and innovative financial instruments create off-balance-sheet risk. Furthermore, many traditional transactions have off-balance-sheet effects, for example,
   a. Operating leases
   b. Unconditional purchase obligations
   c. Transfers of receivables with recourse accounted for as sales
   d. Deferred compensation arrangements, such as pensions, postretirement benefit obligations, and employee stock option plans
   e. Guarantees of indebtedness
   f. Transactions accounted for under SFAS 5, *Accounting for Contingencies*
   g. Certain financial instruments (see subunit F.5. in Study Unit 1).

8. **Purchase Commitments**. A commitment to acquire goods in the future is not recorded at the time of the agreement, e.g., by debiting an asset and crediting a liability, but **ARB 43, Chapter 4**, requires the accrual of a loss in the current year's income statement on goods subject to a firm purchase commitment if the market price of these goods declines below the commitment price.
   a. The rationale for current loss recognition is the same as that for inventory on hand: a decline (but not an increase) in the utility of cost expenditures should be recognized when it occurs. Thus, the LCM rule is followed.
      1) If the losses are expected to arise from firm, noncancelable, and unhedged commitments for the future purchase of inventory items, they should be measured in the same way as inventory losses and, if material, recognized and separately disclosed.
         a) However, the utility of commitments is not impaired, and no loss occurs, if the amounts to be realized from the disposition of the future inventory items are protected by a firm sales contract or if other circumstances reasonably assure against loss.
   b. Under GAAP, the accounting treatment is to debit a loss account and credit a current liability, e.g., allowance for purchase commitment loss.
   c. Under **SFAS 133**, *Accounting for Derivative Instruments and Hedging Activities*, a **firm commitment** is defined as "an agreement with an unrelated party, binding on both parties and usually legally enforceable, with the following characteristics:
      1) The agreement specifies all significant terms, including the quantity to be exchanged, the fixed price, and the timing of the transaction. The fixed price may be expressed as a specified amount of an entity's functional currency or of a foreign currency. It may also be expressed as a specified interest rate or specified effective yield.
      2) The agreement includes a disincentive for nonperformance that is sufficiently large to make performance probable."
      3) When a previously unrecognized firm commitment is designated as a hedged item, an asset or liability is recognized related to the recognition of the gain or loss on the commitment.
9. Stop and review! You have completed the outline for this subunit. Study multiple-choice questions 14 through 23 beginning on page 241.

C. Long-Term Liabilities

1. **Issue of Bonds at a Premium or Discount**
   a. If bonds are issued at a discount or a premium, **APB 21**, *Interest on Receivables and Payables*, requires that the interest method of amortization be used (unless the results of another method are not materially different). Under the interest method, interest expense changes every period, but the interest rate is constant.
      1) Bonds are sold at the sum of the present values of the maturity value and the interest payments (if interest-bearing). The difference between the face value and the selling price of bonds is either a discount or a premium.
         a) Bonds are sold at a discount when they sell for less than face value, that is, when the contract (stated) interest rate is less than the market (effective) interest rate. Bonds are sold at a premium (in excess of face value) when the stated rate exceeds the effective rate.

b) APB 21 requires that bond discount or premium appear as a direct deduction from or addition to the face amount of the bond payable.

2) When bonds are issued between interest payment dates, the price includes accrued interest.

3) Interest expense is equal to the carrying value of the bond at the beginning of the period times the yield (market) interest rate.

4) Interest paid remains constant and is equal to the face value of the bond times the stated rate.

5) The difference between interest expense and interest paid is the discount or premium amortization.

a) When bonds are issued at a discount, interest expense exceeds interest (cash) paid. When bonds are issued at a premium, interest (cash) paid exceeds interest expense.

6) The carrying value of bonds issued at a discount increases as the discount is amortized, resulting in higher interest expense each payment period.

a) Because the discount amortization equals the excess of an increasing interest expense over the constant amount of interest paid, the amount amortized will increase with each payment.

7) For bonds issued at a premium, the carrying value will decrease as the premium is amortized. The result is a lower interest expense each interest payment period.

a) Because the premium amortization is equal to the excess of the constant amount of interest paid over a decreasing amount of interest expense, the amount of premium amortized also will increase with each payment.

8) The periodic reduction of the discount (premium) will cause the net carrying value of the bonds to be higher (lower) than the net carrying value at the previous period-end.

a) At the maturity date, the discount or premium will be fully amortized to zero, and the net carrying value will be equal to the face value of the bonds.

2. **Issue Costs**

a. APB 21 states that issue costs should be reported in the balance sheet as deferred charges and amortized over the life of the bonds. They should not be commingled with bond premiums or discounts.

1) Issue costs are incurred to bring a bond to market and include printing and engraving costs, legal fees, accountants' fees, underwriters' commissions, registration fees, and promotional costs.

2) Although the effective-interest method is theoretically superior, issue costs are customarily amortized using the straight-line method.

3) SFAC 6, which does not supersede any part of APB 21, has suggested that bond issue costs may also be treated as a reduction in the related debt liability, that is, in the same manner as bond discount (an increase in bond discount or a decrease in bond premium). However, the income statement effects of the two methods are identical if the same method is used to amortize the discount (or premium) and the issue costs.

3. **Types of Bonds**

   a. A bond contains a promise to pay an amount of money (face value) at the maturity date plus interest at the stated rate at specified intervals. Bonds may also have the following characteristics:

      1) **Debentures** are backed by the borrower's general credit but not by specific collateral.
      2) **Mortgage bonds** are backed by specific assets, usually real estate.
      3) When all of the bonds in a bond issue mature on the same date, they are called **term bonds**.
      4) When portions of a bond issue mature at different dates, they are called **serial bonds**.
      5) **Registered bonds** are recorded in the name of the owner, who is the only party entitled to payment.
      6) **Coupon bonds** are usually bearer instruments. Whoever presents the periodic interest coupons is entitled to payment.
      7) **Subordinated debentures** and **second mortgage bonds** are junior securities with claims inferior to those of senior bonds.
      8) **Guaranty bonds** are guaranteed by a third party, e.g., the parent of the subsidiary that issued the bonds.
      9) **Zero-coupon** or **deep-discount bonds** are noninterest-bearing.
      10) **Commodity-backed bonds** are payable at prices related to a commodity such as gold.
      11) **Collateral trust bonds** are backed by specific securities.
      12) **Revenue bonds** are issued by governmental units and are payable from specific revenue sources.
      13) **Income bonds** pay interest contingent on the debtor's profitability.
      14) **Callable bonds** may be redeemed by the issuer before maturity.
      15) **Convertible bonds** may be converted into equity securities of the issuer at the option of the holder (buyer) under the conditions specified in the bond indenture.
      16) **Variable rate bonds** pay interest that is dependent on market conditions.
      17) The **bond indenture** (agreement with creditors) often provides for setting aside monies in a sinking fund for payments of interest and principal.

4. **Conversion of Bonds**

   a. There are two approaches to accounting for conversion of convertible debt. One view is that convertible debt has characteristics of both debt and equity and that separate accounting recognition should be given to both at the time of issuance.

      1) The contrary and prevailing view under **APB 14**, *Convertible Debt and Debt Issued with Stock Purchase Warrants*, is that the debt and equity aspects of the convertible debt are inseparable. APB 14 states that all proceeds (usually cash) should be accounted for as debt (a liability) until conversion.

         a) The bond issue price (fair value) is affected, however, by the conversion feature.

b. Under the **book-value method** for recognizing the conversion of outstanding bonds payable to common stock, the stock issued is recorded at the carrying value of the bonds (credit common stock and additional paid-in capital, debit the payable) at the time of issuance, with no recognition of gain or loss. This method is the most common.

   1) Under the **market-value method**, the stock is recorded at the market value of the stock (or of the bonds). A gain or loss is recognized equal to the difference between the market value recorded and the carrying value of the bonds payable.

c. Because the book value is based on all related accounts, the balances of unamortized bond premium or discount, unamortized issue costs, and conversion costs should be considered adjustments of the net carrying value at the time of conversion.

   1) Consequently, these items should be reflected as adjustments of the additional paid-in capital account.

d. According to **SFAS 84**, *Induced Conversions of Convertible Debt*, an issuer of a convertible security may attempt to induce prompt conversion of its convertible debt to equity securities by offering additional securities or other consideration as a sweetener.

   1) The additional consideration used to induce conversion should be reported as an ordinary expense. The amount equals the fair value of the securities or other consideration transferred in excess of the fair value of the securities that would have been issued under the original conversion privilege.

e. The treatment of gains or losses from early extinguishment of convertible debt is the same as for the retirement of ordinary debt.

5. **Detachable Stock Warrants**

a. If debt securities must be surrendered to exercise attached warrants, the securities are substantially equivalent to convertible debt.

   1) Under APB 14, *Convertible Debt and Debt Issued with Stock Purchase Warrants*, no portion of the proceeds from the issuance should be accounted for as attributable to the conversion feature or the warrants.

b. APB 14 requires the proceeds from debt securities issued with detachable warrants to be allocated between the debt securities and the warrants based on their relative fair values at the time of issuance.

   1) The portion allocated to the warrants should be accounted for as paid-in capital.

   2) When the fair value of the warrants but not the bonds is known, paid-in capital from stock warrants should be credited (increased) for the fair value of the warrants, with the remainder credited to the bonds.

6. **Refinancing of Notes Payable**

a. **SFAS 6**, *Classification of Short-term Obligations Expected to Be Refinanced*, states that, if an enterprise intends to refinance short-term obligations on a long-term basis and demonstrates an ability to consummate the refinancing, the obligation should be excluded from current liabilities and classified as noncurrent.

1) The ability to consummate the refinancing may be demonstrated by a post-balance-sheet-date issuance of a long-term obligation or equity securities or by entering into a financing agreement that meets the following criteria:

   a) The agreement does not expire within the longer of 1 year or the operating cycle.

   b) It is noncancelable by the lender.

   c) No violation of the agreement exists at the balance sheet date.

   d) The lender is financially capable of honoring the agreement.

b. The amount of the short-term liability that is reclassified as a long-term liability should not exceed the amount available for refinancing.

c. **SFAS 78**, *Classification of Obligations That Are Callable by the Creditor*, states that long-term obligations callable because of the debtor's violation of the debt agreement at the balance sheet date are current liabilities.

1) These obligations need not be classified as current if it is probable that a violation will be cured within a specified grace period.

   a) If the creditor formally waives the right to demand repayment for a period of more than a year from the balance sheet date, the debt need not be classified as current.

   b) Reclassification is not required if the debtor expects and has the ability to refinance the obligation on a long-term basis.

2) The provisions of this statement also apply to debts that by their terms are callable within the year (or normal operating cycle, if longer).

7. **Other Notes Payable Questions**

a. Notes payable should be measured at their present value. This requirement applies to noninterest-bearing notes, notes that have an unrealistically low rate of interest, and notes that are not due within 1 year. Otherwise, notes payable should be measured at face value.

b. An appropriate interest rate should be determined in accordance with APB 21.

1) Discount or premium, loan origination fees, etc., are amortized using the effective-interest method to arrive at a periodic interest expense that reflects a constant rate of interest when applied to the beginning balance.

2) APB 21 states that discount or premium is not an asset or liability separable from the related note. A discount or premium should therefore be reported as a direct deduction from or addition to the face amount of the note.

8. **Troubled Debt Restructuring**

a. **SFAS 15**, *Accounting by Debtors and Creditors for Troubled Debt Restructurings*, is applicable when "a creditor for economic or legal reasons related to the debtor's financial difficulties grants a concession to the debtor that it would not otherwise consider."

b. **Debtor accounting**. Debtors should recognize an extraordinary gain or loss (carrying amount – settlement amount) as a result of the extinguishment of debt when creditors settle a debt by accepting assets with a fair value different from the book value of the debt.

1) If equity securities are issued to settle a debt, the issuance should be recorded at fair value. The gain equals the carrying amount of the debt minus the fair value of the equity interest.

2) If the terms of the troubled debt are modified, there should be no adjustment of the payable unless the total payments to be made (including interest) are less than the book value of the debt.

a) The effective interest rate should be adjusted to decrease interest expense over the life of the payable.

c. **Creditor accounting**. Creditors should account for assets received as full payment of the debt at fair value with appropriate recognition of gain or loss (the difference between the fair value received and the recorded investment).

d. **SFAS 114**, *Accounting by Creditors for Impairment of a Loan*, amends SFAS 15 with regard to creditor accounting for loans restructured in a troubled debt restructuring involving a modification of terms. All such loans are to be measured under SFAS 114.

1) A loan is impaired if it is probable that the creditor will not collect all amounts due under the contractual terms of the original loan agreement.

2) If a loan is found to be impaired, the impairment is measured based on the present value of the expected future cash flows discounted at the loan's effective interest rate.

a) As a practical expedient, a creditor is also permitted to measure impairment based on a loan's observable market price or the fair value of the collateral if the loan is collateral dependent.

i) If foreclosure is probable, impairment is based on the fair value of the collateral.

3) If the recorded investment in the loan exceeds the present value of the expected future cash flows (or the observable market price of the loan or the fair value of the collateral), the creditor debits bad-debt expense and credits an allowance account. An existing allowance is adjusted appropriately, with a corresponding debit or credit to bad-debt expense.

4) As a result of an amendment by **SFAS 118**, *Accounting by Creditors for Impairment of a Loan–Income Recognition and Disclosures*, SFAS 114 does not address the issues of recognition, measurement, or display of interest income derived from an impaired loan.

e. If a troubled debt restructuring involves both a receipt of assets and a modification of terms, the creditor should account for the assets at fair value and should reduce the recorded investment in the receivable accordingly. The creditor should then account for the remaining portion in accordance with SFAS 114.

f. Repossessions are accounted for by creditors as described above.

g. Debt-restructuring expenses are expensed as incurred, except by debtors issuing equity securities (restructuring expenses reduce paid-in capital from these securities).

9. Stop and review! You have completed the outline for this subunit. Study multiple-choice questions 24 through 43 beginning on page 245.

D. Leases

1. The primary pronouncement applicable to leases is **SFAS 13**, *Accounting for Leases*. A **lease** is an agreement between a lessor (owner) and a lessee that conveys the right to use specific property for a stated period in exchange for a stated payment. The accounting for leases is based on the substance of the transaction. A lease may be, in effect, a financing agreement in which the lessor finances the purchase. Leases may also be, in effect, rental agreements.

2. **Lessee Accounting for Capital Leases**. A lessee classifies a lease as a capital lease or an operating lease. A **capital lease** transfers substantially all of the benefits and risks of ownership of the property.

   a. It should be accounted for as the acquisition of an asset and the incurrence of an obligation by the lessee. In subsequent periods, the lessee depreciates the asset and recognizes interest on the liability.

   b. A lease must be classified as a capital lease by a lessee if, at its inception, any one of four criteria is satisfied. Each of these criteria indicates that a substantial transfer of the benefits and risks of ownership has occurred.

      1) The following are the four criteria:

         a) The lease provides for the transfer of ownership of the leased property.

         b) The lease contains a bargain purchase option.

         c) The lease term is 75% or more of the estimated economic life of the leased property.

         d) The present value of the minimum lease payments (excluding executory costs) is at least 90% of the excess of the fair value of the leased property to the lessor at the inception of the lease over any related investment tax credit.

      2) However, criteria 1)c) and 1)d) are inapplicable if the beginning of the lease term falls within the last 25% of the total estimated economic life.

      3) In the case of a lease agreement covering land only, two of the four criteria may be used in determining whether the agreement constitutes a capital lease. If the lease either transfers ownership at the end of the lease or contains a bargain purchase option, the lessee records a capital lease; otherwise, the lease is an operating lease.

         a) Leases involving both land and buildings are subject to complex rules beyond the scope of this outline.

   c. The lessee must record a capital lease as an asset and an obligation at an amount equal to the present value of the minimum lease payments. The present value cannot exceed the fair value of the leased property at the inception of the lease. Thus, the lessee cannot use an unreasonably low discount rate.

1) The discount rate used is the lower of the **lessor's implicit interest rate** (if known) or the lessee's incremental borrowing rate. The discount rate used by the lessor is the rate implicit in the lease, that is, the rate at which the present value of the minimum lease payments and the unguaranteed residual value at the beginning of the lease term equals the fair value of the leased property at the inception of the lease, minus any ITC expected to be realized by the lessor. This rule prevents use of an unreasonably high discount rate for the purpose of avoiding capitalization under D.2.b.1)d) on the previous page.

d. **Minimum lease payments** include the minimum rental payments (excluding **executory costs** such as insurance, maintenance, and taxes) required during the lease term and the payment called for by a bargain purchase option.

1) If no such option exists, the minimum lease payments equal the sum of the minimum rental payments, the amount of **residual value guaranteed** by the lessee, and any nonrenewal penalty imposed.

a) Accordingly, the lessee's minimum lease payments (the amount at which the lessee capitalizes the transaction) will be lower if the residual value is unguaranteed rather than guaranteed.

2) Minimum lease payments do not include contingent rentals.

a) **SFAS 29**, *Determining Contingent Rentals*, defines contingent rentals as lease payments based on a factor that does not exist or is not measurable at the inception of the lease. For example, future sales do not exist at the inception of the lease. Thus, lease payments based on future sales are contingent rentals.

3) **FASB Interpretation No. 19**, *Lessee Guarantee of the Residual Value of Leased Property*, states that the amount of guaranteed residual value to be included in the determination of minimum lease payments is the determinable amount the lessee is required to make good, even if that amount is materially lower than the expected salvage value.

a) Any guarantee of residual value obtained by the lessee from an unrelated third party for the benefit of the lessor is specifically excluded from the determination of the lessee's minimum lease payments, provided that the lessor explicitly releases the lessee from primary and secondary liability on a residual value deficiency. Furthermore, amounts paid as consideration for this third-party guarantee are treated as executory costs (along with insurance, maintenance, taxes, etc.) and are also excluded.

4) SFAS 13 requires that the future minimum lease payments as of the date of the latest balance sheet presented be disclosed in the aggregate and for each of the 5 succeeding fiscal years. This disclosure is required whether the lease is classified as a capital lease or as an operating lease.

e. A lessee's periodic lease payment has two components: interest and the reduction of the lease obligation.

1) Under the **effective-interest method**, the appropriate interest rate is applied to the carrying value of the lease obligation at the beginning of the interest period to calculate interest. The effect is to produce a constant periodic rate of interest on the remaining balance.

a) The portion of the minimum lease payment that is greater than the amount of interest reduces the balance sheet liability.

b) In a classified balance sheet, the lease liability must be allocated between the current and noncurrent portions. The current portion at a balance sheet date is the reduction of the lease liability in the forthcoming year.

c) A residual guarantee or nonrenewal penalty that does not serve to extend the lease term results in a balance at the end of the lease term equal to the amount of the guarantee or penalty.

f. The **term of a lease** may include more than the fixed noncancellable lease term. However, in no case may the lease term extend beyond the date a bargain purchase option becomes exercisable. The lease term may include any periods

1) Covered by bargain renewal options

2) Covered by ordinary renewal options preceding the date at which a bargain purchase option is exercisable

3) Covered by ordinary renewal options during which a guarantee by the lessee of the lessor's debt or a loan from the lessee to the lessor related to the leased property is expected to be in effect

4) For which failure to renew the lease imposes a penalty on the lessee in an amount such that renewal appears to be reasonably assured

5) Representing renewals or extensions of the lease at the lessor's option

g. An asset recorded under a capital lease on the lessee's books should be amortized in a manner consistent with the lessee's normal depreciation policy. Hence, the accounting for the asset and the obligation involves separate processes.

1) If the lease is capitalized because the lease either transfers ownership to the lessee by the end of the lease term or contains a bargain purchase option, the amortization of the asset should be over its estimated economic life.

2) If the lease is capitalized because the lease term equals or exceeds 75% of the expected remaining life, or the present value of the minimum lease payments is equal to or greater than 90% of the fair value at the inception of the lease, the asset should be amortized over the lease term to its expected value to the lessee, if any, at the end of that term. For example, if the lessee has guaranteed a residual value and has no interest in any excess that might be realized, the maximum expected value to the lessee is the amount of the guarantee.

3. **Lessor Accounting for Capital Leases**. Lessors also classify most leases as operating or capital leases using the criteria in D.2.b.1) on page 219. In addition, although a lease satisfies one of the four capitalization criteria, the lessor may not treat the lease as a capital lease unless **collectibility** of the remaining payments is reasonably predictable and no material **uncertainties** exist regarding unreimbursable costs to be incurred by the lessor. Lessors must then determine whether a capital lease is a direct financing or sales-type lease.

a. In a **direct financing lease**, the lessor does not recognize a manufacturer's or dealer's profit (loss) because the fair value of the leased property and its cost or carrying amount are the same at the inception of the lease. The difference between the **gross investment** (minimum lease payments + unguaranteed residual value) and its cost or carrying amount is recorded as **unearned income**.

1) The unearned income and the **initial direct costs** of a direct financing lease are amortized to income over the lease term using the interest method so as to produce a constant rate of return on the **net investment**, which equals the gross investment, plus unamortized initial direct costs, minus unearned income.

a) Initial direct costs include the lessor's costs to originate a lease incurred in dealings with independent third parties that directly result from, and are essential to, the acquisition of the lease. They also include certain costs directly related to specified activities performed for that lease, e.g., evaluating lessee financial condition and security arrangements, negotiating terms, preparing documents, and closing.

b. In a **sales-type lease**, the lessor recognizes manufacturer's or dealer's profit (loss) because the fair value of the leased property at the lease's inception differs from its cost or carrying amount. The lessor records unearned income equal to the gross investment defined in D.3.a. on page 220 minus the sum of the present values of its two components discounted at the rate implicit in the lease. Moreover, the cost or carrying amount, plus initial direct costs, minus the present value of the unguaranteed residual value, is charged against income in the same period that the sales price (present value of the minimum lease payments, an amount that varies depending on whether residual value is guaranteed) is recognized. The result is the recognition of a profit (loss).

1) The unearned income is amortized to income over the lease term using the interest method so as to produce a constant rate of return on the net investment, which, in the case of a sales-type lease, equals the gross investment minus unearned income.

c. The following are the basic entries:

Direct Financing Lease		
Lease payments receivable	$XXX	
Asset		$XXX
Unearned income		XXX

Sales-Type Lease		
Cost of goods sold	$XXX	
Asset		$XXX
Lease payments receivable	XXX	
Sales revenue		XXX
Unearned income		XXX

d. The **minimum lease payments** calculated by the **lessor** are the same as those for the lessee except that they include any residual value or rental payments beyond the lease term guaranteed by a financially capable third party unrelated to the lessor or the lessee.

1) The effect of this difference may be that the capitalization criterion stated in D.2.b.1)d) on page 219 is met by the lessor but not the lessee.

4. As in the case of lessee accounting, SFAS 13 prescribes complex rules for lessor accounting when the lease involves land or land and buildings. These rules are beyond the scope of this outline.

5. **Operating leases** constitute off-balance-sheet financing because they do not meet the criteria for capitalization. They are transactions in which lessees rent the right to use lessor assets without acquiring a substantial portion of the benefits and risks of ownership of those assets.

a. Under an operating lease, the lessee records no asset or obligation, and the lessor records no sale or financing. The lessee does accrue rental expense at the end of an accounting period. Such accrual is at settlement value rather than present value.

b. Rent is reported as income by the lessor or expense by the lessee under the lease agreement. However, if rentals vary from a straight-line basis, the straight-line basis should be used unless another systematic and rational basis is more representative of the time pattern in which the use benefit is reduced.

c. The lessor records lease income, asset depreciation, maintenance, etc. Also, the lessor reports the leased property near property, plant, and equipment in the balance sheet and depreciates the property according to its normal depreciation policy for owned assets.

1) Initial direct costs should be deferred and amortized over the lease term in proportion to the recognition of rental income.

6. **Sale-leaseback transactions** involve the sale of property by the owner and a lease of the property back to the seller.

a. In a sale-leaseback transaction, if the lease qualifies as a **capital lease**, the profit or loss on the sale is normally deferred and amortized by the seller-lessee in proportion to the amortization of the leased asset, that is, at the same rate at which the leased asset is depreciated.

1) The profit deferred may be reported as an asset valuation allowance (a contra asset with a credit balance).

2) An indicated loss is deferred and amortized as prepaid rent if the carrying amount of the asset sold is greater than the sale price but the fair value exceeds the carrying amount.

3) If the carrying amount is greater than the fair value, the excess is recognized immediately as a loss.

b. A profit or loss on the sale in a sale-leaseback transaction normally should be deferred and amortized in proportion to the gross rental payments expensed over the lease term if the leaseback is classified as an **operating lease** (**SFAS 28**, *Accounting for Sales with Leasebacks*).

1) When the seller-lessee classifies the lease arising from the sale-leaseback as an operating lease, no asset is shown on the balance sheet, and the deferral cannot be presented as a contra asset. Accordingly, the usual practice is to report the profit (loss) as a deferred credit (debit).

c. SFAS 28 provides for certain exceptions to the foregoing rules:

1) One exception applies when the seller-lessee retains more than a minor part (more than 10%), but less than substantially all (less than 90%), of the use of the property through the leaseback.

a) The excess profit is recognized at the date of the sale if the seller-lessee in this situation realizes a profit on the sale in excess of either

i) The present value of the minimum lease payments over the lease term if the leaseback is an operating lease, or

ii) The recorded amount of the leased asset if the leaseback is classified as a capital lease.

b) "Substantially all" has essentially the same meaning as the "90% test" used in determining whether a lease is a capital or operating lease (the present value of the lease payments is 90% or more of the fair value of the leased property). "Minor" refers to a transfer of 10% or less of the use of the property in the lease.

2) Another exception applies when the seller-lessee relinquishes the right to substantially all of the remaining use of the property sold and retains only a minor portion of such use. This exception is indicated if the present value of a reasonable amount of rentals for the leaseback represents a minor part of the use of the property (10% or less of the fair value of the asset sold). In this case, the seller-lessee should account for the sale and the leaseback as separate transactions based upon their respective terms.

7. Stop and review! You have completed the outline for this subunit. Study multiple-choice questions 44 through 60 beginning on page 252.

E. Pensions and Other Postretirement Benefits

1. ***Employers' Accounting for Pensions*** **(SFAS 87)**

a. SFAS 87 is applicable to any arrangement that is similar in substance to a pension plan, regardless of form, the method of financing, or whether the plan is written or implied by the well-defined practice of paying postretirement benefits.

b. SFAS 87 is based on the fundamental assumption that a **defined benefit pension plan** is part of an employee's compensation incurred when the services provided to the employer by the employee are rendered.

1) The defined pension benefit is provided in the form of deferred payments that are not precisely determinable.

a) These payments can only be estimated based on the plan benefit formula and relevant future events such as future compensation levels, mortality rates, ages at retirement, and vesting considerations.

c. SFAS 87 permits the delayed recognition of certain events, the reporting of a net cost, and the offsetting of assets and liabilities.

1) Delayed recognition means that certain changes in the pension obligation and in the value of the plan assets are not recognized as they occur. They are recognized on a systematic and gradual basis over subsequent periods.

2) Net costs means that various pension costs (service cost, interest, actuarial gains and losses, etc.) reflected in income are reported as one expense.

3) The offsetting feature means that the recognized values of the plan assets contributed to the plan are offset in the statement of financial position against the recognized liabilities.

d. The **projected benefit obligation (PBO)** as of a date is equal to the actuarial present value of all benefits attributed by the pension benefit formula to employee services rendered prior to that date. The PBO is measured using assumptions as to future as well as past and current salary levels.

1) The PBO at the end of a period equals the PBO at the beginning of the period, plus service cost, plus retroactive benefits (prior service cost) granted by a plan amendment during the period, minus benefits paid, plus or minus changes in the PBO resulting from changes in assumptions and from experience different from that assumed.

2) The **accumulated benefit obligation (ABO)** is the present value of benefits accrued to date based on past and current compensation levels.

3) Assumptions about discount (interest) rates must be made to calculate the PBO and the ABO.

   a) They reflect the rates at which benefits can be settled. In estimating these rates, it is appropriate to consider current prices of annuity contracts that could be used to settle pension obligations as well as the rates on high-quality fixed investments (SFAS 87).

e. Annual pension expense is the **net periodic pension cost (NPPC)**. It consists of six elements.

1) **Service cost** is the present value of the future benefits earned by the employees in the current period (as calculated according to the plan's benefit formula). This amount is provided by the plan's actuary and is unaffected by the funded status of the plan.

2) **Interest cost** is the increase in the PBO determined by multiplying the PBO at the beginning of the year by the current discount rate (e.g., the interest rate at which annuities could be purchased to settle pension obligations).

   a) This discount rate may change with changes in interest rates.
   b) The PBO and the discount rate are provided by the plan's actuary.

3) The **actual return on plan assets** is based on the fair value of the plan assets at the beginning and end of the accounting period adjusted for contributions and payments during the period (FV at end of the period – FV at beginning of the period – contributions to the plan assets + benefits paid to the employees). The return on plan assets component (given that it is positive) decreases NPPC.

   a) The **expected return on plan assets** is the market-related value of the plan assets at the beginning of the period multiplied by the expected long-term rate of return.

      i) Market-related value may be either fair value or a calculated value that recognizes changes in fair value systematically and rationally over no more than 5 years, such as a 5-year moving average.

         - The purpose of spreading recognition of the changes in fair value is to reduce the volatility of the NPPC. For example, a company may choose to recognize 20% of the last 5 years' gains and losses each year.

   b) The difference between the actual and the expected returns is ultimately included in the gain or loss component of NPPC, but gains and losses (e.g., the difference between the actual and the expected returns) are not required to be recognized in NPPC in the period when they occur.

      i) Thus, the net effect on the required minimum NPPC is to decrease it by the amount of the expected, not the actual, return on plan assets because the current asset gain or loss, that is, the difference between the actual and expected returns, may be deferred.

4) **Gains and losses** arise from changes in the amount of the PBO or plan assets that result from experience different from that expected and from changes in assumptions. SFAS 87 adopts a corridor approach to reduce the volatility of the NPPC caused by gains and losses.

   a) The cumulative unrecognized net gain or loss at the beginning of the year is subject to required amortization in NPPC only to the extent it exceeds 10% of the greater of the PBO or the market-related value of plan assets. Thus, only the amount exceeding the 10% threshold need be amortized.

   b) The minimum required amortization equals the excess described just above divided by the average remaining service period of active employees expected to receive benefits.

   c) Amortization of a net unrecognized gain (loss) decreases (increases) NPPC.

5) **Amortization of prior service cost.** If a pension plan is amended to grant additional benefits for past periods of service, the cost of the retroactive benefits is allocated to the future periods of service of employees active at the date of the amendment who are expected to receive benefits.

   a) The cost of retroactive benefits is the increase in the PBO at the date of the amendment and should be amortized by assigning an equal amount to each future period of service of each employee active at the date of the amendment who is expected to receive benefits under the plan. However, to reduce the burden of these allocation computations, any alternative amortization approach (e.g., averaging) that more rapidly reduces the unrecognized prior service cost is acceptable if applied consistently.

6) **Amortization of any unrecognized transition asset or obligation.** The net obligation or net asset arising when SFAS 87 is first applied (the transition amount) is the difference between (1) the PBO of the plan and (2) an amount equal to the fair value of the plan assets, plus any recognized accrued liability, or minus any prepaid pension cost. Straight-line amortization is to be over the average remaining service period of participating employees (if less than 15 years, a 15-year period may be elected).

   a) For example, if a plan is underfunded by $125,000 (the excess of the PBO over plan assets), but an accrued liability of $50,000 has already been credited because the periodic pension cost of prior periods exceeded funding, the $75,000 unrecognized net obligation is amortized over the remaining service period of participating employees.

   b) Amortization of a net obligation (asset) increases (decreases) NPPC.

f. Unfunded accrued pension cost is recorded as a credit to the **accrued/prepaid pension cost** account when funding is less than the NPPC. Prepaid pension cost (a debit) results from funding the plan in excess of the NPPC.

   1) Assuming an unfunded ABO, the total net liability reported in the balance sheet equals the unfunded ABO (ABO – fair value of plan assets).

a) An **additional minimum pension liability** must be recognized if a portion of the ABO is unfunded and an asset has been recognized as prepaid pension cost or the existing liability (unfunded accrued pension cost) is less than the unfunded ABO.

i) Thus, the additional liability equals the unfunded ABO plus prepaid pension cost or minus accrued pension cost.

ii) Recognition of an additional liability has no effect on earnings. An intangible asset is debited to the extent unrecognized prior service cost exists. If that amount is not adequate, the remainder is reported in other comprehensive income.

g. SFAS 87 emphasizes accounting for a single-employer, defined benefit pension plan, but it also applies to defined contribution plans.

1) A **defined contribution plan** provides benefits in exchange for services, provides an account for each participant, and specifies how contributions are to be determined. Pension benefits depend only on contributions, returns on investment, and allocated forfeitures of other participants' benefits. Thus, employees have the benefit of gain and the risk of loss.

2) Under a defined contribution plan, the periodic pension cost reported by the employer is the contribution called for in that period. The company reports an asset only if the contribution to the pension trust is greater than the defined, required contribution. The company reports a liability only if the contribution is less than the required amount.

2. **SFAS 106**, *Employers' Accounting for Postretirement Benefits Other Than Pensions*, applies principles similar to those of pension accounting.

a. SFAS 106 emphasizes an employer's accounting for a single-employer plan that defines the postretirement benefits other than pensions to be provided to employees (other postretirement employee benefits or OPEB).

1) The OPEB are defined in terms of monetary amounts (e.g., a given dollar value of life insurance) or benefit coverage (e.g., amounts per day for hospitalization).

a) The amount of benefits depends on such factors as the benefit formula, the life expectancy of the retiree and any beneficiaries and covered dependents, and the frequency and significance of events (e.g., illnesses) requiring payments.

2) The costs are expensed over the attribution period, which begins on the date of hire unless the plan's benefit formula grants credit for service only from a later date. The end of the period is the full eligibility date.

3) The basic elements of accounting for OPEB include the **expected postretirement benefit obligation (EPBO)**, which equals the **accumulated postretirement benefit obligation (APBO)** after the full eligibility date.

a) The EPBO for an employee is the actuarial present value at a given date of the OPEB expected to be paid. Its measurement depends on the anticipated amounts and timing of future benefits, the costs to be incurred to provide those benefits, and the extent the costs are shared by the employee and others (such as governmental programs).

b) The APBO for an employee is the actuarial present value at a given date of the future benefits attributable to the employee's service as of that date. Unlike the calculation of the ABO described in SFAS 87, the determination of the APBO (as well as of the EPBO and service cost) implicitly includes the consideration of future salary progression to the extent the benefit formula defines benefits as a function of future compensation levels.

c) SFAS 106 "requires that an employer's obligation for postretirement benefits expected to be provided to or for an employee be fully accrued by the date that employee attains full eligibility for all of the benefits, even if the employee is expected to render additional service beyond that date."

i) The full eligibility date is reached when the employee has rendered all the services necessary to earn all of the benefits expected to be received by that employee.

ii) Prior to that date, the EPBO exceeds the APBO.

4) Unlike SFAS 87, SFAS 106 does not require recognition of a minimum liability.

b. The six possible components included in net periodic postretirement benefit cost (NPPBC) of an employer sponsoring a defined benefit health care plan are service cost, interest on the APBO, return on plan assets, amortization of unrecognized prior service cost, amortization of the transition obligation or asset, and the gain or loss component.

c. **Service cost** is defined as the actuarial present value of benefits attributed to services rendered by employees during the period. It is the portion of the EPBO attributed to service in the period and is not affected by the level of funding.

d. **Interest cost** reflects the change in the APBO during the period resulting solely from the passage of time. It equals the APBO at the beginning of the period times the assumed discount rate used in determining the present value of future cash outflows currently expected to be required to satisfy the obligation.

e. **Prior service cost** is defined as the cost of benefit improvements attributable to plan participants' prior service pursuant to a plan amendment or a plan initiation that provides benefits in exchange for plan participants' prior service.

1) Ordinarily, it is recognized in NPPBC by assigning an equal amount to each remaining year of service to the full eligibility date of each participant active at the amendment date who was not yet fully eligible for benefits.

f. The **gain or loss components** of NPPBC (SFAS 106) and NPPC (SFAS 87) are calculated similarly. Under SFAS 106, however, if an enterprise consistently recognizes gains and losses immediately, gains (losses) that do not offset previously recognized losses (gains) must first reduce any unrecognized transition obligation (asset).

1) The transition obligation (asset) represents an underlying unfunded (overfunded) APBO.

2) The FASB believes that gains (losses) should not be recognized until the unfunded (overfunded) APBO is recognized.

g. **A gain or loss from a temporary deviation** from the substantive plan is immediately recognized in income.

1) For example, under a plan's terms, an excess of benefit payments over the sum of the employer's cost and the employees' contributions for a year may be recovered from increased employees' contributions in the subsequent year. However, for the current year only, the employer may decide not to adjust contributions.

2) Delayed recognition is inappropriate because a temporary deviation is not deemed to provide future economic value and relates to benefits already paid.

3) If the deviation is other than temporary, that is, if the employer decides to continue to bear the burden of increased costs, the implication is that the substantive plan (the plan as understood by the parties, as opposed to the existing written plan) has been amended. An amendment would require accounting for prior service cost.

h. The initial application of SFAS 106 may result in a **transition asset or obligation**.

1) The transition amount is the difference between (1) the APBO and (2) the fair value of plan assets, plus any recognized accrued postretirement benefit cost, or minus any recognized prepaid postretirement benefit cost.

2) Unlike the accounting prescribed by SFAS 87, SFAS 106 permits employers to elect immediate recognition in income of the transition amount as the effect of a change in accounting principle.

3) The amount attributable to the effects of a plan initiation or benefit improvements adopted after 1990 is treated as unrecognized prior service cost and excluded from the transition amount immediately recognized.

4) If employers wish to amortize the transition amount on a delayed basis as part of the NPPBC, straight-line amortization over the average remaining service period of active plan participants is required unless

a) That period is less than 20 years, in which case a 20-year period may be elected, or

b) Almost all plan participants are inactive, in which case the average remaining life expectancy of those participants must be used.

3. Stop and review! You have completed the outline for this subunit. Study multiple-choice questions 61 through 70 beginning on page 258.

F. Deferred Income Taxes

1. Scope and Principles

a. **SFAS 109**, *Accounting for Income Taxes*, adopts the asset and liability method of accounting for income taxes.

1) It establishes standards of accounting and reporting for income taxes currently payable and for the tax consequences of

a) Revenues, expenses, gains, and losses included in taxable income of an earlier or later year than the year in which they are recognized in income for financial reporting purposes

b) Other events that create differences between the tax bases of assets and liabilities and their amounts for financial reporting purposes

c) Operating loss or tax credit carrybacks for refunds of taxes paid in prior years and carryforwards to reduce taxes payable in future years

2) SFAS 109 applies to

a) Taxes based on income, whether foreign, federal, state, or local

b) An enterprise's domestic and foreign operations that are consolidated, combined, or accounted for by the equity method

c) Foreign enterprises in preparing statements based on U.S. GAAP

3) It does not address

a) The investment tax credit
b) Discounting future tax liabilities (recording them at their present value)
c) Income tax accounting for interim periods except for the

i) Standards for recognition of tax benefits
ii) Effects of enacted tax law changes
iii) Changes in valuation allowances

b. **Interperiod tax allocation**. Tax consequences are a transaction's or an event's effects on current and deferred income taxes. Income taxes currently payable or refundable for a particular year usually include the tax consequences of most of the events recognized in the financial statements for the same year.

1) However, certain significant exceptions exist. As a result, the tax consequences of some transactions or events may be recognized in income taxes currently payable or refundable in a year different from that in which their financial-statement effects are recognized. Moreover, some transactions or events may have tax consequences or financial-statement effects but never both.

a) Because of these differences, income taxes currently payable or refundable may differ from (exceed or be less than) income tax expense or benefit. The accounting for these differences is interperiod tax allocation.

c. **Objectives of SFAS 109**. Accrual accounting should recognize taxes payable or refundable for the current year.

1) It should also recognize deferred tax liabilities and assets for the future tax consequences of events that have been previously recognized in the enterprise's financial statements or tax returns.

d. **Basic principles of income tax accounting**

1) A current tax liability or asset is recognized for the estimated taxes payable or refundable on current-year tax returns.

2) A deferred tax liability or asset is recognized for the estimated future tax effects attributable to temporary differences and carryforwards.

3) Measurement of tax liabilities and assets is based on enacted tax law; the effects of future changes in that law are not anticipated.

4) A deferred tax asset is reduced by a valuation allowance if it is more likely than not that some portion will not be realized.

2. **Temporary and Permanent Differences**

a. **Temporary differences (TDs)** include differences between the tax basis of an asset or liability and its reported amount in the financial statements that will result in taxable or deductible amounts in future years when the reported amount of the asset is recovered or the liability is settled.

1) A **future taxable amount** will result from the recovery of an asset related to a revenue or gain that is taxable subsequent to being recognized in financial income.

a) An example is income recognized under the equity method for financial statement purposes and at the time of distribution in taxable income.

2) A future taxable amount also results from the recovery of an asset related to any expense or loss that is deductible for tax purposes prior to being recognized in financial income.

a) An example is a long-term asset that is amortized or depreciated for tax purposes more quickly than for financial reporting.

3) A **future deductible amount** results from the settlement of a liability related to an expense or loss that is deductible for tax purposes subsequent to being recognized in financial income.

a) An example is a warranty liability, which is recognized as an expense in financial income when a product is sold and recognized in taxable income when the expenditures are made in a later period.

4) A future deductible amount also results from the settlement of a liability related to a revenue or gain that is taxable prior to being recognized in financial income.

a) An example is subscriptions revenue received in advance, which is recognized in taxable income when received and recognized in financial income when earned in a later period.

5) TDs may also result from events that have been recognized in the financial statements and will result in taxable or deductible amounts in future years based on provisions in the tax laws but that cannot be identified with a particular asset or liability for financial reporting purposes.

a) A TD relates to a particular asset or liability if the reduction of the asset or liability causes reversal of the TD.

b) An example is organizational costs. They must be expensed when incurred for financial reporting purposes (written off rather than recognized as an asset) but deferred for tax purposes. Another example is an operating loss carryforward.

b. A **permanent difference** arises from an event that is recognized either in pretax financial income or in taxable income but never in the other. It does not result in a deferred tax asset or liability.

1) Examples of items recognized in pretax financial income but never in taxable income are municipal bond interest, premiums on insurance policies for key executives, and the proceeds from such policies. Examples of items recognized in taxable income but never in financial income are the dividends-received deduction and percentage depletion.

a) Under IRC Sec. 197, goodwill acquired after August 10, 1993 is tax deductible on a pro rata basis over a 15-year period. Hence, amortization of such goodwill does not result in a permanent difference. However, goodwill acquired prior to August 11, 1993 is not tax deductible and therefore results in a permanent difference.

3. **Recognition and Measurement**

a. Because recovery of assets and settlement of liabilities are inherent assumptions of GAAP, accrual accounting must recognize deferred tax consequences of TDs (temporary differences).

1) **Basic definitions**

a) **Income tax expense or benefit** is the sum of the current tax expense or benefit and deferred tax expense or benefit.

b) **Current tax expense or benefit** is the amount of taxes paid or payable (or refundable) for the year as determined by applying the enacted tax law to the taxable income or excess of deductions over revenues for that year.

c) **Current tax liability** is equal to taxable income times the applicable tax rate.

d) **Deferred tax expense or benefit** is the net change during the year in an enterprise's deferred tax liabilities and assets.

e) A **deferred tax liability** records the deferred tax consequences attributable to taxable TDs. It is measured using the applicable enacted tax rate and provisions of the enacted tax law.

f) A **deferred tax asset** records the deferred tax consequences attributable to deductible TDs and carryforwards. It is measured using the applicable enacted tax rate and provisions of the enacted tax law.

2) A **valuation allowance** is a contra account to a deferred tax asset. It is used to reduce a deferred tax asset if the weight of the available evidence, both positive and negative, indicates that it is more likely than not (that is, the probability is more than 50%) that some portion will not be realized. The allowance should be sufficient to reduce the deferred tax asset to the amount that is more likely than not to be realized.

a) Future realization of the tax benefit represented by a deferred tax asset ultimately depends on the existence of sufficient taxable income of the proper character (ordinary income or capital gain) within the carryback and carryforward period.

i) For example, federal corporate tax law permits net operating losses to be carried back 2 years and forward 20 years. A company may also choose the carryforward only.

b) The following are sources of taxable income permitting realization of the tax benefit of a deferred tax asset and therefore eliminating or reducing the need for a valuation allowance:

i) Reversals of taxable TDs

ii) Future taxable income without regard to reversing differences and carryforwards

iii) Taxable income in the carryback period

iv) Tax-planning strategies, for example, those that accelerate taxable amounts to permit use of an expiring tax credit carryforward, change the character of income or loss, or switch from tax-exempt to taxable items of income

3) **Determination of deferred taxes**. The process below is followed for each taxpaying entity in each tax jurisdiction:

a) Identify TDs (types and amounts) and operating loss and tax credit carryforwards for tax purposes (nature and amounts, and length of the remaining carryforward period).

b) Measure the total deferred tax liability for taxable TDs using the applicable tax rate.

c) Measure the total deferred tax asset for deductible TDs and operating loss carryforwards using the applicable tax rate.

d) Measure deferred tax assets for each type of tax credit carryforward.

e) Recognize a valuation allowance if necessary.

4) **Applicable tax rates**. A deferred tax liability or asset is measured using the tax rate(s) expected to apply when the liability or asset is expected to be settled or realized.

a) The tax rate used in the measurement of deferred tax liabilities and assets is, in essence, a flat rate if graduated rates are not significant to the enterprise. Otherwise, an average of the applicable graduated rates is used.

5) The basic entry to record taxes in accordance with the asset and liability method required by SFAS 109 is

Income tax expense (or benefit)	debit (or credit)	
Income tax payable (or refundable)		credit (or debit)
Deferred income tax liability (or asset)		credit (or debit)

4. **Additional Issues**

a. SFAS 109 requires **intraperiod tax allocation**. Income tax expense (benefit) is allocated to continuing operations, discontinued operations, extraordinary items, other comprehensive income, and items debited or credited directly to equity.

1) Intraperiod tax allocation requires allocation of a period's income tax expense to the components of net income but does not affect that income.

2) The tax benefits of most operating loss carryforwards and carrybacks are reported in the same manner as the source of the income or loss in the current year.

b. **Enacted changes** in the tax law or rates require an adjustment of a deferred tax liability or asset in the period of the enactment of the tax law or rate. The effect is included in the amount of income tax expense or benefit allocated to continuing operations.

c. **Change in Tax Status.** The resulting effect on deferred taxes is recognized.

1) When an enterprise changes from nontaxable to taxable status, a deferred tax amount reflecting TDs at the time of the change is recognized.

2) When an enterprise changes its status from taxable to nontaxable, any existing deferred tax liability or asset is ordinarily eliminated at the date of the change.

3) For an elective change, the effect is recognized on the approval date (or on the filing date if approval is not needed).

   a) If the change in status results from a change in tax law, the effect is recognized on the enactment date.

4) The effect of recognizing or eliminating the deferred tax liability or asset is included in the amount of income tax expense or benefit allocated to continuing operations.

d. **Business Combinations**. A deferred tax liability or asset is recognized for the differences between the assigned values and the tax bases of assets and liabilities acquired in a purchase business combination.

1) This rule does not apply to nondeductible goodwill, unallocated negative goodwill, leveraged leases, and certain other items.

e. **Financial Statement Presentation**. Deferred tax liabilities and assets should be separated into current and noncurrent components. Whether an item is current or noncurrent depends on the classification of the related asset or liability.

1) A TD relates to a specific asset or liability if the reduction of the asset or liability causes a reversal of the TD. For example, a TD resulting from accounting for a long-term contract using the percentage-of-completion method for financial statement purposes and the completed-contract method for tax purposes does not relate to a specific asset or liability. The TD reverses only when the contract is completed, not when receivables arising from program billings, etc., are collected (SFAS 37).

   NOTE: The completed-contract method is allowed only in limited circumstances for income tax purposes.

2) If a deferred tax item, including a deferred tax asset related to a carryforward, is not related to an asset or liability for financial reporting, it is classified based on the expected reversal date of the TD.

3) A valuation allowance for a particular tax jurisdiction is allocated pro rata between current and noncurrent deferred tax assets.

4) For a given tax-paying entity and within a specific jurisdiction, current deferred tax assets and liabilities are netted. Noncurrent deferred tax assets and liabilities are also offset and shown as a single amount.

5. **Basic Examples**

a. **Deferred tax liability**. For 2000, Pitou Co.'s pretax financial income is $520,000, and its taxable income is $500,000. The $20,000 difference is attributable solely to an excess of tax depreciation over book depreciation that will result in future taxable amounts when the TD reverses. Pitou's applicable tax rate is 34%. Given no beginning deferred tax amounts, the deferred tax liability is $6,800 (34% x $20,000 taxable TD), and the deferred tax expense is also $6,800 ($6,800 year-end deferred tax liability – $0 balance at the beginning of the year). Income tax payable (current tax expense) is $170,000 (34% x $500,000 taxable income). Accordingly, income tax expense is $176,800 ($170,000 current tax expense + $6,800 deferred tax expense). The year-end entry is

Income tax expense	$176,800	
Income tax payable		$170,000
Deferred income tax liability		6,800

For 2001, Pitou Co. has pretax financial income of $442,000 and taxable income of $450,000. The difference reflects an $8,000 excess of book depreciation over tax depreciation. There is no other difference between pretax financial income and taxable income. Hence, the taxable TD is reduced to $12,000 ($20,000 – $8,000), the year-end deferred tax liability is $4,080 (34% x $12,000), and the decrease in the deferred tax liability (the deferred tax benefit arising from reduction in the liability) is $2,720 ($6,800 at the beginning of the year – $4,080 at year-end). Current tax expense (tax payable) is $153,000 (34% x $450,000 taxable income). Consequently, total income tax expense for the year is $150,280 ($153,000 current tax expense – $2,720 deferred tax benefit). The year-end entry is

Income tax expense	$150,280	
Deferred income tax liability	2,720	
Income tax payable		$153,000

b. **Deferred tax asset**. Lunes Co. began operations in the year just ended. It has taxable income of $400,000 and pretax financial income of $385,000. The difference is solely attributable to receipt of unearned subscription revenue (a liability) that was included as revenue in the tax return in the year of collection. Lunes will recognize $9,000 of this unearned revenue as earned in its second year of operations and $6,000 in the third year. The applicable tax rate is 34%. Thus, the deferred tax asset is $5,100 (34% x $15,000 deductible TD), and the deferred tax benefit is also $5,100 ($5,100 year-end deferred tax asset – $0 balance at the beginning of the year). Income tax payable (current tax expense) is $136,000 (34% x $400,000 taxable income). Accordingly, income tax expense is $130,900 ($136,000 current tax expense – $5,100 deferred tax benefit). Based on the evidence (taxable income), no valuation allowance is required for the deferred tax asset. Thus, the year-end entry is

Income tax expense	$130,900	
Deferred income tax asset	5,100	
Income tax payable		$136,000

In its second year of operations, Lunes has taxable income of $600,000, with income tax payable (current tax expense) of $204,000 (34% x $600,000). Taxable income and pretax financial income differ only in that $9,000 of unearned revenue collected in the preceding year is included in the determination of pretax financial income. At the end of the second year, the deferred tax asset is therefore $2,040 [34% x ($15,000 – $9,000)], and the deferred tax expense (the decrease in the deferred tax asset) is $3,060 ($5,100 – $2,040). Total income tax expense is $207,060 ($204,000 current tax expense + $3,060 deferred tax expense). Based on the evidence (taxable income), no valuation allowance is required for the deferred tax asset. Thus, the year-end entry is

Income tax expense	$207,060	
Income tax payable		$204,000
Deferred income tax asset		3,060

c. **Deferred tax asset -- valuation allowance**. Mardi Co. has a $6,000 deductible TD at the end of its current year. The applicable tax rate is 34%. Consequently, Mardi recorded a deferred tax asset of $2,040 (34% x $6,000). However, after weighing all the evidence, Mardi Co. has decided that it is more likely than not (more than 50% probable) that $4,000 of the deductible temporary difference will not be realized. To reflect this determination, a valuation allowance (a contra account) should be credited. The offsetting debit is to income tax expense. The amount of the valuation allowance should be sufficient to reduce the deferred tax asset to the amount that is more likely than not to be realized. Accordingly, Mardi should recognize a $1,360 valuation allowance to reduce the $2,040 deferred tax asset to $680 (34% x $2,000). The entry is

Income tax expense	$1,360	
Deferred tax asset valuation allowance		$1,360

6. Stop and review! You have completed the outline for this subunit. Study multiple-choice questions 71 through 87 beginning on page 262.

MULTIPLE-CHOICE QUESTIONS

A. Current Liabilities, Accruals, and Deferred Revenues

1. On August 1, 1997, a company issued 5-year bonds with a face amount of $10,000,000. The bonds carry a stated interest rate of 10% and interest is payable annually on July 31. Which is the appropriate classification of bonds payable and the related accrued interest payable on the December 31, 2001 balance sheet?

Classification Table

	Bonds Payable	Interest Payable
Classification A	Current liability	Current liability
Classification B	Current liability	Long-term liability
Classification C	Long-term liability	Current liability
Classification D	Long-term liability	Long-term liability

A. Classification A.

B. Classification B.

C. Classification C.

D. Classification D.

The correct answer is (A). *(CIA, adapted)*

REQUIRED: The appropriate classification of bonds payable and the related accrued interest payable on the December 31, 2001 balance sheet.

DISCUSSION: ARB 43, Chapter 3A, *Current Assets and Current Liabilities*, defines a current liability as an obligation that will be either liquidated using current assets or replaced by another current liability. SFAS 78, *Classification of Obligations That Are Callable by the Creditor*, amends ARB 43 to include the following as current liabilities: (1) obligations that, by their terms, are or will be due on demand within 1 year (or the operating cycle if longer), and (2) obligations that are or will be callable by the creditor within 1 year because of a violation of a debt covenant. At the balance sheet date of December 31, 2001, both the principal of the bonds and the interest accrued at the balance sheet date will be due within a year. These amounts are expected to require the use of current assets (there is no evidence to the contrary) and should be classified as current liabilities.

Answer (B) is incorrect because the interest payable should be classified as a current liability. It is due within a year after the December 31, 2001 balance sheet date. Answer (C) is incorrect because the balance of bonds payable should be classified as a current liability. The bonds are due within a year after the December 31, 2001 balance sheet date. Answer (D) is incorrect because both the balance of bonds payable and interest payable should be classified as current liabilities.

2. The selling price of a new company's units is $10,000 each. The buyers are provided with a 2-year warranty that is expected to cost the company $250 per unit in the year of the sale and $750 per unit in the year following the sale. The company sold 80 units in the first year of operation and 100 units in the second year. Actual payments for warranty claims were $10,000 and $65,000 in years one and two, respectively. The amount charged to warranty expense during the second year of operation is

A. $25,000

B. $65,000

C. $85,000

D. $100,000

The correct answer is (D). *(CIA, adapted)*

REQUIRED: The amount charged to warranty expense during the second year of operation.

DISCUSSION: Under the accrual method, the total estimated warranty costs are charged to operating expense in the year of sale. The total estimated warranty cost per unit is $1,000 ($250 + $750). In year two, 100 units were sold, so the warranty expense recognized is $100,000.

Answer (A) is incorrect because $25,000 is the expected amount of warranty claims for the first year of second-year sales. Answer (B) is incorrect because $65,000 is the actual amount of claims in the second year. Answer (C) is incorrect because $85,000 is the expected amount of warranty claims in the second year.

3. Paxton Company started offering a 3-year warranty on its products sold after June 1, 2000. Paxton's actual sales for the year ended May 31, 2001 were $2,695,000. The total cost of the warranty is expected to be 3% of sales. The actual 2001 warranty expenditures were $31,500 in labor and $9,100 in parts. The amount of warranty expense that should appear on Paxton's income statement for the year ended May 31, 2001 is

A. $31,500

B. $40,250

C. $40,600

D. $80,850

The correct answer is (D). *(CMA, adapted)*

REQUIRED: The annual warranty expense.

DISCUSSION: If warranty expense is expected to be 3% of sales, that amount should be recorded as an expense for the year. Consequently, the expense is $80,850 (3% x $2,695,000). The amount of cash expended during the year is irrelevant because the expense is expected to be paid over 3 years. A liability is credited for any portion of the expense not paid during 2001.

Answer (A) is incorrect because $31,500 is the current year's outlay for labor. Answer (B) is incorrect because $40,250 is the liability accrued at year-end. Answer (C) is incorrect because $40,600 is the cash outlay for the current year.

4. An employee has the right to receive compensation for future paid leave, and the payment of compensation is probable. If the obligation relates to rights that vest but the amount cannot be reasonably estimated, the employer should

A. Accrue a liability with proper disclosure.

B. Not accrue a liability nor disclose the situation.

C. Accrue a liability; however, the additional disclosure is not required.

D. Not accrue a liability; however, disclosure is required.

The correct answer is (D). *(CMA, adapted)*

REQUIRED: The treatment of an obligation for future paid leave when the amount cannot be reasonably estimated.

DISCUSSION: SFAS 43 lists four requirements that must be met before a liability is accrued for future compensated absences. These requirements are that the obligation must arise for past services, the employee rights must vest or accumulate, payment is probable, and the amount can be reasonably estimated. If the amount cannot be reasonably estimated, no liability should be recorded. However, the obligation should be disclosed.

Answers (A) and (C) are incorrect because the conditions are not met for accrual of a liability. Answer (B) is incorrect because disclosure is required.

5. The Elam Company has reasonably estimated the following probable costs for the compensated absences of its employees:

Vacation pay (vested)	$5,000
Vacation pay (accumulated but not vested)	3,000
Sick pay (vested)	4,000
Sick pay (accumulated but not vested)	2,000

The costs are attributable to services that have already been rendered. In accordance with SFAS 43, *Accounting for Compensated Absences*, the minimum amount that Elam must accrue as its liability for compensated absences is

A. $5,000

B. $8,000

C. $12,000

D. $14,000

The correct answer is (C). *(Publisher)*

REQUIRED: The minimum amount of liability to be accrued for compensated absences.

DISCUSSION: Vacation pay and vested sick pay should be accrued as liabilities. Thus, the minimum accrual is $12,000 ($5,000 + $3,000 + $4,000).

Answer (A) is incorrect because accumulated vacation pay and vested sick pay should be accrued. Answer (B) is incorrect because SFAS 43 also requires accrual of vested sick pay. Answer (D) is incorrect because SFAS 43 does not require accrual of nonvested sick pay.

6. Pine Company began operations on January 1, Year 1. Pine employs 10 individuals who work 8-hour days and are paid hourly. Each employee earns 10 paid vacation days annually. Vacation days may be taken after January 1 of the year following the year in which they are earned. Additional information is as follows:

Actual Hourly Wage Rate		Vacation Days Used By Each Employee	
Year 1	Year 2	Year 1	Year 2
$8.00	$8.00	0	8

The amounts of compensated absences liability that should have appeared on Pine's balance sheet at December 31, Year 1 and Year 2 were

A. $0 and $6,400.

B. $6,400 and $7,680.

C. $0 and $1,280.

D. $6,400 and $1,280

The correct answer is (B). *(Publisher)*

REQUIRED: The liability for vacation pay at the end of Year 1 and Year 2.

DISCUSSION: Each employee earns 10 vacation days a year at $64 per day (8 hours x $8). Thus, for each employee, the annual expense is $640. The total for 10 workers is $6,400. Because no vacation days were used during Year 1, the entire balance of $6,400 will be a liability at December 31. The workers will earn an additional 10 days of vacation during Year 2, while using up eight days. Consequently, the liability will increase by two days during Year 2, or $1,280 (2 days x 10 workers x $64). Adding the $1,280 to the $6,400 from the preceding year results in a year-end liability of $7,680.

Answers (A) and (C) are incorrect because accumulated vacation pay should be accrued for Year 1. Answer (D) is incorrect because the $6,400 liability from Year 1 should be carried forward to Year 2.

7. Case Cereal Co. frequently distributes coupons to promote new products. On October 1, Case mailed 1 million coupons for $.45 off each box of cereal purchased. Case expects 120,000 of these coupons to be redeemed before the December 31 expiration date. It takes 30 days from the redemption date for Case to receive the coupons from the retailers. Case reimburses the retailers an additional $.05 for each coupon redeemed. As of December 31, Case had paid retailers $25,000 related to these coupons, and had 50,000 coupons on hand that had not been processed for payment. What amount should Case report as a liability for coupons in its December 31 balance sheet?

A. $35,000

B. $29,000

C. $25,000

D. $22,500

The correct answer is (A). *(CPA, adapted)*

REQUIRED: The liability for coupons at year-end.

DISCUSSION: The company pays $.50 ($.45 + $.05) for the redemption of a coupon, and it expects 120,000 to be redeemed at a total cost of $60,000 (120,000 x $.50). Given that payments of $25,000 have been made, the liability at year-end must be $35,000 ($60,000 – $25,000). The cost associated with the unprocessed coupons on hand does not reduce the liability because payment for these coupons has not yet been made.

Answer (B) is incorrect because $29,000 does not include the additional $.05 per coupon paid to retailers. Answer (C) is incorrect because $25,000 is the cost of the coupons on hand that have not yet been processed for payment. Case expects to receive additional redeemed coupons for 30 days after the balance sheet date. Answer (D) is incorrect because $22,500 equals $.45 times 50,000 coupons.

8. In December, Mill Co. began including one coupon in each package of candy that it sells and offering a toy in exchange for $.50 and five coupons. The toys cost Mill $.80 each. Sixty percent of the coupons will eventually be redeemed. During December, Mill sold 110,000 packages of candy, and no coupons were redeemed. In its December 31 balance sheet, what amount should Mill report as estimated liability for coupons?

A. $3,960

B. $10,560

C. $19,800

D. $52,800

The correct answer is (A). *(CPA, adapted)*

REQUIRED: The amount to be reported as a liability for unredeemed coupons at year-end.

DISCUSSION: The liability for coupon redemptions is $3,960 {[(110,000 coupons issued ÷ 5 per toy) x 60% redemption rate] x ($.80 – $.50) set cost per toy}.

Answer (B) is incorrect because $10,560 does not include the $.50 paid by customers for the toy. Answer (C) is incorrect because $19,800 is based on the assumption one coupon can be redeemed for a toy. Answer (D) is incorrect because $52,800 assumes one coupon can be redeemed for a toy, and excludes the $.50 that customers must pay per toy.

9. During Year 1, Rex Co. introduced a new product carrying a two-year warranty against defects. The estimated warranty costs related to dollar sales are 2% within 12 months following sale, and 4% in the second 12 months following sale. Sales and actual warranty expenditures for December 31, Year 1 and Year 2 are as follows:

	Sales	Actual Warranty Expenditures
Year 1	$ 600,000	$ 9,000
Year 2	1,000,000	30,000
	$1,600,000	$39,000

At December 31, Year 2, Rex should report an estimated warranty liability of

A. $0

B. $39,000

C. $57,000

D. $96,000

The correct answer is (C). *(CPA, adapted)*

REQUIRED: The estimated warranty liability at the end of the second year.

DISCUSSION: Because this product is new, the beginning balance in the estimated warranty liability account at the beginning of Year 1 is $0. For Year 1, the estimated warranty costs related to dollar sales are 6% (2% + 4%) of sales, or $36,000 ($600,000 x 6%). For Year 2, the estimated warranty costs are $60,000 ($1,000,000 sales x 6%). These amounts are charged to warranty expense and credited to the estimated warranty liability account. This liability account is debited for expenditures of $9,000 and $30,000 in Year 1 and Year 2, respectively. Hence, the estimated warranty liability at 12/31/Year 2 is $57,000.

Estimated Warranty Liability

Debit		Credit	
		$ 0	1/1/Year 1
Year 1 expenditures	$ 9,000	36,000	Year 1 expense
Year 2 expenditures	30,000	60,000	Year 2 expense
		$57,000	12/31/Year 2

Answer (A) is incorrect because all warranties have not expired. Answer (B) is incorrect because $39,000 equals the total warranty expenditures to date. Answer (D) is incorrect because $96,000 equals the total warranty expense to date.

10. Felicity Press received a total of $180,000 for 3-year subscriptions that began April 1, 2001. It recorded this amount as unearned revenue. Assuming Felicity records adjustments only at the end of the calendar year, the adjusting entry required to reflect the proper balances in the accounts at December 31, 2001 is to

A. Debit subscription revenue for $135,000 and credit unearned revenue for $135,000.

B. Debit unearned revenue for $135,000 and credit subscription revenue for $135,000.

C. Debit subscription revenue for $45,000 and credit unearned revenue for $45,000.

D. Debit unearned revenue for $45,000 and credit subscription revenue for $45,000.

The correct answer is (D). *(Publisher)*

REQUIRED: The year-end adjusting entry for subscriptions revenue given an initial entry to unearned revenue.

DISCUSSION: The initial entry was to debit cash and credit unearned revenue, a liability account, for $180,000. The subscriptions were for 3 years, or 36 months, beginning April 1, 2001. Of this period, 25% (9 months ÷ 36 months) had elapsed as of December 31, 2001. Because the earning process for subscriptions revenue is completed in proportion to the delivery of the subscribed materials over the term of the agreement, Felicity should recognize 25% of the amounts received for subscriptions as revenue at December 31, 2001. The adjusting entry is to debit unearned revenue and credit subscription revenue for $45,000 (25% x $180,000). This entry reduces the liability balance to $135,000, representing the remaining 27 months of subscriptions.

Answers (A) and (C) are incorrect because debiting revenue and crediting unearned revenue assumes the initial entry was to a revenue account. Answer (B) is incorrect because $45,000, not $135,000, is the adjustment needed at year-end.

11. Flyn Press received a total of $180,000 for 3-year subscriptions that began April 1, 2001. It recorded this amount as subscription revenue. Assuming Flyn records adjustments only at the end of the calendar year, the adjusting entry required to reflect the proper balances in the accounts at December 31, 2001 is to

A. Debit subscription revenue for $135,000 and credit unearned revenue for $135,000.

B. Debit unearned revenue for $135,000 and credit subscription revenue for $135,000.

C. Debit subscription revenue for $45,000 and credit unearned revenue for $45,000.

D. Debit unearned revenue for $45,000 and credit subscription revenue for $45,000.

The correct answer is (A). *(Publisher)*

REQUIRED: The year-end adjusting entry given an initial entry to a revenue account.

DISCUSSION: The company initially debited cash and credited subscription revenue, an income-statement account, for $180,000. Of this amount, $45,000 [(9 months ÷ 36 months) x $180,000] had been earned by year-end. Because $45,000 should be the year-end subscription revenue amount, the adjusting entry is to debit subscription revenue and credit unearned revenue (a liability account) for $135,000 ($180,000 – $45,000).

Answers (B) and (D) are incorrect because debiting unearned revenue and crediting revenue assumes the initial entry was to an unearned revenue account. Answer (C) is incorrect because $135,000, not $45,000, is the necessary adjustment needed at year-end.

12. Hopkins Corporation, a manufacturer of industrial fans, accounts for warranty costs under the accrual method. During November 2001, the company sold 500 units at $6,000 each. Each unit had a 1-year warranty. Based on past experience, the company expects future warranty costs to be $150 per unit. As of December 31, 2001, no journal entries involving warranty costs related to these units had been made, and no warranty costs were incurred during November or December. The year-end adjusting entry required at December 31, 2001 to account for estimated future warranty costs is to

A. Make no entry until costs are incurred.

B. Debit sales for $75,000 and credit unearned warranty revenue for $75,000.

C. Debit warranty expenses for $62,500 and credit estimated liability under warranties for $62,500.

D. Debit warranty expenses for $75,000 and credit estimated liability under warranties for $75,000.

The correct answer is (D). *(Publisher)*

REQUIRED: The entry to record estimated future warranty costs.

DISCUSSION: When the warranty is inseparable from the item sold, warranty costs should be treated as a loss contingency to be accrued at the time of sale if their incurrence is probable and their amount can be reasonably estimated. The company sold 500 units, each of which is expected to result in warranty costs of $150. No warranty costs have yet been incurred, so the full $150 per unit should be accrued at year-end. The estimated expense is $75,000 (500 units x $150). The adjusting entry is therefore to debit warranty expense and credit estimated liability under warranties for $75,000.

Answer (A) is incorrect because, under GAAP, warranty costs should be accrued in the year of sale when the warranty is an integral part of the sale. Answer (B) is incorrect because the company is selling a product, not warranties. Thus, a liability and an expense must be accrued for the expected cost of servicing the products, not a liability for unearned revenue. Answer (C) is incorrect because a full year's expense should be recorded, not a prorated amount for the remaining 10 months in the warranty period.

13. Beginning January 1, 2001, Stone Company offered a 3-year warranty from date of sale on any of its products sold after January 1, 2001. The warranty offer was part of a program to increase sales. Meeting the terms of the warranty was expected to cost 4% of sales. Sales made under warranty in 2001 totaled $18 million, and 20% of the units sold were returned. These units were repaired or replaced at a cost of $130,000. The warranty expense reported on Stone's 2001 income statement is

A. $720,000

B. $202,000

C. $240,000

D. $130,000

The correct answer is (A). *(Publisher)*

REQUIRED: The amount of warranty expense for 2001.

DISCUSSION: Given that warranty expense is expected to be 4% of sales, $720,000 (4% x $18,000,000) is recorded as an expense for 2001. How many units were returned in the current year and how much cash was expended for warranty repairs in the current year are not relevant because the warranty will last for 3 years. Warranty expense is recorded in the year of sale because warranty expense represents a selling cost.

Answer (B) is incorrect because $202,000 equals .4% of sales plus the cash outlay. Answer (C) is incorrect because the total cost is deducted in the year of the sale. It is not allocated over 3 years. Answer (D) is incorrect because $130,000 is the cash outlay in the current year.

B. Contingent Liabilities and Commitments

14. The accrual of a contingent liability and the related loss should be recorded when the

A. Loss resulting from a future event may be material in relation to income.

B. Future vent that gives rise to the liability is unusual in nature and nonrecurring.

C. Amount of the loss resulting from the event is reasonably estimated and the occurrence of the loss is probable.

D. Event that gives rise to the liability is unusual and its occurrence is probable.

The correct answer is (C). *(CMA, adapted)*

REQUIRED: The timing of the accrual of a contingent liability and the related loss.

DISCUSSION: SFAS 5 requires a contingent liability to be recorded, along with the related loss, when it is probable that an asset has been impaired or a liability has been incurred, and the amount of the loss can be reasonably estimated. The key words are "probable" and "reasonably estimated."

Answer (A) is incorrect because the loss must be probable and capable of estimation before it is recorded. Answer (B) is incorrect because the terms unusual and nonrecurring apply to extraordinary items, not contingencies. Answer (D) is incorrect because there is no requirement that a contingency be unusual.

15. A company is subject to warranty claims. It is estimated that between $1,000,000 and $3,000,000 will probably be paid out. No estimate of loss within this range is more likely than any other. The company should

A. Make no journal entry at this time.

B. Disclose only a possible loss.

C. Defer a loss of $1,000,000 to $3,000,000.

D. Accrue a loss of $1,000,000.

The correct answer is (D). *(CIA, adapted)*

REQUIRED: The proper accounting for warranty claims.

DISCUSSION: SFAS 5, *Accounting for Contingencies*, requires that a loss from contingencies be accrued when it is probable that, at a balance sheet date, an asset is overstated or a liability has been incurred and the amount of the loss can be reasonably estimated. According to FASB Interpretation No. 14, *Reasonable Estimation of the Amount of a Loss*, if the estimate is stated within a given range and no amount within that range appears to be a better estimate than any other, the minimum of the range should be accrued.

Answer (A) is incorrect because GAAP require accrual of a $1,000,000 loss. Answer (B) is incorrect because the loss is probable. Answer (C) is incorrect because the loss is not deferred; it is accrued.

Questions 16 and 17 are based on the following information. Tonya Corporation entered into a noncancellable, long-term contract with a supplier for the purchase of raw materials beginning in the calendar year 2001. The contract price at December 31, 2001 was $1 million, and the fair value of the raw materials was $1,150,000. This amount was considered material.

---

16. Tonya Corporation's financial statements at December 31, 2001 should

A. Include a contingent liability of $1 million.

B. Disclose the purchase commitment.

C. Include a liability of $1,150,000.

D. Include a deferred liability of $1 million.

The correct answer is (B). *(Publisher)*

REQUIRED: The proper accounting treatment of a purchase commitment on the year-end financial statements.

DISCUSSION: Purchase commitments ordinarily are not recognized because title has not passed to the buyer, but ARB 43 requires that losses on purchase commitments be recorded in the period in which they occur. Gains, however, should not be recorded. Thus, because a gain ($1,150,000 fair value – $1,000,000 price = $150,000 gain) is involved, the accounting treatment is to disclose the material purchase commitment but make no journal entry.

Answers (A) and (C) are incorrect because no liability is recorded as long as the contract is executory. When the other party performs under the contract, Tonya will incur an obligation and must then record a liability. Answer (D) is incorrect because no liability is recognized until the other party performs.

17. Assume the goods were received and the market price of the raw materials is $900,000. For this transaction, Tonya Corporation's financial statements at December 31, 2001 should report

A. Nothing about this commitment.

B. A liability of $1 million.

C. A liability of $100,000.

D. A liability of $900,000.

The correct answer is (B). *(Publisher)*

REQUIRED: The treatment of a loss on a purchase commitment.

DISCUSSION: Tonya should debit inventory (purchases) for $900,000 (assuming this amount is the lower-of-cost-or-market valuation), debit a loss for $100,000 ($1,000,000 price – $900,000 fair value), and credit a liability for the $1 million agreed purchase price. If the goods had not been shipped by the seller, the entry would have been to debit an estimated loss and credit an estimated liability for $100,000. The subsequent entry when the goods are received would then be to debit inventory, debit the estimated liability, and credit a liability.

Answer (A) is incorrect because the executed contract must be recorded. Answer (C) is incorrect because the entire $1 million liability must be recorded for the executed contract. If the contract were executory (unperformed), only the estimated loss and an equal liability would be recognized. Answer (D) is incorrect because $900,000 is the fair value of the inventory.

18. When reporting contingencies

A. Guarantees of others' indebtedness are reported as a loss contingency only if the loss is considered imminent or highly probable.

B. Disclosure of a loss contingency is to be made if there is a remote possibility that the loss has been incurred.

C. Disclosure of a loss contingency must include a dollar estimate of the loss.

D. A loss that is probable but not estimable must be disclosed with a notation that the amount of the loss cannot be estimated.

The correct answer is (D). *(CMA, adapted)*

REQUIRED: The true statement about reporting contingencies.

DISCUSSION: SFAS 5 prescribes the accounting for contingencies. Contingencies are divided into three categories: probable (likely to occur), reasonably possible, and remote. When contingent losses are probable and the amount can be reasonably estimated, the amount of the loss should be charged against income. If the amount cannot be reasonably estimated but the loss is at least reasonably possible, full disclosure should be made, including a statement that an estimate cannot be made.

Answer (A) is incorrect because SFAS 5 requires that a guarantee of another's indebtedness is to be disclosed even if the possibility of loss is remote. Answer (B) is incorrect because remote contingencies ordinarily need not be disclosed. Answer (C) is incorrect because disclosure need not include an amount when that amount cannot be reasonably estimated.

19. A company has been sued for $100,000,000 for producing and selling an unsafe product. Attorneys for the company cannot predict the outcome of the litigation. In its financial statements, the company should

A. Make the following journal entry, and disclose the existence of the lawsuit in a footnote.

Estimated loss from litigation	$100,000,000	
Estimated liability from litigation loss		$100,000,000

B. Disclose the existence of the lawsuit in a footnote without making a journal entry.

C. Neither make a journal entry nor disclose the lawsuit in a footnote because bad publicity will hurt the company.

D. Make the following journal entry, and disclose the existence of the lawsuit in a footnote.

Cost of goods sold	$100,000,000	
Estimated liability from litigation loss		$100,000,000

The correct answer is (B). *(CIA, adapted)*

REQUIRED: The financial statement treatment of a possible loss from litigation.

DISCUSSION: A contingency is "an existing condition, situation, or set of circumstances involving uncertainty as to possible gain or loss to an enterprise that will ultimately be resolved when one or more future events occur or fail to occur." The accounting treatment of loss contingencies is to charge estimated losses to income (and record the liability or asset impairment) when information available prior to issuance of financial statements indicates that it is probable that an asset had been impaired or a liability had been incurred (as of year-end) and the amount of loss can be reasonably estimated. If an accrual is not made, disclosure of the contingency should be made when there is a reasonable possibility that a loss will occur.

Answers (A) and (D) are incorrect because a journal entry is made when the loss contingency is probable and reasonably estimable, not just possible. Answer (C) is incorrect because a disclosure must be made when a loss contingency is possible.

20. For the past 3 months, Kenton Inc. has been negotiating a labor contract with potentially significant wage increases. Before completing the year-end financial statements on November 30, Kenton determined that the contract was likely to be signed in the near future. Kenton has estimated that the effect of the new contract will cost the company either $100,000, $200,000, or $300,000. Also, Kenton believes that each estimate has an equal chance of occurring and that the likelihood of the new contract being retroactive to the fiscal year ended November 30 is probable. According to SFAS 5, Kenton should

A. Do nothing because no loss will occur if the contract is never signed.

B. Disclose each loss contingency amount in the notes to the November 30 financial statements.

C. Accrue $100,000 in the income statement, and disclose the nature of the contingency and the additional loss exposure.

D. Follow conservatism and accrue $300,000 in the income statement, and disclose the nature of the contingency.

The correct answer is (C). *(CMA, adapted)*

REQUIRED: The proper action regarding the recording of a contingency under the provisions of SFAS 5.

DISCUSSION: SFAS 5 prescribes accounting for contingencies. Estimated losses from contingencies should be charged to income when information available prior to issuance of financial statements indicates that it is probable that an asset has been impaired or a liability has been incurred and the amount of loss can be reasonably estimated. "Probable" means that the future event is "likely" to occur. Moreover, if an estimate is stated within a given range, and no amount within the range appears to be a better estimate than any other, the minimum of the range should be accrued. Also, the nature of the contingency, the additional loss exposure, and the amount accrued should be disclosed.

Answer (A) is incorrect because a loss contingency should not be disregarded unless the chance of occurrence is remote. Answer (B) is incorrect because an event that will probably occur should be accrued in the financial statements. Answer (D) is incorrect because the minimum amount in the range should be accrued, unless another amount would give a more accurate estimate. Conservatism does not require accrual of the minimum estimate if another is the most likely.

21. Companies participating in the approach to off-balance-sheet financing known as interest rate swaps

A. Report only original borrowings on the balance sheet.

B. Report any rights to receive interest payments in accordance with the swap in the notes and not on the balance sheet.

C. Report any obligations to make interest payments in accordance with the swap in the notes and not on the balance sheet.

D. Report the effect of the swap on total interest revenues or expenses on the income statement.

The correct answer is (D). *(CIA, adapted)*

REQUIRED: The financial statement effect.

DISCUSSION: Interest rate swaps are derivatives used to alter the terms of original borrowings. For example, a company with variable-rate debt may agree to exchange obligations with a company obligated on fixed-rate debt. Under SFAS 133, derivatives are recognized as assets or liabilities and measured at fair value in the balance sheet as the underlying (for example, a specified interest rate) changes. Consequently, the right to receive interest payments and the obligation to make such payments are reflected on the balance sheet. Moreover, the effect of an interest rate swap is to alter interest revenues or expenses. The interest revenues and expenses reported in the income statement include any effect of swap transactions during the accounting period.

Answers (A), (B), and (C) are incorrect because an interest rate swap is a derivative, and rights to receive interest payments and obligations to make interest payments on swaps are reflected on the balance sheet.

22. Careful reading of an annual report will reveal that off-balance-sheet debt includes

A. Amounts due in future years under operating leases.

B. Transfers of accounts receivable without recourse.

C. Current portion of long-term debt.

D. Amounts due in future years under capital leases.

The correct answer is (A). *(CMA, adapted)*

REQUIRED: The off-balance-sheet debt.

DISCUSSION: Off-balance-sheet debt includes any type of liability that the company is responsible for but that does not appear on the balance sheet. The most common example is the amount due in future years on operating leases. Under SFAS 13, operating leases are not capitalized; instead, only the periodic payments of rent are reported when actually paid. Capital leases (those similar to a purchase) must be capitalized and reported as liabilities.

Answer (B) is incorrect because transfers of accounts receivable without recourse do not create a liability for the company. This transaction is simply a transfer of receivables for cash. Answer (C) is incorrect because the current portion of long-term debt is reported on the balance sheet as a current liability. Answer (D) is incorrect because amounts due in future years under capital leases are required to be capitalized under SFAS 13.

23. Which of the following is not an example of off-balance-sheet financing?

A. Transfers of receivables to third parties with recourse that are deemed to be sales.

B. Guarantees of indebtedness.

C. Unconditional purchase obligations.

D. Capitalized leases.

The correct answer is (D). *(CIA, adapted)*

REQUIRED: The item not off-balance-sheet financing.

DISCUSSION: Off-balance-sheet financing is debt that need not be recognized in the financial statements. One purpose is to improve the balance sheet by reducing the debt-equity ratio. Some common examples of off-balance-sheet financing are transfers of receivables with recourse accounted for as sales, project financing arrangements, take-or-pay contracts, unconditional purchase obligations, pension obligations (amounts in excess of the unfunded accumulated benefit obligation), and operating leases. Capitalized leases are recorded as financial commitments on the balance sheet and are not off-balance-sheet financing.

Answer (A) is incorrect because, when transfers of receivables to third parties with recourse are deemed to be sales, they are not recorded as borrowings. Answer (B) is incorrect because guarantees of indebtedness result in loss contingencies that are disclosed but not accrued unless the loss is probable. Answer (C) is incorrect because an unconditional purchase commitment must be disclosed but not recorded at the time of the agreement.

C. Long-Term Liabilities

24. If the market rate of interest is <List A> the coupon rate when bonds are issued, then the bonds will sell in the market at a price <List B> the face value, and the issuing firm will record a <List C> on bonds payable.

	List A	List B	List C
A.	Equal to	Equal to	Premium
B.	Greater than	Greater than	Premium
C.	Greater than	Less than	Discount
D.	Less than	Greater than	Discount

The correct answer is (C). *(CIA, adapted)*

REQUIRED: The relationship of the market rate, the coupon rate, and the recording of a discount or premium.

DISCUSSION: If the market rate exceeds the coupon rate, the price of the bonds must decline to a level that equates the yield on the bonds with the market rate of interest. Accordingly, the bonds will be recorded by a debit to cash for the proceeds, a debit to discount on bonds payable, and a credit to bonds payable at face value.

Answer (A) is incorrect because, if the market rate equals the coupon rate, the bonds will not sell at a premium or discount. Answer (B) is incorrect because, if the market rate exceeds the coupon rate, the bond issue will sell at a discount. Answer (D) is incorrect because, if the market rate is less than the coupon rate, the bonds will sell at a price in excess of the face value. The issuing company will record a premium.

25. On January 1, a company issued a 10-year $500,000 bond at 96% of face value. The bond bears interest at 12%, payable on January 1 and July 1. The entry to record the issuance of the bond on January 1 would be

A.	Cash	$480,000	
	Bonds payable		$480,000
B.	Cash	$500,000	
	Bonds payable		$500,000
C.	Cash	$480,000	
	Discount on bonds payable	$ 20,000	
	Bonds payable		$500,000
D.	Cash	$500,000	
	Premium on bonds payable		$ 20,000
	Bonds payable		$480,000

The correct answer is (C). *(CIA, adapted)*

REQUIRED: The entry to record the issuance of the bond.

DISCUSSION: The company received $480,000 cash on the issuance of the bond. Its face value is $500,000, the amount to be paid at maturity. Hence, the credit to bonds payable is $500,000. The $20,000 difference is recorded as a discount on bonds payable (a debit) and is amortized over the life of the issue.

Answer (A) is incorrect because the entry to bonds payable is based on the face, or maturity, value of the bond issued. The difference between the amount received on issuance and the face value is recorded as a premium or discount on bonds payable. Answer (B) is incorrect because the discount should be recognized. Answer (D) is incorrect because the debit to cash is $480,000, a $20,000 discount should be debited, and the credit to bonds payable is $500,000.

26. A company issues 10-year bonds with a face value of $1,000,000, dated January 1 and bearing interest at an annual rate of 12% payable semiannually on January 1 and July 1. The full interest amount will be paid each due date. The market rate of interest on bonds of similar risk and maturity, with the same schedule of interest payments, is also 12%. If the bonds are issued on February 1, the amount the issuing company receives from the buyers of the bonds on that date is

A. $990,000

B. $1,000,000

C. $1,010,000

D. $1,020,000

The correct answer is (C). *(CIA, adapted)*

REQUIRED: The amount received when bonds are issued subsequent to the date printed on the face of the bonds.

DISCUSSION: The amount the issuing company receives on February 1 is the face value of the issue plus 1 month of accrued interest, or $1,010,000 {$1,000,000 + [($1,000,000 x 12%) ÷ 12]}.

Answer (A) is incorrect because $990,000 is the result if 1 month of accrued interest is deducted from, rather than added to, the amount received. Answer (B) is incorrect because the purchasers must pay for the accrued interest from the last interest date to the issue date. They will receive 6 months' interest on July 1 despite holding the bonds for 5 months. Answer (D) is incorrect because $1,020,000 results from adding 2 months of accrued interest to the face value.

Questions 27 and 28 are based on the following information. On January 1, Matthew Company issued 7% term bonds with a face amount of $1,000,000 due in 8 years. Interest is payable semiannually on January 1 and July 1. On the date of issue, investors were willing to accept an effective interest rate of 6%.

27. The bonds were issued on January 1 at

A. A premium.

B. An amortized value.

C. Book value

D. A discount.

The correct answer is (A). *(CMA, adapted)*

REQUIRED: The true statement about the issuance of bonds.

DISCUSSION: Because the bonds sold for more than their face value, they were sold at a premium. The premium adjusted the yield of the bonds to the effective rate (presumably, the market rate).

Answer (B) is incorrect because an amortized value is the carrying amount of the bonds after at least one period's amortization has been recorded. Answer (C) is incorrect because book value is the amount at which bonds appear on the financial statements, including any unamortized premium or discount. For a new issue of bonds, no book value existed before issuance (i.e., they did not appear on the books). Answer (D) is incorrect because a discount arises when bonds are sold at less than their face value.

28. Assume the bonds were issued on January 1 for $1,062,809. Using the effective interest amortization method, Matthew Company recorded interest expense for the 6 months ended June 30 in the amount of

A. $35,000

B. $70,000

C. $63,769

D. $31,884

The correct answer is (D). *(CMA, adapted)*

REQUIRED: The interest expense for the first 6 months that the bonds are outstanding.

DISCUSSION: The annual interest cash outlay is $70,000 (7% nominal rate x $1,000,000), or $35,000 each semiannual period. Interest expense is less than $35,000, however, because the bonds were originally issued at a premium. That premium should be amortized over the life of the bond. Thus, interest expense for the first 6 months is $31,884 [$1,062,809 x 6% x (6 months ÷ 12 months)], and premium amortization is $3,116 ($35,000 – $31,884).

Answer (A) is incorrect because the $35,000 is the cash outlay. Answer (B) is incorrect because $70,000 is the cash outlay for a full year. Answer (C) is incorrect because $63,769 is the expense for the first year if interest is paid annually.

29. A bond issue sold at a premium is valued on the statement of financial position at the

A. Maturity value.

B. Maturity value plus the unamortized portion of the premium.

C. Cost at the date of investment.

D. Maturity value less the unamortized portion of the premium.

The correct answer is (B). *(CMA, adapted)*

REQUIRED: The means of valuing a bond issue sold at a premium.

DISCUSSION: A bond liability is shown at its face value (maturity value), minus any related discount, or plus any related premium. Thus, a bond issued at a premium is shown at its maturity value plus the unamortized portion of the premium. The premium account is sometimes called an adjunct account because it is shown as an addition to another account.

Answer (A) is incorrect because the maturity value must be increased by any related unamortized premium. Answer (C) is incorrect because even a bond investment must be adjusted for the related premium or discount. Answer (D) is incorrect because the premium is added to the maturity value of a bond liability.

30. Lister Company intends to refinance a portion of its short-term debt next year and is negotiating a long-term financing agreement with a local bank. This agreement will be noncancelable and will extend for 2 years. The amount of short-term debt that Lister Company can exclude from its statement of financial position at December 31

A. May exceed the amount available for refinancing under the agreement.

B. Depends on the demonstrated ability to consummate the refinancing.

C. Must be adjusted by the difference between the present value and the market value of the short-term debt.

D. Is reduced by the proportionate change in the working capital ratio.

The correct answer is (B). *(CMA, adapted)*

REQUIRED: The amount of short-term debt excluded.

DISCUSSION: If an enterprise intends to refinance short-term obligations on a long-term basis and demonstrates an ability to consummate the refinancing, the obligations should be excluded from current liabilities and classified as noncurrent (SFAS 6, *Classification of Short-Term Obligations Expected to Be Refinanced*). The ability to consummate the refinancing may be demonstrated by a post-balance-sheet-date issuance of a long-term obligation or equity securities, or by entering into a financing agreement that meets certain criteria. These criteria are that the agreement does not expire within 1 year, it is noncancellable by the lender, no violation of the agreement exists at the balance sheet date, and the lender is financially capable of honoring the agreement.

Answer (A) is incorrect because the amount excluded cannot exceed the amount available for refinancing. Answers (C) and (D) are incorrect because SFAS 6 has no provision for adjustments or reductions.

31. A company issues $100,000 of 8% bonds at par. Each $1,000 bond carries five detachable warrants, each of which allows the holder to acquire one share of $5 par value common stock for $30 a share. After issuance, the bonds were quoted at 98 ex-rights, and the warrants were quoted at $6 each. The value assigned to the bonds at issuance should be

A. $97,000

B. $97,029.70

C. $98,000

D. $100,000

The correct answer is (B). *(Publisher)*

REQUIRED: The value assigned to bonds with detachable warrants.

DISCUSSION: After issuance, the bonds are valued at $98,000, and the warrants are worth $3,000 (500 warrants at $6 each). Thus, the value assigned to the bonds at issuance is $97,029.70 [($98,000 ÷ $101,000) x $100,000].

Answer (A) is incorrect because the values are prorated between the two securities instead of the warrants being subtracted from the proceeds. Answer (C) is incorrect because $98,000 is the market value of the bonds, not the issue price. Answer (D) is incorrect because $100,000 is the total of bonds and warrants.

32. According to SFAS 78, *Classification of Obligations That Are Callable by the Creditor*, long-term obligations that are or will become callable by the creditor because of the debtor's violation of a provision of the debt agreement at the balance sheet date should be classified as

A. Long-term liabilities.

B. Current liabilities unless the debtor goes bankrupt.

C. Current liabilities unless the creditor has waived the right to demand repayment for more than 1 year from balance sheet date.

D. Contingent liabilities until the violation is corrected.

The correct answer is (C). *(CMA, adapted)*

REQUIRED: The classification of long-term debt.

DISCUSSION: In these circumstances, the obligation should be classified as current. However, the debt need not be reclassified if the violation will be cured within a specified grace period or if the creditor formally waives or subsequently loses the right to demand repayment for a period of more than a year from the balance sheet date. Also, reclassification is not required if the debtor expects and has the ability to refinance the obligation on a long-term basis.

Answer (A) is incorrect because SFAS 78 requires classification as a current liability. Answer (B) is incorrect because bankruptcy is not an exception. Answer (D) is incorrect because SFAS 78 concerns callable, not contingent, liabilities.

33. On July 1, 20X0, Eagle Corp. issued 600 of its 10%, $1,000 bonds at 99 plus accrued interest. The bonds are dated April 1, 20X0 and mature in ten years. Interest is payable semiannually on April 1 and October 1. What amount did Eagle receive from the bond issuance?

A. $579,000

B. $594,000

C. $600,000

D. $609,000

The correct answer is (D). *(CPA, adapted)*

REQUIRED: The cash received from the issuance of a bond at a discount plus accrued interest.

DISCUSSION: The face value of the bonds is $600,000 (600 bonds x $1,000 face value). Excluding interest, the proceeds from the issuance of the bonds were $594,000 ($600,000 x 99%). Accrued interest for three months was $15,000 ($600,000 face value x 10% coupon rate x 3/12). The net cash received from the issuance of the bonds was therefore equal to $609,000 ($594,000 bond proceeds + $15,000 accrued interest).

Answer (A) is incorrect because $579,000 results from subtracting the $15,000 of interest. Answer (B) is incorrect because $594,000 does not include accrued interest. Answer (C) is incorrect because $600,000 is the face value of the bonds.

34. Hancock Co.'s December 31, 20X0 balance sheet contained the following items in the long-term liabilities section:

Unsecured	
9.375% registered bonds ($25,000 maturing annually beginning in 20X4)	$275,000
11.5% convertible bonds, callable beginning in 20X9, due in 20 years	125,000
Secured	
9.875% guaranty security bonds, due in 20 years	$250,000
10.0% commodity backed bonds ($50,000 maturing annually beginning in 20X4)	200,000

What are the total amounts of serial bonds and debenture bonds?

	Serial Bonds	Debenture Bonds
A.	$475,000	$400,000
B.	$475,000	$125,000
C.	$450,000	$400,000
D.	$200,000	$650,000

The correct answer is (A). *(CPA, adapted)*

REQUIRED: The total amounts of serial bonds and debenture bonds.

DISCUSSION: Serial bonds mature in installments at various dates. Debentures are unsecured bonds. The commodity-backed bonds and the registered bonds are serial bonds. They total $475,000 ($275,000 + $200,000). The registered bonds and the convertible bonds are debentures. They total $400,000 ($275,000 + $125,000).

Answer (B) is incorrect because the registered bonds are also debentures. Answer (C) is incorrect because the registered bonds, not the guaranty security bonds, are serial bonds. Answer (D) is incorrect because the registered bonds are serial bonds and the guaranty security bonds are not debentures.

35. On July 1, 20X0, after recording interest and amortization, York Co. converted $1 million of its 12% convertible bonds into 50,000 shares of $1 par value common stock. On the conversion date, the carrying amount of the bonds was $1.3 million, the market value of the bonds was $1.4 million, and York's common stock was publicly trading at $30 per share. Using the book-value method, what amount of additional paid-in capital should York record as a result of the conversion?

A. $950,000

B. $1,250,000

C. $1,350,000

D. $1,500,000

The correct answer is (B). *(CPA, adapted)*

REQUIRED: The additional paid-in capital from conversion of bonds under the book-value method.

DISCUSSION: Under the book-value method for recognizing the conversion of outstanding bonds payable to common stock, the stock issued is recorded at the carrying value of the bonds, with no recognition of a gain or loss. Accordingly, the conversion should be recorded at $1.3 million. However, this amount must be allocated between common stock and additional paid-in capital. The common stock account is always valued at par value; therefore, $50,000 (50,000 shares x $1) will be credited to common stock and $1,250,000 to additional paid-in capital.

Answer (A) is incorrect because $950,000 equals the face value of the bonds minus the par value of the stock. Answer (C) is incorrect because the carrying value of the bonds is not increased by the par value of the stock. Answer (D) is incorrect because $1,500,000 is the full value of the stock at the market price.

36. At December 31, 2001, a company had the following short-term obligations that were expected to be refinanced:

17% note payable	$140,000
15% note payable	$200,000

The 17% note payable was issued on October 1, 2001 and matures on July 1, 2002. The 15% note payable was issued on May 1, 2001 and matures on May 1, 2002. On February 1, 2002, the $140,000 balance of the 17% note payable was refinanced by issuance of a long-term debt instrument. On February 7, 2002, the company entered into a non-cancellable agreement with a lender to refinance the 15% note payable on a long-term basis. On March 1, 2002, the date of issuance of the December 31, 2001 balance sheet, both parties are financially capable of honoring the agreement and there have been no violations of the provisions of the refinancing agreement. The total amount of short-term obligations that may be properly excluded from current liabilities on the company's December 31, 2001 balance sheet is

A. $0

B. $140,000

C. $200,000

D. $340,000

The correct answer is (D). *(CIA, adapted)*

REQUIRED: The total amount of short-term obligations that may be properly excluded from current liabilities.

DISCUSSION: Under SFAS 6, an enterprise is required to exclude a short-term obligation from current liabilities if the entity has the intent and ability to refinance it on a long-term basis. The ability to consummate the refinancing may be demonstrated either by (1) actually refinancing the short-term obligation by issuance of a long-term obligation or equity securities after the date of the balance sheet but before it is issued, or (2) entering into a financing agreement that clearly permits the enterprise to refinance the debt on a long-term basis. The ability to refinance the 17% note payable is demonstrated by the actual refinancing after the balance sheet date but before the date of issuance of the balance sheet. The ability to refinance the 15% note payable is demonstrated by the borrower's entering into a long-term, noncancellable financing agreement given that both parties are financially capable and no violations of its terms have occurred. Thus, $340,000 ($140,000 17% note + $200,000 15% note) may be excluded from current liabilities.

Answer (A) is incorrect because $340,000 may be excluded from current liabilities. Answer (B) is incorrect because the 15% note is also excluded from current liabilities. Answer (C) is incorrect because the 17% note is also excluded from current liabilities.

37. A company has a $100,000 liability on the books. In 1 year, $110,000 will be due, including 10% interest. The company negotiates settlement of the debt today by exchanging $90,000 of customer receivables. What is the journal entry today?

A.	Liability	$110,000	
	Receivables		$99,000
	Gain		11,000
B.	Liability	$100,000	
	Receivables		$99,000
	Gain		1,000
C.	Liability	$110,000	
	Receivables		$90,000
	Gain		20,000
D.	Liability	$100,000	
	Receivables		$90,000
	Gain		10,000

The correct answer is (D). *(CIA, adapted)*

REQUIRED: The journal entry to record settlement of a liability by exchanging customer receivables.

DISCUSSION: A troubled debt restructuring may occur as an asset exchange, as a modification of terms, or as a combination of these two methods. In this instance, the troubled debt restructuring is effected as an asset exchange. In such an exchange, the asset given up for the troubled debt must first be adjusted from its carrying amount to its fair value, with an ordinary gain or loss being recognized for the adjustment. The fair value of the asset provided must then be compared with the carrying value of the troubled debt to determine the extraordinary item to be recognized. In this question, one must assume that the book and fair values of the receivables are the same. Consequently, the liability should be debited for its $100,000 balance. Receivables with a $90,000 balance are given up, so that account should be credited. The difference is a gain.

Answer (A) is incorrect because the liability and receivables should not be increased by the 10% interest rate. Answer (B) is incorrect because the receivables should not be increased by the 10% interest rate. Answer (C) is incorrect because the liability should not be increased by the 10% interest rate.

38. On March 1, 20X0, Fine Co. borrowed $10,000 and signed a two-year note bearing interest at 12% per annum compounded annually. Interest is payable in full at maturity on February 28, 20X2. What amount should Fine report as a liability for accrued interest at December 31, 20X1?

A. $0

B. $1,000

C. $1,200

D. $2,320

The correct answer is (D). *(CPA, adapted)*

REQUIRED: The amount of accrued interest liability.

DISCUSSION: Given annual compounding, interest for the second year is calculated based on a carrying amount equal to the $10,000 principal plus the $1,200 (12% x $10,000) of first-year interest. Thus, accrued interest for the next 10 months is $1,120 {[($10,000 + $1,200) x 12%] x (10 months ÷ 12 months)}. Total accrued interest after 22 months is $2,320 ($1,200 + $1,120).

Answer (A) is incorrect because interest is accrued annually. Answer (B) is incorrect because $1,000 is the 20X0 interest accrual. Answer (C) is incorrect because $1,200 is the interest for the first 12 months.

Questions 39 through 42 are based on the following information. On January 1, 2001, Nichols Company issued 7% term bonds with a face amount of $2 million due January 1, 2009. Interest is payable semiannually on January 1 and July 1. On the date of issue, investors were willing to accept an effective interest rate of 6%.

---

39. Assume the bonds were issued on January 1, 2001 for $2,125,618. Using the effective interest amortization method, Nichols Company recorded interest expense for the 6 months ended June 30, 2001 in the amount of

A. $70,000

B. $140,000

C. $127,537

D. $63,769

The correct answer is (D). *(Publisher)*

REQUIRED: The interest expense for the first 6 months that the bonds are outstanding.

DISCUSSION: Given that the bonds paid interest at a 7% contract rate, the annual interest outlay is $140,000 on a $2 million issue, or $70,000 each semiannual period. Interest expense is less than $70,000, however, because the bonds were originally issued at a $125,618 premium. That premium, which existed because investors were willing to accept a 6% effective interest rate, should be amortized over the life of the bond. For a semiannual period, that 6% annual effective rate translates to a 3% semiannual rate. Hence, interest expense is $63,769 (3% x $2,125,618 face value plus premium), the cash outlay is $70,000, and premium amortization is $6,231 ($70,000 – $63,769).

Answer (A) is incorrect because $70,000 is the semiannual cash outlay. Answer (B) is incorrect because $140,000 is the cash outlay for a full year. Answer (C) is incorrect because $127,537 would be the expense for the first year if interest were paid on an annual basis instead of semiannually.

40. Assume the bonds were issued on January 1, 2001 for $2,125,618. Using the effective interest amortization method, Nichols Company recorded interest expense for the 6 months ended December 31, 2001 in the amount of

A. $70,000

B. $140,000

C. $63,582

D. $63,769

The correct answer is (C). *(Publisher)*

REQUIRED: The interest expense for the second 6 months that the bonds are outstanding.

DISCUSSION: For a semiannual period, the 6% annual effective rate translates to a 3% semiannual rate. For the first 6-month period (ending June 30), interest expense was $63,769 (3% x $2,125,618 face value plus premium), the cash outlay was $70,000 [7% x $2,000,000 x (6 ÷ 12)], and premium amortization was $6,231 ($70,000 – $63,769). The book value of the bond after 6 months was therefore $2,119,387 ($2,125,618 – $6,231). Consequently, for the second 6-month period (ending December 31, 2001), interest expense was $63,582 (3% x $2,119,387).

Answer (A) is incorrect because $70,000 is the semiannual cash outlay. Answer (B) is incorrect because the $140,000 is the cash outlay for a full year. Answer (D) is incorrect because $63,769 is the expense for the 6-month period ended June 30, 2001.

41. What is the book value of the bonds after the payment of interest on January 1, 2002?

A. $2,000,000

B. $2,125,618

C. $2,119,387

D. $2,112,969

The correct answer is (D). *(Publisher)*

REQUIRED: The book value of the bonds after they have been outstanding for 1 year.

DISCUSSION: For a semiannual period, the 6% annual effective rate translates to a 3% semiannual rate. For the first 6-month period (ending June 30), interest expense was $63,769 (3% x $2,125,618 face value plus premium), the cash outlay was $70,000 [7% x $2,000,000 x (6 ÷ 12)], and premium amortization was $6,231 ($70,000 – $63,769). The book value of the bond after 6 months was therefore $2,119,387 ($2,125,618 – $6,231). Consequently, for the second 6-month period (ending December 31, 2001), interest expense was $63,582 (3% x $2,119,387), amortization was $6,418 ($70,000 – $63,582), and the year-end book value was $2,112,969 ($2,119,387 – $6,418).

Answer (A) is incorrect because $2,000,000 is the face value of the bonds. Answer (B) is incorrect because $2,125,618 is the issue price. Answer (C) is incorrect because $2,119,387 is the book value after 6 months.

42. The bonds were issued on January 1, 2001 at

A. A premium.

B. An amortized value.

C. Book value.

D. A discount.

The correct answer is (A). *(Publisher)*

REQUIRED: The true statement about the bond issue.

DISCUSSION: Because the bonds sold for more than their face value, they were issued at a premium. If they had been sold for less than their face value, they would have been issued at a discount.

Answer (B) is incorrect because an amortized value is the amount at which bonds appear on the books after at least one period's amortization has been recorded. Answer (C) is incorrect because book value is the amount at which bonds appear on the financial statements, net of any premium or discount. Given that these bonds were new, they did not have a book value at the time of issuance (i.e., they did not appear on the books). Answer (D) is incorrect because a discount arises when bonds are sold at less than their face value.

43. On December 30, 20X0, Hale Corp. paid $400,000 cash and issued 80,000 shares of its $1 par value common stock to its unsecured creditors on a pro rata basis pursuant to a reorganization plan under Chapter 11 of the bankruptcy statutes. Hale owed these unsecured creditors a total of $1.2 million. Hale's common stock was trading at $1.25 per share on December 30, 20X0. As a result of this transaction, Hale's total shareholder's equity had a net increase of

A. $1,200,000

B. $800,000

C. $100,000

D. $80,000

The correct answer is (B). *(CPA, adapted)*

REQUIRED: The net increase in shareholder's equity immediately after a Chapter 11 reorganization.

DISCUSSION: According to SFAS 15, a debtor that grants an equity interest in full settlement of a payable should account for the equity interest at fair value. The difference between the fair value of the equity interest and the carrying amount of the payable is an extraordinary gain. The appropriate accounting for this troubled debt restructuring is to debit liabilities for $1.2 million and to credit cash for $400,000, common stock at its par value of $80,000 (80,000 shares x $1), additional paid-in capital for $20,000 [($1.25 fair value per share – $1 par) x 80,000 shares], and an extraordinary gain for $700,000. Accordingly, the net increase in total shareholders' equity is $800,000 ($80,000 + $20,000 + $700,000).

Answer (A) is incorrect because $1,200,000 is the amount of the debt. Answer (C) is incorrect because $100,000 is the increase in contributed capital. Answer (D) is incorrect because $80,000 is the increase in common stock.

D. Leases

44. On January 1, 20X0, Harrow Co. as lessee signed a five-year noncancellable equipment lease with annual payments of $100,000 beginning December 31, 20X0. Harrow treated this transaction as a capital lease. The five lease payments have a present value of $379,000 at January 1, 20X0, based on interest of 10%. What amount should Harrow report as interest for the year ended December 31, 20X0?

A. $37,900

B. $27,900

C. $24,200

D. $0

The correct answer is (A). *(CPA, adapted)*

REQUIRED: The interest to be recognized in the first year of a capital lease.

DISCUSSION: The lease liability at the inception of the lease is $379,000. Under the effective-interest method, the lease liability balance (the carrying value) at the beginning of each year should be multiplied by the implicit interest rate to determine interest for that year. Accordingly, the interest expense for the first year is $37,900 ($10% x $379,000).

Answer (B) is incorrect because $27,900 results from assuming that the initial payment was made immediately. Answer (C) is incorrect because $24,200 is one-fifth of the total interest ($500,000 – $379,000 PV). Answer (D) is incorrect because interest must be accrued.

45. On January 1, 20X0, Babson, Inc. leased two automobiles for executive use. The lease requires Babson to make five annual payments of $13,000 beginning January 1, 20X0. At the end of the lease term, December 31, 20X4, Babson guarantees the residual value of the automobiles will total $10,000. The lease qualifies as a capital lease. The interest rate implicit in the lease is 9%. Present value factors for the 9% rate implicit in the lease are as follows:

For an annuity due with 5 payments	4.240
For an ordinary annuity with 5 payments	3.890
Present value of $1 for 5 periods	0.650

Babson's recorded capital lease liability immediately after the first required payment should be

A. $48,620

B. $44,070

C. $35,620

D. $31,070

The correct answer is (A). *(CPA, adapted)*

REQUIRED: The recorded capital lease liability immediately after the first required payment.

DISCUSSION: SFAS 13 requires that the lessee record a capital lease as an asset and a liability at the present value of the minimum lease payments during the lease term. If no bargain purchase option exists, the minimum lease payments equal the sum of the minimum rental payments, the amount of guaranteed residual value, and any nonrenewal penalty imposed. Accordingly, the present value of the minimum lease payments, minus the first required payment, is $48,620 [($13,000 annual payment x 4.240 PV of an annuity due at 9% for 5 periods) + ($10,000 guaranteed residual value x .650 PV of $1 at 9% for 5 periods) – $13,000 first payment].

Answer (B) is incorrect because $44,070 is based on the interest factor for an ordinary annuity. Answer (C) is incorrect because $35,620 results from deducting the first payment twice. Answer (D) is incorrect because $31,070 is based on the interest factor for an ordinary annuity and on deducting the first payment twice.

46. For a direct-financing lease, the gross investment (lease payments receivable) recorded by the lessor is equal to the

A. Present value of the minimum lease payments minus the unguaranteed residual value accruing to the lessor at the end of the lease term.

B. Lower of 90% of the present value of the minimum lease payments or the fair value of the leased asset.

C. Difference between the fair value of the leased asset and the unearned interest revenue.

D. Minimum lease payments plus the unguaranteed residual value accruing to the lessor at the end of the lease term.

The correct answer is (D). *(CMA, adapted)*

REQUIRED: The gross investment recorded by the lessor for a direct-financing lease.

DISCUSSION: For both sales-type and direct-financing leases, the lessor should record as the gross investment in the lease the amount of the minimum lease payments (which include periodic payments plus guaranteed residual value) plus any amounts of unguaranteed residual value. The net investment in the lease is equal to the gross investment, plus any unamortized initial direct costs, minus unearned income. The unguaranteed residual value is the expected value of the leased asset in excess of the guaranteed residual value at the end of the lease term (SFAS 13).

Answers (A), (B), and (C) are incorrect because the gross investment is not adjusted for the time value of money or fair value.

47. Initial direct costs incurred by the lessor under a sales-type lease should be

A. Deferred and allocated over the economic life of the leased property.

B. Expensed in the period incurred.

C. Deferred and allocated over the term of the lease in proportion to the recognition of rental income.

D. Added to the gross investment in the lease and amortized over the term of the lease as a yield adjustment.

The correct answer is (B). *(CMA, adapted)*

REQUIRED: The accounting for initial direct costs in a sales-type lease.

DISCUSSION: SFAS 91 defines initial direct costs as having two components: (1) the lessor's external costs to originate a lease incurred in dealings with independent third parties and (2) the internal costs directly related to specified activities performed by the lessor for that lease. According to SFAS 13, in a sales-type lease, the cost, or carrying amount if different, plus any initial direct costs, minus the present value of any unguaranteed residual value, is charged against income in the same period that the present value of the minimum lease payments is credited to sales. The result is the recognition of a net profit or loss on the sales-type lease.

Answer (A) is incorrect because initial direct costs are considered an expense in the period of sale. Answers (C) and (D) are incorrect because they describe the proper treatment of initial direct costs in an operating lease and a direct-financing lease, respectively.

48. Howe Co. leased equipment to Kew Corp. on January 2, 20X0 for an eight-year period expiring December 31, 20X7. Equal payments under the lease are $600,000 and are due on January 2 of each year. The first payment was made on January 2, 20X0. The list selling price of the equipment is $3,520,000, and its carrying cost on Howe's books is $2.8 million. The lease is appropriately accounted for as a sales-type lease. The present value of the lease payments at an imputed interest rate of 12% (Howe's incremental borrowing rate) is $3.3 million. What amount of profit on the sale should Howe report for the year ended December 31, 20X0?

A. $720,000

B. $500,000

C. $90,000

D. $0

The correct answer is (B). *(CPA, adapted)*

REQUIRED: The amount of profit on a sales-type lease.

DISCUSSION: Howe Co., the lessor, should report a profit from a sales-type lease. The gross profit equals the difference between the sales price (present value of the minimum lease payments) and the cost. The cost for a sales-type lease is not the same as the fair value. Consequently, the profit on the sale equals $500,000 ($3,300,000 – $2,800,000).

Answer (A) is incorrect because $720,000 is the result of using the list selling price instead of the present value of the lease payments. Answer (C) is incorrect because $90,000 is one-eighth of the difference between the list price and the cost. Answer (D) is incorrect because a profit of $500,000 should be reported.

49. On January 1, 20X0, Wren Company leased a building to Brill under an operating lease for 10 years at $50,000 per year, payable the first day of each lease year. Wren paid $15,000 to a real estate broker as a finder's fee. The annual depreciation on the building is $12,000. For 20X0, Wren incurred insurance and property tax expenses totaling $9,000. Wren's net rental income for 20X0 should be

A. $27,500

B. $29,000

C. $35,000

D. $36,500

The correct answer is (A). *(CPA, adapted)*

REQUIRED: The net rental income that should be recorded for the first year.

DISCUSSION: The net rental income is equal to the $50,000 annual payment minus any expenses to be recorded during the year. These expenses include $12,000 of depreciation, $9,000 for insurance and property taxes, and $1,500 ($15,000 ÷ 10 years) amortization of the finder's fee. The finder's fee is an initial direct cost that should be deferred and allocated over the lease term in proportion to the recognition of rental income (SFAS 13). It should therefore be recorded as a deferred charge and amortized using the straight-line method over the 10-year lease term. Accordingly, the net rental income for 20X0 is $27,500.

Rental income	$50,000
Depreciation	(12,000)
Insurance and property tax expenses	(9,000)
Amortization	(1,500)
Net rental income	$27,500

Answer (B) is incorrect because $29,000 does not include amortization of the finder's fee. Answer (C) is incorrect because $35,000 equals rental income minus the full finder's fee. Answer (D) is incorrect because $36,500 excludes insurance and property taxes from the computation.

50. Equipment covered by a lease agreement is expected by the lessor to have a residual value at the end of the lease term of $20,000. As part of the lease agreement, the lessee guarantees a residual value of $12,000. In the case of excessive usage, the guaranteed residual value is $18,000. What is the amount of guaranteed residual value that should be included in the calculation of the minimum lease payments?

A. $0

B. $12,000

C. $18,000

D. $20,000

The correct answer is (B). *(Publisher)*

REQUIRED: The amount of guaranteed residual value to be included in minimum lease payments.

DISCUSSION: FASB Interpretation No. 19, *Lessee Guarantee of the Residual Value of Leased Property*, states that the amount of guaranteed residual value to be included in the determination of minimum lease payments is the "specified maximum deficiency that the lessee is obligated to make up." In these circumstances, that amount is materially lower than the expected salvage value. Consequently, the $12,000 guarantee should be included. The additional guarantee of $6,000 ($18,000 – $12,000) in the case of excessive usage is similar to a contingent rental payment. Because it is not determinable at the lease's inception, it is not a lessee guarantee of the residual value that is includible in the minimum lease payments.

Answer (A) is incorrect because the guaranteed residual value is included in the determination of minimum lease payments. Answer (C) is incorrect because the additional guarantee of $6,000 ($18,000 – $12,000) is not included. It is contingent and thus nondeterminable. Answer (D) is incorrect because the minimum lease payments include only guaranteed residual value.

51. On August 1, Jones Corporation leased property to Smith Company for a 5-year period. The annual $20,000 lease payment is payable at the end of each year. The expected residual value at the end of the lease term is $10,000. Jones Company's implicit interest rate is 12%. The cost of the property to Jones was $50,000, which is the fair value at the lease date. The present value of an ordinary annuity of 1 for five periods is 3.605. The present value of 1 at the end of five periods is .567. At the inception of the lease, the recorded gross investment is

A. $110,000

B. $100,000

C. $72,100

D. $90,000

The correct answer is (A). *(J.O. Hall)*

REQUIRED: The amount to be recorded.

DISCUSSION: For a direct-financing or a sales-type lease, the lessor should record the gross investment in the lease at the undiscounted sum of the minimum lease payments (the total of the periodic payments and any guaranteed residual value, net of executory costs) and any unguaranteed residual value. The gross investment is the same regardless of whether any residual value is guaranteed. The five periodic payments of $20,000 equal $100,000. The expected residual value including guaranteed and unguaranteed portions equals $10,000. The gross investment should be $110,000 ($100,000 + $10,000).

Answer (B) is incorrect because it fails to include the residual value in the gross investment. Answer (C) is incorrect because the annual lease payments should be recorded at their undiscounted value. Answer (D) is incorrect because the residual value is added to, not subtracted from, the undiscounted lease payments.

52. On December 1, 20X0, Clark Company leased office space for five years at a monthly rental of $60,000. On that date, Clark paid the lessor the following amounts:

First month's rent	$ 60,000
Last month's rent	60,000
Security deposit (refundable at lease expiration)	80,000
Installation of new walls and offices	360,000

Clark's December 20X0 expense relating to its use of this office space is

A. $60,000

B. $66,000

C. $126,000

D. $200,000

The correct answer is (B). *(CPA, adapted)*

REQUIRED: The lessee's expense relating to an operating lease.

DISCUSSION: During 20X0, this operating lease was effective only for the month of December. The 20X0 expenses therefore include the $60,000 monthly rent plus the $360,000 cost of the installation of the new walls and offices allocated over the 60 months of the rental agreement. Thus, the total December expense equals $66,000 [$60,000 + ($360,000 ÷ 60 months)].

Answer (A) is incorrect because $60,000 does not include the allocation of the leasehold improvements. Answer (C) is incorrect because $126,000 includes the last month's rent. Answer (D) is incorrect because $200,000 includes the last month's rent and the security deposit but does not include the allocation of the cost of the leasehold improvements.

53. Which of the following leases would be classified as a capital lease by the lessee?

	Lease A	Lease B	Lease C	Lease D
Contains a bargain purchase option?	Yes	No	No	No
Lease term portion of the economic life of the leased property	60%	70%	80%	90%
Present value of the minimum lease payments as a portion of the fair value of the leased property	60%	70%	80%	90%

A. Lease A only.

B. Lease B only.

C. Leases A, C, and D.

D. Leases C and D only.

The correct answer is (C). *(CIA, adapted)*

REQUIRED: The lease(s) meeting a capitalization criterion.

DISCUSSION: SFAS 13, *Accounting for Leases*, states that a lease must be classified as a capital lease by a lessee if, at its inception, any one of the following criteria is met:

1) A lease provides for the transfer of ownership of the leased property.
2) The lease contains a bargain purchase option.
3) The lease term is 75% or more of the estimated economic life of the leased property.
4) The present value of the minimum lease payments (excluding executory costs) is at least 90% of the excess of the fair value of the leased property to the lessor at the inception of the lease over any related investment tax credit.

Lease A is a capital lease because the terms of the lease include a bargain purchase option. Leases C and D pass the economic life (75%) test, and lease D also passes the recovery of investment (90%) test.

Answer (A) is incorrect because Leases C and D are also capital leases. Answer (B) is incorrect because B is the only operating lease in the set. Answer (D) is incorrect because Lease A contains a bargain purchase option, so it qualifies as a capital lease.

54. Howell Corporation, a publicly traded corporation, is the lessee in a leasing agreement with Brandon Inc. to lease land and a building. If the lease contains a bargain purchase option, Howell should record the land and the building as a(n)

A. Operating lease and capital lease, respectively.

B. Capital lease and operating lease, respectively.

C. Capital lease but recorded as a single unit.

D. Capital lease but separately classified.

The correct answer is (D). *(CMA, adapted)*

REQUIRED: The accounting treatment of a lease agreement that contains a bargain purchase option.

DISCUSSION: A lessee records a lease as a capital lease if it meets any one of four criteria. Existence of a bargain purchase option is one of these criteria. If a lease involving land and a building contains a bargain purchase option or if the lease transfers ownership to the lessee at the end of its term, the lessee separately capitalizes the land and the building.

Answers (A) and (B) are incorrect because the bargain purchase option makes the lease a capital lease. Answer (C) is incorrect because the land and the building should be recorded in separate accounts. The building is depreciable and the land is not.

55. Initial direct costs are incurred by the lessor and may be classified as incremental direct costs and internal direct costs. All of the following costs are examples of initial direct costs except the costs of

A. Closing the lease transaction.

B. Negotiating lease terms.

C. Establishing and monitoring credit policies.

D. Evaluating collateral and security arrangements.

The correct answer is (C). *(CMA, adapted)*

REQUIRED: The item not an initial direct cost.

DISCUSSION: Under SFAS 91, initial direct costs have two components: (1) the lessor's external costs to originate a lease incurred in dealings with independent third parties and (2) the internal costs directly related to specified activities performed by the lessor for that lease, such as evaluating the lessee's financial condition; evaluating guarantees, collateral, and other security arrangements; negotiating lease terms; preparing and processing lease documents; and closing the transaction. Initial direct costs do not include the costs of advertising and other solicitation, servicing of existing leases, establishing and monitoring of credit policies, supervision, and administration.

Answers (A), (B), and (D) are incorrect because they are all components of initial direct costs of a lease.

Questions 56 and 57 are based on the following information. Suki Corporation is the lessor in a lease arrangement with Idrol Associates. At the inception of the lease, Suki incurred legal fees and other initial direct costs for the preparation and processing of the lease contract that were considered material in amount.

56. Assuming the lease is classified as an operating lease by Suki Corporation, the initial direct costs should be

A. Expensed in the year of incurrence by including them in cost of goods sold or by treating them as a selling expense.

B. Deferred and recognized as a reduction in the interest rate implicit in the lease.

C. Deferred and allocated over the lease term in proportion to the recognition of rental income.

D. Deferred and carried on the statement of financial position until the end of the lease term.

The correct answer is (C). *(CMA, adapted)*

REQUIRED: The lessor's accounting treatment of the initial direct costs of an operating lease.

DISCUSSION: SFAS 13, *Accounting for Leases*, requires lessors to capitalize the initial direct costs of an operating lease and allocate them over the term of the lease in proportion to the recognition of rental income.

Answer (A) is incorrect because the initial direct costs of a lease are to be deferred and matched against the future revenues from the lease. Answer (B) is incorrect because the initial direct costs are to be recognized separately. Answer (D) is incorrect because the initial direct costs are to be amortized over the term of the lease.

57. Assuming the lease is classified as a direct-financing capital lease by Suki Corporation, the initial direct costs should be

A. Expensed in the year of incurrence by including them in cost of goods sold or by treating them as a selling expense.

B. Deferred and recognized as a reduction in the interest rate implicit in the lease.

C. Deferred and allocated over the lease term in proportion to the recognition of rental income.

D. Deferred and carried on the statement of financial position until the end of the lease term.

The correct answer is (B). *(CMA, adapted)*

REQUIRED: The lessor's treatment of initial direct costs of a direct-financing lease.

DISCUSSION: SFAS 98, *Accounting for Leases*, states that initial direct costs should be accounted for as an addition to the gross investment in a direct-financing lease. The net investment equals the gross investment, plus unamortized initial direct costs, minus unearned income (gross investment – carrying amount). The unearned income and the initial direct costs are amortized over the lease term to provide a constant rate of return on the net investment.

Answer (A) is incorrect because SFAS 13 does not permit the lessor to expense initial direct costs immediately unless a sales-type lease is involved. Answer (C) is incorrect because the treatment of the initial direct costs of direct-financing and operating leases differs. The former are accounted for as an addition to the gross investment. Answer (D) is incorrect because the costs are allocated over the period of the lease by means of increasing the cost of the investment in the lease.

Questions 58 and 59 are based on the following information. On January 1, Plantation Restaurant is planning to enter as the lessee into the two lease agreements described in the opposite column. Each lease is noncancellable, and Plantation does not receive title to either leased property during or at the end of the lease term. All payments required under these agreements are due on January 1 each year.

Lessor	Hadaway, Inc.	Cutter Electronics
Type of property	Oven	Computer
Yearly rental	$15,000	$4,000
Lease term	10 years	3 years
Economic life	15 years	5 years
Purchase option	None	$3,000
Renewal option	None	None
Fair market value at inception of lease	$125,000	$10,200
Unguaranteed residual value	None	$2,000
Lessee's incremental borrowing rate	10%	10%
Executory costs paid by	Lessee	Lessor
Annual executory costs	$800	$500
Present value factor at 10% (of an annuity due)	6.76	2.74

58. Plantation Restaurant should treat the lease agreement with Hadaway, Inc. as a(n)

A. Capital lease with an initial asset value of $101,400.

B. Operating lease, charging $14,200 in rental expense and $800 in executory costs to annual operations.

C. Operating lease, charging the present value of the yearly rental expense to annual operations.

D. Operating lease, charging $15,000 in rental expense and $800 in executory costs to annual operations.

The correct answer is (D). *(CMA, adapted)*

REQUIRED: The true statement about the lease.

DISCUSSION: The Hadaway lease is an operating lease with a $15,000 annual rental expense with annual executory costs of $800 to be paid by the lessee. An operating lease does not transfer the rights and risks of ownership to the lessee. The Hadaway lease is nothing more than a rental arrangement. SFAS 13 specifies that if any one of the following criteria is met, the lease is a capital lease: the lease transfers title to the lessee, the lease has a bargain purchase option, the lease term is 75% or more of the useful life of the leased asset, or the present value of the minimum lease payments is 90% or more of the asset's fair value. The Hadaway lease meets none of these four criteria.

Answer (A) is incorrect because the Hadaway lease does not meet any of the criteria of a capital lease. Answer (B) is incorrect because rental expense is $15,000. Answer (C) is incorrect because the actual cash outlay for rent, $15,000, is charged to expense.

59. Plantation Restaurant should treat the lease agreement with Cutter Electronics as a(n)

A. Capital lease with an initial asset value of $10,960.

B. Capital lease with an initial asset value of $10,200.

C. Operating lease, charging $3,500 in rental expense and $500 in executory costs to annual operations.

D. Capital lease with an initial asset value of $9,590.

The correct answer is (D). *(CMA, adapted)*

REQUIRED: The true statement about the lease.

DISCUSSION: A capital lease is one in which many of the rights of ownership are transferred to the lessee. For accounting purposes, the lessee treats a capital lease as similar to the purchase of an asset. SFAS 13 specifies that if the present value of the minimum lease payments (excluding executory costs) is 90% or more of the asset's fair value, the lease should be accounted for as a capital lease. Given that the executory costs associated with the lease are to be paid by the lessor, a portion of the lease rental price is for those costs, not for the asset. Executory costs include insurance, maintenance, and similar expenses. Consequently, the annual minimum lease payment equals the annual payment minus the executory costs, or $3,500 ($4,000 yearly rental – $500). The present value of the minimum lease payments is therefore $9,590 (2.74 x $3,500), which is greater than 90% of the fair value of the asset. Thus, the lease should be capitalized. The appropriate amount of the initial asset value is the present value of the minimum lease payments calculated above.

Answer (A) is incorrect because the initial asset value cannot exceed the fair value of the leased asset. Moreover, $10,960 includes the present value of the executory costs. Answer (B) is incorrect because $10,200 is the fair value of the leased asset. Answer (C) is incorrect because the Cutter lease meets the criteria of a capital lease.

60. On January 1, 20X0, Hooks Oil Co. sold equipment with a carrying amount of $100,000 and a remaining useful life of 10 years to Maco Drilling for $150,000. Hooks immediately leased the equipment back under a 10-year capital lease with a present value of $150,000. It will depreciate the equipment using the straight-line method. Hooks made the first annual lease payment of $24,412 in December 20X0. In Hooks's December 31, 20X0 balance sheet, the unearned gain on the equipment sale should be

A. $50,000

B. $45,000

C. $25,588

D. $0

The correct answer is (B). *(CPA, adapted)*

REQUIRED: The unearned gain on the equipment sale one year after a sale-leaseback transaction.

DISCUSSION: A profit or loss on the sale in a sale-leaseback transaction is ordinarily deferred and amortized in proportion to the amortization of the leased asset if the leaseback is classified as a capital lease. At 12/31/X0, a gain proportionate to the lease amortization will be recognized [($150,000 – $100,000) ÷ 10 years = $5,000]. Hence, the deferred gain will be $45,000 ($50,000 – $5,000).

Answer (A) is incorrect because $50,000 is the total deferred gain at the inception of the lease. Answer (C) is incorrect because $25,588 is the difference between the total deferred gain and the periodic lease payment. Answer (D) is incorrect because the seller-lessee has retained substantially all of the use of the property and should therefore defer gain.

E. Pensions and Other Postretirement Benefits

61. The Rice Company sponsors a defined benefit pension plan for its employees. At the beginning of Year 1, Rice had prepaid pension cost of $15,000, pension plan assets with a fair value of $50,000, and a projected benefit obligation (PBO) of $35,000. The accumulated benefit obligation (ABO) equals the PBO. The service cost for Year 1 was $45,000, and the amount funded was $40,000. The discount rate and the expected rate of return on plan assets were 10%. No amortization of prior service cost, previously unrecognized gains or losses, or transition amount is required to determine the minimum net periodic pension cost (NPPC). Thus, for Year 1, Rice reported

A. Interest cost of $5,000.

B. Prepaid pension cost of $15,000.

C. NPPC of $43,500.

D. Accrued pension cost of $16,500.

The correct answer is (C). *(Publisher)*

REQUIRED: The true statement about pension reporting.

DISCUSSION: NPPC equals the sum of service cost and interest cost, minus the expected return on plan assets, or $43,500 [$45,000 + (10% discount rate x $35,000 PBO) – (10% expected rate of return x $50,000 fair value of plan assets)].

Answer (A) is incorrect because the interest cost component of NPPC is $3,500. Answers (B) and (D) are incorrect because prepaid pension cost is $11,500 [$15,000 – ($43,500 NPPC – $40,000 of funding)].

62. According to SFAS 87, *Employer's Accounting for Pension Plans*, the projected benefit obligation (PBO) is best described as the

A. Present value of benefits accrued to date based on future salary levels.

B. Present value of benefits accrued to date based on current salary levels.

C. Increase in retroactive benefits at the date of the amendment of the plan.

D. Amount of the adjustment necessary to reflect the difference between actual and estimated actuarial returns.

The correct answer is (A). *(CMA, adapted)*

REQUIRED: The best description of the PBO.

DISCUSSION: SFAS 87 defines the PBO as the actuarial present value of all future benefits attributable to past employee service at a moment in time. It is based on assumptions as to future compensation if the pension plan formula is based on future compensation.

Answer (B) is incorrect because the accumulated benefit obligation (ABO) is based only on current salary levels. Answer (C) is incorrect because prior service costs reflect the increase in retroactive benefits at the date of the amendment of the plan. Answer (D) is incorrect because the amortization of actuarial gains and losses is the amount of the adjustment necessary to reflect the difference between actual and estimated actuarial returns.

63. The following information pertains to Lee Corp.'s defined benefit pension plan for 20X0:

Service cost	$160,000
Actual and expected gain on plan assets	35,000
Unexpected loss on plan assets related to a 20X0 disposal of a subsidiary	40,000
Amortization of unrecognized prior service cost	5,000
Annual interest on pension obligation	50,000

What amount should Lee report as pension expense in its 20X0 income statement?

A. $250,000

B. $220,000

C. $210,000

D. $180,000

The correct answer is (D). *(CPA, adapted)*

REQUIRED: The pension expense for the year.

DISCUSSION: The six possible components of net periodic pension cost (NPPC) are (1) service cost, (2) interest cost, (3) return on plan assets, (4) gain or loss to the extent recognized, (5) amortization of any unrecognized prior service cost, and (6) amortization of any transition amount. Accordingly, the service cost, gain on plan assets, interest cost, and amortization of prior service cost are included in the computation. Gains and losses arising from changes in the projected benefit obligation or plan assets resulting from experience different from that assumed and from changes in assumptions about discount rates, life expectancies, etc., are not required to be recognized when they occur. Accordingly, the unexpected 20X0 loss on plan assets will be included in the net unrecognized gain or loss balance and will be eligible for amortization in 20X1. NPPC is therefore $180,000 ($160,000 service cost – $35,000 actual and expected return on plan assets + $5,000 prior service cost amortization + $50,000 interest cost).

Answer (A) is incorrect because $250,000 results from adding, not subtracting, the expected gain on plan assets. Answer (B) is incorrect because $220,000 includes the unexpected loss. Answer (C) is incorrect because $210,000 includes the unexpected loss and subtracts, rather than adds, the amortization of prior service cost.

64. At the start of its current fiscal year, Emper Co. amended its defined benefit pension plan, resulting in an increase of $600,000 in the PBO. As of the date of the amendment, Emper had 50 employees. Ten employees are expected to leave at the end of each of the next 5 years (including the current year). The minimum amortization of prior service cost in the first year is

A. $80,000

B. $120,000

C. $160,000

D. $200,000

The correct answer is (D). *(Publisher)*

REQUIRED: The minimum amortization of prior service cost.

DISCUSSION: Prior service cost is amortized by assigning an equal amount to each future period of service of each employee active at the date of the plan amendment who is expected to receive benefits under the plan. If all or almost all of a plan's participants are inactive, the prior service cost is amortized based on the remaining life expectancy of the participants. An alternative amortization approach, such as a straight-line method, that recognizes the cost of retroactive amendments more quickly is also permitted if used consistently. For Emper, total service years rendered during the 5-year period is 150 (50 + 40 + 30 + 20 + 10). The amortization fraction for the first year is thus 50/150, and the minimum amortization is $200,000 ($600,000 x 50/150).

Answer (A) is incorrect because 50, not 20, must be used as the numerator of the amortization fraction. Answer (B) is incorrect because the use of straight-line amortization over 5 years does not recognize the cost of retroactive amendments more quickly, so the method described above must be used. Answer (C) is incorrect because 50, not 40, must be used as the numerator of the amortization fraction for the first year.

65. Deerfield Corporation has the following information available regarding its pension plan:

	May 31, 2000	May 31, 2001
Accumulated benefit obligation (ABO)	$180,000	$280,000
Projected benefit obligation (PBO)	200,000	320,000
Fair value of plan assets	162,000	180,000
Unrecognized prior service cost	68,000	52,000
Prepaid pension cost	30,000	--
Accrued pension cost	--	88,000

In accordance with the requirements of SFAS 87, *Employer's Accounting for Pension Plans*, Deerfield's minimum liability at May 31, 2000 and 2001, respectively, was

A. $38,000 and $140,000.

B. $98,000 and $0.

C. $48,000 and $12,000.

D. $18,000 and $100,000.

The correct answer is (D). *(CMA, adapted)*

REQUIRED: The minimum pension liability at the beginning and end of a period.

DISCUSSION: SFAS 87 requires the recording of a liability if the ABO is underfunded. Thus, if the ABO is greater than the fair value of plan assets, a net liability must be recognized. At May 31, 2000, the $180,000 ABO is $18,000 greater than the $162,000 fair value of plan assets. At May 31, 2001, a liability of $100,000 exists because the $280,000 ABO is $100,000 greater than the $180,000 fair value of plan assets.

Answer (A) is incorrect because $38,000 and $140,000 equal the excess of the PBO over the fair value of plan assets at May 31, 2000 and 2001, respectively. Answer (B) is incorrect because $98,000 is the sum of unrecognized prior service cost and prepaid pension cost, and $0 is the difference between the PBO at May 31, 2001 and the sum of the fair value of the plan assets, the unrecognized prior service cost, and the accrued pension cost. Answer (C) is incorrect because $48,000 is the amount of the entry at May 31, 2000 to record the additional liability needed to reflect the required minimum liability. It equals the excess of the ABO over the fair value of plan assets, plus the prepaid pension cost. The entry is to debit an intangible asset and to credit the additional liability for $48,000. At May 31, 2001, $12,000 equals the amount of the entry to record the additional liability ($280,000 ABO – $180,000 fair value of plan assets – $88,000 accrued pension cost).

66. The following information relates to the 2001 activity of the defined benefit pension plan of Twain Publishers, Ltd., a company whose stock is publicly traded:

Service cost	$120,000
Return on plan assets	30,000
Interest cost on pension benefit obligation	40,000
Amortization of actuarial loss	10,000
Amortization of prior service cost	5,000
Amortization of transition obligation	15,000

Twain's 2001 pension cost is

A. $120,000

B. $140,000

C. $150,000

D. $160,000

The correct answer is (D). *(A. Oddo)*

REQUIRED: The net periodic pension cost (NPPC) for the year.

DISCUSSION: Components of NPPC are service cost, interest cost, the expected return on plan assets, and amortization of any (1) unrecognized prior service cost, (2) net transition asset or obligation, or (3) unrecognized net gain (loss). Service cost, interest cost, and the amortization of actuarial loss, prior service cost, and a net transition obligation increase the net periodic pension cost. The expected return on plan assets decreases NPPC. As indicated below, NPPC is $160,000.

Service cost	$120,000
Return on plan assets	(30,000)
Interest cost	40,000
Amortization of actuarial loss	10,000
Amortization of prior service cost	5,000
Amortization of transition obligation	15,000
Net periodic pension cost	$160,000

Answer (A) is incorrect because $120,000 only includes the service cost component. Answer (B) is incorrect because $140,000 excludes the amortization of prior service cost and the transition obligation. Answer (C) is incorrect because $150,000 excludes the amortization of the actuarial loss.

67. At end of the year, Penny Company's projected benefit obligation (PBO) was determined to be $1,500,000, which was $200,000 higher than had been expected. The market-related value of the defined benefit plan's assets was equal to its fair value of $1,250,000. No other gains and losses have occurred. If the average remaining service life is 20 years, the minimum required amortization of the unrecognized net gain (loss) in the next year will be

A. $20,000

B. $3,750

C. $2,500

D. $0

The correct answer is (C). *(Publisher)*

REQUIRED: The minimum required amortization of unrecognized net gain (loss) next year.

DISCUSSION: At a minimum, amortization of the cumulative unrecognized net gain or loss (excluding asset gains and losses not yet reflected in market-related value) must be included as a component of NPPC for a year if, as of the beginning of the year, that unrecognized gain or loss exceeds 10% of the greater of the PBO or the market-related value (MRV) of plan assets. At year-end, Penny's PBO was $200,000 greater than estimated (a $200,000 liability loss). Because no other gain or loss has occurred, the unrecognized net loss to be amortized beginning next year is $200,000. The corridor amount is $150,000 (10% of the greater of $1,500,000 PBO or $1,250,000 MRV of plan assets). The amount outside the corridor is $50,000 ($200,000 – $150,000), and the amount to be amortized is $2,500 ($50,000 ÷ 20 years of average remaining service life).

Answer (A) is incorrect because $20,000 is the result of using the full $200,000 liability loss without regard to the corridor amount and assumes an amortization period of 10 years instead of 20. Answer (B) is incorrect because $3,750 is the result of using $125,000 (10% x $1,250,000 plan assets) as the corridor amount instead of $150,000. Answer (D) is incorrect because $50,000 of the liability loss must be amortized over the average remaining service life beginning the year following the loss.

68. The following information pertains to Gali Co.'s defined benefit pension plan for 20X0:

Fair value of plan assets, beginning of year	$350,000
Fair value of plan assets, end of year	525,000
Employer contributions	110,000
Benefits paid	85,000

In computing pension expense, what amount should Gali use as actual return on plan assets?

A. $65,000

B. $150,000

C. $175,000

D. $260,000

The correct answer is (B). *(CPA, adapted)*

REQUIRED: The actual return on plan assets.

DISCUSSION: The actual return on plan assets is based on the fair value of plan assets at the beginning and end of the accounting period, adjusted for contributions and payments during the period. The actual return for Gali is $150,000 ($525,000 – $350,000 – $110,000 + $85,000).

Answer (A) is incorrect because $65,000 results when benefits paid to employees are not included. Answer (C) is incorrect because $175,000 is the change in the fair value of plan assets without adjustment for contributions or benefits paid. Answer (D) is incorrect because $260,000 does not deduct employer contributions.

Questions 69 and 70 are based on the following information. On November 30, the Board of Directors of Baldwin Corporation amended its pension plan giving retroactive benefits to its employees. The information to the right is provided at November 30:

Accumulated benefit obligation (ABO)	$825,000
Projected benefit obligation (PBO)	900,000
Accrued pension cost	112,500
Plan assets (fair value)	307,500
Market-related asset value	301,150
Unrecognized prior service cost	190,000
Average remaining service life of employees	10 years
Useful life of pension goodwill	20 years

69. Baldwin Corporation's minimum pension liability at November 30 is

A. $190,000

B. $405,000

C. $517,500

D. $523,850

The correct answer is (C). *(CMA, adapted)*

REQUIRED: The minimum pension liability.

DISCUSSION: Under SFAS 87, a minimum liability must be recognized when the ABO exceeds the fair value of plan assets. Because the ABO exceeds the fair value of plan assets, the minimum liability to be recognized is $517,500 ($825,000 ABO – $307,500 FVPA).

Answer (A) is incorrect because $190,000 is the unrecognized prior service cost, which can be allocated to future periods. Answer (B) is incorrect because $405,000 is the additional liability to be recognized. Answer (D) is incorrect because $523,850 is based on the market-related asset value.

70. Using the straight-line method of amortization, the amount of prior service cost charged to expense during the year ended November 30 is

A. $9,500

B. $19,000

C. $30,250

D. $190,000

The correct answer is (B). *(CMA, adapted)*

REQUIRED: The prior service cost expensed using the straight-line method.

DISCUSSION: Unrecognized prior service cost arises from the awarding of retroactive benefits resulting from plan initiation or amendments. Prior service cost is assigned to the future service periods of active employees using either a straight-line or another acceptable method of allocation. Given that the average remaining service life of the firm's employees is 10 years, the annual charge is $19,000 ($190,000 ÷ 10).

Answer (A) is incorrect because $9,500 is based on a 20-year amortization period. Answer (C) is incorrect because $30,250 equals the sum of unrecognized prior service cost and accrued pension cost, divided by 10 years. Answer (D) is incorrect because unrecognized prior service cost can be amortized over the remaining work life of employees; it does not have to be recorded entirely in the year of origination.

F. Deferred Income Taxes

71. Which one of the following temporary differences will result in a deferred tax asset?

A. Use of the straight-line depreciation method for financial statement purposes and the Modified Accelerated Cost Recovery System (MACRS) for income tax purposes.

B. Installment sale profits accounted for on the accrual basis for financial statement purposes and on a cash basis for income tax purposes.

C. Advance rental receipts accounted for on the accrual basis for financial statement purposes and on a cash basis for tax purposes.

D. Investment gains accounted for under the equity method for financial statement purposes and under the cost method for income tax purposes.

The correct answer is (C). *(CMA, adapted)*

REQUIRED: The TD that will result in a deferred tax asset.

DISCUSSION: A deferred tax asset records the deferred tax consequences attributable to deductible temporary differences and carryforwards. Advance rental receipts accounted for on the accrual basis for financial statement purposes and on a cash basis for tax purposes would give rise to a deferred tax asset. The financial statements would report no income and no related tax expense because the rental payments apply to future periods. The tax return, however, would treat the rent as income when the cash was received, and a tax would be due in the year of receipt. Because the tax is paid prior to recording the income for financial statement purposes, it represents an asset that will be recognized as an expense when income is finally recorded.

Answer (A) is incorrect because using accelerated depreciation on the tax return results in a deferred tax liability. Answer (B) is incorrect because recognizing installment income on the financial statements but not the tax return results in a taxable temporary difference. Answer (D) is incorrect because recognizing investment gains on the financial statements earlier than they are recognized on the tax return gives rise to a deferred tax liability.

72. Barth and Garth, Inc. depreciate equipment over 15 years for financial purposes and over 7 years for federal income tax purposes. As a result of this temporary difference, the deferred income taxes will be reported in its first year of use as a

A. Noncurrent asset.

B. Noncurrent liability.

C. Current liability.

D. Current asset.

The correct answer is (B). *(Publisher)*

REQUIRED: The classification of deferred taxes arising from the excess of tax over book depreciation.

DISCUSSION: When a deferred tax liability or asset is related to an asset or a liability, its classification as current or noncurrent is based on the classification of the related item for financial reporting purposes. Because tax depreciation for the first year is greater than book depreciation, the tax basis of this noncurrent asset differs from (is less than) its book basis. The result is a taxable temporary difference. The related deferred tax liability is classified as noncurrent because the related asset is noncurrent.

Answer (A) is incorrect because a temporary difference related to depreciable equipment results in a liability. Answers (C) and (D) are incorrect because depreciable equipment is classified as a noncurrent asset.

73. According to SFAS 109, when a company reports deferred tax assets and liabilities for 2 consecutive years, a deferred income tax benefit or expense should be reported equal to the

A. Decrease in the deferred tax assets.

B. Sum of the net changes in deferred tax assets and deferred tax liabilities.

C. Increase in the deferred tax liabilities.

D. Amount of the total income tax liability.

The correct answer is (B). *(Publisher)*

REQUIRED: The method of determining deferred income tax expense or benefit.

DISCUSSION: The deferred tax expense or benefit recognized is the sum of the net changes in the deferred tax assets and deferred tax liabilities. The deferred income tax expense or benefit is aggregated with the income taxes currently payable or refundable to determine the amount of income tax expense or benefit for the year to be recorded in the income statement.

Answers (A) and (C) are incorrect because the deferred income tax expense or benefit is equal to the sum of the net changes in the deferred tax assets and deferred tax liabilities. Answer (D) is incorrect because the total income tax liability includes both the current and deferred income tax expense or benefit for the year.

74. At the end of the current year, its first year of operation, the Fratzie Corporation reported $45,000 taxable income and $38,000 pretax financial income as a result of a single temporary difference. Because of uncertain economic times, the company believes that only 75% of the deductible temporary difference is more likely than not to be realized. The tax rate for the current year is 30%, and no change has been enacted for future years. On the year-end balance sheet, the deferred tax asset will be reported at a net balance of

A. $7,000

B. $5,250

C. $2,100

D. $1,575

The correct answer is (D). *(Publisher)*

REQUIRED: The amount of deferred tax asset.

DISCUSSION: The deferred tax asset is based on the difference ($7,000) between taxable income ($45,000) and financial income ($38,000). However, there is an expectation only 75% of the tax benefit is more likely than not to be realized. Thus, the amount of the future deductible amounts will be $5,250 (75% x $7,000). The deferred tax asset is $1,575 (30% enacted tax rate x $5,250).

Answers (A) and (B) are incorrect because they represent differences in income before application of the tax rate. Answer (C) is incorrect because $2,100 is based on the full benefit without consideration that 25% of the benefit will never be realized.

75. In its 20X0 income statement, Cere Co. reported income before income taxes of $300,000. Cere estimated that, because of permanent differences, taxable income for 20X0 would be $280,000. During 20X0, Cere made estimated tax payments of $50,000, which were debited to income tax expense. Cere is subject to a 30% tax rate. What amount should Cere report as income tax expense?

A. $34,000

B. $50,000

C. $84,000

D. $90,000

The correct answer is (C). *(CPA, adapted)*

REQUIRED: The amount to be reported for income tax expense.

DISCUSSION: Income tax expense or benefit is the sum of current tax expense or benefit and deferred tax expense or benefit. A deferred tax expense or benefit is the change in an entity's deferred tax assets and liabilities. However, a permanent difference does not result in a change in a deferred tax asset or liability. Thus, income tax expense equals the current income tax expense, which is the amount of taxes paid or payable for the year. Income taxes payable for 20X0 equal $84,000 ($280,000 taxable income x 30%).

Answer (A) is incorrect because $34,000 equals the $84,000 of income taxes payable minus the $50,000 of income taxes paid. Answer (B) is incorrect because $50,000 equals income taxes paid, not the total current income tax expense. Answer (D) is incorrect because $90,000 is equal to the reported income of $300,000 multiplied by the tax rate.

76. West Corp. leased a building and received the $36,000 annual rental payment on June 15, 20X0. The beginning of the lease was July 1, 20X0. Rental income is taxable when received. West's tax rates are 30% for 20X0 and 40% thereafter. West had no other permanent or temporary differences. West determined that no valuation allowance was needed. What amount of deferred tax asset should West report in its December 31, 20X0 balance sheet?

A. $5,400

B. $7,200

C. $10,800

D. $14,400

The correct answer is (B). *(CPA, adapted)*

REQUIRED: The amount of deferred tax asset reported at year-end.

DISCUSSION: The $36,000 rental payment is taxable in full when received in 20X0, but only $18,000 ($36,000 x 6/12) should be recognized in financial accounting income for the year. The result is a deductible temporary difference (deferred tax asset) arising from the difference between the tax basis ($0) of the liability for unearned rent and its reported amount in the year-end balance sheet ($36,000 – $18,000 = $18,000). The income tax payable for 20X0 based on the rental payment is $10,800 (30% tax rate for 20X0 x $36,000), the deferred tax asset is $7,200 (40% enacted tax rate applicable after 20X0 when the asset will be realized x $18,000 future deductible amount), and the income tax expense is $3,600 ($10,800 current tax expense – $7,200 deferred tax benefit). The deferred tax benefit equals the net change during the year in the enterprise's deferred tax liabilities and assets ($7,200 deferred tax asset recognized in 20X0 – $0).

Answer (A) is incorrect because $5,400 is based on a 30% tax rate. Answer (C) is incorrect because $10,800 is the income tax payable. Answer (D) is incorrect because $14,400 would be the income tax payable if the 40% tax rate applied in 20X0.

77. Based on its current operating levels, Glucose Corporation estimates that its annual level of taxable income in the foreseeable future will be $200,000 annually. Enacted tax rates for the tax jurisdiction in which Glucose operates are 15% for the first $50,000 of taxable income, 25% for the next $50,000 of taxable income, and 35% for taxable income in excess of $100,000. Which tax rate should Glucose use to measure a deferred tax liability or asset in accordance with SFAS 109?

A. 15%

B. 25%

C. 27.5%

D. 35%

The correct answer is (C). *(Publisher)*

REQUIRED: The tax rate applicable to the measurement of a deferred tax liability or asset.

DISCUSSION: In measuring a deferred tax liability or asset, the objective is to use the enacted tax rate(s) expected to apply to taxable income in the periods in which the deferred tax liability or asset is expected to be settled or realized. If graduated tax rates are a significant factor for an enterprise, the applicable tax rate is the average graduated tax rate applicable to the amount of estimated future annual taxable income. As indicated, the applicable tax rate is 27.5% ($55,000 ÷ $200,000).

Taxable Income		Tax Rate		
$ 50,000	×	15%	=	$ 7,500
50,000	×	25%	=	12,500
100,000	×	35%	=	35,000
$200,000				$55,000

Answer (A) is incorrect because 15% is the tax rate for the first $50,000 of income. Answer (B) is incorrect because 25% is the tax rate for income over $50,000 but less than $100,000. Answer (D) is incorrect because 35% is the tax rate for income over $100,000.

Questions 78 and 79 are based on the following information. Bearings Manufacturing Company Inc. purchased a new machine on January 1, 2001 for $100,000. The company uses the straight-line depreciation method with an estimated equipment life of 5 years and a zero salvage value for financial statement purposes, and uses the 3-year Modified Accelerated Cost Recovery System (MACRS) with an estimated equipment life of 3 years for income tax reporting purposes. Bearings is subject to a 35% marginal income tax rate. Assume that the deferred tax liability at the beginning of the year is zero and that Bearings has a positive earnings tax position. The MACRS depreciation rates for 3-year equipment are shown below.

Year	Rate
1	33.33%
2	44.45
3	14.81
4	7.41

78. What is the deferred tax liability at December 31, 2001 (rounded to the nearest whole dollar)?

A. $7,000

B. $33,330

C. $11,666

D. $4,666

The correct answer is (D). *(CMA, adapted)*

REQUIRED: The deferred tax liability assuming tax rates will not change.

DISCUSSION: For financial reporting purposes, the reported amount (cost – accumulated depreciation) of the machine at year-end, assuming straight-line depreciation and no salvage value, will be $80,000 [$100,000 cost – ($100,000 ÷ 5 years)]. The tax basis of this asset will be $66,670 [$100,000 – (33.33% x $100,000)]. A taxable temporary difference has arisen because the excess of the reported amount over the tax basis will result in a net future taxable amount over the recovery period. A taxable temporary difference requires recognition of a deferred tax liability. Assuming the 35% rate applies during the asset's entire life, the deferred tax liability equals the applicable enacted tax rate times the temporary difference, or $4,666 [35% x ($80,000 – $66,670)].

Answer (A) is incorrect because $7,000 is the tax benefit provided by the $20,000 depreciation expense on the books. Answer (B) is incorrect because $33,330 is the depreciation deduction on the tax return. Answer (C) is incorrect because $11,666 is the tax shield based on MACRS depreciation.

79. For Bearings Manufacturing Company Inc., assume that the following new corporate income tax rates will go into effect:

2002-2004	40%
2005	45%

What is the amount of the deferred tax asset/liability at December 31, 2001 (rounded to the nearest whole dollar)?

A. $0

B. $9,000

C. $2,668

D. $6,332

The correct answer is (D). *(CMA, adapted)*

REQUIRED: The deferred tax liability assuming tax rates will change.

DISCUSSION: When one tax rate does not apply to all relevant years, a more complex calculation is necessary. In this question, different rates apply during the recovery period. During the years 2002-2004, book depreciation will equal $60,000 [3 x ($100,000 ÷ 5)], and tax depreciation will equal $66,670 (the tax basis at December 31, 2001 will be recovered in full by December 31, 2004). Based on the applicable enacted 40% tax rate, the net deferred tax asset for 2002-2004 will be $2,668 [40% x ($66,670 – $60,000)]. However, the excess of book over tax depreciation in 2001 will be $20,000 ($20,000 – $0). Based on the applicable enacted 45% tax rate, the deferred tax liability for 2005 will be $9,000 (45% x $20,000). Accordingly, the net deferred tax liability at December 31, 2001 is $6,332 ($9,000 – $2,668).

Answer (A) is incorrect because a deferred tax liability of $6,332 is recorded for a taxable temporary difference. Answer (B) is incorrect because $9,000 is the deferred tax liability for 2001 reflecting the excess of book over tax depreciation. Answer (C) is incorrect because $2,668 is the deferred tax asset for 2002-2004 resulting from the excess of tax over book depreciation during that period.

80. In preparing its December 31 financial statements, Irene Corp. must determine the proper accounting treatment of a $180,000 loss carryforward available to offset future taxable income. There are no temporary differences. The applicable current and future income tax rate is 30%. Available evidence is not conclusive as to the future existence of sufficient taxable income to provide for the future realization of the tax benefit of the $180,000 loss carryforward. However, based on the available evidence, Irene believes that it is more likely than not that future taxable income will be available to provide for the future realization of only $100,000 of this loss carryforward. In its statement of financial condition, Irene should recognize what amounts?

	Deferred Tax Asset	Valuation Allowance
A.	$0	$0
B.	$30,000	$0
C.	$54,000	$24,000
D.	$54,000	$30,000

The correct answer is (C). *(Publisher)*

REQUIRED: The amounts to be recognized as a deferred tax asset and related valuation allowance.

DISCUSSION: The applicable tax rate should be used to measure a deferred tax asset for an operating loss carry-forward that is available to offset future taxable income. Irene should therefore recognize a $54,000 ($180,000 x 30%) deferred tax asset. A valuation allowance should be recognized to reduce the deferred tax asset if, based on the weight of the available evidence, it is more likely than not that some portion or all of a deferred tax asset will not be realized. Based on the available evidence, Irene believes that it is more likely than not that the tax benefit of $100,000 of the operating loss will be realized. Thus, the company should recognize a $24,000 valuation allowance to reduce the $54,000 deferred tax asset to $30,000 ($100,000 x 30%), the amount of the deferred tax asset that is more likely than not to be realized.

Answer (A) is incorrect because a deferred tax asset equal to $54,000 should be recognized and a valuation allowance should be recognized equal to $24,000 to reduce the deferred tax asset to $30,000. Answer (B) is incorrect because a deferred tax asset of $30,000 results from netting the valuation allowance against the deferred tax asset. Answer (D) is incorrect because $30,000 is the deferred tax asset, not the valuation allowance, after the two are netted.

Questions 81 through 83 are based on the following information. Sarasota Manufacturing Company (SMC) purchased a new machine on January 1, 2001 for $200,000. For financial statement purposes, the company uses the straight-line depreciation method with an estimated equipment life of 5 years and a $0 salvage value. For federal income tax purposes, it uses the 3-year Modified Accelerated Cost Recovery System (MACRS). SMC is subject to a 35% marginal income tax rate for all relevant years. Assume that SMC had no deferred tax assets or liabilities at the beginning of the year, and that it has positive earnings for book and tax purposes at all relevant times. Also assume that the MACRS tax rates for 3-year equipment are given below:

Year	Rate
1	33.33%
2	44.45
3	14.81
4	7.41

81. What is the deferred tax liability at December 31, 2001 (rounded to the nearest whole dollar)?

A. $14,000

B. $66,660

C. $23,331

D. $9,331

The correct answer is (D). *(Publisher)*

REQUIRED: The deferred tax liability at December 31, 2001.

DISCUSSION: In the first year of its use of an accelerated tax depreciation method, SMC has a taxable temporary difference (TD) because tax depreciation exceeds book depreciation. This difference between the tax basis and the reported amount of the asset is temporary because it will reverse in the future when book depreciation exceeds tax depreciation. It is taxable because in the future it will cause taxable income to exceed book income. Thus, the entity must recognize a deferred tax liability. Book depreciation for each year of the 5-year life is $40,000 [($200,000 – $0 salvage) x (1 year ÷ 5 years)]. MACRS depreciation for the first year is $66,660 [($200,000 – $0) x 33.33%]. Accordingly, the taxable TD at the end of the first year (the future taxable amount) is $26,660 ($66,660 – $40,000). At the applicable tax rate, the deferred tax liability at the end of 2001 is $9,331 (35% x $26,660).

Answer (A) is incorrect because $14,000 is the tax shield provided by depreciation of $40,000 (straight-line). Answer (B) is incorrect because $66,660 is the depreciation expense on the tax return. Answer (C) is incorrect because $23,331 is the tax shield provided by depreciation of $66,660 (MACRS).

82. Assuming no other transactions involving depreciable assets, what is the balance of the deferred tax liability at December 31, 2002 (rounded to the nearest whole dollar)?

A. $17,115

B. $26,446

C. $ 7,784

D. $ 9,331

The correct answer is (B). *(Publisher)*

REQUIRED: The deferred tax liability at December 31, 2002.

DISCUSSION: After 2 years, accumulated straight-line depreciation is $80,000 [($200,000 – $0) x (2 years ÷ 5 years)], and accumulated MACRS depreciation is $155,560 [($200,000 – $0) x (33.33% + 44.45%)]. Accordingly, the taxable TD (the amount by which future taxable income will exceed book income) after 2 years is $75,560 ($155,560 – $80,000). At the applicable tax rate, the deferred tax liability at the end of 2000 is $26,446 (35% x $75,560).

Answer (A) is incorrect because the $17,115 is the increase in the deferred tax liability for 2002. Answer (C) is incorrect because $7,784 equals the increase in 2000 minus the beginning balance. Answer (D) is incorrect because $9,331 is the balance at the end of 2001.

83. Assume that new corporate income tax rates will go into effect as follows:

2002-2004	40%
2005	45%

What is the amount of the deferred tax liability at December 31, 2001 (rounded to the nearest whole dollar)?

A. $11,997

B. $10,664

C. $14,000

D. $12,664

The correct answer is (D). *(Publisher)*

REQUIRED: The deferred tax liability at December 31, 2001, assuming that the tax rates in later years will be higher than the current rate.

DISCUSSION: Deferred tax amounts are measured using the enacted future tax rates that will apply when related future taxable or deductible amounts arise from temporary differences. The following is the pattern of these amounts for SMC:

Year	Book Depreciation	MACRS Depreciation ($200,000 × Annual Rate)	Annual Taxable (Deductible) TD
2001	$40,000	$66,660	$(26,660)
2002	40,000	88,900	(48,900)
2003	40,000	29,620	10,380
2004	40,000	14,820	25,180
2005	40,000	0	40,000

The table above indicates that the temporary difference at December 31, 2001 arising from using different depreciation methods for tax and book purposes will reverse over the next 4 years ($40,000 + $25,180 + $10,380 – $48,900 = $26,660). The deferred tax liability at December 31, 2001 is therefore measured as follows:

Year	Taxable (Deductible) Amount		Enacted Tax Rate		Annual Tax Expense (Benefit)
2002	$(48,900)	×	40%	=	$(19,560)
2003	10,380	×	40%	=	4,152
2004	25,180	×	40%	=	10,072
2005	40,000	×	45%	=	18,000
					$ 12,664

Answer (A) is incorrect because $11,997 assumes a 45% rate applies to all relevant years. Answer (B) is incorrect because $10,664 assumes a 40% rate applies to all relevant years. Answer (C) is incorrect because $14,000 equals the annual tax shield provided by the straight-line method at a 35% rate.

84. Quinn Co. reported a net deferred tax asset of $9,000 in its December 31, 20X0 balance sheet. For 20X1, Quinn reported pretax financial statement income of $300,000. Temporary differences of $100,000 resulted in taxable income of $200,000 for 20X1. At December 31, 20X1, Quinn had cumulative taxable temporary differences of $70,000. Quinn's effective income tax rate is 30%. In its December 31, 20X1 income statement, what should Quinn report as deferred income tax expense?

A. $12,000

B. $21,000

C. $30,000

D. $60,000

The correct answer is (C). *(CPA, adapted)*

REQUIRED: The deferred income tax expense.

DISCUSSION: Deferred tax expense or benefit is the net change in an entity's deferred tax liabilities and assets during the year. Quinn had a net deferred tax asset of $9,000 at the beginning of 20X1, and a net deferred tax liability of $21,000 ($70,000 x 30%) at the end of 20X1. The net change (a deferred tax expense in this case) is $30,000 ($9,000 reduction in the deferred tax asset + $21,000 increase in deferred tax liabilities).

Answer (A) is incorrect because $12,000 results from offsetting the deferred tax liability and the deferred tax asset. Answer (B) is incorrect because $21,000 is the deferred tax liability. Answer (D) is incorrect because $60,000 is the income tax expense for the year ($200,000 x .30).

85. As a result of differences between depreciation for financial reporting purposes and tax purposes, the financial reporting basis of Noor Co.'s sole depreciable asset, acquired in 20X0, exceeded its tax basis by $250,000 at December 31, 20X0. This difference will reverse in future years. The enacted tax rate is 30% for 20X0 and 40% for future years. Noor has no other temporary differences. In its December 31, 20X0 balance sheet, how should Noor report the deferred tax effect of this difference?

A. As an asset of $75,000.

B. As an asset of $100,000.

C. As a liability of $75,000.

D. As a liability of $100,000.

The correct answer is (D). *(CPA, adapted)*

REQUIRED: The deferred tax effect of the difference between the financial reporting basis and the tax basis.

DISCUSSION: The temporary difference arises because the excess of the reported amount of the depreciable asset over its tax basis will result in taxable amounts in future years when the reported amount is recovered. A taxable temporary difference results in a deferred tax liability. Because the enacted tax rate for future years is 40%, the deferred income tax liability is $100,000 ($250,000 x 40%).

Answers (A) and (B) are incorrect because the deferred income tax effect is a liability. The temporary difference results in taxable, not deductible, amounts. Answer (C) is incorrect because $75,000 is based on the 20X0 tax rate.

86. Taft Corp. uses the equity method to account for its 25% investment in Flame, Inc. During 20X0, Taft received dividends of $30,000 from Flame and recorded $180,000 as its equity in the earnings of Flame. Additional information follows:

- All the undistributed earnings of Flame will be distributed as dividends in future periods.
- The dividends received from Flame are eligible for the 80% dividends-received deduction.
- There are no other temporary differences.
- Enacted income tax rates are 30% for 20X0 and thereafter.

In its December 31, 20X0 balance sheet, what amount should Taft report for deferred income tax liability?

A. $9,000

B. $10,800

C. $45,000

D. $54,000

The correct answer is (A). *(CPA, adapted)*

REQUIRED: The deferred income tax liability reported on the balance sheet.

DISCUSSION: According to SFAS 109, the deferred tax liability constitutes the "deferred tax consequences attributable to taxable temporary differences. A deferred tax liability is measured using the applicable enacted tax rate and provisions of the enacted tax law." Taft's recognition of $180,000 of equity-based earnings creates a temporary difference that will result in taxable amounts in future periods when dividends are distributed. The deferred tax liability arising from this temporary difference is measured using the 30% enacted tax rate and the dividends-received deduction. Accordingly, given that all the undistributed earnings will be distributed, a deferred tax liability of $9,000 [($180,000 equity – $30,000 dividends received) x 20% not deductible x 30% tax rate applicable after 20X0] should be reported.

Answer (B) is incorrect because $10,800 equals 30% of 20% of the equity in the earnings of Flame. Answer (C) is incorrect because $45,000 is the net increase in Taft's investment in Flame account under the equity method multiplied by the 30% tax rate. Answer (D) is incorrect because $54,000 equals 30% of $180,000.

87. Mill, which began operations on January 1, 20X0, recognizes income from long-term construction contracts under the percentage-of-completion method in its financial statements and under the completed-contract method for income tax reporting. Income under each method follows:

Year	Completed-Contract	Percentage-of-Completion
20X0	$ --	$300,000
20X1	400,000	600,000
20X2	700,000	850,000

There are no other temporary differences. If the applicable tax rate is 25%, Mill should report in its balance sheet at December 31, 20X2 a deferred income tax liability of

A. $37,500

B. $105,000

C. $162,500

D. $195,000

The correct answer is (C). *(CPA, adapted)*

REQUIRED: The deferred tax liability arising from differences in reporting income from long-term contracts.

DISCUSSION: In its financial statements issued through 12/31/X2, Mill has reported $1,750,000 ($300,000 + $600,000 + $850,000) of income from long-term contracts. In its tax returns for the same period, it has reported $1,100,000 ($400,000 + $700,000) of income from the same sources. The result is a taxable temporary difference. Thus, Mill expects to have future taxable amounts of $650,000 and should recognize a deferred tax liability of $162,500 (25% applicable tax rate x $650,000).

Answer (A) is incorrect because $37,500 is the amount of the liability arising from the excess of percentage-of-completion over completed-contract revenue for 2000, assuming a 25% rate. Answer (B) is incorrect because $105,000 is the amount of the liability arising from the excess of percentage-of-completion over completed-contract revenue for 20X1 and 20X2, assuming a 30% rate. Answer (D) is incorrect because $195,000 is based on a 30% rate.

STUDY UNIT 6: EQUITY

13 pages of outline
55 multiple-choice questions

Study Unit 6 is one of seven pertaining to preparation of financial statements, a major topic that has been assigned a relative weight range of 50% to 70% of Part 2. This and the preceding study unit concern the financing structure of the entity.

A. Equity

1. Equity of a business enterprise consists of contributed capital, retained earnings, and accumulated other comprehensive income.

Preferred stock (cumulative and participating)	$XXX		
Additional paid-in capital	XXX	$XXX	
Donated capital		XXX	
Common (preferred) stock subscribed		XXX	
Common stock dividends distributable		XXX	
Stock warrants outstanding		XXX	
Common stock	$XXX		
Additional paid-in capital	XXX	XXX	
Total contributed capital			$XXX
Appropriation of retained earnings		$XXX	
Unappropriated retained earnings		XXX	
Total retained earnings			XXX
Accumulated other comprehensive income			XXX
Subscriptions receivable			(XXX)
Treasury stock (at cost)			(XXX)
Total equity			$XXX

2. An important concept is **legal capital**, which in many states is the par or stated value of preferred and common stock.
   a. Par or stated value is an arbitrary amount per share established in the corporate charter.
   b. Legal capital cannot be distributed to shareholders as dividends.
   c. Legal capital also represents the maximum liability of the shareholders.
3. **Contributed capital** represents amounts invested by owners in exchange for stock (common or preferred).
   a. The stated capital (capital stock) shows the par or stated value of all shares issued and outstanding (if stock has no par or stated value, the amount received is given).
      1) Amounts for common and preferred stock are separately listed.

b. Paid-in capital in excess of par or stated value (additional paid-in capital) consists of the sources of contributed capital in excess of legal capital. These sources may include

1) Amounts in excess of par or stated value received for the company's stock

2) A debit item for receipts that are less than par or stated value, for example, discount on common stock

3) Amounts attributable to treasury stock transactions

4) Transfers at fair value from retained earnings upon the issuance of stock dividends

c. **Donated assets**. In general, **SFAS 116**, *Accounting for Contributions Received and Contributions Made*, requires that contributions received be recognized as revenues or gains in the period of receipt and as assets, decreases of liabilities, or expenses depending on their form. They are measured at fair value.

1) **APB 9**, *Reporting the Results of Operations*, states that "adjustments or charges or credits resulting from transactions in the company's own capital stock" are excluded from the determination of net income or the results of operations. Thus, the receipt of a contribution of a company's own stock is recorded at fair value as increases in both additional paid-in capital and treasury stock. Because these accounts offset, the net effect on equity is $0.

2) SFAS 116 does not apply to tax exemptions, abatements, or incentives, or to transfers of assets from a government to a business enterprise. Hence, a credit to donated capital may be appropriate in these cases. Nevertheless, consistency suggests that these transactions also be accounted for in accordance with SFAS 116.

4. **Common Stock**. The common shareholders are the owners of the corporation, and their rights as owners, although reasonably uniform, depend on the laws of the state in which the firm is incorporated. Equity ownership involves risk because holders of common stock are not guaranteed a return and are last in priority in a liquidation. Shareholders' capital provides the cushion for creditors if any losses occur on liquidation.

a. Advantages

1) Common stock does not require a fixed dividend; i.e., dividends are paid from profits when available.

2) There is no fixed maturity date for repayment of the capital.

3) The sale of common stock increases the creditworthiness of the firm by providing more equity.

4) Common stock is frequently more attractive to investors than debt because it grows in value with the success of the firm.

a) The higher the common stock value, the more advantageous equity financing is over debt financing.

b. Disadvantages

1) Control (voting rights) is usually diluted as more common stock is sold.

2) New common stock sales dilute earnings available to existing shareholders because of the greater number of shares outstanding.

3) Underwriting costs are typically higher for common stock issues.

4) Too much equity may raise the average cost of capital of the firm above its optimal level.

5) Common stock cash dividends are not deductible as an expense and are after-tax cash deductions to the firm.

5. **Shareholder Rights.** Shareholders participate indirectly in corporate policy and management by meeting annually and electing directors. In addition, shareholders must approve fundamental changes: amendments to the articles of incorporation or bylaws; all actions of merger or consolidation; and any proposal by directors to sell, lease, or exchange all or substantially all of the corporation's assets. However, the shareholders have little control over the day-to-day operation of the corporation.

a. **Voting rights.** The articles may provide for more or less than one vote per share.

1) Usually, each shareholder is entitled to one vote for each share owned for each new director to be elected, i.e., straight voting. Shareholders also have the right to remove directors by vote.

2) **Cumulative voting** is mandatory in almost 50% of the states that allow it.

a) Cumulative voting entitles each shareholder who has one vote per share owned per director to accumulate votes and either give one candidate as many votes as the number of directors to be elected multiplied by the number of shares owned or distribute that number of votes among as many candidates as (s)he wishes.

b) *Number of directors to be elected × Number of shares of the shareholder = Number of votes the shareholder may allocate to any one or more candidates*

c) Cumulative voting allows minority shareholders to obtain representation on the board, if they own a certain minimum number of shares. It can preclude the holders of more than 50% of the voting stock from electing the entire board of directors.

3) Different voting rights for different classes of shares are permitted. Thus, each class may have the right to elect one director. This results in **class voting**.

4) A **voting agreement**, whereby shareholders contract how they will vote their shares, may be perpetual and secret.

5) **Voting trusts.** Shareholders transfer their shares to one or more voting trustees in exchange for voting trust certificates. The trustees elect directors based on instructions from the shareholders.

a) The term of a voting trust is initially limited to 10 years.

i) Shareholders can agree to continue it beyond 10 years.

b) A voting trust indenture (document) must be made public, and copies must be available for inspection at the corporate offices.

6) A **proxy** is an authorization by a shareholder for someone else to vote the shares. Typically, a proxy must be written and is revocable at any time.

a) A proxy is effective for no more than 11 months, unless otherwise permitted by statute and specifically included in the writing or unless the proxy is coupled with an interest; e.g., the shares are collateral for a loan or the shareholder enters into a buy/sell agreement or a voting agreement. The proxy coupled with an interest may be irrevocable.

b) An otherwise irrevocable proxy is revocable by a bona fide purchaser of the shares who has no notice of the proxy.

c) A general proxy permits a holder to vote on all corporate proposals other than fundamental corporate changes. A limited proxy permits a holder to vote only on matters specified in the proxy.

b. Common shareholders may have **preemptive rights** to purchase any additional stock issuances in proportion to their current ownership percentages.

c. **Meetings**. Ordinarily, shareholders may act only at a meeting.

1) Annual shareholders' meetings are required and must be held at a time fixed in the bylaws. The purpose is to elect new directors and to conduct other necessary business. Lack of notice or defective notice voids action taken at the meeting.

2) Special shareholder meetings, e.g., to approve a merger, may be called by the board of directors, the owner(s) of at least 10% of the issued and outstanding common stock, or any other persons authorized in the articles of incorporation. Special meetings require written notice.

3) A quorum must be represented in person or by proxy to conduct business at a shareholders' meeting. A quorum is defined as a majority of shares outstanding. Most state statutes permit the articles to establish a greater percentage (supermajority).

4) Shareholders can act without a meeting if all shareholders entitled to vote consent in writing to the action.

6. **Preferred Stock**

a. Advantages from the issuer's (firm's) view

1) It is a form of equity and therefore builds the creditworthiness of the firm.

2) Control is still held by common shareholders.

3) Preferred stock is more flexible than bond issues because it has no maturity date or sinking fund schedule.

4) Superior earnings of the firm are usually still reserved for the common shareholders.

b. Disadvantages of issuing preferred stock

1) Preferred stock cash dividends are not tax deductible and are paid with taxable income. The result is substantially greater cost relative to bonds.

2) In periods of economic difficulty, accumulated dividends may create major managerial and financial problems for the firm.

c. Typical provisions of preferred stock issues

1) **Priority** in assets and earnings. If the firm goes bankrupt, the preferred shareholders have priority over common shareholders.

2) **Cumulative dividends** (See C.1.c.)

3) **Convertibility**. Preferred stock issues may be convertible into common stock at the option of the shareholder.

4) **Participation** (See C.1.d.)

5) An issue of preferred stock that specifies that it will be redeemed within a few years (e.g., 5 to 10 years) is known as **transient preferred stock**.

d. The **dividends-received deduction**. Holding common or preferred stock rather than bonds provides corporations a major tax advantage: At least 70% of the dividends received is tax deductible, whereas all bond interest received is taxable.

7. **Retained earnings** is increased by net income and decreased by net losses, dividends, and certain treasury stock transactions.

a. Prior-period adjustments (error corrections) are taken directly to retained earnings.

8. **Other Equity Accounts**

a. Treasury stock (See subunit E.)

b. **Accumulated other comprehensive income** is a separate component of equity that reports items included in comprehensive income but excluded from the determination of net income. See Study Unit 2, B.5.

9. Stop and review! You have completed the outline for this subunit. Study multiple-choice questions 1 through 8 beginning on page 282.

B. Issuance and Retirement of Stock.

1. **Issuance of Stock**. Upon issuance of stock, cash is debited and common stock is credited for the par or stated value.

a. The difference is credited to additional paid-in capital.

b. A discount is unlikely but would be debited to stock discount.

c. When stock is subscribed, the corporation recognizes an obligation to issue stock, and the subscriber undertakes the legal obligation to pay for the shares subscribed.

1) At this date, if collection of the price is reasonably assured, the corporation should debit subscriptions receivable, credit common (preferred) stock subscribed, and credit additional paid-in capital for any excess of the contract price over the par value of the common (preferred) stock subscribed.

Subscriptions receivable	$XXX	
Common (preferred) stock subscribed		$XXX
Additional paid-in capital		XXX

a) Subscriptions receivable should be reported as a contra equity account. The SEC requires this treatment unless collection has occurred before issuance of the financial statements. In that case, the account may be reported as an asset.

2) When the subscription price is paid and the common (preferred) stock is issued, the corporation should debit cash, debit the common (preferred) stock subscribed account, credit subscriptions receivable, and credit the common (preferred) stock account.

Cash	$XXX	
Common (preferred) stock subscribed	XXX	
Subscriptions receivable		$XXX
Common (preferred) stock		XXX

a) Thus, additional paid-in capital is increased when the stock is subscribed and is not affected when the stock is subsequently issued.

3) When a subscriber defaults, the entry to record the subscription must be reversed.

a) State laws and corporate policies vary with regard to the treatment of defaults. The possibilities range from complete refund to complete forfeiture.

b) To the extent that payment has been received and is forfeited, additional paid-in capital from stock subscription default is credited for the amount forfeited.

2. The charter (articles of incorporation) filed with the secretary of state of the state of incorporation indicates the classes of stock that may be issued and their authorized amounts in terms of shares or total dollar value.

a. When authorized shares are issued, the effect is to increase the amount of that class of stock outstanding.

b. If a company does not hold any stock as treasury stock, the number of shares of each type of stock may be determined by dividing the value allocated to each stock account by the related par value or stated value.

3. Stock may be issued in exchange for services or property as well as for cash.

a. The transaction should be recorded at the more clearly determinable of the fair values of the stock or the property or services received.

b. The fair value used is that in effect at the date of the agreement.

4. Stock may be issued upon the conversion of convertible securities such as bonds or preferred stock.

a. The customary method of accounting for the conversion of convertible debt is to record the newly issued stock at the book value of the converted securities. No gain or loss is recognized. However, a gain or loss would be recognized under the market-value method.

b. No gain or loss is recognized on transactions with owners of an enterprise's own stock, including the conversion of convertible preferred stock. Accordingly, the book value method must be used for conversion of preferred stock to common stock.

5. The proceeds of the combined issuance of different classes of securities should be allocated based on the relative fair values of the securities.
   a. If the fair value of one of the classes of securities is not known, the other securities should be recorded at their fair values, with the remainder of the proceeds credited to the securities for which the fair value is not determinable.
6. **Retirement**. When stock is retired, cash (or treasury stock) is credited. The stock account is debited for the par or stated value.
   a. Additional paid-in capital is debited to the extent additional paid-in capital exists from the original stock issuance.
      1) Any remainder is debited to retained earnings or credited to additional paid-in capital from stock retirement.
   b. As noted in B.4.b. on the previous page, no gain or loss is reported on transactions with owners of an enterprise's own stock, but the transfer of nonmonetary assets in exchange for stock requires recognition of any holding gain or loss on the nonmonetary assets.
   c. Preferred stock may be subject to a **call provision**, that is, mandatory redemption at the option of the company at a specified price.
7. Stop and review! You have completed the outline for this subunit. Study multiple-choice questions 9 through 14 beginning on page 284.

C. Dividends

1. **Cash dividends** are distributed to shareholders in the form of cash. Dividends provide information to the stock market. Thus, companies generally have an active policy strategy with respect to dividends.
   a. In practice, dividends usually exhibit greater stability than earnings.
   b. When cash dividends are declared, a liability to the shareholders is created because the dividends must be paid once they are declared.
      1) At the declaration date, retained earnings must be debited, resulting in a decrease in retained earnings.

Retained earnings	$XXX	
Dividends payable		$XXX

      2) When the cash dividends are subsequently paid, the dividends payable account is debited and a cash account credited. Thus, at the payment date, retained earnings is not affected.

Dividends payable	$XXX	
Cash		$XXX

      3) Unlike stock dividends, cash dividends cannot be rescinded.
   c. Preferred dividends may be **cumulative**.
      1) If the preferred stock is cumulative, dividends in arrears and the preferred dividends for the current period must be paid before common shareholders may receive dividends. Dividends in arrears are not a liability of the company until they are declared and are not recognized in the financial statements. However, the aggregate and per-share amounts of dividends in arrears should be disclosed on the face of the balance sheet or in the notes.

d. Preferred stock may also be **participating**.

1) Preferred stock may be fully participating; that is, it may share equally in a cash dividend after a basic return has been paid to holders of both common and preferred stock at the preference rate for the preferred. The remainder is allocated in proportion to the par values of the outstanding shares. But nonparticipating preferred receives only the preference rate.

2) Preferred stock may also be partially participating, for example, up to a ceiling rate or after a specified higher rate has been paid to the common shareholders.

e. A residual dividend policy will pay dividends only if earnings exceed the amount needed to support an optimal capital budget (i.e., a firm will pay higher dividends when it has fewer attractive investment opportunities).

2. **Property Dividends**. **APB 29**, *Accounting for Nonmonetary Transactions*, requires that a nonreciprocal transfer of nonmonetary assets to owners, other than one made "in a spinoff or other form of reorganization or liquidation or in a plan that is in substance the rescission of a prior business combination," be recorded at the fair value of the asset transferred on the declaration date.

a. For example, if the property has appreciated, it should first be written up to fair value and a gain recognized.

Property A	$XXX	
Gain on disposition		$XXX

1) The dividend should then be recognized as a decrease in (debit to) retained earnings and a corresponding increase in (credit to) a dividend payable.

Retained earnings	$XXX	
Property dividend payable		$XXX

a) The distribution of the property dividend is recognized by a debit to property dividend payable and a credit to the asset account.

Property dividend payable	$XXX	
Property A		$XXX

3. **Scrip dividends** may be declared when a corporation has sufficient retained earnings but is short of cash. Scrip is a form of note payable.

a. When a scrip dividend is declared, retained earnings is debited and scrip dividend payable is credited.

b. When the scrip dividend is paid, scrip dividend payable and interest expense are debited, and cash is credited.

4. **Liquidating dividends** are repayments of capital. They are distributions in excess of the corporation's retained earnings.

a. Because the effect of a liquidating dividend is to decrease contributed capital, additional paid-in capital is debited first to the extent available before the other contributed capital accounts are charged.

1) Thus, declaration of a dividend, a portion of which is liquidating, may decrease both additional paid-in capital and retained earnings.

5. **Stock dividends and stock splits** do not increase net assets. They also do not change the proportionate interests of shareholders.
   a. A **stock dividend** is an issuance of a company's own common stock for no consideration to its common shareholders. The purpose is to provide the shareholders with additional evidence of their interests in the retained earnings of the business without distribution of cash or other assets.
   b. A **stock split** is an issuance of a company's own common stock to its common shareholders for no consideration. The purpose is to reduce materially the market price per share by increasing the number of shares outstanding, thereby obtaining wider distribution and improved marketability.
   c. According to **ARB 43, Chapter 7B**, a stock dividend is recognized by capitalizing retained earnings in an amount equal to the fair value of the additional shares distributed. Capitalizing retained earnings results in a debit to retained earnings and credits to common stock and additional paid-in capital. Moreover, the par or stated value of each common share is unaffected. Thus, a stock dividend increases the aggregate par or stated value of shares outstanding.
      1) A stock split is recognized by a decrease in the par or stated value of each common share, resulting in a proportionate increase in the number of shares outstanding. Thus, a stock split does not change the aggregate par or stated value of shares outstanding.
      2) In some circumstances, legal requirements of the state in which an enterprise is incorporated may require the capitalization of retained earnings when a stock split occurs. Under these circumstances, the stock split preferably should be described as a **split-up effected in the form of a dividend**, and retained earnings should be capitalized in an amount equal to the legal requirement, usually the par or stated value of the additional shares distributed.
      3) The enterprise's description of the intent of the distribution normally determines whether the distribution should be accounted for as a stock dividend or a stock split. However, an issuance of shares less than **20% or 25%** of the previously outstanding shares usually should be recognized as a stock dividend. The SEC provides that an issuance of less than 25% should be treated as a stock dividend.
   d. The recipient of a stock dividend should not recognize income. After receipt of the dividend, the shareholder has the same proportionate interest in the corporation and the same total book value as before the declaration of the stock dividend.
   e. Stock dividends often require the issuance of **fractional share rights**. When they are issued as part of a stock dividend, retained earnings is debited and the stock rights outstanding account is credited. If the stock rights are forfeited, the entry is to debit stock rights outstanding and credit additional paid-in capital from forfeiture of stock rights.
   f. Stock dividends are **revocable**. Nevertheless, undistributed stock dividends are normally reported in the equity section. At the declaration date, the debit is to retained earnings and the credits are to stock dividends distributable and additional paid-in capital.
   g. **Treasury stock** may be adjusted for stock dividends and splits depending on the intended use of the treasury stock. Thus, the adjustment is more likely if the stock is held to meet obligations under an employee stock ownership plan. However, some states prohibit the payment of stock dividends on treasury stock.
   h. A **reverse stock split** reduces the number of shares outstanding, which serves to increase the market value per share of those shares still outstanding.

6. **Important Dates Concerning the Declaration of Dividends**
   a. **Date of declaration** -- the date the directors meet and formally vote to declare a dividend. On this date, the dividend becomes a liability of the corporation.
   b. **Date of record** -- the date as of which the corporation determines the shareholders who will receive the declared dividend. Essentially, the corporation closes its shareholder records on this date. Only those shareholders who own the stock on the date of record will receive the dividend. It typically falls anywhere from 2 to 6 weeks after the declaration date.
   c. **Date of payment** -- the date on which the dividend is actually paid (when the checks are put into the mail to the investors). The payment date is usually from 2 to 4 weeks after the date of record.
   d. **Ex-dividend date** -- a date established by the stock exchanges, such as 4 days before the date of record. Unlike the other dates mentioned above, it is not established by the corporate board of directors. The period between the ex-dividend date and the date of record gives the stock exchange members time to process any transactions so that new shareholders will receive the dividends to which they are entitled. An investor who buys a share of stock before the ex-dividend date will receive the dividend that has been previously declared. An investor who buys the stock after the ex-dividend date (but before the date of record or payment date) will not receive the declared dividend. Instead, the individual who sold the stock will receive the dividend because (s)he owned it on the ex-dividend date.
      1) Usually, a stock price will drop on the ex-dividend date by the amount of the dividend because the new investor will not receive it.
7. Stop and review! You have completed the outline for this subunit. Study multiple-choice questions 15 through 37 beginning on page 287.

D. Retained Earnings Entries

1. Few entries are made to the retained earnings account. Annually, net income or loss is closed to retained earnings. Occasionally, a prior-period adjustment will be entered in retained earnings.
2. **Appropriations of Retained Earnings**. Retained earnings is sometimes appropriated to a special account to disclose that earnings retained in the business (not paid out in dividends) are being used for special purposes.
   a. A company may restrict (appropriate) retained earnings for such purposes as compliance with the terms of a bond indenture (bond contract), retention of assets for internally financed expansion, anticipation of losses, or adherence to legal restrictions (for example, a state law restricting retained earnings by an amount equal to the cost of treasury stock).
      1) The appropriation does not set aside assets. Rather, it has the effect of limiting the amount available for dividends, decreasing unappropriated retained earnings. A formal entry (debit RE, credit RE appropriated) may be used, or the restriction may be disclosed in a footnote.
      2) According to APB 9, "transfers to and from accounts properly designated as appropriated retained earnings (such as general purpose contingency reserves or provisions for replacement costs of fixed assets)" are always excluded from the determination of net income. However, appropriation of retained earnings is permitted if it is report-ed within equity and is clearly identified (SFAS 5).

3. A **quasi-reorganization** is accomplished by closing out the retained earnings account (which in a cumulative loss situation would have a debit balance). In subsequent years, any balance in retained earnings will be dated (e.g., an account may be entitled "Retained Earnings Since December 31, 1996").

4. Stop and review! You have completed the outline for this subunit. Study multiple-choice questions 38 through 40 beginning on page 294.

E. Accounting for Treasury Stock

1. Treasury stock consists of shares of the entity's own stock reacquired for various purposes, e.g., mergers, stock options, stock dividends, or the elimination of a particular ownership interest. Treasury stock is commonly accounted for at cost, but the par value method is also acceptable.

2. The **cost method** of accounting for treasury stock transactions records the acquisition of treasury stock as a debit to a treasury stock account and a credit to cash. No other accounts are affected.

   a. When the treasury stock is subsequently reissued for cash at a price in excess of its acquisition cost, the difference between the cash received and the carrying value (acquisition cost) of the treasury stock is credited to an account titled "additional paid-in capital from treasury stock transactions" and not to "additional paid-in capital."

   b. If the treasury stock is subsequently reissued at less than acquisition cost, the deficiency is first treated as a reduction of additional paid-in capital related to previous reissuances of treasury stock of the same class.

      1) After additional paid-in capital from previous reissuances of treasury stock is reduced to a zero balance, the remaining debit is to retained earnings.

   c. Treasury stock accounted for at cost is a contra equity account. It is reported on the balance sheet as an unallocated reduction of total equity. Moreover, in most states, the cost of treasury stock is deemed to be a restriction of retained earnings.

   d. Treasury stock is not an asset, no dividends are paid on it, and no gains and losses are recognized on treasury stock transactions.

3. The **par value method** treats the acquisition of treasury stock as a constructive retirement and the resale as a new issuance.

   a. Upon acquisition, the entry originally made to issue stock is effectively reversed. Treasury stock at par value (a debit) is recorded as an offset to the contributed capital account representing issued shares of the same type, and the additional paid-in capital recorded when the stock was originally issued is removed.

      1) Any difference between the original issuance price and the reacquisition price is ordinarily adjusted through additional paid-in capital accounts and retained earnings. Hence, gains are credited to additional paid-in capital from treasury stock transactions, and losses are debited to the same account but only to the extent of prior gains.

         a) If the credit balance in the account is insufficient to absorb the loss, retained earnings will be debited for the remainder.

b. The subsequent reissuance removes the treasury stock at par value and reestablishes additional paid-in capital for any excess of the reissuance price over par value.

   1) If the reissuance price is less than par, the debit is to an additional paid-in capital account or to retained earnings.

c. Under the par value method, treasury stock is shown in the balance sheet as a direct reduction of common (preferred) stock, not of total equity.

4. **Cost Method vs. Par Value Method**

   a. EXAMPLE: Rhone Company has the following balances in its shareholders' equity section on December 31, 2001:

Common stock, $10 par value, 200,000 shares outstanding	$2,000,000
Additional paid-in capital ($2 per share)	$600,000
Retained earnings	$2,000,000

4/15/99 -- Rhone reacquired 30,000 shares for $600,000 ($20 per share).

Cost Method			Par Method		
Treasury stock	$600,000		Treasury stock ($10 × 30,000)	$300,000	
Cash		$600,000	Additional paid-in capital ($2 × 30,000)	60,000	
			Retained earnings	240,000	
			Cash		$600,000

7/28/99 -- Rhone reissued 10,000 shares of treasury stock for $30 per share.

Cost Method			Par Method		
Cash	$300,000		Cash	$300,000	
Treasury stock ($20 × 10,000)		$200,000	Treasury stock ($10 × 10,000)		$100,000
Additional paid-in capital from treasury stock		100,000	Additional paid-in capital from treasury stock		200,000

10/2/99 -- Rhone reissued 15,000 shares of treasury stock for $8 per share.

Cost Method			Par Method		
Cash	$120,000		Cash	$120,000	
Additional paid-in capital from treasury stock	100,000		Additional paid-in capital from treasury stock	30,000	
Retained earnings	80,000		Treasury stock ($10 × 15,000)		$150,000
Treasury stock ($20 × 15,000)		$300,000			

5. Stop and review! You have completed the outline for this subunit. Study multiple-choice questions 41 through 49 beginning on page 295.

F. Stock Rights

1. The **preemptive right** safeguards a shareholder's proportionate ownership. Thus, it is the right to purchase a pro rata amount of a new issuance of the same class of stock. However, many companies have eliminated the preemptive right because it may inhibit the large issuances of stock that are often needed in business combinations.

2. In a **rights offering**, each shareholder is issued a certificate or **warrant** that is an option to buy a certain number of shares at a fixed price.

   a. If the rights are exercised and stock is issued, the issuer will reflect the proceeds received as a credit to (an increase in) common (preferred) stock at par value, with any remainder credited to additional paid-in capital.

      1) However, if the rights previously issued without consideration are allowed to lapse, contributed capital is unaffected.

b. From the time the rights offering is announced to the issue date, the stock trades **rights-on**. After the issue date, it trades **ex-rights** because the rights can be sold separately.

c. The recipient of stock rights must allocate the carrying value of the shares owned between those shares and the rights based on their relative fair values at the time the rights are received, for example, by debiting available-for-sale securities (rights) and crediting available-for-sale securities for the appropriate amount. The recipient then has three options: exercise the rights, sell them, or let them expire.

1) If the rights are exercised, the amount allocated to them becomes part of the carrying value of the acquired shares.

2) If the rights are sold, their carrying value is credited, cash is debited, and a gain (loss) is credited (debited).

3) If the rights expire, a loss is recorded.

3. A stock option plan may or may not be intended to compensate employees for their work. The compensation expense for compensatory stock option plans should be recognized in the periods that the employee performs the service.

a. **SFAS 123**, *Accounting for Stock-Based Compensation*, recommends but does not require that stock-based compensation be accounted for using a **fair-value-based method**, such as might be determined using an option-pricing model. However, entities may continue to apply APB 25, which allows the use of **intrinsic values** to measure compensation (market price – option price when the number of shares employees are entitled to and the option or purchase price are known). Entities that elect to apply APB 25 must nevertheless make certain fair-value-based disclosures.

b. According to **APB 25**, *Accounting for Stock Issued to Employees*, noncompensatory stock option plans have all of the following characteristics:

1) Participation by substantially all full-time employees who meet limited employment qualifications

2) Equal offers of stock to all eligible employees

3) A limited amount of time permitted to exercise the option

4. **Stock warrants** (certificates evidencing options to buy stock at a given price within a certain period) not only may be issued to employees (as compensation) or to shareholders but also may be attached to bonds or preferred stock.

a. The proceeds of securities issued with **detachable warrants** are allocated between the warrants and the securities based on their relative fair values. If the fair value of one but not the other is known, the proceeds are allocated incrementally. For example, if the fair value of the securities but not the warrants is known, the securities are recorded at fair value, and the remainder of the proceeds is assigned to the warrants. If warrants are not detachable, they are not accounted for separately.

5. Transaction costs associated with the redemption of stock rights reduce equity.

6. Stop and review! You have completed the outline for this subunit. Study multiple-choice questions 50 through 55 beginning on page 298.

MULTIPLE-CHOICE QUESTIONS

A. Equity

1. At December 31, a company has total assets at book value of $300,000. Liabilities are $120,000. Also, on December 31, the stock is selling at $20 per share, and there are 10,000 shares outstanding. As a result, the company should take the difference between the book value and fair value of the stock and

A. Capitalize as an asset (and amortize over the estimated useful life not to exceed 40 years), with the offset to shareholders' equity.

B. Capitalize as an asset (and amortize over the estimated useful life), with the offset to revenue.

C. Capitalize as an asset (and amortize over 5 years), with the offset to shareholders' equity.

D. Not capitalize any asset, record any revenue, or change shareholders' equity at this time.

The correct answer is (D). *(CIA, adapted)*

REQUIRED: The proper accounting when the value of stock exceeds its book value.

DISCUSSION: In most instances, the fair value of a company's stock exceeds its book value. Unless the company is being acquired or undergoing a reorganization, the difference in stock values (book and fair values) is ignored for financial reporting purposes.

Answers (A), (B), and (C) are incorrect because the difference between book and fair values does not result in a journal entry.

2. Issues of preferred stock that specify redemption of the issues over relatively short periods such as 5 to 10 years are called

A. Transient preferreds.

B. Short-term preferreds.

C. Preferred stock obligations.

D. Temporary preferreds.

The correct answer is (A). *(CIA, adapted)*

REQUIRED: The term for issues of preferred stock that specify redemption of the issues over relatively short periods.

DISCUSSION: Some preferred stock may be redeemed at a given time or at the option of the holder or otherwise at a time not controlled by the issuer. This feature makes preferred stock more nearly akin to debt, particularly in the case of transient preferred stock, which must be redeemed within a short time (e.g., 5 to 10 years). The SEC requires a separate presentation of redeemable preferred, nonredeemable preferred, and common stock.

Answer (B) is incorrect because short-term preferreds is not a term in common usage. Answer (C) is incorrect because preferred stock obligations is not a term in common usage. Answer (D) is incorrect because temporary preferreds is not a term in common usage.

3. Which type of voting disallows a freeze-out of minority shareholders?

A. Straight voting.

B. Cumulative voting.

C. Proxy voting.

D. Trustee voting.

The correct answer is (B). *(Publisher)*

REQUIRED: The true statement about minority shareholder voting rights.

DISCUSSION: In straight voting, a majority shareholder has the ability to elect the entire board of directors because each shareholder has a single vote for each share owned for each director to be elected, resulting in a "freeze-out" of minority shareholders. Cumulative voting, on the other hand, enables a shareholder to cast his total number of votes for any director. Thus, minority shareholders can obtain representation on the board of directors.

Answer (A) is incorrect because straight voting allows a freeze-out. Answer (C) is incorrect because proxy voting allows management to gain control of minority shareholder votes. Answer (D) is incorrect because trustee voting refers to transferring voting rights to a trustee to allow a group of owners not to lose control of a corporation.

4. Which of the following is usually not a feature of cumulative preferred stock?

A. Has priority over common stock with regard to earnings.

B. Has priority over common stock with regard to assets.

C. Has voting rights.

D. Has the right to receive dividends in arrears before common stock dividends can be paid.

The correct answer is (C). *(CIA, adapted)*

REQUIRED: The item not usually a feature of cumulative preferred stock.

DISCUSSION: Preferred stock does not usually have voting rights. Preferred shareholders are usually given the right to vote for directors only if the company has not paid the preferred dividend for a specified period of time, such as ten quarters. Such a provision is an incentive for management to pay preferred dividends.

Answer (A) is incorrect because preferred stock has priority over common stock with regard to earnings, so dividends must be paid on preferred stock before they can be paid on common stock. Answer (B) is incorrect because preferred stock has priority over common stock with regard to assets. In the event of liquidation, for example, because of bankruptcy, the claims of preferred shareholders must be satisfied in full before the common shareholders receive anything. Answer (D) is incorrect because cumulative preferred stock has the right to receive any dividends not paid in prior periods before common stock dividends are paid.

5. Unless specifically restricted, each share of common stock carries all of the following rights except the right to share proportionately in

A. The vote for directors.

B. Corporate assets upon liquidation.

C. Cumulative dividends.

D. New issues of stock of the same class.

The correct answer is (C). *(CMA, adapted)*

REQUIRED: The item that is not a right of common shareholders.

DISCUSSION: Common stock does not have the right to accumulate unpaid dividends. This right is often attached to preferred stock.

Answers (A), (B), and (D) are incorrect because common shareholders have the right to share proportionately in dividends (but only after preferred shareholders have been paid), in voting (although different classes of shares may have different privileges), in corporate assets upon liquidation (but only after other claims have been satisfied), and in any new issues of stock of the same class (this latter right is known as the preemptive right).

6. In comparing an investment in preferred stock to an investment in bonds, one substantial advantage to a corporation investing in preferred stock is the

A. Taxable interest received.

B. Voting power acquired.

C. Set maturity date.

D. Dividends-received deduction.

The correct answer is (D). *(Publisher)*

REQUIRED: The major advantage associated with an investment in preferred stock rather than in bonds.

DISCUSSION: By investing in preferred stock instead of bonds, a corporation receives a significant tax advantage in the form of the dividends-received deduction. Under the dividends-received deduction, at least 70% of dividends received from preferred stock is deductible for tax purposes. With bonds, any interest received is fully taxable. Furthermore, the dividends-received deduction also applies when a corporation holds an investment in common stock.

Answer (A) is incorrect because interest is not paid on preferred stock. Taxability of interest is a disadvantage of bonds. Answer (B) is incorrect because an investment in preferred stock usually does not confer voting rights. Answer (C) is incorrect because an investment in preferred stock does not include a maturity date.

7. The following excerpt was taken from a company's financial statements: ". . . 10% convertible participating . . . $10,000,000." What is most likely being referred to?

A. Bonds.

B. Common stock.

C. Stock options.

D. Preferred stock.

The correct answer is (D). *(CIA, adapted)*

REQUIRED: The securities most likely referred to as convertible participating.

DISCUSSION: Preferred shareholders have priority over common shareholders in the assets and earnings of the enterprise. If preferred dividends are cumulative, any past preferred dividends must be paid before any common dividends. Preferred stock may also be convertible into common stock, and it may be participating. For example, 10% fully participating preferred stock will receive additional distributions at the same rates as other shareholders if dividends paid to all shareholders exceed 10%.

Answer (A) is incorrect because bonds normally have a coupon yield stated in percentage and may be convertible but are not participating. Answer (B) is incorrect because common stock is not described as convertible or participating on the financial statements. Answer (C) is incorrect because common stock options are not participating and do not have a stated yield rate.

8. Preferred and common stock differ in that

A. Failure to pay dividends on common stock will not force the firm into bankruptcy, while failure to pay dividends on preferred stock will force the firm into bankruptcy.

B. Common stock dividends are a fixed amount, while preferred stock dividends are not.

C. Preferred stock has a higher priority than common stock with regard to earnings and assets in the event of bankruptcy.

D. Preferred stock dividends are deductible as an expense for tax purposes, while common stock dividends are not.

The correct answer is (C). *(CIA, adapted)*

REQUIRED: The difference between preferred and common stock.

DISCUSSION: In the event of bankruptcy, the claims of preferred shareholders must be satisfied before common shareholders receive anything. The interests of common shareholders are secondary to those of all other claimants.

Answer (A) is incorrect because failure to pay dividends will not force the firm into bankruptcy, whether the dividends are for common or preferred stock. Only failure to pay interest will force the firm into bankruptcy. Answer (B) is incorrect because preferred dividends are fixed. Answer (D) is incorrect because neither common nor preferred dividends are tax deductible.

B. Issuance and Retirement of Stock

9. On February 1 of the current year, King Corp., a newly formed company, had the following stock issued and outstanding:

- Common stock, no par, $1 stated value, 10,000 shares originally issued for $15 per share
- Preferred stock, $10 par value, 3,000 shares originally issued for $25 per share

King's February 1 statement of shareholders' equity should report

	Common Stock	Preferred Stock	Additional Paid-in Capital
A.	$150,000	$30,000	$45,000
B.	$150,000	$75,000	$0
C.	$10,000	$75,000	$140,000
D.	$10,000	$30,000	$185,000

The correct answer is (D). *(CPA, adapted)*

REQUIRED: The amounts of common stock, preferred stock, and additional paid-in capital to be reported in the statement of shareholders' equity.

DISCUSSION: The common stock was issued for a total of $150,000 (10,000 shares x $15). Of this amount, $10,000 (10,000 shares x $1 stated value) should be allocated to the common stock, with the remaining $140,000 ($150,000 – $10,000) credited to additional paid-in capital. The preferred stock was issued for $75,000 (3,000 shares x $25), of which $30,000 (3,000 shares x $10 par value) should be allocated to the preferred stock and $45,000 ($75,000 – $30,000) to additional paid-in capital. In the February 1 statement of shareholders' equity, King therefore should report $10,000 in the common stock account, $30,000 in the preferred stock account, and $185,000 ($140,000 + $45,000) as additional paid-in capital.

Answers (A), (B), and (C) are incorrect because the excess of the issue price of the common stock over its stated value is credited to additional paid-in capital, not common stock, and the excess of the issue price of the preferred stock over its par value is credited to additional paid-in capital, not preferred stock.

10. The par value of a common stock represents

A. The estimated market value of the stock when it was issued.

B. The liability ceiling of a shareholder when a company undergoes bankruptcy proceedings.

C. The total value of the stock that must be entered in the issuing corporation's records.

D. The amount that must be recorded on the issuing corporation's record as paid-in capital.

The correct answer is (B). *(CMA, adapted)*

REQUIRED: The amount represented by the par value of common stock.

DISCUSSION: Par value represents a stock's legal capital. It is an arbitrary value assigned to stock before it is issued. Par value represents a shareholder's liability ceiling because, as long as the par value has been paid in to the corporation, the shareholders obtain the benefits of limited liability.

Answer (A) is incorrect because par value is rarely the same as market value. Normally, market value will be equal to or greater than par value, but there is no relationship between the two. Answer (C) is incorrect because all assets received for stock must be entered into a corporation's records. The amount received is very rarely the par value. Answer (D) is incorrect because all assets received for stock represent paid-in capital. Thus, paid-in capital may exceed par value.

11. At December 31, 2000, a corporation has the following account balances:

Common stock ($10 par, 50,000 shares issued)	$500,000
8% preferred stock ($50 par, 10,000 shares issued)	500,000
Paid-in capital in excess of par on common stock	640,000
Paid-in capital in excess of par on preferred stock	20,000
Retained earnings	600,000

The preferred stock is cumulative, nonparticipating, and has a call price of $55 per share. The journal entry to record the redemption of all preferred stock on January 2, 2001 pursuant to the call provision is

A.

Preferred stock	$500,000	
Paid-in capital in excess of par: preferred	20,000	
Discount on preferred stock	30,000	
Cash		$550,000

B.

Preferred stock	$500,000	
Paid-in capital in excess of par: preferred	20,000	
Loss on redemption of preferred stock	30,000	
Cash		$550,000

C.

Preferred stock	$500,000	
Loss on redemption of preferred stock	50,000	
Retained earnings	300,000	
Cash		$550,000
Paid-in capital in excess of par: preferred		300,000

D.

Preferred stock	$500,000	
Paid-in capital in excess of par: preferred	20,000	
Retained earnings	30,000	
Cash		$550,000

The correct answer is (D). *(CIA, adapted)*

REQUIRED: The journal entry to record the redemption of preferred stock pursuant to the call provision.

DISCUSSION: The exercise of the call provision resulted in the redemption of the 10,000 shares of preferred stock issued and outstanding at the call price of $550,000 (10,000 shares x $55 call price per share). To eliminate the carrying value of the preferred stock and recognize the cash paid in this transaction, the required journal entry is to debit preferred stock for $500,000, debit paid-in capital in excess of par: preferred for $20,000, and credit cash for $550,000. The difference of $30,000 ($550,000 cash – $520,000 carrying value of the preferred stock) is charged to retained earnings. No loss is reported because GAAP do not permit the recognition of a gain or loss on transactions involving a company's own stock.

Answers (A), (B), and (C) are incorrect because the $30,000 excess of cash paid over the carrying value of the redeemed stock should be debited to retained earnings.

12. Mouse Co. issued 1,000 shares of its $5 par common stock to Howe as compensation for 1,000 hours of legal services performed. Jason usually bills $160 per hour for legal services. On the date of issuance, the stock was trading on a public exchange at $140 per share. By what amount should the additional paid-in capital account increase as a result of this transaction?

A. $135,000

B. $140,000

C. $155,000

D. $160,000

The correct answer is (A). *(CPA, adapted)*

REQUIRED: The increase in additional paid-in capital.

DISCUSSION: When stock is issued for property or services, the transaction is recorded at the fair value of the stock or of the property or services received. In this case, the value of the stock is used because it is more definite. The $140,000 should be allocated as follows: $5,000 ($5 par x 1,000 shares) to common stock and $135,000 to additional paid-in capital.

Answer (B) is incorrect because $5,000 should be allocated to common stock. Answers (C) and (D) are incorrect because the value of the stock should be used to record the transaction.

13. Purple Corp. had outstanding 2,000 shares of 11% preferred stock, $50 par. On August 8 of this year, Purple redeemed and retired 25% of these shares for $22,500. On that date, Purple's additional paid-in capital from preferred stock totaled $30,000. To record this transaction, Purple should debit (credit) its capital accounts as follows:

	Preferred Stock	Additional Paid-in Capital	Retained Earnings
A.	$25,000	$ 7,500	$(10,000)
B.	$25,000	--	$ (2,500)
C.	$25,000	$(2,500)	--
D.	$22,500	--	--

The correct answer is (C). *(CPA, adapted)*

REQUIRED: The accounting for redemption and retirement of preferred stock.

DISCUSSION: Under the cost method, the entry to record a treasury stock purchase is to debit treasury stock at cost ($22,500) and credit cash. The entry to retire this stock is to debit preferred stock at par [(25% x 2,000 shares) x $50 = $25,000], debit additional paid-in capital from the original issuance (25% x $30,000 = $7,500), credit treasury stock at cost ($22,500), and credit additional paid-in capital from stock retirement ($10,000). No entry to retained earnings is necessary.

Answers (A) and (B) are incorrect because, if the reacquisition price is less than the issuance price, a credit is made to additional paid-in capital, not retained earnings. Answer (D) is incorrect because preferred stock must be debited for the par value of the retired shares.

14. The equity section of Smith Corporation's statement of financial position is presented below.

Preferred stock, $100 par	$12,000,000
Common stock, $5 par	10,000,000
Paid-in capital in excess of par	18,000,000
Retained earnings	9,000,000
Net worth	$49,000,000

The common shareholders of Smith Corporation have preemptive rights. If Smith Corporation issues 400,000 additional shares of common stock at $6 per share, a current holder of 20,000 shares of Smith Corporation's common stock must be given the option to buy

A. 1,000 additional shares.

B. 3,774 additional shares.

C. 4,000 additional shares.

D. 3,333 additional shares.

The correct answer is (C). *(CMA, adapted)*

REQUIRED: The new shares that a shareholder may buy given preemptive rights.

DISCUSSION: Common shareholders usually have preemptive rights, which means they have the right to purchase any new issues of stock in proportion to their current ownership percentages. The purpose of a preemptive right is to allow shareholders to maintain their current percentages of ownership. Given that Smith had 2,000,000 shares outstanding ($10,000,000 ÷ $5 par), an investor with 20,000 shares has a 1% ownership. Hence, this investor must be allowed to purchase 4,000 (1% x 400,000 shares) of the additional shares.

Answer (A) is incorrect because the investor would be allowed to purchase 1% of any new issues. Answers (B) and (D) are incorrect because preferred shareholders do not share in preemptive rights.

C. Dividends

15. Treating dividends as an active policy strategy assumes that

A. Dividends provide information to the market.

B. Dividends are irrelevant.

C. Dividend payments should be made to common shareholders first.

D. Dividends are costly, and the firm should retain earnings and issue stock dividends.

The correct answer is (A). *(CMA, adapted)*

REQUIRED: The assumption made when dividends are treated as an active policy strategy.

DISCUSSION: Stock prices often move in the same direction as dividends. Moreover, companies dislike cutting dividends. They tend not to raise dividends unless anticipated future earnings will be sufficient to sustain the higher payout. Thus, some theorists have proposed the information content or signaling hypothesis. According to this view, a change in dividend policy is a signal to the market regarding management's forecast of future earnings. Consequently, the relation of stock price changes to changes in dividends reflects not an investor preference for dividends over capital gains but rather the effect of the information conveyed.

Answer (B) is incorrect because an active dividend policy suggests management assumes that dividends are relevant to investors. Answer (C) is incorrect because preferred shareholders always receive their dividends ahead of common shareholders. Answer (D) is incorrect because an active dividend policy recognizes that investors want dividends.

16. In practice, dividends

A. Usually exhibit greater stability than earnings.

B. Fluctuate more widely than earnings.

C. Tend to be a lower percentage of earnings for mature firms.

D. Are usually set as a fixed percentage of earnings.

The correct answer is (A). *(CMA, adapted)*

REQUIRED: The true statement about dividends and their relation to earnings.

DISCUSSION: Dividend policy determines the portion of net income distributed to shareholders. Corporations normally try to maintain a stable level of dividends, even though profits may fluctuate considerably, because many shareholders buy stock with the expectation of receiving a certain dividend every year. Thus, management tends not to raise dividends if the payout cannot be sustained. The desire for stability has led theorists to propound the information content or signaling hypothesis: a change in dividend policy is a signal to the market regarding management's forecast of future earnings. This stability often results in a stock that sells at a higher market price because shareholders perceive less risk in receiving their dividends.

Answer (B) is incorrect because most companies try to maintain stable dividends. Answer (C) is incorrect because mature firms have less need of earnings to reinvest for expansion; thus, they tend to pay a higher percentage of earnings as dividends. Answer (D) is incorrect because dividend payout ratios normally fluctuate with earnings to maintain stable dividends.

17. On December 1, Charles Company's board of directors declared a cash dividend of $1.00 per share on the 50,000 shares of common stock outstanding. The company also has 5,000 shares of treasury stock. Shareholders of record on December 15 are eligible for the dividend, which is to be paid on January 1. On December 1, the company should

A. Make no accounting entry.

B. Debit retained earnings for $50,000.

C. Debit retained earnings for $55,000.

D. Debit retained earnings for $50,000 and paid-in capital for $5,000.

The correct answer is (B). *(CMA, adapted)*

REQUIRED: The proper journal entry on the declaration date of a dividend.

DISCUSSION: Dividends are recorded on their declaration date by a debit to retained earnings and a credit to dividends payable. The dividend is the amount payable to all shares outstanding. Treasury stock is not eligible for dividends because it is not outstanding. Thus, the December 1 entry is to debit retained earnings and credit dividends payable for $50,000 (50,000 x $1).

Answer (A) is incorrect because a liability should be recorded. Answer (C) is incorrect because the treasury stock is not eligible for a dividend. Answer (D) is incorrect because paid-in capital is not affected by the declaration of a dividend.

18. At December 31, 20X1 and 20X2, Maui Co. had 3,000 shares of $100 par, 5% cumulative preferred stock outstanding. No dividends were in arrears as of December 31, 20X0 Maui did not declare a dividend during 20X1. During 20X2, Maui paid a cash dividend of $10,000 on its preferred stock. Maui should report dividends in arrears in its 20X2 financial statements as a(n)

A. Accrued liability of $15,000.

B. Disclosure of $15,000.

C. Accrued liability of $20,000.

D. Disclosure of $20,000.

The correct answer is (D). *(CPA, adapted)*

REQUIRED: The amount and means of reporting preferred dividends in arrears.

DISCUSSION: Dividends in arrears on preferred stock are not an obligation of the company and are not recognized in the financial statements. However, the aggregate and per-share amounts of arrearages in cumulative preferred dividends should be disclosed on the face of the balance sheet or in the notes (APB 10). The aggregate amount in arrears is $20,000 [(2 years x 5% x $100 par x 3,000 shares) – $10,000 paid in 20X2].

Answers (A) and (C) are incorrect because dividends in arrears do not meet recognition criteria. Answer (B) is incorrect because $15,000 is the arrearage for one year.

19. Frasier Corp.'s outstanding capital stock at December 15 consisted of the following:

- 30,000 shares of 5% cumulative preferred stock, par value $10 per share, fully participating as to dividends. No dividends were in arrears.
- 200,000 shares of common stock, par value $1 per share

On December 15, Frasier declared dividends of $100,000. What was the amount of dividends payable to Frasier's common shareholders?

A. $10,000

B. $34,000

C. $40,000

D. $60,000

The correct answer is (C). *(CPA, adapted)*

REQUIRED: The dividends to common shareholders.

DISCUSSION: The stated rate of dividends must be paid to preferred shareholders before any amount is paid to common shareholders. Given no dividends in arrears, this amount is $15,000 (5% x $10 par x 30,000 shares). The preferred stock will also participate equally in the cash dividend after a 5% return is paid on the common. The basic return to common shareholders is $10,000 (5% x 200,000 shares x $1 par). The remaining $75,000 ($100,000 – $15,000 – $10,000) will be shared in proportion to the par values of the shares outstanding.

The aggregate par value of the preferred is $300,000 ($10 par x 30,000 shares). The aggregate par value of the common is $200,000 ($1 par x 200,000 shares). The distribution will therefore be in the ratio of 3:2, and $45,000 ($75,000 x 60%) is the participating share of the preferred shareholders. The balance of $30,000 ($75,000 – $45,000) will be paid to the common shareholders. The total dividends on the common stock is $40,000 ($10,000 + $30,000).

Answer (A) is incorrect because $10,000 is the basic return to common shareholders. Answer (B) is incorrect because $34,000 results from assuming that no basic return is paid to the common shareholders. Answer (D) is incorrect because $60,000 is paid to the preferred shareholders.

20. Brady Corporation has 6,000 shares of 5% cumulative, $100 par value preferred stock outstanding and 200,000 shares of common stock outstanding. Brady's board of directors last declared dividends for the year ended May 31, 1999, and there were no dividends in arrears. For the year ended May 31, 2001, Brady had net income of $1,750,000. The board of directors is declaring a dividend for common shareholders equivalent to 20% of net income. The total amount of dividends to be paid by Brady at May 31, 2001 is

A. $350,000

B. $380,000

C. $206,000

D. $410,000

The correct answer is (D). *(CMA, adapted)*

REQUIRED: The total amount of dividends to be paid given cumulative preferred stock.

DISCUSSION: If a company has cumulative preferred stock, all preferred dividends for the current and any unpaid prior years must be paid before any dividends can be paid on common stock. The total preferred dividends that must be paid equal $60,000 (2 years x 5% x $100 par x 6,000 shares), and the common dividend is $350,000 ($1,750,000 x 20%), for a total of $410,000.

Answer (A) is incorrect because $350,000 is the common stock dividend. Answer (B) is incorrect because $380,000 omits the $30,000 of cumulative dividends for 2000. Answer (C) is incorrect because $206,000 is based on a flat rate of $1 per share of stock.

21. If a company uses the residual dividend policy, it will pay

A. A fixed cash dividend each quarter and use the residual as retained earnings.

B. A fixed stock dividend each quarter and retain all earnings as a residual.

C. All earnings as dividends each year.

D. Dividends only if earnings exceed the amount needed to support an optimal capital budget.

The correct answer is (D). *(CIA, adapted)*

REQUIRED: The definition of a residual dividend policy.

DISCUSSION: Under the residual theory of dividends, the amount (residual) of earnings paid as dividends depends on the available investment opportunities and the debt-equity ratio at which cost of capital is minimized. The rational investor should prefer reinvestment of retained earnings when the return exceeds what the investor could earn on investments of equal risk. However, the firm may prefer to pay dividends when investment opportunities are poor and the use of internal equity financing would move the firm away from its ideal capital structure.

Answer (A) is incorrect because the cash dividend would not be stable, but a residual. Answer (B) is incorrect because the residual theory concerns cash dividends. Answer (C) is incorrect because all earnings are not distributed as dividends.

22. Residco Inc. expects net income of $800,000 for the next fiscal year. Its targeted and current capital structure is 40% debt and 60% common equity. The director of capital budgeting has determined that the optimal capital spending for next year is $1.2 million. If Residco follows a strict residual dividend policy, what is the expected dividend payout ratio for next year?

A. 90.0%

B. 66.7%

C. 40.0%

D. 10.0%

The correct answer is (D). *(CMA, adapted)*

REQUIRED: The expected dividend payout ratio assuming a strict residual dividend policy.

DISCUSSION: Under the residual theory of dividends, the residual of earnings paid as dividends depends on the available investments and the debt-equity ratio at which cost of capital is minimized. The rational investor should prefer reinvestment of retained earnings when the return exceeds what the investor could earn on investments of equal risk. However, the firm may prefer to pay dividends when investment returns are poor and the internal equity financing would move the firm away from its ideal capital structure. If Residco wants to maintain its current structure, 60% of investments should be financed from equity. Hence, it needs $720,000 (60% x $1,200,000) of equity funds, leaving $80,000 of net income ($800,000 NI – $720,000) available for dividends. The dividend payout ratio is therefore 10% ($80,000 ÷ $800,000 NI).

Answer (A) is incorrect because 90% is the reinvestment ratio. Answer (B) is incorrect because 66.7% is the ratio between earnings and investment. Answer (C) is incorrect because 40% is the ratio of debt in the ideal capital structure.

23. A stock dividend

A. Increases the debt-to-equity ratio of a firm.

B. Decreases future earnings per share.

C. Decreases the size of the firm.

D. Increases shareholders' wealth.

The correct answer is (B). *(CMA, adapted)*

REQUIRED: The true statement about a stock dividend.

DISCUSSION: A stock dividend is a transfer of equity from retained earnings to paid-in capital. The debit is to retained earnings, and the credits are to common stock and additional paid-in capital. More shares are outstanding following the stock dividend, but every shareholder maintains the same percentage of ownership. In effect, a stock dividend divides the pie (the corporation) into more pieces, but the pie is still the same size. Hence, a corporation will have a lower EPS and a lower book value per share following a stock dividend, but every shareholder will be just as well off as previously.

Answers (A), (C), and (D) are incorrect because a stock dividend has no effect except on the composition of the equity section of the balance sheet.

24. A company declares and pays both a $200,000 cash dividend and a 10% stock dividend. The effect of the <List A> dividend is to <List B>.

	List A	List B
A.	Cash	Increase retained earnings
B.	Cash	Decrease retained earnings and increase equity
C.	Stock	Decrease retained earnings
D.	Stock	Decrease retained earnings and decrease equity

The correct answer is (C). *(CIA, adapted)*

REQUIRED: The effect of a dividend.

DISCUSSION: A stock dividend results in a transfer from retained earnings to paid-in capital equal to the fair value of the stock.

Answer (A) is incorrect because cash dividends reduce retained earnings. Answer (B) is incorrect because cash dividends decrease both retained earnings and equity. Answer (D) is incorrect because stock dividends have no net effect on equity.

Questions 25 through 27 are based on the following information. Excerpts from the statement of financial position for Markham Corporation as of April 30, 2001 are presented as follows:

Cash	$ 725,000
Accounts receivable (net)	1,640,000
Inventories	2,945,000
Total current assets	$5,310,000
Accounts payable	$1,236,000
Accrued liabilities	831,000
Total current liabilities	$2,067,000

The board of directors of Markham met on May 5, 2001 and declared a quarterly cash dividend in the amount of $800,000 ($.50 per share). The dividend was paid on May 28, 2001 to shareholders of record as of May 15, 2001.

Assume that the only transactions that affected Markham during May 2001 were the dividend transactions and that the closing entries have been made.

---

25. Markham's total equity would be

A. Increased by the dividend declaration and unchanged by the dividend payment.

B. Unchanged by the dividend declaration and decreased by the dividend payment.

C. Unchanged by either the dividend declaration or the dividend payment.

D. Decreased by the dividend declaration and unchanged by the dividend payment.

The correct answer is (D). *(CMA, adapted)*

REQUIRED: The effect on a firm's total equity resulting from the declaration and payment of a dividend.

DISCUSSION: The declaration of a dividend results in an increase in current liabilities and a corresponding decrease in retained earnings (a shareholders' equity account). Thus, the declaration of a dividend decreases equity. The subsequent payment of the dividend has no effect on equity because that transaction involves using cash (a current asset) to pay the previously recorded current liability.

Answers (A), (B), and (C) are incorrect because equity is decreased by the declaration of a dividend, but the payment of a previously declared dividend has no effect on equity.

26. If the dividend declared by Markham had been a 10% stock dividend instead of a cash dividend, Markham's current liabilities would have been

A. Decreased by the dividend declaration and increased by the dividend distribution.

B. Unchanged by the dividend declaration and increased by the dividend distribution.

C. Unchanged by the dividend declaration and decreased by the dividend distribution.

D. Unchanged by either the dividend declaration or the dividend distribution.

The correct answer is (D). *(CMA, adapted)*

REQUIRED: The effect of the declaration and distribution of a stock dividend on a firm's current liabilities.

DISCUSSION: The declaration and distribution of a stock dividend involves transferring some amount from retained earnings to permanent equity. No liability account is affected by either the declaration or the distribution because shareholders are not receiving anything that they did not already have. A stock dividend merely divides the corporate pie into more pieces.

Answers (A), (B), and (C) are incorrect because a current liability account is not affected by either the declaration or the payment of a stock dividend.

27. If the dividend declared by Markham Corporation had been a 10% stock dividend instead of a cash dividend, Markham's total equity would have been

A. Decreased by the dividend declaration and increased by the dividend distribution.

B. Unchanged by the dividend declaration and increased by the dividend distribution.

C. Increased by the dividend declaration and unchanged by the dividend distribution.

D. Unchanged by either the dividend declaration or the dividend distribution.

The correct answer is (D). *(CMA, adapted)*

REQUIRED: The effect on total equity of the declaration and distribution of a stock dividend.

DISCUSSION: The entry to record the declaration of a stock dividend involves a debit to one equity account (retained earnings) and a credit to one or more other equity accounts (common stock dividend distributable and possibly additional paid-in capital) for the fair value of the stock. Consequently, the declaration has no effect on total equity because the entry merely entails a transfer from retained earnings to permanent capital. The subsequent distribution of a stock dividend requires only a debit to common stock dividend distributable and a credit to common stock. Because both are equity accounts, the distribution has no effect on total shareholders' equity.

Answers (A) and (C) are incorrect because the declaration of a stock dividend has no effect on total equity. Answer (B) is incorrect because the distribution of a stock dividend has no effect on total equity.

28. Which one of the following items would likely increase earnings per share (EPS) of a corporation?

A. Purchase of treasury stock.

B. Declaration of a stock split.

C. Declaration of a stock dividend.

D. A reduction in the amount of cash dividends paid to common shareholders.

The correct answer is (A). *(CMA, adapted)*

REQUIRED: The item that would likely increase EPS.

DISCUSSION: A purchase of treasury stock would increase earnings per share because fewer shares would be outstanding. The numerator of the EPS fraction (income available to common shareholders) would remain unchanged, but the denominator (weighted-average number of shares outstanding) would decrease.

Answer (B) is incorrect because a stock split reduces EPS. More shares are outstanding after the split. Answer (C) is incorrect because a stock dividend increases the shares outstanding and thus decreases EPS. Answer (D) is incorrect because a change in cash dividends paid to common shareholders has no effect on EPS. Dividends on common shares are declared out of income available to common shareholders.

29. Which of the following types of dividends do not reduce equity in the corporation?

A. Cash dividends.

B. Property dividends.

C. Liquidating dividends.

D. Stock dividends and split-ups in the form of a dividend.

The correct answer is (D). *(CIA, adapted)*

REQUIRED: The dividends that do not reduce shareholders' equity.

DISCUSSION: The issuance of a stock dividend results in a debit to retained earnings and credits to contributed capital for the fair value of the stock. A split-up effected in the form of a dividend requires capitalization of retained earnings equal to the amount established by the issuer's state of incorporation (usually par value). Consequently, neither a stock dividend nor a split-up effected in the form of a dividend has a net effect on equity.

Answers (A), (B), and (C) are incorrect because cash, property, and liquidating dividends reduce equity. They involve an immediate or promised future nonreciprocal distribution of assets.

30. Stock dividends and stock splits differ in that

A. Stock splits involve a bookkeeping transfer from retained earnings to the capital stock account.

B. Stock splits are paid in additional shares of common stock, whereas a stock dividend results in replacement of all outstanding shares with a new issue of shares.

C. In a stock split, a larger number of new shares replaces the outstanding shares.

D. A stock dividend results in a decline in the par value per share.

The correct answer is (C). *(CIA, adapted)*

REQUIRED: The difference between stock dividends and stock splits.

DISCUSSION: A stock split does not involve any accounting entries. Instead, a larger number of new shares are issued to replace and retire all outstanding shares.

Answer (A) is incorrect because stock dividends involve a bookkeeping transfer. Stock splits do not involve a change in the capital accounts. Answer (B) is incorrect because stock dividends are paid in additional shares of common stock. In stock splits, all outstanding shares are replaced with a new issue of shares. Answer (D) is incorrect because, in a stock split, there is a large decline in the book value, and in the market value, per share. A stock dividend does not affect the par value of stock.

31. On May 28, a company announced that its directors had met on May 26 and declared a dividend of 25 cents per share, payable to shareholders of record on June 20, with payment to be made on July 5. The date on which the declared dividend becomes a liability of the company is

A. May 26.

B. May 28.

C. June 20.

D. July 5.

The correct answer is (A). *(CIA, adapted)*

REQUIRED: The date on which the declared dividend becomes a liability.

DISCUSSION: The dividend becomes a liability of the company on the declaration date (May 26), which is the date the directors meet and formally vote to declare a dividend.

Answer (B) is incorrect because May 28 is the announcement date. The dividend becomes a liability as soon as it is declared. Answer (C) is incorrect because June 20 is the record date, on which the list of shareholders owning the shares who will receive the dividend payments is determined. Answer (D) is incorrect because July 5 is the dividend payment date. The declared dividend is no longer a liability after the payment is made.

Questions 32 and 33 are based on the following information. A company has 1,000 shares of $10 par value common stock and $5,000 of retained earnings. Two proposals are under consideration. The first is a stock split giving each shareholder two new shares for each share formerly held. The second is to declare and distribute a 50% split-up effected in the form of a dividend.

32. The stock split proposal will <List A> earnings per share by <List B> than will the stock dividend proposal for a split-up effected in the form of a dividend.

	List A	List B
A.	Increase	More
B.	Increase	Less
C.	Decrease	More
D.	Decrease	Less

The correct answer is (C). *(CIA, adapted)*

REQUIRED: The effect of a stock split and a split-up effected in the form of a dividend on earnings per share.

DISCUSSION: The stock split will double the number of shares outstanding to 2,000. The 50% split-up effected in the form of a dividend will increase the number of outstanding shares to 1,500. The higher number of shares in the stock split will result in a lower earnings per share than will result from the split-up effected in the form of a dividend.

Answers (A), (B), and (D) are incorrect because the stock split results in a greater number of shares outstanding and a lower EPS.

33. Under the <List A>, the par value per outstanding share will <List B>.

	List A	List B
A.	Split-up effected in the form of a dividend	Increase
B.	Stock split	Increase
C.	Split-up effected in the form of a dividend	Decrease
D.	Stock split	Decrease

The correct answer is (D). *(CIA, adapted)*

REQUIRED: The effect of a stock split and a split-up effected in the form of a dividend on par value.

DISCUSSION: A stock split results in a lower par value per share because the total number of shares increases but the total par value of outstanding stock does not change.

Answers (A) and (C) are incorrect because par value per share does not change following a split-up effected in the form of a dividend. Answer (B) is incorrect because par value per share decreases following a stock split.

34. The policy decision that by itself is least likely to affect the value of the firm is the

A. Investment in a project with a large net present value.

B. Sale of a risky division that will now increase the credit rating of the entire company.

C. Distribution of stock dividends to shareholders.

D. Use of a more highly leveraged capital structure that resulted in a lower cost of capital.

The correct answer is (C). *(CIA, adapted)*

REQUIRED: The policy decision that is least likely to affect the value of the firm.

DISCUSSION: A stock dividend does not significantly affect the value of the firm. It simply divides ownership interests into smaller pieces without changing any shareholder's proportionate share of ownership.

Answer (A) is incorrect because a positive NPV project should increase the value of the firm. Answer (B) is incorrect because the higher credit rating should reduce the cost of capital and therefore increase the value of the firm. Answer (D) is incorrect because the lower cost of capital should reduce the required rate of return and increase the value of the firm.

35. When a company desires to increase the market value per share of common stock, the company will

A. Sell treasury stock.

B. Implement a reverse stock split.

C. Sell preferred stock.

D. Split the stock.

The correct answer is (B). *(CMA, adapted)*

REQUIRED: The transaction that increases the market value per share of common stock.

DISCUSSION: A reverse stock split decreases the number of shares outstanding, thereby increasing the market price per share. A reverse stock split may be desirable when a stock is selling at such a low price that management is concerned that investors will avoid the stock because it has an undesirable image.

Answer (A) is incorrect because a sale of treasury stock increases the supply of shares and could lead to a decline in market price. Answer (C) is incorrect because a sale of preferred stock will take dollars out of investors' hands, thereby reducing funds available to invest in common stock. Hence, market price per share of common stock will not increase. Answer (D) is incorrect because a stock split increases the shares issued and outstanding. The market price per share is likely to decline as a result.

36. Natural Co. had 100,000 shares of common stock issued and outstanding at January 1, 20X0. During 20X0, Natural took the following actions:

March 15	-- declared a 2-for-1 stock split, when the fair value of the stock was $80 per share
December 15	-- declared a $.50 per share cash dividend

In Natural's statement of shareholders' equity for 20X0, what amount should Natural report as dividends?

A. $50,000

B. $100,000

C. $850,000

D. $950,000

The correct answer is (B). *(CPA, adapted)*

REQUIRED: The amount to be reported as dividends.

DISCUSSION: The 100,000 shares of common stock split 2-for-1, leaving 200,000 shares at year-end. The dividends declared equaled $100,000 (200,000 shares x $0.50).

Answer (A) is incorrect because $50,000 does not reflect the stock split. Answer (C) is incorrect because $850,000 equals the fair value of the stock on March 15 plus the dividend, assuming no stock split. Answer (D) is incorrect because $950,000 equals the fair value of the stock on March 15 plus the dividend on 200,000 shares.

37. The date when the right to a dividend expires is called the

A. Declaration date.

B. Ex-dividend date.

C. Holder-of-record date.

D. Payment date.

The correct answer is (B). *(CIA, adapted)*

REQUIRED: The date when the right to a dividend expires.

DISCUSSION: The ex-dividend date is 4 days before the date of record. Unlike the other relevant dates, it is not established by the corporate board of directors but by the stock exchanges. The period between the ex-dividend date and the date of record gives the stock exchange members time to process any transactions in time for the new shareholders to receive the dividend to which they are entitled. An investor who buys a share of stock before the ex-dividend date will receive the dividend that has been previously declared. An investor who buys after the ex-dividend date (but before the date of record or payment date) will not receive the declared dividend.

Answer (A) is incorrect because, on the declaration date, the directors formally vote to declare a dividend. Answer (C) is incorrect because, on the date of record, the corporation determines which shareholders will receive the declared dividend. Answer (D) is incorrect because, on the date of payment, the dividend is actually paid.

D. Retained Earnings Entries

38. Items reported as prior-period adjustments

A. Do not include the effect of a mistake in the application of accounting principles as this is accounted for as a change in accounting principle rather than as a prior-period adjustment.

B. Do not affect the presentation of prior-period comparative financial statements.

C. Do not require further disclosure in the body of the financial statements.

D. Are reflected as adjustments of the opening balance of the retained earnings of the earliest period presented.

The correct answer is (D). *(CMA, adapted)*

REQUIRED: The true statement about items reported as prior-period adjustments.

DISCUSSION: Prior-period adjustments are made for the correction of errors. According to SFAS 16, *Prior Period Adjustments*, the effects of errors on prior-period financial statements are reported as adjustments to beginning retained earnings for the earliest period presented in the retained earnings statement. Such errors do not affect the income statement for the current period.

Answer (A) is incorrect because accounting errors of any type are corrected by a prior-period adjustment. Answer (B) is incorrect because a prior-period adjustment will affect the presentation of prior-period comparative financial statements. Answer (C) is incorrect because prior-period adjustments should be fully disclosed in the notes or elsewhere in the financial statements.

39. An appropriation of retained earnings by the board of directors of a corporation for future plant expansion will result in

A. The establishment of a fund to help finance future plant expansion.

B. The setting aside of cash to be used for future plant expansions.

C. A decrease in cash on the balance sheet with an equal increase in the investments and funds section of the balance sheet.

D. The disclosure that management does not intend to distribute, in the form of dividends, assets equal to the amount of the appropriation.

The correct answer is (D). *(CMA, adapted)*

REQUIRED: The effect of an appropriation of retained earnings.

DISCUSSION: An appropriation of retained earnings simply transfers a portion of the retained earnings balance into a separate retained earnings account. The sole purpose of such an event is to disclose that earnings retained in the business are to be used for special purposes and will not be available for dividends. The same result could be obtained as effectively by a note. No funds are set aside by an appropriation of retained earnings.

Answer (A) is incorrect because no fund is established by the appropriation of retained earnings. Answers (B) and (C) are incorrect because no cash is involved in an appropriation of retained earnings.

40. Page Co. had retained earnings of $200,000 on December 31, 20X0. On April 20, 20X1, Page reacquired 2,000 shares of its common stock at $10 per share. On October 3, 20X1, Page sold 500 of these shares of treasury stock for $12 per share. Page uses the cost method to record treasury stock. During 20X1, Page had paid cash dividends of $70,000. Also, Page had distributed property dividends of $20,000. Its net income for the year ended December 31, 20X1 was $80,000. On December 31, 20X1, how much should Page report as retained earnings?

A. $190,000
B. $191,000
C. $210,000
D. $211,000

The correct answer is (A). *(Publisher)*

REQUIRED: The amount to be reported as retained earnings.

DISCUSSION: Retained earnings is increased by net income and can be decreased by net losses, certain treasury stock transactions, and dividends. Therefore, retained earnings is $190,000 ($200,000 – $70,000 – $20,000 + $80,000). The $1,000 excess of proceeds over the cost of treasury stock does not affect retained earnings because Page uses the cost method to account for treasury stock. Under the cost method, the excess should be a credit to additional paid-in capital.

Answer (B) is incorrect because $191,000 includes the $1,000 excess from the sale of treasury stock. Answer (C) is incorrect because $210,000 results from a failure to subtract $20,000 due to the distribution of the property dividends. Answer (D) is incorrect because $211,000 is the result of erroneously including the $1,000 excess from the sale of treasury stock and failing to subtract $20,000 in distributed property dividends.

E. Accounting for Treasury Stock

41. Corporations purchase their outstanding stock for all of the following reasons except to

A. Meet employee stock compensation contracts.
B. Increase earnings per share by reducing the number of shares outstanding.
C. Make a market in the stock.
D. Improve short-term cash flow.

The correct answer is (D). *(CMA, adapted)*

REQUIRED: The item not a reason for a company to buy treasury stock.

DISCUSSION: The acquisition of treasury stock does not improve a company's short-term cash flow. Cash must be expended to purchase the shares.

Answers (A), (B), and (C) are incorrect because a corporation purchases its own stock to facilitate possible acquisitions, to allow shareholders to receive capital gains rather than dividends, to comply with employee stock compensation contracts, to avoid a hostile takeover, to increase EPS and book value, to support the market for the stock, to eliminate dissident shareholders, and to reduce the size of the business.

42. The purchase of treasury stock with a firm's surplus cash

A. Increases a firm's assets.
B. Increases a firm's financial leverage.
C. Increases a firm's interest coverage ratio.
D. Dilutes a firm's earnings per share.

The correct answer is (B). *(CMA, adapted)*

REQUIRED: The true statement about a purchase of treasury stock.

DISCUSSION: A purchase of treasury stock involves a decrease in assets (usually cash) and a corresponding decrease in shareholders' equity. Thus, equity is reduced and the debt-to-equity ratio and financial leverage increase.

Answer (A) is incorrect because assets decrease when treasury stock is purchased. Answer (C) is incorrect because a firm's interest coverage ratio is unaffected. Earnings, interest expense, and taxes will all be the same regardless of the transaction. Answer (D) is incorrect because the purchase of treasury stock is antidilutive; the same earnings will be spread over fewer shares. Some firms purchase treasury stock for this reason.

43. At December 31, 2000, a company had the following equity accounts:

Common stock, $10 par, 100,000 shares authorized, 40,000 shares issued and outstanding	$ 400,000
Additional paid-in capital from issuance of common stock	640,000
Retained earnings	1,000,000
Total equity	$2,040,000

Each of the 40,000 shares of common stock outstanding was issued at a price of $26. On January 2, 2001, 2,000 shares were reacquired for $30 per share. The cost method is used in accounting for this treasury stock. Which of the following correctly describes the effect of the acquisition of the treasury stock?

A. Common stock is reduced by $20,000.

B. Additional paid-in capital from issuance of common stock is reduced by $32,000.

C. The retained earnings account balance is reduced by $8,000.

D. Total equity is reduced by $60,000.

The correct answer is (D). *(CIA, adapted)*

REQUIRED: The effect of the acquisition of the treasury stock under the cost method.

DISCUSSION: Using the cost method, the journal entry to record the acquisition of the treasury stock includes a debit to treasury stock for $60,000. The balance of the treasury stock account is classified as a contra equity item. Thus, the acquisition of the treasury stock reduces total equity by $60,000 ($30 x 2,000 shares = $60,000).

Answer (A) is incorrect because the common stock account balance is not affected when treasury stock is acquired. Answer (B) is incorrect because additional paid-in capital is not affected when treasury stock is acquired and accounted for by the cost method. Answer (C) is incorrect because the retained earnings account is not affected by treasury stock acquisitions when the cost method is used.

Questions 44 and 45 are based on the following information. On January 5, 2000, Norton Company issued 5,000 shares of common stock with a par value of $100. The proceeds received were at the issue price of $120 per share. On June 4, 2001, the company reacquired 500 shares at $115 per share.

---

44. Under the cost method of accounting for treasury stock, the amount debited to the treasury stock account is

A. $57,500

B. $50,000

C. $60,000

D. $7,500

The correct answer is (A). *(CMA, adapted)*

REQUIRED: The amount debited to treasury stock under the cost method.

DISCUSSION: Under the cost method, the amount debited to treasury stock is the amount paid. The cost is $115 per share, or $57,500 for 500 shares.

Answer (B) is incorrect because $50,000 is the amount recorded under the par value method. Answer (C) is incorrect because $60,000 was the original issuance price of the reacquired shares. Answer (D) is incorrect because $7,500 is the amount in excess of par. The full amount paid for the treasury stock is debited to treasury stock under the cost method.

45. Under the par value method of accounting for treasury stock, the amount debited to the treasury stock account is

A. $57,500

B. $50,000

C. $60,000

D. $10,000

The correct answer is (B). *(CMA, adapted)*

REQUIRED: The amount debited to treasury stock under the par value method.

DISCUSSION: Under the par value method, only the par value of stock is debited to treasury stock. The par value of 500 shares at $100 each is $50,000.

Answer (A) is incorrect because $57,500 is the cost of the treasury stock. Answer (C) is incorrect because $60,000 was the original issuance price of the reacquired shares. Answer (D) is incorrect because $10,000 is the difference between the issuance price and par value.

Questions 46 and 47 are based on the following information. On January 4, 20X1, Plant Co. was organized with 5,000 authorized shares of $50 par common stock. During 20X1, Plant had the following capital transactions:

January 7 -- issued 2,000 shares at $60 per share
June 20 -- reacquired 500 shares at $65 per share
November 19 -- reissued 400 shares held in treasury at $70 per share
December 3 -- retired the 100 shares of treasury stock

These were the only transactions affecting Plant's treasury stock.

46. Under the cost method of accounting for treasury stock, what amount should Plant report as total additional paid-in capital on its December 31, 20X1 balance sheet?

A. $20,500

B. $21,000

C. $22,000

D. $23,000

The correct answer is (B). *(Publisher)*

REQUIRED: The total additional paid-in capital reported under the cost method.

DISCUSSION: Under the cost method, additional paid-in capital is credited for $20,000 (2,000 shares x $10 excess over par) for the initial sale of common stock. Additional paid-in capital from treasury stock transactions is then credited for $2,000 (400 shares x $5 excess over the cost of shares) for the sale of treasury stock. Additional paid-in capital is then debited for $1,000 (100 shares x $10 excess over par) for the retirement of the remaining treasury stock. Thus, total ending additional paid-in capital is $21,000 ($20,000 + $2,000 – $1,000).

Answer (A) is incorrect because $20,500 includes the $500 debit to retained earnings on the retirement of treasury stock. Answer (C) is incorrect because $22,000 does not include the $1,000 debit from the retirement of treasury stock. Answer (D) is incorrect because $23,000 includes a $5,000 debit from purchase of treasury stock and an $8,000 credit from sale of treasury stock.

47. Under the par-value method of accounting for treasury stock, what amount should Plant report as additional paid-in capital on its December 31, 20X1 balance sheet?

A. $15,000

B. $20,500

C. $21,000

D. $23,000

The correct answer is (D). *(Publisher)*

REQUIRED: The additional paid-in capital reported under the par-value method.

DISCUSSION: Under the par-value method, additional paid-in capital is credited for $20,000 (2,000 shares x $10 excess over par) for the initial sale of common stock. It is then debited for $5,000 (500 shares x $10 excess over par) for the purchase of treasury stock. Additional paid-in capital is then credited for $8,000 (400 shares x $20 excess over par) for the reissuance of treasury stock. Thus, ending additional paid-in capital is $23,000 ($20,000 – $5,000 + $8,000).

Answer (A) is incorrect because $15,000 excludes the $8,000 credit from the reissuance of treasury stock. Answer (B) is incorrect because $20,500 includes the $2,500 debit to retained earnings on the acquisition of treasury stock. Answer (C) is incorrect because $21,000 includes a $2,000 credit from the sale of treasury stock and a $1,000 debit from the retirement of treasury stock.

Questions 48 and 49 are based on the following information. On January 3, 2000, Greenlee Company issued 5,000 shares of common stock with a par value of $50. The proceeds received were at the issue price of $60 per share. On June 4, 2001, the company reacquired 500 shares at $57.50 per share. These transactions were the only ones affecting Greenlee's treasury stock.

48. Under the cost method of accounting for treasury stock, the amount debited to treasury stock is

A. $28,750

B. $25,000

C. $30,000

D. $3,750

The correct answer is (A). *(Publisher)*

REQUIRED: The amount debited to treasury stock under the cost method.

DISCUSSION: The cost method debits treasury stock for the amount paid. In this case, the cost is $57.50 per share, or $28,750 for 500 shares.

Answer (B) is incorrect because $25,000 is the aggregate par value of 500 shares. It is the amount debited to treasury stock under the par value method. Answer (C) is incorrect because $30,000 was the original issuance price of the reacquired shares. Answer (D) is incorrect because $3,750 is the amount paid in excess of par.

49. Under the par value method of accounting for treasury stock, the amount debited to treasury stock is

A. $28,750

B. $25,000

C. $30,000

D. $3,750

The correct answer is (B). *(Publisher)*

REQUIRED: The amount debited to treasury stock under the par value method.

DISCUSSION: The par value method debits the par value of reacquired stock to treasury stock. The par value of 500 shares at $50 each is $25,000.

Answer (A) is incorrect because $28,750 is the cost of the treasury stock. This amount is debited to treasury stock under the cost method. Answer (C) is incorrect because $30,000 was the original issuance price of the reacquired shares. Answer (D) is incorrect because $3,750 is the amount paid in excess of par. It is debited to additional paid-in capital.

F. Stock Rights

50. When stock rights are issued without consideration and are allowed to lapse, the following occurs on the books of the issuing company:

A. Common stock at par value is increased.

B. Additional paid-in capital is credited.

C. Investment in stock warrants is debited.

D. None of the answers are correct.

The correct answer is (D). *(Publisher)*

REQUIRED: The effect on the issuing company when stock rights without consideration are allowed to lapse.

DISCUSSION: When rights are issued without consideration, such as in a dividend distribution, only a memorandum entry is made by the issuer. If the rights are exercised and stock is issued, the effect on the books of the issuing company is an increase in common stock at par value with any remainder credited to additional paid-in capital. However, if the rights are allowed to lapse, contributed capital is unaffected.

Answers (A), (B), and (C) are incorrect because, when rights previously issued without consideration are allowed to lapse, there is no effect on contributed capital.

51. SFAS 123, *Accounting for Stock-Based Compensation*, applies to stock-based compensation arrangements involving employees and others. With regard to accounting for employee compensation, it

A. Requires a fair-value-based method.

B. Requires an intrinsic-value-based method.

C. Measures compensation cost as the difference between the quoted market price and the exercise price at the grant date.

D. Permits entities to continue measuring compensation cost using intrinsic values.

The correct answer is (D). *(Publisher)*

REQUIRED: The true statement about SFAS 123.

DISCUSSION: SFAS 123, *Accounting for Stock-Based Compensation*, is an alternative to APB 25. It applies to stock purchase plans, stock options, restricted stock, and stock appreciation rights. Fair-value-based accounting for stock compensation plans is not required. An entity may continue to apply APB 25. Nevertheless, the fair-value-based method is preferable for purposes of justifying a change in accounting principle. However, initial adoption of an accounting principle for a new transaction is not a change in principle. Thus, an entity that is already measuring stock-based employee compensation cost using the intrinsic-value method stated in APB 25 need not change its accounting.

Answer (A) is incorrect because an entity that already uses the intrinsic value method need not change to the fair-value-based method described in SFAS 123. Answers (B) and (C) are incorrect because SFAS 123 encourages use of a fair-value-based method. The differences between quoted market price and the exercise price at the grant date is the intrinsic value.

52. According to APB 25, *Accounting for Stock Issued to Employees*, noncompensatory stock option plans have all of the following characteristics except

A. Participation by substantially all full-time employees who meet limited employment qualifications.

B. Equal offers of stock to all eligible employees.

C. A limited amount of time permitted to exercise the option.

D. A provision related to the achievement of certain performance criteria.

The correct answer is (D). *(CMA, adapted)*

REQUIRED: The item that is not a characteristic of a noncompensatory stock option plan.

DISCUSSION: Issuance of stock to employees pursuant to a noncompensatory plan does not result in an expense. A noncompensatory plan is defined as one in which substantially all full-time employees participate, the stock available to each employee is equal or is based on salary, the option exercise period is reasonable, and the discount from market is not greater than reasonable in an offer to shareholders or others. Noncompensatory plans do not provide for the achievement of certain performance criteria.

Answer (A) is incorrect because participation by all full-time employees is a characteristic of noncompensatory plans. Answer (B) is incorrect because noncompensatory plans should make offers of stock equally to all employees or be based on salary levels. Answer (C) is incorrect because a limited exercise period is a characteristic of noncompensatory plans.

53. According to APB 25, *Accounting for Stock Issued to Employees*, a stock option plan may or may not be intended to compensate employees for their work. The compensation expense for compensatory stock option plans should be recognized in the periods the

A. Employees become eligible to exercise the options.

B. Employees perform services.

C. Stock is issued.

D. Options are granted.

The correct answer is (B). *(CMA, adapted)*

REQUIRED: The true statement about recognition of compensation expense for compensatory stock option plans.

DISCUSSION: A compensatory stock option plan involves the issuance of stock in whole or in part for employee services. Accordingly, a contributed capital account such as stock options outstanding should be credited. The compensation cost should be recognized as an expense of one or more periods in which the employee performed services. If the measurement date precedes the rendering of services, a debit is made to deferred compensation expense, a contra equity account that will be amortized as employee services are rendered and expenses are recognized.

Answer (A) is incorrect because recognition in the periods the employees become eligible to exercise the options violates the matching concept. Answer (C) is incorrect because recognition when the stock is issued might result in an expense being recorded years after the benefits of the employee's service had accrued. Answer (D) is incorrect because recognition in the periods the options are granted might result in recording the expense prior to services being performed.

54. When bonds with detachable stock warrants are purchased, the price should be allocated between the warrants and the bonds based upon their relative fair values at issuance. The amount debited to investment in stock warrants relative to the total amount paid

A. Increases the premium on the investment in bonds.

B. Increases the discount on investment in bonds.

C. Increases either any premium on the bonds or any discount on the bonds.

D. Has no effect on the investment of bond premium or discount as the warrants are purchased separately.

The correct answer is (B). *(Publisher)*

REQUIRED: The effect on the carrying value of bonds of debiting investment in stock warrants.

DISCUSSION: The portion of the price allocated to the detachable stock warrants decreases the allocation to investment in bonds. Thus, amounts debited to investment in stock warrants increase the discount or decrease the premium recorded for the investment in bonds.

Answers (A), (C), and (D) are incorrect because the allocation to detachable stock warrants decreases the premium or increases any discount.

55. Early in its fiscal year, Starr Co. purchased 1,000 shares of Pack Co. common stock for $54,000. In the same transaction, Starr acquired 2,000 detachable stock warrants. Two of the warrants are required to purchase one additional share of Pack Co. common stock. The market price of the stock without the warrants was $49 per share. The market price of the warrants was $3.50 per warrant. Starr sold 50% of the warrants several weeks later. If the proceeds received by Starr equaled $4,000, it recognized a realized gain of

A. $3,000

B. $625

C. $500

D. $0

The correct answer is (B). *(Publisher)*

REQUIRED: The gain on sale of detachable warrants.

DISCUSSION: The recipient of stock rights must allocate the carrying value of the shares owned between those shares and the rights based on their relative fair values at the time the rights are received. Thus, the amounts to be allocated to the common stock and warrants are $47,250 ({($49 x 1,000) ÷ [($49 x 1,000) + ($3.50 x 2,000)]} x $54,000) and $6,750 ($54,000 – $47,250), respectively. The realized gain is therefore $625 [$4,000 – ($6,750 x 50%)].

Answer (A) is incorrect because $3,000 is the excess of the fair value of 2,000 rights over the sale price of 1,000 rights. Answer (C) is incorrect because $500 equals the excess of the sale price of 1,000 rights over their fair value. Answer (D) is incorrect because Starr should recognize a realized gain for the excess of the price over the carrying amount.

STUDY UNIT 7: OTHER INCOME ITEMS

14 pages of outline
64 multiple-choice questions

This study unit, one of seven devoted to advanced topics on the preparation of financial statements, addresses income statement captions appearing beneath operating income; EPS disclosures; the effects of early extinguishment of debt; and such foreign currency issues as translation, remeasurement, and accounting for transaction gains and losses.

A. Discontinued Operations

1. The results of operations of a segment that has been or will be discontinued, together with any gain or loss on disposal, should be reported separately as a component of income before extraordinary items and the cumulative effect of accounting changes. Income from discontinued operations and the gain or loss on disposal should be disclosed net of tax.
   a. **APB 30**, *Reporting the Results of Operations*, defines a **segment** as a component of an entity whose activities represent a separate major product line or class of customer and whose assets, results of operations, and activities can be physically and operationally distinguished from the remainder of the entity for financial reporting purposes.
2. Discontinued operations should be presented as two subcategories.
   a. The first is operating income or loss of the segment prior to the measurement date.
      1) The **measurement date** is the date on which management commits itself to a formal plan to dispose of a segment of a business, whether by sale or abandonment.
   b. The second is the gain or loss on disposal.
      1) The **gain or loss on disposal** includes estimated operating income or loss of the segment from the measurement date to the disposal date, any direct disposal costs incurred during the phaseout period, and the estimated gain or loss on the actual disposal.
         a) An estimated loss from the disposal of a segment is recognized at the measurement date.
            i) An adjustment in the current period of an estimated loss on disposal recognized in a prior period should be accounted for as a change in estimate.

b) A gain on disposal is recognized when realized, which is ordinarily in the period when the disposal occurs.

i) However, if the measurement and disposal dates are in different periods, the portion of a net gain on disposal realized in the period in which the measurement date occurs may be recognized in that period. For example, if the operating income from the measurement date to the balance sheet date exceeds an expected net loss for the balance of the phaseout period, the excess is a realized gain.

c) EXAMPLE: Shadow Corporation manufactures computers. The South Division manufactured typewriters, but its profits were declining. Consequently, Shadow Corporation decided on November 15, 2001 to sell the assets of the South Division on January 31, 2002. The following is Shadow Corporation's income statement after South Division was discontinued.

Shadow Corporation
INCOME STATEMENT
For the Year Ended 12/31/01

Revenue:		
Net sales	$1,500,000	
Other revenue	40,000	
Total revenue		$1,540,000
Expenses:		
Cost of goods sold	$ 750,000	
Selling expense	75,000	
Administrative expense	90,000	
Interest expense	70,000	
Total expenses		(985,000)
Net income from continuing operations before taxes		$ 555,000
Income taxes		(206,000)
Net income from continuing operations		$ 349,000
Discontinued operations:		
Income from operations of South Division (net of $12,000 tax)	$ 34,000	
Loss on disposal of South Division including provision for loss of $14,000 on operations during phaseout period (net of $15,000 tax savings)	(52,000)	
Total loss from discontinued operations		(18,000)
Net income		$ 331,000

3. When a business presents comparative financial statements, and the current and prior years include results of operations before the measurement date, it should disclose the results of operations of the disposed segment, net of tax, in a separate component of income before extraordinary items for each year presented. Thus, prior years' amounts must be reclassified from continuing operations to discontinued operations.

4. Adjustments, costs, and expenses that are clearly a direct result of the decision to dispose should be included in the gain or loss on disposal if they are clearly not adjustments, costs, and expenses associated with normal business activities that should have been recognized on a going-concern basis up to the measurement date.
   a. Costs and expenses directly associated with the disposal decision include such items as severance pay, additional pension costs, employee relocation costs, and future rentals on long-term leases not offset by sub-rentals (APB 30).
5. The BEPS and DEPS amounts for a discontinued operation should be presented on the face of the income statement or in the related notes.
6. Stop and review! You have completed the outline for this subunit. Study multiple-choice questions 1 through 6 beginning on page 315.

B. Extraordinary Items

1. According to APB 30, a material transaction or event that is unusual in nature and infrequent in occurrence in the environment in which the entity operates should be reported as an extraordinary item.
   a. These criteria, however, do not apply when a pronouncement, for example, **SFAS 4**, *Reporting Gains and Losses from Extinguishment of Debt*, specifically defines certain gains and losses as extraordinary items.
      1) Even if early extinguishment is frequent, it is still extraordinary.
      2) An **in-substance defeasance** does not operate as an extinguishment of debt (**SFAS 140**, *Accounting for Transfers and Servicing of Financial Assets and Liabilities and Extinguishments of Debt*).
   b. Extraordinary items should be shown separately in the income statement, net of tax, after results of discontinued operations but before the cumulative effect of a change in accounting principle.
      1) The BEPS and DEPS amounts for an extraordinary item should be presented on the face of the income statement or in the related notes.
   c. A transaction or event is **unusual** if it has a high degree of abnormality and is of a type clearly unrelated to, or only incidentally related to, the ordinary and typical activities of the entity.
   d. A transaction or event is **infrequent** if it is not reasonably expected to recur in the foreseeable future; e.g., earthquakes are extraordinary in Florida, not Japan.
   e. If only one criterion is met, the item should be reported, but not net of tax, as a separate component of income from continuing operations.
   f. APB 30 gives specific examples of items that are not extraordinary.
      1) Write-downs of receivables, inventories, and intangibles
      2) Gains and losses from exchange or translation of foreign currencies, including those resulting from major devaluations and revaluations
      3) Gains and losses on disposal of a segment
      4) Other gains and losses from sale or abandonment of property, plant, and equipment used in the business
      5) Effects of strikes, including those against competitors and major suppliers
      6) Adjustments of accruals on long-term contracts

g. In rare cases, however, an event or transaction that is material, unusual, and infrequent may result in an extraordinary gain or loss that includes one or more of the gains or losses listed in B.1.f. In such a case, gains and losses such as those in B.1.f.1) and 4) should be included in the extraordinary item if they directly result from a major casualty, an expropriation, or a prohibition under a newly enacted law or regulation.

1) Any portion of the losses resulting from valuation of assets on a going-concern basis (such as the loss from writing down assets to fair value) is not included in the extraordinary item.

h. Extraordinary gains and losses should be recorded in the interim financial statements in the quarters in which they occur. They should not be prorated.

i. Any insurance reimbursements reduce the related loss.

Loss	$XXX	
Receivable from insurance company	XXX	
Assets		$XXX
Liability (for repairs, etc.)		XXX

2. Stop and review! You have completed the outline for this subunit. Study multiple-choice questions 7 through 10 beginning on page 317.

C. Accounting Changes

1. An **accounting change** is defined in **APB 20**, *Accounting Changes*, as a change in an accounting principle, an accounting estimate, or the reporting entity. A change from an accounting principle that is not generally accepted to one that is generally accepted is the correction of an error and is treated as a prior-period adjustment, not as an accounting change.

a. Prior-period adjustments are made directly to retained earnings.

2. **Changes in Estimate**

a. A change in accounting estimate is a normal, recurring correction or adjustment. The effect of a change in accounting estimate is accounted for in the period of change, if the change affects that period only, or in the period of change and in future periods, if the change affects both the current period and future periods.

1) Examples of items that require estimates are uncollectible receivables, inventory obsolescence, service lives and salvage values of depreciable assets, warranty costs, periods benefited by a deferred cost, and recoverable mineral reserves.

2) Under APB 20, when the effect of a change in accounting principle cannot be separated from the effect of a change in accounting estimate, the change is accounted for as a change in estimate. The effect of the change should be reflected in current and future periods only.

a) An example of such a change is the change from deferring and amortizing a cost to recording it as an expense when incurred because future benefits of the cost have become doubtful. Because the new method is adopted to recognize a change in estimated future benefits, the effect of the change in principle is inseparable from the change in estimate.

3. **Cumulative-Effect Changes**

a. With certain exceptions, a change from one generally accepted accounting principle to another, such as a change in depreciation methods, should be reported as a cumulative-effect type change in accounting principle.

1) The cumulative effect of the change on beginning retained earnings, based on a retroactive computation, should appear as a separate component after extraordinary items in the income statement, net of tax effect.

a) Prior-period statements presented for comparative purposes should not be restated.

b) However, pro forma data for income before extraordinary items and net income should be shown on the face of the income statement as supplementary disclosures for all periods presented as if the newly adopted principle had been applied during all periods affected.

c) The BEPS and DEPS amounts of the cumulative effect should be presented on the face of the income statement or in the related notes.

2) According to **SFAS 3**, *Reporting Accounting Changes in Interim Financial Statements*, if an accounting change occurs in other than the first quarter of the enterprise's fiscal year, the proper treatment is to calculate the cumulative effect on retained earnings at the beginning of the year and include it in restated net income presented in the first quarter financial statements. In addition, all previously issued interim financial statements of the current year must be restated to reflect the new accounting method.

b. The category of accounting principles includes not only accounting principles and practices but also the methods of applying them. APB 20 establishes a presumption that, once adopted, an accounting principle should not be changed in accounting for events and transactions of a similar type.

1) This presumption in favor of continuity may be overcome only if the enterprise justifies the use of an alternative acceptable principle on the basis that it is preferable, i.e., that financial reporting will improve.

a) For example, justification may be established if an SFAS creates a new principle, expresses preference for a principle not being used, or rejects a principle being used.

c. In certain instances, the cumulative effect of an accounting change may not be determinable and will not be included in the income statement in the year of the change.

1) Disclosure will be made of the effect of the change in the current period.
2) The best example of such a change is a change to LIFO.

a) In most cases, determining the LIFO inventory valuation retroactively would be impossible. Information concerning the composition of inventory throughout the history of the entity, as well as all the individual unit prices, usually cannot be reconstructed.

4. **Special Changes**

   a. Accounting changes are accounted for by retroactive restatement only in special cases. Unless otherwise noted, the following changes in principle require retroactive restatement of financial statements with full disclosure in the year of the change:

      1) Change from LIFO to another inventory method

      2) Change from the completed-contract to the percentage-of-completion method (or vice versa)

      3) Change to or from the full-cost method used in the extractive industries

      4) Change in the reporting entity

         a) APB 20 defines this change as a "special type of change in accounting principle."

         b) APB 20 describes the following as changes in the reporting entity: presenting consolidated or combined statements in place of statements of individual companies, changing the specific subsidiaries included in the group for which consolidated statements are presented, changing the companies included in combined statements, and effecting a business combination accounted for by the pooling-of-interests method.

      5) Change from one acceptable principle to another by a closely held company when its financial statements are issued for the first time for any of the following purposes: obtaining additional equity capital, effecting a business combination, or registering securities

         a) Under APB 20, retroactive restatement is permitted (not required) in these circumstances as a one-time exemption from cumulative-effect treatment.

      6) Change from a nonequity method to the equity method of accounting for investments in common stock.

      7) Change to the method of accounting required or permitted by a new pronouncement

         a) A pronouncement may not only mandate use of a new principle, but also require its retroactive application. One example was SFAS 73, which required retroactive restatement for a change from retirement-replacement-betterment accounting to depreciation accounting for railroad track structures.

         b) Another possibility is that a pronouncement may permit the entity to elect either the retroactive or cumulative-effect method of accounting for the change. For example, SFAS 109 permitted this election for the change from the deferred to the asset-liability method of accounting for income taxes.

5. **Prior-Period Adjustments**

   a. According to **SFAS 16**, *Prior Period Adjustments*, items of profit or loss related to **corrections of errors** in prior-period statements are accounted for as prior-period adjustments. They are debited or credited (net of tax) to retained earnings and reported as adjustments in the statement of changes in equity or in the statement of retained earnings. They are not included in the determination of net income for the current period.

b. Prior-period adjustments reported in single-period statements are reflected as adjustments of the opening balance of retained earnings. According to **APB 9**, *Reporting the Results of Operations*, if comparative statements are presented, corresponding adjustments should be made to the amounts of net income (and its components) and retained earnings balances (as well as other affected balances) for all periods reported to reflect the retroactive application of the prior-period adjustments.

c. According to APB 20, errors in financial statements include mathematical mistakes, mistakes in applying accounting principles, and oversight or misuse of facts existing when the statements were issued.

1) A change in estimate differs from an error correction because it is based on new information or subsequent developments. Hence, the former is accounted for in the appropriate income statement accounts, and the latter is treated as a prior-period adjustment.

2) A change to a generally accepted accounting principle from one that is not is an error correction.

6. **Error Analysis**

a. A correcting journal entry combines the reversal of the error with the correct entry. Thus, it requires a determination of the

1) Journal entry originally recorded

2) Event or transaction that occurred

3) Correct journal entry

4) EXAMPLE: If the purchase of a fixed asset on account had been debited to purchases:

Incorrect Entry	Correct Entry	Correcting Entry
Purchases	Fixed asset	Fixed asset
A/P	A/P	Purchases

If cash had been incorrectly credited:

Incorrect Entry	Correct Entry	Correcting Entry
Purchases	Fixed asset	Cash
Cash	A/P	Purchases
		Fixed asset
		A/P

b. The analysis of accounting errors addresses such issues as whether an error affects prior-period financial statements, the timing of error detection, whether comparative financial statements are presented, and whether the error is counterbalancing.

1) An error affecting prior-period statements may or may not affect net income. For example, misclassifying an item as a gain rather than a revenue does not affect income and is readily correctable. No prior-period adjustment to retained earnings is required.

2) An error that affects prior-period net income is counterbalancing if it self-corrects over two periods. For example, understating ending inventory for one period (and the beginning inventory of the next period) understates the net income and retained earnings of the first period but overstates the net income and retained earnings of the next period by the same amount (assuming no tax changes). However, despite the self-correction, the financial statements remain misstated. They should be restated if presented comparatively in a later period.

a) An example of a noncounterbalancing error is a misstatement of depreciation. Such an error does not self-correct over two periods. Thus, a prior-period adjustment will be necessary.

b) In principle, a counterbalancing error requires no correcting entry if detection occurs two or more periods afterward (assuming no tax changes). Earlier detection necessitates a correcting entry.

7. Stop and review! You have completed the outline for this subunit. Study multiple-choice questions 11 through 31 beginning on page 319.

D. Earnings per Share (EPS)

1. According to **SFAS 128**, *Earnings per Share*, **EPS** is the amount of earnings attributable to a share of common stock. Investors commonly use this ratio to measure the performance of an entity over an accounting period. SFAS 128 prescribes two forms of EPS -- basic (BEPS) and diluted (DEPS). When a loss is reported, applicable loss-per-share figures are presented.

2. **BEPS** measures the entity's earnings performance during the reporting period based on common stock outstanding during all or part of the period. BEPS equals income available to common shareholders divided by the weighted-average number of shares of common stock outstanding.

   a. **Income available to common shareholders** is equal to either income from continuing operations (if that number is reported in the income statement) or net income, minus dividends on cumulative preferred stock or dividends declared on noncumulative preferred stock. When either a loss from continuing operations or a net loss is reported, dividends on preferred stock (if applicable) increase the amount of the loss.

      1) When a discontinued operation is not reported but the entity has an extraordinary item or an accounting change, SFAS 128 states that the line item to be used is income before extraordinary item (or an accounting change) instead of income from continuing operations.

   b. **The weighted-average number of common shares outstanding** is determined by relating the portion of the reporting period that the shares were outstanding to the total time in the period. Weighting is necessary because some shares may have been issued or reacquired during the period.

3. **DEPS** measures the entity's earnings performance during the reporting period based on both common stock and dilutive potential common stock.

   a. DEPS is computed by

      1) Increasing the denominator of BEPS to include the weighted-average number of additional shares of common stock that would have been outstanding if dilutive potential common stock had been issued.

2) Increasing the numerator of BEPS for any dividends on convertible preferred stock and the after-tax interest related to any convertible debt.

a) The numerator is also adjusted for other changes in income or loss, such as profit-sharing expenses, that would result from the assumed issuance of potential common stock.

b. **Potential common stock** is a security or other contract that may entitle the holder to obtain common stock. Examples include convertible securities (convertible preferred stock and convertible debt), stock options and warrants (and their equivalents), and contingently issuable common stock.

1) Option and warrant equivalents include nonvested stock granted to employees, stock purchase contracts, and partially paid stock subscriptions.

c. Potential common stock is **dilutive** if its inclusion in the calculation of EPS results in a reduction of EPS (or an increase in loss per share). In determining whether potential common stock is dilutive, each issue or series of issues is considered separately and in sequence from the most dilutive to the least dilutive. The issue with the lowest earnings per incremental share is included in DEPS before issues with higher earnings per incremental share. If the issue with the lowest earnings per incremental share is found to be dilutive with respect to BEPS, it is included in a trial calculation of DEPS. If the issue with the next lowest earnings per incremental share is dilutive with respect to the first trial calculation of DEPS, it is included in a new DEPS calculation. This process continues until all issues of potential common shares have been tested.

1) The calculation of DEPS does not assume the conversion, exercise, or contingent issuance of **antidilutive** securities, i.e., securities that increase EPS or decrease loss per share amounts.

d. DEPS is based on the most advantageous conversion rate or exercise price from the perspective of the holder. Moreover, previously reported DEPS is not retroactively adjusted for subsequent conversions or subsequent changes in the market price of the common stock.

e. The **if-converted method** is used to determine the dilutive effect of convertible securities. Conversion is not assumed if the effect is antidilutive. The if-converted method assumes that the convertible security was converted at the beginning of the period or time of issuance, if later. As a result, to arrive at the DEPS denominator, the BEPS denominator is increased by the weighted-average number of shares of common stock assumed to be issued.

1) To determine the DEPS numerator, the BEPS numerator is increased by the dividends related to convertible preferred stock and by the after-tax amounts of interest related to convertible debt for which the denominator was increased. The BEPS numerator is also adjusted for other after-tax changes in income or loss, such as profit-sharing or royalty expenses, that would result from the assumed issuance of common shares.

f. The **treasury stock method** is used to determine the dilutive effect of outstanding call options and warrants issued by the reporting entity. Dilution occurs if the average market price for the period exceeds the exercise price.

1) The treasury stock method assumes that

a) The options and warrants were converted at the beginning of the period or time of issuance, if later.

b) The proceeds were used to purchase common stock at the average market price during the period.

c) To arrive at the DEPS denominator, the BEPS denominator is increased by the difference between the number of shares issued and the number of shares purchased.

2) The **reverse treasury stock method** is used when the entity has entered into contracts to repurchase its own stock, for example, when it has **written put options**. When the contracts are in the money (the exercise price exceeds the average market price), the potential dilutive effect on EPS is calculated by

a) Assuming the issuance at the beginning of the period of sufficient shares to raise the proceeds needed to satisfy the contracts

b) Assuming those proceeds are used to repurchase shares

c) Including the excess of shares assumed to be issued over those assumed to be repurchased in the DEPS denominator

3) Options held by the entity on its own stock, whether they are puts or calls, are not included in the DEPS denominator because their effect is antidilutive.

g. The **control number** for determining whether potential common shares are dilutive is income from continuing operations adjusted for preferred dividends if that number is reported [See D.2.a.1)]. Thus, if a potential common stock has a dilutive effect on the calculation of DEPS for income from continuing operations, the same number of shares used to adjust the denominator for that calculation is used to adjust the denominator for the calculation of DEPS for all other reported earnings figures, including discontinued operations, extraordinary items, cumulative effect of a change in accounting principle, and either net income or net loss.

1) If a loss from continuing operations or a loss from continuing operations available to common shareholders is reported, potential common stock is not included in the calculation of DEPS for any reported earnings figure.

h. If the number of common shares outstanding changes because of a stock dividend, a stock split, or a reverse stock split, EPS figures for all periods presented are adjusted retroactively to reflect the change in capital structure. Adjustments are made for such changes in capital structure even if they occur after the close of the current period but before the issuance of the financial statements.

i. All entities must present BEPS amounts for both income from continuing operations [See D.2.a.1)] and net income on the face of the income statement. An entity with a simple capital structure (only common stock outstanding) reports BEPS amounts only.

1) An entity with a complex capital structure presents BEPS and DEPS amounts for income from continuing operations and net income with equal prominence on the face of the income statement.

2) An entity that reports a discontinued operation, an extraordinary item, or the cumulative effect of an accounting change reports the applicable BEPS and DEPS amounts for these components of income on the face of the income statement or in the notes to the financial statements.

j. For all periods for which an income statement or earnings summary is presented, disclosures must include EPS data and the following items:

1) A reconciliation by individual security of the numerators and denominators of the BEPS and DEPS computations for income from continuing operations

2) The effect of preferred dividends on the BEPS numerator

3) Potential common shares not included in DEPS because their inclusion would have had an antidilutive effect in the periods reported

k. If DEPS data are reported for at least one period, they are reported for all periods reported, even if they are equal to BEPS amounts.

l. For the latest period for which an income statement is presented, an entity must disclose any transaction occurring after the end of the most recent period but before the issuance of the financial statements that would have had a material effect on EPS had the transaction occurred prior to the balance sheet date.

m. **SFAS 129**, *Disclosure of Information about Capital Structure*, applies to all entities. It continues and consolidates previously existing guidance.

1) Rights and privileges of outstanding securities must be disclosed along with information about shares issued.

2) The equity section of the balance sheet should disclose information about liquidation preferences of preferred stock.

3) Redemption requirements for the next 5 years must also be disclosed.

4. Stop and review! You have completed the outline for this subunit. Study multiple-choice questions 32 through 45 beginning on page 326.

E. Early Extinguishment of Debt

1. **APB 26**, *Early Extinguishment of Debt*, applies to all extinguishments of debt except for troubled debt restructurings and conversions to equity securities of the debtor pursuant to conversion privileges granted at the date of issuance of the debt.

a. Gains or losses from early extinguishment should be recognized in income in the period of extinguishment.

1) The rationale for current recognition is that such gains or losses reflect a change in the value of the old debt caused by a change in the market rate of interest not recognized in the accounts.

2. Under **SFAS 140**, *Accounting for Transfers and Servicing of Financial Assets and Extinguishments of Liabilities*, a debtor derecognizes a liability only if it has been extinguished. One of the following must occur to extinguish a liability:

a. The debtor pays the creditor and is relieved of its obligation with respect to the liability. Paying the creditor includes delivering cash, financial assets, goods, or services, or reacquiring the outstanding debt securities.

b. The debtor is legally released from being the primary obligor, either judicially or by the creditor.

3. **SFAS 4**, *Reporting Gains and Losses from Extinguishment of Debt*, requires that they be aggregated and, if material, classified as **extraordinary items** net of related tax effect.
    a. However, according to **SFAS 64**, *Extinguishment of Debt Made to Satisfy Sinking-Fund Requirements*, gains and losses from extinguishments of debt made to satisfy sinking-fund requirements that must be met within 1 year of the date of extinguishment should be treated as ordinary (not extraordinary) gains or losses.
        1) This classification is determined without regard to the means (cash or otherwise) of extinguishment.
4. The gain or loss on the retirement of debt is equal to the difference between the proceeds paid (including any call premium and miscellaneous costs of reacquisition) and the carrying value of the debt.
    a. The carrying value of the debt is equal to the face value plus any unamortized premium or minus any unamortized discount.
    b. In addition, any unamortized issue costs are considered in effect a reduction of the carrying value even though they are accounted for separately from the discount or premium.
5. **In-substance defeasance** is an arrangement in which a company places purchased securities in an irrevocable trust in order to provide assets for the future repayment of a long-term debt issuance as it matures.
    a. In-substance defeasance does not meet the derecognition criteria of **SFAS 140** because the liability is still outstanding and the debtor has not obtained a legal release from being the primary obligor.
6. APB 26 states that if an early extinguishment of debt is achieved by a direct exchange of new securities (a **refunding**), the reacquisition price is accounted for at the present value of the new securities.
7. Stop and review! You have completed the outline for this subunit. Study multiple-choice questions 46 through 51 beginning on page 332.

F. Foreign Currency Issues

1. Currently, accounting data for foreign operations are consolidated into domestic financial statements using a functional currency approach.
    a. An entity's **functional currency** is the currency of the primary economic environment in which it operates. The functional currency is normally that of the environment in which the entity primarily expends and generates cash. For example, the functional currency of a British subsidiary would be the pound.
        1) A highly inflationary currency, that is, one with a 3-year inflation rate of 100% or more, is not considered stable enough to be a functional currency. Instead, the financial statements of the foreign entity are remeasured as if the reporting currency were the functional currency.
        2) Indications that the subsidiary's currency is the functional currency include the following:
            a) Its cash flows are primarily in that foreign currency,
            b) They do not affect the parent's cash flows,
            c) Labor and materials are obtained in the local market of the foreign subsidiary,

d) Subsidiary financing is obtained from local foreign sources and from the subsidiary's operations, and

e) Few intercompany transactions occur between the foreign subsidiary and the parent.

3) However, sales prices that are responsive to exchange rate fluctuations and international competition suggest that the functional currency is the parent's currency.

b. The following are the steps in the **functional currency translation approach**:

1) Identify the functional currency.

2) Measure financial statement amounts in the functional currency; e.g., a Swiss company may prepare its statements in Swiss francs even though it conducts most of its business in euros (the euro is the functional currency).

a) If the subsidiary's financial statements are not maintained in the functional currency, they must be **remeasured** into that currency using the temporal rate method.

i) Remeasurement presents statements as if they had been originally prepared in the functional currency.

ii) The **current exchange rate** is used to remeasure all accounts except those specified in **SFAS 52**, *Foreign Currency Translation*.

iii) **Historical rates** should be used for the specified accounts, which include common nonmonetary balance sheet items and related revenue, expense, gain, and loss accounts, e.g., inventory; property, plant, and equipment; prepaid expenses; deferred charges and credits; cost of sales; intangible assets; amortization of intangibles; and common stock.

b) Gains and losses arising from remeasurement of monetary assets and liabilities are recognized currently in income.

c) An entity can be in any form, including subsidiary, division, branch, or joint venture.

3) Once the financial statement elements have been measured in terms of the functional currency, a **current exchange rate** is used to **translate** assets and liabilities from the functional currency into the reporting currency of the parent.

a) In theory, revenues, expenses, gains, and losses are translated at the rate in effect when they were recognized, but they are so numerous that a weighted-average rate for the period may be used.

4) **Translation adjustments** for a foreign operation that is relatively self-contained and integrated within its environment do not affect cash flows of the reporting enterprise and should be excluded from net income. Thus, they are reported in **other comprehensive income**.

5) **FASB Interpretation No. 37**, *Accounting for Translation Adjustments upon Sale of Part of an Investment in a Foreign Entity*, clarifies SFAS 52. A pro rata portion of the accumulated translation adjustment attributable to an investment shall be recognized in measuring the gain or loss on the sale of all or part of a company's interest in a foreign entity.

2. When a foreign currency transaction gives rise to a receivable or a payable that is fixed in terms of the amount of foreign currency to be received or paid, a change in the exchange rate between the functional currency and the currency in which the transaction is denominated results in a gain or loss that ordinarily should be included in determining net income in the period in which the exchange rate changes. The same treatment applies when the transaction is settled. **Transaction gains and losses** are reported in the aggregate in the income statement and should be disclosed.

   a. EXAMPLE: Assume that inventory was purchased for 10,000 foreign currency units (FCUs) at a time when the FCU was worth $.25. The entry for the purchase would be

Purchases	$2,500	
Accounts payable		$2,500

      1) If the FCU strengthens compared with the dollar before the payment date, the company will have to pay more to obtain the 10,000 FCUs necessary to make payment to the supplier. If the price of the FCU rises to $.26, the entry for payment will be

Accounts payable	$2,500	
Transaction loss	100	
Cash		$2,600

      2) If the dollar strengthens during the intervening period, a gain is recorded. If the FCU falls to $.22, the entry for payment is

Accounts payable	$2,500	
Cash		$2,200
Transaction gain		300

   b. Certain transaction gains and losses are excluded from the determination of net income and are reported in the same way as translation adjustments, that is, in other comprehensive income:

      1) Transactions that are designated and effective as economic hedges of a net investment in a foreign entity

      2) Long-term investments in foreign entities to be consolidated, combined, or accounted for by the equity method

   c. The subject of **foreign currency hedging** is treated in Study Unit 8, D.

3. Stop and review! You have completed the outline for this subunit. Study multiple-choice questions 52 through 64 beginning on page 334.

MULTIPLE-CHOICE QUESTIONS

A. Discontinued Operations

1. When reporting the discontinuance of a business segment, APB 30, *Reporting the Results of Operations*, specifies that

A. The results of the segment operations during the phaseout period are reported as part of the gain or loss from continuing operations.

B. The income (loss) from segment operations is calculated from the date the segment started operations.

C. The gain or loss on discontinued operations should be reported net of tax as a separate item before extraordinary items.

D. The costs directly associated with discontinuance should be included as an expense of continuing operations.

The correct answer is (C). *(CMA, adapted)*

REQUIRED: The true statement about discontinued operations reporting requirements.

DISCUSSION: The results of operations of a segment that has been or will be discontinued, together with any gain or loss on disposal, should be reported separately as a component of income before extraordinary items and the cumulative effect of accounting changes. Income from discontinued operations and the gain or loss on disposal should each be disclosed net of tax.

Answer (A) is incorrect because operating results during the phaseout period are part of the gain (loss) on disposal. Answers (B) and (D) are incorrect because discontinued operations should be presented as two subcategories. The first is operating income (loss) of the segment in the current period up to the measurement date. The second is the gain (loss) on disposal. The gain (loss) on disposal includes estimated operating income (loss) of the segment from the measurement date to the disposal date plus the estimated gain (loss) on the actual disposal. The direct costs of discontinuance are included in the gain (loss) on the actual disposal and should thus not be included as an expense of continuing operations.

2. The gain or loss from disposal of a segment

A. Includes the operating gain or loss realized by the segment from the beginning of the fiscal year to the disposal date.

B. Is reported as an addition or subtraction for the beginning balance of retained earnings on the statement of retained earnings.

C. Is reported as an extraordinary item on the income statement.

D. Is reported as a component of net income and distinguished from the operating gain or loss realized by the segment prior to the measurement date.

The correct answer is (D). *(CMA, adapted)*

REQUIRED: The true statement about the gain or loss from disposal of a segment.

DISCUSSION: Discontinued operations should be presented as two subcategories. The first is operating income or loss of the segment prior to the measurement date. The second is the gain or loss on disposal. The gain or loss on disposal includes estimated operating income or loss of the segment from the measurement date to the disposal date and any disposal costs incurred during the phaseout period, plus the estimated gain or loss on the actual disposal.

Answer (A) is incorrect because the operating gain or loss for the partial period is not combined with the gain or loss on disposal. Answer (B) is incorrect because gain or loss on disposal is reported on the income statement, not the retained earnings statement. Answer (C) is incorrect because gain or loss on disposal is reported in a discontinued operations section prior to extraordinary items.

Questions 3 and 4 are based on the following information. On December 31, 2001, the board of directors of Gator Manufacturing, Inc. committed to a plan to discontinue the operations of its Jersey Division in 2002. Gator estimated that Jersey's 2002 operating loss would be $900,000 and that Jersey's facilities would be sold for $400,000 less than their carrying amounts. Jersey's 2001 operating loss was $1,700,000. Gator's effective tax rate is 35%.

3. In its 2001 income statement, what amount should Gator report as loss from discontinued operations?

A. $1,105,000

B. $1,690,000

C. $1,700,000

D. $2,600,000

The correct answer is (A). *(CPA, adapted)*

REQUIRED: The loss from discontinued operations at year-end.

DISCUSSION: The results of operations of a segment that has been or will be discontinued, together with any gain or loss on disposal, should be reported separately as a component of income before extraordinary items and the cumulative effect of accounting changes. Income or loss from discontinued operations and the gain or loss on disposal should each be disclosed net of tax. Accordingly, the loss from discontinued operations, net of tax effect, is $1,105,000 [$1,700,000 loss prior to the 12/31/01 measurement date x (1.0 – 35% tax rate)].

Answer (B) is incorrect because $1,690,000 equals the after-tax 2001 loss from discontinued operations, plus the estimated after-tax operating loss for 2002. Answer (C) is incorrect because $1,700,000 is the pretax 2001 loss from discontinued operations. Answer (D) is incorrect because $2,600,000 equals the pretax 2001 loss from discontinued operations, plus the estimated pretax operating loss for 2002.

4. In its 2001 income statement, what amount should Gator report as loss on disposal of discontinued operations?

A. $260,000

B. $400,000

C. $845,000

D. $1,300,000

The correct answer is (C). *(CPA, adapted)*

REQUIRED: The loss on disposal of discontinued operations reported on the income statement.

DISCUSSION: The gain or loss on disposal should include not only the gain or loss on disposal of the assets but also any income or loss from operations during the phaseout period. If a net loss is expected, it should be provided for at the measurement date (12/31/01). Thus, loss on disposal of discontinued operations, net of taxes, is $845,000 [($900,000 expected operating loss + $400,000 estimated loss on asset sale) x (1 – 35%)].

Answer (A) is incorrect because $260,000 does not include the expected operating loss. Answer (B) is incorrect because $400,000 is a pretax amount that does not include the expected operating loss. Answer (D) is incorrect because the loss on disposal of discontinued operations should be reported net of tax.

5. During January 1999, Doe Corp. agreed to sell the assets and product line of its Hart division. The sale was completed on January 15, 2000, and resulted in a gain on disposal of $900,000. Hart's operating losses were $600,000 for 1999 and $50,000 for the period January 1 through January 15, 2000. Disregarding income taxes, what amount of net gain (loss) should be reported in Doe's comparative 2000 and 1999 income statements?

	2000	1999
A.	$0	$250,000
B.	$250,000	$0
C.	$850,000	$(600,000)
D.	$900,000	$(650,000)

The correct answer is (B). *(CPA, adapted)*

REQUIRED: The amounts reported in comparative statements for discontinued operations.

DISCUSSION: A gain or loss on disposal includes estimated income or loss from the measurement date (January 1999) to the disposal date (January 15, 2000), any disposal costs incurred, and the estimated gain or loss on the actual disposal. A gain on disposal is recognized when realized. If the measurement and disposal dates are in different periods, the portion of a net gain realized in the period in which the measurement date occurs may be recognized in that period. Doe's net gain on disposal is $250,000 ($900,000 gain on actual disposal – $600,000 operating losses in 1999 – $50,000 operating losses in 2000). Because no part of the gain on disposal is realized in 1999, Doe should not recognize a gain or a loss on disposal in the 1999 income statement. The entire $250,000 gain on disposal should therefore be recognized in 2000.

Answer (A) is incorrect because a gain is reported in the period in which it is realized. Answers (C) and (D) are incorrect because the gains and losses during the phaseout period are treated as one transaction. Hence, they are offset.

6. On October 1, 2000, Host Co. approved a plan to dispose of a segment of its business. Host expected that the sale would occur on April 1, 2001 at an estimated gain of $350,000. The segment had actual and estimated operating losses as follows:

1/1/00 to 9/30/00	$(300,000)
10/1/00 to 12/31/00	(200,000)
1/1/01 to 3/31/01	(400,000)

In its 2000 income statement, what should Host report as a loss on disposal of the segment before income taxes?

A. $200,000

B. $250,000

C. $500,000

D. $600,000

The correct answer is (B). *(CPA, adapted)*

REQUIRED: The loss on disposal.

DISCUSSION: The segment is expected to be sold for a gain of $350,000. However, $600,000 in operating losses is estimated during the phaseout period (measurement date through the disposal date). Thus, a net loss of $250,000 should be recognized. APB 30 states that if a loss is expected on disposal, the estimated loss should be reported at the measurement date and recognized in the period of the measurement date.

Answer (A) is incorrect because $200,000 is the operating loss from 10/1/00 to 12/31/00. Answer (C) is incorrect because $500,000 is the operating loss for 2000. Answer (D) is incorrect because the $600,000 loss is offset by the $350,000 gain on sale.

B. Extraordinary Items

7. When reporting extraordinary items,

A. Each item (net of tax) is presented on the face of the income statement separately as a component of net income for the period.

B. Each item is presented exclusive of any related income tax.

C. Each item is presented as an unusual item within income from continuing operations.

D. All extraordinary gains or losses that occur in a period are summarized as total gains and total losses, then offset to present the net extraordinary gain or loss.

The correct answer is (A). *(CMA, adapted)*

REQUIRED: The true statement about the reporting of extraordinary items.

DISCUSSION: Extraordinary items should be presented net of tax after income from operations. APB 30 states, "Descriptive captions and the amounts for individual extraordinary events or transactions should be presented, preferably on the face of the income statement, if practicable; otherwise, disclosure in related notes is acceptable."

Answer (B) is incorrect because extraordinary items are to be reported net of the related tax effect. Answer (C) is incorrect because extraordinary items are not reported in the continuing operations section of the income statement. Answer (D) is incorrect because each extraordinary item is to be reported separately.

8. Which one of the following material events would be classified as an extraordinary item on an income statement?

A. A write-down of inventories.

B. A loss due to the effects of a strike against a major supplier.

C. A gain or loss on the disposal of a portion of the business.

D. A gain or loss from the extinguishment of debt.

The correct answer is (D). *(CMA, adapted)*

REQUIRED: The event that would be classified as an extraordinary item on the income statement.

DISCUSSION: APB 30 gives examples of certain transactions that are not to be considered extraordinary items. These include write-downs of receivables and inventories, translation of foreign exchange, disposal of a business segment, disposal of productive assets, the effects of strikes, and the adjustments of accruals on long-term contracts. A gain or loss on the early extinguishment of debt is to be shown as an extraordinary item under the provisions of SFAS 4.

Answers (A), (B), and (C) are incorrect because APB 30 specifically excludes a write-down of inventories, a loss due to the effects of a strike against a major supplier, and a gain or loss on the disposal of a portion of the business from the definition of extraordinary items.

9. On January 1, 2000, Hart, Inc. redeemed its 15-year bonds of $500,000 par value for 102. They were originally issued on January 1, 1988 at 98 with a maturity date of January 1, 2003. The bond issue costs relating to this transaction were $20,000. Hart amortizes discounts, premiums, and bond issue costs using the straight-line method. What amount of extraordinary loss should Hart recognize on the redemption of these bonds?

A. $16,000

B. $12,000

C. $10,000

D. $0

The correct answer is (A). *(CPA, adapted)*

REQUIRED: The extraordinary loss on the redemption of bonds.

DISCUSSION: The gain or loss on the retirement of debt is equal to the difference between the proceeds paid and the carrying value of the debt. The carrying value of the debt is equal to the face value plus any unamortized premium or minus any unamortized discount. In addition, any unamortized issue costs are considered, in effect, a reduction of the carrying value, even though they are accounted for separately from the bond discount or premium. The unamortized discount is $2,000 {3/15 x [(1 – 98%) x $500,000]}, and the unamortized bond issue costs equal $4,000 (3/15 x $20,000). Hence, the effective carrying amount is $494,000 ($500,000 – $2,000 – $4,000), and the extraordinary loss on this early extinguishment of debt is $16,000 [(102% x $500,000 redemption price) – $494,000].

Answer (B) is incorrect because $12,000 does not consider the issue costs. Answer (C) is incorrect because $10,000 does not consider the issue costs or the discount. Answer (D) is incorrect because an extraordinary loss should be recognized.

10. Strand, Inc. incurred the following infrequent losses during 2000:

- A $90,000 write-down of equipment leased to others
- A $50,000 adjustment of accruals on long-term contracts
- A $75,000 write-off of obsolete inventory

In its 2000 income statement, what amount should Strand report as total infrequent losses that are not considered extraordinary?

A. $215,000

B. $165,000

C. $140,000

D. $125,000

The correct answer is (A). *(CPA, adapted)*

REQUIRED: The amount to be reported as total infrequent losses not considered extraordinary.

DISCUSSION: To be classified as an extraordinary item, a transaction must be both unusual in nature and infrequent in occurrence in the environment in which the business operates. APB 30 specifies six items that are not considered extraordinary. These items include the write-down of equipment, the adjustment of accruals on long-term contracts, and the write-off of obsolete inventory. Thus, Strand should report $215,000 ($90,000 + $50,000 + $75,000) of total infrequent losses as a component of income from continuing operations.

Answer (B) is incorrect because $165,000 improperly excludes the adjustment of accruals. Answer (C) is incorrect because $140,000 improperly excludes the write-off of inventory. Answer (D) is incorrect because $125,000 improperly excludes the write-down of equipment.

C. Accounting Changes

11. On January 1, 1997, Flax Co. purchased a machine for $528,000 and depreciated it by the straight-line method, using an estimated useful life of 8 years with no salvage value. On January 1, 2000, Flax determined that the machine had a useful life of 6 years from the date of acquisition and will have a salvage value of $48,000. An accounting change was made in 2000 to reflect the additional data. The accumulated depreciation for this machine should have a balance at December 31, 2000 of

A. $292,000

B. $308,000

C. $320,000

D. $352,000

The correct answer is (A). *(CPA, adapted)*

REQUIRED: The accumulated depreciation 1 year following a change in estimate.

DISCUSSION: For each of the first 3 years (1997 - 1999), depreciation expense was recorded as $66,000 ($528,000 cost ÷ 8 years). Accumulated depreciation at 1/1/00 was $198,000 ($66,000 x 3), and the carrying value of the machine was $330,000 ($528,000 cost – $198,000 accumulated depreciation). For 2000, the depreciation expense is $94,000 [($330,000 carrying amount – $48,000 estimated salvage value) ÷ 3 remaining years of expected useful life]. Consequently, the accumulated depreciation at 12/31/00 is $292,000 ($198,000 accumulated depreciation at December 31, 1999 + $94,000 depreciation for 2000).

Answer (B) is incorrect because $308,000 is based on the new estimated life, but without consideration of salvage value. Answer (C) is incorrect because $320,000 assumes that the machine was depreciated from the beginning, based on a 6-year life and a $48,000 salvage value. Answer (D) is incorrect because $352,000 assumes that the machine was depreciated from the beginning, based on a 6-year life and no salvage value.

12. During 2000, Orca Corp. decided to change from the FIFO method of inventory valuation to the weighted-average method. Inventory balances under each method were as follows:

	FIFO	Weighted-Average
January 1, 2000	$71,000	$77,000
December 31, 2000	79,000	83,000

Orca's income tax rate is 30%. In its 2000 financial statements, what amount should Orca report as the cumulative effect of this accounting change?

A. $2,800

B. $4,000

C. $4,200

D. $6,000

The correct answer is (C). *(CPA, adapted)*

REQUIRED: The cumulative income statement effect.

DISCUSSION: A change in accounting principle usually requires that the cumulative effect of the change on beginning retained earnings, based on a retroactive computation, be reported separately in the income statement of the year of the change. In this case, the cumulative effect results from the increase in beginning inventory. This change increases net income for prior periods by decreasing aggregate cost of goods sold (net of tax) by $4,200 [($77,000 – $71,000) x (1.0 – .30)].

Answer (A) is incorrect because $2,800 results from using the ending inventory instead of the beginning inventory. Answer (B) is incorrect because $4,000 results from using the ending inventory and does not consider taxes. Answer (D) is incorrect because $6,000 is the increase before income taxes.

13. Milton Co. began operations on January 1, 1998. On January 1, 2000, Milton changed its inventory method from LIFO to FIFO for both financial and income tax reporting. If FIFO had been used in prior years, Milton's inventories would have been higher by $60,000 and $40,000 at December 31, 2000 and 1999, respectively. Milton has a 30% income tax rate. What amount should Milton report as the cumulative effect of this accounting change in its income statement for the year ended December 31, 2000?

A. $0

B. $14,000

C. $28,000

D. $42,000

The correct answer is (A). *(CPA, adapted)*

REQUIRED: The cumulative effect of the accounting change.

DISCUSSION: Under APB Opinion No. 20, a change from LIFO to any other method of inventory pricing is a special change in accounting principle that must be accounted for as a prior-period adjustment. The financial statements for all periods presented must be restated. The adjustment should be made directly to the balance of beginning retained earnings. Consequently, the change does not result in the recognition of the cumulative effect in income in the year of change.

Answers (B), (C), and (D) are incorrect because the cumulative effect is a direct adjustment to beginning retained earnings.

14. On January 1, 1998, a company purchased a piece of equipment for $250,000, which was originally estimated to have a useful life of 10 years with no salvage value. Depreciation has been recorded for 3 years on a straight-line basis. On January 1, 2001, the estimated useful life was revised so that the equipment is considered to have a total life of 20 years. Assume that the depreciation method and the useful life for financial reporting and tax purposes are the same. The depreciation expense in 2001 on this equipment would be

A. $8,750

B. $10,294

C. $12,500

D. $14,706

The correct answer is (B). *(CIA, adapted)*

REQUIRED: The depreciation expense in 2001 after a change in estimate.

DISCUSSION: In 2001, the book value at the start of the period will be amortized over the revised estimated years of useful life. The depreciation recognized during 1998-2000 was $75,000 [3 years x ($250,000 ÷ 10)]. Thus, the book value at the beginning of 2001 was $175,000, and 2001 depreciation based on the revised estimated useful life is $10,294 [$175,000 ÷ (20 – 3)].

Answer (A) is incorrect because $8,750 is the result of depreciating the remaining carrying value over 20 years rather than the remaining 17 years. Answer (C) is incorrect because $12,500 results from accounting for the change in estimate retroactively. Answer (D) is incorrect because $14,706 results from depreciating the original book value over the revised estimate of remaining useful life.

15. Jordan Company signed a new $136,800 3-year lease beginning March 1, 2001 for a storage facility for finished goods inventory. Jordan recorded the first year's payment of $45,600 in the prepaid rent account. The balance in the prepaid rent account prior to this entry was $30,780. This prior balance relates to the previous lease for this facility that had expired February 28, 2001. Jordan records adjustments only at May 31, the end of the fiscal year. At May 31, 2001, the adjusting entry needed to reflect the correct balances in the prepaid rent and rent expense accounts is to debit

A. Prepaid rent for $11,400 and credit rent expense for $11,400.

B. Rent expense for $11,400 and credit prepaid rent for $11,400.

C. Prepaid rent for $42,180 and credit rent expense for $42,180.

D. Rent expense for $42,180 and credit prepaid rent for $42,180.

The correct answer is (D). *(CMA, adapted)*

REQUIRED: The entry necessary to correct the prepaid rent and rent expense accounts.

DISCUSSION: The existing balance ($30,780) in prepaid rent at March 1, 2001 reflects a prepayment for the first 9 months of the fiscal year that should now be expensed. The initial payment on the new lease is for the last 3 months of the current fiscal year and the first 9 months of the next. Accordingly, 25% (3 months ÷ 12 months) of this initial payment should be expensed. The entry is therefore to debit rent expense and credit prepaid rent for $42,180 [$30,780 + (25% x $45,600)].

Answer (A) is incorrect because prepaid rent should be credited for $42,180. Answer (B) is incorrect because the existing amount in prepaid rent also needs to be expensed. Answer (C) is incorrect because prepaid rent should be credited for $42,180.

16. An accounting change requiring the cumulative effect of the adjustment to be presented on the income statement is a change in the

A. Life of equipment from 10 to 7 years.

B. Depreciation method from straight-line to double-declining-balance.

C. Specific subsidiaries included in the group for which consolidated statements are presented.

D. Estimated liability for warranty costs.

The correct answer is (B). *(CMA, adapted)*

REQUIRED: The accounting change that should be reported as a cumulative-effect-type change.

DISCUSSION: A change in depreciation methods is reported as a change in accounting principle. The cumulative effect on beginning retained earnings, based on a retroactive calculation, should be reflected as a component of net income between extraordinary items and net income.

Answers (A) and (D) are incorrect because each is a change in estimate and is accounted for currently and prospectively. Answer (C) is incorrect because a change in the reporting entity requires a retroactive restatement of the financial statements.

17. According to APB 20, a change from last-in, first-out (LIFO) costing to first-in, first-out (FIFO) costing requires

A. Retroactive treatment in the financial statements.

B. Prospective treatment in the financial statements.

C. An entry in the income statement recording the cumulative effect of the change.

D. Disclosure in the notes only.

The correct answer is (A). *(CMA, adapted)*

REQUIRED: The proper treatment of a change from LIFO to FIFO.

DISCUSSION: Most changes in accounting principle should be recognized by including the cumulative effect, based on a retroactive computation, of changing to a new accounting principle in net income of the period of the change. However, a change from LIFO to any other method of inventory pricing is a special change in accounting principle that requires a retroactive restatement of financial statements with full disclosure in the year of change.

Answer (B) is incorrect because prospective treatment applies only to changes in estimates. Answer (C) is incorrect because a change from LIFO to FIFO is a special exception to which the general rule does not apply. Answer (D) is incorrect because the change must be shown on the face of the statements, not just in the notes.

18. When a company changes to the last-in, first-out (LIFO) method of inventory valuation, there is no restatement of prior years' income because

A. Restatement would be impracticable.

B. Restatement would reduce the usefulness of prior-period statements.

C. Restatement would not change the reported result.

D. Restatement would reduce prior years' income.

The correct answer is (A). *(CIA, adapted)*

REQUIRED: The reason for not restating prior years' income for a change to LIFO.

DISCUSSION: Restatement may be impracticable for a change to LIFO because determining the LIFO inventory valuation retroactively may not be feasible. Information concerning the composition of inventory throughout the history of the entity, as well as all individual unit prices, usually cannot be reconstructed. Accordingly, a change to LIFO may result in no recognition of the cumulative effect of the change. Disclosure is limited to showing the effect on current results and to an explanation of the reason for omitting accounting for the cumulative effect (APB 20).

Answer (B) is incorrect because prior-period and current statements would be more comparable if the latter were restated. Answer (C) is incorrect because restatement is likely to change reported results. Answer (D) is incorrect because restatement could decrease, increase, or not change prior years' income.

19. An example of an item that should be reported as a prior-period adjustment in a company's annual financial statements is

A. A settlement resulting from litigation.

B. An adjustment of income taxes.

C. A correction of an error that occurred in a prior period.

D. An adjustment of utility revenue because of rate revisions ordered by a regulatory commission.

The correct answer is (C). *(CMA, adapted)*

REQUIRED: The item that should be treated as a prior-period adjustment.

DISCUSSION: The correction of an error in the financial statements of a prior period is accounted for and reported as a prior-period adjustment and excluded from the determination of net income for the current period (SFAS 16, *Prior Period Adjustments*).

Answers (A), (B), and (D) are incorrect because, under SFAS 16, these items are prior interim (not annual) period adjustments.

20. According to APB 20, *Accounting Changes*, a change in the liability for warranty costs requires

A. Presenting prior-period financial statements as previously reported.

B. Presenting the effect of pro forma data on income and earnings per share for all prior periods presented.

C. Reporting an adjustment to the beginning retained earnings balance in the statement of retained earnings.

D. Reporting current and future financial statements on the new basis.

The correct answer is (D). *(CMA, adapted)*

REQUIRED: The accounting treatment of a change in the liability for warranty costs.

DISCUSSION: A change in the liability is merely a change in an estimate; it is not a change in principle. APB 20 requires changes in estimate to be accounted for prospectively, that is, in the current and future periods. The cumulative effect of the change is not recognized in the income statement, and retroactive adjustment of the financial statements is not permitted.

Answer (A) is incorrect because prior-period statements are not adjusted for changes in estimates. Answer (B) is incorrect because APB 20 specifically prohibits the reporting of pro forma amounts for prior periods as a result of a change in estimate. Answer (C) is incorrect because only prior-period adjustments are accounted for through an adjustment of retained earnings.

21. According to APB 20, *Accounting Changes*, a change from the sum-of-the-years'-digits depreciation method to the straight-line depreciation method is an example of a(n)

A. Accounting estimate change.

B. Accounting principle change.

C. Error correction.

D. Prior-period adjustment.

The correct answer is (B). *(CMA, adapted)*

REQUIRED: The type of change typified by switching from sum-of-the-years'-digits depreciation to straight-line.

DISCUSSION: Switching depreciation methods is an ordinary change in accounting principle. Such changes are accounted for by using the new principle in the period of change and by recognizing the cumulative effect of the change for all prior periods as the last item in the income statement (before per-share amounts).

Answer (A) is incorrect because a change in the life of a depreciable asset is an example of a change in estimate. Answer (C) is incorrect because changing from one generally accepted method to another is not an error correction. Answer (D) is incorrect because only error corrections result in prior-period adjustments.

22. Items reported as prior-period adjustments

A. Do not include the effect of a mistake in the application of accounting principles as this is accounted for as a change in accounting principle rather than as a prior-period adjustment.

B. Do not affect the presentation of prior-period comparative financial statements.

C. Do not require further disclosure in the body of the financial statements.

D. Are reflected as adjustments of the opening balance of the retained earnings of the earliest period presented.

The correct answer is (D). *(CMA, adapted)*

REQUIRED: The true statement about items reported as prior-period adjustments.

DISCUSSION: Prior-period adjustments are made for the correction of errors. Prior-period adjustments reported in single-period statements are reflected as adjustments of the opening balance of retained earnings. According to APB 9, *Reporting the Results of Operations*, if comparative statements are presented, corresponding adjustments should be made to the amounts of net income (and its components) and retained earnings balances (as well as other affected balances) for all periods reported to reflect the retroactive application of the prior-period adjustments.

Answer (A) is incorrect because errors of any type are corrected by a prior-period adjustment. Answer (B) is incorrect because a prior-period adjustment will affect the presentation of prior-period comparative financial statements. Answer (C) is incorrect because prior-period adjustments should be fully disclosed in the notes or elsewhere in the financial statements.

23. According to APB 20, *Accounting Changes*, a change from the cash basis of accounting to the accrual basis for financial statement purposes requires

A. Retroactive treatment in the financial statements.

B. Prospective treatment in the financial statements.

C. An entry in the income statement recording the cumulative effect of the change.

D. Retroactive treatment on a pro forma basis only.

The correct answer is (A). *(CMA, adapted)*

REQUIRED: The proper treatment in the financial statements of a change from the cash to the accrual basis.

DISCUSSION: Presentation of financial statements in accordance with GAAP ordinarily requires use of the accrual basis. Accordingly, the change from the cash to the accrual basis was the correction of an error that necessitated a prior-period adjustment. In comparative financial statements, all prior periods affected by the prior-period adjustment should be restated (SFAS 16).

Answer (B) is incorrect because prospective treatment applies only to changes in estimates. Answer (C) is incorrect because an error correction requires retroactive treatment. Answer (D) is incorrect because retroactive treatment on a pro forma basis is not required.

24. In a review of the May 31, 2001 financial statements during the normal year-end closing process, it was discovered that the interest income accrual on Simpson Company's notes receivable was omitted. The amounts omitted were calculated as follows:

May 31, 2000	$ 91,800
May 31, 2001	100,200

The May 31, 2001 entry to correct for these errors, ignoring the effect of income taxes, includes a

A. Credit to retained earnings for $91,800.

B. Credit to interest revenue for $91,800.

C. Debit to interest revenue for $100,200.

D. Credit to interest receivable for $100,200.

The correct answer is (A). *(CMA, adapted)*

REQUIRED: The entry to correct the failure to accrue interest income at the end of the preceding year.

DISCUSSION: SFAS 16 requires prior-period adjustments (error corrections) to be accounted for through retained earnings, not the income statement. Thus, the beginning balance of retained earnings should be credited for revenue that was erroneously not accrued in a prior period. The amount of the credit at May 31, 2001 is $91,800 (2000 accrued interest revenue).

Answer (B) is incorrect because the prior-period adjustment is to retained earnings. Answer (C) is incorrect because the 2001 credit to interest revenue is $100,200. Answer (D) is incorrect because $100,200 is debited to interest receivable.

25. While preparing its 2000 financial statements, Dek Corp. discovered computational errors in its 1999 and 1998 depreciation expense. These errors resulted in overstatement of each year's income by $25,000, net of income taxes. The following amounts were reported in the previously issued financial statements:

	1999	1998
Retained earnings, 1/1	$700,000	$500,000
Net income	150,000	200,000
Retained earnings, 12/31	$850,000	$700,000

Dek's 2000 net income is correctly reported at $180,000. Which of the following amounts should be reported as prior-period adjustments and net income in Dek's 2000 and 1999 comparative financial statements?

	Year	Prior-Period Adjustment	Net Income
A.	1999	--	$150,000
	2000	$(50,000)	180,000
B.	1999	$(50,000)	$150,000
	2000	—	180,000
C.	1999	$(25,000)	$125,000
	2000	--	180,000
D.	1999	--	$125,000
	2000	--	180,000

The correct answer is (C). *(CPA, adapted)*

REQUIRED: The amounts that should be reported as prior-period adjustments and net income in comparative financial statements.

DISCUSSION: A prior-period adjustment is necessary to correct an error. In the comparative financial statements presented for 1999 and 2000, all prior periods affected by the prior-period adjustment should be restated to reflect the adjustment. Consequently, the beginning balance of retained earnings for 1999 should be debited to correct the $25,000 overstatement of after-tax income for 1998, a year for which financial statements are not presented. Because the statements for 1999 should be restated to reflect the correction of the error in 1999 net income, this amount will be correctly reported in the 2000 and 1999 comparative financial statements as $125,000 ($150,000 in the previously issued 1999 statements – $25,000 overstatement). No prior-period adjustment to the 2000 financial statements is necessary. The 1999 statements, including the ending retained earnings balance, will have been revised to correct the errors. Hence, the 2000 beginning retained earnings (1999 ending retained earnings) will need no further revision.

Answer (A) is incorrect because 1999 net income is $125,000, and the prior-period adjustment is made to the beginning balance of retained earnings for 1999. Answer (B) is incorrect because the prior-period adjustment is for $25,000 (the overstatement of 1998 net income). Answer (D) is incorrect because a prior-period adjustment must be made in the 1999 statements.

26. Separate disclosure in the statement of retained earnings would be required for

A. Repurchase and cancellation of long-term debt at an amount different from its carrying value.

B. An extraordinary loss.

C. Resale of treasury stock at an amount greater than the price at which it was purchased.

D. Discovery that estimated warranty expense for machines sold last year was recorded twice.

The correct answer is (D). *(CMA, adapted)*

REQUIRED: The item that would be separately disclosed in the retained earnings statement.

DISCUSSION: The only items that appear on a retained earnings statement are dividends, net income, and prior-period adjustments. Prior-period adjustments are essentially defined as clerical errors. Thus, the discovery that estimated warranty expense had been recorded twice would result in a prior-period adjustment.

Answers (A) and (B) are incorrect because they would appear on the income statement. Answer (C) is incorrect because the resale of treasury stock at a price greater than cost would result in a credit to a paid-in capital account, not to retained earnings. Thus, this transaction would not appear on the retained earnings statement.

27. The failure to record an accrued expense at year-end will result in which of the following overstatement errors in the financial statements prepared at that date?

	Net Income	Working Capital	Cash
A.	No	No	Yes
B.	No	Yes	No
C.	Yes	No	No
D.	Yes	Yes	No

The correct answer is (D). *(CIA, adapted)*

REQUIRED: The overstatement errors resulting from the failure to record an accrued expense at year-end.

DISCUSSION: An accrued expense is an expense that has been incurred but not paid. The appropriate adjusting entry to record an accrued expense will increase an expense account and increase a liability account. The failure to record an accrued expense will result in an understatement of expenses leading to an overstatement of net income. The failure to record the increase in a liability account will result in an understatement of current liabilities leading to an overstatement of working capital. There will be no effect on cash.

Answer (A) is incorrect because the failure to record an accrued expense will result in an overstatement of net income and an overstatement of working capital, and will have no effect on cash. Answer (B) is incorrect because the failure to record an accrued expense will result in an overstatement of net income. Answer (C) is incorrect because the failure to record an accrued expense will result in an overstatement of working capital.

28. If ending inventory is underestimated due to an error in the physical count of items on hand, the cost of goods sold for the period will be <List A>, and net earnings will be <List B>.

	List A	List B
A.	Underestimated	Underestimated
B.	Underestimated	Overestimated
C.	Overestimated	Underestimated
D.	Overestimated	Overestimated

The correct answer is (C). *(CIA, adapted)*

REQUIRED: The effect on cost of goods sold and net earnings when ending inventory is underestimated.

DISCUSSION: Cost of goods sold equals beginning inventory, plus purchases, minus ending inventory. If the ending inventory is underestimated, the cost of goods sold will be overestimated. If cost of goods sold is overestimated, net earnings will be underestimated.

Answer (A) is incorrect because the cost of goods sold will be overestimated. Answer (B) is incorrect because the cost of goods sold will be overestimated, and net earnings will be underestimated. Answer (D) is incorrect because net earnings will be underestimated.

29. Suppose that a company pays one of its liabilities twice during the year, in error. What are the effects of this mistake?

A. Assets, liabilities, and owners' equity will be understated.

B. Assets, net income, and owners' equity will be unaffected.

C. Assets and liabilities will be understated.

D. Assets and net income and owners' equity will be understated, and liabilities will be overstated.

The correct answer is (C). *(CIA, adapted)*

REQUIRED: The effects of paying a liability twice.

DISCUSSION: When a liability is paid, an entry debiting accounts payable and crediting cash is made. If a company erroneously pays a liability twice, the accounts payable and cash accounts will be understated by the amount of the liability. Hence, assets and liabilities will be understated.

Answer (A) is incorrect because the double payment of a liability does not affect expenses of the period, so it does not affect net income and owners' equity. Answer (B) is incorrect because assets will be reduced. Answer (D) is incorrect because both assets and liabilities will be understated, whereas net income and owners' equity will be unaffected.

30. Which of the following errors is not self-correcting over two accounting periods?

A. Failure to record accrued wages.

B. Failure to record depreciation.

C. Overstatement of inventory.

D. Failure to record prepaid expenses.

The correct answer is (B). *(CIA, adapted)*

REQUIRED: The error that is not self-correcting over two accounting periods.

DISCUSSION: A failure to record depreciation must be corrected as it does not correct itself over two periods. It is a noncounterbalancing error.

Answer (A) is incorrect because a failure to record accrued wages will correct itself when the wages are paid in the following period and represents a counterbalancing error. Answer (C) is incorrect because the overstatement of inventory will correct itself over two periods and is therefore a counterbalancing error. Answer (D) is incorrect because a failure to record prepaid expenses will correct itself in the next period when the prepaid expense is consumed and is therefore a counterbalancing error.

31. A company had sales in both 2000 and 2001 of $100,000. Cost of sales for 2000 was $70,000. In computing cost of sales for 2000, an item of inventory purchased in 2000 for $50 was incorrectly written down to current replacement cost of $35. The item is currently selling in 2001 for $100, its normal selling price. As a result of this error,

A. Income for 2000 is overstated.

B. Cost of sales for 2001 will be overstated.

C. Income for 2001 will be overstated.

D. Income for 2001 will be unaffected.

The correct answer is (C). *(Publisher)*

REQUIRED: The effect of an inventory understatement.

DISCUSSION: The effect of erroneously writing down inventory is to understate inventory at the end of 2000. The understatement of ending inventory causes cost of goods sold to be overstated in 2000. The overstatement of cost of goods sold in turn causes 2000 income to be understated. The understatement of 2001 beginning inventory causes cost of goods sold to be understated and income to be overstated in 2001.

Answer (A) is incorrect because 2000 income is understated as a result of the understatement of ending inventory. Answer (B) is incorrect because the understatement of 2000 ending inventory results in understated 2001 beginning inventory and understated 2001 cost of sales. Answer (D) is incorrect because the 2001 income will be overstated due to the understatement of beginning inventory.

D. Earnings per Share (EPS)

Questions 32 through 38 are based on the following information. Pubco is a public company that uses a calendar year and has a complex capital structure. In the computation of its basic and diluted earnings per share (BEPS and DEPS, respectively) in accordance with SFAS 128, *Earnings per Share*, Pubco uses income before extraordinary items as the control number. Pubco reported no cumulative effect of accounting changes or discontinued operations, but it had an extraordinary loss (net of tax) of $1,200,000 in the first quarter when its income before the extraordinary item was $1,000,000.

The average market price of Pubco's common stock for the first quarter was $25, the shares outstanding at the beginning of the period equaled 300,000, and 12,000 shares were issued on March 1.

At the beginning of the quarter, Pubco had outstanding $2,000,000 of 5% convertible bonds, with each $1,000 bond convertible into 10 shares of common stock. No bonds were converted.

At the beginning of the quarter, Pubco also had outstanding 120,000 shares of preferred stock paying a quarterly dividend of $.10 per share and convertible to common stock on a one-to-one basis. Holders of 60,000 shares of preferred stock exercised their conversion privilege on February 1.

Throughout the first quarter, warrants to buy 50,000 shares of Pubco's common stock for $28 per share were outstanding but unexercised.

Pubco's tax rate was 30%.

32. The weighted-average number of shares used to calculate BEPS amounts for the first quarter is

A. 444,000

B. 372,000

C. 344,000

D. 300,000

The correct answer is (C). *(Publisher)*

REQUIRED: The weighted-average number of shares used to calculate BEPS amounts for the first quarter.

DISCUSSION: The number of shares outstanding at January 1 was 300,000, 12,000 shares were issued on March 1, and 60,000 shares of preferred stock were converted to 60,000 shares of common stock on February 1. Thus, the weighted-average number of shares used to calculate BEPS amounts for the first quarter is 344,000 {300,000 + [12,000 x (1 ÷ 3)] + [60,000 x (2 ÷ 3)]}.

Answer (A) is incorrect because 444,000 is the adjusted weighted-average number of shares used in the DEPS calculation. Answer (B) is incorrect because 372,000 is the total outstanding at March 31. Answer (D) is incorrect because 300,000 equals the shares outstanding at January 1.

33. The control number for determining whether potential common shares are dilutive or antidilutive is

A. $1,000,000

B. $994,000

C. $(206,000)

D. $(1,200,000)

The correct answer is (B). *(Publisher)*

REQUIRED: The control number for determining whether potential common shares are dilutive or antidilutive.

DISCUSSION: If a company reports discontinued operations, extraordinary items, or accounting changes, it uses income from continuing operations (in Pubco's case, income before extraordinary item), adjusted for preferred dividends, as the control number for determining whether potential common shares are dilutive or antidilutive. Hence, the number of potential common shares used in calculating DEPS for income from continuing operations is also used in calculating the other DEPS amounts even if the effect is antidilutive with respect to the corresponding BEPS amounts. However, if the entity has a loss from continuing operations available to common shareholders, no potential common shares are included in the calculation of any DEPS amount (SFAS 128). The control number for Pubco is $994,000 {$1,000,000 income before extraordinary item – [$.10 per share dividend x (120,000 preferred shares – 60,000 preferred shares converted)]}.

Answer (A) is incorrect because $1,000,000 is unadjusted income from continuing operations. Answer (C) is incorrect because $(206,000) is the net loss available to common shareholders after subtracting the extraordinary loss. Answer (D) is incorrect because $(1,200,000) is the extraordinary loss.

34. The BEPS amount for the net income or loss available to common shareholders after the extraordinary item is

A. $2.89

B. $(0.46)

C. $(0.60)

D. $(3.49)

The correct answer is (C). *(Publisher)*

REQUIRED: The BEPS amount for the net income or loss available to common shareholders after the extraordinary item.

DISCUSSION: The weighted-average of shares used in the BEPS denominator is 344,000. The numerator equals income before extraordinary item, minus preferred dividends, minus the extraordinary loss. Thus, it equals the control number minus the extraordinary loss, or $(206,000) [$994,000 – $1,200,000]. The BEPS amount for the net income or loss available to common shareholders after the extraordinary item is $(0.60) [$(206,000) ÷ 344,000 shares].

Answer (A) is incorrect because $2.89 is the BEPS amount for income available to common shareholders before the extraordinary item. Answer (B) is incorrect because $(0.46) uses the denominator of the DEPS calculation. Answer (D) is incorrect because $(3.49) is the BEPS amount for the extraordinary loss.

35. The difference between BEPS and DEPS for the extraordinary item is

A. $2.89

B. $2.10

C. $.79

D. $.60

The correct answer is (C). *(Publisher)*

REQUIRED: The difference between BEPS and DEPS for the extraordinary item.

DISCUSSION: BEPS for the extraordinary loss is $(3.49) [$(1,200,000) ÷ 344,000]. DEPS for the extraordinary item is $(2.70) [$(1,200,000) ÷ 444,000 shares].

Answer (A) is incorrect because $2.89 is the difference between DEPS and BEPS for the extraordinary loss. Answer (B) is incorrect because $2.10 is the difference between DEPS for the extraordinary loss and the BEPS for the net loss available to common shareholders after the extraordinary loss. Answer (D) is incorrect because $.60 is the BEPS for the net loss available to common shareholders after the extraordinary loss.

36. The weighted-average number of shares used to calculate DEPS amounts for the first quarter is

A. 444,000

B. 438,000

C. 372,000

D. 344,000

The correct answer is (A). *(Publisher)*

REQUIRED: The weighted-average number of shares used to calculate DEPS amounts for the first quarter.

DISCUSSION: The denominator of DEPS equals the weighted-average number of shares used in the BEPS calculation (344,000) plus dilutive potential common shares (assuming the control number is not a loss). The incremental shares from assumed conversion of warrants is zero because they are antidilutive. The $25 market price is less than the $28 exercise price. The assumed conversion of all the preferred shares at the beginning of the quarter results in 80,000 incremental shares {[120,000 shares x (3 ÷ 3)] – [60,000 shares x (2 ÷ 3)]}. The assumed conversion of all the bonds at the beginning of the quarter results in 20,000 incremental shares [($2,000,000 ÷ $1,000 per bond) x 10 common shares per bond]. Consequently, the weighted-average number of shares used to calculate DEPS amounts for the first quarter is 444,000 (344,000 + 0 + 80,000 + 20,000).

Answer (B) is incorrect because 438,000 assumes the hypothetical exercise of all the warrants at the beginning of the period at a price of $28 and the repurchase of shares using the proceeds at a price of $25. Answer (C) is incorrect because 372,000 is the total outstanding at March 31. Answer (D) is incorrect because 344,000 is the denominator of the BEPS fraction.

37. Refer to the information preceding question 32 on page 326. The effect of assumed conversions on the numerator of the DEPS fraction is

A. $31,000

B. $25,000

C. $23,500

D. $17,500

The correct answer is (C). *(Publisher)*

REQUIRED: The effect of assumed conversions on the numerator of the DEPS fraction.

DISCUSSION: If all of the convertible preferred shares are assumed to be converted on January 1, $6,000 of dividends [$.10 x (120,000 – 60,000) preferred shares] will not be paid. Furthermore, if the bonds are assumed to be converted on January 1, interest of $17,500 {[5% x $2,000,000 ÷ 4] x (1.0 – .3 tax rate)} will not be paid. Accordingly, the effect of assumed conversions on the numerator of the DEPS fraction is an addition of $23,500 ($6,000 + $17,500) to the income available to common shareholders.

Answer (A) is incorrect because $31,000 disregards the tax shield provided by bond interest. Answer (B) is incorrect because $25,000 equals one quarter's bond interest payment. Answer (D) is incorrect because $17,500 is the effect of the assumed conversion of the bonds alone.

38. Refer to the information preceding question 32 on page 326. The DEPS amount for the net income or loss available to common shareholders after the extraordinary item is

A. $2.29

B. $(0.41)

C. $(0.53)

D. $(2.70)

The correct answer is (B). *(Publisher)*

REQUIRED: The DEPS amount for the net income or loss available to common shareholders.

DISCUSSION: The numerator equals the income available to common shareholders (the control number), plus the effect of the assumed conversions, minus the extraordinary loss. The denominator equals the weighted average of shares outstanding plus the dilutive potential common shares. Hence, the DEPS amount for the net income or loss available to common shareholders after the extraordinary item is $(.41) [($994,000 + $23,500 – $1,200,000) ÷ 444,000].

Answer (A) is incorrect because $2.29 is the DEPS amount for income before the extraordinary item. Answer (C) is incorrect because $(0.53) is based on the BEPS denominator. Answer (D) is incorrect because $(2.70) is the DEPS for the extraordinary item.

Questions 39 through 42 are based on the following information. Spark Automotive uses a calendar year for financial reporting. The company is authorized to issue 10 million shares of $10 par common stock. At no time has Spark issued any potential common stock. Listed below is a summary of Spark's common stock activities:

- Number of common shares issued and outstanding at December 31, 1998 = 2,000,000 shares.
- Shares issued as a result of a 10% stock dividend on September 30, 1999 = 200,000 shares.
- Shares issued for cash on March 31, 2000 = 2,000,000 shares.
- Number of common shares issued and outstanding at December 31, 2000 = 4,200,000 shares.

A two-for-one stock split of Spark's common stock took place on March 31, 2001.

---

39. The weighted-average number of common shares used in computing basic earnings per common share for 1999 on the 2000 comparative income statement was

A. 2,200,000

B. 2,100,000

C. 2,050,000

D. 4,200,000

The correct answer is (A). *(Publisher)*

REQUIRED: The weighted-average number of shares used in computing basic earnings per common share for 1999 on the 2000 comparative income statement.

DISCUSSION: There were 2 million shares outstanding at the beginning of 1999. Another 200,000 were issued as a result of a stock dividend on September 30. Because a stock dividend merely divides existing shares into more pieces, the dividend is assumed to have occurred at the beginning of the year. Thus, on the 1999 income statement, the number of shares outstanding throughout the year would have been 2.2 million. No subsequent changes were made in those 2.2 million shares in 2000 (no stock dividends or stock splits). Consequently, the comparative statements for 1999 and 2000 will report basic earnings per share using the same weighted-average number of common shares for 1999 as the 1999 income statement.

Answers (B) and (C) are incorrect because no weighting is required. Common stock outstanding during 1999 did not change as a result of 2000 transactions. Answer (D) is incorrect because the stock split does not occur until 2001.

40. The weighted-average number of common shares used in computing basic earnings per common share for 2000 on the 2000 comparative income statement was

A. 3,150,000

B. 3,700,000

C. 4,200,000

D. 7,400,000

The correct answer is (B). *(Publisher)*

REQUIRED: The weighted-average number of shares used in computing basic EPS for 2000 on the 2000 income statement.

DISCUSSION: At the beginning of 2000, 2.2 million shares were outstanding. This figure remained unchanged for 3 months until March 31 when an additional 2 million shares were issued. Thus, for the last 9 months of the year, 4.2 million shares were outstanding. Hence, the weighted-average number of shares outstanding throughout the year was 3,700,000 {[2,200,000 x (3 ÷ 12)] + [4,200,000 x (9 ÷ 12)]}.

Answer (A) is incorrect because 3,150,000 is the weight assigned to 4,200,000 shares for 9 months. Answer (C) is incorrect because 4,200,000 shares were not outstanding during the first 3 months of the year. Answer (D) is incorrect because the stock split did not occur until the following year.

41. The weighted-average number of common shares to be used in computing basic earnings per common share for 2000 on the 2001 comparative income statement is

A. 3,700,000

B. 4,200,000

C. 7,400,000

D. 8,400,000

The correct answer is (C). *(Publisher)*

REQUIRED: The weighted-average number of common shares to be used in computing basic EPS for 2000 on the 2001 comparative income statement.

DISCUSSION: The number of shares used in computing the 2000 basic EPS on the 2000 income statement was 3.7 million (see solution to previous question). However, because of the stock split on March 31, 2001, those shares were doubled. Thus, the basic EPS calculation for 2000 on the 2001 comparative income statement is 7.4 million shares (2 x 3,700,000 shares).

Answer (A) is incorrect because 3,700,000 is the number of shares used on the 2000 income statement. Answers (B) and (D) are incorrect because the shares outstanding must be weighted. The full 4,200,000 shares were not outstanding during the first 3 months of 2000.

42. Refer to the information at the bottom of page 328. The weighted-average number of common shares to be used in computing basic earnings per common share for 2001 on the 2001 comparative income statement is

A. 4,200,000

B. 6,300,000

C. 7,350,000

D. 8,400,000

The correct answer is (D). *(Publisher)*

REQUIRED: The weighted-average number of shares used in computing basic EPS for 2001 on the 2001 comparative income statement.

DISCUSSION: At the beginning of 2001, 4.2 million shares were outstanding. However, the March 31 stock split increased that number to 8.4 million. Because a stock split is assumed to have occurred on the first day of the year, the number of shares outstanding throughout 2001 is 8.4 million.

Answer (A) is incorrect because 4,200,000 does not consider the stock split. Answers (B) and (C) are incorrect because stock splits do not require a weighting of the shares outstanding; stock splits and stock dividends are assumed to have occurred on the first day of the fiscal year.

Questions 43 through 45 are based on the following information. Peters Corp.'s capital structure was as follows:

	December 31 1999	December 31 2000
Outstanding shares of stock:		
Common	100,000	100,000
Convertible preferred	10,000	10,000
9% convertible bonds	$1,000,000	$1,000,000

During 2000, Peters paid dividends of $3.00 per share on its preferred stock. The preferred shares are convertible into 20,000 shares of common stock, and the 9% bonds are convertible into 30,000 shares of common stock. Assume that the income tax rate is 30%.

43. If net income for 2000 is $350,000, Peters should report DEPS as

A. $3.20

B. $2.95

C. $2.92

D. $2.75

The correct answer is (D). *(CPA, adapted)*

REQUIRED: The DEPS, given convertible preferred stock and convertible bonds outstanding and net income of $350,000.

DISCUSSION: Potential common stock is included in the calculation of DEPS if it is dilutive. When two or more issues of potential common stock are outstanding, each issue is considered separately in sequence, from the most to the least dilutive. This procedure is necessary because a convertible security may be dilutive on its own, but antidilutive when included with other potential common shares in the calculation of DEPS.

The incremental effect on EPS determines the degree of dilution. The lower the incremental effect, the more dilutive. The incremental effect of the convertible preferred stock is $1.50 [($3 preferred dividend x 10,000) ÷ 20,000 potential common shares]. The incremental effect of the convertible debt is $2.10 {[$1,000,000 x 9% x (1.0 – 30%)] ÷ 30,000 potential common shares}. Because the $1.50 incremental effect of the convertible preferred is lower, it is the more dilutive, and its incremental effect is compared with the BEPS amount, which equals $3.20 [($350,000 – $30,000) ÷ 100,000]. Because $1.50 is lower than $3.20, the convertible preferred is dilutive and is included in a trial calculation of DEPS. The result is $2.92 [($350,000 – $30,000 + $30,000) ÷ (100,000 + 20,000)]. However, the $2.10 incremental effect of the convertible debt is lower than the $2.92 trial calculation, so the convertible debt is also dilutive and should be included in the calculation of DEPS. Thus, the DEPS amount is $2.75 as indicated below.

$$\frac{\$350{,}000 - \$30{,}000 + \$30{,}000 + \$63{,}000}{100{,}000 + 20{,}000 + 30{,}000} = \$2.75$$

Answer (A) is incorrect because $3.20 equals BEPS. Answer (B) is incorrect because $2.95 excludes the convertible preferred stock. Answer (C) is incorrect because $2.92 excludes the convertible debt.

44. If net income for 2000 is $245,000, Peters should report DEPS as

A. $2.15

B. $2.14

C. $2.05

D. $2.04

The correct answer is (D). *(Publisher)*

REQUIRED: The DEPS, given convertible preferred stock and convertible debt outstanding and net income of $245,000.

DISCUSSION: As calculated in question 38, the incremental effect of the convertible preferred is $1.50 and of the convertible debt is $2.10. Given net income of $245,000, the BEPS amount equals $2.15 [($245,000 – $30,000) ÷ 100,000]. The $1.50 incremental effect of the convertible preferred stock is lower than BEPS, so it is dilutive and should be included in a trial calculation of DEPS. The result is $2.04 [($245,000 – $30,000 + $30,000) ÷ (100,000 + 20,000)]. Because the $2.10 incremental effect of the convertible debt is higher than $2.04, the convertible debt is antidilutive and should not be included in the DEPS calculation. Thus, DEPS should be reported as $2.04.

Answer (A) is incorrect because $2.15 equals BEPS. Answer (B) is incorrect because $2.14 excludes the convertible preferred stock. Answer (C) is incorrect because $2.05 includes the convertible debt.

45. If net income for 2000 is $170,000, Peters should report DEPS as

A. $1.40

B. $1.42

C. $1.55

D. $1.70

The correct answer is (A). *(Publisher)*

REQUIRED: The DEPS, given convertible preferred stock and convertible debt outstanding and net income of $170,000.

DISCUSSION: Given net income of $170,000, the BEPS amount equals $1.40 [($170,000 – $30,000) ÷ 100,000]. This amount is lower than both the $2.10 incremental effect of the convertible debt and the $1.50 incremental effect of the convertible preferred. Thus, both convertible securities are antidilutive, and Peters should report that DEPS is equal to BEPS. This dual presentation can be presented in one line on the income statement.

Answer (B) is incorrect because $1.42 includes the convertible preferred stock. Answer (C) is incorrect because $1.56 includes the convertible debt. Answer (D) is incorrect because $1.70 results from not adjusting the $170,000 of net income for the $30,000 of preferred dividends when determining income available to common shareholders.

E. Early Extinguishment of Debt

46. A liability may be derecognized in the financial statements in all of the following situations except

A. The debtor pays off the obligation with financial assets (other than cash) and is relieved of its obligation for the liability.

B. The debtor places purchased securities into an irrevocable trust and uses the principal and interest to pay off the liability as it matures.

C. The judicial system legally releases the debtor from being the primary obligor of the liability.

D. The debtor reacquires the outstanding debt from the creditor and holds the securities as treasury bonds.

The correct answer is (B). *(Publisher)*

REQUIRED: The situation in which a liability cannot be derecognized in the financial statements.

DISCUSSION: SFAS 140 does not allow the debtor to derecognize a liability unless the liability is considered extinguished. A liability is extinguished if either of the following conditions is met: (1) The debtor pays the creditor and is relieved of its obligation for the liability, or (2) the debtor is legally released from being the primary obligor of the liability, either judicially or by the creditor. Creating an irrevocable trust and using the proceeds (principal and interest) to pay off the debt securities as they mature is called "in-substance defeasance." In-substance defeasance does not meet the derecognition criteria. First, the debtor is not legally released as the primary obligor of the liability. Second, the debtor has not been relieved of its obligation for the liability because the creditor has not been paid. In many cases, the creditor is not even aware that the trust has been created.

Answers (A) and (D) are incorrect because paying the creditor includes the delivery of cash, other financial assets, goods, or services or the reacquisition of the outstanding debt securities whether the securities are canceled or held as so-called treasury bonds. Answer (C) is incorrect because a debtor may be legally released as the primary obligor of the liability either judicially or by the creditor.

47. An entity should not derecognize an existing liability under which of the following circumstances?

A. The entity exchanges convertible preferred stock for its outstanding debt securities. The debt securities are not canceled but are held as treasury bonds.

B. Because of financial difficulties being experienced by the entity, a creditor accepts a parcel of land as full satisfaction of an overdue loan. The value of the land is less than 50% of the loan balance.

C. The entity irrevocably places cash into a trust that will be used solely to satisfy scheduled principal and interest payments of a specific bond obligation. Because the trust investments will generate a higher return, the amount of cash is less than the carrying amount of the debt.

D. As part of the agreement to purchase a shopping center from the entity, the buyer assumes without recourse the mortgage for which the center serves as collateral.

The correct answer is (C). *(Publisher)*

REQUIRED: The circumstances under which an existing liability should not be derecognized.

DISCUSSION: SFAS 140, *Accounting for Transfers and Servicing of Financial Assets and Extinguishments of Liabilities*, prescribes the derecognition of a liability only if it has been extinguished. Extinguishment occurs when either (1) the debtor pays the creditor and is relieved of its obligation for the liability, or (2) the debtor is legally released from being the primary obligor under the liability, either judicially or by the creditor.

Answers (A), (B), and (D) are incorrect because they describe the circumstances under which debt may be extinguished.

48. According to SFAS 4, *Reporting Gains and Losses from Extinguishment of Debt*, gains or losses from extinguishment of debt should be aggregated and, if material, classified in the income statement as an extraordinary item, net of related income tax effect. Which one of the following types of extinguishments would not be classified as an extraordinary item?

A. Extinguishment of debt at more than the net carrying amount.

B. Cash purchases of debt made to satisfy current sinking-fund requirements.

C. Refinancing existing debt with new debt.

D. Extinguishment of debt at less than the net carrying amount.

The correct answer is (B). *(CMA, adapted)*

REQUIRED: The type of extinguishment not classified as an extraordinary item.

DISCUSSION: Extinguishment of debt may arise from the reacquisition of debt instruments. Gains or losses from early extinguishment are customarily treated as extraordinary. However, SFAS 64 emphasizes that gains and losses on early extinguishments made to satisfy current (due within 1 year) sinking-fund requirements are not extraordinary.

Answers (A) and (D) are incorrect because gains or losses from extinguishments at more or less than carrying value are treated as extraordinary under SFAS 4. Answer (C) is incorrect because APB 26 and SFAS 4 state that gains or losses on refinancing are treated as extraordinary.

49. On December 1, 1998, Catfish Company issued its 10%, $2 million face value bonds for $2.3 million. Interest is payable on November 1 and May 1. On December 31, 2000, the book value of the bonds, inclusive of the unamortized premium, was $2.1 million. On July 1, 2001, Catfish reacquired the bonds at 97, plus accrued interest. Catfish appropriately uses the straight-line method of amortization. The gain on Catfish's extinguishment of debt is

A. $48,000

B. $52,000

C. $112,000

D. $160,000

The correct answer is (C). *(Publisher)*

REQUIRED: The gain on extinguishment of debt.

DISCUSSION: The gain is the difference in carrying (book) value at the date of extinguishment and the price paid. As of December 31, 2000, the bonds had been outstanding 25 months. Since $200,000 ($2.3 million – $2.1 million) had been amortized over those 25 months, the straight-line rate is apparently $8,000 per month ($200,000 ÷ 25 months). Therefore, during the first half of 2001, an additional $48,000 (6 x $8,000) would be amortized, leaving a book value of $2,052,000. Subtracting the $1,940,000 (97% x $2 million) from the $2,052,000 carrying value results in a gain of $112,000.

Answer (A) is incorrect because $48,000 is the amortization for the final 6 months. Answer (B) is incorrect because $52,000 is the unamortized premium on July 1, 2001; it would be the gain if the bonds had been purchased at face value. Answer (D) is incorrect because $160,000 is the result of including the amount to be amortized during the first half of the year into the gain.

50. When reporting gains and losses from extinguishment of debt that are treated as extraordinary items, all of the following disclosures on the face of, or in the notes to, the financial statements are required except

A. A description of the extinguishment transactions, including the sources, if practicable, of the cash used to extinguish the debt.

B. The interest expense that would have been recorded in the period ignoring extinguishment.

C. The income tax effect in the period of extinguishment.

D. The per-share amount of the aggregate gain or loss, net of related tax effect.

The correct answer is (B). *(CMA, adapted)*

REQUIRED: The disclosure not required with respect to extraordinary gains and losses from extinguishment of debt.

DISCUSSION: APB 26, *Early Extinguishment of Debt*, as amended by SFAS 4, *Reporting Gains and Losses from Extinguishment of Debt*, requires that gains or losses on early extinguishment of debt be reported as extraordinary items. However, no pronouncement requires that interest expense avoided be disclosed.

Answers (A), (C), and (D) are incorrect because SFAS 4 requires disclosure of a description of the extinguishment transactions, including the sources, if practicable, of the cash used to extinguish the debt, the income tax effect in the period of extinguishment, and the per-share amount of the aggregate gain or loss, net of related tax effect.

51. On January 2, 2001, Wright Corporation entered into an in-substance debt defeasance transaction by placing cash of $875,000 into an irrevocable trust. The trust assets are to be used solely for satisfying the interest and principal payments on Wright's 6%, $1,100,000, 30-year bond payable. Wright has not been legally released under the bond agreement, but the probability is remote that Wright will be required to place additional cash in the trust. On December 31, 2000, the bond's carrying amount was $1,050,000 and its fair value was $800,000. Disregarding income taxes, what amount of extraordinary gain (loss) should Wright report in its 2001 income statement?

A. $(75,000)

B. $0

C. $175,000

D. $225,000

The correct answer is (B). *(Publisher)*

REQUIRED: The amount of extraordinary gain (loss) to be recognized on an in-substance defeasance.

DISCUSSION: SFAS 140 prohibits the recognition of a gain (loss) from an in-substance defeasance.

Answers (A), (C), and (D) are incorrect because an in-substance defeasance does not result in the derecognition of a liability.

F. Foreign Currency Issues

52. SFAS 52, *Foreign Currency Translation*, requires the application of the functional currency concept. Before the financial statements of a foreign subsidiary may be translated into the parent company's currency, the functional currency of the foreign subsidiary must be determined. All of the following factors indicate that a foreign subsidiary's functional currency is the foreign currency rather than the parent's currency except when

A. Its cash flows are primarily in foreign currency and do not affect the parent's cash flows.

B. Its sales prices are responsive to exchange rate changes and to international competition.

C. Its labor, material, and other costs are obtained in the local market of the foreign subsidiary.

D. Its financing is primarily obtained from local foreign sources and from the subsidiary's operations.

The correct answer is (B). *(CMA, adapted)*

REQUIRED: The factor not indicating that a foreign subsidiary's functional currency is the foreign currency rather than the parent's currency.

DISCUSSION: SFAS 52 states that the functional currency is that of the primary economic environment in which an entity operates. Thus, it is usually the currency in which cash is generated and expended by the entity whose financial statements are being translated. Indications that the subsidiary's currency is the functional currency include the following: Its cash flows are primarily in that foreign currency, they do not affect the parent's cash flows, labor and materials are obtained in the local market of the foreign subsidiary, subsidiary financing is obtained from local foreign sources and from the subsidiary's operations, and few intercompany transactions take place between the foreign subsidiary and the parent. However, sales prices that are responsive to exchange rate fluctuations and international competition suggest that the functional currency is the parent's currency.

Answers (A), (C), and (D) are incorrect because they are factors indicating that the functional currency is the foreign currency.

53. If an entity's books of account are not maintained in its functional currency, SFAS 52 requires remeasurement into the functional currency prior to the translation process. An item that should be remeasured by use of the current exchange rate is

A. An investment in bonds to be held until maturity.

B. A plant asset and the associated accumulated depreciation.

C. A patent and the associated accumulated amortization.

D. The revenue from a long-term construction contract.

The correct answer is (A). *(CMA, adapted)*

REQUIRED: The item that should be remeasured into the functional currency using the current exchange rate.

DISCUSSION: The current rate should be used for all items except common nonmonetary balance sheet accounts and their related revenues, expenses, gains, and losses, which are remeasured at historical rates. Thus, most monetary items, such as an investment in bonds, are remeasured at the current exchange rate.

Answer (B) is incorrect because plant assets are not monetary assets. They should be remeasured at historical rates. Answer (C) is incorrect because a patent is remeasured at historical rates. Answer (D) is incorrect because the revenue from a long-term construction contract is one of the exceptions for which the current rate is not to be used.

54. SFAS 52 requires that, in a highly inflationary economy, the financial statements of a foreign entity be remeasured as if the functional currency were the reporting currency. For this requirement, a highly inflationary economy is one that has

A. An inflation rate of at least 33% in the most recent past year.

B. An inflation rate of at least 50% in the most recent past year.

C. An inflation rate of at least 100% in the most recent past year.

D. A cumulative inflation rate of at least 100% over a 3-year period.

The correct answer is (D). *(CMA, adapted)*

REQUIRED: The definition of a highly inflationary economy.

DISCUSSION: SFAS 52 recognized that the currency in a highly inflationary economy is not stable enough to be a functional currency. Instead, the more stable currency of the parent corporation should be used as the functional currency. A highly inflationary economy has a cumulative inflation rate over a 3-year period of at least 100%.

Answers (A), (B), and (C) are incorrect because SFAS 52 specifies an inflation rate of at least 100% over a 3-year period.

55. SFAS 52 states that transaction gains and losses have direct cash flow effects when foreign-denominated monetary assets are settled in amounts greater or less than the functional currency equivalent of the original transactions. These transaction gains and losses should be reflected in income

A. At the date the transaction originated.

B. On a retroactive basis.

C. In the period the exchange rate changes.

D. Only at the year-end balance sheet date.

The correct answer is (C). *(CMA, adapted)*

REQUIRED: The time when foreign currency transaction gains and losses should be reflected in income.

DISCUSSION: A foreign currency transaction is one whose terms are denominated in a currency other than the entity's functional currency. When a foreign currency transaction gives rise to a receivable or a payable that is fixed in terms of the amount of foreign currency to be received or paid, a change in the exchange rate between the functional currency and the currency in which the transaction is denominated results in a gain or loss that ordinarily should be included as a component of income from continuing operations in the period in which the exchange rate changes.

Answer (A) is incorrect because the extent of any gain or loss cannot be known at the date of the original transaction. Answer (B) is incorrect because retroactive recognition is not permitted. Answer (D) is incorrect because gains and losses are recognized in the period of the rate change.

56. FASB 52, *Foreign Currency Translation*, defines foreign currency transactions as those denominated in other than an entity's functional currency. Transaction gains and losses are reported as

A. Extraordinary items.

B. Adjustments to the beginning balance of retained earnings.

C. A component of equity.

D. A component of income from continuing operations.

The correct answer is (D). *(CMA, adapted)*

REQUIRED: The proper treatment of foreign currency transaction gains (losses).

DISCUSSION: When a foreign currency transaction gives rise to a receivable or a payable, a change in the exchange rate between the measurement currency and the currency in which the transaction is denominated is a foreign currency transaction gain (loss) that should be included as a component of income from continuing operations.

Answer (A) is incorrect because transaction gains (losses) are not so unusual as to warrant extraordinary status. Answer (B) is incorrect because adjustments to retained earnings are made only for prior-period adjustments, and transaction gains (losses) do not meet the criteria for such treatment. Answer (C) is incorrect because foreign currency translation gains and losses (not transaction gains and losses) are reported in other comprehensive income, a component of equity.

57. On September 22, 2000, Yumi Corp. purchased merchandise from an unaffiliated foreign company for 10,000 units of the foreign company's local currency. On that date, the spot rate was $.55. Yumi paid the bill in full on March 20, 2001, when the spot rate was $.65. The spot rate was $.70 on December 31, 2000. What amount should Yumi report as a foreign currency transaction loss in its income statement for the year ended December 31, 2000?

A. $0

B. $500

C. $1,000

D. $1,500

The correct answer is (D). *(CPA, adapted)*

REQUIRED: The amount of foreign currency transaction loss to be reported in the income statement.

DISCUSSION: The FASB requires that a receivable or payable denominated in a foreign currency be adjusted to its current exchange rate at each balance sheet date. The resulting gain or loss should ordinarily be reflected in current income. It is the difference between the spot rate on the date the transaction originates and the spot rate at year-end. Thus, the 2000 transaction loss for Yumi Corp. is $1,500 [($0.55 – $0.70) x 10,000 units].

Answer (A) is incorrect because a loss resulted when the spot rate increased. Answer (B) is incorrect because $500 results from using the spot rates at 12/31/00 and 3/20/01. Answer (C) is incorrect because $1,000 results from using the spot rates at 9/22/00 and 3/20/01.

58. SFAS 52, *Foreign Currency Translation*, requires the use of different methods to translate or remeasure foreign currency financial statements. When the foreign affiliate's functional currency is not the reporting currency of the parent (or investor), the

A. Current/noncurrent method should be used to translate the foreign affiliate's financial statements.

B. Monetary/nonmonetary method should be used to translate the foreign affiliate's financial statements.

C. Temporal method should be used to remeasure the foreign affiliate's financial statements.

D. Current exchange rate method should be used to translate the foreign affiliate's financial statements.

The correct answer is (D). *(CMA, adapted)*

REQUIRED: The method that should be used to translate or remeasure when the foreign affiliate's functional currency is not the reporting currency of the parent.

DISCUSSION: SFAS 52 requires that the affiliate's statements first be remeasured into its functional currency. Then, a current exchange rate is used to translate the foreign entity's financial statements into U.S. dollars. This method applies the current exchange rate to all elements of the financial statements. The resulting adjustments are reported in other comprehensive income to be recognized in income upon the sale or liquidation of the foreign entity.

Answer (A) is incorrect because SFAS 52 requires translation using a current exchange rate. Noncurrent (historical) rates are used in the remeasurement of certain items. Answer (B) is incorrect because consideration of whether items are monetary or nonmonetary is a factor in remeasurement, not translation. Thus, nonmonetary balance sheet items and related revenues and expenses are remeasured at historical exchange rates. Answer (C) is incorrect because, although the temporal method should be used for remeasurement, the question does not state whether the financial statements are presented in a currency other than the functional currency.

59. Unrealized foreign currency gains and losses included in the other comprehensive income section of a consolidated balance sheet represent

A. Foreign currency transaction gains and losses.

B. The amount resulting from translating foreign currency financial statements into the reporting currency.

C. Remeasurement gains and losses.

D. Accounting not in accordance with generally accepted accounting principles.

The correct answer is (B). *(CMA, adapted)*

REQUIRED: The meaning of unrealized foreign currency gains and losses reported as other comprehensive income.

DISCUSSION: Unrealized foreign currency gains and losses in the other comprehensive income section of the balance sheet can arise from unrealized gains and losses on available-for-sale securities, from certain hedging transactions (cash flow hedges), and from translation of foreign currency financial statements. SFAS 52 requires that foreign currency translation adjustments resulting from translation of an entity's financial statements into the reporting currency be reported on the balance sheet in other comprehensive income. Accumulated currency translation gains or losses remain in that section until the foreign entity is sold or liquidated. At that time, translation gains or losses will be recognized in the income statement.

Answer (A) is incorrect because transaction gains and losses (as opposed to translation gains and losses) are recognized in the income statement as they occur. Answer (C) is incorrect because remeasurement gains and losses are included in net income. Answer (D) is incorrect because SFAS 52 states the GAAP for reporting of translation adjustments.

60. When restating financial statements originally recorded in a foreign currency,

A. Income taxes are ignored in calculating and disclosing the results of foreign currency translations.

B. A component of annual net income, "Adjustment from Foreign Currency Translation," should be presented in the notes to the financial statements or in a separate schedule.

C. The aggregate transaction gain or loss included in net income should be disclosed in the financial statements or in the notes to the financial statements.

D. The financial statements should be adjusted for a rate change that occurs after the financial statement date but prior to statement issuance.

The correct answer is (C). *(CMA, adapted)*

REQUIRED: The true statement about restating financial statements originally recorded in a foreign currency.

DISCUSSION: SFAS 52 adopts the functional currency translation approach. Translation adjustments resulting from translating the functional currency into U.S. dollars are not reported in the income statement but are reported in other comprehensive income and will be recognized in income upon the sale or liquidation of the foreign entity. However, foreign currency transaction gains or losses are ordinarily recognized in the income statement of the period in which the exchange rate changes. Accordingly, the aggregate transaction gain or loss included in earnings shall be disclosed.

Answer (A) is incorrect because allocation of income tax expense is required, including those income taxes related to translation adjustments and those transaction gains and losses recorded in a separate component of equity. Answer (B) is incorrect because the adjustment for foreign currency translation is reported in other comprehensive income. Answer (D) is incorrect because an enterprise's financial statements are not adjusted for rate changes after their effective date or after the date of foreign currency statements of a foreign entity if they are consolidated, combined, or accounted for under the equity method in the enterprise's financial statements.

61. Prior to SFAS 52, there was significant disagreement among informed observers regarding the basic nature, information content, and meaning of results produced by various methods of translating amounts from foreign currencies into the reporting currency. SFAS 52 directs that organizations

A. Change the accounting model to recognize currently the effects of all changing prices in the primary statements.

B. Defer any recognition of changing currency prices until they are realized by an actual exchange of foreign currency into the reporting currency.

C. Recognize currently the effect of changing currency prices on the carrying amounts of designated foreign assets and liabilities.

D. Recognize currently the effect of changing currency prices on the carrying amounts of all foreign assets, liabilities, revenues, expenses, gains, and losses.

The correct answer is (D). *(CMA, adapted)*

REQUIRED: The true statement about the requirements of SFAS 52.

DISCUSSION: The elements of the financial statements of separate entities within an enterprise must be consolidated if the performance, financial position, and cash flows of the enterprise are to be presented. If those statements are in different currencies, they must be translated into the reporting currency. According to SFAS 52, the functional currency translation approach is appropriate for use in accounting for and reporting the financial results and relationships of foreign subsidiaries in consolidated statements. It involves identifying the functional currency of the entity (the currency of the primary economic environment in which the entity operates), measuring all elements of the financial statements in the functional currency, and using a current exchange rate for translation from the functional currency to the reporting currency.

Answer (A) is incorrect because the primary financial statements are based on historical cost and nominal dollar accounting. They do not reflect changes in general or specific price levels, except for changes in foreign exchange rates. Answer (B) is incorrect because SFAS 52 ordinarily requires immediate recognition of changes in exchange rates. Answer (C) is incorrect because SFAS 52 also applies to revenues, expenses, gains, and losses.

62. The Brinjac Company owns a foreign subsidiary. Included among the subsidiary's liabilities for the year just ended are 400,000 LCU of revenue received in advance, recorded when $.50 was the dollar equivalent per LCU, and a deferred tax liability for 187,500 LCU, recognized when $.40 was the dollar equivalent per LCU. The rate of exchange in effect at year-end was $.35 per LCU. If the accounting is in accordance with SFAS 52 and SFAS 109 and the dollar is the functional currency, what total should be included for these two liabilities on Brinjac's consolidated balance sheet at year-end?

A. $205,625

B. $215,000

C. $265,625

D. $275,000

The correct answer is (D). *(C.J. Skender)*

REQUIRED: The total of two liability accounts of a foreign subsidiary in the consolidated statements.

DISCUSSION: When a foreign entity's functional currency is the U.S. dollar, the financial statements of the entity recorded in a foreign currency must be remeasured in terms of the U.S. dollar. In accordance with SFAS 52, revenue received in advance (deferred income) is considered a nonmonetary balance sheet item and is remeasured at the applicable historical rate (400,000 LCU x $.50/LCU = $200,000). Deferred charges and credits (except policy acquisition costs for life insurance companies) are also remeasured at historical exchange rates. Deferred taxes were formerly not subject to this rule, but SFAS 109 amended SFAS 52 to eliminate the exception. Consequently, the deferred tax liability (a deferred credit) should be remeasured at the historical rate (187,500 LCU x $.40/LCU) = $75,000). The total for these liabilities is therefore $275,000 ($200,000 + $75,000).

Answer (A) is incorrect because $205,625 results from applying the year-end rate to the total liabilities. Answer (B) is incorrect because the historical, not current, rate should be used to remeasure the deferred income. Answer (C) is incorrect because the historical rate is used to remeasure nonmonetary balance sheet items, including deferred tax assets and liabilities.

63. A widely diversified U.S. corporation sold portions of three wholly owned foreign subsidiaries in the same year. The functional currency of each subsidiary was the currency of the country in which it was located. The percentage sold and the amount of the translation adjustment attributable to each subsidiary at the time of sale follow:

	% Sold	Translation Adjustment
Sub A	100%	$90,000 credit
Sub B	50%	40,000 debit
Sub C	10%	25,000 debit

What total amount of the translation adjustment should be reported as part of the gain on sale of the three subsidiaries?

A. $90,000 credit.

B. $70,000 net credit.

C. $67,500 net credit.

D. $0

The correct answer is (C). *(Publisher)*

REQUIRED: The total translation adjustment included in the gain on the sale of subsidiaries.

DISCUSSION: FASB Interpretation No. 37, *Accounting for Translation Adjustments upon Sale of Part of an Investment in a Foreign Entity*, clarifies SFAS 52. A pro rata portion of the accumulated translation adjustment attributable to an investment shall be recognized in measuring the gain or loss on the sale of all or part of a company's interest in a foreign entity. Here, the total amount to be reported is a $67,500 net credit [(100% x $90,000) – (50% x $40,000) – (10% x $25,000)].

Answer (A) is incorrect because a $90,000 credit fails to consider Subs B and C. Answer (B) is incorrect because a $70,000 net credit fails to consider Sub C. Answer (D) is incorrect because a translation adjustment is recognized as part of the gain on the sale of the subsidiaries.

64. A U.S. company and a German company purchased the same stock on the German stock exchange and held the stock for 1 year. The value of the euro weakened against the dollar over this period. Comparing the returns of the two companies, the United States company's return will be

A. Lower.

B. Higher.

C. The same.

D. Indeterminate from the information provided.

The correct answer is (A). *(CIA, adapted)*

REQUIRED: The effect of the exchange rate movement.

DISCUSSION: The returns on the stock are presumably paid in euros. Hence, the change in the value of the euro relative to the dollar does not affect the German company's return. However, the weakening of the euro reduces the number of dollars it will buy, and the U.S. company's return in dollars is correspondingly reduced.

Answer (B) is incorrect because the return to the U.S. company is adversely affected by the exchange rate movement. Answers (C) and (D) are incorrect because the return to the U.S. company was directly affected by the exchange rate movement, but the return to the German company was not.

Study Unit 8: Other Reporting Issues

25 pages of outline
56 multiple-choice questions

A. Business Combinations
B. Consolidated Financial Statements
C. Segment Reporting
D. Derivatives and Hedging

Study Unit 8 is the last of seven covering preparation of financial statements, a major topic that has been assigned a relative weight range of 50% to 70% of Part 2. This study unit emphasizes circumstances in which the reporting entity is redefined through business combinations. However, the final section concerns disaggregated disclosures.

A. Business Combinations

1. **Legal Perspective on Business Combinations**
   a. **Merger**. Only one of the combining companies survives. The assets and liabilities of the other combining companies are merged into the surviving company. The three types of mergers are
      1) **Vertical merger** -- union of two companies, one of which supplies inputs (e.g., raw materials) for the other
      2) **Horizontal merger** -- union of two companies that engage in the same or similar activities
      3) **Conglomerate merger** -- union of two unrelated companies
   b. **Consolidation**. A new company is organized to take over the combining companies.
   c. **Acquisition**. One company exchanges cash, equity securities, or debt securities for the majority of the outstanding stock of another company, and both companies continue to operate separately.
2. The **tax perspective** on growth is to consider whether a business combination is a tax-free or a taxable event.
   a. Certain exchanges of stock are tax-free exchanges, which permit the owners of one company to exchange their stock for the stock of the purchaser without paying taxes.
   b. Inheritance-tax problems of owners force the sale of many closely held businesses.
3. The **accounting perspective** on growth must consider the type of accounting to be used for acquisition-type combinations -- either purchase or pooling accounting.
   a. **Purchase accounting**. The acquisition is considered to be a purchase of net assets, and the assets and liabilities of the purchased company are recorded at their fair value on the consolidated books, usually resulting in increased depreciation charges.
      1) The book value of most assets is usually less than fair value because of inflation and accounting depreciation policies.
      2) The tax issues that arise when a combination is accounted for as a purchase, e.g., whether to file a consolidated return, the determination of tax bases and book values, and whether the event is taxable, are beyond the scope of this book.

b. **Pooling accounting**. The acquisition is considered to be a combining of ownership interests, and the assets of the combining companies retain their old book values.

1) The result is usually a higher accounting income under the pooling method.
2) Depreciation remains the same for tax purposes.

4. The **financial perspective** on growth is the most important, encompassing all the previous perspectives; the legal, tax, and accounting perspectives all have economic impact.

a. Additional factors determining the terms of business combinations

1) Earning levels and growth rates
2) Sales levels and growth rates
3) Dividends
4) Market values
5) Book values
6) Net current assets

b. The exchanges of stock in business combinations involving public companies often result in a greater market value than the sum of the market values of the individual companies.

1) Qualitative considerations not reflected in the historical financial data may operate to create a synergistic effect.

a) For example, a firm needing stronger management expertise, a better distribution network, or a research and development capacity may seek a complementary merger partner.

5. **Holding companies** -- companies that hold investments in the stock of other operating companies

a. The acquisition method of business combination is pertinent.

b. Holding-company pyramiding results in control of assets with a very small percentage of ownership.

1) The potential profits (and losses) are high.

c. Advantages

1) Control can often be obtained with small percentages of total stock ownership if there are no other large shareholders.

2) Risk is isolated; i.e., if one investee has problems, it can be sold.

3) The investment does not require the approval of shareholders or the investee's board of directors.

a) The stock may be purchased in public markets or directly from current shareholders.

4) Alternatively, a **tender offer** may be made to the shareholders of the potential investee with or without the approval of the potential investee management.

a) If the potential investee management does not cooperate, the potential investor can advertise the offer, e.g., in the *Wall Street Journal*.

b) A tender offer asks shareholders to tender their shares for a specified price, subject to a certain number of shares being tendered.

5) If a question of antitrust arises, it is easier to be forced to liquidate a stock investment than an internal operating division.

d. Disadvantage

1) If the entity meets the criteria of a personal holding company (PHC), undistributed PHC income is subject to a 39.6% tax rate. A company is a PHC if five or fewer shareholders own 50% or more of the shares and 60% or more of the adjusted ordinary gross income is PHC income (essentially, passive income). However, certain organizations are exempt from treatment as PHCs, e.g., S corporations, banks, and insurance companies.

6. **Purchase Accounting**

a. Under **APB 16**, *Business Combinations*, the purchase method must be used to account for a business combination that does not involve all of the distinctive conditions that require a pooling of interests.

1) The purchase method treats the combination as an acquisition of one company by another.

2) The purchase method normally follows historical-cost accounting. APB 16 states general principles that govern the application of the historical-cost basis to a purchase. The choice of principle depends on the nature of the transaction:

a) An asset acquired by exchanging cash or other assets is recorded at cost, that is, at the amount of cash disbursed or the fair value of other assets distributed.

b) An asset acquired by incurring liabilities is recorded at cost, that is, at the present value of the amounts to be paid.

c) An asset acquired by issuing shares of stock of the acquiring corporation is recorded at the fair value of the asset; that is, shares of stock issued are recorded at the fair value of the consideration received for the stock.

3) The acquirer records the identifiable assets obtained and liabilities assumed at their fair values.

a) Under the general guidance in APB 16, the fair value amounts assigned to the assets or liabilities are as follows:

Assets Obtained/ Liabilities Assumed	Fair Value Amounts
Marketable securities	Fair values
Receivables	Present values at current interest rates, minus allowances for collectibility and collection costs
Finished goods and merchandise	Estimated selling prices, minus disposal costs and a reasonable profit allowance for the selling effort of the acquiring corporation
Work-in-process	Estimated selling prices, minus costs to complete, disposal costs, and a reasonable profit allowance for the completing and selling effort of the acquiring corporation
Raw materials	Current replacement costs
Fixed assets to be used	Replacement costs unless expected use indicates a lower value to the acquirer
Fixed assets to be sold	Fair values minus costs to sell
Identifiable intangibles	Appraised values
Other assets, e.g., land	Appraised values
Liabilities	Present values at current interest rates

4) Income of the acquiring company includes its share of the earnings of the acquired company after acquisition (cash flows are also consolidated after acquisition).

a) **ARB 51**, *Consolidated Financial Statements*, states that, when a subsidiary is purchased during the year, the preferred method of presenting the results of operations is to include the subsidiary's operations in the consolidated income statement as though it had been acquired at the beginning of the year and to deduct from the total earnings the preacquisition earnings. The minority interest income for the entire year is also deducted.

b. **Goodwill** is the purchase price of a group of assets or an investee minus the sum of the assigned costs (fair values) of the net identifiable assets (identifiable tangible assets + identifiable intangible assets – liabilities assumed).

1) Goodwill is amortized over its estimated useful life, not exceeding 40 years.

2) **Negative goodwill** arises when a company purchases another organization at a price less than the fair value of the net identifiable assets. Negative goodwill should be eliminated through a pro rata reduction of all noncurrent assets, except long-term investments in marketable securities. Any remainder is a deferred credit amortized over the period benefitted, not exceeding 40 years.

3) EXAMPLE: A company has assets with a fair value of $5 million and liabilities with a fair value of $3 million. If a purchaser acquires 80% of its common stock for $1.5 million, the excess of cost over the fair value of the net identifiable assets acquired is $100,000. The fair value of the net identifiable assets of the company is $2,000,000 ($5,000,000 of assets – $3,000,000 of liabilities). Because 80% of $2 million was purchased for $1.5 million, the excess of $100,000 is treated as negative goodwill.

c. The **equity method** is required to be used by an investor that can exert significant influence over the investee. A rebuttable presumption of significant influence exists when the investor owns at least 20% of the investee's outstanding voting common stock. Generally, the cost method is used when the investor's share of the investee is 20% or less.

1) The equity method requires the investor to recognize its share of investee income in an investment account. Dividends received from the investee are a credit to this account.

a) Amortization of any excess of cost over book value purchased is required.

d. When a stock investment includes more than 50% but less than 100% of the outstanding stock of a company, a minority interest exists.

1) The method of computation of that minority interest is identical under the pooling-of-interests and the purchase methods.

e. Three types of costs may be incurred in effecting a purchase combination: direct costs of acquisition, costs of registering and issuing equity securities, and indirect and general expenses.

1) Direct costs of acquisition, such as legal, accounting, consulting, and finder's fees, are included in the cost of the company acquired.

2) The costs of registration and issuance of equity securities reduce the otherwise determinable fair value of the securities, ordinarily as a debit to additional paid-in capital.

3) Indirect and general expenses are deducted as incurred in determining net income. Examples are time spent by combining company executives negotiating the combination and other normal business expenses involving a combination.

NOTE: In pooling accounting, all of the above costs are expensed as incurred.

7. **Pooling Accounting**

a. The pooling-of-interests method of accounting is intended to present, as a single interest, two or more common shareholder interests that were previously independent and to combine the rights and risks represented by those interests. The shareholders neither withdraw nor invest assets but, in effect, exchange voting common stock in a ratio that determines their respective interests in the combined entity.

1) A business combination that meets 12 specific conditions should be accounted for by the pooling-of-interests method. The 12 criteria are grouped into three categories in APB 16:

a) Combining companies

NOTE: The FASB is currently re-deliberating whether to eliminate the pooling-of-interests method.

i) Each combining company is autonomous.

ii) Each company is independent of the other combining companies; that is, an intercorporate investment at the time of initiation and consummation of the pooling may not exceed 10% of the voting common stock of any combining company.

b) Combining interests

i) A combination is a single transaction or is completed within 1 year of initiation.

ii) An issuance is made solely of common stock for at least 90% of the outstanding voting common stock of the other company.

iii) No change in shareholders' equities is made in contemplation of the combination.

iv) No reacquisition of more than a normal number of shares prior to the combination occurs.

v) The ratio of ownership among individual shareholders remains the same.

vi) Voting rights of shareholders are not restricted.

vii) No contingent stock issuances, payments, etc., exist after the combination is consummated.

c) Absence of planned transactions

i) There are no plans to retire any of the common stock issued in the combination.

ii) No special arrangements exist to benefit former shareholders.

iii) There is no intention to dispose of significant assets, except duplicate facilities or excess capacity, for 2 years.

b. Under the pooling-of-interests method of accounting for a business combination, assets and liabilities are recorded by the combined entity at their carrying (book) value, a treatment compatible with historical cost.

1) If the separate companies recorded assets and liabilities using different methods, the amounts may be adjusted to the same basis of accounting if the change would have been appropriate for the separate company.
   a) This change is retroactive, and prior-period statements should be restated including adjustments to retained earnings.
2) Because no acquisition is deemed to have occurred, no goodwill is recognized.

c. In a pooling of interests, the surviving corporation will issue stock to one or more combining companies.
   1) After the pooling, the balance in the capital stock account should equal the par or stated value of the stock outstanding as a result of the pooling.
   2) The total consolidated contributed capital should equal the sum of the contributed capital amounts of the combining entities. Accordingly, capital stock will be credited for the par or stated value of the shares issued, with a balancing credit to additional paid-in capital.
      a) However, if the par or stated value of the shares issued in the combination is greater than the contributed capital of the subsidiary, additional paid-in capital must be debited. Because additional paid-in capital may not be reduced below zero, a debit to retained earnings will be necessary if additional paid-in capital is insufficient.
   3) The retained earnings of the consolidated entity should equal the sum of the retained earnings of the combining entities, except for the effects of the foregoing adjustment and elimination of any intercompany transactions.
   4) These and other pooling entries are made on a worksheet containing a column of accounts for each combining entity.
      a) If only one set of books will exist for the pooled entity, the entries are made on the books of the surviving company when the business combination is effected and only one corporation exists.
         i) The books of the other combining companies are closed out; i.e., debits are credited and credits are debited.

d. In accounting for a business combination by the pooling method, operations of the combined entities must be reported for all periods presented as if the pooling had occurred prior to the earliest statement presented.
   1) The restatement requirement covers balance sheet and income statement data, including EPS calculations.
   2) Thus, the results of operations for the year of combination include the combined results of operations of the separate companies for the entire year whether or not the combination occurred at the beginning of the year.
   3) The effects of intercompany transactions on current assets, current liabilities, revenue, and cost of sales for the periods presented and on retained earnings at the beginning of the periods presented should be eliminated to the extent possible.
      a) The effects on EPS of nonrecurring intercompany transactions involving long-term assets and liabilities need not be eliminated.

e. APB 16 states that all costs incurred to effect a business combination accounted for as a pooling of interests should be treated as expenses of the combined entity.

1) These expenses include fees of finders and consultants, registration fees, salaries and other expenses related to services of employees, costs of providing information to shareholders, and costs and losses of combining operations and instituting efficiencies.

2) These costs should be deducted to determine net income of the combined entity in the period in which the costs were incurred.

8. Stop and review! You have completed the outline for this subunit. Study multiple-choice questions 1 through 22 beginning on page 364.

B. Consolidated Financial Statements

1. **SFAS 94**, *Consolidation of All Majority-Owned Subsidiaries*, requires consolidation of all companies in which a parent has a controlling financial interest through direct or indirect ownership of a majority voting interest (over 50% of the outstanding voting shares).

   a. However, consolidation is not required if control is likely to be temporary or does not rest with the majority owner, for example, because the subsidiary is in bankruptcy or in legal reorganization or is subject to foreign exchange restrictions or other government-imposed restrictions that preclude exercise of control.

   b. If the conditions dictating consolidation are met, subsidiaries should be shown on a consolidated basis with the parent company.

2. Consolidation is an accounting process for a business combination when the combined companies remain legally separate. It should not be confused with a business combination effected as a consolidation, that is, one in which a new company is formed to account for the assets and liabilities of the combining companies.

3. Consolidated statements are intended to present the results of operations, financial position, and cash flows of a parent company and its subsidiaries as if they constituted a single economic entity.

   a. When consolidated financial statements are prepared, the normal procedure is to start with the output of the formal accounting systems of the parent and the subsidiary(ies) and, on a worksheet only, prepare the informal (worksheet) adjusting and eliminating entries necessary to prepare the consolidated financial statements.

      1) These consolidating adjusting entries must be cumulative because previous worksheet entries were not recorded in the accounts of either the parent or the subsidiary.

      2) The working papers can be based on balances after year-end closing or on trial balances before closing. Thus, the latter includes revenue and expense accounts.

   b. There are two main approaches to valuing a business combination when there is less than 100% ownership of the subsidiary.

      1) Under the **entity theory**, goodwill is established as if 100% of the subsidiary was purchased, regardless of the parent's actual ownership percentage in the subsidiary.

      2) Under the **proprietary theory**, the goodwill amount is the difference between the amount actually paid for a percentage of a subsidiary and the value of that percentage of the subsidiary.

   c. The basis of consolidation is a significant accounting policy that should be disclosed in the financial statements (APB 22). Normally, the disclosure is made either as the first footnote to the financial statements or in a separate summary preceding the notes.

4. The guidance provided by authoritative pronouncements regarding consolidations is not extensive. However, ARB 51 gives the following description of the general consolidation procedures:

   a. Intercompany balances and transactions, such as open account balances (receivables and payables), the parent's investment in the subsidiary, sales and purchases, interest, holdings of securities, dividends, etc., should be eliminated in full even if a minority interest exists.

      1) Elimination means debits are credited and credits are debited.

      2) Retained earnings or deficits of a purchased subsidiary at the date of acquisition are excluded from consolidated retained earnings in the entry eliminating the parent's investment account and the subsidiary's equity accounts.

      3) Shares of the parent held by a subsidiary should not be treated as outstanding in the consolidated balance sheet. They are eliminated.

   b. Intercompany profits and losses are completely eliminated, but the procedure varies with the direction of the sale.

      1) Parent to subsidiary (downstream): The entire profit or loss not realized by sale outside of the consolidated entity is subtracted from the parent's income. The minority interest is unaffected by the elimination.

      2) Subsidiary to parent (upstream): The entire profit or loss not realized by sale outside of the consolidated entity is subtracted from the subsidiary's income. In the upstream case, the effect is to allocate the elimination of the intercompany profit or loss between the parent (or consolidated entity) and the minority interest. The upstream case is relevant only if the subsidiary (or a combining company in a pooling) has a minority interest. However, if the asset is sold to someone outside the group, the original intercompany profit will be realized and will no longer need to be eliminated.

   c. The amount of the minority interest recognized at the date of the combination equals a proportionate share of the subsidiary's book value.

      1) Subsequently, the minority interest is adjusted for its share of the subsidiary's income and dividends. On consolidating worksheets, an adjustment to minority interest is also needed for unrealized intercompany profits and losses on upstream sales of inventory and fixed assets and purchases of combining company debt.

   d. In the income statement, the minority interest's adjusted share of the subsidiary's income is usually treated as a deduction in arriving at consolidated income. The parent's investment in subsidiary account and its proportionate share of the subsidiary's equity accounts, which include retained earnings, are eliminated in a consolidation. The remainder of the subsidiary's equity is reported separately as the minority interest.

   e. In consolidated statements, the parent's net income equals the consolidated net income because the parent should account for the investment using the equity method. Consolidated net income is also equal to the parent's net income, plus subsidiary net income, minus minority interest net income, minus adjustments for intercompany profit (the latter involve certain inventory, fixed assets, and debt as described in 5.c., 5.d., and 5.e. on pages 347 and 348). In a pooling, no parent-subsidiary relationship exists, but some o all of the combining companies may have a minority interest and intercompany profit transactions (inventory, fixed assets, or debt).

   f. In the consolidated balance sheet, the equity section should reflect the parent's equity section. Placement of the minority interest is in dispute, although SFAC 6 indicates a preference for treating it as part of equity.

5. **Consolidating Journal Entries for Purchase Combinations**

a. Basic elimination entry. This entry eliminates investment account and subsidiary equity accounts attributable to the parent.

Common stock (sub)	$XXX	
Additional paid-in capital (sub)	XXX	
Retained earnings (sub)	XXX	
Dividends (sub)		$XXX
Investment (parent)		XXX
Minority interest		XXX

The above entries to the subsidiary's accounts effectively allocate the subsidiary's net assets between the parent's "investment in investee" account and the minority interest.

b. Elimination of directly offsetting intercompany accounts. They are reciprocal and do not affect consolidated net income or minority interest.

Sales	$XXX	
Cost of sales		$XXX
Payables	XXX	
Receivables		XXX
Interest income	XXX	
Interest expense		XXX

c. Elimination of intercompany profit from inventory. If ending inventory of a combining company includes purchased goods from another combining company that were sold at a profit, unrealized profit exists from a consolidated point of view because the goods have not been sold outside the consolidated group.

Cost of sales	$XXX	
Inventory		$XXX

This writes the inventory down to cost and decreases consolidated net income. Part of this reduction of income should be allocated to the minority interest if the sale is upstream (sale by a combining company with a minority interest).

d. Elimination of intercompany profit in fixed asset purchase/sale transactions

1) In the period of the purchase/sale, eliminate any gain recognized on the sale of a fixed asset between combining companies.

Gain on sale	$XXX	
Fixed asset		$XXX

2) Eliminate any depreciation taken by the purchaser representing an amount different from what would have been taken if the seller had retained and depreciated the fixed asset.

Accumulated depreciation	$XXX	
Depreciation expense		$XXX

3) In subsequent periods, first eliminate the previously reported gain that is now in retained earnings and then eliminate the excess depreciation taken in the period and in all prior periods (i.e., a cumulative adjustment).

Retained earnings	$XXX	
Fixed asset		$XXX
Accumulated depreciation	XXX	
Depreciation expense		XXX
Retained earnings		XXX

4) If the seller has a minority interest, adjust minority interest and minority interest income as appropriate. Note that all adjustments for intercompany profit elimination flow through to consolidated totals unless explicitly adjusted to minority interest.

e. Elimination of intercompany debt transactions

1) The debt issued by one combining company of a consolidated group may be purchased by another combining company of the group from a third party so that the debt accounts are not reciprocal (i.e., the purchase price is not equal to the book value of the debt on the books of the issuer, which is another combining company).

2) The gain on extinguishment of debt from a consolidated point of view must be recognized in the period the debt is purchased by a combining company. There are five issues to resolve.

a) Maturity or face value of the debt
b) Interest receivable/payable at period-end
c) Interest income/expense based on the maturity value and stated rate
d) Discount or premium on the books of the issuer (debtor)
e) Discount or premium on the books of the purchaser (creditor)

3) The maturity value, interest receivable/payable, and interest income/expense are direct eliminations and should be so handled.

4) The premium or discount on the debtor's and creditor's books and any related amortization should be eliminated and recognized as a gain or loss on extinguishment in the period of purchase and as an adjustment of retained earnings in each period thereafter.

a) Debit or credit the "investment in debt" account of the investor/creditor to bring the balance to zero (after the maturity value is eliminated) and eliminate any amortization of that balance that was adjusted to interest income during the period.

i) If the purchase was at a premium (discount), amortization requires a debit (credit) to interest income. Thus, the elimination entry is to credit (debit) interest income.

ii) The balance of the journal entry is to gain or loss in the period of debt acquisition and to retained earnings in all remaining periods.

b) Debit or credit the premium or discount on the books of the debtor and eliminate any related amortization of premium or discount that was adjusted to interest expense during the period.

i) If the purchase was at a premium (discount), amortization results in a credit (debit) to interest expense that must be reversed.

ii) The balance of the journal entry is to gain or loss in the period of debt acquisition and to retained earnings in all remaining periods.

c) The cumulative adjustments to retained earnings decrease because amortization of the gain or loss flows into retained earnings.

f. All upstream intercompany profit items require an adjustment to minority interest.

1) Adjustments are made to retained earnings and current minority interest income.

2) In the preceding journal entries, adjustments to retained earnings can individually be made pro rata to retained earnings and minority interest; e.g., if minority interest is 10%, 10% of every entry to retained earnings would not be made to retained earnings but, rather, to minority interest.

a) Alternatively, one summary entry can be made to retained earnings to adjust minority interest (which was established with the first elimination entry).

3) All entries to nominal accounts involving upstream transactions (those from combining companies with minority interest) require an adjustment to minority interest income.

a) The entry to establish minority interest net income is to debit a contra consolidated net income account and credit minority interest income.

Consolidated net income	$XXX	
Minority interest income		$XXX

b) The amount is the minority interest percentage times the subsidiary's/combining company's net income adjusted for any upstream transactions.

c) For example, if inventory, which includes $1,000 of gross profit sold upstream by a 10% minority interest combining company, has not been resold out of the consolidated group, the previous minority interest entry would be reduced by $100 (10% of $1,000) in the period of the sale.

i) In periods subsequent to the sale, a previous period's unrealized upstream gain would be removed from the beginning balances of the seller by a debit to retained earnings and a credit to cost of sales.

6. Stop and review! You have completed the outline for this subunit. Study multiple-choice questions 23 through 36 beginning on page 373.

C. Segment Reporting

1. **SFAS 131**, *Disclosure about Segments of an Enterprise and Related Information*, applies to the interim financial reports and annual financial statements of public business enterprises.

2. The objective of segment reporting is to provide information about the different types of business activities of the entity and the economic environments in which it operates. This information is reported on an operating segment basis.

3. SFAS 131 defines an **operating segment** as "a component of an enterprise

a. "That engages in business activities from which it may earn revenues and incur expenses (including revenues and expenses relating to transactions with other components of the same enterprise),

b. "Whose operating results are regularly reviewed by the enterprise's chief operating decision maker to make decisions about resources to be allocated to the segment and assess its performance, and

c. "For which discrete financial information is available."

4. **Aggregation Criteria**. Operating segments may be aggregated if doing so is consistent with the objective of SFAS 131; if they have similar economic characteristics; and if they have similar products and services, production processes, classes of customers, distribution methods, and regulatory environments.
5. **Reportable segments** are those that have been identified in accordance with sections 2. through 4. above and on the previous page and also meet any of the quantitative thresholds described below. However, SFAS 131 does not define how these quantitative thresholds are calculated. Instead, the amounts of reported segment items are the measures that are reviewed by the enterprises's chief operating decision maker. Furthermore, if an operating segment does not meet any of the quantitative thresholds, management has the discretion to treat it as reportable if such information would be useful to readers of the financial statements.
   a. **Revenue test**. Reported revenue, including sales to external customers and intersegment sales or transfers, is at least 10% of the combined revenue of all operating segments.
   b. **Asset test**. Assets are at least 10% of the combined assets of all operating segments.
   c. **Profit (loss) test**. The absolute amount of reported profit or loss is at least 10% of the greater, in absolute amount, of either the combined reported profit of all operating segments that did not report a loss, or the combined reported loss of all operating segments that did report a loss.
6. Information about operating segments not meeting the quantitative thresholds may be combined to produce a reportable segment only if the operating segments share a majority of the aggregation criteria.
7. If the total external revenue of the operating segments is less than 75% of consolidated revenue, additional operating segments are identified as reportable until the 75% level is reached.
8. Information about nonreportable activities and segments is combined and disclosed in an "all other" category as a reconciling item.
9. As the number of reportable segments increases above 10, the enterprise may decide that it has reached a practical limit.
10. **Disclosures** include the following:
    a. Such general information as the factors used to identify the reportable segments, including the basis of organization, and the types of revenue-generating products and services for each reportable segment
    b. A measure of profit or loss and total assets for each reportable segment and, if the amounts are included in the measure of segment profit or loss reviewed by the chief operating decision maker, such other items as revenues from external customers, revenues from other operating segments, interest revenue, interest expense, depreciation, depletion, amortization, unusual items, equity in the net income of equity-based investees, income tax expense or benefit, extraordinary items, and other significant noncash items
    c. The amount of investment in equity-based investees and total expenditures for additions to most long-lived assets for each reportable segment if they are included in segment assets reviewed by the chief operating decision maker
11. If a majority of a segment's revenues are from interest, and net interest revenue is the primary basis for assessing its performance and the resources allocated to it, net interest revenue may be reported given proper disclosure.

12. **Measurement**. The general principle is that the information reported is measured in the same way as the internal information used to evaluate a segment's performance and to allocate assets to it.
    a. If the chief operating decision maker uses more than one measure of a segment's profit or loss or assets, the reported measures are those most consistent with the consolidated financial statements. Explanations of the measurements of segment profit or loss and segment assets should be given for each reportable segment.
13. **Reconciliations** should be provided for the total reportable segments' revenues and consolidated revenues, the total of the reportable segments' measures of profit or loss and pretax consolidated operating income (but if the enterprise allocates other items, such as income taxes, the reconciliation may be to income after those items), the total reportable segments' assets and consolidated assets, and the total reportable segments' amounts for every other significant item of information disclosed and the consolidated amount. Significant reconciling items should be separately identified and described.
14. **Interim period information** is disclosed for each reportable segment in condensed financial statements. Disclosures include external revenues, intersegment revenues, a measure of segment profit or loss, total assets that have materially changed since the last annual report, differences from the last annual report in the basis of segmentation or of segment profit or loss, and a reconciliation of the total reportable segments' profit or loss and consolidated pretax income.
15. **Restatement of previously reported information** is required if changes in internal organization cause the composition of reportable segments to change. However, an enterprise must restate only items of disclosure that it can practicably restate.
    a. In these circumstances, if segment information for earlier periods, including interim periods, is not restated, segment information for the year of the change must be disclosed under the old basis and the new basis of segmentation if practicable.
16. Certain **enterprise-wide disclosures** must be provided only if they are not given in the reportable operating segment information.
    a. **Information about products and services**. Revenues from external customers for each product and service or each group of similar products and services are reported if practicable based on the financial information used to produce the general-purpose financial statements.
    b. The following information about **geographic areas** is also reported if practicable: external revenues attributed to the home country, external revenues attributed to all foreign countries, material external revenues attributed to an individual foreign country, the basis for attributing revenues from external customers, and certain information about assets.
    c. If 10% or more of revenue is derived from sales to any **single customer**, that fact, the amount of revenue from each such customer, and the segment(s) reporting the revenues must be disclosed. Single customers include entities under common control and each federal, state, local, or foreign government.
17. Stop and review! You have completed the outline for this subunit. Study multiple-choice questions 37 through 43 beginning on page 377.

D. Derivatives and Hedging

1. **SFAS 133**, *Accounting for Derivative Instruments and Hedging Activities*, as amended by **SFAS 138**, *Accounting for Certain Derivative Instruments and Certain Hedging Activities*, applies to all entities, including not-for-profit organizations and defined benefit pension plans. The standards it establishes for derivative instruments, including those embedded in other contracts, and hedging activities are based on four principles:
   a. Derivatives should be recognized as **assets or liabilities** in the statement of financial position.
   b. **Fair value** is the only relevant measure for derivatives. Moreover, the carrying amount of a hedged item should reflect any changes in its fair value while the hedge is in effect that are attributable to the hedged risk.
      1) Derivatives usually have no value at inception but result in positive or negative fair value as the price of the underlying item changes.
   c. Only items that are assets and liabilities should be recognized as such.
   d. Designated hedged items should receive special accounting treatment only if they meet qualifying criteria, for example, the likelihood of effectiveness of the hedge in producing offsetting fair value or cash flow changes during the term of the hedge for the risk being hedged.
2. A derivative is defined informally as an investment transaction in which the buyer purchases the right to a potential gain with a commitment for a potential loss. It is a wager on whether the value of something will go up or down. The purpose of the transaction is either to speculate (incur risk) or to hedge (avoid risk).
   a. Thus, a derivative is an executory contract that results in cash flow between two **counterparties** based on the change in some other indicator of value. Examples of these indicators include prices of financial instruments, such as common shares or government bonds; currency exchange rates; interest rates; commodity prices; or indexes, such as the S&P 500 or the Dow Jones Industrial Average.
3. Derivative instruments (derivatives) should be contrasted with financial instruments, which include cash, accounts receivable, notes receivable, bonds, preferred shares, common shares, etc. The following are examples of derivative instruments:
   a. A **call option** is the right to purchase something (e.g., a commodity, foreign currency, etc.) at an exercise (strike) price. The purchaser pays a premium for the opportunity to benefit from the appreciation in the underlying item. An American call option is a right to purchase during the term of the option. A European call option permits purchase at a given date.
   b. A **forward contract** is an agreement negotiated between two parties for the purchase and sale of a stated amount of a commodity, foreign currency, or financial instrument at a stated price, with delivery or settlement at a stated future date. Unlike futures contracts, forward contracts are usually specifically negotiated agreements and are not traded on regulated exchanges. Thus, the parties are subject to default risk (i.e., that the other party will not perform).

c. A **futures contract** is a forward-based agreement to make or receive delivery or make a cash settlement that involves a specified quantity of a commodity, foreign currency, or financial instrument during a specified time interval. Futures contracts are usually standardized and exchange traded. They are therefore less risky than forward contracts. Another reason for their lesser risk is that they are "marked to market" daily; that is, money must be paid to cover any losses as they occur. Furthermore, unlike forward contracts, futures contracts very rarely result in actual delivery. The parties customarily make a net settlement in cash on the expiration date.

d. An **interest rate swap** is an exchange of one party's interest payments based on a fixed rate for another party's interest payments based on a floating rate. The maturity value may or may not be swapped. Moreover, most interest rate swaps permit net settlement because they do not require delivery of interest-bearing assets with a principal equal to the contracted amount. Thus, an interest rate swap is appropriate when one counterparty prefers the payment pattern of the other. For example, if a firm with fixed-rate debt has revenues that vary with interest rates, it may prefer floating rate debt so that its debt service burden will correlate directly with its revenues.

e. A **put option** is the right to sell something at an exercise (strike) price. The gain is the excess of the exercise price over the market price of the underlying item. An American put option is the right to sell during the term of the option. A European put option is the right to sell at a given date.

4. **Hedging** is not defined in SFAS 133. However, *The CPA Letter* (October 2000) defines a hedge as "a defensive strategy designed to protect an entity against the risk of adverse price or interest-rate movements on certain of its assets, liabilities, or anticipated transactions. A hedge is used to avoid or reduce risks by creating a relationship by which losses on certain positions are expected to be counterbalanced in whole or in part by gains on separate positions in another market."

   a. Thus, the purchase or sale of a derivative or other instrument is a hedge if it is expected to neutralize the risk of a recognized asset or liability, an unrecognized firm commitment, a forecasted transaction, etc. For example, if a flour company buys and uses 1 million bushels of wheat each month, it may wish to guard against increases in wheat costs when it has committed to sell at a price related to the current cost of wheat. If so, the company will purchase wheat futures contracts that will result in gains if the price of wheat increases (offsetting the actual increased costs).

5. SFAS 133 formally defines a **derivative** as a financial instrument or other contract with certain characteristics. It states that a derivative, including one embedded in another contract, has at least one **underlying** (interest rate, exchange rate, price index, etc.) and at least one **notional amount** (number of units specified in the contract) or payment provision, or both. The terms of a derivative also permit or require net settlement or provide for the equivalent. Moreover, no **initial net investment**, or one smaller than that necessary for contracts with similar responses to the market, is required.

   a. **Net settlement** means that the derivative can be readily settled with only a net delivery of assets. Thus, neither party need deliver an asset associated with its underlying or an asset that has a principal, stated amount, etc., equal to the notional amount (possibly adjusted for discount or premium). If one party must deliver such an asset, the net settlement criterion is still met if a market mechanism exists to facilitate net settlement, or the asset is readily convertible to cash or is a derivative.

6. The following are not within the **scope** of SFAS 133:
   a. "Regular-way" security trades (contracts lacking a provision for net settlement or a market mechanism to facilitate net settlement)
   b. Normal purchases and sales (contracts providing for purchase or sale of nonfinancial assets—even if readily convertible to cash—that will be delivered in quantities expected to be used or sold over a reasonable period in the normal course of business)
   c. Traditional life, property, and casualty insurance contracts
   d. Certain guarantee contracts
   e. Certain contracts that are not exchange traded
   f. Derivatives that impede recognition of a sale (for example, a call option that permits a transferor to repurchase financial assets that are not readily available)
7. The following are NOT deemed to be derivatives for purposes of SFAS 133:
   a. Contracts issued or held that are indexed to the entity's own shares and classified in equity in its balance sheet
   b. Contracts issued that are related to stock-based compensation (SFAS 123)
   c. Contracts issued as contingent consideration in a business combination by an entity accounting for the transaction using the purchase method

   NOTE: The exclusions in a., b., and c. apply only to the issuer, not to the counterparty.
8. **Gains and losses** from changes in the fair value of a derivative, whether or not it is designated and qualifies as a hedging instrument, are included in earnings in the period of change (except for certain gains and losses on a derivative designated as a cash flow hedge or as a hedge of a net investment in a foreign operation).
9. **Types of Hedges**. Hedge accounting ordinarily is limited to derivatives. Provided that the hedging derivatives (and the hedged items) meet the complex criteria in SFAS 133, such derivatives, for example, formal documentation of the hedging relationship and the entity's risk management objective and strategy (as well as many other criteria beyond the scope of this outline), may qualify and be designated as hedges of
   a. Changes in the fair value of a recognized asset or liability (or part thereof) or of an unrecognized firm commitment that are attributable to a specified risk (fair value hedge)
      1) A **firm commitment** is an agreement with an unrelated party that is binding on both parties and is usually legally enforceable. It specifies all significant terms, and its performance is probable because it contains a sufficiently large disincentive for nonperformance.
   b. The variable cash flows of a recognized asset or liability or of a forecasted transaction that are attributable to a specified risk (cash flow hedge)
      1) A **forecasted transaction** is expected, although no firm commitment exists. It does not confer current rights to future benefits or impose a current obligation for future sacrifices because no transaction or event has occurred. When such a transaction or event occurs, it will be at the prevailing market price.
   c. Certain foreign currency exposures [see D.11.a.3)].

10. An exception to the rule limiting hedging instruments to derivatives is permitted for a nonderivative financial instrument that is designated as a fair value hedge of the foreign currency exposure of an unrecognized firm commitment. The same exception applies to hedges of the foreign currency exposure of a net investment in a foreign operation. The nonderivative hedging instrument in these cases is one that may result in foreign currency transaction gain or loss accounted for under SFAS 52 (see Study Unit 7, F.).

11. **Accounting for Hedging Gain or Loss**

    a. **Fair value hedges** reduce risk when a recognized asset or liability or a firm commitment has fixed cash flows. For example, fixed rate investments and debt and firm commitments to purchase or sell assets or incur liabilities may be subject to fair value hedging.

        1) The gain or loss on the hedged item attributable to the risk being hedged is an adjustment to the carrying amount of the item and is recognized currently in earnings.

            a) When the hedged item is a previously unrecognized firm commitment, the recognition of the gain or loss on the firm commitment includes debiting an asset or crediting a liability, respectively. Accordingly, the phrase "asset and liability" used in SFAS 133 includes a firm commitment.

        2) The loss or gain on the hedging instrument (normally, a derivative) is also recognized currently in earnings.

        3) SFAS 133 (as amended) permits a **fair value hedge** of certain types of **foreign currency exposures**. They include

            a) An unrecognized firm commitment

            b) A recognized asset or liability (including an available-for-sale security) for which a foreign currency transaction gain or loss is recognized in earnings under SFAS 52

        4) Accordingly, the gain or loss on the hedging derivative or hedging nonderivative instrument in a fair value hedge of a foreign-currency-denominated firm commitment and the offsetting loss or gain on the hedged firm commitment attributable to the hedged risk are recognized in earnings in the same period.

        5) Similarly, the gain or loss on the hedging derivative instrument in a fair value hedge of a recognized asset or liability (one for which a foreign currency transaction gain or loss is recognized) and the offsetting loss or gain on the hedged recognized asset or liability attributable to the hedged risk also are recognized in earnings in the same period.

    b. **Cash-flow hedges** reduce risk when a recognized asset or liability (for example, all or certain interest payments on variable rate debt) or a forecasted transaction (for example, an anticipated purchase, sale, or issue of debt) has variable cash flows.

        1) Because the gain or loss on the hedged item will not occur until a future period, the **effective** portion of the loss or gain on the designated hedging instrument is reported in **other comprehensive income (OCI)**. It will be recognized in earnings (**reclassified** from OCI) when the gain or loss on the intended transaction is recognized in earnings. The ineffective portion is recognized in earnings immediately.

            a) The **effectiveness** of a hedge is the percentage of gain or loss on the hedged item that is offset by the hedging instrument's loss or gain. Hedges should be highly effective.

2) A nonderivative instrument may not be the hedging instrument in a **foreign currency cash flow hedge**. However, a derivative instrument may be designated as a hedge of "the foreign currency exposure to variability in the functional-currency-equivalent cash flows associated with a forecasted transaction, a recognized asset or liability, an unrecognized firm commitment, or a forecasted intercompany transaction" (e.g., a forecasted sale to a foreign subsidiary).

a) Thus, the effective portion of the gain or loss on the hedging derivative instrument in a foreign currency cash flow hedge is recognized as a component of OCI, and the ineffective portion is recognized in earnings in the period in which the gain or loss is recognized. The gain or loss recognized as a component of OCI is reclassified into earnings in the same period(s) during which the hedged item affects earnings.

c. Gains and losses on a derivative designated as a hedge of a foreign currency exposure of a **net investment in a foreign operation** are reported as part of the cumulative translation adjustment in OCI to the extent the hedge is effective. If the hedging instrument is a nonderivative financial instrument, the foreign currency transaction gain or loss determined under SFAS 52 is treated in the same manner.

12. Embedded Derivatives

a. A common example of an embedded derivative is the conversion feature of convertible debt. It represents a call option on the issuer's stock. Embedded derivatives must be accounted for separately from the related **host contract** if the following conditions are met:

1) The economic characteristics and risks of the embedded derivative instrument are **not clearly and closely related** to the economic characteristics of the host.

2) The hybrid instrument is **not remeasured at fair value** under otherwise applicable GAAP, with changes in fair value reported in earnings as they occur.

3) A freestanding instrument with the same terms as the embedded derivative would be subject to the requirements of SFAS 133.

b. If an embedded derivative is accounted for separately, the host contract is accounted for based on the accounting standards that are applicable to instruments of its type. The separated derivative should be accounted for under SFAS 133.

1) If separating the two instruments is impossible, the entire contract must be measured at fair value, with gains and losses recognized in earnings. It may not be designated as a hedging instrument because nonderivatives usually do not qualify as hedging instruments.

13. The accounting for changes in fair value of a derivative depends, as indicated above, on the reasons for holding it. The accounting also depends on whether the entity has elected to **designate** it as part of a hedging relationship and whether it meets the **qualifying criteria** for the particular type of accounting.

a. All or part of a derivative may be designated as a hedging instrument. The proportion must be expressed as a percentage of the entire derivative.

b. SFAS 133 establishes qualifying criteria that are numerous and complex and, accordingly, are not reproduced here. They relate to effectiveness, the degree of formal documentation needed regarding the hedging relationship, requirements for particular hedging instruments and hedged items, etc.

1) A reporting entity that elects hedge accounting must, among other things, formally determine at the hedge's inception the methods (consistent with the entity's risk management strategy) for determining the effectiveness and ineffectiveness of the hedge. Thus, an entity must specify whether all of the gain or loss on the hedging instrument will be included in the assessment of effectiveness. For example, an entity may exclude all or part of the time value from the assessment of effectiveness.

14. A **not-for-profit organization** or other entity not reporting earnings separately recognizes the change in fair value of all derivatives as a change in net assets (unless a derivative hedges a foreign currency exposure of a net investment in a foreign operation). In a fair value hedge, the change in fair value of the hedged item attributable to the risk being hedged is recognized as a change in net assets. These entities may not use cash flow hedge accounting.

15. The following are among the **disclosures** required for derivatives and hedging:

a. Objectives for holding or issuing derivatives

b. Context for understanding the objectives

c. Strategies for achieving the objectives

d. Risk management policies

e. Details about fair value hedges, cash flow hedges, and hedges of a net investment in a foreign operation

f. Display within OCI of a separate classification for net gain or loss on derivatives designated and qualifying as cash flow hedges to the extent they are reported in comprehensive income.

16. **Examples of Hedging Transactions**

a. **Fair value hedge**. A company wishes to hedge the fair value of its investment in an inventory of Commodity A by selling futures contracts on August 1, 2001 for delivery on February 1, 2002, the date on which it intends to sell the inventory. The following information is available about spot and futures prices and the company's estimates of changes in the fair value of the inventory (changes in spot rates adjusted for its transportation costs, storage costs, etc.):

	Spot Rate	Futures Rate for February 1 Delivery	Change in Fair Value of Inventory
August 1, 2001	$.51	$.53	
December 31, 2001	.49	.51	$(21,000)
February 1, 2002	.52	.52	32,000

The company sold futures contracts for 1 million pounds of Commodity A at $.53 per pound, its inventory had an average cost of $.38 per pound, and it sold the entire inventory of Commodity A on February 1, 2002 at the spot rate of $.52 per pound. The company also bought offsetting February 2002 futures contracts on February 1, 2002 for 1 million pounds of Commodity A at $.52 per pound. This transaction closed out its futures position. The following journal entries should be made (ignoring the margin deposit with the broker):

August 1, 2001

The fair value of the futures contracts is zero at the inception date. Thus, no entry is made to record their fair value.

December 31, 2001

Loss	$21,000	
Inventory -- Commodity A		$21,000

(The company estimates a loss of $21,000.)

Receivable from/liability to broker	$20,000	
Gain on the hedge		$20,000

[The gain on the futures contract is $.02 per pound ($.53 futures rate at August 1, 2001 – $.51 futures rate at December 31, 2001 for February 1, 2002 delivery) times 1,000,000 pounds, or a $20,000 gain.]

February 1, 2002

Inventory -- Commodity A	$32,000	
Gain		$32,000

(The company estimates a gain of $32,000.)

Loss on the hedge	$10,000	
Receivable from/liability to broker		$10,000

[The loss on the futures contracts is $.01 per pound ($.52 rate at February 1, 2002 – $.51 futures rate at December 31, 2001 for February 1, 2002 delivery) times 1,000,000 pounds, or a $10,000 loss.]

Cash	$10,000	
Receivable from/liability to broker		$10,000

(This entry records settlement of the futures contracts.)

Accounts receivable	$520,000	
Cost of goods sold	391,000	
Sales		$520,000
Inventory -- Commodity A		391,000

[The revenue from the sale equaled the spot rate ($.52) times 1,000,000 pounds, or $520,000. The inventory equaled the average cost ($.38) times 1,000,000 pounds, minus the fair value loss on December 31, 2001 ($21,000), plus the fair value gain on February 1, 2002 ($32,000), or $391,000.]

b. **Cash flow hedge**. At January 2, 2001, a company determines that it will need to purchase 100,000 pounds of Commodity B in June 2001. The purchase is expected to be at the spot rate. To hedge this forecasted transaction, the company agrees to purchase futures contracts for 100,000 pounds of Commodity B at the June 2001 futures price of $3.05 per pound. Hedge effectiveness will be determined by comparing the total change in the fair value of the futures contracts with the changes in the cash flows of the anticipated purchase. In June, the company buys 100,000 pounds of Commodity B at the spot rate of $3.20 per pound. Ignoring the margin deposit for the futures contracts, the following are the journal entries for this transaction:

January 2001

Because the margin deposit is ignored in this problem, no journal entry is made. The futures contract is not recorded because, at its inception, its fair value is zero.

June 2001

Commodity B inventory	$320,000	
Cash		$320,000

[The quantity purchased (100,000 pounds) times the spot rate ($3.20 per pound) equals $320,000.]

Futures contracts	$15,000	
Other comprehensive income		$15,000

[The gain, which will subsequently be reclassified into earnings when the inventory is sold, equals the difference between the spot rate and the futures contract rate ($3.20 – $3.05 = $.15) times 100,000 pounds, or $15,000.]

Cash	$15,000	
Futures contracts		$15,000

(This entry records the net cash settlement. In practice, futures contracts are settled daily.)

c. **Hedge of a net investment in a foreign operation**. Parent, Inc., a U.S. company, has a net investment in its Xenadian subsidiary, Subco, of 100 million foreign currency units (FCU), the subsidiary's functional currency. At November 1, 2001, Parent sells a forward exchange contract for the delivery of 100 million FCU on February 1, 2002. This contract is designated as a hedge of the net investment in Subco. The contract rate equals the forward rate at November 1, 2001 of $1.15 per FCU. On that date, the spot rate is $1.17 per FCU. Parent records the premium on the forward contract [($1.17 – $1.15) x 100,000,000 FCU = $2,000,000] as a translation adjustment. Moreover, Parent records the change in fair value of the forward contract at fair value in its statement of financial position, with the effective portion of the hedge (100% in this case) recorded in other comprehensive income (OCI). In accordance with SFAS 52, Parent also translates its net investment in Subco into U.S. dollars, and it reports the effects of changes in exchange rates as a cumulative translation adjustment in OCI.

The following table provides information about exchange rates, the forward contract's changes in fair value, and the translation adjustments (change in spot rates x the notional amount). Measuring the fair value of a foreign currency forward contract requires discounting the estimated future cash flows. This estimate of cash flows is based on the changes in the forward rate, not in the spot rate.

	Gain (Loss) – Forward Contract's Change in Fair Value (Discounted)	Gain (Loss) – Cumulative Translation Adjustment	Spot Rates per FCU	Forward Rates per FCU for 2/1 Delivery
November 1, 2001			$1.17	$1.15
December 31, 2001	$3,920,000	$(4,000,000)	1.13	1.11
February 1, 2002	2,080,000	(4,000,000)	1.09	1.09
	$6,000,000	$ 8,000,000		

The following are the basic journal entries:

November 1, 2001

No entry is made because the forward rate and the contract rate were the same.

December 31, 2001

Receivable -- forward contract	$3,920,000	
OCI		$3,920,000

[The change in fair value of the contract (discounted future cash flows based on changes in the forward rate) is recorded in OCI in the same manner as a translation adjustment. Parent determined that the estimated change in cash flows equaled the change in forward rates ($1.15 – $1.11 = $0.04) times 100,000,000 FCU, or $4,000,000. It then determined that the present value of that change was $3,920,000 (given).]

OCI	$4,000,000	
Net investment -- Subco		$4,000,000

[The translation adjustment in accordance with SFAS 52 is the change in spot rates ($1.17 – $1.13 = $.04) times 100,000,000 FCU, or a loss of $4,000,000.]

February 1, 2002

Receivable -- forward contract	$2,080,000	
OCI		$2,080,000

[The total change in fair value of the contract is the change in forward rates ($1.15 – $1.09 = $.06) times 100,000,000 FCU, or a gain of $6,000,000. Of this amount, $3,920,000 (discounted) was recognized at December 31, 2001. Thus, to record the fair value of the contract on the settlement date requires an additional credit to OCI of $2,080,000 ($6,000,000 gain – $3,920,000).]

OCI	$4,000,000	
Net investment - Subco		$4,000,000

[The translation adjustment is the change in spot rates ($1.13 – $1.09) times 100,000,000 FCU, or a loss of $4,000,000.]

Cash	$6,000,000	
Receivable - forward contract		$6,000,000

(This entry reflects the net cash settlement of the foreign currency forward contract.)

d. **Fair value hedge using an interest-rate swap**. Major Manufacturer borrowed $1 million on December 31, 2001 for 3 years at 8% fixed interest. The debt is not prepayable, and interest is due semiannually. On the same date, Major entered into an interest-rate swap by which it receives 8% fixed interest on $1 million and pays variable interest on the same amount in accordance with an agreed index of standard interest rates. Payments on the debt and settlement of the swap are on the same dates, with no premium/discount resulting from the swap. Major designates the swap as a fair value hedge, and the risk hedged is stated to be the change in market interest rates. Furthermore, the hedge is assumed to be completely effective because all of the criteria in SFAS 133 are met; i.e., the swap's fair value at its inception is zero, the notional amount of the swap equals the principal amount of the debt, the expiration date of the swap equals the maturity date of the debt, etc. Given that the hedge is completely effective, changes in its fair value are used to measure the changes in the fair value of the debt. The following are illustrative data at the inception date and the first two reset dates:

	Fair Value of the Debt	Fair Value of the Interest Rate Swap Based on Dealer Quotes (After Settlement)	Index Variable Rate (Rate Changed on Indicated Date)
December 31, 2001	$1,000,000	$ 0	6.5%
June 30, 2002	970,000	(30,000)	7.5%
December 31, 2002	1,010,000	10,000	6.0%

Under the shortcut method described in SFAS 133, the variable rate paid on the swap is combined with the difference between the fixed rates paid and received (in this case, zero). The result is multiplied by the principal of the debt to determine the annual interest expense. The following are illustrative journal entries:

December 31, 2001

Cash	$1,000,000	
Debt		$1,000,000

(The swap's fair value at its inception is given as zero. Thus, no entry is made.)

June 30, 2002

Interest expense	$40,000	
Interest payable		$40,000
Interest payable	$40,000	
Cash		$40,000

(The interest on the debt is $1,000,000 times the 8% fixed rate for 6 months.)

Cash	$7,500	
Interest expense		$7,500

[The semiannual interest expense equals the 6.5% variable rate for the first 6 months of 2002 times $1,000,000 times 6 divided by 12 months, or $32,500. Accordingly, Major receives a net settlement of $7,500 ($40,000 paid on the debt – $32,500 semiannual interest expense).]

Debt	$30,000	
Gain from hedge		$30,000

(The increase in interest rates at June 30, 2002 reduced the debt's fair value.)

Loss from hedge	$30,000	
Interest rate swap contract		$30,000

(The swap's fair value decreased.)

December 31, 2002

(The entries to accrue and pay the $40,000 interest on the debt are the same.)

Cash	$2,500	
Interest expense		$2,500

[The semiannual interest expense equals the 7.5% variable rate for the last 6 months of 2002 times $1,000,000 times 6 divided by 12 months, or $37,500. Accordingly, Major receives a net settlement of $2,500 ($40,000 paid on the debt – $37,500 semiannual interest expense).]

Loss from hedge	$40,000	
Debt		$40,000

(The decrease in interest rates at December 31, 2002 increased the debt's fair value.)

Interest rate swap contract	$40,000	
Gain from hedge		$40,000

(The swap's fair value increased.)

e. **Embedded derivative used as a cash flow hedge of a forecasted transaction**. Aviatrix Co. bought a one-year crude oil knock-in note on January 1, 2001 for $20,000,000. Such a note combines an interest-bearing instrument with a series of options. This note had a 1% coupon rate and provided for investor gains if specified oil prices rose. The contingency was not separable from the note. In effect, part of the normal coupon rate purchased an option tied to changes in oil prices. This embedded option should be accounted for separately because it is not clearly and closely related to the economic characteristics of the host contract (a fixed rate note); the option is indexed to the price of oil and is not related to interest rates. Moreover, the host contract is not remeasured at fair value, and the option qualifies as a derivative instrument.

Aviatrix appropriately designated the option as a hedge of fuel purchases it expects to make on January 1, 2002, and it has ascertained that the option should be highly effective as a hedge because the intrinsic value of the option is closely correlated with the expected cash outflows for fuel purchases. Under SFAS 133, an entity that elects hedge accounting must determine at the outset the methods for assessing the effectiveness and ineffectiveness of the hedge. Aviatrix has decided to assess hedge effectiveness based on the option's intrinsic value; hence, the change in time value is excluded from the assessment of hedge effectiveness (paragraph 63 of SFAS 133).

The note had a fair value on January 1, 2001 of $18,800,000, and the option had a fair value of $1,200,000 (but a $0 intrinsic value). If the option's maturity value (an intrinsic, not a time, value) was $1,500,000, the journal entries made by Aviatrix in accordance with SFAS 133 are as follows:

January 1, 2001

Investment in knock-in note	$18,800,000	
Option	1,200,000	
Cash		$20,000,000

(To record the note's purchase.)

December 31, 2001

Investment in knock-in note	$1,200,000	
Interest income		$1,200,000

(To amortize the discount on the note.)

Interest receivable	$200,000	
Interest income		$200,000

[This entry accrues annual interest at the nominal rate of 1% (1% x $20,000,000).]

Option	$1,500,000	
Other comprehensive income		$1,500,000

[To record the change in the intrinsic value of the option ($1,500,000 – $0 = $1,500,000). The credit is to OCI because the option is a cash flow hedge of a forecasted transaction. This gain will be reclassified into earnings when the fuel purchases are recorded.]

Loss from hedge	$1,200,000	
Option		$1,200,000

[To record the extent of ineffectiveness of the hedge, that is, the change in the time value. Because the effectiveness of the option is assessed based only on intrinsic value, the change in time value ($1,200,000 – $0 = $1,200,000 loss) is debited to a loss. The ineffective portion of the gain or loss on a derivative designated as a cash flow hedge is reported in earnings.]

January 1, 2002

Cash	$21,700,000	
Investment in knock-in note		$20,000,000
Option		1,500,000
Interest receivable		200,000

17. Stop and review! You have completed the outline for this subunit. Study multiple-choice questions 44 through 56 beginning on page 380.

MULTIPLE-CHOICE QUESTIONS

A. Business Combinations

1. A business combination may be legally structured as a merger, a consolidation, or an acquisition. Which of the following describes a business combination that is legally structured as a merger?

A. The surviving company is one of the two combining companies.

B. The surviving company is neither of the two combining companies.

C. An investor-investee relationship is established.

D. A parent-subsidiary relationship is established.

The correct answer is (A). *(Publisher)*

REQUIRED: The characteristic of a business combination legally structured as a merger.

DISCUSSION: In a business combination legally structured as a merger, the assets and liabilities of one of the combining companies are transferred to the books of the other combining company (the surviving company). The surviving company continues to exist as a separate legal entity. The nonsurviving company ceases to exist as a separate entity. Its stock is canceled, and its books are closed.

Answer (B) is incorrect because it describes a consolidation, in which a new firm is formed to account for the assets and liabilities of the combining companies. Answers (C) and (D) are incorrect because they describe an acquisition. A parent-subsidiary relationship exists when the investor company holds more than 50% of the outstanding stock of the investee company.

2. A horizontal merger is a merger between

A. Two or more firms from different and unrelated markets.

B. Two or more firms at different stages of the production process.

C. A producer and its supplier.

D. Two or more firms in the same market.

The correct answer is (D). *(CMA, adapted)*

REQUIRED: The example of a horizontal merger.

DISCUSSION: A horizontal merger is one between competitors in the same market. From the viewpoint of the Justice Department, it is the most closely scrutinized type of merger because it has the greatest tendency to reduce competition.

Answer (A) is incorrect because a merger between firms in different and unrelated markets is a conglomerate merger. Answers (B) and (C) are incorrect because a merger between two or more firms at different stages of the production process, or between a producer and a supplier, is a vertical merger.

3. Which type of acquisition does not require shareholders to have a formal vote to approve?

A. Merger.

B. Acquisition of stock.

C. Acquisition of all of the firm's assets.

D. Consolidation.

The correct answer is (B). *(Publisher)*

REQUIRED: The type of acquisition that does not require a formal vote by shareholders for approval.

DISCUSSION: Purchasing the stock of another company is advantageous when management and the board of directors of the purchased company are hostile to the combination because the acquisition does not require a formal vote by the shareholders. Thus, the management and the board of directors cannot influence shareholders. Also, after the acquisition, both companies continue to operate separately.

Answer (A) is incorrect because a merger is not an acquisition. In a merger, only one of the combining companies survives. Answer (C) is incorrect because an acquisition of all of the firm's assets requires a vote from the shareholders. Answer (D) is incorrect because in a consolidation, a new company is formed and neither of the merging companies survives.

4. Which of the following is a combination involving the absorption of one firm by another?

A. Merger.

B. Consolidation.

C. Proxy fight.

D. Acquisition.

The correct answer is (A). *(Publisher)*

REQUIRED: The combination involving the absorption of one firm by another.

DISCUSSION: A merger is a business combination in which an acquiring firm absorbs another firm. The acquiring firm remains in business as a combination of the two merged firms. Thus, the acquiring firm maintains its name and identity. However, approval of the merger is required by votes of the shareholders of each firm.

Answer (B) is incorrect because a consolidation merges two companies and forms a new company in which neither of the two merging firms survives. It is similar to a merger, but one firm is not absorbed by another. Answer (C) is incorrect because a proxy fight is an attempt by dissident shareholders to gain control of the corporation by electing directors. Answer (D) is incorrect because both companies continue to operate separately after an acquisition.

5. The acquisition of a retail shoe store by a shoe manufacturer is an example of

A. Vertical integration.

B. A conglomerate.

C. Market extension.

D. Horizontal integration.

The correct answer is (A). *(CMA, adapted)*

REQUIRED: The type of transaction represented.

DISCUSSION: The acquisition of a shoe retailer by a shoe manufacturer is an example of vertical integration. Vertical integration is typified by a merger or acquisition involving companies that are in the same industry but at different levels in the supply chain. In other words, one of the companies supplies inputs for the other.

Answer (B) is incorrect because a conglomerate is a company made up of subsidiaries in unrelated industries. Answer (C) is incorrect because market extension involves expanding into new market areas. Answer (D) is incorrect because horizontal integration involves a merger between competing firms in the same industry.

6. In a business combination that is accounted for as a purchase and does not create negative goodwill, the acquiring company records the assets of the acquired company at the

A. Original cost.

B. Original cost minus accumulated depreciation.

C. Fair value.

D. Book value.

The correct answer is (C). *(CMA, adapted)*

REQUIRED: The accounting for a business combination not resulting in negative goodwill that is accounted for as a purchase.

DISCUSSION: Business combinations are accounted for either as a purchase or as a pooling of interests. Under purchase accounting, the cost of the acquired company is allocated to the assets acquired and liabilities assumed on the basis of their fair values. Any excess of the cost over the fair value of the identifiable net assets acquired is allocated to goodwill. If the fair value of the identifiable net assets acquired is greater than cost, the excess (negative goodwill) is allocated proportionately to reduce the values assigned to noncurrent assets (except long-term investments in marketable securities). Any remainder is classified as a deferred credit (APB 16).

Answers (A) and (B) are incorrect because assets are recorded at their fair value in a purchase. Answer (D) is incorrect because book value is the method used to record assets in a pooling of interests.

7. Under the purchase method of accounting, the value of long-lived assets of the acquired company

A. Is the book value in the ledger and the consolidated financial statements.

B. Is the fair value in the ledger and book value in the consolidated financial statements.

C. Is the current fair value.

D. Depends upon the purchase price paid for the assets on the date of acquisition.

The correct answer is (D). *(CMA, adapted)*

REQUIRED: The true statement about the value of long-lived assets of an acquired company.

DISCUSSION: The purchase method follows principles normally applied under historical-cost accounting. Assets acquired for cash or other assets are recorded at cost (cash paid or the fair value of the other assets). Assets acquired by incurring liabilities are also recorded at cost (the present value of the amounts to be paid). Assets acquired by issuing stock are recorded at their fair value. Whatever the form of the price paid, it must then be allocated to the individual assets acquired and liabilities assumed.

Answer (A) is incorrect because a pooling of interests records assets acquired at their book values. Answer (B) is incorrect because the old book values are not carried forward unless they are equal to the fair values at the time of acquisition. Answer (C) is incorrect because the fair values may be written down if the purchase price is less than the fair value, that is, if negative goodwill exists.

8. APB 16 states the principles to be followed in allocating the cost of an acquired company when using the purchase method for a business combination. If the current fair value of the net assets acquired exceeds the total cost, the difference should be

A. Added directly to shareholders' equity at the date of acquisition.

B. Treated as goodwill to be amortized over the period benefitted, not to exceed 40 years.

C. Allocated on a pro rata basis to the assets acquired.

D. Applied pro rata to reduce, but not below zero, the amounts initially assigned to noncurrent assets other than long-term investments in marketable securities.

The correct answer is (D). *(CMA, adapted)*

REQUIRED: The proper treatment of the excess of the current fair value of net assets acquired over their total cost.

DISCUSSION: APB 16 requires that the excess (negative goodwill) be allocated proportionately based on their fair values to all noncurrent assets except long-term investments in marketable securities. Any excess remaining after noncurrent assets are adjusted to zero should be classified as a deferred credit to be amortized over a period not exceeding 40 years.

Answer (A) is incorrect because negative goodwill is not added to shareholders' equity. Answer (B) is incorrect because the difference is not goodwill, which is the excess of cost over the fair value of the identifiable net assets, but negative goodwill. Answer (C) is incorrect because allocations are made only to noncurrent assets.

9. Under accounting for consolidations, the purchase method is characterized by all of the following attributes except that the

A. Assets and liabilities are recorded at fair value or the purchase price of the acquired company, whichever is less.

B. Excess of the purchase price over the fair value of identifiable assets and liabilities is recorded as goodwill.

C. Goodwill of the acquired company is always carried forward to the balance sheet of the consolidated entity.

D. Fair value of the shares issued by the acquiring company is added to the paid-in capital of the consolidated entity.

The correct answer is (C). *(CMA, adapted)*

REQUIRED: The item not a characteristic of the purchase method.

DISCUSSION: When a business combination is accounted for as a purchase, the cost is allocated to the specifically identifiable assets acquired and liabilities assumed based on their fair values. If the cost exceeds the sum of the amounts assigned to the net identifiable assets, the excess is recorded as goodwill, an intangible that is not specifically identifiable. Thus, the acquiring company will seldom record goodwill equal to the amount on the acquired company's balance sheet. Indeed, goodwill may not be recorded because the fair value of the identifiable net assets exceeds the cost.

Answer (A) is incorrect because historical-cost accounting for purchase method transactions requires the identifiable net assets to be recorded at fair value or the purchase price of the acquired company, whichever is less. Answer (B) is incorrect because goodwill is the excess of the price over the fair value of the identifiable net assets. Answer (D) is incorrect because the stock issued by the parent is recorded at its fair value, just as in any purchase transaction.

10. Which form of accounting for a business combination must result in recognition of goodwill when the amount paid exceeds the fair value of the identifiable net assets?

A. Consolidation.

B. Aggregation.

C. Purchase.

D. Pooling.

The correct answer is (C). *(Publisher)*

REQUIRED: The form of accounting for a business combination that creates goodwill.

DISCUSSION: The purchase method treats the combination as an acquisition of one company by another. The acquirer records the identifiable assets obtained and liabilities assumed at their fair values. Goodwill is the excess of the purchase price of the assets or an investee over the sum of the assigned costs (fair values) of the net identifiable assets (sum of the identifiable tangible and identifiable intangible assets, minus liabilities assumed).

Answer (A) is incorrect because a consolidation may be accounted for as a pooling, a method that records only book values. Answer (B) is incorrect because aggregation is a nonsense term in this context. Answer (D) is incorrect because, in a pooling, assets and liabilities are recorded at book value, so goodwill is not recognized.

11. What form of accounting is used when the assets of the acquired firm are added to the assets of the acquiring firm at book value after business combination?

A. Consolidation.

B. Aggregation.

C. Purchase.

D. Pooling.

The correct answer is (D). *(Publisher)*

REQUIRED: The form of accounting used when the assets of the acquired firm are added to the assets of the acquiring firm at book value after business combination.

DISCUSSION: In pooling of interests, assets and liabilities are recorded by the combined entity at their carrying (book) value, a treatment compatible with historical cost. If the separate companies recorded assets and liabilities using different methods, the amounts may be adjusted to the same basis of accounting if the change would have been appropriate for the separate company.

Answer (A) is incorrect because a consolidation may be accounted for as a purchase wherein assets are recorded at fair values. Answer (B) is incorrect because aggregation is a nonsense term in this context. Answer (C) is incorrect because purchase accounting records fair, not book, values.

12. Under accounting for consolidations, the pooling method is characterized by all of the following attributes except that the

A. Assets and liabilities of the acquired company are recorded at book value for consolidation reporting purposes.

B. Business combination expenses for acquiring a company under the pooling method are capitalized.

C. Newly created goodwill, rather than goodwill that was already on the books of the subsidiary, is not recognized.

D. Retained earnings of the acquired company are carried forward to the consolidated financial statements.

The correct answer is (B). *(CMA, adapted)*

REQUIRED: The attribute not a characteristic of the pooling method.

DISCUSSION: Costs incurred to effect a business combination accounted for as a pooling of interests are expenses of the combined corporation, not additions to assets or direct reductions of shareholders' equity. Consequently, they are deducted in determining the net income of the combined company for the period in which they are incurred (APB 16).

Answers (A) and (D) are incorrect because pooling-of-interests accounting assumes a combining of ownership interests, not a purchase, and no basis exists for revaluing assets. No readjustment of asset and liability balances occurs except to conform the accounting principles of the pooled companies. Accordingly, the retained earnings of the acquired company are also carried forward to the consolidated financial statements. Answer (C) is incorrect because no goodwill is recorded in a pooling unless it was already on the books of a combining company. Goodwill is recognized only if a purchase has occurred to establish an objective valuation.

13. The 12 conditions established by the Accounting Principles Board (APB) that must be present in order to use the pooling accounting method for business combinations include all of the following except

A. Each of the constituent companies is independent of the other companies.

B. The constituent companies combine in a single transaction or in accordance with a specific plan within 1 year of initiating the plan.

C. None of the constituent companies change the equity interest of their voting common stock either within 2 years of initiating the combination or between the date of initiation and consummation of the combination.

D. The combined enterprise agrees to retire or acquire all of the common stock issued to effect the combination.

The correct answer is (D). *(CMA, adapted)*

REQUIRED: The item that is not a criterion to use the pooling-of-interest method.

DISCUSSION: Under APB 16, all 12 of the following criteria must be met: (1) The combining companies are autonomous; i.e., one has not been a subsidiary of the other during the past 2 years. (2) Not more than 10% of the stock of any combining company is held by the other combining companies before the pooling. (3) The combination is effected in a single transaction within 1 year after the plan is initiated. (4) Only common stock of the surviving company is issued for at least 90% of the outstanding voting stock of the other combining companies. (5) The combining companies do not change the composition of shareholders' equity or the amount of common stock in contemplation of the combination. (6) The combining companies reacquire treasury stock only for purposes other than the business combination. (7) The ratio of ownership of individual common shareholders to that of other common shareholders remains the same after the exchange of stock; i.e., each shareholder maintains his/her relative percentage of ownership. (8) The new shareholders are not deprived of or restricted in exercising the voting rights of their stock. (9) The combination is resolved when initiated, and there are no provisions for contingent issuances of securities or for the payment of other contingent consideration. (10) There is no plan to retire any stock issued to effect the combination. (11) No special financial arrangements are made to benefit former shareholders of the combining companies. (12) There is no plan to dispose of a significant amount of the combining companies' assets for the 2 years following the combination, except to eliminate duplicate facilities or excess capacity. As noted above, an agreement to directly or indirectly retire or acquire all of the common stock issued to effect the combination would rule out the use of the pooling method.

Answers (A), (B), and (C) are incorrect because these are all pooling criteria specified in APB 16.

14. Poe, Inc. acquired 100% of Shaw Co. in a business combination on September 30, 2000. During 2000, Poe declared quarterly dividends of $25,000, and Shaw declared quarterly dividends of $10,000. Under each of the following methods of accounting for the business combination, what amount should be reported as dividends declared in the December 31, 2000 consolidated statement of retained earnings?

	Purchase	Pooling of Interests
A.	$100,000	$130,000
B.	$100,000	$140,000
C.	$130,000	$130,000
D.	$130,000	$140,000

The correct answer is (A). *(CPA, adapted)*

REQUIRED: The dividends declared to be reported under the purchase and pooling methods.

DISCUSSION: Under the purchase method, no part of the shareholders' equity of the acquired company is carried forward after the combination. Thus, only the $100,000 of dividends declared by Poe will be included in the statement of retained earnings. Under the pooling-of-interests method, the retained earnings balances of the combining companies at the time of the combination are carried forward. Accordingly, the dividends declared by Shaw prior to the combination date plus the dividends declared by Poe ($100,000 + $30,000 = $130,000) will be reported in the consolidated statement of retained earnings.

Answer (B) is incorrect because $140,000 erroneously includes the $10,000 dividend declared by Shaw after the combination date. Answer (C) is incorrect because only the dividends declared by Poe should be reported under the purchase method. Answer (D) is incorrect because $130,000 should be the amount declared under the pooling of interests method rather than the purchase method, and $140,000 erroneously includes the dividends declared by Shaw after the combination date.

Questions 15 and 16 are based on the following information. These costs were incurred in completing a business combination.

Direct acquisition expenses	$120,000
Indirect acquisition expenses	60,000
Costs to register and issue stock	40,000

15. Assuming that this business combination is appropriately accounted for as a purchase, the amount charged to the expenses of business combination account is

A. $40,000

B. $60,000

C. $100,000

D. $120,000

The correct answer is (B). *(CMA, adapted)*

REQUIRED: The amount charged to expense assuming a business combination is treated as a purchase.

DISCUSSION: In applying the purchase method of accounting for a business combination, the cost to the purchasing entity of acquiring another entity is the amount of cash or the fair value of other assets given up in the transaction. In addition, any direct fees paid related to the combination are added to the consideration given. Costs of registering and issuing equity securities are a reduction of the otherwise determinable fair value of the securities. The amount charged to expenses of business combination is therefore the indirect acquisition expense of $60,000.

Answers (A) and (C) are incorrect because the costs to register and issue stock reduce its fair value. Answer (D) is incorrect because direct fees are added to the consideration given.

16. Assuming that this business combination is appropriately accounted for as a pooling of interests, the amount charged to the expenses of business combination account is

A. $40,000

B. $60,000

C. $100,000

D. $220,000

The correct answer is (D). *(CMA, adapted)*

REQUIRED: The amount charged to expense assuming a business combination is treated as a pooling.

DISCUSSION: According to APB 16, *Business Combinations*, "The pooling of interests method records neither the acquiring of assets nor the obtaining of capital. Therefore, costs incurred to effect a combination accounted for by that method and to integrate the continuing operations are expenses of the combined corporation rather than additions to assets or direct reductions of shareholders' equity. Accordingly, all expenses related to effecting a business combination accounted for by the pooling of interests method should be deducted in determining the net income of the resulting combined corporation for the period in which the expenses are incurred. Those expenses include, for example, registration fees, costs of furnishing information to shareholders, fees of finders and consultants, salaries and other expenses related to services of employees, and costs and losses of combining operations of the previously separate companies and instituting efficiencies." Thus, $220,000 ($120,000 + $60,000 + $40,000) should be expensed.

Answers (A), (B), and (C) are incorrect because all of the listed costs should be expensed.

Questions 17 and 18 are based on the following information. On July 1, Pushway Corporation issued 200,000 shares of $5 par value common stock in exchange for all of Stroker Company's common stock. This stock had a fair value that was $200,000 in excess of the equity of Stroker Company on the date of exchange. This difference was attributed to the excess of the fair value of Stroker Company's equipment over its book value. The equipment has an estimated remaining life of 10 years. Pushway Corporation and Stroker Company reported depreciation expense for the year of the combination of $400,000 and $100,000 respectively before consolidation and before any adjustment for the exchange. For financial reporting purposes, both companies use a calendar year and the straight-line depreciation method with depreciation calculated on a monthly basis beginning with the month of acquisition.

17. Assuming the business combination is appropriately accounted for as a purchase, consolidated depreciation expense reported for the year of the combination would have been

A. $400,000

B. $500,000

C. $510,000

D. $460,000

The correct answer is (D). *(CMA, adapted)*

REQUIRED: The consolidated depreciation expense assuming purchase accounting.

DISCUSSION: Under the purchase method, depreciation expense consists of that recorded by each of the companies, plus depreciation on written-up assets. Allocating the $200,000 write-up over 10 years results in extra depreciation on the consolidated worksheet (appearing on neither company's individual books) of $20,000 per year. Because the combination occurred at midyear, only one-half year's extra depreciation should be recorded, or $10,000. Thus, the consolidated depreciation expense is $460,000 ($400,000 + $50,000 Stroker depreciation for 6 months + $10,000).

Answer (A) is incorrect because $400,000 equals Pushway's depreciation for the year of the combination. Answer (B) is incorrect because $500,000 assumes a pooling of interests. Answer (C) is incorrect because $510,000 includes Pushway's depreciation, Stroker's depreciation, and 6 months of the extra depreciation.

18. Assuming the business combination is appropriately accounted for as a pooling of interests, consolidated depreciation expense reported for the year of the combination would have been

A. $400,000

B. $500,000

C. $510,000

D. $520,000

The correct answer is (B). *(CMA, adapted)*

REQUIRED: The consolidated depreciation expense assuming a pooling of interests.

DISCUSSION: In a pooling of interests, assets are recorded at the book values at which they appeared on the investee's books. Accordingly, no goodwill or write-up of assets is recognized, and depreciation expense simply consists of the $500,000 ($400,000 + $100,000) recorded on the books of the separate companies.

Answer (A) is incorrect because $400,000 equals Pushway's depreciation for the year of the combination. Answer (C) is incorrect because $510,000 assumes a write-up of the equipment for half of the current year. Answer (D) is incorrect because $520,000 assumes a write-up of the equipment.

Questions 19 and 20 are based on the following information. On June 30, 2000, Pane Corp. exchanged 150,000 shares of its $20 par value common stock for all of Sky Corp.'s common stock. At that date, the fair value of Pane's common stock issued was equal to the book value of Sky's net assets. Both corporations continued to operate as separate businesses, maintaining accounting records with years ending December 31. Information from separate company operations follows:

	Pane	Sky
Retained earnings -- 12/31/99	$3,200,000	$925,000
Net income -- 6 months ended 6/30/00	800,000	275,000
Dividends paid -- 3/25/00	750,000	--

19. If the business combination is accounted for as a pooling of interests, what amount of retained earnings would Pane report in its June 30, 2000 consolidated balance sheet?

A. $5,200,000

B. $4,450,000

C. $3,525,000

D. $3,250,000

The correct answer is (B). *(CPA, adapted)*

REQUIRED: The retained earnings at the date of acquisition after a pooling of interests.

DISCUSSION: In a pooling of interests, the contributed capital of the surviving entity should be equal to the total of the contributed capital for the combining entities. The retained earnings for the surviving entity should also be equal to the total of the retained earnings of the combining entities, except in certain circumstances, e.g., when an allocation of retained earnings was made to contributed capital, or the effects of intercompany transactions must be eliminated. The total of the retained earnings of the combining companies on June 30, 2000 is $4,450,000 ($3,200,000 Pane's RE at 12/31/99 + $800,000 Pane's NI at 6/30/00 + $925,000 Sky's RE at 12/31/99 + $275,000 Sky's NI at 6/30/00 – $750,000 dividends paid by Pane on 3/25/00).

Answer (A) is incorrect because $5,200,000 includes the dividends paid by Pane. Answer (C) is incorrect because $3,525,000 does not include Sky's beginning retained earnings. Answer (D) is incorrect because $3,250,000 equals Pane's separate retained earnings on June 30, 2000.

20. If the business combination is accounted for as a purchase, what amount of retained earnings would Pane report in its June 30, 2000 consolidated balance sheet?

A. $5,200,000

B. $4,450,000

C. $3,525,000

D. $3,250,000

The correct answer is (D). *(CPA, adapted)*

REQUIRED: The retained earnings at the date of a business combination accounted for as a purchase.

DISCUSSION: A purchase is viewed as an acquisition of net assets. Thus, only the fair value of the net assets of a subsidiary is included in a consolidated balance sheet prepared using the purchase method. The shareholders' equity, including retained earnings, is excluded. Pane's separate retained earnings is therefore equal to the amount in the consolidated balance sheet, i.e., $3,250,000 ($3,200,000 beginning RE + $800,000 NI – $750,000 dividends).

Answer (A) is incorrect because $5,200,000 includes Sky's retained earnings at 6/30/00 and does not deduct the dividends paid. Answer (B) is incorrect because $4,450,000 equals the consolidated retained earnings if the combination is accounted for as a pooling. Answer (C) is incorrect because $3,525,000 includes Sky's net income through 6/30/00.

Questions 21 and 22 are based on the following information. On December 31, 2000, Saxe Corporation was merged into Poe Corporation. In the business combination, Poe issued 200,000 shares of its $10 par common stock, with a market price of $18 a share, for all of Saxe's common stock.

The shareholders' equity section of each company's balance sheet immediately before the combination was

	Poe	Saxe
Common stock	$3,000,000	$1,500,000
Additional paid-in capital	1,300,000	150,000
Retained earnings	2,500,000	850,000
	$6,800,000	$2,500,000

21. Assume that the merger qualifies for treatment as a purchase. In the December 31, 2000 consolidated balance sheet, additional paid-in capital should be reported at

A. $950,000

B. $1,300,000

C. $1,450,000

D. $2,900,000

The correct answer is (D). *(CPA, adapted)*

REQUIRED: The additional paid-in capital to be reported in the consolidated balance sheet assuming a purchase.

DISCUSSION: A business combination accounted for as a purchase is treated as an acquisition. To effect the acquisition, the 200,000 shares were issued for $3,600,000 (200,000 shares x $18 market price per share). Of this amount, $2,000,000 (200,000 shares x $10 par) should be allocated to the common stock of Poe, with the remaining $1,600,000 ($3,600,000 – $2,000,000) allocated to additional paid-in capital. The additional paid-in capital recorded on Poe's (the parent company's) books is $2,900,000 ($1,300,000 + $1,600,000). This balance is also reported on the 2000 consolidated balance sheet.

Answer (A) is incorrect because $950,000 is the additional paid-in capital reported under the pooling of interests method. Answer (B) is incorrect because $1,300,000 is the amount reported by Poe immediately before the combination. Answer (C) is incorrect because $1,450,000 is the sum of the amounts reported by Poe and Saxe immediately before the combination.

22. Assume that the merger qualifies for treatment as a pooling of interests. In the December 31, 2000 consolidated balance sheet, additional paid-in capital should be reported at

A. $950,000

B. $1,300,000

C. $1,450,000

D. $2,900,000

The correct answer is (A). *(CPA, adapted)*

REQUIRED: The additional paid-in capital to be reported in the consolidated balance sheet for a merger qualifying as a pooling of interests.

DISCUSSION: If the transaction is accounted for as a pooling of interests, the contributed capital for the combined entity is equal to the sum of the contributed capital for the combining entities. Poe's contributed capital is $4,300,000 ($3,000,000 common stock + $1,300,000 additional paid-in capital). Saxe's contributed capital is $1,650,000 ($1,500,000 common stock + $150,000 additional paid-in capital). Contributed capital for the consolidated entity is therefore equal to $5,950,000. Of this total, $3,000,000 should be allocated to the common stock account for the Poe stock outstanding prior to the combination. An additional $2,000,000 (200,000 shares x $10 par value) should also be allocated to common stock because of the issuance of stock to effect the combination. Hence, the total recorded in common stock is $5,000,000. The remaining $950,000 ($5,950,000 total contributed capital – $5,000,000 total common stock) is allocated to additional paid-in capital for Poe as the parent and for the consolidated entity.

Answer (B) is incorrect because $1,300,000 is the amount reported by Poe immediately before the combination. Answer (C) is incorrect because $1,450,000 is the sum of the amounts reported by Poe and Saxe immediately before the combination. Answer (D) is incorrect because $2,900,000 is the additional paid-in capital reported under the purchase method.

B. Consolidated Financial Statements

23. When issuing consolidated financial statements,

A. The notes must show how the gross consolidated income tax return expense is allocated to the entities comprising the consolidation.

B. The consolidation policy must be disclosed either in the body of the financial statements or in a note to the financial statements.

C. Parent company statements and consolidated statements should not be presented in the same set of statements in a comparative format.

D. The consolidation policy must be presented in the notes to the financial statements as the first item in the accounting policies note.

The correct answer is (B). *(CMA, adapted)*

REQUIRED: The true statement about the issuance of consolidated financial statements.

DISCUSSION: A description of all significant accounting policies should be included as an integral part of the financial statements. An example of a required disclosure is the basis of consolidation. This disclosure is normally made in the first footnote to the financial statements or in a separate summary preceding the notes (APB 22).

Answer (A) is incorrect because the provisions requiring taxes to be allocated among entities relates only to financial accounting income tax expense, not the tax return income tax expense. Answer (C) is incorrect because there are no prohibitions against reporting parent company and consolidated statements in a comparative format. Answer (D) is incorrect because consolidation policies may be shown on the face of the financial statements.

24. When preparing consolidated financial statements, the entity being accounted for is the

A. Legal entity.

B. Parent company.

C. Minority interest.

D. Economic entity.

The correct answer is (D). *(CMA, adapted)*

REQUIRED: The entity being accounted for when consolidated financial statements are prepared.

DISCUSSION: The preparation of consolidated financial statements is based upon the concept of economic entity, not legal entity. Each of the corporations in a consolidated group is a separate legal entity, but consolidated statements are prepared because all of the corporations are under common economic control.

Answer (A) is incorrect because each corporation is a separate legal entity, but no legal entity represents the entire group. Answer (B) is incorrect because consolidated financial statements are for the parent company and all of its subsidiaries. Answer (C) is incorrect because the financial statements represent the holdings of the consolidated group, not the minority interest. The minority interest has equity only in certain subsidiaries.

25. Panco, Inc. owns 90% of the voting stock of Spany Corporation. After consolidated financial statements have been prepared, the entries to eliminate intercompany payables and receivables will

A. Be reflected only in the accounts of Panco.

B. Be reflected only in the accounts of Spany.

C. Be reflected in the accounts of both Panco and Spany.

D. Not be reflected in the accounts of either company.

The correct answer is (D). *(CMA, adapted)*

REQUIRED: The accounts, if any, affected by elimination entries.

DISCUSSION: Elimination entries appear only in the working papers used to consolidate a parent and its subsidiaries. They never appear on the books of either the parent or the subsidiary. Each corporation is a separate entity, and individual company books should show intercompany payables and receivables without adjustment for the effect of elimination entries.

Answers (A), (B), and (C) are incorrect because elimination entries appear only in the working papers.

26. Allocation of the differential in connection with the investment elimination for preparing consolidated statements is unnecessary if

A. The elimination entry is being made in the first year after the business combination.

B. The business combination was recorded as a pooling of interests.

C. The cost method of accounting for the investment has been used.

D. The equity method of accounting for the investment has been used.

The correct answer is (B). *(CMA, adapted)*

REQUIRED: The circumstance in which allocation of the investment elimination differential is unnecessary.

DISCUSSION: When a business combination is recorded as a purchase, the cost of the net assets acquired and their fair value will usually differ. The purchase price is allocated to the specifically identifiable assets acquired and liabilities assumed based on their fair values. The excess of cost over the fair value of net assets received is designated as goodwill. In a pooling of interests, the assets acquired and liabilities assumed are recorded at their book values prior to consolidation. In a pooling, no goodwill and no differential will exist to allocate.

Answer (A) is incorrect because an elimination entry will always have to be made when a consolidation is recorded as a purchase, regardless of the year. Answers (C) and (D) are incorrect because allocations must be made whenever a purchase is involved under either method.

27. In the preparation of consolidated financial statements, the investment in subsidiary account should not be eliminated against the

A. Retained earnings of the subsidiary.

B. Par value of capital stock of the subsidiary.

C. Paid-in capital above par value of the subsidiary.

D. Intercompany accounts receivable.

The correct answer is (D). *(CMA, adapted)*

REQUIRED: The account against which the investment in subsidiary account is not eliminated.

DISCUSSION: Intercompany accounts receivable must be eliminated (credited) in the consolidation working papers, but the offsetting debit is to intercompany payables. In the preparation of consolidated financial statements, the investment in subsidiary account has to be eliminated (credited) in the working papers against the accounts of the subsidiaries. In addition to this elimination entry, other entries eliminate intercompany receivables, payables, sales, and purchases.

Answers (A), (B), and (C) are incorrect because all shareholders' equity accounts of the subsidiary are eliminated against the investment account.

28. In the process of preparing consolidated financial statements, which one of the following items does not need to be eliminated?

A. Intercompany profit in beginning inventory.

B. Intercompany profit on intercompany sale of a fixed asset.

C. Intercompany dividends receivable/payable.

D. Intercompany profit on inventory sold to a nonaffiliated company.

The correct answer is (D). *(CMA, adapted)*

REQUIRED: The item that is not eliminated in the preparation of consolidated financial statements.

DISCUSSION: Intercompany profits must be eliminated whenever the assets sold are still within the consolidated group. For example, if the parent sells equipment to a subsidiary at a profit, the intercompany profit must be eliminated before the consolidated statements are prepared or the assets will not be recorded (on the consolidated balance sheet) at historical cost to the group. If the subsidiary subsequently sells the assets to someone outside the group, the original intercompany profit will be realized (through sale to the outsider) and no longer will need to be eliminated.

Answers (A) and (B) are incorrect because intercompany profits in inventory, or any other assets still within the group, must be eliminated. Answer (C) is incorrect because intercompany dividends receivable/payable must be eliminated. Otherwise, the consolidated company would report an asset receivable from itself.

29. If a parent company purchases a 90% interest in a subsidiary accounted for by the entity theory, and if the investment cost exceeds book value of the subsidiary's net assets, the minority interest will

A. Be the same amount as if the parent company used the proprietary theory in preparing consolidated financial statements.

B. Be less in amount than if the parent company used the proprietary theory in preparing consolidated financial statements.

C. Be more in amount than if the parent company used the proprietary theory in preparing consolidated financial statements.

D. Not be separately disclosed in the consolidated financial statements.

The correct answer is (C). *(CMA, adapted)*

REQUIRED: The true statement about minority interest under the entity theory if a subsidiary is purchased at an amount in excess of the book value of its net assets.

DISCUSSION: The issue is whether goodwill is recognized only on the portion of the subsidiary bought by the parent (proprietary theory), or whether goodwill should be recognized in total for the subsidiary, i.e., on the portion of assets bought by the parent plus the portion retained by the minority shareholders (the entity theory). For example, if a subsidiary's net assets are $100,000 and the parent pays $99,000 for a 90% interest, goodwill is $9,000 under the proprietary theory. In other words, equity of $90,000 in identifiable assets was acquired for $99,000. Hence, goodwill must be $9,000. However, if $9,000 of goodwill is attributable to the $90,000 of assets acquired by the parent, the entity theory argues that $1,000 of goodwill should be attributable to the $10,000 (10%) of identifiable assets owned by the minority shareholders. Because the consolidated assets are greater under the entity theory ($10,000 of goodwill versus $9,000 under the proprietary theory), the minority interest is also greater.

Answers (A) and (B) are incorrect because the entity theory results in greater assets and a larger minority interest than the proprietary theory. Answer (D) is incorrect because the minority interest is always separately disclosed in the consolidated balance sheet.

30. Palmer Inc. purchased 75% of the outstanding shares of Weller Inc. for $3,900,000. At that time, Weller had $7,200,000 of total recorded liabilities, and total recorded assets of $10,500,000, while the fair value of all Weller's assets was $11,800,000. The amount of goodwill purchased by Palmer Inc. is

A. $1,425,000

B. $1,500,000

C. $975,000

D. $450,000

The correct answer is (D). *(CMA, adapted)*

REQUIRED: The amount of goodwill purchased.

DISCUSSION: The fair value of the subsidiary's net assets was $4,600,000 ($11,800,000 – $7,200,000). Palmer acquired 75% of these assets, or $3,450,000. Subtracting the $3,450,000 of net identifiable assets from the purchase price of $3,900,000 results in goodwill value of $450,000.

Answers (A), (B), and (C) are incorrect because the goodwill is $450,000.

31. On September 1, 1999, Mickey Corporation acquired the net assets of Smith Corporation. Smith had a fair value of $10,992,000 on the acquisition date. The purchase price was paid in the form of $8 million of cash and $4 million of notes payable. Mickey's management believes that the goodwill acquired has an indefinite life and should be amortized over the longest allowable period. During the December 31, 2001 year-end audit after all adjusting entries have been made, the remaining goodwill is determined to be worthless. The amount of the write-off as of December 31, 2001 should be

A. $1,008,000

B. $957,600

C. $932,400

D. $949,200

The correct answer is (D). *(Publisher)*

REQUIRED: The amount of goodwill written off.

DISCUSSION: APB 17 requires that goodwill be amortized over a period of 40 years or less. Given that the company paid $12 million for identifiable net assets with a fair value of $10,992,000, goodwill is $1,008,000. Over 40 years, annual amortization is $25,200 ($1,008,000 ÷ 40). For 1999, the amortization is $8,400 [$25,200 x (4 months ÷ 12 months)]. For 2000 and 2001, total amortization was $50,400 (2 x $25,200). The book value of the goodwill after adjusting entries at December 31, 2001 is therefore $949,200 ($1,008,000 – $8,400 – $50,400). This amount is written off when the goodwill is determined to be worthless.

Answer (A) is incorrect because $1,008,000 is the initial asset balance. Answer (B) is incorrect because it omits the 1999 amortization of $8,400. Answer (C) is incorrect because the 1999 amortization was $8,400, not $25,200.

32. Sun, Inc. is a wholly owned subsidiary of Patton, Inc. On June 1, 2000, Patton declared and paid a $1 per share cash dividend to shareholders of record on May 15, 2000. On May 1, 2000, Sun bought 10,000 shares of Patton's common stock for $700,000 on the open market, when the book value per share was $30. What amount of gain should Patton report from this transaction in its consolidated income statement for the year ended December 31, 2000?

A. $0

B. $390,000

C. $400,000

D. $410,000

The correct answer is (A). *(CPA, adapted)*

REQUIRED: The amount of gain to be reported from the purchase of parent's stock by a subsidiary.

DISCUSSION: Subsidiary stockholdings in a parent are normally treated as treasury stock on the consolidated balance sheet. Gains and losses on treasury stock are not recognized. Thus, no gain is recognized in the consolidated income statement when a subsidiary purchases the parent's stock on the open market.

Answer (B) is incorrect because $390,000 equals the $700,000 paid, minus the $300,000 book value, minus the $10,000 dividend. Answer (C) is incorrect because $400,000 equals the $700,000 paid minus the $300,000 book value. Answer (D) is incorrect because $410,000 equals the $700,000 paid, minus the $300,000 book value, plus the $10,000 dividend.

Questions 33 through 35 are based on the following information. On January 2, 2000, Pare Co. purchased 75% of Kidd Co.'s outstanding common stock. Selected balance sheet data at December 31, 2000, is as follows:

	Pare	Kidd
Total assets	$420,000	$180,000
Liabilities	$120,000	$ 60,000
Common stock	100,000	50,000
Retained earnings	200,000	70,000
	$420,000	$180,000

During 2000, Pare and Kidd paid cash dividends of $25,000 and $5,000, respectively, to their shareholders. There were no other intercompany transactions.

---

33. In its December 31, 2000, consolidated statement of retained earnings, what amount should Pare report as dividends paid?

A. $5,000

B. $25,000

C. $26,250

D. $30,000

The correct answer is (B). *(CPA, adapted)*

REQUIRED: The amount reported as dividends paid.

DISCUSSION: In consolidated statements, the amount of dividends paid equals the parent's dividends paid. The subsidiary's dividends paid to the parent (75% x $5,000 = $3,750) are eliminated as an intercompany transaction. The remaining $1,250 of the subsidiary's dividends reduces the amount reported as the minority interest.

Answer (A) is incorrect because $5,000 is the subsidiary's dividends paid. Answer (C) is incorrect because $26,250 includes the minority interest. Answer (D) is incorrect because $30,000 includes the subsidiary's dividends paid.

34. In Pare's December 31, 2000 consolidated balance sheet, what amount should be reported as minority interest in net assets?

A. $0

B. $30,000

C. $45,000

D. $105,000

The correct answer is (B). *(CPA, adapted)*

REQUIRED: The minority interest in net assets.

DISCUSSION: Given that 25% of the stock is held by minority interests, $30,000 equals the minority interest in net assets [($180,000 – $60,000) x 25%].

Answers (A), (C), and (D) are incorrect because the minority interest in net assets is $30,000 [($180,000 – $60,000) x 25%].

35. In its December 31, 2000 consolidated balance sheet, what amount should Pare report as common stock?

A. $50,000

B. $100,000

C. $137,500

D. $150,000

The correct answer is (B). *(CPA, adapted)*

REQUIRED: The amount reported as common stock.

DISCUSSION: In consolidated statements, the parent's common stock equals the consolidated common stock.

Answers (A), (C), and (D) are incorrect because, in consolidated statements, the parent's common stock equals the consolidated common stock.

36. Clark Co. had the following transactions with affiliated parties during 2000:

- Sales of $50,000 to Dean, Inc., with $20,000 gross profit. Dean had $15,000 of this inventory on hand at year-end. Clark owns a 15% interest in Dean and does not exert significant influence.
- Purchases of raw materials totaling $240,000 from Kent Corp., a wholly owned subsidiary. Kent's gross profit on the sale was $48,000. Clark had $60,000 of this inventory remaining on December 31, 2000.

Before eliminating entries, Clark had consolidated current assets of $320,000. What amount should Clark report in its December 31, 2000 consolidated balance sheet for current assets?

A. $320,000

B. $314,000

C. $308,000

D. $302,000

The correct answer is (C). *(CPA, adapted)*

REQUIRED: The amount reported on the consolidated balance sheet for current assets.

DISCUSSION: When a parent buys inventory from a subsidiary (an upstream transaction), the inventory on the consolidated balance sheet must be adjusted to the price paid by the subsidiary until the inventory is sold to an outside party. Hence, the gross profit made by Kent, which was included in the $60,000 of inventory held by Clark, must be reduced by the pro rata share of profit made on the sale by Kent, reducing the inventory to Kent's original cost. The reduction is $12,000 [($60,000 EI ÷ $240,000 purchases) x $48,000 gross profit]. Thus, current assets equal $308,000 ($320,000 – $12,000). Because Kent is wholly owned, no allocation of the reduction in gross profit to a minority interest is necessary. The transaction with Dean requires no elimination. Dean is not consolidated.

Answer (A) is incorrect because $320,000 does not eliminate intercompany transactions. Answer (B) is incorrect because $314,000 does not involve eliminating the effect of the transactions with Kent but does involve deducting the gross profit included in the inventory held by Dean. Answer (D) is incorrect because $302,000 treats the sales to Dean as occurring between a parent and a consolidated subsidiary.

C. Segment Reporting

37. SFAS 131, *Disclosures about Segments of an Enterprise and Related Information*, requires reporting of information about

A. Industry segments.

B. Operating segments.

C. For-profit and not-for-profit organizations.

D. Public and nonpublic enterprises.

The correct answer is (B). *(Publisher)*

REQUIRED: The reporting required by SFAS 131.

DISCUSSION: The objective of segment reporting is to provide information about the different types of business activities of the entity and the economic environments in which it operates. This information is reported on an operating segment basis. SFAS 131 defines an operating segment as "a component of an enterprise that engages in business activities from which it may earn revenues and incur expenses (including revenues and expenses relating to transactions with other components of the same enterprise), whose operating results are regularly reviewed by the enterprise's chief operating decision maker to make decisions about resources to be allocated to the segment and assess its performance, and for which discrete financial information is available." A reportable segment is one that satisfies the foregoing definition and also meets one of three quantitative thresholds.

Answer (A) is incorrect because SFAS 131 superseded SFAS 14, which required line-of-business information classified by industry segment. Instead, SFAS 131 defines segments based on the entity's internal organization. Answers (C) and (D) are incorrect because SFAS 131 applies to public business enterprises.

38. Company M has identified four operating segments. Which of the following segments meet(s) the quantitative threshold for reported profit or loss?

Segment	Reported Profit (Loss)
S	$ 90,000
T	(100,000)
U	910,000
V	(420,000)

A. Segment U only.

B. Segments U and V.

C. Segments T, U, and V.

D. Segments S, T, U, and V.

The correct answer is (C). *(Publisher)*

REQUIRED: The segment(s) meeting the quantitative threshold for reported profit or loss.

DISCUSSION: Under SFAS 131, information must be reported separately about an operating segment that reaches one of three quantitative thresholds. Under the profit or loss test, if the absolute amount of the reported profit or loss equals at least 10% of the greater, in absolute amount, of (1) the combined profit of all operating segments not reporting a loss, or (2) the combined loss of all operating segments reporting a loss, the segment meets the threshold.

Segments T, U, and V are reportable segments. As shown below, the sum of the reported profits of S and U ($1,000,000) is greater than the sum of the losses of T and V ($520,000). Consequently, the test criterion is $100,000 (10% x $1,000,000).

Segment	Reported Profit	Reported Loss
S	$ 90,000	$ 0
T	0	100,000
U	910,000	0
V	0	420,000
	$1,000,000	$520,000

Answers (A), (B), and (D) are incorrect because Segments T, U, and V each meet the profit or loss test, but Segment S does not.

39. In accordance with SFAS 131, *Disclosures about Segments of an Enterprise and Related Information*, what ordinarily must be reported for each reportable segment?

A. Segment cash flow.

B. Interest revenue net of interest expense.

C. A measure of profit or loss.

D. External revenues from export sales if they are 10% or more of consolidated sales.

The correct answer is (C). *(Publisher)*

REQUIRED: The item ordinarily reported for each reportable segment.

DISCUSSION: For each reportable segment, an enterprise must report a measure of profit or loss, certain items included in the determination of that profit or loss, total segment assets, and certain related items. Segment cash flow need not be reported.

Answer (A) is incorrect because segment cash flow need not be reported. Answer (B) is incorrect because interest revenue and expense are reported separately unless a majority of revenues derive from interest and the chief operating decision maker relies primarily on net interest revenue for assessing segment performance and allocating resources. Answer (D) is incorrect because, if practicable, geographic information is reported for external revenues attributed to the home country and to all foreign countries in total. If external revenues attributed to a foreign country are material, they are disclosed separately.

40. For each of the following groups of customers, purchases amounted to 10% or more of the revenue of a publicly held company. For which of these groups must the company disclose information about major customers?

A. Federal governmental agencies, 6%; state governmental agencies, 4%.

B. French governmental agencies, 6%; German governmental agencies, 4%.

C. Parent company, 6%; subsidiary of parent company, 4%.

D. Federal governmental agencies, 6%; foreign governmental agencies, 4%.

The correct answer is (C). *(Publisher)*

REQUIRED: The set of circumstances requiring disclosure about major customers.

DISCUSSION: For purposes of SFAS 131, a group of customers under common control must be regarded as a single customer in determining whether 10% or more of the revenue of an enterprise is derived from sales to any single customer. A parent and a subsidiary are under common control, and they should be regarded as a single customer. Major customer disclosure is required in situation (C) because total combined revenue is 10% (6% + 4%).

Answers (A), (B), and (D) are incorrect because each governmental unit is to be treated as a separate customer in applying the 10% revenue test.

41. Correy Corp. and its divisions are engaged solely in manufacturing operations. The following data (consistent with prior years' data) pertain to the industries in which operations were conducted for the year ended December 31:

Operating Segment	Total Revenue	Profit	Assets at 12/31
A	$10,000,000	$1,750,000	$20,000,000
B	8,000,000	1,400,000	17,500,000
C	6,000,000	1,200,000	12,500,000
D	3,000,000	550,000	7,500,000
E	4,250,000	675,000	7,000,000
F	1,500,000	225,000	3,000,000
	$32,750,000	$5,800,000	$67,500,000

In its segment information for the year, how many reportable operating segments does Correy have?

A. Three.

B. Four.

C. Five.

D. Six.

The correct answer is (C). *(CPA, adapted)*

REQUIRED: The number of reportable operating segments.

DISCUSSION: Four operating segments (A, B, C, and E) have revenue equal to or greater than 10% of the $32,750,000 total revenue of all operating segments. These four segments also have profit equal to or greater than 10% of the $5,800,000 total profit of all operating segments that did not report a loss. Five segments (A, B, C, D, and E) have assets greater than 10% of the $67,500,000 total assets of all operating segments. Because an operating segment is reportable if it meets one or more of the three tests established by SFAS 131, Correy Corp. has five reportable operating segments for the year.

Answers (A), (B), and (D) are incorrect because segments A, B, C, D, and E, but not F, meet at least one of the tests.

42. Terra Co.'s total revenues from its three operating segments were as follows:

Segment	Sales to External Customers	Intersegment Sales	Total Revenues
Lion	$ 70,000	$30,000	$100,000
Monk	22,000	4,000	26,000
Nevi	8,000	16,000	24,000
Combined	$100,000	$50,000	$150,000
Elimination	–	(50,000)	(50,000)
Consolidated	$100,000	$ –	$100,000

Which operating segment(s) is (are) deemed to be (a) reportable segment(s)?

A. None.

B. Lion only.

C. Lion and Monk only.

D. Lion, Monk, and Nevi.

The correct answer is (D). *(CPA, adapted)*

REQUIRED: The reportable operating segments in conformity with the revenue test.

DISCUSSION: For the purpose of identifying reportable operating segments, SFAS 131 defines revenue to include sales to external customers and intersegment sales or transfers. In accordance with the revenue test, a reportable operating segment has revenue equal to 10% or more of the total combined revenue, internal and external, of all of the enterprise's operating segments. Given combined revenues of $150,000, Lion, Monk, and Nevi all qualify because their revenues are at least $15,000 (10% x $150,000).

Answers (A), (B), and (C) are incorrect because Lion, Monk, and Nevi all qualify as reportable operating segments.

43. Hyde Corp. has three manufacturing divisions, each of which has been determined to be a reportable operating segment. In the year just ended, Clay division had sales of $3,000,000, which was 25% of Hyde's total sales, and had traceable operating costs of $1,900,000. Hyde incurred operating costs of $500,000 that were not directly traceable to any of the divisions. In addition, Hyde incurred interest expense of $300,000. The calculation of the measure of segment profit or loss reviewed by Hyde's chief operating decision maker does not include an allocation of interest expense incurred by Hyde. However, it does include traceable costs. It also includes nontraceable operating costs allocated based on the ratio of divisional sales to aggregate sales. In reporting segment information, what amount should be shown as Clay's profit for the year?

A. $875,000

B. $900,000

C. $975,000

D. $1,100,000

The correct answer is (C). *(CPA, adapted)*

REQUIRED: The amount to be shown as profit for a reportable operating segment.

DISCUSSION: The amount of a segment item reported, such as profit or loss, is the measure reported to the chief operating decision maker for purposes of making resource allocation and performance evaluation decisions regarding the segment. However, SFAS 131 does not stipulate the specific items included in the calculation of that measure. Consequently, allocation of revenues, expenses, gains, and losses are included in the determination of reported segment profit or loss only if they are included in the measure of segment profit or loss reviewed by the chief operating decision maker. Given that this measure for Clay reflects traceable costs and an allocation of nontraceable operating costs, the profit is calculated by subtracting the $1,900,000 traceable costs and the $125,000 ($500,000 x 25%) of the allocated costs from the division's sales of $3,000,000. The profit for the division is $975,000.

Sales	$ 3,000,000
Traceable costs	(1,900,000)
Allocated costs (25%)	(125,000)
Profit	$ 975,000

Answer (A) is incorrect because no amount of interest expense should be included in the calculation. Answer (B) is incorrect because Clay's share of interest expense (25% x $300,000 = $75,000) is excluded from the calculation of profit. Answer (D) is incorrect because the allocated nontraceable operating costs must also be subtracted.

D. Derivatives and Hedging

44. To the extent the hedge is effective, a loss arising from the decrease in fair value of a derivative is included in current earnings if the derivative qualifies and is designated as a

	Fair-value Hedge	Cash-flow Hedge
A.	Yes	No
B.	No	Yes
C.	Yes	Yes
D.	No	No

The correct answer is (A). *(Publisher)*

REQUIRED: The treatment of a loss arising from a decrease in fair value of a derivative qualified and designated as either a fair-value or a cash-flow hedge.

DISCUSSION: A fair-value hedge includes a hedge of an exposure to changes in the fair value of a recognized asset or liability or of an unrecognized firm commitment. Changes in both (1) the fair value of a derivative that qualifies and is designated as a fair-value hedge and (2) the fair value of the hedged item attributable to the hedged risk are included in earnings in the period of change. Thus, the net effect on earnings is limited to the ineffective portion, i.e., the difference between the changes in fair value. A cash-flow hedge includes a hedge of an exposure to variability in the cash flows of a recognized asset or liability or a forecasted transaction. Changes in the fair value of a derivative that qualifies and is designated as a cash-flow hedge are recognized as a component of other comprehensive income to the extent the hedge is effective. The ineffective portion of the hedge is recognized in current earnings. The changes accumulated in other comprehensive income are reclassified to earnings in the period(s) the hedged transaction affects earnings. For example, accumulated amounts related to a forecasted purchase of equipment are reclassified as the equipment is depreciated.

Answers (B), (C), and (D) are incorrect because, to the extent a hedge is effective, only the changes in fair value of a hedge qualified and designated as a fair-value hedge are included in earnings in the periods the changes take place.

45. Herbert Corporation was a party to the following transactions during November and December 2001. Which of these transactions most likely resulted in an investment in a derivative subject to the accounting prescribed by SFAS 133, Accounting for Derivative Instruments and Hedging Activities?

A. Purchased 1,000 shares of common stock of a public corporation based on the assumption that the stock would increase in value.

B. Purchased a term life insurance policy on the company's chief executive officer to protect the company from the effects of an untimely demise of this officer.

C. Agreed to cosign the note of its 100%-owned subsidiary to protect the lender from the possibility that the subsidiary might default on the loan.

D. Based on its forecasted need to purchase 300,000 bushels of wheat in 3 months, entered into a 3-month forward contract to purchase 300,000 bushels of wheat to protect itself from changes in wheat prices during the period.

The correct answer is (D). *(Publisher)*

REQUIRED: The transaction resulting in an investment in a derivative instrument.

DISCUSSION: SFAS 133 defines a derivative as a financial instrument or other contract that (1) has (a) one or more underlyings and (b) one or more notional amounts or payment provisions, or both; (2) requires either no initial net investment or an immaterial net investment; and (3) requires or permits net settlement. An underlying may be a specified interest rate, security price, commodity price, foreign exchange rate, index of prices or rates, or other variable. A notional amount is a number of currency units, shares, bushels, pounds, or other units specified. Settlement of a derivative is based on the interaction of the notional amount and the underlying. The purchase of the forward contract as a hedge of a forecasted need to purchase wheat meets the criteria prescribed by SFAS 133.

Answer (A) is incorrect because it involves a net investment equal to the fair value of the stock. Answers (B) and (C) are incorrect because each is based on an identifiable event, not an underlying.

46. Garcia Corporation has entered into a binding agreement with Hernandez Company to purchase 400,000 pounds of Colombian coffee at $2.53 per pound for delivery in 90 days. This contract is accounted for as a

A. Financial instrument.

B. Firm commitment.

C. Forecasted transaction.

D. Fair value hedge.

The correct answer is (B). *(Publisher)*

REQUIRED: The type of transaction defined.

DISCUSSION: A firm commitment is an agreement with an unrelated party, binding on both parties and usually legally enforceable, that specifies all significant terms and includes a disincentive for nonperformance.

Answer (A) is incorrect because a financial instrument does not involve the delivery of a product. Answer (C) is incorrect because a forecasted transaction is a transaction that is expected to occur for which no firm commitment exists. Answer (D) is incorrect because the purchase commitment is an exposure to risk, not a hedge of an exposure to risk.

47. On October 1, 2001, Bordeaux, Inc., a calendar-year-end firm, invested in a derivative designed to hedge the risk of changes in fair value of certain assets, currently valued at $1.5 million. The derivative is structured to result in an effective hedge. However, some ineffectiveness may result. On December 31, 2001, the fair value of the hedged assets has decreased by $350,000; the fair value of the derivative has increased by $325,000. Bordeaux should recognize a net effect on 2001 earnings of

A. $0

B. $25,000

C. $325,000

D. $350,000

The correct answer is (B). *(Publisher)*

REQUIRED: The net effect on earnings of a partially effective hedge of changes in fair value of a recognized asset.

DISCUSSION: A hedge of an exposure to changes in the fair value of a recognized asset or liability is classified as a fair value hedge. Gains and losses arising from changes in fair value of a derivative classified as a fair value hedge are included in the determination of earnings in the period of change. They are offset by losses or gains on the hedged item attributable to the risk being hedged. Thus, earnings of the period of change are affected only by the net gain or loss attributable to the ineffective aspect of the hedge. The ineffective portion is equal to $25,000 ($350,000 – $325,000).

Answer (A) is incorrect because the effect on earnings is equal to the ineffective portion of the hedge. Answers (C) and (D) are incorrect because each is a gross effect.

Questions 48 and 49 are based on the following information. As part of its risk management strategy, a copper mining company sells futures contracts to hedge changes in fair value of its inventory. On March 12, the commodity exchange spot price is $0.81/lb.; the futures price for mid-June is $0.83/lb. On that date, the company, a calendar year-end firm, sells 200 futures contracts on the commodity exchange at $0.83/lb. for delivery in June. Each contract is for 25,000 lbs. The company designates these contracts as a fair-value hedge of 5 million lbs. of current inventory for which a mid-June sale is expected. The average cost of this inventory is $0.58/lb. The company documents (1) the hedging relationship between the futures contracts and its inventory, (2) its objectives and strategy for undertaking the hedge, and (3) its conclusion that the hedging relationship will be highly effective.

48. On March 31, the mid-June commodity exchange futures price is $0.85/lb. In the March 31 statement of financial position, the company should record the value of the futures contracts as a(n)

A. $100,000 asset.

B. $100,000 liability.

C. $4,250,000 liability.

D. $4,250,000 asset.

The correct answer is (B). *(Publisher)*

REQUIRED: The amount at which the futures contracts should be recorded on the March 31 statement of financial position.

DISCUSSION: SFAS 133 requires that derivative instruments be recorded as assets and liabilities and measured at fair value. At March 12, the inception of the futures contracts, the fair value of the futures contracts was $0 because the contracts were entered into at the futures price at that date. On March 31, the fair value of the futures contract is equal to the change in the futures price between the inception price and the March 31 price. Given that the futures contracts created an obligation to deliver 5 million lbs. (25,000 lbs. x 200 contracts) of copper at $0.83/lb. and that the price had risen to $0.85/lb. at the date of the financial statements, the company should record a loss and a liability of $100,000 [5 million lbs. x ($0.83 – $0.85)].

Answers (A) and (D) are incorrect because the futures contracts should be recorded as a liability. Answers (C) and (D) are incorrect because the contracts should be measured at the $100,000 change in the futures price rather than at the March 31 futures price.

49. If, on March 31, the company concluded that the hedge was 100% effective, the company should record the value of the hedged copper inventory in the March 31 statement of financial position at

A. $4,350,000

B. $4,250,000

C. $3,000,000

D. $2,900,000

The correct answer is (C). *(Publisher)*

REQUIRED: The amount at which the hedged copper inventory should be recorded on the statement of financial position.

DISCUSSION: For a fair-value hedge, changes in the fair value of the hedged item attributable to the hedged risk are reflected as adjustments to the carrying value of the hedged recognized asset or liability or the previously unrecognized firm commitment on the statement of financial position. The adjustments to carrying value are accounted for in the same manner as other components of the carrying value of the asset or liability. Thus the inventory should be recorded at $3,000,000 [(5 million lbs. x $0.58) original cost + $100,000 gain in fair value].

Answers (A), (B), and (D) are incorrect because the hedged copper inventory should be recorded at its $2,900,000 original cost plus the $100,000 gain in fair value attributable to the hedged risk.

50. At the beginning of period 1, Forecast Corporation enters into a qualifying cash flow hedge of a transaction it expects to occur at the beginning of period 4. Forecast assesses hedge effectiveness by comparing the change in present value (PV) of the expected cash flows associated with the forecasted transaction with all of the hedging derivative's gain or loss (change in fair value). The change in those cash flows that occurs for any reason has been designated as the hedged risk. The following information about the periodic changes hedging relationship is available:

Period	Change in Fair Value of the Derivative	Change in PV of Expected Cash Flows from the Forecasted Transaction
1	$50,000	$(48,000)
2	47,000	(51,000)
3	(81,000)	80,000

Given that the hedge is effective to the extent it offsets the change in the present value of the expected cash flows on the forecasted transaction, Forecast should

A. Recognize a loss of $2,000 in earnings for period 1.

B. Report a balance in other comprehensive income (OCI) of $16,000 at the end of period 3.

C. Recognize a gain of $47,000 in earnings for period 2.

D. Record other comprehensive income of $97,000 for period 2.

The correct answer is (B). *(Publisher)*

REQUIRED: The appropriate accounting for a cash flow hedge of a forecasted transaction.

DISCUSSION: The effective portion of a cash flow hedge of a forecasted transaction is included in OCI until periods in which the forecasted transaction affects earnings. At the end of period 3, the net change in the hedging derivative's fair value is $16,000 ($50,000 + $47,000 – $81,000), and the change in the PV of the expected cash flows on the forecasted transaction is –$19,000 ($80,000 – $48,000 – $51,000). Thus, the hedge is effective at the end of period 3 to the extent it offsets $16,000 of the net $19,000 decrease in the cash flows of the forecasted transaction that are expected to occur in period 4.

Answer (A) is incorrect because Forecast should recognize earnings for period 1 of $2,000. The increase in fair value of the derivative exceeds the decrease in PV of the cash flows by $2,000. The derivative is adjusted to fair value by a $50,000 debit, OCI is credited for $48,000, and earnings is credited for $2,000. Answers (C) and (D) are incorrect because the entry for period 2 is to debit the derivative for $47,000, debit earnings for $2,000, and credit OCI for $49,000 ($50,000 + $47,000 – $48,000 credit in period 1). At the end of period 2, OCI should have a credit balance of $97,000 (the extent of the hedge's effectiveness).

51. According to SFAS 133, *Accounting for Derivative Instruments and Hedging Activities*, as amended by SFAS 138, *Accounting for Certain Derivative Instruments and Certain Hedging Activities*, the effective portion of a loss associated with a change in fair value of a derivative instrument shall be reported as a component of other comprehensive income only if the derivative is appropriately designated as a

A. Cash flow hedge of the foreign currency exposure of a forecasted transaction.

B. Fair value hedge of the foreign currency exposure of an unrecognized firm commitment.

C. Fair value hedge of the foreign currency exposure of a recognized asset or liability for which a foreign currency transaction gain or loss is recognized in earnings.

D. Speculation in a foreign currency.

The correct answer is (A). *(Publisher)*

REQUIRED: The derivative for which the effective portion of a loss associated with its change in fair value is reported as a component of other comprehensive income.

DISCUSSION: The hedge of the foreign currency exposure of a forecasted transaction is designated as a cash flow hedge. The effective portion of gains and losses associated with changes in fair value of a derivative instrument designated and qualifying as a cash flow hedging instrument is reported as a component of other comprehensive income.

Answers (B) and (C) are incorrect because a hedge of the foreign currency exposure of either an unrecognized firm commitment or of a recognized asset or liability for which a foreign currency transaction gain or loss is recognized in earnings may be a fair value hedge or a cash flow hedge. The effective portion of gains and losses arising from changes in fair value of a derivative classified as a fair value hedge is included in earnings of the period of change. It is offset by losses and gains on the hedged item that are attributable to the risk being hedged. Answer (D) is incorrect because gains and losses associated with changes in fair value of a derivative used as a speculation in a foreign currency are included in earnings of the period of change.

52. The effective portion of a gain arising from an increase in the fair value of a derivative is included in earnings in the period of change if the derivative is appropriately designated and qualifies as a hedge of

A. A foreign currency exposure of a net investment in a foreign operation.

B. A foreign currency exposure of a forecasted transaction.

C. A foreign currency exposure of an available-for-sale security.

D. The variable cash flows of a forecasted transaction.

The correct answer is (C). *(Publisher)*

REQUIRED: The derivative for which the effective portion of a gain is included in earnings in the period in which a change in fair value occurs.

DISCUSSION: A fair value hedge includes a hedge of an exposure to changes in the fair value of a recognized asset or liability or an unrecognized firm commitment. Such a hedge minimizes the risk associated with fixed cash flows. A foreign currency fair value hedge includes a hedge of a foreign currency exposure of an unrecognized firm commitment. It also includes a hedge of a foreign currency exposure of a recognized asset or liability (including an available-for-sale security) for which a foreign currency transaction gain or loss is recognized in earnings under SFAS 52. Gains and losses arising from changes in fair value of a derivative classified as either a fair value or a foreign fair value hedge are included in the determination of earnings in the period of change. They are offset by losses or gains on the hedged item attributable to the risk being hedged. Thus, earnings of the period of change are affected only by the net gain or loss attributable to the ineffective aspect of the hedge.

Answer (A) is incorrect because the effective portion of gains and losses on this hedge is reported as a component of the cumulative translation adjustment in other comprehensive income. Answers (B) and (D) are incorrect because the effective portion of gains and losses on these hedges is included in other comprehensive income until periods in which the forecasted transaction affects earnings.

Questions 53 and 54 are based on the following information. On November 15, 2001, Hector Corp., a calendar-year-end U.S. company, signed a legally binding contract to purchase equipment from Diego Corp., a foreign company. The negotiated price is FC1,000,000. The scheduled delivery date is February 15, 2002. Terms require payment by Hector Corp. upon delivery. The terms also impose a 10% penalty on Diego Corp. if the equipment is not delivered by February 15, 2002.

To hedge its commitment to pay FC1,000,000, Hector entered into a forward-exchange contract on November 15, 2001 to receive FC1,000,000 on February 15, 2002 at an exchange rate of FC1.00 = U.S.$0.36. Additional exchange rate information:

Date	Spot Rates	Forward Rates for February 15, 2002
11/15/01	1 FC = $0.35 U.S.	1 FC = $0.36 U.S.
12/31/01	1 FC = $0.36 U.S.	1 FC = $0.38 U.S.
02/15/02	1 FC = $0.39 U.S.	1 FC = $0.39 U.S.

Quotes obtained from dealers indicate the following incremental changes in the fair values of the forward-exchange contract based on the changes in forward rates discounted on a net-present-value basis:

Date	Gain/(Loss)
11/15/01	$0
12/31/01	$19,600
02/15/02	$10,400

Hector formally documented its objective and strategy for entering into this hedge. Hector also decided to assess hedge effectiveness based on an assessment of the difference between changes in value of the forward-exchange contract and the U.S.-dollar equivalent of the firm commitment. Because both changes are based on changes in forward rates, Hector further determined that the hedge is 100% effective.

53. The contract signed by Hector Corp. to purchase the equipment from Diego Corp. meets the definition of a

	Firm Commitment	Forecasted Transaction
A.	Yes	Yes
B.	No	No
C.	Yes	No
D.	No	Yes

The correct answer is (C). *(Publisher)*

REQUIRED: The type of contract described.

DISCUSSION: SFAS 133 defines a firm commitment as an agreement between unrelated parties, binding on both and usually legally enforceable, that specifies all significant terms and includes a disincentive for nonperformance. SFAS 133 defines a forecasted transaction as a transaction that is expected to occur for which there is no firm commitment.

Answers (A), (B), and (D) are incorrect because the contract meets the definition of a firm commitment. Thus, it cannot be a forecasted transaction.

54. What are the amounts reported for the forward contract receivable and the firm commitment liability at December 31, 2001 and February 15, 2002 (prior to the settlement of the contract)?

	12/31/01	02/15/02
A.	$10,000	$40,000
B.	$19,600	$30,000
C.	$19,600	$10,400
D.	$20,000	$30,000

The correct answer is (B). *(Publisher)*

REQUIRED: The amounts to be recorded for a forward contract receivable and a firm commitment at 12/31/01 and 02/15/02 (prior to the settlement of the contract).

DISCUSSION: This hedge is a foreign currency fair value hedge because it hedges a foreign currency exposure of an unrecognized firm commitment whose cash flows are fixed. Thus, unlike a foreign currency cash flow hedge, it does not hedge the foreign currency exposure to variability in the functional-currency-equivalent cash flows associated with an unrecognized firm commitment. SFAS 133 requires recognition of the forward contract receivable as an asset at fair value, with the changes in fair value recognized in earnings. SFAS 133 further requires recognition of the changes in the fair value of the firm commitment that are attributable to the changes in exchange rates. These changes in fair value are recognized in earnings and as entries to a liability. Fair values should reflect changes in the forward exchange rates on a net-present-value basis. Thus, the forward contract receivable should be debited and a gain credited for $19,600 at 12/31/01. A loss should be debited and a firm commitment liability should be credited in the same amount at the same date. (NOTE: Under current GAAP, no asset or liability is recognized for a firm commitment when the contract is signed.) At 2/15/02, a further $10,400 forward contract gain and firm commitment loss should be recorded. Because the changes in value of both the forward contract and the U.S.-dollar equivalent of the firm commitment are based on changes in forward rates, the hedge is completely effective; the changes in fair values ($19,600 and $10,400) of the forward contract receivable (gains) and the firm commitment (losses) offset each other in the income statement.

Answer (A) is incorrect because the balance sheet amounts should be based on the discounted changes in forward rates, not the undiscounted changes in spot rates. Answer (C) is incorrect because $19,600 and $10,400 are the respective income statement effects. Answer (D) is incorrect because $20,000 is the undiscounted change in the forward rates at 12/31/01.

55. As a result of this hedging transaction, at what amount should Hector recognize the equipment on February 15, 2002?

A. $350,000

B. $360,000

C. $390,000

D. $420,000

The correct answer is (B). (Publisher)

REQUIRED: The amount at which the equipment should be recognized as a result of the hedging transaction.

DISCUSSION: The equipment should be recorded at $360,000. This amount equals $390,000 (FC1,000,000 x $0.39 spot rate at 2/15/02) minus the $30,000 balance in the firm commitment liability account. The entry is to debit equipment for $360,000, debit the firm commitment liability for $30,000, and credit a payable for $390,000. On the same date, Hector will debit the payable for $390,000, credit the forward contract receivable for $30,000, and credit cash for $360,000. The latter entry reflects settlement of the payable and of the forward contract.

Answer (A) is incorrect because $350,000 is the amount that would have been recognized if the equipment had been delivered on 11/15/01. Answer (C) is incorrect because $390,000 is the amount that would have been recognized if the firm commitment had not been hedged. Answer (D) is incorrect because $420,000 equals $390,000 plus the $30,000 balance in the firm commitment liability account.

56. On October 1, 2001, Weeks Co., a calendar-year-end U.S. company, forecasts that, near the end of March 2002, Sullivan Corp., a foreign entity, will purchase 50,000 gallons of Weeks's primary product for FC500,000. Sullivan has not firmly committed to the purchase. However, based on Sullivan's purchasing pattern, Weeks believes that the sale is probable. Weeks's risk-management policy includes avoiding foreign currency exposure through the use of foreign currency forward contracts. Thus, on October 1, Weeks enters into a 6-month foreign currency forward contract to sell FC500,000 to a dealer on March 31. Weeks designates the contract as a hedge and determines that hedge effectiveness will be based on changes in forward rates. The following information is available:

	Value of FC500,000 Based on Spot Rates	Value of FC500,000 Based on Forward Rates for 03/31/02	Incremental Discounted Changes in Value of Forward Contract Based on Changes in Forward Rates
10/01/01	$570,000	$500,000	$0
12/31/01	$540,000	$490,000	$9,800
03/31/02	$475,000	$475,000	$15,200

At what amounts should Weeks record the forward contract on December 31, 2001 and March 31, 2002?

	12/31/01	03/31/02
A.	$9,800	$25,000
B.	$10,000	$25,000
C.	$540,000	$475,000
D.	$490,000	$475,000

The correct answer is (A). *(Publisher)*

REQUIRED: The amounts at which the forward contract should be recognized.

DISCUSSION: Weeks should record the forward contract as a receivable at fair value. Fair value is based on changes in forward rates discounted on a net present value basis. Thus, the receivable should be recorded at $9,800 on December 31, 2001 and $25,000 ($9,800 + $15,200) on March 31, 2002. Because a hedge of the foreign currency exposure of a forecasted transaction is a cash flow hedge, Weeks should also credit these amounts to other comprehensive income. On March 31, the sale should be recorded at $500,000 ($475,000 value based on the spot rate at March 31 + $25,000 balance in other comprehensive income). The amount of cash received also is equal to $500,000 ($475,000 + $25,000 balance in the forward contract receivable).

Answer (B) is incorrect because the change in forward rates should be adjusted for the time value of money. Answer (C) is incorrect because $540,000 and $475,000 reflect the value of FC500,000 at spot rates. Answer (D) is incorrect because $490,000 and $475,000 reflect the value of FC500,000 at forward rates.

STUDY UNIT 9: FINANCIAL STATEMENT ANALYSIS

11 pages of outline
61 multiple-choice questions

A. Ratio Analysis
B. Limitations of Ratio Analysis
C. Comparative Analysis

The essence of financial statement analysis is the calculation of financial ratios. These ratios establish relationships among financial statement accounts at a moment in time or for a given accounting period. Once calculated, the firm's ratios can be compared with its historical data and with its projections for the future. Moreover, ratios can also be evaluated by comparison with those for other firms or with industry averages. The relative weight range assigned to this major topic is 10% to 15%.

A. Ratio Analysis

1. Ratio analysis addresses such issues as the firm's liquidity, use of leverage, asset management, cost control, profitability, growth, and valuation.
2. Ratio analysis permits determination of standards and trends.
   a. Normal or average ratios can be computed for broad industrial categories.
   b. Ratios for individual firms can be compared with those of competitors, especially industry leaders.
   c. Changes in ratios over time provide insight about the future (trend analysis).
3. When a balance sheet amount is related to an income statement amount in computing a ratio, the balance sheet amount should be an average for the period. For example, ratios such as inventory turnover and return on assets use a balance sheet figure that is an average for the period.
4. **Liquidity ratios** measure the relationship of a firm's liquid assets to current liabilities. Thus, such ratios provide information about the short-term viability of the business, i.e., the firm's ability to pay its current obligations and to continue operations.
   a. The **current ratio** (working capital ratio) equals current assets divided by current liabilities and is the most common measure of near-term solvency.
      1) $\frac{\textit{Current assets}}{\textit{Current liabilities}}$
         a) **Current assets** include cash; net accounts receivable; certain held-to-maturity, available-for-sale, and trading securities; inventories; and prepaid items.
         b) **Current liabilities** include accounts payable, notes payable, current maturities of long-term debt, unearned revenues, taxes payable, wages payable, and other accruals.
      2) A low ratio indicates a possible solvency problem. An overly high ratio indicates that management may not be investing idle assets productively.
      3) The general principle is that the current ratio should be proportional to the operating cycle. Thus, a shorter cycle may justify a lower ratio.

4) The quality of accounts receivable and merchandise inventory should be considered before evaluating the current ratio. Accordingly, a low receivables turnover (net credit sales ÷ average accounts receivable) and a low inventory turnover (cost of sales ÷ average inventory) indicate a need for a higher current ratio.

5) Use of LIFO understates the current ratio.

b. A conservative version of the current ratio is the **acid test or quick ratio**, which divides the quick assets (cash, net receivables, and marketable securities) by current liabilities.

1) $$\frac{\textit{Cash + Net receivables + Marketable securities}}{\textit{Current liabilities}}$$

2) This ratio measures the firm's ability to pay its short-term debts from its most liquid assets and avoids the problem of inventory valuation.

3) A less conservative variation divides the difference between current assets and inventory by current liabilities.

4) A more conservative variation is the cash ratio [(cash equivalents + marketable securities) ÷ current liabilities].

c. **Working capital** is the excess of current assets over current liabilities.

1) *Current assets – Current liabilities*

2) Working capital is a less useful measure than the current and quick ratios because it is the absolute difference between current assets and liabilities and therefore does not facilitate comparisons.

d. The **sales-to-working-capital ratio** (working capital turnover) is sales divided by average working capital.

1) $$\textit{Sales to working capital} = \frac{\textit{Sales}}{\textit{Average working capital}}$$

2) A high sales-to-working-capital ratio may indicate either very high sales (good) or a low supply of working capital (potentially bad). For example, a high ratio could indicate that a firm is undercapitalized and does not have the resources to invest in working capital.

e. The **defensive interval** equals the sum of cash equivalents, net receivables, and marketable securities, divided by the expected daily operating cash outflows.

1) $$\frac{\textit{Cash equivalents + Net receivables + Marketable securities}}{\textit{Daily operating cash outflow}}$$

5. **Activity ratios** measure the firm's use of assets to generate revenue and income. The ratios also evaluate liquidity because it determines how quickly assets are turned into cash.

a. The **receivables turnover ratio** equals net credit sales divided by average accounts receivable. (However, net sales is often used because credit sales data may be unavailable.)

1) $$\frac{\textit{Net credit sales}}{\textit{Average accounts receivable}}$$

2) This ratio measures the efficiency of accounts receivable collection.

3) A high turnover is preferable.

4) As in the case of inventory, cyclical factors may cause the average of the beginning and ending balances to be unrepresentative. In that event, a monthly or quarterly average should be used.

b. The **number of days of receivables** (days' sales in average receivables or the average collection period) equals the number of days in the period divided by the receivables turnover ratio.

1) $$\frac{\text{365, 360, } \textit{or} \text{ 300}}{\textit{Receivables turnover ratio}}$$

2) This ratio is the average number of days to collect a receivable.

3) It may also be computed as average accounts receivable divided by average daily sales.

   a) Average daily sales are net credit sales divided by the number of days in the period.

   b) Another possibility is to calculate days' sales in ending receivables. This ratio equals ending receivables divided by the average daily sales.

4) The number of days of receivables should be compared with the company's credit terms to determine whether the average customer is paying within the credit period.

5) The **operating cycle** of an enterprise may be estimated by adding days' sales in average inventory to days' sales in average receivables.

c. The **inventory turnover ratio** equals cost of sales divided by average inventory.

1) $$\frac{\textit{Cost of sales}}{\textit{Average inventory}}$$

2) If the average of the beginning and ending inventory is not representative because of cyclical factors, a monthly or quarterly average is preferable.

3) A high turnover implies that the firm does not hold excessive stocks of inventories that are unproductive and that lessen the firm's profitability.

4) A high turnover also implies that the inventory is truly marketable and does not contain obsolete goods.

5) The ratio of a firm that uses LIFO may not be comparable with that of a firm with a higher inventory valuation.

d. The **number of days of inventory** (days' sales in average inventory) equals the number of days in the year divided by the inventory turnover ratio.

1) $$\frac{\text{365, 360, } \textit{or} \text{ 300}}{\textit{Inventory turnover ratio}}$$

2) This ratio measures the average number of days that inventory is held before sale. Thus, it reflects the efficiency of inventory management.

3) It may also be computed as average inventory divided by average daily cost of sales.

4) Still another possibility is to calculate the days' sales in ending inventory. This ratio equals ending inventory divided by the average daily cost of sales.

e. The **fixed assets turnover ratio** equals net sales divided by average net fixed assets.

1) $\dfrac{\textit{Net sales}}{\textit{Average net fixed assets}}$

2) This ratio measures the level of use of property, plant, and equipment.

a) It is largely affected by the capital intensiveness of the company and its industry, by the age of the assets, and by the depreciation method used.

3) A high turnover is preferable to a low turnover.

f. The **total asset turnover ratio** equals net sales divided by average total assets.

1) $\dfrac{\textit{Net sales}}{\textit{Average total assets}}$

2) This ratio measures the level of capital investment relative to sales volume.

3) For all turnover ratios, high turnover is preferable because it implies effective use of assets to generate sales.

4) Certain assets, for example, investments, do not relate to net sales. Their inclusion decreases the ratio.

6. **Profitability ratios** measure earnings relative to some base, for example, productive assets, sales, or capital. Increased profits benefit shareholders not only because they make additional funds available for dividend payments but also because they may result in appreciation of the firm's stock price. Profits also provide a cushion for debt coverage. Hence, profitability ratios are used by investors, creditors, and others to evaluate management's stewardship of the firm's assets.

a. The **profit margin on sales** equals net income divided by sales.

1) $\dfrac{\textit{Net income after interest and taxes}}{\textit{Net sales}}$

2) The numerator may also be stated in terms of the net income available to common shareholders.

3) Another form of the ratio excludes nonrecurring items from the numerator, e.g., unusual or infrequent items, discontinued operations, extraordinary items, and effects of accounting changes. The result is sometimes called the **net profit margin**. This adjustment may be made for any ratio that includes net income.

a) Still other numerator refinements are to exclude equity-based earnings and items in the other income and other expense categories.

b. The ratio of **net operating income to sales** may be defined as earnings before interest and taxes (EBIT) divided by sales.

1) $\dfrac{\textit{EBIT}}{\textit{Net sales}}$

2) Use of EBIT emphasizes operating results and more nearly approximates cash flows than other income measures.

c. The **return on investment** or **ROI** (also called **return on total assets**) may be defined as net income divided by average total assets.

1) $$\frac{\textit{Net income after interest and taxes}}{\textit{Average total assets}}$$

2) The numerator may be defined in various ways. One possibility is net income available to common shareholders. Another is found in the **basic earning power ratio**, which divides EBIT by average total assets. This ratio enhances comparability of firms with different capital structures and tax planning strategies. The denominator may be defined to include only operating assets. Investments, intangibles, and the other asset category would be excluded.

d. The **Du Pont equation** relates the return on total assets, the total asset turnover, and the profit margin on sales.

1) $$\frac{\textit{Net income after interest and taxes}}{\textit{Average total assets}} = \frac{\textit{Net sales}}{\textit{Average total assets}} \times \frac{\textit{Net income after interest and taxes}}{\textit{Net sales}}$$

2) This formula emphasizes that ROI may be explained in terms of the efficiency of asset management and the profit margin. The effects of modifying the Du Pont equation to reflect net operating income (EBIT) and operating assets should be understood.

3) The formula above may be multiplied by the **equity multiplier** (also known as the leverage factor) to determine the return on common equity. See page 395.

e. The ratio of **net operating income to total capital** is a variation of the return on total assets that excludes noninterest-bearing debt from total assets.

1) $$\frac{\textit{EBIT}}{\textit{Equity + Interest-bearing debt}}$$

2) Total capital is defined in the same way as in the section on asset management. A variation is the **marginal profitability rate** (change in EBIT ÷ change in total capital).

f. The **return on common equity** equals the net income available to common shareholders divided by their average equity.

1) $$\frac{\textit{Net income after interest and taxes - Preferred dividends}}{\textit{Average common equity}}$$

2) The average common equity includes total equity minus the preferred shareholders' capital and any minority interest.

3) This ratio and the next one measure the return on the book value of equity.

4) A variation of the return on common equity is the **marginal return on common equity** (change in net income ÷ change in common equity).

g. The **return on total equity** equals net income minus dividends on redeemable preferred stock, divided by average total equity.

1) $$\frac{\textit{Net income after interest and taxes - Dividends on redeemable preferred stock}}{\textit{Average total equity}}$$

2) Redeemable preferred stock is usually considered to be equivalent to debt. Indeed, the SEC requires it to be reported separately from other equity.

h. In accordance with SFAS 128, **basic earnings per share (BEPS)** equals net income available to common shareholders divided by the weighted-average number of shares outstanding (see SU 7).

1) $$\frac{\textit{Net income available to common shareholders}}{\textit{Average outstanding shares}}$$

2) Net income available to common shareholders is income from continuing operations or net income, minus preferred dividends.

3) If the enterprise has dilutive potential common stock outstanding, it must report **dilutive earnings per share (DEPS)**.

a) DEPS measures the entity's earnings performance during the reporting period, based on both common stock and dilutive potential common stock. DEPS is computed by

i) Increasing the denominator of BEPS for the weighted-average number of shares of common stock that would have been issued if dilutive potential common stock had been issued.

ii) Increasing the numerator of BEPS for convertible preferred dividends and after-tax amounts of interest related to the potential common stock. The numerator is also adjusted for other changes in income or loss, such as profit-sharing expenses, that would result from the assumed issuance of potential common stock.

b) **Potential common stock** is a security or other contract that may entitle the holder to obtain common stock. Examples include convertible securities (convertible preferred stock and convertible debt), stock options and warrants (and their equivalents), and contingently issuable common stock.

i. The **price-earnings (P-E) ratio** equals the market price per share of common stock divided by EPS.

1) $$\frac{\textit{Market price}}{\textit{EPS}}$$

2) Most analysts prefer to use diluted EPS.

3) Growth companies are likely to have high P-E ratios. A high ratio may also indicate that the firm is relatively low risk or that its choice of accounting methods results in a conservative EPS.

j. The **dividend payout ratio** equals dividends per common share divided by EPS.

1) $$\frac{\textit{Dividends per common share}}{\textit{EPS}}$$

2) The most conservative version of this ratio uses a diluted EPS amount that excludes nonrecurring items. Firms develop dividend policies based on recurring earnings because they usually prefer a stable pattern of dividends.

3) The appropriate ratio depends on the firm's unique circumstances, including shareholder preferences regarding dividend income and capital gains. The general principle, however, is that growth companies have a low payout.

4) A related ratio is the **dividend yield**. It equals dividends per share of common stock divided by the market price per share of common stock.

7. **Coverage ratios** help measure the long-run solvency of the firm.

a. **Book value per share** equals the amount of net assets available to the shareholders of a given type of stock divided by the number of those shares outstanding.

1) $\frac{\textit{Equity}}{\textit{Shares outstanding}}$

2) When a company has preferred stock as well as common stock outstanding, the computation of book value per common share must consider potential claims by preferred shareholders, such as whether the preferred stock is cumulative and in arrears or participating. It must also consider whether the call price (or possibly the liquidation value) exceeds the carrying amount of the preferred stock.

3) Book value per share is ordinarily based on historical cost expressed in nominal dollars. Accordingly, it may be misleading because book values ordinarily differ materially from fair values.

b. The book value per share is used to calculate the **market-to-book ratio**.

1) $\frac{\textit{Market price per share}}{\textit{Book value per share}}$

2) Well-managed firms should sell at high multiples of their book value, which reflects historical cost.

c. The **times-interest-earned ratio** equals earnings before interest and taxes (EBIT), divided by interest.

1) $\frac{\textit{EBIT}}{\textit{Interest expense}}$

2) This ratio is an income statement approach to evaluating debt-payment ability. It indicates the margin of safety for payment of fixed interest charges, so a consistently high ratio is desirable.

3) Interest is tax deductible. Hence, interest and tax must be added to net income to determine the amount available to pay interest.

4) The most accurate calculation of the numerator includes only earnings expected to recur. Consequently, unusual or infrequent items, extraordinary items, discontinued operations, and the effects of accounting changes should be excluded. Undistributed equity earnings should also be excluded because they are not available to cover interest. However, the minority income exclusion should be added back. Interest expense of a consolidated entity is included in consolidated income, so the income of that entity should be included.

5) The denominator should include capitalized interest.

d. **Cash flow per share** equals net cash provided by operations minus preferred dividends, divided by common shares outstanding.

1) $$\frac{\textit{Cash provided by operations - Preferred dividends}}{\textit{Common shares outstanding}}$$

2) This ratio is a better indicator of short-term capacity to make capital outlays and dividend payments than EPS. However, it is not a substitute for EPS as a measure of profitability. Hence, the FASB has stated that cash flow per share is not to be reported in the financial statements.

3) The denominator is the same as that used in the EPS calculation.

e. The **debt ratio** equals total liabilities divided by total assets.

1) $$\frac{\textit{Total liabilities}}{\textit{Total assets}}$$

2) The debt ratio measures the percentage of funds provided by creditors. It determines long-term debt-payment ability and the degree to which creditors are protected from the firm's insolvency. Hence, creditors prefer this ratio to be low as a cushion against losses.

3) The conservative approach to calculation of this ratio is to include short-term liabilities, contingencies, deferred taxes, the minority interest, and redeemable preferred stock in the numerator.

f. The **debt-to-equity ratio** equals total debt divided by total equity.

1) $$\frac{\textit{Total liabilities}}{\textit{Equity}}$$

2) It compares the resources provided by creditors with resources provided by owners.

3) Like the debt ratio, the debt-to-equity ratio determines long-term debt-payment ability, and the conservative approach is to include all liabilities and near liabilities in the numerator.

g. The **fixed charge coverage ratio** extends the times-interest-earned ratio to include the interest portion associated with long-term lease obligations.

1) $$\frac{\textit{EBIT + Interest portion of operating leases}}{\textit{Interest + Interest portion of operating leases}}$$

2) Other items, e.g., the entire amount of annual lease payments instead of the interest component, preferred dividends, pension payments, or depreciation may be included. Furthermore, the adjustments made to the times-interest-earned ratio may also be made.

h. The **operating cash flow to total debt ratio** equals the net cash provided by operations divided by total debt.

1) $$\frac{\textit{Operating cash flow}}{\textit{Total debt}}$$

2) A high ratio is desirable. Moreover, the most conservative approach is to include all debt items in the denominator.

i. The **equity multiplier (leverage factor)** equals total assets divided by common equity.

1) $\frac{\textit{Total assets}}{\textit{Common equity}}$

2) The equity multiplier is a component of the return-on-equity calculation. It measures the extent to which debt financing enhances equity financing.

a) $\frac{\textit{Net income}}{\textit{Net sales}} \times \frac{\textit{Net sales}}{\textit{Total assets}} \times \frac{\textit{Total assets}}{\textit{Common equity}} = \frac{\textit{Net income}}{\textit{Common equity}}$

3) **Leverage ratios** measure the firm's use of debt to finance assets and operations. As leverage increases, the risk that the firm may not be able to meet its maturing obligations and the risk borne by creditors increase. Nevertheless, interest is tax deductible, so leverage increases the firm's return when it is profitable. Furthermore, debt financing permits the owners to retain control.

8. Stop and review! You have completed the outline for this subunit. Study multiple-choice questions 1 through 56 beginning on page 398.

B. Limitations of Ratio Analysis

1. Although ratio analysis provides useful information pertaining to the efficiency of operations and the stability of financial condition, it has inherent limitations.

   a. Development of ratios for comparison with industry averages is more useful for firms that operate within a particular industry than for conglomerates (firms that operate in a variety of industries).

   b. The effects of inflation on fixed assets and depreciation, inventory costs, long-term debt, and profitability cause misstatement of a firm's balance sheet and income statement. For example, fixed assets and depreciation will be understated, and inventory also will be understated if LIFO is used. Moreover, the interest-rate increases that accompany inflation will decrease the value of outstanding long-term debt. Many assets are recorded at historical cost, so their true value may not be reflected on the balance sheet.

   c. Ratio analysis may be affected by seasonal factors. For example, inventory and receivables may vary widely, and year-end balances may not reflect the averages for the period.

   d. A firm's management has an incentive to **window dress** financial statements to improve results.

   e. Comparability of financial statement amounts and the ratios derived from them is impaired if different firms choose different accounting policies. Also, changes in a firm's own accounting policies may create some distortion in the comparison of the results over a period of years.

   f. Generalizations about which ratios are strong indicators of a firm's financial position may change from industry to industry, firm to firm, and division to division.

   g. Ratios are constructed from accounting data, much of which is subject to estimation.

h. Current performance and trends may be misinterpreted if sufficient years of historical analysis are not considered.

i. Ratio analysis may be distorted by failing to use an average or weighted average.

j. Misleading conclusions may result if improper comparisons are selected.

k. Whether a certain level of a ratio is favorable depends on the underlying circumstances. For example, a high quick ratio indicates high liquidity, but it may also imply that excessive cash is being held.

l. Different ratios may yield opposite conclusions about a firm's financial health. Thus, the net effects of a set of ratios should be analyzed.

m. Industry averages may include data from capital-intensive and labor-intensive firms. They may also include data from firms with greatly divergent policies regarding leverage.

n. Some industry averages may be based on small samples.

o. Different sources of information may compute ratios differently.

p. Some data may be presented either before or after taxes.

q. Comparability among firms may be impaired if they have different fiscal years.

r. The geographical locations of firms may affect comparability because of differences in labor markets, price levels, governmental regulation, taxation, and other factors.

s. Size differentials among firms affect comparability because of differences in access to and cost of capital, economies of scale, and width of markets.

2. Stop and review! You have completed the outline for this subunit. Study multiple-choice questions 57 and 58 on page 415.

C. Comparative Analysis

1. Comparative analysis involves both horizontal and vertical analysis. Horizontal (trend) analysis compares analytical data over a period of time. Vertical analysis makes comparisons among a single year's data. GAAP recommends that comparative financial statements be prepared for at least the current and the prior year.

   a. Comparison with competitors and industry averages.

      1) Comparing a company's performance with respect to its industry may identify the company's strengths and weaknesses. Horizontal analysis of the industry may identify industrywide trends and practices.

      2) Common-size financial statements are used to compare firms of different sizes.

         a) Items on common-size financial statements are expressed as percentages of corresponding base-year figures. The base amount is assigned the value of 100%.

            i) The **horizontal** form of common-size (percentage) analysis is useful for evaluating trends. The amounts for subsequent years are stated in percentages of a base-year amount.

ii) **Vertical** common-size (percentage) analysis presents figures for a single year expressed as percentages of a base amount on the balance sheet (e.g., total assets) and on the income statement (e.g., sales).

b. Many sources of standards for evaluating a firm's ratios are available, including the financial statements of individual firms. Researching many of the sources of comparative ratios is facilitated by the Standard Industrial Classification (SIC), a categorization of firms by industry that was developed for use in generating governmental financial statistics. However, a user of information organized based on the SIC should be aware that not every firm clearly fits one of the categories.

1) The following are some of the major sources of financial data:

a) *The Department of Commerce Financial Report* is a quarterly publication for manufacturing, mining, and trading firms. It provides financial statement data reported in industry dollars. It also includes a variety of ratios and industrywide common-size vertical financial statements.

b) *Robert Morris Associates Annual Statement Studies* is published by an organization of bank loan and credit officers. The data relate to thousands of firms in more than 350 industries. Included are common-size statements, certain ratios, and 5-year comparative historical information.

c) Dun & Bradstreet publishes *Industry Norms and Key Business Ratios*, which covers over 1 million firms in over 800 lines of business.

d) *Value Line Investment Service* provides financial data and rates the stocks of over 1,700 firms.

e) Standard & Poor's, Moody's Investors' Service, and various brokerages compile industry studies.

2. Stop and review! You have completed the outline for this subunit. Study multiple-choice questions 59 through 61 beginning on page 415.

MULTIPLE-CHOICE QUESTIONS

A. Ratio Analysis

1. When a balance sheet amount is related to an income statement amount in computing a ratio,

A. The balance sheet amount should be converted to an average for the year.

B. The income statement amount should be converted to an average for the year.

C. Both amounts should be converted to market value.

D. Comparisons with industry ratios are not meaningful.

The correct answer is (A). *(CMA, adapted)*

REQUIRED: The true statement about relating balance sheet to income statement amounts in a ratio.

DISCUSSION: In ratios such as inventory turnover, asset turnover, receivables turnover, and return on assets, the balance sheet figure should be an average for the period. The reason is that the income statement amounts represent activity over a period. Thus, the balance sheet figure should be adjusted to reflect assets available for use throughout the period.

Answer (B) is incorrect because the income statement amount is a single figure for an entire year; there is nothing to average. Answer (C) is incorrect because traditional financial statements and the ratios computed from the data they present are mostly stated in historical cost terms. Answer (D) is incorrect because comparison is the purpose of ratio usage. All ratios are meaningless unless compared to something else, such as an industry average.

2. Windham Company has current assets of $400,000 and current liabilities of $500,000. Windham Company's current ratio would be increased by

A. The purchase of $100,000 of inventory on account.

B. The payment of $100,000 of accounts payable.

C. The collection of $100,000 of accounts receivable.

D. Refinancing a $100,000 long-term loan with short-term debt.

The correct answer is (A). *(CMA, adapted)*

REQUIRED: The transaction that would increase a current ratio of less than 1.0.

DISCUSSION: The current ratio equals current assets divided by current liabilities. An equal increase in both the numerator and denominator of a current ratio less than 1.0 causes the ratio to increase. Windham Company's current ratio is .8 ($400,000 ÷ $500,000). The purchase of $100,000 of inventory on account would increase the current assets to $500,000 and the current liabilities to $600,000, resulting in a new current ratio of .833.

Answers (B) and (D) are incorrect because each transaction decreases the current ratio. Answer (C) is incorrect because the current ratio would be unchanged.

3. Given an acid test ratio of 2.0, current assets of $5,000, and inventory of $2,000, the value of current liabilities is

A. $1,500

B. $2,500

C. $3,500

D. $6,000

The correct answer is (A). *(CIA, adapted)*

REQUIRED: The value of current liabilities given the acid test ratio, current assets, and inventory.

DISCUSSION: The acid test or quick ratio equals the ratio of the quick assets (cash, net accounts receivable, and marketable securities) divided by current liabilities. Current assets equal the quick assets plus inventory and prepaid expenses. This question assumes that the entity has no prepaid expenses. Given current assets of $5,000, inventory of $2,000, and no prepaid expenses, the quick assets must be $3,000. Because the acid test ratio is 2.0, the quick assets are double the current liabilities. Current liabilities therefore are equal to $1,500 ($3,000 quick assets ÷ 2.0).

Answer (B) is incorrect because $2,500 results from dividing the current assets by 2.0. Current assets includes inventory, which should not be included in the calculation of the acid test ratio. Answer (C) is incorrect because $3,500 results from adding inventory to current assets rather than subtracting it. Answer (D) is incorrect because $6,000 results from multiplying the quick assets by 2 instead of dividing by 2.

4. The ratio of sales to working capital is a measure of

A. Collectibility.

B. Financial leverage.

C. Liquidity.

D. Profitability.

The correct answer is (C). *(CMA, adapted)*

REQUIRED: The quality measured by the ratio of sales to working capital.

DISCUSSION: Like most ratios involving working capital, the working capital turnover (sales ÷ average working capital) is a measure of liquidity, which is the ability to meet obligations as they mature. However, it is also an activity measure, and a high turnover is preferable.

Answer (A) is incorrect because working capital includes cash and inventory, neither of which involves collectibility. Answer (B) is incorrect because financial leverage concerns the relationship between the use of debt capital and equity capital. Answer (D) is incorrect because profitability measures incorporate costs as well as revenues, assets, and liabilities.

5. The number of days' sales in receivables is a measure of

A. Asset value.

B. Sales performance.

C. Profitability.

D. Liquidity.

The correct answer is (D). *(CMA, adapted)*

REQUIRED: The characteristic measured by the number of days' sales in receivables.

DISCUSSION: Turnover ratios are activity ratios that measure management's efficiency in using assets. However, the number of days' sales in receivables (days in the period divided by the receivables turnover ratio), also known as the average collection period, and other turnover ratios are a measure of liquidity because these statistics show how long it will take to turn inventory into cash.

Answer (A) is incorrect because valuation is not measured. Answer (B) is incorrect because sales performance is measured by profitability ratios. Answer (C) is incorrect because profitability ratios measure a firm's return on its investment. An example is earnings per share.

6. A high sales-to-working-capital ratio could indicate

A. Unprofitable use of working capital.

B. Sales are not adequate relative to available working capital.

C. The firm is undercapitalized.

D. The firm is not susceptible to liquidity problems.

The correct answer is (C). *(CMA, adapted)*

REQUIRED: The meaning of a high sales-to-working-capital ratio.

DISCUSSION: A high sales-to-working-capital ratio is usually favorable because working capital, by itself, is an unprofitable use of resources. A firm does not earn money by holding cash, inventory, or receivables. Such assets should be minimized. However, a high ratio of sales to working capital may indicate either very high sales (a good situation) or a low supply of working capital (a potentially bad situation). Thus, a high ratio could indicate that a firm is undercapitalized and does not have the resources to invest in working capital.

Answers (A) and (B) are incorrect because a high ratio means low levels of working capital compared to sales. The firm may be using its current assets effectively. Answer (D) is incorrect because a high ratio may indicate insufficient working capital to support the company's sales level, with resulting liquidity problems.

Questions 7 through 10 are based on the following information. Tosh Enterprises reported the following account information:

Accounts receivable	$400,000
Accounts payable	160,000
Bonds payable, due in 10 years	600,000
Cash	200,000
Interest payable, due in 3 months	20,000
Inventory	800,000
Land	500,000
Notes payable, due in 6 months	100,000
Prepaid expenses	80,000

The company has a normal operating cycle of 6 months.

7. The current ratio for Tosh Enterprises is

A. 1.68

B. 2.14

C. 5.00

D. 5.29

The correct answer is (D). *(Publisher)*

REQUIRED: The current ratio.

DISCUSSION: The current ratio equals current assets divided by current liabilities. Current assets consist of accounts receivable, cash, inventory, and prepaid expenses, a total of $1,480,000 ($400,000 + $200,000 + $800,000 + $80,000). Current liabilities consist of accounts payable, interest payable, and notes payable, a total of $280,000 ($160,000 + $20,000 + $100,000). Hence, the current ratio is 5.29 ($1,480,000 ÷ $280,000).

Answer (A) is incorrect because 1.68 includes long-term bonds payable among the current liabilities. Answer (B) is incorrect because 2.14 is the quick ratio. Answer (C) is incorrect because 5.00 excludes prepaid expenses from current assets.

8. What is the company's quick (acid-test) ratio?

A. 0.68

B. 1.68

C. 2.14

D. 2.31

The correct answer is (C). *(Publisher)*

REQUIRED: The quick ratio.

DISCUSSION: The quick ratio equals quick assets divided by current liabilities. For Tosh, quick assets consist of cash ($200,000) and accounts receivable ($400,000), a total of $600,000. Current liabilities consist of accounts payable ($160,000), interest payable ($20,000), and notes payable ($100,000), a total of $280,000. Hence, the quick ratio is 2.14 ($600,000 ÷ $280,000).

Answer (A) is incorrect because 0.68 includes long-term bonds payable among the current liabilities. Answer (B) is incorrect because 1.68 includes long-term bonds payable among the current liabilities and inventory and prepaid expenses among the quick assets. Answer (D) is incorrect because 2.31 excludes interest payable from the current liabilities.

9. What will happen to the ratios below if Tosh Enterprises uses cash to pay 25% of the accounts payable?

	Current Ratio	Quick Ratio
A.	Increase	Increase
B.	Decrease	Decrease
C.	Increase	Decrease
D.	Decrease	Increase

The correct answer is (A). *(Publisher)*

REQUIRED: The effect on the current and quick ratios of using cash to pay a portion of accounts payable.

DISCUSSION: Tosh's current ratio is 5.29 ($1,480,000 current assets ÷ $280,000 current liabilities), and its quick ratio is 2.14 ($600,000 quick assets ÷ $280,000 current liabilities). Using cash to pay 25% of the accounts payable decreases the numerator and denominator by $40,000 (25% x $160,000 accounts payable). The new current ratio will be 6.00 ($1,440,000 ÷ $240,000), and the new quick ratio will be 2.33 ($560,000 ÷ $240,000). If a ratio exceeds 1.0, equal decreases in the numerator and denominator increase the ratio.

Answers (B), (C), and (D) are incorrect because, given that both ratios initially exceeded 1.0, decreasing cash and accounts payable by equal amounts will increase both ratios.

10. The amount of working capital is

A. $600,000

B. $1,120,000

C. $1,200,000

D. $1,220,000

The correct answer is (C). *(Publisher)*

REQUIRED: The amount of working capital.

DISCUSSION: Working capital equals current assets minus current liabilities. For Tosh Enterprises, current assets consist of accounts receivable, cash, inventory, and prepaid expenses, a total of $1,480,000 ($400,000 + $200,000 + $800,000 + $80,000). Current liabilities consist of accounts payable, interest payable, and notes payable, a total of $280,000 ($160,000 + $20,000 + $100,000). Accordingly, working capital is $1,200,000 ($1,480,000 – $280,000).

Answer (A) is incorrect because $600,000 includes long-term bonds payable among the current liabilities. Answer (B) is incorrect because $1,120,000 excludes prepaid expenses from current assets. Answer (D) is incorrect because $1,220,000 excludes interest payable from current liabilities.

11. Rice, Inc. uses the allowance method to account for uncollectible accounts. An account receivable that was previously determined uncollectible and written off was collected during May. The effect of the collection on Rice's current ratio and total working capital is

	Current Ratio	Working Capital
A.	None	None
B.	Increase	Increase
C.	Decrease	Decrease
D.	None	Increase

The correct answer is (A). *(CMA, adapted)*

REQUIRED: The effect on the current ratio and working capital of collecting an account previously written off to the allowance account.

DISCUSSION: The entry to record this transaction is to debit receivables, credit the allowance, debit cash, and credit receivables. The result is to increase both an asset (cash) and a contra asset (allowance for bad debts). These appear in the current asset section of the balance sheet. Thus, the collection changes neither the current ratio nor working capital because the effects are offsetting. The credit for the journal entry is made to the allowance account on the assumption that another account will become uncollectible. The company had previously estimated its bad debts and established an appropriate allowance. It then (presumably) wrote off the wrong account. Accordingly, the journal entry reinstates a balance in the allowance account to absorb future uncollectibles.

Answers (B), (C), and (D) are incorrect because neither the current ratio nor working capital is affected.

12. Merit, Inc. uses the direct write-off method to account for uncollectible accounts receivable. If the company subsequently collects an account receivable that was written off in a prior accounting period, the effect of the collection of the account receivable on Merit's current ratio and total working capital would be

	Current Ratio	Working Capital
A.	None	None
B.	Increase	Increase
C.	Increase	None
D.	None	Decrease

The correct answer is (B). *(CMA, adapted)*

REQUIRED: The effect on the current ratio and working capital of collecting an account written off in a prior period under the direct write-off method.

DISCUSSION: Because the company uses the direct write-off method, the original entry involved a debit to a bad debt expense account (closed to retained earnings). The subsequent collection required a debit to cash and a credit to bad debt expense or retained earnings. Thus, only one current asset account was involved in the collection entry, and current assets (cash) increased as a result. If current assets increase, and no change occurs in current liabilities, the current ratio and working capital both increase.

Answers (A), (C), and (D) are incorrect because the current ratio and working capital increase.

13. Accounts receivable turnover ratio will normally decrease as a result of

A. The write-off of an uncollectible account (assume the use of the allowance for doubtful accounts method).

B. A significant sales volume decrease near the end of the accounting period.

C. An increase in cash sales in proportion to credit sales.

D. A change in credit policy to lengthen the period for cash discounts.

The correct answer is (D). *(CMA, adapted)*

REQUIRED: The event that will cause the accounts receivable turnover ratio to decrease.

DISCUSSION: The accounts receivable turnover ratio equals net credit sales divided by average receivables. Hence, it will decrease if a company lengthens the credit period or the discount period because the denominator will increase as receivables are held for longer times.

Answer (A) is incorrect because write-offs do not reduce net receivables (gross receivables – the allowance) and will not affect the receivables balance and therefore the turnover ratio if an allowance system is used. Answer (B) is incorrect because a decline in sales near the end of the period signifies fewer credit sales and receivables, and the effect of reducing the numerator and denominator by equal amounts is to increase the ratio if the fraction is greater than 1.0. Answer (C) is incorrect because an increase in cash sales with no diminution of credit sales will not affect receivables.

14. The days' sales-in-receivables ratio will be understated if the company

A. Uses a natural business year for its accounting period.

B. Uses a calendar year for its accounting period.

C. Uses average receivables in the ratio calculation.

D. Does not use average receivables in the ratio calculation.

The correct answer is (A). *(CMA, adapted)*

REQUIRED: The reason the days' sales-in-receivables ratio will be understated.

DISCUSSION: The days' sales-in-receivables ratio equals the days in the year divided by the receivables turnover ratio (sales ÷ average receivables). Days' sales may also be computed based only on ending receivables. In either case, use of the natural business year tends to understate the ratio because receivables will usually be at a low point at the beginning and end of the natural year. For example, a ski resort may close its books on May 31, a low point in its operating cycle.

Answer (B) is incorrect because using a calendar year will not necessarily affect the usefulness of the days' sales ratio. Answers (C) and (D) are incorrect because using average receivables would not always understate the ratio. The ratio could be higher or lower depending on changes in sales volume or the percentage of credit to cash sales, or other factors.

Questions 15 through 21 are based on the following information. Depoole Company is a manufacturer of industrial products and uses a calendar year for financial reporting purposes. These questions present several of Depoole's transactions during the year. Assume that total quick assets exceeded total current liabilities both before and after each transaction described. Further assume that Depoole has positive profits during the year and a credit balance throughout the year in its retained earnings account.

15. Payment of a trade account payable of $64,500 would

A. Increase the current ratio, but the quick ratio would not be affected.

B. Increase the quick ratio, but the current ratio would not be affected.

C. Increase both the current and quick ratios.

D. Decrease both the current and quick ratios.

The correct answer is (C). *(CMA, adapted)*

REQUIRED: The effect of paying a trade account payable on the current and quick ratios.

DISCUSSION: Given that the quick assets exceed current liabilities, both the current and quick ratios exceed one because the numerator of the current ratio includes other current assets in addition to the quick assets of cash, net accounts receivable, and short-term marketable securities. An equal reduction in the numerator and the denominator, such as a payment of a trade payable, will cause each ratio to increase.

Answers (A), (B), and (D) are incorrect because both the current ratio and the quick ratio would increase.

16. The purchase of raw materials for $85,000 on open account would

A. Increase the current ratio.

B. Decrease the current ratio.

C. Increase net working capital.

D. Decrease net working capital.

The correct answer is (B). *(CMA, adapted)*

REQUIRED: The effect of a credit purchase of raw materials on the current ratio and/or working capital.

DISCUSSION: The purchase increases both the numerator and denominator of the current ratio by adding inventory to the numerator and payables to the denominator. Because the ratio before the purchase was greater than one, the ratio is decreased.

Answer (A) is incorrect because the current ratio is decreased. Answers (C) and (D) are incorrect because the purchase of raw materials on account has no effect on working capital (current assets and current liabilities change by the same amount).

17. The collection of a current accounts receivable of $29,000 would

A. Increase the current ratio.

B. Decrease the current ratio and the quick ratio.

C. Increase the quick ratio.

D. Not affect the current or quick ratios.

The correct answer is (D). *(CMA, adapted)*

REQUIRED: The effect of collection of a current account receivable on the current and quick ratios.

DISCUSSION: Collecting current accounts receivable has no effect on either the current ratio or the quick ratio because assets (both current and quick) are reduced for the collection of receivables and increased by the same amount for the receipt of cash. Current liabilities are unchanged by the transaction.

Answers (A), (B), and (C) are incorrect because collecting current accounts receivable does not create a net change in current assets, quick assets, or current liabilities, which means the current and quick ratios are not changed.

18. Obsolete inventory of $125,000 was written off during the year. This transaction

A. Decreased the quick ratio.

B. Increased the quick ratio.

C. Increased net working capital.

D. Decreased the current ratio.

The correct answer is (D). *(CMA, adapted)*

REQUIRED: The effect of writing off obsolete inventory.

DISCUSSION: Writing off obsolete inventory reduced current assets, but not quick assets (cash, receivables, and marketable securities). Thus, the current ratio was reduced and the quick ratio was unaffected.

Answers (A) and (B) are incorrect because the quick ratio was not affected. Answer (C) is incorrect because working capital was decreased.

19. The issuance of new shares in a five-for-one split of common stock

A. Decreases the book value per share of common stock.

B. Increases the book value per share of common stock.

C. Increases total shareholders' equity.

D. Decreases total shareholders' equity.

The correct answer is (A). *(CMA, adapted)*

REQUIRED: The effect of a five-for-one split of common stock.

DISCUSSION: Given that five times as many shares of stock are outstanding, the book value per share of common stock is one-fifth of the former value after the split.

Answer (B) is incorrect because the book value per share is decreased. Answers (C) and (D) are incorrect because the stock split does not change the amount of shareholders' equity.

20. The issuance of serial bonds in exchange for an office building, with the first installment of the bonds due late this year,

A. Decreases net working capital.

B. Decreases the current ratio.

C. Decreases the quick ratio.

D. Affects all of the answers as indicated.

The correct answer is (D). *(CMA, adapted)*

REQUIRED: The effect of issuing serial bonds with the first installment due late this year.

DISCUSSION: The first installment is a current liability; thus the amount of current liabilities increases with no corresponding increase in current assets. The effect is to decrease working capital, the current ratio, and the quick ratio.

Answer (A) is incorrect because the bond issuance would also decrease the current ratio and the quick ratio. Answer (B) is incorrect because the bond issuance would also decrease net working capital and the quick ratio. Answer (C) is incorrect because the bond issuance would also decrease net working capital and the current ratio.

21. Refer to the information preceding question 15 on page 402. The early liquidation of a long-term note with cash affects the

A. Current ratio to a greater degree than the quick ratio.

B. Quick ratio to a greater degree than the current ratio.

C. Current and quick ratio to the same degree.

D. Current ratio but not the quick ratio.

The correct answer is (B). *(CMA, adapted)*

REQUIRED: The effect of an early liquidation of a long-term note with cash.

DISCUSSION: The numerators of the quick and current ratios are decreased when cash is expended. Early payment of a long-term liability has no effect on the denominator (current liabilities). Since the numerator of the quick ratio, which includes cash, net receivables, and marketable securities, is less than the numerator of the current ratio, which includes all current assets, the quick ratio is affected to a greater degree.

Answers (A), (C), and (D) are incorrect because the quick ratio is affected to a greater degree than the current ratio.

22. To determine the operating cycle for a retail department store, which one of the following pairs of items is needed?

A. Days' sales in accounts receivable and average merchandise inventory.

B. Cash turnover and net sales.

C. Accounts receivable turnover and inventory turnover.

D. Asset turnover and return on sales.

The correct answer is (C). *(CMA, adapted)*

REQUIRED: The pair of items needed to determine the operating cycle for a retailer.

DISCUSSION: The operating cycle is the time needed to turn cash into inventory, inventory into receivables, and receivables back into cash. For a retailer, it is the time from purchase of inventory to collection of cash. Thus, the operating cycle of a retailer is equal to the sum of the number of days' sales in inventory and the number of days' sales in receivables. Inventory turnover equals cost of goods sold divided by average inventory. The days' sales in inventory equals 365 (or another period chosen by the analyst) divided by the inventory turnover. Accounts receivable turnover equals net credit sales divided by average receivables. The days' sales in receivables equals 365 (or other number) divided by the accounts receivable turnover.

Answer (A) is incorrect because cost of sales must be known to calculate days' sales in inventory. Answers (B) and (D) are incorrect because they are insufficient to permit determination of the operating cycle.

23. If the ratio of total liabilities to shareholders' equity increases, a ratio that must also increase is

A. Times interest earned.

B. Total liabilities to total assets.

C. Return on equity.

D. The current ratio.

The correct answer is (B). *(CMA, adapted)*

REQUIRED: The ratio that will increase if the ratio of total liabilities to shareholders' equity increases.

DISCUSSION: Because total assets will be the same as the sum of liabilities and equity, an increase in the liabilities-to-equity ratio will simultaneously increase the liabilities-to-assets ratio.

Answer (A) is incorrect because no determination can be made of the effect on interest coverage without knowing the amounts of income and interest expense. Answer (C) is incorrect because the return on equity may be increased or decreased as a result of an increase in the liabilities-to-equity ratio. Answer (D) is incorrect because the current ratio equals current assets divided by current liabilities, and additional information is necessary to determine whether it would be affected. For example, an increase in current liabilities from short-term borrowing would increase the liabilities-to-equity ratio but decrease the current ratio.

Questions 24 through 26 are based on the following information. The selected data pertain to a company at December 31:

Quick assets	$208,000
Acid test ratio	2.6 to 1
Current ratio	3.5 to 1
Net sales for the year	$1,800,000
Cost of sales for the year	$990,000
Average total assets for the year	$1,200,000

24. The company's current liabilities at December 31 equal

A. $59,429

B. $80,000

C. $134,857

D. $187,200

The correct answer is (B). *(CIA, adapted)*

REQUIRED: The current liabilities at year-end.

DISCUSSION: The acid test ratio is equal to quick assets divided by current liabilities. Thus, current liabilities equal the $208,000 of quick assets divided by the 2.6 acid test ratio. Hence, current liabilities equal $80,000.

Answers (A), (C), and (D) are incorrect because the current liabilities at year-end are determined using the quick assets total and the acid test ratio: Current liabilities equals the quick assets divided by the acid test ratio.

25. The company's inventory balance at December 31 is

A. $72,000

B. $187,200

C. $231,111

D. $282,857

The correct answer is (A). *(CIA, adapted)*

REQUIRED: The inventory balance at year-end.

DISCUSSION: Inventory is equal to the difference between current assets and quick assets (assuming no prepaid expenses are included in current assets). The current ratio is equal to current assets divided by current liabilities. Accordingly, multiplying the current liabilities of $80,000 (determined in the previous question) by the current ratio of 3.5 gives current assets of $280,000. Subtracting the $208,000 of quick assets from the $280,000 of current assets results in an inventory balance of $72,000.

Answers (B), (C), and (D) are incorrect because inventory equals the difference between current assets and quick assets (assuming no prepaid expenses). Multiplying the current liabilities by the current ratio gives the current assets. Subtracting the quick assets from the current assets gives the inventory balance.

26. The company's asset turnover ratio for the year is

A. .675

B. .825

C. 1.21

D. 1.50

The correct answer is (D). *(CIA, adapted)*

REQUIRED: The asset turnover ratio for the year.

DISCUSSION: The asset turnover ratio equals $1,800,000 of net sales divided by $1,200,000 of average total assets. The asset turnover ratio is therefore equal to 1.5.

Answers (A), (B), and (C) are incorrect because asset turnover ratio equals net sales divided by average total assets.

27. Which one of the following inventory cost flow assumptions will result in a higher inventory turnover ratio in an inflationary economy?

A. FIFO.

B. LIFO.

C. Weighted average.

D. Specific identification.

The correct answer is (B). *(CMA, adapted)*

REQUIRED: The cost flow assumption that will result in a higher inventory turnover ratio in an inflationary economy.

DISCUSSION: The inventory turnover ratio equals the cost of goods sold divided by the average inventory. LIFO assumes that the last goods purchased are the first goods sold and that the oldest goods purchased remain in inventory. The result is a higher cost of goods sold and a lower average inventory than under other inventory cost flow assumptions if prices are rising. Because cost of goods sold (the numerator) will be higher and average inventory (the denominator) will be lower than under other inventory cost flow assumptions, LIFO produces the highest inventory turnover ratio.

Answers (A), (C), and (D) are incorrect because, when prices are rising, LIFO results in a higher cost of goods sold and a lower average inventory than under other inventory cost flow assumptions.

28. Based on the data presented below, what is Beta Corporation's cost of sales for the year?

Current ratio	3.5
Acid test ratio	3.0
Year-end current liabilities	$600,000
Beginning inventory	$500,000
Inventory turnover	8.0

A. $1,600,000

B. $2,400,000

C. $3,200,000

D. $6,400,000

The correct answer is (C). *(CMA, adapted)*

REQUIRED: The cost of sales given various ratios, ending liabilities, and beginning inventory.

DISCUSSION: Inventory turnover equals cost of sales divided by average inventory. The turnover ratio and the beginning inventory are known. If ending inventory can be determined, average inventory and cost of sales can also be calculated. The relationship among the current ratio, acid test ratio, and current liabilities facilitates this calculation. The current ratio is the ratio of current assets to current liabilities. Thus, Beta's current assets are 3.5 times its current liabilities. Given that current liabilities at year-end are $600,000, current assets at year-end must be $2,100,000 (3.5 x $600,000). The acid test ratio is equal to the ratio of the sum of cash, net accounts receivable, and short-term marketable securities to current liabilities. Accordingly, Beta's quick assets are 3.0 times its current liabilities. If current liabilities at year-end are $600,000, the quick assets are $1,800,000 (3.0 x $600,000). The difference between current assets and quick assets is equal to inventory (assuming no prepaid expenses are included in current assets). Because current assets at year-end are $2,100,000 and quick assets are $1,800,000, ending inventory must be $300,000. Average inventory is equal to $400,000 [($500,000 beginning inventory + $300,000 ending inventory) ÷ 2]. An inventory turnover (cost of sales ÷ average inventory) of 8.0 indicates that cost of sales is 8.0 times average inventory. Cost of sales is therefore equal to $3,200,000 (8.0 x $400,000).

Answers (A), (B), and (D) are incorrect because cost of sales equals average inventory times inventory turnover.

29. Return on investment may be calculated by multiplying total asset turnover by

A. Average collection period.

B. Profit margin.

C. Debt ratio.

D. Fixed-charge coverage.

The correct answer is (B). *(CIA, adapted)*

REQUIRED: The method of calculating return on investment.

DISCUSSION: Return on investment is equal to profit divided by the average total assets. Asset turnover is equal to net sales divided by average total assets. Profit margin is equal to the profit divided by net sales. Thus, multiplying the asset turnover by the profit margin results in the cancellation of net sales from both ratios, leaving a ratio composed of profit in the numerator and average total assets in the denominator, which equals return on investment.

Answers (A), (C), and (D) are incorrect because return on investment cannot be determined using the average collection period, debt ratio, or fixed-charge coverage.

30. Return on investment (ROI) is a term often used to express income earned on capital invested in a business unit. A company's ROI is increased if

A. Sales increase by the same dollar amount as expenses and total assets.

B. Sales remain the same and expenses are reduced by the same dollar amount that total assets increase.

C. Sales decrease by the same dollar amount that expenses increase.

D. Net profit margin on sales increases by the same percentage as total assets.

The correct answer is (B). *(CMA, adapted)*

REQUIRED: The change that would increase a company's ROI.

DISCUSSION: If equal amounts are added to the numerator and denominator of a fraction that is less than one, the ratio will increase. Assuming that the ROI (net income ÷ total assets) is less than one, keeping sales constant while reducing expenses and increasing total assets by equal amounts will increase the ROI because the increase in net income equals the increase in total assets.

Answer (A) is incorrect because increasing sales and expenses by the same amount does not change net income (sales – expenses). Increasing the denominator without increasing the numerator reduces the ratio. Answer (C) is incorrect because decreasing the numerator without changing the denominator reduces the ratio. Answer (D) is incorrect because equal percentage changes in its elements neither increase nor decrease the ratio.

31. What type of ratio is earnings per share?

A. Profitability ratio.

B. Activity ratio.

C. Liquidity ratio.

D. Leverage ratio.

The correct answer is (A). *(Publisher)*

REQUIRED: The proper classification of the earnings per share ratio.

DISCUSSION: Earnings per share is a profitability ratio. It measures the level of profitability of the firm on a per-share basis.

Answer (B) is incorrect because activity ratios measure management's efficiency in using specific resources. Answer (C) is incorrect because liquidity ratios indicate the ability of a company to meet short-term obligations. Answer (D) is incorrect because leverage or equity ratios concern the relationship of debt to equity and measure the impact of the debt on profitability and risk.

32. If a company is profitable and is effectively using leverage, which one of the following ratios is likely to be the largest?

A. Return on total assets.

B. Return on operating assets.

C. Return on common equity.

D. Return on total equity.

The correct answer is (C). *(CMA, adapted)*

REQUIRED: The ratio that is likely to be largest if a profitable company is effectively using leverage.

DISCUSSION: The purpose of leverage is to use creditor capital to earn income for shareholders. If the return on the resources provided by creditors or preferred shareholders exceeds the cost (interest or fixed dividends), leverage is used effectively, and the return to common equity will be higher than the other measures. The reason is that common equity provides a smaller proportion of the investment than in an unleveraged company.

Answers (A), (B), and (D) are incorrect because return on total assets, return on operating assets, and return on total equity will be lower than the return on common equity if the firm is profitable and using leverage effectively.

33. Which one of the following statements about the price-earnings (P-E) ratio is correct?

A. A company with high growth opportunities ordinarily has a high P-E ratio.

B. A P-E ratio has more meaning when a firm has losses than when it has profits.

C. A P-E ratio has more meaning when a firm has abnormally low profits in relation to its asset base.

D. A P-E ratio expresses the relationship between a firm's market price and its net sales.

The correct answer is (A). *(CMA, adapted)*

REQUIRED: The true statement about the P-E ratio.

DISCUSSION: A company with high growth opportunities typically has a high P-E ratio because investors are willing to pay a price for the stock higher than that justified by current earnings. In effect, they are trading current earnings for potential future earnings.

Answer (B) is incorrect because a P-E ratio cannot be computed when a firm has losses. Answer (C) is incorrect because a firm with abnormally low profits could have an extremely high, and thus meaningless, P-E ratio. Answer (D) is incorrect because the P-E ratio expresses the relationship between market price and a firm's EPS.

34. Watson Corporation computed the following items from its financial records for the year:

Price-earnings ratio	12
Payout ratio	.6
Asset turnover ratio	.9

The dividend yield on Watson's common stock is

A. 5.0%

B. 7.2%

C. 7.5%

D. 10.8%

The correct answer is (A). *(CMA, adapted)*

REQUIRED: The dividend yield given the P-E ratio, payout ratio, and asset turnover ratio.

DISCUSSION: Dividend yield is computed by dividing the dividend per share by the market price per share. The payout ratio (.6) is computed by dividing dividends by net income per share (EPS). The P-E ratio (12) is computed by dividing the market price per share by net income per share. Thus, assuming that net income per share (EPS) is $X, the market price must be $12X and the dividends per share $.6X (.6 x $X net income per share). Consequently, the dividend yield is 5.0% ($.6X dividend ÷ $12X market price per share).

Answer (B) is incorrect because 7.2% equals 12% times the payout ratio. Answer (C) is incorrect because 7.5% equals asset turnover divided by the P-E ratio. Answer (D) is incorrect because 10.8% equals 12% times the asset turnover ratio.

35. A drop in the market price of a firm's common stock will immediately increase its

A. Return on equity.

B. Dividend payout ratio.

C. Market-to-book ratio.

D. Dividend yield.

The correct answer is (D). *(CMA, adapted)*

REQUIRED: The effect of a drop in the market price of a firm's common stock.

DISCUSSION: Dividend yield equals dividends per common share divided by the market price per common share. Hence, a drop in the market price of the stock will increase this ratio, holding all else constant.

Answers (A), (B), and (C) are incorrect because these ratios are based on book values in their calculation rather than the market price of the common stock.

36. The following information is provided about the common stock of Evergreen Inc. at the end of the fiscal year:

Number of shares outstanding	1,800,000
Par value per share	$ 10.00
Dividends paid per share (last 12 months)	12.00
Market price per share	108.00
Basic earnings per share	36.00
Diluted earnings per share	24.00

The price-earnings ratio for Evergreen's common stock is

A. 3.0 times.

B. 4.5 times.

C. 9.0 times.

D. 10.8 times.

The correct answer is (B). *(CMA, adapted)*

REQUIRED: The price-earnings ratio.

DISCUSSION: The price-earnings ratio is

$$\frac{\textit{Market price}}{\textit{Diluted EPS}} = \frac{\$108}{\$24} = 4.5$$

Answer (A) is incorrect because 3.0 is based on BEPS rather than DEPS in the denominator. Answer (C) is incorrect because 9.0 is based on dividends rather than DEPS in the denominator. Answer (D) is incorrect because 10.8 is based on par value rather than DEPS in the denominator.

37. Baylor Company paid out one-half of last year's earnings in dividends. Baylor's earnings increased by 20%, and the amount of its dividends increased by 15% in the current year. Baylor's dividend payout ratio for the current year was

A. 50%

B. 57.5%

C. 47.9%

D. 78%

The correct answer is (C). *(CMA, adapted)*

REQUIRED: The dividend payout ratio given earnings and dividend increases.

DISCUSSION: The prior-year dividend payout ratio was 50%. Hence, if prior-year net income was X, the total dividend payout would have been 50%X. If earnings increase by 20%, current-year income will be 120%X. If dividends increase by 15%, the total dividends paid out will be 57.5%X (115% x 50%X), and the new dividend payout ratio will be 47.9% (57.5%X ÷ 120%X).

Answer (A) is incorrect because 50% is the prior-year payout ratio. Answer (B) is incorrect because 57.5% is 115% of the prior-year payout ratio. Answer (D) is incorrect because 78% equals 65% of 120%.

38. Book value per common share represents the amount of equity assigned to each outstanding share of common stock. Which one of the following statements about book value per common share is correct?

A. Market price per common share usually approximates book value per common share.

B. Book value per common share can be misleading because it is based on historical cost.

C. A market price per common share that is greater than book value per common share is an indication of an overvalued stock.

D. Book value per common share is the amount that would be paid to shareholders if the company were sold to another company.

The correct answer is (B). *(CMA, adapted)*

REQUIRED: The true statement about book value per common share.

DISCUSSION: Book value is based on the financial statements, which are stated in terms of historical cost and nominal dollars. The figure can be misleading because fair values may differ substantially from book figures.

Answer (A) is incorrect because market price may be more or less than book value. Answer (C) is incorrect because fair value may be more accurate than the carrying values if the historical cost figures are out of date. Answer (D) is incorrect because the amount another company would pay would be based on fair values, not book values.

39. The book value per share calculation of a corporation is usually significantly different from the market value of the stock's selling price due to the

A. Use of accrual accounting in preparing financial statements.

B. Omission of the number of preferred shares outstanding at year-end in the calculation.

C. Use of historical costs in preparing financial statements.

D. Omission of total assets from the numerator in the calculation.

The correct answer is (C). *(CMA, adapted)*

REQUIRED: The reason the book value of a corporation's stock is usually different from its market value.

DISCUSSION: A stock's book value is the amount of net assets available to the holders of a given type of stock, divided by the number of those shares outstanding. The market price is the amount that a stock market investor is willing to pay for the stock. The two values are normally different because the book value is based primarily on historical cost expressed in nominal dollars. Accordingly, the book value may be misleading because book values of assets may differ materially from the fair values of those same assets.

Answer (A) is incorrect because stock market investors base their decisions on fair values, and accrual accounting contributes to the determination of fair values. Thus, both book value and market value rely on accrual accounting. Answer (B) is incorrect because preferred shares are not omitted when book value per share of preferred stock is calculated. Answer (D) is incorrect because net, not total, assets are available to shareholders. Hence, the numerator in the book value calculation is based on net assets.

40. A measure of long-term debt-paying ability is a company's

A. Length of the operating cycle.

B. Return on assets.

C. Inventory turnover ratio.

D. Times-interest-earned ratio.

The correct answer is (D). *(CMA, adapted)*

REQUIRED: The measure of a company's long-term debt-paying ability.

DISCUSSION: The times-interest-earned ratio is one measure of a firm's ability to pay its debt obligations out of current earnings. This ratio equals earnings before interest and taxes divided by interest expense.

Answer (A) is incorrect because the length of the operating cycle does not affect long-term debt-paying ability. By definition, long-term means longer than the normal operating cycle. Answer (B) is incorrect because return on assets measures only how well management uses the assets that are available. It does not compare the return with debt service costs. Answer (C) is incorrect because the inventory turnover ratio is a measure of how well a company is managing one of its current assets.

Questions 41 through 46 are based on the following information. The Statement of Financial Position for King Products Corporation for the fiscal years ended June 30, 2001 and June 30, 2000 is presented below. Net sales and cost of goods sold for the year ended June 30, 2001 were $600,000 and $440,000, respectively.

King Products Corporation
Statement of Financial Position
(in thousands)

	June 30	
	2001	2000
Cash	$ 60	$ 50
Trading securities (at fair value)	40	30
Accounts receivable (net)	90	60
Inventories (at lower of cost or market)	120	100
Prepaid items	30	40
Total current assets	340	280
Land (at cost)	200	190
Building (net)	160	180
Equipment (net)	190	200
Patents (net)	70	34
Goodwill (net)	40	26
Total long-term assets	660	630
Total assets	$1,000	$910
Notes payable	$ 46	$24
Accounts payable	94	56
Accrued interest	30	30
Total current liabilities	170	110
Notes payable, 10% due 12/31/06	20	20
Bonds payable, 12% due 6/30/09	30	30
Total long-term debt	50	50
Total liabilities	220	160
Preferred stock - 5% cumulative, $100 par, nonparticipating, authorized, issued and outstanding, 2,000 shares	200	200
Common stock - $10 par, 40,000 shares authorized, 30,000 shares issued and outstanding	300	300
Additional paid-in capital - common	150	150
Retained earnings	130	100
Total equity	780	750
Total liabilities & equity	$1,000	$910

41. King Products Corporation's inventory turnover ratio for the fiscal year ended at June 30, 2001 was

A. 3.7

B. 4.0

C. 4.4

D. 6.0

The correct answer is (B). *(CMA, adapted)*

REQUIRED: The inventory turnover ratio for 2001.

DISCUSSION: The inventory turnover ratio equals cost of sales divided by the average inventory. Consequently, the inventory turnover is 4 times per year {$440,000 ÷ [($120,000 + $100,000) ÷ 2]}.

Answer (A) is incorrect because 3.7 is based on year-end inventory. Answer (C) is incorrect because 4.4 is based on beginning inventory. Answer (D) is incorrect because 6.0 is based on sales and beginning inventory.

42. King Products Corporation's receivables turnover ratio for this period was

A. 4.9

B. 5.9

C. 6.7

D. 8.0

The correct answer is (D). *(CMA, adapted)*

REQUIRED: The receivables turnover ratio for 2001.

DISCUSSION: The receivables turnover ratio equals net credit sales divided by the average receivables balance. In this question, net sales must be used because the amount of net credit sales is not given. Thus, the receivables turnover is 8 times per year {$600,000 ÷ [($90,000 + $60,000) ÷ 2]}.

Answer (A) is incorrect because 4.9 is based on cost of sales and year-end receivables. Answer (B) is incorrect because 5.9 is based on cost of sales. Answer (C) is incorrect because 6.7 is based on year-end receivables.

43. King Products Corporation's average collection period for the fiscal year ended June 30, 2001 using a 360-day year was

A. 36 days.

B. 45 days.

C. 54 days.

D. 61 days.

The correct answer is (B). *(CMA, adapted)*

REQUIRED: The average collection period for 2001.

DISCUSSION: The average collection period equals the number of days in a year divided by the receivables turnover ratio. The receivables turnover was 8 times per year (see preceding question). Thus, the average collection period is 45 days (360 ÷ 8).

Answer (A) is incorrect because 36 days assumes a turnover of 10 times per year. Answer (C) is incorrect because 54 days assumes a turnover of 6.7 times per year. Answer (D) is incorrect because 61 days assumes a turnover of 5.9 times per year.

44. King Products Corporation's quick (acid test) ratio at June 30, 2001 was

A. 0.6

B. 1.1

C. 1.8

D. 2.0

The correct answer is (B). *(CMA, adapted)*

REQUIRED: The quick (acid-test) ratio at June 30, 2001.

DISCUSSION: The quick ratio equals quick assets divided by current liabilities. King's quick assets consist of cash, receivables, and trading securities. Accordingly, the quick ratio is 1.11 [($60 cash + $40 trading securities + $90 accounts receivable) ÷ $170 current liabilities].

Answer (A) is incorrect because 0.6 omits receivables. Answer (C) is incorrect because 1.8 includes inventories. Answer (D) is incorrect because 2.0 is the current ratio.

45. Assuming that King Products Corporation's net income for the year ended June 30, 2001 was $70,000 and there are no preferred stock dividends in arrears, King Products' return on common equity was

A. 7.8%

B. 10.6%

C. 10.9%

D. 12.4%

The correct answer is (B). *(CMA, adapted)*

REQUIRED: The return on common equity for 2001.

DISCUSSION: The preferred stock dividend requirement is $10,000 (5% x $200,000 par value), so the net income available to common shareholders is $60,000 ($70,000 NI – $10,000). The return on common equity equals income available to common shareholders divided by the average common shareholders' equity. Given that preferred shareholders' equity was $200,000 at all relevant times, beginning and ending common shareholders' equity was $550,000 ($750,000 total – $200,000) and $580,000 ($780,000 total – $200,000), an average of $565,000 [($580,000 + $550,000) ÷ 2]. The return on common equity was therefore 10.6% ($60,000 ÷ $565,000).

Answer (A) is incorrect because 7.8% includes preferred equity in the denominator. Answer (C) is incorrect because 10.9% is based on beginning-of-the-year equity. Answer (D) is incorrect because 12.4% does not subtract the preferred dividend requirement from net income.

46. Assuming that there are no preferred stock dividends in arrears, King Products Corporation's book value per share of common stock at June 30, 2001 was

A. $10.00

B. $14.50

C. $18.33

D. $19.33

The correct answer is (D). *(CMA, adapted)*

REQUIRED: The book value per share of common stock assuming no preferred dividends in arrears.

DISCUSSION: Book value equals equity attributable to a class of stock divided by the number of shares outstanding. At year-end, 30,000 shares of common stock are outstanding. Equity attributable to the common shareholders includes all equity except preferred stock. Thus, the book value of a share of common stock is $19.33 [($780,000 total equity – $200,000 preferred stock) ÷ 30,000 shares of common stock].

Answer (A) is incorrect because $10 is the par value per share of the common stock; book value includes additional paid-in capital and retained earnings. Answer (B) is incorrect because $14.50 is based on 40,000 authorized shares. Answer (C) is incorrect because $18.33 was the book value at the end of 2000.

47. A debt-to-equity ratio is

A. About the same as the debt-to-assets ratio.

B. Higher than the debt-to-assets ratio.

C. Lower than the debt-to-assets ratio.

D. Not correlated with the debt-to-assets ratio.

The correct answer is (B). *(CMA, adapted)*

REQUIRED: The true statement comparing the debt-to-equity and debt-to-assets ratios.

DISCUSSION: Because debt plus equity equals assets, a debt-to-equity ratio would have a lower denominator than a debt-to-assets ratio. Thus, the debt-to-equity ratio would be higher than the debt-to-assets ratio.

Answer (A) is incorrect because the ratios would always be different unless either debt or equity equaled zero. Answer (C) is incorrect because the lower denominator in the debt-to-equity ratio means that it would always be higher than the debt-to-assets ratio. Answer (D) is incorrect because the two ratios are related in that they always move in the same direction.

Questions 48 through 53 are based on the following information about Devlin Company.

Statement of Financial Position as of May 31 (in thousands)

	2001	2000
Assets		
Current assets		
Cash	$ 45	$ 38
Trading securities	30	20
Accounts receivable (net)	68	48
Inventory	90	80
Prepaid expenses	22	30
Total current assets	255	216
Investments, at equity	38	30
Property, plant, and equipment (net)	375	400
Intangible assets (net)	80	45
Total assets	$748	$691
Liabilities and equity		
Current liabilities		
Notes payable	$ 35	$ 18
Accounts payable	70	42
Accrued expenses	5	4
Income taxes payable	15	16
Total current liabilities	125	80
Long-term debt	35	35
Deferred taxes	3	2
Total liabilities	163	117
Equity		
Preferred stock, 6%, $100 par value, cumulative	150	150
Common stock, $10 par value	225	195
Additional paid-in capital - common stock	114	100
Retained earnings	96	129
Total equity	585	574
Total liabilities and equity	$748	$691

Income Statement for the year ended May 31
(in thousands)

	2001	2000
Net sales	$480	$460
Costs and expenses		
Cost of goods sold	330	315
Selling, general, and administrative	52	51
Interest expense	8	9
Income before taxes	90	85
Income taxes	36	34
Net income	$ 54	$ 51

48. Devlin Company's acid-test ratio at May 31, 2001 was

A. 0.60 to 1.

B. 0.90 to 1.

C. 1.14 to 1.

D. 1.86 to 1.

The correct answer is (C). *(CMA, adapted)*

REQUIRED: The acid-test ratio.

DISCUSSION: The acid-test, or quick, ratio equals quick assets (cash, trading securities, and accounts receivable) divided by current liabilities. Quick assets total $143 ($45 + $30 + $68), so the acid-test ratio is 1.14 ($143 ÷ $125 current liabilities).

Answer (A) is incorrect because 0.60 to 1 omits receivables. Answer (B) is incorrect because 0.90 to 1 omits trading securities. Answer (D) is incorrect because 1.86 to 1 includes inventory among quick assets.

49. Assuming there are no preferred stock dividends in arrears, Devlin Company's return on common equity for the year ended May 31, 2001 was

A. 6.3%

B. 7.5%

C. 7.8%

D. 10.5%

The correct answer is (D). *(CMA, adapted)*

REQUIRED: The return on common equity.

DISCUSSION: The return on common equity equals income available to common shareholders divided by average common equity. Net income available to common shareholders is $45 [$54 – (6% x $150 par value of preferred stock)]. Average common equity is $429.5 {[$574 – $150 preferred stock) + ($585 – $150 preferred stock)] ÷ 2}. Thus, the return is 10.5% ($45 ÷ $429.5).

Answer (A) is incorrect because 6.3% is based on average total assets. Answer (B) is incorrect because 7.5% equals net income divided by average total assets. Answer (C) is incorrect because 7.8% equals net income divided by beginning total assets.

50. Devlin Company's inventory turnover for the year ended May 31, 2001 was

A. 3.67 times.

B. 3.88 times.

C. 5.33 times.

D. 5.65 times.

The correct answer is (B). *(CMA, adapted)*

REQUIRED: The inventory turnover.

DISCUSSION: Inventory turnover equals cost of goods sold divided by average inventory. Hence, the inventory turnover is 3.88 times per year {$330 CGS ÷ [($90 + $80) ÷ 2]}.

Answer (A) is incorrect because 3.67 times is based on ending inventory. Answer (C) is incorrect because 5.33 times equals sales divided by ending inventory. Answer (D) is incorrect because 5.65 times is based on sales, not cost of goods sold.

51. Devlin Company's asset turnover for the year ended May 31, 2001 was

A. 0.08 times.

B. 0.46 times.

C. 0.67 times.

D. 0.83 times.

The correct answer is (C). *(CMA, adapted)*

REQUIRED: The asset turnover.

DISCUSSION: Asset turnover equals net sales divided by average total assets. Consequently, the asset turnover is .67 times per year {$480 net sales ÷ [($748 + $691) ÷ 2]}.

Answer (A) is incorrect because 0.08 times is based on net income. Answer (B) is incorrect because 0.46 times uses cost of goods sold in the numerator. Answer (D) is incorrect because 0.83 times is based on average total shareholders' equity.

52. Devlin Company's rate of return on assets for the year ended May 31, 2001 was

A. 7.2%

B. 7.5%

C. 7.8%

D. 11.2%

The correct answer is (B). *(CMA, adapted)*

REQUIRED: The rate of return on assets.

DISCUSSION: The rate of return on assets equals net income divided by average total assets. Accordingly, the rate of return is 7.5% {$54 ÷ [($748 + $691) ÷ 2]}.

Answer (A) is incorrect because 7.2% uses ending total assets instead of average total assets. Answer (C) is incorrect because 7.8% equals net income divided by beginning total assets. Answer (D) is incorrect because 11.2% is the return on sales.

53. Devlin Company's times-interest-earned ratio for the year ended May 31, 2001 was

A. 6.75 times.

B. 11.25 times.

C. 12.25 times.

D. 18.75 times.

The correct answer is (C). *(CMA, adapted)*

REQUIRED: The times-interest-earned ratio.

DISCUSSION: The times-interest-earned ratio equals income available to pay interest (net income + income taxes + interest) divided by interest. The ratio is therefore 12.25 [($54 + $36 + $8) ÷ $8].

Answer (A) is incorrect because 6.75 times uses after-tax income in the numerator. Answer (B) is incorrect because 11.25 times equals income before taxes divided by interest. Answer (D) is incorrect because 18.75 times results from adding selling, general, and administrative expenses to the numerator.

Questions 54 and 55 are based on the following information. Selected data from Ostrander Corporation's financial statements for the years indicated are presented in thousands.

	Year 2 Operations
Net sales	$4,175
Cost of goods sold	2,880
Interest expense	50
Income tax	120
Gain on disposal of a segment (net of tax)	210
Administrative expense	950
Net income	385

	December 31	
	Year 2	Year 1
Cash	$ 32	$ 28
Trading securities	169	172
Accounts receivable (net)	210	204
Merchandise inventory	440	420
Tangible fixed assets	480	440
Total assets	1,397	1,320
Current liabilities	370	368
Total liabilities	790	750
Common stock outstanding	226	210
Retained earnings	381	360

54. The times-interest-earned ratio for Ostrander Corporation for year 2 is

A. .57 times.

B. 7.70 times.

C. 3.50 times.

D. 6.90 times.

The correct answer is (D). *(CMA, adapted)*

REQUIRED: The times-interest-earned ratio for year 2.

DISCUSSION: The interest coverage ratio is computed by dividing net income from operations before taxes and interest by interest expense. Net income of $385, minus the disposal gain of $210, is added to income taxes of $120 and interest expense of $50 to produce a ratio numerator of $345. Dividing $345 by $50 results in an interest coverage of 6.90 times.

Answer (A) is incorrect because .57 is the debt ratio. Answer (B) is incorrect because 7.70 times is based on net income from operations after taxes and interest. Answer (C) is incorrect because 3.50 times results from not adding interest and taxes to net income after the gain on disposal is subtracted.

55. The total debt-to-equity ratio for Ostrander Corporation in year 2 is

A. 3.49

B. 0.77

C. 2.07

D. 1.30

The correct answer is (D). *(CMA, adapted)*

REQUIRED: The total debt-to-equity ratio for year 2.

DISCUSSION: Total equity consists of the $226 of capital stock and $381 of retained earnings, or $607. Debt is given as the $790 of total liabilities. Thus, the ratio is 1.30 ($790 ÷ $607).

Answer (A) is incorrect because 3.49 equals total liabilities divided by common stock outstanding. Answer (B) is incorrect because 0.77 equals equity divided by debt. Answer (C) is incorrect because 2.07 equals total liabilities divided by retained earnings.

56. The relationship of the total debt to the total equity of a corporation is a measure of

A. Liquidity.

B. Profitability.

C. Creditor risk.

D. Solvency.

The correct answer is (C). *(CMA, adapted)*

REQUIRED: The characteristic measured by the relationship of total debt to total equity.

DISCUSSION: The debt-to-equity ratio is a measure of risk to creditors. It indicates how much equity cushion is available to absorb losses before the interests of debt holders would be impaired. The less leveraged the company, the safer the creditors' interests.

Answer (A) is incorrect because liquidity concerns how quickly cash can be made available to pay debts as they come due. Answer (B) is incorrect because the debt-to-equity ratio evaluates a company's capital structure and is thus oriented toward the balance sheet. It does not measure the use (profits) made of assets. Answer (D) is incorrect because solvency implies asset availability to pay debts. Technically, whenever the debt-to-equity ratio can be computed with a meaningful answer, it can be said that the firm is solvent because assets, by definition, have to exceed debts.

B. Limitations of Ratio Analysis

57. Which of the following is not a limitation of ratio analysis affecting comparability among firms?

A. Different accounting policies.

B. Different fiscal years.

C. Different sources of information.

D. All of the above are limitations of ratio analysis.

The correct answer is (D). *(Publisher)*

REQUIRED: The factor that is not a limitation of ratio analysis affecting comparability among firms.

DISCUSSION: Ratio analysis provides useful information regarding the efficiency of operations and the stability of financial condition. Nevertheless, it has several inherent limitations, such as firms using different accounting policies, different fiscal years, and different sources of information. Each of these factors impairs the comparability of financial statement amounts and the ratios derived from them.

Answers (A), (B), and (C) are incorrect because each represents a limitation of ratio analysis.

58. Which of the following is the worst limitation of ratio analysis affecting comparability from one interim period to the next within a firm?

A. Management has an incentive to window dress financial statements to improve results.

B. In a seasonal business, inventory and receivables may vary widely with year-end balances not reflecting the averages for the period.

C. Comparability is impaired if different firms use different accounting policies.

D. Generalizations about which ratios are strong indicators of a firm's financial position may change from industry to industry and firm to firm.

The correct answer is (B). *(Publisher)*

REQUIRED: A limitation of ratio analysis affecting comparability from one interim period to the next within a firm.

DISCUSSION: Ratio analysis may be affected by seasonal factors. For example, inventory and receivables may vary widely, and the year-end balances may not reflect the averages for the period or the balances at the end of various interim periods.

Answer (A) is incorrect because management has less incentive to window dress on interim statements and for internal purposes. Answer (C) is incorrect because comparability limitations resulting from different firms using different accounting policies are a concern when making industry comparisons; it would not be a problem for intrafirm comparisons. Answer (D) is incorrect because intrafirm comparability is not affected by questions about whether alternative industries have different ratios, which are strong indicators of financial health.

C. Comparative Analysis

59. Under GAAP, comparative financial statements are

A. Required for at least the current and the prior year.

B. Required for at least the current and the prior 2 years.

C. Recommended for at least the current and the prior year.

D. Neither required nor recommended.

The correct answer is (C). *(S. Rubin)*

REQUIRED: The position of GAAP concerning comparative financial statements.

DISCUSSION: ARB 43, Ch. 2A, states that in any 1 year it is ordinarily desirable that financial statements of two or more periods be presented. This position is generally understood to be a recommendation rather than a requirement.

Answers (A) and (B) are incorrect because comparative financial statements are not required. Answer (D) is incorrect because comparative financial statements are recommended.

60. In financial statement analysis, expressing all financial statement items as a percentage of base-year amounts is called

A. Horizontal common-size analysis.

B. Vertical common-size analysis.

C. Trend analysis.

D. Ratio analysis.

The correct answer is (A). *(CMA, adapted)*

REQUIRED: The term for expressing all financial statement items as a percentage of base-year amounts.

DISCUSSION: Expressing financial statement items as percentages of corresponding base-year figures is a horizontal form of common-size (percentage) analysis that is useful for evaluating trends. The base amount is assigned the value of 100%, and the amounts for other years are denominated in percentages compared to the base year.

Answer (B) is incorrect because vertical common-size (percentage) analysis presents figures for a single year expressed as percentages of a base amount on the balance sheet (e.g., total assets) and on the income statement (e.g., sales). Answer (C) is incorrect because the term "trend analysis" is most often applied to the quantitative techniques used in forecasting to fit a curve to given data. Answer (D) is incorrect because it is a general term.

61. In assessing the financial prospects for a firm, financial analysts use various techniques. Which of the following is an example of vertical common-size analysis?

A. An assessment of the relative stability of a firm's level of vertical integration.

B. A comparison in financial ratio form between two or more firms in the same industry.

C. A statement that current advertising expense is 2% greater than in the prior year.

D. A statement that current advertising expense is 2% of sales.

The correct answer is (D). *(CMA, adapted)*

REQUIRED: The example of vertical common-size analysis.

DISCUSSION: Vertical common-size analysis compares the components within a set of financial statements. A base amount is assigned a value of 100%. For example, total assets on a common-size balance sheet and net sales on a common-size income statement are valued at 100%. Common-size statements permit evaluation of the efficiency of various aspects of operations. An analyst who states that advertising expense is 2% of sales is using vertical common-size analysis.

Answer (A) is incorrect because vertical integration occurs when a corporation owns one or more of its suppliers or customers. Answer (B) is incorrect because vertical common-size analysis restates financial statement amounts as percentages. Answer (C) is incorrect because a statement that advertising expense is 2% greater than in the previous year results from horizontal analysis.

STUDY UNIT 10: EXTERNAL AUDITING

34 pages of outline
64 multiple-choice questions

Study Unit 10 provides an overview of the attest function performed by independent public accountants (CPAs). It contains the standard audit report, the 10 generally accepted auditing standards (GAAS), outlines of the AICPA *Code of Professional Conduct* and Statements on Auditing Standards (SASs), a section on audit evidence, and material on audit sampling methods. It also includes outlines of pronouncements governing services other than the traditional audit of financial statements. Nevertheless, the financial statement audit remains the most vital function of independent accountants. The relative weight range assigned to Study Unit 10 is 10% to 15% of Part 2.

A. Generally Accepted Auditing Standards (GAAS)

1. The 10 GAAS are categorized as general, field work, and reporting standards.
2. **General Standards**
   a. The audit is to be performed by a person or persons having adequate technical training and proficiency as an auditor.
   b. In all matters relating to the assignment, an independence in mental attitude is to be maintained by the auditor or auditors.
   c. Due professional care is to be exercised in the planning and performance of the audit and the preparation of the report.
3. **Standards of Field Work**
   a. The work is to be adequately planned and assistants, if any, are to be properly supervised.
   b. A sufficient understanding of internal control is to be obtained to plan the audit and to determine the nature, timing, and extent of tests to be performed.
   c. Sufficient competent evidential matter is to be obtained through inspection, observation, inquiries, and confirmations to afford a reasonable basis for an opinion regarding the financial statements under audit.
4. **Standards of Reporting**
   a. The report shall state whether the financial statements are presented in accordance with GAAP.
   b. The report shall identify circumstances in which GAAP have not been consistently observed in the current period in relation to the preceding period.
   c. Informative disclosures in the financial statements are to be regarded as reasonably adequate unless otherwise stated in the report.

d. The report shall contain either an expression of opinion regarding the financial statements, taken as a whole, or an assertion to the effect that an opinion cannot be expressed. When an overall opinion cannot be expressed, the reasons therefor should be stated. In all cases in which an auditor's name is associated with financial statements, the report should contain a clear-cut indication of the character of the auditor's work, if any, and the degree of responsibility the auditor is taking.

5. Stop and review! You have completed the outline for this subunit. Study multiple-choice questions 1 through 3 on page 451.

B. AICPA *Code of Professional Conduct*

1. The *Code of Professional Conduct* was formally adopted on January 12, 1988. It consists of two sections: Principles and Rules. The Principles are goal-oriented and aspirational but nonbinding. The Rules are mandatory. When the Code was adopted, the AICPA membership also voted to make changes regarding peer review, membership requirements, the disciplinary process, and CPE standards.

   a. The following are the Principles:

      Article I - Responsibilities. "In carrying out their responsibilities as professionals, members should exercise sensitive professional and moral judgments in all their activities."

      Article II - The Public Interest. "Members should accept the obligation to act in a way that will serve the public interest, honor the public trust, and demonstrate commitment to professionalism."

      Article III - Integrity. "To maintain and broaden public confidence, members should perform all professional responsibilities with the highest sense of integrity."

      Article IV - Objectivity and Independence. "A member should maintain objectivity and be free of conflicts of interest in discharging professional responsibilities. A member in public practice should be independent in fact and appearance when providing auditing and other attestation services."

      Article V - Due Care. "A member should observe the profession's technical and ethical standards, strive continually to improve competence and the quality of services, and discharge professional responsibility to the best of the member's ability."

      Article VI - Scope and Nature of Services. "A member in public practice should observe the Principles of the Code of Professional Conduct in determining the scope and nature of services to be provided."

   b. The following are the Rules:

      Rule 101 - Independence. "A member in public practice shall be independent in the performance of professional services as required by standards promulgated by bodies designated by Council."

1) Independence is impaired by the following transactions, interests, and relationships. However, this list is not all-inclusive. Independence is impaired if, during the engagement or at the time of expressing an opinion, a member or his/her firm had a direct financial interest or a material indirect financial interest in the client; was a trustee of any trust or executor of any estate that had a direct or material indirect financial interest in the client; had any joint, closely held business investment with the client or any officer, director, or principal shareholder that was material in relation to the member's net worth or the member's firm's net worth; or had a loan to or from a client or any officer, director, or principal shareholder except as permitted in other interpretations.

Rule 102 - Integrity and Objectivity. "In the performance of any professional service, a member shall maintain objectivity and integrity, shall be free of conflicts of interest, and shall not knowingly misrepresent facts or subordinate his or her judgment to others."

Rule 201 - General Standards. "A member shall comply with the following standards and with any interpretation thereof by bodies designated by Council:

"**Professional Competence**. Undertake only those professional services that the member or the member's firm can reasonably expect to be completed with professional competence.

"**Due Professional Care**. Exercise due professional care in the performance of professional services.

"**Planning and Supervision**. Adequately plan and supervise the performance of professional services.

"**Sufficient Relevant Data**. Obtain sufficient relevant data to afford a reasonable basis for conclusions or recommendations in relation to any professional services performed."

Rule 202 - Compliance with Standards. "A member who performs auditing, review, compilation, management advisory, tax, or other professional services shall comply with standards promulgated by Council."

Rule 203 - Accounting Principles. "A member shall not (1) express an opinion or state affirmatively that the financial statements or other financial data of any entity are presented in conformity with generally accepted accounting principles or (2) state that he or she is not aware of any material modifications that should be made to such statements or data in order for them to be in conformity with generally accepted accounting principles, if such statements or data contain any departure from an accounting principle promulgated by bodies designated by Council to establish such principles that has a material effect on the statements or data taken as a whole. If, however, the statements or data contain such a departure and the member can demonstrate that, due to unusual circumstances, the financial statements or data would otherwise have been misleading, the member can comply with the rule by describing the departure, its approximate effects, if practicable, and the reasons why compliance with the principle would result in a misleading statement."

Rule 301 - Confidential Client Information. "A member in public practice shall not disclose any confidential client information without the specific consent of the client. This rule shall not be construed (1) to relieve a member of his or her professional obligations under rules 202 and 203, (2) to affect in any way the member's obligation to comply with a validly issued and enforceable subpoena or summons, or to prohibit a member's compliance with applicable laws and government regulations, (3) to prohibit review of a member's professional practice under AICPA or state CPA society or Board of Accountancy authorization, or (4) to preclude a member from initiating a complaint with, or responding to any inquiry made by, the ethics division or trial board of the Institute or a duly constituted investigative or disciplinary body of a state CPA society or Board of Accountancy.

"Members of any of the bodies identified in (4) above and members involved with professional practice reviews identified in (3) above shall not use to their own advantage or disclose any member's confidential client information that comes to their attention in carrying out those activities. This prohibition shall not restrict members' exchange of information in connection with the investigative or disciplinary proceedings described in (4) above or the professional practice reviews described in (3) above."

Rule 302 - Contingent Fees. "A member in public practice shall not:

"(1) Perform for a contingent fee any professional services for, or receive such a fee from, a client for whom the member or the member's firm performs:

(a) an audit or review of a financial statement; or,

(b) a compilation of a financial statement when the member expects, or reasonably might expect, that a third party will use the financial statement and the member's compilation report does not disclose a lack of independence; or,

(c) an examination of prospective financial information; or,

"(2) Prepare an original or amended tax return or claim for a tax refund for a contingent fee for any client.

"The prohibition in (1) applies during the period in which the member or the member's firm is engaged to perform any of the services listed and the period covered by any historical financial statements involved in any such listed services.

"Except as stated in the next sentence, a contingent fee is a fee established for the performance of any service pursuant to an arrangement in which no fee will be charged unless a specified finding or result is attained, or in which the amount of the fee is otherwise dependent upon the finding or result of such service. Solely for purposes of this rule, fees are not regarded as being contingent if fixed by courts or other public authorities, or, in tax matters, if determined based on the results of judicial proceedings or the findings of governmental agencies.

"A member's fees may vary depending, for example, on the complexity of services rendered."

Rule 501 - Acts Discreditable. "A member shall not commit an act discreditable to the profession."

Rule 502 - Advertising and Other Forms of Solicitation. "A member in public practice shall not seek to obtain clients by advertising or other forms of solicitation in a manner that is false, misleading, or deceptive. Solicitation by the use of coercion, overreaching, or harassing conduct is prohibited."

Rule 503 - Commissions and Referral Fees
"A. Prohibited commissions
A member in public practice shall not for a commission recommend or refer to a client any product or service, or for a commission recommend or refer any product or service to be supplied by a client, or receive a commission, when the member or the member's firm also performs for that client:
(a) an audit or review of a financial statement; or
(b) a compilation of a financial statement when the member expects, or reasonably might expect, that a third party will use the financial statement and the member's compilation report does not disclose a lack of independence; or
(c) an examination of prospective financial information.
This prohibition applies during the period in which the member is engaged to perform any of the services listed above and the period covered by any historical financial statements involved in such listed services.
"B. Disclosure of permitted commissions
A member in public practice who is not prohibited by this rule from performing services for or receiving a commission and who is paid or expects to be paid a commission shall disclose that fact to any person or entity to whom the member recommends or refers a product or service to which the commission relates.
"C. Referral fees
Any member who accepts a referral fee for recommending or referring any service of a CPA to any person or entity or who pays a referral fee to obtain a client shall disclose such acceptance or payment to the client."

Rule 505 - Form of Organization and Name. "A member may practice public accounting only in a form of organization permitted by law or regulation whose characteristics conform to resolutions of Council.

"A member shall not practice public accounting under a firm name that is misleading. Names of one or more past owners may be included in the firm name of a successor organization.

"A firm may not designate itself as 'Members of the American Institute of Certified Public Accountants' unless all of its CPA owners are members of the Institute."

NOTE: According to the pertinent resolution of the AICPA Council, a majority of the firm's ownership in terms of financial interests and voting rights must belong to CPAs, and each non-CPA owner must be actively engaged in providing services to clients as his/her principal occupation. A CPA must have ultimate responsibility for all the services provided by the firm and by each business unit performing audits and other engagements under SASs, reviews, examinations of prospective financial information, and compilation services. Moreover, non-CPA owners must abide by the Code and complete CPE and educational requirements.

2. Stop and review! You have completed the outline for this subunit. Study multiple-choice questions 4 through 6 on page 452.

C. AICPA Statements on Auditing Standards

1. The Auditing Standards Board of the AICPA issues Statements interpreting the 10 GAAS. These Statements are considered to have the status of GAAS. Accordingly, they must be followed by independent auditors. They are issued as separate pronouncements in sequence but are also codified and organized into sections.
2. The following summaries of the SASs are listed by their codified numbers for ease of reference to the AICPA Professional Standards. Although the summaries do not need to be memorized, the basic concept set forth in each pronouncement should be noted; it may be a topic on the CMA exam.

AU SECTIONS Relevant to the CMA Exam

110 - Responsibilities and Functions of the Independent Auditor

The object of independent audits is to express an opinion on whether the financial statements, in all material respects, are presented fairly in conformity with GAAP. Thus, the auditors must plan and perform the audit to obtain reasonable assurance about whether the financial statements are free of material misstatement, whether caused by error or fraud. Both the financial statements and the internal controls are the responsibility of management. Auditors must comply with professional standards and have adequate education and experience.

150 - Generally Accepted Auditing Standards (GAAS)

Standards concern the quality of performance of audit procedures and the objectives to be attained by the use of those procedures (see page 417).

161 - The Relationship of Generally Accepted Auditing Standards to Quality Control Standards

Under Conduct Rule 202, individual auditors are responsible for complying with GAAS. Firms of auditors should also establish quality control policies and procedures. The type and extent of these procedures are dependent upon the firm's size, organizational structure, nature of the practice, cost-benefit considerations, and the separation between personnel and practice departments. Whereas GAAS relate to individual audits, quality control standards relate to overall audit practice, but quality control should affect both individual audits and overall practice.

201 - Nature of the General Standards

The general standards refer to the qualifications of the auditor and the quality of his/her work.

210 - Training and Proficiency of the Independent Auditor

Both education and experience, as well as proper supervision, are necessary. An auditor must have experience and seasoned judgment to accept final responsibility for an audit opinion. Objectivity and independent judgment are necessary in the preparation of the audit opinion.

220 - Independence

An auditor must always have an independent state of mind. (S)he must also be independent in appearance. Many companies encourage independence by having the auditors appointed by the board of directors or elected by shareholders.

230 - Due Professional Care in the Performance of Work

Due professional care relates to the auditor's activities and how well (s)he performs them. An auditor should have the degree of skill commonly possessed by other auditors and must exercise it with reasonable care and diligence. An auditor should also exercise professional skepticism. The exercise of due professional care allows the auditor to obtain reasonable, not absolute, assurance.

310 - Relationship between the Auditor's Appointment and Planning

It is more efficient and effective to appoint the auditor as early as possible. If appointment comes near or after the close of the period being audited, the auditor must determine whether an adequate audit can be made or whether a qualified opinion or a disclaimer is necessary. Early appointment allows a significant portion of the audit to be carried out before year-end. The auditor should establish an understanding with the client regarding the services to be performed. An understanding ordinarily includes, for example, 1) the objective of the audit, 2) management's responsibility for the financial statements and internal control, 3) management's responsibility for ensuring that the entity complies with laws and regulations, 4) management's responsibility for providing all financial records and information to the auditor, 5) management's responsibility for correcting material misstatements, and 6) management's willingness to provide a representation letter at the conclusion of the audit. These and other matters may be communicated in an engagement letter.

311 - Planning and Supervision

Planning and supervision relate to the first standard of field work with respect to preparing audit programs, obtaining knowledge of the client's business, and dealing with differences of opinion among firm personnel. Audit planning requires developing an overall strategy for the audit. The nature, extent, and timing of planning varies with the size of the entity and other factors. A written audit program aids and instructs assistants in work to be done, and details necessary audit procedures. The audit program should be based on the auditor's knowledge of the client's business, including the methods used for computer processing of significant accounting information. The auditor may need to consider whether specialized skills are needed, e.g., to consider the effects of computer processing. Supervision, the directing and evaluating of subordinates, relates to all aspects of an audit. Assistants should know what is expected of them and procedures to follow concerning disagreements on accounting and auditing issues. Procedures should be adequate for the documentation and resolution of such disagreements.

312 - Audit Risk and Materiality in Conducting an Audit

Audit risk and materiality relate to the nature, timing, and extent of audit procedures and their evaluation. **Audit risk** is the risk that the auditor may unknowingly fail to modify the opinion on materially misstated financial statements. It includes inherent risk, control risk, and detection risk. **Inherent risk** is the susceptibility of an assertion to material misstatement assuming that there are no related controls. **Control risk** is the risk that a material misstatement could occur that will not be prevented or detected on a timely basis by the entity's internal control. **Detection risk** is the risk that the auditor will not detect a material misstatement that exists in an assertion. Financial statements are materially misstated if they contain misstatements that, singly or in the aggregate, are important enough to cause them not to be fairly presented, in all material respects, in conformity with GAAP. Misstatements may arise from errors or fraud. Materiality is based on the auditor's professional judgment as to the needs of a reasonable person who will rely on the financial statements. The FASB defines **materiality** as the "magnitude of an omission or misstatement of accounting information that, in the light of surrounding circumstances, makes it probable that the judgment of a reasonable person relying on the information would have been changed or influenced by the omission or misstatement." Auditors must consider audit risk and materiality during the entire audit. The audit should be planned to limit risk to a level low enough to permit expression of an opinion. Audit planning should consider the auditor's preliminary judgment about materiality levels. The auditor must balance the inherent risk and control risk believed to exist and the acceptable detection risk. The auditor should consider this balance when evaluating the fairness of the financial statements in view of the aggregation of likely misstatements.

313 - Substantive Tests prior to the Balance Sheet Date

Application of substantive tests at interim dates, i.e., prior to year-end, increases the risk that undetected misstatements may exist at year-end. Accordingly, auditors should apply some substantive tests to the remaining period (from the date substantive tests were performed to year-end). But, if control risk is assessed at the maximum, the auditor must consider whether the effectiveness of the tests covering the remaining period will be impaired. Also, all auditing procedures must be coordinated, e.g., those applied to related party transactions. In other words, the tests applied during the remaining period and at year-end need to be based on the interim work.

315 - Communications between Predecessor and Successor Auditors

A successor auditor is required to communicate with the predecessor auditor before accepting an auditing engagement. The successor should request permission from the client to make an inquiry of the predecessor before final acceptance of the engagement. Thus, the successor should ask the client to authorize the predecessor to respond fully to inquiries. The successor auditor should inquire about reasons for the change in auditors; disagreements with management about accounting principles and auditing procedures; facts bearing on management's integrity; and communications to audit committees or others regarding fraud, illegal acts by clients, and internal-control-related matters. The predecessor should respond promptly and fully, but, if circumstances require a limited response, the limited nature of that response must be clearly indicated. The successor should also request the client to permit review of the predecessor's working papers. The predecessor auditor ordinarily permits the successor to review working papers. The successor auditor's communications with the predecessor auditor may have a bearing on the audit of opening balances and the evaluation of the consistency of application of accounting principles. An auditor who is considering accepting an engagement for a reaudit is a successor auditor, and the previous auditor is a predecessor auditor.

316 - Consideration of Fraud in a Financial Statement Audit

The auditor must plan and perform the audit to obtain reasonable assurance about whether the financial statements are free of material misstatement, whether caused by error or fraud. The auditor must also specifically assess the risk of material misstatement due to fraud. Fraud involves misstatements arising from fraudulent financial reporting and misappropriation of assets. The auditor should consider fraud risk factors related to specified categories for each of the types of misstatement. Communications about fraud may need to be made not only to management and the audit committee but also to parties outside the entity.

317 - Illegal Acts by Clients

The auditor is required to design the audit to provide reasonable assurance of detecting illegal acts that have a direct and material effect on the financial statements. This responsibility is the same as that for material errors and fraud. The auditor's responsibility for illegal acts having material but indirect financial statement effects is to be aware that they may have occurred. However, the auditor is not obligated to apply specific procedures to detect them unless information comes to his/her attention indicating their existence.

319 - Consideration of Internal Control in a Financial Statement Audit

In all audits, the auditor should obtain a sufficient understanding of internal control to plan the audit and to determine the nature, timing, and extent of tests to be performed. Internal control is a process--effected by an entity's board of directors, management, and other personnel--designed to provide reasonable assurance regarding the achievement of objectives related to reliability of financial reporting, effectiveness and efficiency of operations, and compliance with applicable laws and regulations. Internal control consists of five interrelated components (a useful mnemonic is "Controls stop **CRIME**" with the E representing Environment). **Control activities** are the policies and procedures that help ensure that management directives are carried out. **Risk assessment** is the entity's identification, analysis, and management of relevant risks. **Information and communication** include the identification, capture, and exchange of information in a form and time frame that enable people to carry out their responsibilities. **Monitoring** is a process that assesses the quality of internal control performance over time. **Control environment** sets the tone of an organization, influencing the control consciousness of its people. It is the foundation for all other components.

Due to inherent limitations, internal control can provide only **reasonable assurance** that control objectives are met. Thus, human judgment is faulty, and controls may fail because of simple error or mistake. Controls can be circumvented by collusion, or management may override internal control. Another limitation is that the costs should not exceed the benefits of control, but their precise measurement is not feasible. Audits in accordance with generally accepted auditing standards (GAAS) require the auditor to obtain an understanding of the five components of internal control and to assess control risk. Controls most likely to be relevant to an audit pertain to the entity's objective of preparing financial statements for external purposes that are fairly presented in conformity with GAAP or another comprehensive basis of accounting. Certain controls ordinarily are not relevant and need not be considered, for example, controls concerning the effectiveness and efficiency of certain management decisionmaking processes, such as product pricing or some expenditures for R&D or advertising. **Assessing control risk at below the maximum** requires identifying specific controls relevant to specific assertions that are likely to prevent or detect misstatements and testing of controls to evaluate effectiveness. **Tests of controls** are directed toward the effectiveness of the design or operation of internal controls. The lower the assessed level of control risk (the more closely it approaches zero), the more assurance audit evidence must provide that controls relevant to an assertion are effective. The ultimate purpose of assessing control risk (and inherent risk) is to contribute to the evaluation of the overall risk that the financial statements contain material misstatements. The assessed levels of control risk and inherent risk determine the acceptable level of detection risk for financial statement assertions. The acceptable level of detection risk determines the nature, timing, and extent of substantive tests. **Documentation of the assessed level of control risk** is required. When control risk for an assertion is assessed at the maximum, the auditor should document the conclusion but need not document its basis.

322 - The Auditor's Consideration of the Internal Audit Function in an Audit of Financial Statements

External auditors should obtain an understanding of the internal audit function as part of the understanding of internal control and may consider its existence in determining the nature, timing, and extent of audit work. If some of those activities are relevant, the auditor should determine whether it is efficient to consider further how the internal audit function may affect the audit work. If it is efficient, the auditor should assess the competence and objectivity of the internal audit function. (S)he must also evaluate and test the internal auditors' work that significantly affects the auditor's procedures. Even if the internal auditors' work is expected to affect the audit procedures, the reporting responsibility continues to rest solely with the external auditor. Moreover, the external auditor must make judgments about whether and to what extent (s)he must directly test financial statement assertions after considering the work of the internal auditors. Issues of materiality, inherent and control risk, and the subjectivity involved in the evaluation of audit evidence must be weighed. Even if the internal audit function is deemed not to be relevant to the audit, the external auditor must assess the competence and objectivity of the internal auditors and evaluate and supervise their work if their direct assistance is sought.

324 - Reports on the Processing of Transactions by Service Organizations

This section concerns audits of service organizations and of clients of service organizations. It applies to a financial statement audit of an entity that uses another organization's services as part of its own information system. Such services affect the initiation of transactions; accounting records, supporting information, and accounts; accounting processing; and the financial reporting process.

325 - Communication of Internal Control Related Matters Noted in an Audit

An auditor must communicate all reportable conditions related to any of the internal control components. The report states the purpose of an audit, defines reportable conditions (and possibly material weaknesses), describes deficiencies found, and includes a restriction on use. No report is issued if no reportable conditions were identified in the audit.

326 - Evidential Matter

Most audit work entails obtaining and evaluating evidence about financial statement assertions. Auditors develop audit objectives and design substantive tests based on these assertions. Objectives do not vary depending on whether processing is manual or electronic, but audit procedures are influenced by the type of processing. In many cases, auditors must use information technology to access certain information, and the nature of electronic processing may require tests of controls. The evidence supporting the financial statements consists of the underlying accounting data and corroborating information. It is increasingly found in the form of electronic messages, for example, as a result of the use of EDI. Evidence, whether written or electronic, must be competent and sufficient. However, the auditor most often relies on persuasive rather than convincing evidence.

329 - Analytical Procedures

This standard is intended to improve the effectiveness of audits by requiring that analytical procedures be applied in the planning and overall review phases of an audit. Use of analytical procedures as substantive tests of particular financial statement assertions is discretionary. Analytical procedures consist of evaluations of financial information made by a study of plausible relationships among both financial and nonfinancial data. The procedures identify such things as the existence of unusual transactions and events and amounts, ratios, and trends that might indicate matters that have financial statement and audit planning ramifications.

330 - The Confirmation Process

Confirmation is "the process of obtaining and evaluating a direct communication from a third party in response to a request for information about a particular item affecting financial statement assertions." This pronouncement defines confirmation, relates confirmation procedures to the assessment of audit risk, discusses the design of the confirmation request and the performance of procedures, describes alternative procedures, states the factors used in evaluating the evidence obtained, and provides specific guidance with respect to confirmation of accounts receivable.

331 - Inventories

Observation of physical inventories is a generally accepted auditing procedure. Auditors must make test counts when observing physical inventories. Inventories in public warehouses may be verified by direct confirmation. In addition, if the inventories are material, the auditors must evaluate the warehouse's internal controls (or obtain a report thereon from an independent accountant).

332 - Auditing Derivative Instruments, Hedging Activities, and Investments in Securities

The guidance provided concerns planning and performing audit procedures to test assertions about derivatives and hedging activities accounted for under SFAS 133. The guidance also applies to all debt and equity securities, as defined by SFAS 115, but it extends to assertions about securities not accounted for under SFAS 115, e.g., equity-based investments. An auditor may require **special skill or knowledge** regarding some assertions, for example, an understanding of GAAP for derivatives or of the measurement and disclosure issues for derivatives with complex features. The **assessment of inherent risk** for derivatives and securities depends on such factors as their complexity, management's objectives, whether the pertinent transactions involved a cash exchange, the extent of the entity's experience with derivatives and securities, whether a derivative is embedded in a host contract, external matters (credit risk, market risk, hedging ineffectiveness, legal risk, etc.), the further evolution of derivatives and relevant GAAP, the entity's reliance on the expertise of outsiders, and assumptions required by GAAP. The **assessment of control risk** requires considering whether controls, including those of service organizations, have been implemented that provide for independent monitoring of derivatives activities, independent approval when derivatives personnel wish to exceed limits, senior management's attention to situations in which limits are exceeded and divergences from approved strategies, reconciliations over the full range of derivatives, and high-level review of the identified controls and the results of derivatives activities. The **design of substantive procedures based on the risk assessments** addresses types of assertions about derivatives and securities (existence or occurrence, completeness, rights and obligations, valuation, and presentation and disclosure). Examples are confirmations with issuers, holders, or counterparties; confirmation of settled and unsettled transactions; physical inspection of contracts and other documentation; analytical procedures; inquiries of frequently used counterparties or holders; confirmation of significant terms with a counterparty or holder; tests of valuation based on the method required by GAAP for the measurement or disclosure, such as cost, the investee's financial results, or fair value; and evaluation of whether presentation and disclosure requirements have been met, such as classification of securities and reporting of changes in fair value in either earnings or other comprehensive income. The auditor should perform procedures to determine whether **hedging activities**, including the designation and documentation requirements, have been carried out in accordance with GAAP and therefore qualify for hedge accounting. The auditor must also gather evidence about **management's intent and ability**, for example, to hold debt securities to maturity, to exercise significant influence over an equity-based investee, to enter into a forecasted transaction, or to dispose of securities classified as trading in the near term. Furthermore, the auditor must obtain written **management representations** confirming various aspects of derivatives and securities transactions.

333 - Management Representations

Auditors are required to obtain written representations from management. These representations vary with the circumstances but ordinarily include such items as availability and completeness of all financial data, management's acceptance of responsibility for compliance with GAAP, management's belief that the effects of uncorrected misstatements aggregated by the auditor are immaterial, related party transactions, subsequent events, absence of unrecorded transactions, fraud, gain and loss contingencies, significant estimates and material concentrations related to certain risks and uncertainties, unasserted claims or assessments, title to assets, encumbrances, assets pledged as collateral, violations of laws or regulations, and plans affecting carrying values of assets and liabilities. If management refuses to provide written representations, an unqualified audit opinion cannot be expressed because of the scope limitation.

334 - Related Parties

SFAS 57, *Related Party Disclosures*, requires material related party transactions to be disclosed in the financial statements. Also, these transactions should be accounted for to reflect their substance. Auditors must therefore undertake procedures, e.g., inquiries of management, to determine the existence of related parties and to identify and examine related party transactions.

336 - Using the Work of a Specialist

Specialists under this section include appraisers; engineers; actuaries; attorneys not engaged to provide services related to litigation, claims, or assessments; geologists; etc. The auditor may decide to use a specialist for various reasons, for example, to establish valuation, determine physical characteristics, determine amounts derived through special techniques, and interpret technical requirements, regulations, or agreements. The auditor must consider the specialist's qualifications, obtain an understanding of his/her work, and evaluate any relationship the specialist may have with the client. When using the work of the specialist, the auditor must understand the methods and assumptions used, test the data given to the specialist (in the light of the assessed control risk), and evaluate whether the findings of the specialist support the related assertions in the financial statements. An auditor ordinarily should not refer to the work or findings of a specialist. However, "The auditor may, as a result of the report or findings of the specialist, decide to add explanatory language to his/her standard report or depart from an unqualified opinion." The specialist may be identified "if the auditor believes the reference will facilitate an understanding of the reason for the explanatory paragraph or the departure from the unqualified opinion."

337 - Inquiry of a Client's Lawyer Concerning Litigation, Claims, and Assessments

Auditors should question management about the existence of contingent liabilities. The client should send a letter to its attorneys describing all of the contingent liabilities (litigation, claims, and assessments), including unasserted claims. The letter should request that the attorney confirm the correctness of the client's understanding regarding these claims (reflected in the letter of audit inquiry). The letter should also ask for confirmation that the attorney will advise the client when unasserted claims require disclosure.

339 - Working Papers

Working papers assist auditors in performing audit procedures, supporting the audit opinion, and documenting compliance with GAAS. They include analyses, confirmations, client document abstracts, memoranda, representations, and audit programs. They are the records of the conclusions reached based upon procedures and tests. The structure and content of working papers are dependent upon the type of audit report presented; the nature of the financial statements, schedules, and other information reported on; the nature and condition of the client's records; the assessed level of control risk; and review and supervision requirements. Working papers also may be in the form of tapes, films, or other media. Working papers are the property of the auditor, and disclosure of the contents is limited by the client confidentiality rule.

341 - The Auditor's Consideration of an Entity's Ability to Continue as a Going Concern

The auditor is required to evaluate whether "there is a substantial doubt about the entity's ability to continue as a going concern for a reasonable period of time." Whereas the auditor need not apply auditing procedures specifically designed for this purpose, (s)he may have to obtain additional evidence as well as information about management's plans to mitigate the effects of the conditions or events indicative of the substantial doubt. A substantial doubt requires an explanatory paragraph following the opinion paragraph. The terms "substantial doubt" and "going concern" must be included in the explanatory paragraph.

342 - Auditing Accounting Estimates

Accounting estimates are specifically addressed in the scope paragraph of the standard audit report (see subunit G).

350 - Audit Sampling

See subunit E. for an outline.

380 - Communication with Audit Committees

This standard is intended to improve internal reporting by requiring that certain audit matters be communicated to those who oversee the entity's financial reporting process. It applies if the entity has an audit committee or its equivalent or if the audit constitutes an SEC engagement. Among the matters to be communicated are (1) the auditor's responsibility under GAAS; (2) selection of, changes in, or application of significant accounting policies; (3) management's judgments about sensitive accounting estimates; (4) audit adjustments, including those that management determined to be immaterial either individually or in the aggregate; (5) other information in documents containing audited financial statements; (6) disagreements with management; (7) management's consultations with other accountants; (8) major issues discussed with management prior to accepting the engagement; and (9) difficulties in performing the audit. In an SEC engagement, the auditor should discuss with the audit committee his/her judgments about the quality of the accounting principles applied in the auditee's financial reports.

390 - Consideration of Omitted Procedures after the Report Date

Once (s)he has reported, an auditor has no responsibility to carry out any retrospective review. However, reports and working papers relating to particular engagements may be subjected to post-issuance review for various reasons, and the omission of a necessary procedure may be disclosed. When the auditor concludes that a necessary procedure was omitted, (s)he should assess its importance. If the auditor concludes that the omission of a necessary procedure impairs his/her current ability to support the previously expressed opinion, and (s)he believes there are persons currently relying, or likely to rely, on the report, (s)he should promptly undertake to apply the omitted procedure(s) that would provide a satisfactory basis for the opinion. If (s)he cannot apply the omitted procedure, (s)he should seek advice about his/her legal responsibilities.

410 - Adherence to GAAP

Auditors must express an opinion as to whether the client's statements adhere to GAAP.

411 - The Meaning of "Present Fairly in Conformity with GAAP" in the Independent Auditor's Report

GAAP are the "conventions, rules, and procedures necessary to define accepted accounting practice at a particular time." The nongovernmental GAAP hierarchy is given in SU 1, E. The GAAP hierarchy for state and local governments has five tiers. The first tier [category (a)] consists of sources of officially established accounting principles (GASB Statements and Interpretations, and, if specifically made applicable to state and local governments by GASB Statements or Interpretations, AICPA and FASB pronouncements). The next three tiers contain other sources of established accounting principles. The fifth tier includes other accounting literature. The federal hierarchy has a similar structure, but the Federal Accounting Standards Advisory Board (FASAB) is the source of category (a) guidance.

420 - Consistency of Application of GAAP

If comparability among periods has been materially affected by changes in accounting principles, the auditor should appropriately modify the report. Consistency is not mentioned in the report, however, if no change with a material effect has occurred. Accounting changes that affect consistency and require recognition in audit reports include changes in principle, changes in the reporting entity not resulting from a transaction or event, correction of an error in principle, and changes in principle that are inseparable from a change in estimate. Modification of the report for an inconsistency is not necessary when a pooling of interests is not accounted for by restating prior period financial statements presented comparatively, but a qualified or adverse opinion would be expressed for the departure from GAAP. A change in the policy for determining the items treated as cash equivalents in a statement of cash flows is a change in principle requiring retroactive restatement. The audit report should recognize this change in an explanatory paragraph. Changes that do not affect consistency and do not require modification of the audit report include changes in estimate, error corrections not involving accounting principles, changes in classification, substantially different transactions or events, changes having a material future but not current effect, and changes in the reporting entity resulting from a transaction or event.

431 - Adequacy of Disclosure in Financial Statements

Fairness contemplates adequate disclosure relating to form, content, arrangement of statements, terminology, classifications, and detail. If disclosure is not adequate, the auditor must express a qualified or adverse opinion.

504 - Association with Financial Statements

This section is intended to prevent misinterpretation of the accountant's responsibility when his/her name is associated with financial statements. Accountants should not allow their names to be associated with unaudited financial statements unless the statements are clearly marked "unaudited" and an indication is provided that the accountants do not express an opinion. Negative assurance should never be given if a disclaimer of opinion is expressed. A disclaimer of opinion is appropriate when an accountant is not independent.

508 - Reports on Audited Financial Statements

This standard describes the auditor's report and the conditions for modification. The introductory paragraph refers to an audit and explicitly states management's and the auditor's responsibilities regarding the identified statements. The scope paragraph includes a description of an audit. This paragraph states that the conduct of the audit is intended to provide reasonable assurance about the existence of material misstatements. It also clarifies that the auditor examines evidence on a test basis, assesses accounting principles and estimates, and evaluates statement presentation. The opinion paragraph states whether the financial statements are presented fairly, in all material respects, in conformity with GAAP. The country of origin of GAAS and GAAP also is identified. The auditor may express an unqualified, qualified, or adverse opinion; disclaim an opinion; or add explanatory language to the report while expressing an unqualified opinion. For example, a lack of consistency having material effects and a substantial doubt about an entity's ability to continue as a going concern require explanatory language, but an uncertainty, by itself, does not.

530 - Dating of the Independent Auditor's Report

Audit reports should be dated as of the last day of field work. If events or transactions that occur after completion of the field work are reflected in the financial statements, the report should be dual-dated, i.e., dated as of the last day of field work except for the additional disclosure, which is dated as of its discovery. If audit reports are reissued, they should use the last day of field work.

532 - Restricting the Use of an Auditor's Report

An auditor's "general-use report" is one that is not restricted as to specified parties. An example is an audit report on financial statements prepared in accordance with GAAP or another comprehensive basis of accounting. An auditor's "restricted-use report" is intended for specified parties. Examples are reports on subject matter or presentations based on measurement or disclosure criteria in contracts or regulatory provisions, reports based on procedures performed to meet the needs of specified parties who accept responsibility for their sufficiency, and reports that are by-products of a financial statement audit. A restricted-use report should indicate that the report is intended solely for the information and use of specified parties, identify those parties, and state that the report is not intended to be used and should not be used by anyone other than the specified parties.

534 - Reporting on Financial Statements Prepared for Use in Other Countries

A U.S. auditor may be engaged to report on the financial statements of a U.S. entity that have been prepared in conformity with accounting principles accepted in another country for use outside the U.S. The auditor should understand, and obtain written representations about, the purpose and uses of such financial statements. If the auditor uses the standard report of another country, and the financial statements will have general distribution in that country, (s)he should consider whether any additional legal responsibilities are involved. The auditor should perform the procedures that are necessary to comply with the general and field work standards of U.S. GAAS, although they may need to be modified because the assertions in the statements differ from those prepared according to GAAP. The auditor should understand the accounting principles generally accepted in the other country. The auditor may also be requested to apply the auditing standards of the other country and should thus comply with that nation's general and field work standards. A modified U.S.-style report or the report form of the other country may be used. The auditor may report on two sets of statements for the entity: one based on GAAP and the other on principles generally accepted in the other country. The other country's reporting standards must be complied with.

543 - Part of Audit Performed by Other Independent Auditors

The principal auditor makes a basic decision whether to accept responsibility for the other auditor. If responsibility is accepted, there is no mention of the other auditor in the audit report. To divide responsibility, the audit report indicates the magnitude of the portion of the financial statements audited by the other auditor as a percentage of total assets, income, or other criterion. Reference to the work of another auditor does not affect the nature of the opinion expressed by the principal auditor.

544 - Lack of Conformity with GAAP

If financial statements of regulated companies depart from GAAP, a qualified or adverse opinion will ordinarily be expressed. However, an additional paragraph should express an opinion as to conformity with the basis of accounting prescribed by the regulator.

550 - Other Information in Documents Containing Audited Financial Statements

The auditor should read the other financial information in the annual reports to determine that there is no inconsistency between the other material and the financial statements. Any material misstatements, inconsistencies, etc., require modification by the client, modification of the audit report (an additional paragraph), or withdrawal.

551 - Reporting on Information Accompanying the Basic Financial Statements in Auditor-Submitted Documents

Auditors should report on all information included in the documents submitted to clients that include audited financial statements. This accompanying information typically includes schedules that support the financial statement accounts. The auditor's report should identify this information and state that it is not part of the basic financial statements. The audit opinion should be modified to cover the accompanying information. If the auditor disclaims an opinion on the accompanying information, it should be clearly marked "unaudited."

552 - Reporting on Condensed Financial Statements and Selected Financial Data

This pronouncement concerns reporting in a client-prepared document on condensed statements derived from audited statements of a public entity required to file complete audited statements with a regulatory agency. It also concerns reporting on selected financial data derived from audited statements of any entity presented either in a client-prepared document that includes audited statements or, with respect to a public entity, in a client-prepared document that incorporates audited statements by reference to regulatory agency filings. The auditor's report on condensed statements or selected data should indicate that the auditor has audited and expressed an opinion on the complete statements, state the type of opinion expressed, and provide an opinion as to whether the information set forth is fairly stated in all material respects in relation to the complete statements from which it was derived. In the case of condensed statements, the report should also indicate the date of the report on the complete statements. If the selected data include other information not derived from the complete statements, the auditor should specifically identify the data on which (s)he is reporting.

558 - Required Supplementary Information

Auditors report (i.e., add an additional paragraph to the standard report) on the supplementary disclosures required by the FASB or GASB only when they are omitted, they contain material misstatements, the auditor is unable to complete the prescribed procedures, the auditor is unable to remove substantial doubts about whether the information conforms to prescribed guidelines, or the supplementary data are not clearly marked "unaudited."

560 - Subsequent Events

Some subsequent events require reflection in the financial statements and some require disclosure only. Events that merely confirm situations existing at the balance sheet date should be reflected in the financial statements; e.g., the receivables of a bankrupt debtor should be written off on the statements even though the debtor went bankrupt after the year-end. Other events should be merely disclosed, e.g., the bankruptcy of a debtor arising from a fire that occurred after year-end.

561 - Subsequent Discovery of Facts Existing at the Date of the Auditor's Report

Subsequent to the date of the report, an auditor may become aware of information affecting the financial statements and/or the audit report that existed at the report date. In these circumstances, the report should be reissued. If the client refuses to cooperate, the auditor should notify the client, regulatory agencies, and others relying on the statements.

623 - Special Reports

This pronouncement establishes the auditor's responsibility for reports on financial statements that are prepared in conformity with a comprehensive basis of accounting other than GAAP. It also provides guidance for an engagement to express an opinion on specified elements, accounts, or items of a financial statement. Other topics covered are compliance reports required by contractual agreements and regulatory agencies (AU 801 applies when the auditor tests compliance with laws and regulations in accordance with *Government Auditing Standards*), special-purpose financial presentations required by contractual agreements or regulatory agencies, and financial information presented in prescribed forms or schedules.

625 - Reports on the Application of Accounting Principles

AU 625 applies to an accountant in public practice (reporting accountant), either in connection with a proposal to obtain a new client or, otherwise, in relation to the preparation of a written report on the application of accounting principles to specified transactions, either completed or proposed. It also applies when the accountant is requested to provide a written report on the type of opinion that may be rendered on a specific entity's financial statements. Another application is the preparation of a written report to intermediaries on the application of accounting principles not involving facts or circumstances of a particular principal. AU 625 also governs oral advice on the application of accounting principles to a specific transaction and the type of opinion that may be expressed on financial statements when the reporting accountant concludes the advice is intended to be used by a principal to the transaction as an important decision factor.

634 - Letters for Underwriters and Certain Other Requesting Parties

AU 634 concerns "comfort letters." It states whether independent accountants acting in their professional capacity may comment on specified matters, and, if so, what the form of comment should be. Practical suggestions are offered on such matters as forms of comfort letters suitable to various circumstances, the way in which a particular form of letter may be agreed upon, the dating of letters, and the steps that may be taken when information requiring special mention in a letter comes to the accountants' attention. Also, ways are suggested to reduce or avoid the uncertainties regarding the nature and extent of accountants' responsibilities. AU 634 has been amended to reflect changes pursuant to AT 700, *Management's Discussion and Analysis*.

711 - Filings under Federal Securities Statutes

An accountant has a defense against lawsuits regarding false or misleading statements if (s)he had reasonable grounds, after reasonable investigation, to believe and did believe that statements were true and not misleading at the effective date of the registration statement. The accountant should extend procedures from the date of the report to the effective date of the registration statement. The investigation consists of reading statements, making inquiries, and obtaining a written representation letter from the client about subsequent events. Although the accountant has not expressed an opinion on the unaudited interim information, (s)he still must comment on any noncompliance with GAAP in the report. A predecessor accountant also has subsequent event responsibility and must read the applicable portions of any prospectus and registration statement.

722 - Interim Financial Information

The review of interim financial information provides the accountant, based on application of his/her knowledge of reporting practices to significant accounting matters of which (s)he becomes aware through inquiries and analytical procedures, with a basis for reporting whether material modifications should be made for such information to conform with GAAP (negative assurance). This objective differs significantly from that of an audit, which is to provide a basis for expressing an opinion. This pronouncement provides guidance on the procedures to be applied and on the appropriate reports to be prepared. It also establishes requirements for communication with audit committees. If, prior to the filing of interim financial information with a regulator, the accountant has identified during a review matters to be communicated in accordance with AU 380, (s)he should attempt to discuss these matters with the audit committee (or at least its chair) and financial management prior to the filing.

801 - Compliance Auditing Considerations in Audits of Governmental Entities and Recipients of Governmental Financial Assistance

AU 801 provides general guidance on the auditor's responsibilities under GAAS, *Government Auditing Standards*, and federal requirements for audits of governmental entities or recipients of federal awards. It states the standards for reporting on compliance with laws and regulations and on internal control.

901 - Public Warehouses -- Controls and Auditing Procedures for Goods Held

This pronouncement describes public warehouse operations and related controls. It also describes audit procedures for goods in the warehouse's custody and the audit procedures by the auditor of the owner of the goods.

AT SECTIONS

Statements on Standards for Attestation Engagements (SSAEs). AICPA bodies issue standards for a variety of attest services other than the traditional financial statement audit. The summaries of the standards given below are presented in their codified numerical AT sequence.

100 - Attestation Standards

An attest engagement is one in which a practitioner (a CPA in the practice of public accounting) expresses a conclusion about the reliability of a written assertion that is the responsibility of another party based on an examination, a review, or the application of agreed-upon procedures. AT 100 permits two levels of attest assurance in general distribution reports. Positive assurance should be given in reports that express conclusions on the basis of an **examination**. Negative assurance should be given in reports that express conclusions on the basis of a **review**. Standards for all attest engagements, which are a natural extension of (but do not supersede) the 10 GAAS, are given as follows.

General Standards

a. *The engagement shall be performed by a practitioner or practitioners having adequate technical training and proficiency in the attest function.*

b. *The engagement shall be performed by a practitioner or practitioners having adequate knowledge in the subject matter of the assertion.*

c. *The practitioner shall perform an engagement only if (s)he has reason to believe that the following two conditions exist:*

   1) *The assertion is capable of evaluation against reasonable criteria that either have been established by a recognized body or are stated in the assertion in a sufficiently clear and comprehensive manner for a knowledgeable reader to be able to understand them.*

      a) For example, an engagement to attest that "workers recorded an average of 40 hours per week on a project" could be accepted by a CPA because "recorded" and "40 hours" are measurable (objectively determinable).

      b) However, an engagement to attest that "workers worked very hard on the project" could not be accepted because "very hard" is not measurable.

   2) *The assertion is capable of reasonably consistent estimation or measurement using such criteria.*

      a) Others applying the same measurement criteria to the issues should reach substantially the same conclusions.

d. *In all matters relating to the engagement, independence in mental attitude shall be maintained by the practitioner(s).*

e. *Due professional care shall be exercised in the performance of the engagement.*

Standards of Field Work

a. *The work shall be adequately planned and assistants, if any, shall be properly supervised.*

b. *Sufficient evidence shall be obtained to provide a reasonable basis for the conclusion that is expressed in the report.*

Standards of Reporting

a. *The report shall identify the assertion being reported on and state the character of the engagement.*

b. *The report shall state the practitioner's conclusion about the reliability of the assertion based on the established or stated criteria against which it was measured.*

c. *The report shall state all of the practitioner's significant reservations about the engagement and the assertion.*

d. *The report on an engagement to evaluate an assertion that has been prepared based on agreed-upon criteria or on an engagement to apply agreed-upon procedures should contain a statement limiting its use to the parties who have agreed upon such criteria or procedures.*

The practitioner should establish an understanding with the client regarding the services to be performed. The understanding should include the objectives of the engagement, management's responsibilities, the CPA's responsibilities, and limitations of the engagement. Practitioners performing attestation engagements should prepare and maintain working papers appropriate for the circumstances of the engagement. The working papers should ordinarily indicate that the engagement was adequately planned and supervised and that sufficient evidence was gathered to support the conclusions expressed in the practitioner's report. The working papers are the property of the practitioner.

When an attest service is included in a management advisory services engagement, the SSAEs apply only to the attest service.

200 - Financial Forecasts and Projections

An accountant who either (1) submits to clients or others prospective financial statements (PFSs) that (s)he has assembled or assisted in assembling or (2) reports on PFSs should either compile, examine, or apply agreed-upon procedures to them if those statements are, or reasonably might be, expected to be used by another (third) party.

A **financial forecast** presents an entity's expected financial position, results of operations, and changes in financial position. It is based on the responsible party's assumptions reflecting conditions it expects to exist and the course of action it expects to take. It may be expressed in specific monetary amounts as a single point estimate of forecasted results or as a range, if the responsible party selects key assumptions to form a range within which it reasonably expects, to the best of its knowledge and belief, the item or items subject to the assumptions to actually fall. Certain minimum presentation guidelines apply.

A **financial projection** differs from a forecast in that it is based on the responsible party's assumptions reflecting conditions it expects would exist and the course of action it expects would be taken, given one or more hypothetical assumptions. A projection is sometimes prepared to present one or more hypothetical courses of action for evaluation, as in response to a question such as "What would happen if . . . ?"

300 - Reporting on Pro Forma Financial Information

This pronouncement is applicable to an accountant who examines or reviews and reports on pro forma financial information (PFFI). It does not apply to post-balance-sheet-date transactions reflected in the historical financial statements or to PFFI required by GAAP.

PFFI indicates what the effects on historical information might have been if a consummated or proposed transaction or event, such as a business combination, had occurred earlier.

An accountant may report on an examination (positive assurance) or review (negative assurance) of PFFI if three conditions are met: the appropriate complete historical financial statements are included in the document; the pertinent historical financial statements have been examined or reviewed, and the assurance given by the accountant is commensurate with that given on those statements; and the reporting accountant has appropriate knowledge of the accounting and reporting practices of each significant constituent part of the combined entity.

400 - Reporting on an Entity's Internal Control over Financial Reporting

This statement (as amended by SSAE 9) is primarily concerned with an engagement to examine management's written assertion about the effectiveness of an entity's internal control over financial reporting and to issue a report on such an examination. It states the conditions for performance of the engagement, defines the components of internal control, and describes the limitations of a system. This pronouncement also provides guidance for planning an engagement to express an opinion on whether the entity's internal control is effective based on the control criteria or on whether management's assertion about the effectiveness of internal control is fairly stated. AT 400 also provides guidance about obtaining an understanding of internal control, evaluating the effectiveness of the design and operation of controls, and forming an opinion. Moreover, AT 400 establishes reporting standards and describes the practitioner's responsibility to communicate deficiencies of which (s)he becomes aware.

500 - Compliance Attestation

Compliance attestation engagements and the accompanying reporting obligations should be conducted in accordance with the basic standards set forth by AT 100. The practitioner may perform an examination leading to an opinion on whether an entity is in compliance or whether management's assertions about such compliance is fairly stated. Agreed-upon procedures (but not a review) may also be performed. These engagements concern (a) the entity's compliance with specified requirements (e.g., covenants of a contract either financial or otherwise) or (b) the effectiveness of the entity's internal control over compliance.

The standard does not relate to engagements subject to *Government Auditing Standards*, which requires reporting on an entity's compliance with laws and regulations as well as on internal control.

If management's written assertion is in a representation letter and not in a separate report that will accompany the practitioner's report, the practitioner should state that assertion in the introductory paragraph. The report will ordinarily be for general use, but the practitioner may restrict use of the report.

600 - Agreed-Upon Procedures Engagements

This attestation standard describes agreed-upon procedure engagements in which a practitioner reports findings based on specific procedures performed on the subject matter of an assertion. An assertion is any declaration or set of declarations by a party responsible for the declaration(s). Unlike an audit or review, the practitioner provides neither positive nor negative assurance. The report should be in the form of procedures performed and the findings based on those procedures. Furthermore, the client, not the practitioner, determines the nature, timing, and extent of the procedures performed. The practitioner must be independent, the assertion must be in writing, and the agreed-upon procedures should not be overly subjective or open to varying interpretations (e.g., general review, check, or test). NOTE: The ASB has approved SSAE 10. In part, it removes the requirement that the assertion be written.

700 - Management's Discussion and Analysis

This standard provides guidance to a practitioner performing an attestation engagement on management's discussion and analysis (MD&A) of financial position and results of operations. The MD&A may be presented in an annual report and other documents. The MD&A section of an entity's financial statements discloses information regarding liquidity, capital resources, results of operations, and the effects of inflation and changing prices. It also presents forward-looking information. The MD&A presentation, in accordance with SEC rules, constitutes a written assertion that may be examined or reviewed. However, a report on a review engagement cannot be filed with the SEC.

ASSURANCE SERVICES

Assurance services are independent professional services that improve the quality of information, or its context, for decision makers. They encompass audit and other attestation services but also other, nonstandard, services. However, unless they fall under the AICPA's attestation standards, assurance services do not require written assertions. Also, they do not encompass consulting services. Assurance and consulting services are delivered using a similar body of knowledge and skills, but assurance services differ in two ways: They focus on improving information rather than providing advice, and they usually involve situations in which one party wants to monitor another (often within the same company) rather than the two-party arrangements common in consulting engagements. The AICPA has identified six assurance services: risk assessment; evaluation of performance measurement systems; assessment of information systems reliability; evaluation of care for the elderly; assurance about health care effectiveness; and assessment of the security, privacy, and reliability of electronic commerce.

GOVERNMENT AUDITING STANDARDS

Audits of certain governmental entities are required to be performed in accordance with the 1994 revision of *Government Auditing Standards* (the Yellow Book). It was promulgated by the General Accounting Office (GAO) and applies not only to financial audits (financial statement and financial related audits) but also to performance audits (economy and efficiency audits and program audits). *Government Auditing Standards*, including the two amendments issued to date, incorporate GAAS for reporting and field work for financial audits and any relevant new AICPA standards unless formally excluded by the GAO. Government Auditing Standards also states supplementary standards. They require either separate reports on internal control over financial reporting and on compliance with laws and regulations or one report integrated into the overall report on the audit.

3. Stop and review! You have completed the outline for this subunit. Study multiple-choice questions 7 through 24 beginning on page 453.

D. **Audit Evidence and Procedures**. The third standard of field work states, "Sufficient competent evidential matter is to be obtained through inspection, observation, inquiries, and confirmations to afford a reasonable basis for an opinion regarding the financial statements under audit." Similarly, internal auditors are expected to collect, analyze, interpret, and document sufficient, competent, relevant, and useful information to support audit results. Thus, this section applies to both external and internal auditing.

1. AU 326, *Evidential Matter*, is the basis for most of this outline. According to AU 326, the audit work consists primarily of obtaining and evaluating evidence about the assertions in the financial statements.

    a. **Evidence** is anything that provides a basis for belief; it tends to prove or disprove something. Documentary evidence is considered more reliable when it has been prepared by someone outside the control of the client, for example, a bank statement prepared by a bank.

    b. **Assertions** are explicit or implicit management representations contained in the financial statements. The five assertions (use the mnemonic COVES to help you remember) are classified as follows:

        1) **C**ompleteness -- whether all transactions and accounts that should be presented in the financial statements are included

        2) Rights and **O**bligations -- whether, at a given date, all assets are the rights of the entity and all liabilities are the obligations of the entity

        3) **V**aluation or Allocation -- whether the assets, liabilities, revenues, and expenses of an entity have been included in the financial statements at the appropriate amounts in conformity with GAAP

        4) **E**xistence or Occurrence -- whether assets/liabilities exist at a given date and whether recorded transactions have occurred during a given period

        5) **S**tatement Presentation and Disclosure -- whether financial statement components have been properly classified, described, and disclosed

    c. For example, because inherent risk is high for cash, most audit procedures are directed toward existence.

        1) A bank reconciliation verifies the agreement of the bank statements obtained directly from the institution and the amount of cash reported in the financial statements. These amounts should be equal after adjustment for deposits in transit, outstanding checks, bank charges, etc.

        2) **Proof of cash**. When control risk is high, that is, when control activities for the transaction process are not effective, a proof of cash may be prepared. It provides direct evidence that both the beginning and ending balances, as well as the deposit and disbursement transactions recorded by the bank, reconcile with the transactions recorded in the accounting records for a period of time, typically a month.

2. **Audit objectives** are determined with regard to the assertions.

    a. Audit objectives also depend on the nature of the auditee's economic activity, industry accounting practices, and other specific circumstances of the engagement.

    b. **Audit procedures** do not necessarily have a one-to-one correspondence with audit objectives; one procedure may bear upon several objectives, or several procedures may be needed to attain one objective.

3. **Substantive tests** must be designed to achieve the audit objectives.
   a. Substantive tests are tests of details and analytical procedures intended to detect material misstatements in the account balance, transaction class, and disclosure components of the financial statements. The primary concern when performing substantive tests is the incorrect acceptance of a materially misstated account balance.
   b. The nature, timing, and extent of substantive tests will depend on audit risk (inherent, control, and detection risk) and materiality (AU 312). Considerations will include the
      1) Effectiveness of the particular procedures
      2) Efficiency of the particular procedures (cost-benefit ratio)
      3) Nature of items tested
      4) Kinds and competence of available evidence
      5) Nature of the specific objective
      6) Type of processing (manual or computer) of the accounting data
      7) Effectiveness of the auditee's internal controls
4. The audit effort devoted to gathering evidence through substantive tests is determined in part by the evidence obtained regarding the effectiveness of internal control. Evidence must be gathered permitting assessment of inherent risk and control risk. These assessments permit determination of the allowable level of detection risk for a particular assertion given the level to which the auditor seeks to restrict overall audit risk.
   a. If control risk is to be assessed at less than the maximum, **tests of controls** must be performed. These tests are directed toward the design or operation of specific controls. Their purpose is to obtain evidence permitting an assessment of effectiveness in preventing or detecting material misstatements.
   b. The reasonable basis for the opinion is therefore a body of evidence provided by a combination of the consideration of the internal controls and substantive tests.
5. Evidence includes underlying accounting data and corroborating information.
   a. **Underlying accounting data** consist of the books of original entry (e.g., journals and registers), ledgers, accounting manuals, and records, such as worksheets and spreadsheets, often in electronic form, that support cost allocations, computations, and reconciliations. However, accounting data alone cannot be considered sufficient support for the financial statements.
   b. **Corroborating information** comes from written and electronic information such as checks, records of electronic funds transfers, invoices, contracts, and minutes; from confirmations; from the auditor's own inquiry, observation, inspection, and physical examination; and from any other information permitting conclusions to be drawn.
   c. Confirmations of account receivables are required to be performed under GAAP unless the amount is immaterial, confirmations would be ineffective, or risk of misstatement based on other procedures is judged sufficiently low. The independent auditor can receive direct assistance from the internal auditor in the confirmation process, as long as the independent auditor maintains control over confirmation requests and responses.

1) A **positive confirmation** requests a reply regardless of whether the respondent agrees with the information stated.

2) A **negative confirmation** requests the recipient to respond only if (s)he disagrees with the information stated.

d. The auditor analyzes and reviews the accounting data, retraces the steps in the accounting process and in the preparation of worksheets and allocations, recalculates amounts, and performs reconciliations.

e. The foregoing procedures permit the auditor to determine whether the accounting system has the internal consistency that is persuasive evidence of the fair presentation, in all material respects, of the financial statements.

6. Evidence must be both competent and sufficient.

a. Professional judgment is the measure of the validity of audit evidence.

1) The auditor is permitted a broad discretion not available in the consideration of legal evidence, which is narrowly limited by admissibility criteria.

b. **Competent** evidence is valid and relevant.

1) Pertinence, objectivity, timeliness, and the existence of corroborating matter are aspects of the competence of audit evidence.

2) Evidence is more likely to be reliable if

a) It is gathered from independent sources external to the auditee.

b) The internal controls are effective.

c) It is obtained directly through the auditor's own physical examination, observation, computation, and inspection.

c. What constitutes **sufficient** evidence to provide a reasonable basis for the opinion is a matter of professional judgment.

1) Judgment and attention to the unique circumstances of a specific audit are necessary because obtaining convincing rather than merely persuasive evidence to support the opinion is often not feasible.

2) Evidence gathering is subject to time and cost constraints, and the auditor must adhere to a cost-benefit criterion.

a) However, the difficulty and expense of an audit procedure are not, by themselves, grounds for its omission.

7. The **evaluation** of audit evidence entails determining whether audit objectives have been attained and considering relevant evidence regardless of whether it supports or contradicts assertions in the financial statements.

a. The auditor must avoid forming an opinion until (s)he has obtained sufficient competent evidence to remove substantial doubt about the assertion.

8. Stop and review! You have completed the outline for this subunit. Study multiple-choice questions 25 through 39 beginning on page 459.

E. Audit Sampling

1. **Definition**. Audit sampling applies an audit procedure to less than 100% of the items within an account balance or class of transactions for the purpose of evaluating some characteristic of the balance or class (AU 350).

2. **Audit Sampling Approaches**

   a. **Judgment (nonstatistical) sampling** uses the auditor's subjective judgment to determine the sample size (number of items examined) and sample selection (which items to examine). This subjectivity is not always a weakness. The auditor, based on other audit work, may be able to test the most material and to emphasize those subject to high control risk.

   b. **Statistical (probability or random) sampling** provides an objective method of determining sample size and selecting the items to be examined. Unlike judgment sampling, it also provides a means of quantitatively assessing precision (how closely the sample represents the population) and reliability (confidence level, the percentage of times the sample will adequately reflect the population). Random-based selection is the primary characteristic of statistical sampling.

      1) Statistical sampling helps the auditor to design an efficient sample, to measure the sufficiency of the evidence obtained, and to evaluate the sample results. The third standard of field work requires auditors to obtain sufficient competent evidence. **Sufficiency** relates to the design and size of the sample. Statistical sampling permits the auditor to measure sampling risk and therefore to design more efficient samples (i.e., the minimum samples necessary to provide sufficient evidence).

      2) The **competence** of evidence is a matter of judgment and is not determined by the design and evaluation of the sample. The sample evaluation relates only to the likelihood that existing misstatements or deviations are proportionately included in the sample. Thus, the choice of nonstatistical or statistical sampling does not directly affect the auditor's decisions about the auditing procedures to be applied, the competence of the evidence obtained with respect to individual sample items, or the actions that might be taken given the nature and cause of particular misstatements or deviations.

3. **Uncertainty**. Some uncertainty is implied in the "reasonable basis for an opinion" language in the third standard of field work.

   a. The justification for accepting uncertainty arises because of the need to balance such factors as the cost and time required to examine all data against the adverse consequences of examining only a sample. If these factors do not justify accepting some uncertainty, the only alternative is a complete audit.

   b. The uncertainty inherent in audit procedures is **audit risk**. Audit risk consists of inherent risk, control risk, and detection risk.

      1) The risk that these adverse events will occur jointly is a function of the respective individual risks. Using professional judgment, the auditor assesses inherent risk and control risk (assessing control risk at less than the maximum requires tests of controls), and performs substantive tests (analytical procedures and tests of details of balances or classes) to limit detection risk.

2) Audit risk includes uncertainties caused by sampling and nonsampling factors.

a) **Sampling risk** arises from the possibility that the auditor's conclusions may differ from the conclusions reached if the test were applied in the same way to all items in the balance or class. Hence, a sample may contain proportionately more or fewer misstatements or deviations than exist in the balance or class as a whole. Given a specific design, sampling risk varies inversely with sample size.

i) Statistical sampling permits efficient sampling plans and quantification of sample precision and reliability.

b) **Nonsampling risk** embraces all aspects of audit risk that are not caused by sampling. Nonsampling risk includes selecting audit procedures that are not appropriate to achieve the specific objective and failing to recognize misstatements included in documents examined.

i) Nonsampling risk can be reduced through adequate planning, supervision, and quality control.

4. The auditor should apply professional judgment in assessing sampling risk.

a. In performing substantive tests of details, the auditor is concerned with

1) **The risk of incorrect acceptance**, which "is the risk that the sample supports the conclusion that the recorded account balance is not materially misstated when it is materially misstated"

2) **The risk of incorrect rejection**, which "is the risk that the sample supports the conclusion that the recorded account balance is materially misstated when it is not materially misstated"

b. The auditor is also concerned with two aspects of sampling risk in performing tests of controls.

1) **The risk of assessing control risk too low**, which "is the risk that the assessed level of control risk based on the sample is less than the true operating effectiveness of the internal control policy or procedure"

2) **The risk of assessing control risk too high**, which "is the risk that the assessed level of control risk based on the sample is greater than the true operating effectiveness of the internal control policy or procedure"

c. The risks of incorrect rejection and of assessing control risk too high relate to audit efficiency. These risks are also termed Type I errors or Alpha risk.

d. The risks of incorrect acceptance and of assessing control risk too low relate to audit effectiveness (critical risk). These risks are also termed Type II errors or Beta risk.

e. The **confidence level**, also termed the reliability level, is the complement of the applicable sampling risk factor. Thus, for a test of controls, if the risk of assessing control risk too low is 5%, the auditor's confidence level is 95% (100% – 5%). For a substantive test, if the risk of incorrect rejection is 5%, the auditor's confidence level is 95% (100% – 5%).

5. **Sampling and Substantive Tests**
   a. Planning the sample requires consideration of
      1) The relevant audit objectives and characteristics of the population
      2) Preliminary materiality judgments
         a) **Tolerable misstatement** for a balance or class is defined in view of the maximum misstatement that may exist without causing the financial statements to be materially misstated.
      3) Allowable risk of incorrect acceptance
         a) As the assessed levels of inherent risk, control risk, and detection risk for other substantive procedures directed toward the same audit objective decrease, the auditor's allowable risk of incorrect acceptance for the substantive test of details increases and the required sample size decreases.
   b. **Sampling methods**
      1) **Random-based selection** (random sampling, stratified random sampling, etc.) should be conducted so that the sample represents the population. Consequently, all items should have an opportunity to be chosen.
      2) A **systematic sample** selects a starting point and then takes every nth item in the population.
      3) **Attribute sampling** is used to determine an estimated occurrence rate for a particular characteristic in a population.
      4) **Block sampling (or cluster sampling)** selects groups of items rather than individual items. If blocks of homogenous samples are selected, the sample will be biased.
      5) A **haphazard sample** is a judgment (nonstatistical) sample.
      6) **Discovery sampling** is used when looking for critical errors or fraud. One critical error is enough to stop the use of the technique because the presumption is that no errors should exist.
   c. Performance and evaluation
      1) Appropriate procedures are applied to each sample item.
         a) If documentation for selected items is missing, the auditor must consider the impact on the evaluation of the sample and the possible need for alternative procedures.
      2) The auditor must project the quantitative misstatement results of the sample to the population and compare it with tolerable misstatement.
         a) Qualitative aspects of misstatements should also be considered.
      3) Projected misstatements, known misstatements detected by nonsampling tests, and other audit evidence should be considered in the aggregate in determining whether the financial statements are materially misstated.

6. **Sampling and Tests of Controls**
   a. Planning the sample requires consideration of the
      1) Relation of the sample to the objective of the test
         a) Some tests of controls do not involve sampling.

2) **Tolerable rate** of deviations that would support the assessed level of control risk
   a) The auditor must consider the planned assessed level of control risk and the degree of assurance sought from the evidence in the sample. (S)he must also consider that deviations from policies or procedures do not necessarily cause misstatements.
3) Allowable risk of assessing control risk too low
4) Characteristics of the population

b. Sample selection should be representative, and all items should have an opportunity to be selected.
   1) The selection method should have the potential for choosing items from the entire period.

c. Performance and evaluation
   1) The effects of limitations on tests of controls should be considered.
   2) The sample deviation rate is the best estimate of the population deviation rate.
      a) Qualitative aspects of the deviations should also be considered.
   3) If the sample does not support the planned assessed level of control risk for an assertion, the nature, timing, and extent of substantive procedures may need to be reevaluated.

7. **The Primary Methods of Variables Sampling**. Variables sampling applies to dollar values or other quantities rather than the binary propositions tested by attribute sampling.

   a. **Mean-per-unit** averages the audit values of the sample items and multiplies the average by the number of items in the population to estimate the population value. An allowance for sampling risk is then determined.

   b. **Difference estimation and ratio estimation**
      1) Difference estimation (of population misstatement) determines differences between the audit and book values for items in the sample, adding the differences, calculating the mean difference, and multiplying the mean by the number of items in the population. An allowance for sampling risk (achieved precision at the desired level of confidence based on the normal distribution) is also calculated.
      2) Ratio estimation is similar to difference estimation except that it estimates the population misstatement by multiplying the book value of the population by the ratio of the total audit value of the sample items to their total book value.

   c. **Probability-proportional-to-size (PPS) or dollar-unit sampling (DUS)** uses the dollar as the sampling unit. PPS sampling is appropriate for testing account balances (typically assets) for overstatement when some items may be far larger than others in the population. In effect, it stratifies the population because the larger account balances have a greater chance of being selected. PPS is most useful if few misstatements are expected.

8. Stop and review! You have completed the outline for this subunit. Study multiple-choice questions 40 through 55 beginning on page 464.

F. Compilation and Review

1. Accountants may not be associated with unaudited financial statements of nonpublic companies unless they are reviewed or compiled.
   a. Unaudited statements of public companies are covered by AU 504.
   b. The AICPA has issued eight Statements on Standards for Accounting and Review Services (SSARSs) that apply to unaudited statements of nonpublic entities. They have been codified in section AR of AICPA Professional Standards (Vol. II).
2. **AR 100**, *Compilation and Review of Financial Statements*
   a. Accountants may compile financial statements from client information without performing any procedures to verify, corroborate, or review that information.
      1) **Compilation** involves presenting the representations of management (owners) without expressing any assurance on the statements.
      2) The accountant should have knowledge of the accounting principles and practices of the industry. (S)he also should have a general understanding of the entity's business, its accounting records, the qualifications of its accountants, the accounting basis of the statements, and the form and content of the statements.
      3) Before submission of the financial statements, the accountant must read them and determine whether their form is appropriate and whether they contain obvious material errors.
      4) When an accountant reports on a compilation or submits statements **reasonably expected to be used by a third party**, a report should be included stating
         a) That the statements were compiled in accordance with SSARSs issued by the AICPA.
         b) What a compilation is, that no audit or review was undertaken, and that no opinion or other assurance is expressed.
      5) When an accountant submits financial statements that are **not reasonably expected to be used by a third party**, the required communication may consist either of a compilation report or of the **documentation of an understanding** with the client.
         a) A **submission** is a presentation to a client or a third party of statements the accountant has prepared either manually or through use of computer software. A **third party** is anyone other than managers who are knowledgeable about the procedures applied and the basis of accounting and assumptions used.
   b. When CPAs undertake review engagements, they express limited assurance based upon inquiry and analytical procedures.
      1) A review does not include
         a) Evaluation of internal control
         b) Tests of transactions and account balances
         c) Other auditing procedures

2) An accountant's review report consists of three paragraphs.

a) The introductory paragraph states that a **review** was performed in accordance with SSARSs and that the information is the representation of management.

b) The scope paragraph states that a review consists principally of inquiries of company personnel and analytical procedures applied to the financial data. The accountant is also required to obtain a representation letter from management. It does not constitute an audit in accordance with GAAS, and thus no opinion is expressed.

c) The accountant states that (s)he is not aware of any material modifications that should be made to the financial statements to conform with GAAP.

c. If accountants undertaking compilation and review engagements believe that the financial statements are not in conformity with GAAP, they must have the client make necessary corrections or make the necessary disclosures in their compilation or review report.

3. **AR 200**, *Reporting on Comparative Statements,* establishes standards for reporting on comparative financial statements of nonpublic entities when financial statements of one or more periods presented have been compiled or reviewed.

4. **AR 300**, *Compilation Reports on Financial Statements Included in Certain Prescribed Forms,* provides an alternative compilation report for financial statements included in a prescribed form (e.g., of a regulatory body) that calls for a departure from GAAP. It also provides further guidance applicable to reports on financial statements included therein.

5. **AR 400**, *Communications between Predecessor and Successor Accountants,* concerns communications by a successor accountant with his/her predecessor regarding acceptance of an engagement to compile or review financial statements of a nonpublic entity.

6. **AR 600**, *Reporting on Personal Financial Statements Included in Written Personal Financial Plans,* provides an exemption from AR 100 for personal financial statements included in written personal financial plans prepared by an accountant if the statement will be used solely by the client and his/her advisers and will not be used for any other purpose than to develop the client's personal financial goals and objectives.

7. Stop and review! You have completed the outline for this subunit. Study multiple-choice questions 56 and 57 on page 469.

G. Audit Reports

1. The Auditor's Standard Report

Standard Audit Report

> Independent Auditor's Report
>
> To: <------------ Addressed to the Board of Directors or Shareholders
>
> We have audited the accompanying balance sheets of X Company as of December 31, 20x2 and 20x1, and the related statements of income, retained earnings, and cash flows for the years then ended. These financial statements are the responsibility of the Company's management. Our responsibility is to express an opinion on these financial statements based on our audits.
>
> We conducted our audits in accordance with auditing standards generally accepted in the United States of America. Those standards require that we plan and perform the audit to obtain reasonable assurance about whether the financial statements are free of material misstatement. An audit includes examining, on a test basis, evidence supporting the amounts and disclosures in the financial statements. An audit also includes assessing the accounting principles used and significant estimates made by management, as well as evaluating the overall financial statement presentation. We believe that our audits provide a reasonable basis for our opinion.
>
> In our opinion, the financial statements referred to above present fairly, in all material respects, the financial position of X Company as of [at] December 31, 20x2 and 20x1, and the results of its operations and its cash flows for the years then ended in conformity with accounting principles generally accepted in the United States of America.
>
> Signature <------------ May be signed, typed, or printed
>
> Date <------------ Date of completion of field work

2. Types of Reports

a. **Unqualified opinion**. An unqualified opinion states that the financial statements present fairly, in all material respects, the financial position, results of operations, and cash flows of the entity in conformity with GAAP.

b. **Explanatory language added to the auditor's standard report**. Certain circumstances, although not affecting the auditor's unqualified opinion, may require that the auditor add an explanatory paragraph (or other explanatory language) to the report.

1) Explanatory language not affecting an unqualified opinion must be added in circumstances that include the following: The opinion is based in part on the report of another auditor, the statements contain a departure from GAAP necessary to prevent them from being misleading, the auditor changes the opinion on a prior period when reporting on current statements in comparative form, substantial doubt about the going-concern assumption exists, GAAP are applied inconsistently, and the auditor chooses to emphasize a matter.*

*NOTE: SAS 79 (an amendment of AU 508) eliminated the requirement that, when certain criteria are met, the auditor add an explanatory paragraph for an uncertainty. However, the auditor has the option to add an explanatory paragraph to emphasize a matter, e.g., unusually important risks or uncertainties associated with contingencies, significant estimates, or concentrations.

c. **Qualified opinion**. A qualified opinion states that, **except for** the effects of the matter(s) to which the qualification relates, the financial statements present fairly, in all material respects, the financial position, results of operation, and cash flows of the entity in conformity with GAAP.

1) A qualified opinion is expressed when a lack of sufficient evidence or a scope limitation precludes an unqualified opinion but the auditor has chosen not to disclaim an opinion or when a material departure from GAAP exists but the auditor has decided not to express an adverse opinion. Departures from GAAP include use of a principle at variance with GAAP, inadequate disclosure, and an accounting change if the newly adopted principle is not generally accepted, the method of accounting for the change is not in conformity with GAAP, or the change is not reasonably justified.

d. **Adverse opinion**. An adverse opinion states that the financial statements do not present fairly the financial position, results of operations, or cash flows of the entity in conformity with GAAP. An adverse opinion is expressed when the financial statements as a whole are not presented fairly in conformity with GAAP.

e. **Disclaimer of opinion**. A disclaimer of opinion states that the auditor does not express an opinion on the financial statements. A disclaimer of opinion is expressed because the audit has not been sufficient in scope to permit the formation of an opinion.

3. If only single-year financial statements are presented, the report is adjusted to refer only to those statements.

4. Unless otherwise required, an explanatory paragraph may precede or follow the opinion paragraph in the auditor's report.

5. Statements prepared in accordance with GAAP and audited in accordance with GAAS may be disseminated outside the U.S. Thus, the standard report refers to the country of origin of the accounting and auditing standards.

6. **Other Audit Report Concepts**

a. Financial statements that disclose segment data (see **SFAS 131**, *Disclosures about Segments of an Enterprise and Related Information*) require special audit procedures. However, the auditor need not refer to segment information in the report unless the audit reveals a material misstatement or omission, or unless the audit was subject to a scope limitation.

b. If a qualified opinion or disclaimer of opinion is expressed, negative assurance is inappropriate. Thus, a statement that "nothing has come to our attention indicating the financial statements are not fairly presented" should not be included.

c. Audit reports are usually dated as of the last day of field work.

d. Auditors have a responsibility to determine that other data appearing in documents containing audited financial statements do not conflict with the data in the audited statements.

e. Auditors are responsible for events occurring subsequent to year-end and prior to the issuance of the audit report.

f. Auditors also have a responsibility for making disclosures after issuance of audit reports if information comes to their attention that would have affected their audit report had they known it at the time of issuance.

g. Instead of the standard report, a longer, more analytical report may be issued.

h. Auditors may issue reports on

1) Financial statements prepared on a comprehensive basis of accounting other than GAAP
2) Specific elements, accounts, or items of statements
3) Compliance with contractual or regulatory provisions
4) Information on prescribed forms
5) Internal control
6) The application of accounting principles
7) Financial statements prepared for use in other countries
8) Information accompanying the basic financial statements in auditor-submitted documents
9) Condensed financial statements and selected financial data
10) Required supplementary information
11) Application of agreed-upon procedures to specified elements, accounts, or items of a financial statement

i. Auditors may be requested to provide special letters to underwriters that are issuing securities of a client.

j. Accountants may undertake limited reviews of interim statements based on inquiry and analytical procedures.

7. Stop and review! You have completed the outline for this subunit. Study multiple-choice questions 58 through 64 beginning on page 469.

MULTIPLE-CHOICE QUESTIONS

A. Generally Accepted Auditing Standards (GAAS)

1. An audit of the financial statements of Camden Corporation is being conducted by an external auditor. The external auditor is expected to

A. Express an opinion as to the fairness of Camden's financial statements.

B. Express an opinion as to the attractiveness of Camden for investment purposes.

C. Certify to the correctness of Camden's financial statements.

D. Critique the wisdom and legality of Camden's business decisions.

The correct answer is (A). *(CMA, adapted)*

REQUIRED: The responsibility of an external auditor for an audit of financial statements.

DISCUSSION: The fourth standard of reporting requires the auditor to express an opinion regarding the financial statements taken as a whole or to assert that an opinion cannot be expressed. The opinion concerns the fairness with which the statements have been presented in conformity with GAAP.

Answer (B) is incorrect because the external auditor does not interpret the financial statement data for investment purposes. Answer (C) is incorrect because the external audit normally cannot be so thorough as to permit a guarantee of correctness. Answer (D) is incorrect because the independent audit attests to the fair presentation of the data in the financial statements, not an evaluation of management decisions.

2. The primary reason for an audit by an independent, external audit firm is

A. To guarantee that there are no misstatements in the financial statements.

B. To relieve management of responsibility for the financial statements.

C. To provide increased assurance to users as to the fairness of the financial statements.

D. To insure that any fraud will be discovered.

The correct answer is (C). *(CMA, adapted)*

REQUIRED: The primary reason for an audit by an independent auditor.

DISCUSSION: External auditors express an opinion on the fairness of the financial statements. The independent auditor's opinion provides assurance to third parties, e.g., creditors and investors, that the statements are fairly presented.

Answer (A) is incorrect because auditors do not guarantee the absence of misstatements. Answer (B) is incorrect because management is responsible for the financial statements. Answer (D) is incorrect because external auditors are not in a position to guarantee discovery of fraud since their opinion is based only upon examination and tests of sample transactions, not 100% verification.

3. Generally accepted auditing standards consist of general standards, standards of field work, and standards of reporting. The standards of field work include which one of the following?

A. The audit is to be performed by a person or persons having adequate technical training.

B. In all matters relating to the assignment, an independence of mental attitude is essential.

C. The work is to be adequately planned, and assistants, if any, are to be properly supervised.

D. Due professional care is to be exercised in the planning and performance of the audit.

The correct answer is (C). *(CMA, adapted)*

REQUIRED: The answer that is a generally accepted auditing standard of field work.

DISCUSSION: The three standards of field work concern 1) adequate planning and supervision, 2) understanding internal control, and 3) sufficient competent evidential matter.

Answer (A) is incorrect because, according to the first general standard, the audit is to be performed by a person or persons having adequate technical training. Answer (B) is incorrect because, according to the second general standard, in all matters relating to the assignment, an independence of mental attitude is essential. Answer (D) is incorrect because, according to the third general standard, due professional care is to be exercised in the planning and performance of the audit.

B. AICPA Code of Professional Conduct

4. The independence of the external audit firm will be considered to be impaired if

A. The audit firm has served as the external auditor for many years.

B. The partner in charge of the audit is a personal friend of the chair of the board of the client corporation.

C. The audit firm provides consulting services to the client.

D. The partner in charge of the audit owns an insignificant amount of stock in the client corporation.

The correct answer is (D). *(CMA, adapted)*

REQUIRED: The situation that impairs the independence of an external audit firm.

DISCUSSION: The AICPA *Code of Professional Ethics* requires CPAs to be independent of their audit clients. They cannot have financial or management relationships with the client. Thus, any amount of stock ownership impairs independence or creates a presumption of impairment.

Answer (A) is incorrect because a continuing relationship between the client and the external auditor is not considered to impair independence; auditor rotation is not required. Answer (B) is incorrect because personal friendship between audit personnel and client personnel does not impair independence. Answer (C) is incorrect because there is no current prohibition against offering both audit and consulting services to clients.

5. An external auditor is not permitted to discuss confidential information obtained in the course of a professional engagement except with the consent of the client. This ethical proscription

A. Is unenforceable.

B. Will prevent the auditor from engaging another auditing firm to conduct a peer review.

C. Will not preclude the auditor from complying with a validly issued court subpoena.

D. Is often used by a client to blunt the auditor's efforts to modify the standard auditor's report.

The correct answer is (C). *(CMA, adapted)*

REQUIRED: The effect of the prohibition against discussing confidential client information.

DISCUSSION: Conduct Rule 301 does not prohibit a CPA from disclosing confidential information (1) to comply with a valid and enforceable subpoena or summons issued by a court or with applicable laws and government regulations, (2) to properly discharge the CPA's responsibilities in accordance with his/her profession's standards, (3) to permit a review of the CPA's professional practice under AICPA or state CPA society or Board of Accountancy authorization, or (4) to initiate a complaint with, or to respond to an inquiry made by, the ethics division or trial board of the AICPA or a duly constituted investigative or disciplinary body of a state CPA society or Board of Accountancy.

Answer (A) is incorrect because ethics rules are enforceable through state CPA societies, etc. Answer (B) is incorrect because an exception is made for peer reviews. Answer (D) is incorrect because the CPA would not be independent if the client could dictate the content of the opinion. However, the auditor should not ordinarily disclose, without the client's specific consent, information not required to be disclosed in financial statements to comply with GAAP (AU 431).

6. The communication between an external auditor and a client is confidential. Ordinarily,

A. The client is not required to answer an external auditor's questions in certain circumstances.

B. An external auditor is not permitted to testify in a court of law without the permission of the client.

C. An external auditor is not required to divulge client information even if demanded by a subpoena.

D. An external auditor should not disclose information obtained in the course of the engagement without the client's permission.

The correct answer is (D). *(CMA, adapted)*

REQUIRED: The meaning of confidentiality of communication between an external auditor and a client.

DISCUSSION: Ethics Rule 301 of the AICPA *Code of Professional Ethics* prohibits disclosure of confidential information obtained in the course of a professional engagement except with the consent of the client. Certain exceptions are allowed: responses to a subpoena or summons, peer review activities, participation in disciplinary matters, and the actions necessary for the proper discharge of professional responsibilities.

Answer (A) is incorrect because confidentiality is intended to encourage communication so as to avoid limitations on the scope of the audit. Answers (B) and (C) are incorrect because an auditor can be forced to testify against a client in a federal court (except in certain tax proceedings) and in most state courts.

C. AICPA Statements on Auditing Standards

7. The responsibility for the proper preparation of a company's financial statements rests with its

A. Management.

B. Audit committee.

C. Internal auditors.

D. External auditors.

The correct answer is (A). *(CMA, adapted)*

REQUIRED: The persons ultimately responsible for the proper preparation of a company's financial statements.

DISCUSSION: According to AU 110, management has the responsibility for adopting sound accounting policies and for establishing and maintaining internal controls that will record, process, summarize, and report financial data consistent with the assertions in the financial statements. The fairness of the representations made therein is the responsibility of management alone because the transactions and the related assets and liabilities reflected are within management's direct knowledge and control.

Answers (B), (C), and (D) are incorrect because management is ultimately responsible for the assertions in the financial statements.

8. The risk that an external auditor may not detect a material error or fraud during an audit is increased by the possibility of

A. Executive appeal.

B. Late appointment of the auditor.

C. Management override of internal control.

D. Audit committee review of the management letter.

The correct answer is (C). *(CMA, adapted)*

REQUIRED: The item that increases detection risk.

DISCUSSION: Management can direct subordinates to record or conceal transactions and thereby cause a material misstatement of the financial statements. Management can thus perpetrate fraud by overriding controls that would otherwise have detected the fraud. The auditor must therefore be aware of any circumstances that might predispose management to misstate financial statements. Management's integrity is vital to the effective operation of internal controls.

Answer (A) is incorrect because the term "executive appeal" is not meaningful in this context. Answer (B) is incorrect because a late appointment of the auditor should not reduce the scope of the audit. Answer (D) is incorrect because the management letter includes recommendations for improvements but would not affect detection risk.

9. In planning an audit, the auditor considers audit risk. Audit risk is the

A. Susceptibility of an assertion to material misstatement assuming there are no related controls.

B. Risk that a material misstatement in an assertion will not be prevented or detected on a timely basis by the client's internal control.

C. Risk that the auditor's procedures for verifying account balances will not detect a material misstatement that in fact exists.

D. Risk that the auditor may unknowingly fail to appropriately modify the opinion on financial statements that are materially misstated.

The correct answer is (D). *(CMA, adapted)*

REQUIRED: The true statement about audit risk.

DISCUSSION: According to AU 312, "Audit risk is the risk that the auditor may unknowingly fail to modify the opinion on financial statements that are materially misstated." It includes inherent risk, which is "the susceptibility of an assertion to material misstatement, assuming there are no related controls." It also includes control risk, "the risk that a material misstatement that could occur in an assertion will not be prevented or detected on a timely basis by the entity's internal control." The third component of audit risk is detection risk, "the risk that the auditor will not detect a material misstatement that exists in an assertion."

Answer (A) is incorrect because inherent risk is the susceptibility of an assertion to material misstatement assuming there are no related controls. Answer (B) is incorrect because control risk is the risk that a material misstatement in an assertion will not be prevented or detected on a timely basis by the client's internal control. Answer (C) is incorrect because detection risk is the risk that the auditor's procedures for verifying account balances will not detect a material misstatement that in fact exists.

10. Audit risk is composed of

A. Tolerable error risk, sampling error risk, and inherent risk.

B. Tolerable rate risk, sampling risk, and inherent risk.

C. Allowance for sampling risk, allowance for nonsampling risk, and allowance for inherent risk.

D. Inherent risk, control risk, and detection risk.

The correct answer is (D). *(CMA, adapted)*

REQUIRED: The components of audit risk.

DISCUSSION: Audit risk is composed of inherent risk, control risk, and detection risk (AU 312 and AU 350). Inherent risk is the susceptibility of an assertion to material misstatement in the absence of related controls. Control risk is the risk that a material misstatement in an assertion may occur and not be detected on a timely basis by internal control. Detection risk is the risk that an auditor may not detect a material misstatement in an assertion.

Answer (A) is incorrect because tolerable error and sampling error are terms that no longer appear in the applicable professional standards. They have been replaced by tolerable misstatement and sampling risk, respectively. Also, control risk and detection risk are omitted. Answer (B) is incorrect because control risk and detection risk are omitted. Answer (C) is incorrect because the elements of audit risk are inherent risk, control risk, and detection risk.

11. Inherent risk is

A. The susceptibility of an assertion to a material misstatement, assuming that there are no related controls.

B. The risk that the auditor may unknowingly fail to appropriately modify his or her opinion on financial statements that are materially misstated.

C. The risk that a material misstatement that could occur in an assertion will not be prevented or detected on a timely basis by the entity's internal control.

D. The risk that the auditor will not detect a material misstatement that exists in an assertion.

The correct answer is (A). *(CMA, adapted)*

REQUIRED: The definition of inherent risk.

DISCUSSION: According to AU 312, "Inherent risk is the susceptibility of an assertion to a material misstatement, assuming that there are no related controls. The risk of such misstatement is greater for some assertions and related balances or classes than for others." Unlike detection risk, inherent risk and control "are independent of the audit." Furthermore, inherent risk and control risk are inversely related to detection risk. Thus, the lower the inherent risk, the higher the acceptable detection risk.

Answer (B) is incorrect because the risk that the auditor may unknowingly fail to appropriately modify his or her opinion on financial statements that are materially misstated is audit risk. Answer (C) is incorrect because the risk that a material misstatement that could occur in an assertion will not be prevented or detected on a timely basis by the entity's internal control is control risk. Answer (D) is incorrect because the risk that the auditor will not detect a material misstatement that exists in an assertion is detection risk.

12. The components of audit risk include inherent risk, control risk, and detection risk. Detection risk is the

A. Risk that a material misstatement that could occur in an assertion will not be prevented by the entity's internal control or detected on a timely basis.

B. Risk that the sample supports the conclusion that the recorded account balance is materially misstated when it is not.

C. Susceptibility of an assertion to a material misstatement, assuming that there are no related controls.

D. Risk that the auditor will not find a material misstatement that exists in an assertion.

The correct answer is (D). *(CMA, adapted)*

REQUIRED: The definition of detection risk.

DISCUSSION: According to AU 312, one component of audit risk is detection risk, which is the risk that the auditor will not detect a material misstatement that exists in an assertion. Detection risk for a substantive test of details has two elements: (1) the risk that analytical procedures and other relevant substantive tests will fail to detect misstatements at least equal to tolerable misstatement and (2) the allowable risk of incorrect acceptance for the substantive test of details.

Answer (A) is incorrect because control risk is the risk that a material misstatement that could occur in an assertion will not be prevented by the entity's internal control or detected on a timely basis. Answer (B) is incorrect because sampling risk is the risk that the sample supports the conclusion that the recorded account balance is materially misstated when it is not (AU 350). Answer (C) is incorrect because inherent risk is the susceptibility of an assertion to a material misstatement, assuming that there are no related controls.

13. The steps that an audit firm should take prior to accepting an audit engagement include all of the following except

A. Obtaining a thorough understanding of the client's business.

B. Evaluating independence.

C. Assessing the firm's competence to perform the audit.

D. Determining the firm's ability to use due professional care.

The correct answer is (A). *(CMA, adapted)*

REQUIRED: The step not included in an audit firm's analysis of a potential client.

DISCUSSION: A successor auditor should obtain the permission of the prospective client to make inquiries of the predecessor auditor regarding matters pertinent to acceptance of the engagement, e.g., facts bearing on management's integrity, disagreements with management about accounting principles or auditing procedures, and reasons for the change in auditors (AU 315). However, the auditor would probably not obtain a thorough understanding of the client's business until the audit was scheduled.

Answers (B), (C), and (D) are incorrect because the AICPA's *Code of Professional Conduct* requires an external auditor to be independent in the performance of attestation services, to undertake only those professional services that (s)he can reasonably expect to complete with professional competence, and to use due professional care in the planning and performance of the audit and the preparation of the report.

14. Which of the following best describe the interrelated components of internal control?

A. Organizational structure, management philosophy, and planning.

B. Control environment, risk assessment, control activities, information and communication systems, and monitoring.

C. Risk assessment, backup facilities, responsibility accounting, and natural laws.

D. Legal environment of the firm, management philosophy, and organizational structure.

The correct answer is (B). *(CMA, adapted)*

REQUIRED: The components of internal control.

DISCUSSION: Internal control includes five components: the control environment, risk assessment, control activities, information and communication, and monitoring. The control environment sets the tone of an organization, influences control consciousness, and provides a foundation for the other components. Risk assessment is the identification and analysis of relevant risks to achievement of objectives. Control activities help ensure that management directives are executed. Information and communication are the identification, capture, and exchange of information in a form and time frame that allow people to meet their responsibilities. Monitoring assesses the performance of internal control over time (AU 319).

Answer (A) is incorrect because planning is not a component of internal control. Organizational structure and management philosophy are factors in the control environment component. Answer (C) is incorrect because risk assessment is the only component listed. Answer (D) is incorrect because the legal environment of the firm, management philosophy, and organizational structure are factors in the control environment component.

15. Which one of the following statements does not correctly describe the relationship of the internal auditor and the scope of the external audit of a company's financial statements?

A. The nature, timing, and extent of the external auditor's substantive tests may depend upon the work of the internal auditors.

B. The internal auditors may assist the external auditor in performing substantive tests under certain circumstances.

C. The internal auditors may assist the external auditor in performing tests of controls under certain circumstances.

D. The internal auditors may determine the extent to which audit procedures should be employed by the external auditor.

The correct answer is (D). *(CMA, adapted)*

REQUIRED: The false statement about the relationship of internal auditing and the scope of the external audit.

DISCUSSION: AU 322 states that the independent auditor should obtain an understanding of the internal audit function. If the independent auditor concludes that the work of the internal auditors is relevant to the audit, (s)he should then determine whether it is efficient to consider how that work might affect the nature, timing, and extent of audit procedures. If the internal audit function is found to be sufficiently competent and objective, the external auditor may be able to reduce the scope of both tests of controls and substantive tests. However, the external auditor must make all decisions in matters requiring judgment.

Answer (A) is incorrect because, if certain criteria are met, the auditor must consider how the internal audit function may affect the audit effort devoted to substantive testing. Answers (B) and (C) are incorrect because internal auditors may directly assist the independent external auditor in performing substantive tests and tests of controls if their work is properly supervised, reviewed, evaluated, and tested.

16. An external auditor will use internal auditors to assist in the audit of accounts receivable. Of the following procedures, the one that would be most appropriate for the internal auditors to perform is the

A. Assessment of control risk for accounts receivable.

B. Determination of the number of positive confirmation requests to be mailed to substantiate the existence of accounts receivable.

C. Preparation of an aged trial balance of accounts receivable.

D. Establishment of the dollar amount of accounts receivable that is considered material.

The correct answer is (C). *(CMA, adapted)*

REQUIRED: The procedure most appropriate for the internal auditor to perform in assisting the external auditor.

DISCUSSION: The independent auditor may use internal auditors to provide direct assistance in performing both substantive tests and tests of controls provided that (s)he assesses their competence and objectivity; supervises, reviews, evaluates, and tests their work; and makes all judgments regarding matters that affect the report on the financial statements. Preparing aging schedules is a clerical activity related to a substantive test that an internal auditor may perform under the supervision of the independent auditor.

Answer (A) is incorrect because assessment of control risk for accounts receivable is a matter of judgment to be decided by the external auditor. Answer (B) is incorrect because determination of the number of positive confirmation requests to be mailed to substantiate the existence of accounts receivable is a matter of judgment to be decided by the external auditor. Answer (D) is incorrect because establishment of the dollar amount of accounts receivable that is considered material is a matter of judgment to be decided by the external auditor.

17. Gill & Co., CPAs, are the external auditors for Auto Mufflers, Inc. (AM). AM has a well-trained internal audit staff, including several former Gill staff auditors. Which of the following is most accurate?

A. Gill is precluded from relying on any of AM's internal audit reports because to do so would be a breach of Gill's independence.

B. Gill may use AM's internal audit staff members to perform certain steps in Gill's accounts receivable audit program.

C. AM's internal audits performed during the past year will contribute almost nothing to Gill's compliance testing.

D. Gill may omit substantive testing on one of AM's small subsidiaries because of the extent of the internal audits performed during the year.

The correct answer is (B). *(CMA, adapted)*

REQUIRED: The most accurate statement concerning the external auditor and the client's well-trained internal audit staff.

DISCUSSION: AU 322 permits CPAs to use the client's internal auditors to perform both tests of compliance and substantive tests under appropriate supervision.

Answers (A) and (C) are incorrect because external auditors may also rely on the work of the internal auditor in determining the nature, timing, and extent of audit procedures. Answer (D) is incorrect because substitution of internal audit results for substantive audit procedures is not contemplated by GAAS. Even if a small subsidiary were not visited by the external auditors, the subsidiary's accounts should be analytically reviewed for reasonableness, fluctuations, etc.

18. The effect of a satisfactory internal audit function upon the work of the independent auditor will most likely be

A. A reduction in the scope of audit procedures necessary by the independent auditor.

B. A substitution of the work of the internal auditor for the work of the independent auditor.

C. A substitution of the internal auditor's opinion of the financial statements in place of the independent auditor's opinion.

D. An acceptance of the financial statements as a fair representation of financial position and results of operations.

The correct answer is (A). *(CMA, adapted)*

REQUIRED: The effect of a satisfactory internal audit function on the work of the internal auditor.

DISCUSSION: A satisfactory internal audit function is a significant component of internal control. Before significantly reducing the scope of audit procedures due to a satisfactory internal audit function, the external auditor should review the competency and objectivity of the internal auditor and evaluate his/her work. If the work of the internal auditor is significant, the auditor should review and test the internal auditor's working papers.

Answers (B), (C), and (D) are incorrect because the work of the internal auditor cannot be substituted for the work of the external auditor since external auditors must make all judgments concerning items affecting the audit report, including the expression of an opinion.

19. Analytical procedures are audit methods of evaluating financial statement accounts by studying and comparing relationships among financial and nonfinancial data. The purpose of analytical procedures is to

A. Decide on matters to be covered in an engagement letter.

B. Identify the appropriate schedules to be prepared by the client.

C. Identify the types of errors or fraud that can occur in transactions.

D. Identify unusual conditions that deserve additional audit effort.

The correct answer is (D). *(CMA, adapted)*

REQUIRED: The purpose of analytical procedures in auditing.

DISCUSSION: Analytical procedures "identify such things as the existence of unusual transactions and events and amounts, ratios, and trends that might indicate matters that have financial statement and audit planning ramifications" (AU 329).

Answers (A) and (B) are incorrect because analytical procedures have nothing to do with engagement letters or with schedules prepared by the client. Answer (C) is incorrect because analytical procedures do not identify specific errors.

20. The primary purpose of the representation letter prescribed by AU 333, *Management Representations*, is the

A. Acceptance of the auditor's engagement letter.

B. Evaluation by management of the auditor's performance.

C. Acknowledgment of management's responsibility for the financial statements.

D. Agreement by management to engage the auditor for the next annual audit.

The correct answer is (C). *(CMA, adapted)*

REQUIRED: The primary purpose of the management representation letter.

DISCUSSION: The auditor uses the letter of representation to remind management that the primary responsibility for the overall fairness of financial statements rests with management, not the auditor. AU 333 states that such representations are part of the evidential matter, but they are not a substitute for the application of those auditing procedures necessary to afford a reasonable basis for the opinion.

Answers (A) and (D) are incorrect because the representation letter is not a response to the engagement letter, which is a statement of the parties' contractual understanding. Answer (B) is incorrect because management does not write a letter evaluating the auditor's performance.

21. According to generally accepted auditing standards, the audit report identifies those circumstances in which accounting principles have not been followed consistently except

A. Changes in business conditions, such as the acquisition of a subsidiary company.

B. A change from a principle that is generally accepted to one that is not generally accepted.

C. Changes in the reporting of subsidiaries from individual subsidiary reporting to consolidated financial statements.

D. A change from capitalizing and amortizing a cost to recording it as an expense when incurred because future benefits are now doubtful.

The correct answer is (A). *(CMA, adapted)*

REQUIRED: The consistency exception that is not reported in the auditor's standard report.

DISCUSSION: An auditor must identify circumstances in which accounting principles have not been consistently observed in the current period in relation to the preceding period. Accounting changes that, if material, affect consistency and require recognition in audit reports include a change in accounting principle, a change in the reporting entity not resulting from a transaction or event, correction of an error in principle, a change in principle inseparable from a change in estimate, and a change in the policy for determining which items are cash equivalents. A change in the reporting entity is a special type of change in accounting principle. However, a change in the reporting entity that results "from a transaction or event, such as a pooling of interests, or the creation, cessation, or complete or partial purchase or disposition of a subsidiary or other business unit" does not require inclusion in the audit report of an explanatory paragraph about consistency (AU 420).

Answer (B) is incorrect because correction of an error in principle is a change affecting consistency. Answer (C) is incorrect because presenting consolidated statements in place of the statements of individual companies is a change in the reporting entity not resulting from a transaction or event. Such a change affects consistency. Answer (D) is incorrect because a change in principle inseparable from a change in estimate affects consistency.

Questions 22 and 23 are based on the following information. Fisher Company's fiscal year ended on December 31, 2001, and Fisher issued its annual report on March 15, 2002. On January 2, 2002, a fire occurred at Fisher's warehouse, destroying its contents, which represented 80% of Fisher's inventory. Fisher's fire insurance policy provided minimum coverage only for the facility. On January 20, 2002, a customer who had been in deteriorating financial health entered bankruptcy proceedings; the amount due was considered material.

22. Fisher Company's accounts receivable balance as reported in its annual report at December 31, 2001

A. Includes the amount due for insurance proceeds related to the fire.

B. Reflects the estimated write-down of the receivable from the bankrupt customer.

C. Is unchanged by these events after its year-end.

D. Is higher than at the beginning of the year.

The correct answer is (B). *(CMA, adapted)*

REQUIRED: The true statement regarding the accounts receivable balance in the year-end financial statements.

DISCUSSION: AU 560 states that there are two types of subsequent events: (1) those that require reflection in the financial statements and (2) those that require disclosure only. Events that provide additional evidence about conditions existing at the balance sheet date result in adjustments of the financial statements. For example, the receivable from the bankrupt debtor should be written off in the 2001 statements even though the debtor did not file for bankruptcy until after year-end.

Answer (A) is incorrect because the fire had not yet occurred by the balance sheet date; thus, there were no insurance proceeds to be considered. Answer (C) is incorrect because the receivables balance should be written down. The bankruptcy merely confirmed something that existed at the balance sheet date. Answer (D) is incorrect because no information is given about the beginning accounts receivable balance.

23. Included in Fisher Company's financial statements at December 31, 2001 is

A. A write-off of inventory lost in the fire.

B. A note disclosing the effect of the warehouse fire on Fisher's operations but no inventory adjustment.

C. Nothing related to the bankruptcy or the fire.

D. A description of the causes of the customer's bankruptcy.

The correct answer is (B). *(CMA, adapted)*

REQUIRED: The subsequent event that would be included on the 2001 financial statements.

DISCUSSION: AU 560 states that there are two types of subsequent events: (1) those that require reflection in the financial statements and (2) those that require disclosure only. Events such as losses from a fire or flood do not concern conditions at the balance sheet date. Thus, they should be disclosed as significant subsequent events but do not result in adjustments of the financial statements.

Answer (A) is incorrect because the inventory should not be written off in the 2001 statements. It existed at the balance sheet date. Answer (C) is incorrect because the effect of the bankruptcy should be recorded, and the fire should be disclosed. Answer (D) is incorrect because the causes of the customer's bankruptcy need not be described.

24. An external auditor cannot

A. Express an opinion on whether internal control is effective, in all material respects, based on the control criteria.

B. Express an opinion on the fairness of the financial statements of a nonpublic entity.

C. Make specific recommendations to a client with respect to internal control weaknesses.

D. Report to outside parties regarding a client's compliance with the internal control provisions of the Foreign Corrupt Practices Act.

The correct answer is (D). *(CMA, adapted)*

REQUIRED: The function that an external auditor cannot perform.

DISCUSSION: The FCPA requires companies subject to the Securities Exchange Act of 1934 to maintain an adequate system of internal accounting control. According to AT 400, the auditor should not issue a report providing assurance on compliance with the internal control provision of the act. Whether a firm is in compliance is a legal determination not within the professional capabilities of external auditors.

Answer (A) is incorrect because an engagement to report on the effectiveness of an entity's internal control over financial reporting may include the expression of an opinion (AT 400). Answer (B) is incorrect because GAAS do not distinguish between public and nonpublic entities. Answer (C) is incorrect because the auditor should communicate internal control related matters noted in an audit (AU 325). Reportable conditions as well as material weaknesses must be communicated.

D. Audit Evidence and Procedures

25. Documentary evidence is one of the principal types of corroborating information used by an auditor to substantiate an opinion. Which one of the following examples of documentary evidence would be the most reliable?

A. Time tickets.

B. Material requisition slips.

C. Copies of sales invoices.

D. Bank statements.

The correct answer is (D). *(CMA, adapted)*

REQUIRED: The most reliable documentary evidence.

DISCUSSION: Documentary evidence is considered more reliable when it has been prepared by someone outside the control of the client, for example, a bank statement prepared by a bank. The auditor should obtain the bank statement directly from the bank. Documents to which the client has had access are less reliable (competent) than externally generated documents obtained directly from their sources.

Answer (A) is incorrect because time tickets are generated within the client company. Answer (B) is incorrect because material requisition slips are generated within the client company. Answer (C) is incorrect because copies of sales invoices are generated within the client company.

26. An internal control objective in the revenue cycle is to insure that recorded sales are valid and documented. Which evidence is least likely to satisfy that objective?

A. Bills of lading exist for all invoices.

B. Customer purchase orders support invoices.

C. Shipping documents exist for all invoices.

D. Credit sales have been approved by the credit department.

The correct answer is (D). *(CMA, adapted)*

REQUIRED: The evidence least likely to satisfy the objective that recorded sales are valid and documented.

DISCUSSION: Documentation should exist to provide evidence that valid orders were received, goods sold were shipped, and goods shipped were billed. These documents include examining customer purchase orders, bills of lading and other shipping documents, and copies of billings (invoices) mailed to customers. The approval of credit, however, would not assure that a sale had been made.

Answers (A) and (C) are incorrect because bills of lading and other shipping documents are evidence that goods sold were shipped. Answer (B) is incorrect because a customer purchase order is evidence that an order was received.

27. The most reliable forms of documentary evidence are those documents that are

A. Prenumbered.

B. Internally generated.

C. Issued sequentially.

D. Authorized by a responsible official.

The correct answer is (D). *(CMA, adapted)*

REQUIRED: The most reliable documentary evidence.

DISCUSSION: Documentary evidence from internal sources is more likely to be competent (valid and relevant) if it is generated subject to effective internal controls. Authorization by appropriate parties is essential to effective control.

Answers (A) and (C) are incorrect because the use of prenumbered and sequentially issued documents is a good internal control tool, but such documents may be within the control of an employee who is perpetrating fraud. Answer (B) is incorrect because internally generated documents are easily available to those attempting to commit fraud.

28. An auditor should be able to collect and evaluate documentary evidence. When evaluating and interpreting evidence, the auditor must be concerned about drawing unwarranted conclusions. An example of a valid conclusion is

A. Correct inventory valuation determined from observation of physical inventory counts.

B. Proper accounts payable cutoff at year-end determined from a review of raw materials requisitions.

C. Existence of a company car determined from the examination of a paid invoice.

D. Client ownership determined from outside inquiries about consigned goods.

The correct answer is (D). *(CMA, adapted)*

REQUIRED: The valid conclusion regarding the interpretation of audit evidence.

DISCUSSION: What constitutes sufficient evidence to provide a reasonable basis for the auditor's opinion is a matter of professional judgment. Attention to the unique circumstances of a specific audit are necessary because obtaining convincing rather than merely persuasive evidence is often not feasible. Evidence is more likely to be reliable if it is gathered from independent sources external to the auditee. Evidence is also more likely to be reliable if it is obtained directly through the auditor's own physical examination, observation, or inspection. Obtaining information regarding client ownership of consigned goods from outside parties should be evidence of sufficient weight to reach a valid conclusion regarding ownership (an assertion about rights).

Answer (A) is incorrect because observing inventory primarily tests the existence assertion. Other procedures are required to test the valuation assertion. Answer (B) is incorrect because a review of raw materials requisitions would not be a means of determining the proper cutoff of accounts payable at year-end. Answer (C) is incorrect because the purchase invoice is not sufficient evidence that a car exists; the auditor should also examine the car and determine that the serial number of the car is the same as on the invoice.

29. Which of the following audit tests or procedures would generally be performed during year-end field work?

A. Examination of employee authorizations for medical insurance withholdings.

B. Count of petty cash.

C. Examination of lease agreements.

D. Analysis of a cutoff bank statement.

The correct answer is (D). *(CMA, adapted)*

REQUIRED: The audit test normally performed during year-end field work.

DISCUSSION: A cutoff bank statement is a bank statement requested in the middle of a month to be picked up directly by the auditor. The purpose of obtaining a cutoff bank statement is to determine that there were no unrecorded checks. The unrecorded checks would not be listed as outstanding at year-end but would be returned with the cutoff bank statement. Thus, the cutoff bank statement helps determine the cash balance at year-end and must be part of the year-end work.

Answers (A) and (C) are incorrect because neither has the year-end urgency that cutoff bank statements do. Answer (B) is incorrect because counting of petty cash is not as urgent at year-end since the amounts involved are usually small.

30. The five broad categories of financial statement assertions include all of the following except

A. Existence or occurrence.

B. Materiality or risk.

C. Rights and obligations.

D. Valuation or allocation.

The correct answer is (B). *(CMA, adapted)*

REQUIRED: The item not a category of financial statement assertions.

DISCUSSION: According to AU 326, assertions are explicit or implicit management representations contained in the financial statements. Audit objectives are determined with regard to these assertions. Materiality or risk is not one of the assertions. "Audit risk is the risk that the auditor may unknowingly fail to appropriately modify the opinion on financial statements that are materially misstated. The concept of materiality recognizes that some matters, either individually or in the aggregate, are important for fair presentation of financial statements in conformity with GAAP, while others are not" (AU 312). Thus, materiality is the threshold for recognition of items included in assertions, and audit risk is the degree of probability that assertions are materially misstated.

Answers (A), (C), and (D) are incorrect because financial statement assertions are classified as follows: (1) existence or occurrence, (2) completeness, (3) rights and obligations, (4) valuation or allocation, and (5) presentation and disclosure.

31. A proof of cash used by an auditor

A. Proves that the client's year-end balance of cash is fairly stated.

B. Confirms that the client has properly separated the custody function from the recording function with respect to cash.

C. Validates that the client's bank did not make an error during the period being examined.

D. Determines if there were any unauthorized disbursements or unrecorded deposits for the given period.

The correct answer is (D). *(CMA, adapted)*

REQUIRED: The function of the proof of cash.

DISCUSSION: The proof of cash is a four-column worksheet that consists of a bank reconciliation in the first and fourth columns and a reconciliation of receipts and disbursements in the middle two columns. Thus the reconciliations are both vertical and horizontal. They are horizontal in that the beginning figures plus receipts and minus disbursements equal ending figures. Accordingly, unauthorized disbursements and unrecorded deposits are detected by using a proof of cash (they would not normally be detected by using a bank reconciliation).

Answer (A) is incorrect because a proof of cash reconciles only one bank account, and the fairness of the year-end cash balance is determined by schedules of bank transfers, accessibility of cash in foreign countries, cash on hand, etc. Answer (B) is incorrect because the worksheet reconciles only cash flows and balances and provides no insight as to the separation of functional responsibilities. Answer (C) is incorrect because a proof of cash merely detects and reconciles client and bank errors. One can be prepared when there are bank (or client) errors.

32. All of the following are examples of substantive tests to verify the valuation of net accounts receivable except the

A. Recomputation of the allowance for bad debts.

B. Inspection of accounts for current versus noncurrent status in the statement of financial position.

C. Inspection of the accounts receivable aging schedule.

D. Comparison of the allowance for bad debts with past periods.

The correct answer is (B). *(CMA, adapted)*

REQUIRED: The item not a substantive test.

DISCUSSION: A substantive test is a test of details or an analytical procedure performed to detect material misstatements in the account balance, transaction class, and disclosure components of the financial statements. A test of controls is a test directed toward the design or operation of an internal control policy or procedure to assess its effectiveness in preventing or detecting material misstatements in a financial statement assertion. An external auditor considers the internal controls to determine necessary auditing procedures. The nature, timing, and extent of substantive tests may therefore depend on the effectiveness of the internal controls. The inspection of accounts to determine whether they are current is a matter of classification, not valuation.

Answers (A), (C), and (D) are incorrect because each tests the amount of an account balance to determine whether it is misstated.

33. In verifying a November 30 sales cutoff date, an auditor would be most concerned with comparing records of

A. November cash receipts with December bank deposits.

B. November purchases with December shipments.

C. November accounts receivable with November sales.

D. November sales with November shipping documents.

The correct answer is (D). *(CMA, adapted)*

REQUIRED: The concern when verifying sales cutoff dates.

DISCUSSION: When the auditor analyzes transactions that occurred within a few days before and after the end of the month, (s)he can determine if they have been recorded in the proper accounting periods. The cutoff test compares sales records with sales invoices, purchase orders, and shipping documents. Thus, a comparison of November sales with November shipping documents should help assure that goods recorded as sold were actually shipped.

Answer (A) is incorrect because a cash cutoff is not at issue. Answer (B) is incorrect because purchases do not necessarily correspond to sales. Answer (C) is incorrect because the accounts receivable do not include cash sales or accounts already settled.

34. In performing an audit, which one of the following procedures would be considered a substantive test?

A. Comparing last year's interest expense with this year's interest expense.

B. Comparing signatures on checks with the signatures of authorized check signers.

C. Reviewing initials on receiving documents.

D. Reviewing procedures, followed in receiving, depositing, and disbursing of cash.

The correct answer is (A). *(CMA, adapted)*

REQUIRED: The substantive test.

DISCUSSION: Substantive tests are examinations of transactions and account balances to determine that (1) all transactions occurring during the period are properly reflected in the financial statements, and (2) the statements reflect only the transactions that occurred during the period. Substantive tests are in contrast with compliance tests undertaken to determine that internal controls are operating as prescribed and are effective. Comparing last year's interest expense with this year's interest expense is a form of analytical procedure that will point out any unreasonable relationships or amounts.

Answers (B), (C), and (D) are incorrect because comparing signatures on checks with the signatures of authorized check signers, reviewing initials on receiving documents, and reviewing procedures, followed in receiving, depositing, and disbursing of cash are compliance tests. They determine whether control procedures are being followed.

35. The most reliable form of evidence, other than subsequent cash receipts, concerning the validity of a note receivable balance is a(n)

A. Bill of lading.

B. Confirmation.

C. Customer purchase order.

D. Sales invoice.

The correct answer is (B). *(CMA, adapted)*

REQUIRED: The second most reliable form of evidence.

DISCUSSION: Although subsequent collection is the best form of evidence as to the validity of a note receivable, a confirmation from a customer (or borrower) is the next best evidence. It provides independent, external verification of the balance.

Answer (A) is incorrect because a bill of lading relates to inventory, not notes receivable. Answer (C) is incorrect because a purchase order indicates that a customer placed an order, not that the balance is unpaid. Answer (D) is incorrect because a sales invoice is an internally generated document. A confirmation is external to the auditee.

36. To have sufficient, competent evidential matter, an auditor must have both underlying accounting data and corroborating information. Corroborating information includes

A. Books of original entry.

B. Informal and memorandum records such as worksheets.

C. General and subsidiary ledgers.

D. Documents such as checks and invoices.

The correct answer is (D). *(CMA, adapted)*

REQUIRED: The item included in the category of corroborating information.

DISCUSSION: Audit evidence may be viewed as consisting of the underlying accounting data and corroborating information. Underlying accounting data consist of the books of original entry (e.g., journals and registers), the general and subsidiary ledgers, related accounting manuals, and records such as work sheets and spreadsheets supporting cost allocations, computations, and reconciliations, often in electronic form. Corroborating evidential matter includes both written and electronic information (e.g., checks, invoices, EFTs, contracts, and minutes of meetings); confirmations and other written representations by knowledgeable people; information obtained by the auditor from inquiry, observation, inspection, and physical examination; and other information developed by, or available to, the auditor that permits conclusions through valid reasoning (AU 326).

Answers (A), (B), and (C) are incorrect because books of original entry, informal and memorandum records, and ledgers are the underlying data.

37. Which of the following statements regarding the confirmation of accounts payable is true?

A. The confirmation of accounts payable must be done exclusively by the internal audit staff.

B. The confirmation of accounts payable contributes little or nothing to determining whether unrecorded accounts payable exist.

C. The confirmation of accounts payable must be done exclusively by the independent auditor.

D. The confirmation of accounts payable is an important method of establishing the existence of unrecorded accounts payable.

The correct answer is (B). *(CMA, adapted)*

REQUIRED: The true statement concerning the confirmation of accounts payable.

DISCUSSION: The confirmation of accounts payable asks creditors to confirm the amount owed to them. If there are unrecorded liabilities, the identities of the creditors are unknown and they cannot be sent confirmation.

Answer (A) is incorrect because GAAP require the independent auditor to perform the confirmation procedures. Answer (C) is incorrect because the independent auditor can receive direct assistance from the internal auditor, as long as the independent auditor maintains control over confirmation requests and responses. Answer (D) is incorrect because confirmations are useless when the auditor does not know the identity of the creditors.

38. Confirming accounts receivable is an audit procedure that generally is performed exclusively by the independent auditor or by

A. The internal auditor exclusively.

B. Regulatory auditors exclusively.

C. Both independent and internal auditors.

D. Neither independent nor internal auditors.

The correct answer is (C). *(CMA, adapted)*

REQUIRED: The type of auditor who confirms accounts receivable as an audit procedure.

DISCUSSION: AU 330 states that an independent auditor should maintain control over the confirmation requests and responses while performing the confirmation procedures. However, the need to maintain control does not preclude direct assistance from the internal auditors.

Answers (A) and (B) are incorrect because an independent auditor must maintain control over the confirmation procedures. Answer (D) is incorrect because account receivable confirmations are required unless the amount is immaterial, confirmations would be ineffective, or risk of misstatement based on other procedures is judged sufficiently low.

39. Which of the following statements best describes a positive request for confirmation of an accounts receivable balance?

A. The confirmee will be asked to indicate to the auditor the current balance in the account.

B. The confirmee will be asked to respond to the confirmation request only if the balance indicated in the request is incorrect.

C. The confirmee will be asked to inform the auditor whether the balance indicated in the request is correct and to respond regardless of whether such stated balance is correct.

D. The confirmee will be asked to indicate to the auditor the balance in his/her account only if it is positive (i.e., greater than zero).

The correct answer is (C). *(CMA, adapted)*

REQUIRED: The description of a positive confirmation for accounts receivable.

DISCUSSION: Positive confirmations are in contrast with negative confirmations, which request debtors to notify the independent auditor only if the debtor disagrees with the client's receivable balance. Positive confirmations request debtors to confirm whether the receivable balance is correct or incorrect.

Answers (A) and (D) are incorrect because a positive confirmation requests a response regarding the accuracy of the account as of the confirmation date regardless of the nature of the balance. Answer (B) is incorrect because it describes a negative confirmation.

E. Audit Sampling

40. In performing audit tests, the auditor may use either nonstatistical or statistical sampling. The critical difference between the two types of sampling is that

A. The sampling plan for nonstatistical sampling eliminates procedures required for statistical sampling.

B. Statistical sampling enables quantification and control of sampling risk.

C. Nonsampling risk is lower in statistical sampling.

D. Statistical sampling eliminates both sampling and nonsampling risk.

The correct answer is (B). *(CMA, adapted)*

REQUIRED: The critical difference between nonstatistical and statistical sampling.

DISCUSSION: AU 350, *Audit Sampling*, discusses both statistical and nonstatistical sampling. Statistical sampling allows the auditor to control and measure (quantify) risk associated with observing only a portion of a population. However, the choice of nonstatistical or statistical sampling does not directly affect the auditor's decisions about the auditing procedures to be applied, the competence of the evidential matter obtained with respect to the individual items in the sample, or the actions that might be taken in light of the nature and causes of particular errors. Either approach, when properly applied, can provide sufficient competent evidential matter.

Answer (A) is incorrect because the auditor may use random sampling or other statistical sampling procedures but select specific items on a nonrandom basis. Answer (C) is incorrect because nonsampling risk is the same regardless of the method of sampling used. Answer (D) is incorrect because sampling risk exists with statistical sampling, but the degree of that risk can be measured. Nonsampling risk cannot be eliminated regardless of the methods used.

41. Which one of the following statements concerning sampling risk and nonsampling risk is correct?

A. Neither sampling risk nor nonsampling risk can be reduced by the auditor.

B. Sampling risk, but not nonsampling risk, can be reduced by the auditor.

C. Nonsampling risk, but not sampling risk, can be reduced by the auditor.

D. Both sampling risk and nonsampling risk can be reduced by the auditor.

The correct answer is (D). *(CMA, adapted)*

REQUIRED: The true statement about sampling risk and nonsampling risk.

DISCUSSION: When a test is restricted to a sample, sampling risk arises from the possibility that the auditor's conclusions may be different from those reached if the test were applied in the same way to all items in the account balance or class of transactions. A sample may thus contain more or fewer monetary misstatements or control deviations than exist in the population as a whole (AU 350). Nonsampling risk includes all other aspects of audit risk, such as selecting inappropriate procedures or failing to recognize misstatements in a document that is examined, which would make the procedure ineffective even if applied to all items in the population. Sampling risk can be reduced, for example, by increasing the sample size. Nonsampling risk can be reduced by adequate planning and supervision.

Answers (A), (B), and (C) are incorrect because both types of risk can be reduced by the auditor.

42. Alpha risk in statistical sampling is

A. Related to nonsampling risk.

B. The risk that a material misstatement will occur in a financial statement assertion and the audit will not detect it.

C. The risk of deciding a book balance is materially misstated when it is fairly stated.

D. The risk of selecting a sample that is too small.

The correct answer is (C). *(CMA, adapted)*

REQUIRED: The true statement about alpha risk.

DISCUSSION: Rejection of a correct hypothesis is an alpha or type I error. Acceptance of an incorrect hypothesis is a beta or type II error. Rejecting a book balance as materially misstated when it is correct is an alpha error. Because the auditor will seek additional audit evidence regarding a rejected hypothesis, an alpha error is not as serious as a beta error. If an account balance is incorrectly accepted as fair based upon a sample (a beta error), additional audit work will probably be minimal and the chances of exposing the mistake will be correspondingly reduced.

Answer (A) is incorrect because an alpha error may also arise from sampling risk. Answer (B) is incorrect because AU 312 and AU 319 apply the term detection risk to this kind of risk. It is a beta risk. Answer (D) is incorrect because selecting too small a sample, that is, misapplying a sampling technique, is a form of nonsampling risk. It may result in either an alpha or a beta error.

43. The probability that an auditor's conclusion based on a sample might be different from the conclusion based on an audit of the entire population is the concept of

A. Sampling risk.

B. Control risk.

C. Overreliance.

D. Tolerable rate.

The correct answer is (A). *(CMA, adapted)*

REQUIRED: The term meaning a conclusion based on a sample might be different if based on the entire population.

DISCUSSION: Audit risk includes sampling and nonsampling risk. Sampling risk arises from the possibility that the auditor's conclusions based on a sample may differ from the conclusions reached if the test were applied in the same way to the entire population. Sampling risk varies inversely with sample size.

Answer (B) is incorrect because control risk is the risk that a material misstatement will not be prevented or detected on a timely basis by the entity's controls. Answer (C) is incorrect because the risk of overreliance is an archaic term in the AICPA's auditing pronouncements. It has been replaced by the risk of assessing control risk too low. Answer (D) is incorrect because the tolerable rate is the maximum rate of deviations from a prescribed control that the auditor is willing to accept without changing an assessment of control risk for the assertions related to the control (AU 350).

44. The upper precision limit in statistical sampling is

A. A statistical measure, at a specified reliability level, of the maximum rate of occurrence of an attribute.

B. The percentage of items in a sample that possess a particular attribute.

C. The percentage of items in a population that possess a particular attribute.

D. The maximum rate of exception that the auditor would be willing to accept in the population without altering the planned reliance on the attribute.

The correct answer is (A). *(CMA, adapted)*

REQUIRED: The true statement about the upper precision limit.

DISCUSSION: Precision (the confidence interval) is a range about the sample statistic that is expected to contain the true value of the population at the specified level of reliability (the confidence level) set by the auditor. The size of the precision interval is determined by the acceptable tolerable misstatement or rate of deviations and is based on materiality considerations. The upper precision limit is a measure of the maximum acceptable amount of a variable or rate of occurrence of an attribute.

Answer (B) is incorrect because a sample statistic is the percentage of items in a sample that possess a particular attribute. Answer (C) is incorrect because a population parameter is the percentage of items in a population that possess a particular attribute. Answer (D) is incorrect because the tolerable rate is the maximum rate of exception that the auditor would be willing to accept in the population without altering the planned reliance on the attribute.

45. When the auditor performs substantive tests of balances, the primary concern is

A. Assessing control risk too high.

B. Assessing control risk too low.

C. Incorrect rejection of an account balance.

D. Incorrect acceptance of an account balance.

The correct answer is (D). *(CMA, adapted)*

REQUIRED: The auditor's primary concern when performing substantive tests of account balances.

DISCUSSION: An auditor's primary concern when performing a substantive test is that an account balance will be accepted when it is materially misstated. Such a misstatement could be costly because the financial statement might not be fairly presented. Alternatively, if an account balance is incorrectly rejected, the result will be to expand testing. This result might be costly and inefficient but should not impair the effectiveness of the audit.

Answers (A) and (B) are incorrect because they both relate to sampling risk in performing tests of controls. Answer (C) is incorrect because rejection of an account balance will result in an inefficient audit, but that is not as severe as an ineffective audit.

46. Attribute sampling in statistical sampling is

A. A method of sampling that divides the population into strata and then selects random samples from the strata.

B. A procedure used to determine an estimated occurrence rate of a particular characteristic in a population.

C. A method of sampling in which individual items are drawn at random from a population so that each sample of a given size has an equal chance of being selected.

D. A procedure in which each characteristic selected permits a specified probability of locating an occurrence in a population.

The correct answer is (B). *(CMA, adapted)*

REQUIRED: The true statement about attribute sampling.

DISCUSSION: Attribute sampling asks the question, "How many?" It is used primarily to test controls. The objective is to determine an estimated occurrence rate of deviations and to determine whether estimated rates are within an acceptable range.

Answer (A) is incorrect because it describes stratified random sampling. Answer (C) is incorrect because it describes simple random sampling. Answer (D) is incorrect because it is a nonsense answer.

47. A sample selected so that every combination of the same number of items in the population has an equal probability of selection is a

A. Systematic sample.

B. Random sample.

C. Stratified sample.

D. Block sample.

The correct answer is (B). *(CMA, adapted)*

REQUIRED: The sample selected so that every combination of the same number of items in the population has an equal probability of selection.

DISCUSSION: Probability sampling is possible if each item in the population has a known and nonzero chance of being drawn. A simple random sample is a special case of probability sampling in which every combination of sample items equal to n has the same probability of being chosen. Simple random sampling may occur with or without replacement.

Answer (A) is incorrect because systematic sampling selects a starting point and then takes every nth item in the population. Except for selection of the starting point, this process is not random. Answer (C) is incorrect because stratifying a population means dividing it into subpopulations, thereby permitting application of different sampling techniques to each stratum. Larger or more important items have a greater chance of selection. Answer (D) is incorrect because a block (cluster) sample selects every item in a certain block and no items in other blocks. If blocks of homogeneous samples are selected, the sample will be biased.

48. In determining the sample size for a test of controls using attribute sampling, an auditor would be least concerned with the

A. Expected rate of occurrence.

B. Results of substantive audit procedures.

C. Upper precision limit.

D. Acceptable risk of assessing control risk too low.

The correct answer is (B). *(CMA, adapted)*

REQUIRED: The auditor's least concern in determining sample size for a test of controls using attribute sampling.

DISCUSSION: Although some substantive tests may be made before or concurrent with tests of controls, the essential purpose of the latter is to provide evidence that may allow the auditor to assess control risk at less than the maximum. Such an assessment may permit the auditor to reduce the effort subsequently devoted to substantive testing. Hence, sample size is least likely to be influenced by results of substantive tests not yet performed.

Answer (A) is incorrect because attribute sampling measures error rates in a population rather than values. Answer (C) is incorrect because precision is an interval about the sample statistic within which the true value of the population is expected to fall. Answer (D) is incorrect because inaccurate assessments of inherent risk and control risk lead to a miscalculation of the acceptable level of detection risk and therefore of the degree of assurance to be provided by substantive testing.

49. A sample consisting of contiguous transactions in the population is a

A. Systematic sample.

B. Random sample.

C. Haphazard sample.

D. Block sample.

The correct answer is (D). *(CMA, adapted)*

REQUIRED: The sample consisting of contiguous transactions in the population.

DISCUSSION: Block sampling (also termed cluster sampling) selects groups of items rather than individual items. For this plan to be effective, dispersion within clusters should be greater than dispersion between clusters. An example of block sampling is the inclusion in the sample of all cash disbursements for the months of May and September. If blocks of homogeneous samples are selected, the sample will be biased.

Answer (A) is incorrect because a systematic sample selects every nth item in the population, not contiguous items. Answer (B) is incorrect because, in a simple random sample, every sample of size n has an equal chance of being selected. Answer (C) is incorrect because a haphazard sample is a judgment (nonstatistical) sample.

50. A sample consisting of every nth item in the population is a

A. Systematic sample.

B. Random sample.

C. Stratified sample.

D. Haphazard sample.

The correct answer is (A). *(CMA, adapted)*

REQUIRED: The sample in which every nth item in the population is selected.

DISCUSSION: Systematic sampling is accomplished by selecting a random start and taking every nth item in the population. The value of n is computed by dividing the number in the population by the size of the sample. The random start should be in the first interval. A systematic sample can be effectively used whenever the items in the population are already prenumbered in order (such as sales invoices to be audited).

Answer (B) is incorrect because, in a simple random sample, every sample of size n has an equal chance of being selected. Answer (C) is incorrect because, in a stratified sample, items in different strata (items of different sizes) have different chances of being selected. Answer (D) is incorrect because a haphazard sample is a judgment (nonstatistical) sample.

51. If fraud or gross error is suspected in the population, the auditor would most likely use

A. Variables sampling.

B. Attribute sampling.

C. Discovery sampling.

D. Dollar-unit sampling.

The correct answer is (C). *(CMA, adapted)*

REQUIRED: The type of sampling most likely used when fraud or gross error is suspected.

DISCUSSION: Discovery sampling is used when looking for critical deviations or fraud. As in acceptance sampling, the objective is to be able to state that the deviation rate is below a certain level with a stated degree of confidence. If the auditor finds one critical error, however, (s)he stops sampling and takes appropriate action because the presumption regarding critical deviations is that none should exist. In other words, one discovery is enough to end the use of the technique.

Answer (A) is incorrect because variables sampling is used when sampling for amounts, not an attribute such as fraud. Answer (B) is incorrect because attribute sampling is used to determine the overall deviation rate in a population. It would not be used in the case of expected fraud because the auditor is not concerned with the rate of fraud; even a single episode of fraud is unacceptable. Answer (D) is incorrect because it is a combination of attribute and variables sampling.

52. When the auditor performs tests of controls, the primary concern is

A. Incorrect acceptance of an account balance.

B. Incorrect rejection of an account balance.

C. Assessing control risk too low.

D. Assessing control risk too high.

The correct answer is (C). *(CMA, adapted)*

REQUIRED: The primary concern in tests of controls.

DISCUSSION: An auditor's primary concern when testing controls is that (s)he will assess control risk too low. This risk relates to the effectiveness of the audit because it may incorrectly lead to a reduction in the audit effort devoted to substantive tests.

Answers (A) and (B) are incorrect because they both relate to sampling risk for substantive testing. Answer (D) is incorrect because assessing control risk too high affects the efficiency, not the effectiveness, of the audit. The result is likely to be an increase in the effort devoted to substantive tests.

53. The tolerable rate of occurrence in statistical sampling is

A. A statistical measure, at a specified reliability level, of the maximum rate of occurrence of an attribute.

B. The percentage of items in a sample that possess a particular attribute.

C. The percentage of items in a population that possess a particular attribute.

D. The maximum rate of exception that the auditor would be willing to accept in the population without altering the planned reliance on the attribute.

The correct answer is (D). *(CMA, adapted)*

REQUIRED: The true statement about the tolerable rate of occurrence.

DISCUSSION: The tolerable (to the auditor) rate is the maximum rate at which the auditor would still believe the item measured to be reliable. For example, if the rate of deviations in the population is believed to be 3% (expected rate) and a maximum rate of 5% (tolerable rate) is acceptable, the auditor might set the precision equal to plus or minus 2%.

Answer (A) is incorrect because it describes the upper precision limit. Answer (B) is incorrect because it describes a sample statistic. Answer (C) is incorrect because it describes a population parameter.

54. An auditor may use either of two statistical sampling approaches in substantive testing, probability-proportional-to-size (PPS) sampling and classical variables sampling. PPS sampling is primarily applicable in testing for

A. The number of errors in a year-end sales cutoff.

B. An overstatement of accounts receivable.

C. A credit balance in accounts receivable.

D. An understatement of accounts payable.

The correct answer is (B). *(CMA, adapted)*

REQUIRED: The situation in which probability-proportional-to-size (PPS) sampling is appropriate.

DISCUSSION: PPS sampling (dollar-unit sampling) is a modified version of attribute sampling applied to dollar amounts. It uses the dollar as the sampling unit. PPS sampling is appropriate for testing account balances, such as those for inventory and receivables, in which some items may be far larger than others in the population. In effect, it stratifies the population because the larger account balances have a greater chance of being selected. PPS is most useful if few misstatements are expected and overstatement is more likely than understatement. One disadvantage of PPS sampling is that it is designed to detect overstatements. It is not effective for estimating understatements.

Answer (A) is incorrect because PPS sampling tests account balances for dollar amounts of misstatements, not numbers of misstatements. Traditional attribute sampling tests for error rates. Answers (C) and (D) are incorrect because PPS sampling is not primarily designed to handle understatements effectively.

55. An auditor would use variables sampling to

A. Determine the total estimated value of ending merchandise inventory.

B. Determine the number of inventory items improperly costed.

C. Determine how often credit sales of a certain magnitude were not approved.

D. Estimate how often sales invoices were not verified for mathematical accuracy.

The correct answer is (A). *(CMA, adapted)*

REQUIRED: The circumstances in which variables sampling should be used.

DISCUSSION: Variables sampling is used to estimate a variable, such as an account balance. Attribute sampling is concerned with binary (yes/no) propositions. For example, attribute sampling is used to ascertain whether some attribute of internal control, such as the presence of two signatures on a check, is in place and operating effectively.

Answers (B), (C), and (D) are incorrect because each involves a binary proposition for which estimation of an error rate by attribute sampling is appropriate.

F. Compilation and Review

56. Other than a full financial statement audit, which is the highest level of assurance that an accountant provides regarding the financial statements of a nonpublic entity?

A. A review.

B. A confirmation.

C. A compilation.

D. A submission of unaudited financial statements meeting only minimum requirements.

The correct answer is (A). *(Publisher)*

REQUIRED: The highest level of assurance provided by an accountant other than an audit.

DISCUSSION: An accountant may provide two levels of service below that of a full audit: a review and a compilation. The highest level of assurance, other than an audit, is a review. A review consists principally of inquiries of company personnel and analytical procedures applied to the financial data. A review does not include an evaluation of internal control, tests of transactions and account balances, or other auditing procedures.

Answer (B) is incorrect because a confirmation is a nonsense term in this context; there is no specific level of service by this name offered by accountants. Answer (C) is incorrect because a compilation is the lowest level of service with which an accountant may be associated. It results in the expression of no assurance. Answer (D) is incorrect because an accountant may not submit unaudited statements unless, as a minimum, (s)he complies with the requirements of a compilation.

57. Which of the following steps would an accountant perform when conducting a review but not a compilation of financial statements?

A. Test transactions and account balances.

B. Evaluate internal control.

C. Check clerical accuracy of financial statements.

D. Obtain a representation letter from management.

The correct answer is (D). *(Publisher)*

REQUIRED: The audit step that an accountant would perform during a review engagement but not during a compilation engagement.

DISCUSSION: When accountants undertake review engagements, they express limited assurance based upon inquiry and analytical procedures. These inquiries include obtaining a representation letter from management personnel. A compilation is a lower-level engagement in which the accountant compiles financial statements from client data without performing any auditing or other procedures.

Answer (A) is incorrect because testing transactions is not performed for either type of engagement. Answer (B) is incorrect because evaluating internal control is not a required step for either a review or a compilation. Answer (C) is incorrect because checking clerical accuracy is a requirement for all types of engagements.

G. Audit Reports

58. When two or more auditing firms participate in an audit, one firm should be the principal auditor. If the principal auditor refers to another auditor in a report on an audit that would otherwise result in an unqualified opinion, the audit report issued should contain a(n)

A. Unqualified opinion.

B. Qualified opinion.

C. Except for opinion.

D. Disclaimer of opinion.

The correct answer is (A). *(CMA, adapted)*

REQUIRED: The audit opinion expressed when the principal auditor refers to the work of another auditor.

DISCUSSION: The principal auditor must decide whether to accept responsibility for the work of the other auditors. If the principal auditor does not accept responsibility, the introductory and opinion paragraphs of the report should state the division of responsibility. However, the nature of the opinion expressed is not affected. If the statements are fairly presented in accordance with GAAP, an unqualified opinion is indicated (AU 543).

Answers (B), (C), and (D) are incorrect because referring to the work of another auditor does not preclude an unqualified opinion.

59. An external auditor discovers that a payroll supervisor of the firm being audited has misappropriated $10,000. The firm's total assets and before-tax net income are $14 million and $3 million, respectively. Assuming there are no other issues that will affect the report, the external auditor's report will most likely contain a(n)

A. Disclaimer of opinion.

B. Adverse opinion.

C. Scope qualification.

D. Unqualified opinion.

The correct answer is (D). *(CMA, adapted)*

REQUIRED: The opinion an auditor should express if a misappropriation is discovered.

DISCUSSION: An unqualified opinion will probably be expressed because $10,000 is not a material amount in this case. Also, the amount is known and will be disclosed as either a loss or as a receivable from a bonding company, etc.

Answer (A) is incorrect because a disclaimer of opinion is appropriate when the auditor has not performed an audit sufficient in scope to permit formation of an opinion or when the auditor is not independent of the client. Answer (B) is incorrect because adverse opinions are expressed when financial statements are materially misstated. Answer (C) is incorrect because a scope qualification refers to a restriction in necessary auditing procedures.

60. The auditor may express an unqualified opinion with an explanatory paragraph under all of the following circumstances except

A. A scope limitation resulting from the client's refusal to permit confirmation of receivables.

B. For uncertainty accounted for in conformity with generally accepted accounting principles.

C. A substantial doubt about an entity's going-concern status accounted for in conformity with generally accepted accounting principles.

D. An opinion based in part on the report of another auditor.

The correct answer is (A). *(CMA, adapted)*

REQUIRED: The item that does not warrant an unqualified opinion with an explanatory paragraph.

DISCUSSION: Restrictions on the audit may be imposed by the client or by circumstances, such as the timing of the work, inadequacy of the accounting records, or an inability to obtain sufficient competent evidence. They result in either a qualified opinion or a disclaimer. When restrictions that significantly limit the scope of the audit are imposed by the client, the auditor normally should disclaim an opinion (AU 508).

Answer (B) is incorrect because, absent a scope limitation or a departure from GAAP, an uncertainty does not preclude an unqualified opinion. Moreover, an explanatory paragraph regarding an uncertainty is permitted but not required. Answers (C) and (D) are incorrect because an auditor who expresses an unqualified opinion must include explanatory language in the standard report when the opinion is based in part on the report of another auditor, when there is substantial doubt about the entity's ability to continue as a going concern, when a material change in accounting principles or in the method of their application has occurred between periods, and when certain other circumstances exist.

61. A firm wants to obtain an unqualified opinion from its external auditor. Which one of the following situations would most likely lead to a firm's external auditor's issuance of a qualified opinion, assuming the amounts involved are material?

A. The client agreed to disclose illegal kickbacks in the financial statements.

B. The client's financial statements reflected the use of an accounting principle that had substantial authoritative support but was not an officially established principle, and the external auditor agreed with the client's presentation.

C. The client changed the method of accounting for machinery depreciation from the units-of-production method to the sum-of-the-years'-digits method without providing reasonable justification.

D. The external auditor was unable to determine with certainty the fairness of the allowance for doubtful accounts using normal procedures because of the large volume of customer accounts; consequently, extended procedures were employed by the external auditor.

The correct answer is (C). *(CMA, adapted)*

REQUIRED: The situation most likely to require a qualified opinion.

DISCUSSION: The opinion may be qualified as the result of an accounting change when the new principle is not generally accepted, the method of accounting for the change is not in conformity with GAAP, or management has not provided reasonable justification for the change.

Answer (A) is incorrect because financial statements are fairly presented when illegal kickbacks are properly disclosed in the financial statements. Answer (B) is incorrect because principles with substantial authoritative support are GAAP even though they are not officially established [category (a) in the hierarchy]. Answer (D) is incorrect because the auditor can be satisfied with the allowance for doubtful accounts using extended (other than normal) audit procedures.

62. If the financial statements contain a departure from an official pronouncement of the Financial Accounting Standards Board that has a material effect on the financial statements, the auditor must express a(n)

A. Adverse opinion.

B. Qualified opinion.

C. Disclaimer of opinion.

D. An adverse opinion or a qualified opinion.

The correct answer is (D). *(CMA, adapted)*

REQUIRED: The type of opinion an auditor must express when financial statements contain a material departure from an official pronouncement of the FASB.

DISCUSSION: A qualified opinion states that the financial statements are fairly presented except for the effects of a certain matter. A qualified opinion is expressed when the statements contain a material, unjustified departure from GAAP, but only if an adverse opinion is not appropriate. An adverse opinion is expressed when the financial statements, taken as a whole, are not presented fairly in accordance with GAAP.

Answers (A) and (B) are incorrect because a departure from GAAP may justify either a qualified or an adverse opinion, depending on the circumstances. Answer (C) is incorrect because a disclaimer states that the auditor does not express an opinion. A disclaimer is not appropriate given a material departure from GAAP.

63. If the financial statements taken as a whole are not presented fairly in conformity with generally accepted accounting principles, the auditor must express a(n)

A. Unqualified opinion.

B. Qualified opinion.

C. Except for opinion.

D. Adverse opinion.

The correct answer is (D). *(CMA, adapted)*

REQUIRED: The opinion if the statements as a whole are not presented fairly in conformity with GAAP.

DISCUSSION: An auditor must express an adverse opinion when the financial statements taken as a whole are not presented fairly in conformity with GAAP. "An adverse opinion states that the financial statements do not present fairly the financial position or the results of operations or cash flows in conformity with GAAP" (AU 508).

Answer (A) is incorrect because an unqualified opinion can be expressed only when statements are fairly presented in accordance with GAAP. Answers (B) and (C) are incorrect because a qualified (except for) opinion is expressed when, except for the matter to which the qualification relates, the financial statements are presented fairly, in all material respects, in conformity with GAAP. Possible bases for a qualified opinion are a scope limitation not sufficient for a disclaimer, a lack of sufficient competent evidence, or a material departure from GAAP that the auditor concludes is not a basis for an adverse opinion.

64. When an auditor for some reason is not independent of the client, the report issued should be a(n)

A. Unqualified report.

B. Unqualified report with explanatory language.

C. Qualified report.

D. Disclaimer.

The correct answer is (D). *(CMA, adapted)*

REQUIRED: The appropriate report when an auditor lacks independence.

DISCUSSION: A disclaimer of opinion states that the auditor does not express an opinion. It is appropriate when the auditor has not performed an audit sufficient in scope to permit formation of an opinion or when the auditor is not independent of the client. A disclaimer is not appropriate when the financial statements contain material departures from GAAP (AU 508).

Answers (A) and (B) are incorrect because an auditor must be independent to express an unqualified opinion. Answer (C) is incorrect because a qualified opinion states that the financial statements are fairly presented except for the effects of a certain matter. It cannot be expressed when the auditor lacks independence.

APPENDIX A: ETHICS AS TESTED ON THE CMA/CFM EXAMS

6 pages of outline
17 multiple-choice questions

ETHICS

Questions containing ethical issues can appear on any part of the examination, presented within the context of specific subject areas. Candidates should be familiar with:

> *Statement on Management Accounting Number 1C (Revised),* "Standards of Ethical Conduct for Practitioners of Management Accounting and Financial Management," *Institute of Management Accountants, Montvale, N.J., 1997.*

Current references to business ethics are also found in recent periodicals and newspapers.

A. Ethics

1. Definitions

a. Corporate ethics -- an organization's policies and standards established to assure certain kinds of behavior by its members

b. Individual ethics -- principles of conduct adhered to by an individual

2. Increased Concern for Business Ethics

a. Electrical-equipment conspiracy cases in 1960 caused public concern and creation of the Business Ethics Advisory Council (BEAC) in 1961 under the Secretary of Commerce.

b. BEAC pointed out areas needing self-evaluation by the business community:

1) General business understanding of ethical issues

2) Compliance with laws

3) Conflicts of interest

4) Entertainment and gift expenses

5) Relations with customers and suppliers. Should gifts or kickbacks be given or accepted?

6) Social responsibilities

c. BEAC's recommendations generated business interest, especially from big business, in problems of ethical behavior.

3. **Factors That May Lead to Unethical Behavior**
    a. In any normal population, some people have less than desirable levels of ethics. If these people hold leadership positions, they will adversely influence subordinates.
    b. Organizational factors may lead to unethical behavior.
        1) Pressures for short-run performance in decentralized return on investment (ROI) centers may inhibit ethical behavior.
        2) Emphasis on strict adherence to chain-of-command authority may provide excuses for ignoring ethics when following orders.
        3) Informal work-group loyalties may subvert ethical behavior.
        4) Committee decision processes may make it possible to abstain from or dodge ethical obligations.
    c. External factors may lead to unethical behavior.
        1) Pressure of competition may compromise ethics in the interest of survival.
        2) Unethical behavior of others may force a compromise of ethics.
        3) Definitions of ethical behavior may vary from one culture to another.
            a) Bribes to overseas officials or buyers may be consistent with some countries' customary business practices, but such a practice is not considered ethical among U.S. purchasing agents.
                i) Bribes are now considered illegal under the Foreign Corrupt Practices Act.
            b) The propriety of superimposing our cultural ethical standards (by refusing to bribe) on another culture may be controversial.
4. **General Guides to Ethics**
    a. Golden Rule -- Do unto others as you would have others do unto you.
    b. Maximize good -- Act to provide the greatest good for the greatest number.
    c. Fairness -- Act in ways that are fair or just to all concerned.
    d. Maximize long-run outcomes -- Act to provide the best long-range benefits to society and its resources.
    e. General respect -- Act to respect the planet all humans share and the rights of others because corporate and individual decisions affect them.
5. **Simplified Criteria for Evaluating Ethical Behavior**
    a. Would this behavior be acceptable if people I respect knew I was doing this?
    b. What are the consequences of this behavior for myself, other employees, customers, and society?
6. Ethics are individual and personal, influenced by
    a. Life experiences (rewards for doing right, punishment for doing wrong)
    b. Friendship groups (professional associations, informal groups)
    c. Organizational pressures (responsibilities to superiors and the organization)

B. Codes of Ethical Conduct

1. An organization's code of ethical conduct is the established general value system the organization wishes to apply to its members' activities through
   a. Communicating organizational purposes and beliefs
   b. Establishing uniform ethical guidelines for members
      1) Including guidance on behavior for members in making decisions
2. Laws and written rules cannot cover all situations. However, organizations can benefit from having an established ethical code because it
   a. Effectively communicates acceptable values to all members
      1) Including recruits and subcontractors
   b. Provides a method of policing and disciplining members for violations
      1) Through review panels (formal)
      2) Through group pressure (informal)
   c. Establishes high standards against which individuals can measure their own performance
   d. Communicates to those outside the organization the value system from which the organization's members must not be asked to deviate
3. A typical code for accounting activities (note similarities to the Standards for the Professional Practice of Internal Auditing, GAAP, GAAS, etc.) holds that a financial manager must have
   a. Independence from conflicts of economic interest
   b. Independence from conflicts of professional interest
      1) Responsibility to present information fairly to shareholders/owners and not intentionally protect management
      2) Responsibility to present data to all appropriate managers and not play favorites with information or cover up bad news
      3) Responsibility to exercise an ethical presence in the conduct of professional activities
         a) Ensuring organizational compliance with spirit as well as letter of pertinent laws and regulations
         b) Conducting oneself according to the highest moral and legal standards
         c) Reporting to appropriate internal or external authority any illegal or fraudulent organizational act
   c. Integrity in not compromising professional values for the sake of personal goals
   d. Objectivity in presenting information, preparing reports, and making analyses

C. IMA Code of Ethics

1. The National Association of Accountants (now the Institute of Management Accountants or IMA), through its Management Accounting Practices Committee, issued a revised code of ethics for management accountants in April 1997. This code reflects the official position of the organization. Candidates are urged to study the provisions of the code closely because it is tested. The code is printed below and on the following page in its entirety. (Source: Statement on Management Accounting 1C (Revised), Objectives: Standards of Ethical Conduct for Practitioners of Management Accounting and Financial Management, April 1997, pp. 69-70). The mnemonic CCIO (competence, confidentiality, integrity, and objectivity) is useful. The final section, Resolution of Ethical Conflict, is especially significant.

STANDARDS OF ETHICAL CONDUCT FOR PRACTITIONERS OF MANAGEMENT ACCOUNTING AND FINANCIAL MANAGEMENT

Practitioners of management accounting and financial management have an obligation to the public, their profession, the organizations they serve, and themselves, to maintain the highest standards of ethical conduct. In recognition of this obligation, the Institute of Management Accountants has promulgated the following standards of ethical conduct for practitioners of management accounting and financial management. Adherence to these standards, both domestically and internationally, is integral to achieving the Objectives of Management Accounting. Practitioners of management accounting and financial management shall not commit acts contrary to these standards nor shall they condone the commission of such acts by others within their organizations.

Competence

Practitioners of management accounting and financial management have a responsibility to:

- *Maintain an appropriate level of professional competence by ongoing development of their knowledge and skills.*
- *Perform their professional duties in accordance with relevant laws, regulations, and technical standards.*
- *Prepare complete and clear reports and recommendations after appropriate analyses of relevant and reliable information.*

Confidentiality

Practitioners of management accounting and financial management have a responsibility to:

- *Refrain from disclosing confidential information acquired in the course of their work except when authorized, unless legally obligated to do so.*
- *Inform subordinates as appropriate regarding the confidentiality of information acquired in the course of their work and monitor their activities to assure the maintenance of that confidentiality.*
- *Refrain from using or appearing to use confidential information acquired in the course of their work for unethical or illegal advantage either personally or through third parties.*

Integrity

Practitioners of management accounting and financial management have a responsibility to:

- *Avoid actual or apparent conflicts of interest and advise all appropriate parties of any potential conflict.*
- *Refrain from engaging in any activity that would prejudice their ability to carry out their duties ethically.*
- *Refuse any gift, favor, or hospitality that would influence or would appear to influence their actions.*
- *Refrain from either actively or passively subverting the attainment of the organization's legitimate and ethical objectives.*
- *Recognize and communicate professional limitations or other constraints that would preclude responsible judgment or successful performance of an activity.*
- *Communicate unfavorable as well as favorable information and professional judgments or opinions.*
- *Refrain from engaging in or supporting any activity that would discredit the profession.*

Objectivity

Practitioners of management accounting and financial management have a responsibility to:

- *Communicate information fairly and objectively.*
- *Disclose fully all relevant information that could reasonably be expected to influence an intended user's understanding of the reports, comments, and recommendations presented.*

Resolution of Ethical Conflict

In applying the standards of ethical conduct, practitioners of management accounting and financial management may encounter problems in identifying unethical behavior or in resolving an ethical conflict. When faced with significant ethical issues, practitioners of management accounting and financial management should follow the established policies of the organization bearing on the resolution of such conflict. If these policies do not resolve the ethical conflict, such practitioners should consider the following courses of action:

- *Discuss such problems with the immediate superior except when it appears that the superior is involved, in which case the problem should be presented initially to the next higher managerial level. If satisfactory resolution cannot be achieved when the problem is initially presented, submit the issues to the next higher managerial level. If the immediate superior is the chief executive officer, or equivalent, the acceptable reviewing authority may be a group such as the audit committee, executive committee, board of directors, board of trustees, or owners. Contact with levels above the immediate superior should be initiated only with the superior's knowledge, assuming the superior is not involved. Except where legally prescribed, communication of such problems to authorities or individuals not employed or engaged by the organization is not considered appropriate.*
- *Clarify relevant ethical issues by confidential discussion with an objective advisor (e.g., IMA Ethics Counseling Service) to obtain a better understanding of possible courses of action.*
- *Consult your own attorney as to legal obligations and rights concerning the ethical conflict.*
- *If the ethical conflict still exists after exhausting all levels of internal review, there may be no other recourse on significant matters than to resign from the organization and to submit an informative memorandum to an appropriate representative of the organization. After resignation, depending on the nature of the ethical conflict, it may also be appropriate to notify other parties.*

D. Conflict of Interest

1. Conflict of interest is a conflict between the private and the official responsibilities of a person in a position of trust, sufficient to affect judgment, independence, or objectivity in conducting the affairs of the business.
2. **Examples of Conflict of Interest**
   a. Having a substantial financial interest in a supplier, customer, or distributor
   b. Using privileged information gained from one's official position to enter transactions for personal gain
3. **Methods for Control**
   a. Provide a code of conduct provision applying to conflicts of interest.
   b. Require full financial disclosure by managers.
   c. Require prior notification of any transaction that may raise conflict of interest.
   d. Prohibit financial ties to any supplier, customer, or distributor.
   e. Encourage adherence to strong ethical behavior through corporate actions, policies, and public communications.

E. Legal Aspects of Social Responsibility

1. The **Racketeer Influenced and Corrupt Organization (RICO) Act** was passed in 1970 as an attempt to combat the problem of organized crime and its infiltration of legitimate enterprises.
   a. Its goals were to eliminate organized crime by concentrating on the illegal monies through the use of civil and criminal forfeitures.
   b. Criminal penalties can be levied up to $25,000 and 20 years in jail. Civil penalties include the awarding of treble damages and attorney's fees to the successful plaintiff.
   c. RICO specifically makes the following activities unlawful:
      1) Using income derived from a pattern of racketeering activity to acquire an interest in an enterprise.
      2) Acquiring or maintaining an interest in an enterprise through a pattern of racketeering activity.
      3) Conducting the affairs of an enterprise through a pattern of racketeering activity.
      4) Conspiring to commit any of these offenses.
   d. RICO has been used against white-collar criminals, terrorists, Wall Street insider trading, anti-abortion protesters, local law enforcement agencies, and public accounting firms -- none of which was intended by Congress when the law was passed.
2. The **Foreign Corrupt Practices Act (FCPA) of 1977** regulates payments by U.S. firms operating in other nations.
   a. The act is a reaction to publicity over questionable foreign payments.
   b. The FCPA makes it a criminal offense to make payments to a foreign government or representative thereof to secure or retain business.
   c. It prohibits payments of sales commissions to independent agents, if the commissions are knowingly passed to foreign officials.
   d. Corporations are required to establish internal accounting controls to assure that all overseas payments are proper.
   e. The FCPA applies even if payment is legal in the nation where it is made.
   f. The rationale for the FCPA is that the international reputation of the United States is affected by its international business conduct, which should reflect the best of the United States' ethics.
3. The SEC mandates that the composition of boards of directors include outside directors.
   a. To create diversity and broaden the overview of a company's place in the market and in society
4. Courts are increasingly willing to hold boards of directors and auditors liable for problems.
5. Stop and review! The following 17 multiple-choice questions cover the topic of ethics as it may be tested on the CMA/CFM exams. They are not divided by subunits. We anticipate some "case" questions that describe situations and are followed by one or more questions; e.g., to whom should the financial manager report an ethics violation?

MULTIPLE-CHOICE QUESTIONS

1. If a financial manager/management accountant has a problem in identifying unethical behavior or resolving an ethical conflict, the first action (s)he should normally take is to

A. Consult the board of directors.

B. Discuss the problem with his/her immediate superior.

C. Notify the appropriate law enforcement agency.

D. Resign from the company.

The correct answer is (B). *(Publisher)*

REQUIRED: The proper ethical behavior by a financial manager/management accountant.

DISCUSSION: The Standards of Ethical Conduct for Practitioners of Management Accounting and Financial Management state that the financial manager/management accountant should first discuss an ethical problem with his/her immediate superior. If the superior is involved, the problem should be taken initially to the next higher managerial level.

Answer (A) is incorrect because the board would be consulted initially only if the immediate superior is the chief executive officer and that person is involved in the ethical conflict. Answer (C) is incorrect because unless "legally prescribed, communication of such problems to authorities or individuals not employed or engaged by the organization is not considered appropriate." Answer (D) is incorrect because resignation is a last resort.

2. Sheila is a financial manager who has discovered that her company is violating environmental regulations. If her immediate superior is involved, her appropriate action is to

A. Do nothing since she has a duty of loyalty to the organization.

B. Consult the audit committee.

C. Present the matter to the next higher managerial level.

D. Confront her immediate superior.

The correct answer is (C). *(Publisher)*

REQUIRED: The proper action when a financial manager/management accountant's immediate superior is involved in an ethical problem.

DISCUSSION: To resolve an ethical problem, the financial manager/management accountant's first step is usually to consult his/her immediate superior. If that individual is involved, the matter should be taken to the next higher level of management.

Answer (A) is incorrect because "practitioners of management accounting and financial management have an obligation to the public, their profession, the organization they serve, and themselves, to maintain the highest standards of ethical conduct." Answer (B) is incorrect because the audit committee would be consulted first only if it were the next higher managerial level. Answer (D) is incorrect because if the superior is involved, the next higher managerial level should be consulted first.

3. If a financial manager/management accountant discovers unethical conduct in his/her organization and fails to act, (s)he will be in violation of which ethical standard(s)?

A. "Actively or passively subvert the attainment of the organization's legitimate and ethical objectives."

B. "Communicate unfavorable as well as favorable information."

C. "Condone the commission of such acts by others within their organizations."

D. All of the answers are correct.

The correct answer is (D). *(Publisher)*

REQUIRED: The ethical standard(s) violated by failure to disclose unethical behavior.

DISCUSSION: A financial manager/management accountant displays his/her competence and objectivity and maintains integrity by taking the appropriate action within the organization to resolve an ethical problem. Failure to act would condone wrongful acts, breach the duty to convey unfavorable as well as favorable information, undermine the organization's legitimate aims, discredit the profession, and violate the duty of objectivity owed to users of the subordinate's work product.

Answers (A), (B), and (C) are incorrect because each standard is violated by a financial manager/management accountant who fails to act upon discovering unethical conduct.

4. Corporate social responsibility is

A. Effectively enforced through the controls envisioned by classical economics.

B. Defined as the obligation to shareholders to earn a profit.

C. More than the obligation to shareholders to earn a profit.

D. Defined as the obligation to serve long-term, organizational interests.

The correct answer is (C). *(Publisher)*

REQUIRED: The true statement about corporate social responsibility.

DISCUSSION: The concept of corporate social responsibility involves more than serving the interests of the organization and its shareholders. Rather, it is an extension of responsibility to embrace service to the public interest in such matters as environmental protection, employee safety, civil rights, and community involvement.

Answer (A) is incorrect because a perfectly competitive market was envisioned by classical economics. Answers (B) and (D) are incorrect because the concept embraces the public or societal interest.

5. A common argument against corporate involvement in socially responsible behavior is that

A. It encourages government intrusion in decision making.

B. As a legal person, a corporation is accountable for its conduct.

C. It creates goodwill.

D. In a competitive market, such behavior incurs costs that place the company at a disadvantage.

The correct answer is (D). *(Publisher)*

REQUIRED: The common argument against corporate involvement in socially responsible behavior.

DISCUSSION: Socially responsible behavior clearly has immediate costs to the entity, for example, the expenses incurred in affirmative action programs, pollution control, and improvements in worker safety. When one firm incurs such costs and its competitor does not, the other may be able to sell its products or services more cheaply and increase its market share at the expense of the socially responsible firm. The rebuttal argument is that in the long run the socially responsible company may maximize profits by creating goodwill and avoiding or anticipating governmental regulation.

Answer (A) is incorrect because such behavior may prevent governmental action. Answers (B) and (C) are incorrect because each is an argument for such behavior.

6. The IMA Code of Ethics requires a financial manager/management accountant to follow the established policies of the organization when faced with an ethical conflict. If these policies do not resolve the conflict, the financial manager/management accountant should

A. Consult the board of directors immediately.

B. Discuss the problem with the immediate superior if (s)he is involved in the conflict.

C. Communicate the problem to authorities outside the organization.

D. Contact the next higher managerial level if initial presentation to the immediate superior does not resolve the conflict.

The correct answer is (D). *(Publisher)*

REQUIRED: The proper action when organizational policies do not resolve an ethical conflict.

DISCUSSION: In these circumstances, the problem should be discussed with the immediate superior unless (s)he is involved. In that case, initial presentation should be to the next higher managerial level. If the problem is not satisfactorily resolved after initial presentation, the question should be submitted to the next higher level.

Answer (A) is incorrect because this course of action would be appropriate only for the chief executive officer or for his/her immediate subordinate when the CEO is involved in the conflict. Answer (B) is incorrect because the proper action would be to present the matter to the next higher managerial level. Answer (C) is incorrect because such action is inappropriate unless legally prescribed.

7. Financial managers/management accountants are obligated to maintain the highest standards of ethical conduct. Accordingly, the IMA Code of Ethics explicitly requires that they

A. Obtain sufficient competent evidence when expressing an opinion.

B. Not condone violations by others.

C. Comply with generally accepted auditing standards.

D. Adhere to generally accepted accounting principles.

The correct answer is (B). *(Publisher)*

REQUIRED: The conduct required of financial managers/management accountants.

DISCUSSION: The preamble to the IMA Code of Ethics states, "Practitioners of management accounting and financial management have an obligation to the public, their profession, the organizations they serve, and themselves, to maintain the highest standards of ethical conduct. In recognition of this obligation, the Institute of Management Accountants has promulgated the following standards of ethical conduct for practitioners of management accounting and financial management. Adherence to these standards, both domestically and internationally, is integral to achieving the Objectives of Management Accounting. Practitioners of management accounting and financial management shall not commit acts contrary to these standards nor shall they condone the commission of such acts by others within their organizations."

Answers (A), (C), and (D) are incorrect because each applies to external auditors. The IMA Code of Ethics does not expressly use such language.

8. Integrity is an ethical requirement for all financial managers/management accountants. One aspect of integrity requires

A. Performance of professional duties in accordance with applicable laws.

B. Avoidance of conflict of interest.

C. Refraining from improper use of inside information.

D. Maintenance of an appropriate level of professional competence.

The correct answer is (B). *(Publisher)*

REQUIRED: The aspect of the integrity requirement.

DISCUSSION: According to the IMA Code of Ethics, financial managers/management accountants must "avoid actual or apparent conflicts of interest and advise all appropriate parties of any potential conflict."

Answers (A) and (D) are incorrect because each states an aspect of the competence requirement. Answer (C) is incorrect because it states an aspect of the confidentiality requirement.

9. Under the express terms of the IMA Code of Ethics, a financial manager/management accountant may not

A. Advertise.

B. Encroach on the practice of another financial manager/management accountant.

C. Disclose confidential information unless authorized or legally obligated.

D. Accept other employment while serving as a financial manager/management accountant.

The correct answer is (C). *(Publisher)*

REQUIRED: The action explicitly proscribed by the IMA Code of Ethics.

DISCUSSION: Financial managers/management accountants may not disclose confidential information acquired in the course of their work unless authorized or legally obligated to do so. They must inform subordinates about the confidentiality of information and monitor their activities to maintain that confidentiality. Moreover, financial managers/management accountants should avoid even the appearance of using confidential information to their unethical or illegal advantage.

Answers (A) and (B) are incorrect because the code does not address these matters. Answer (D) is incorrect because other employment may be accepted unless it constitutes a conflict of interest.

10. A financial manager/management accountant discovers a problem that could mislead users of the firm's financial data and has informed his/her immediate superior. (S)he should report the circumstances to the audit committee and/or the board of directors only if

A. The immediate superior, who reports to the chief executive officer, knows about the situation but refuses to correct it.

B. The immediate superior assures the financial manager/management accountant that the problem will be resolved.

C. The immediate superior reports the situation to his/her superior.

D. The immediate superior, the firm's chief executive officer, knows about the situation but refuses to correct it.

The correct answer is (D). *(Publisher)*

REQUIRED: The situation in which the financial manager/management accountant must report to the audit committee and/or board of directors.

DISCUSSION: According to the IMA Code of Ethics, the financial manager/management accountant should "discuss such problems with the immediate superior except when it appears that the superior is involved, in which case the problem should be presented initially to the next higher managerial level. If satisfactory resolution cannot be achieved when the problem is initially presented, submit the issues to the next higher managerial level. If the immediate superior is the chief executive officer, or equivalent, the acceptable reviewing authority may be a group such as the audit committee, executive committee, board of directors, board of trustees, or owners."

Answer (A) is incorrect because, in this situation, the chief executive officer is the next higher managerial level. Answers (B) and (C) are incorrect because the immediate superior has promised or taken action toward satisfactory resolution.

11. In which situation is a financial manager/management accountant permitted to communicate confidential information to individuals or authorities outside the firm?

A. There is an ethical conflict and the board has refused to take action.

B. Such communication is legally prescribed.

C. The financial manager/management accountant knowingly communicates the information indirectly through a subordinate.

D. An officer at the financial manager/management accountant's bank has requested information on a transaction that could influence the firm's stock price.

The correct answer is (B). *(Publisher)*

REQUIRED: The situation in which a financial manager/management accountant may disclose information to those outside the firm.

DISCUSSION: According to the IMA Code of Ethics, financial managers/management accountants are responsible for observing the standard of confidentiality. Thus, the financial manager/management accountant should "refrain from disclosing confidential information acquired in the course of his/her work except when authorized, unless legally obligated to do so."

Answer (A) is incorrect because the IMA Code of Ethics states that "except where legally prescribed, communication of such [ethical conflict] problems to authorities or individuals not employed or engaged by the organization is not considered appropriate." Answer (C) is incorrect because the financial manager/management accountant should "inform subordinates as appropriate regarding the confidentiality of information acquired in the course of their work and monitor their activities to assure the maintenance of that confidentiality." Answer (D) is incorrect because the financial manager/management accountant is required to "refrain from using or appearing to use confidential information acquired in the course of his/her work for unethical or illegal advantage either personally or through third parties."

12. Which ethical standard is most clearly violated if a financial manager/management accountant knows of a problem that could mislead users but does nothing about it?

A. Competence.

B. Legality.

C. Objectivity.

D. Confidentiality.

The correct answer is (C). *(Publisher)*

REQUIRED: The ethical standard most clearly violated when a financial manager/management accountant does nothing about information that is misleading to users.

DISCUSSION: Objectivity is the fourth part of the IMA Code of Ethics. It requires that information be communicated "fairly and objectively," and that all information that could reasonably influence users be fully disclosed.

Answer (A) is incorrect because the competence standard pertains to the financial manager/management accountant's responsibility to maintain his/her professional skills and knowledge. It also pertains to the performance of activities in a professional manner. Answer (B) is incorrect because legality is not addressed in the IMA Code of Ethics. Answer (D) is incorrect because the confidentiality standard concerns the financial manager/management accountant's responsibility not to disclose or use the firm's confidential information.

13. The IMA Code of Ethics includes an integrity standard, which requires the financial manager/management accountant to

A. Identify and make known anything that may hinder his/her judgment or prevent satisfactory completion of any duties.

B. Report any relevant information that could influence users of financial statements.

C. Disclose confidential information when authorized by his/her firm or required under the law.

D. Refuse gifts from anyone.

The correct answer is (A). *(Publisher)*

REQUIRED: The action required of the financial manager/management accountant by the integrity standard.

DISCUSSION: One of the responsibilities of the financial manager/management accountant under the integrity standard is to "recognize and communicate professional limitations or other constraints that would preclude responsible judgment or successful performance of an activity."

Answer (B) is incorrect because the objectivity standard requires the financial manager/management accountant to "disclose fully all relevant information that could reasonably be expected to influence an intended user's understanding of the reports, comments, and recommendations presented." Answer (C) is incorrect because the confidentiality standard requires the financial manager/management accountant to "refrain from disclosing confidential information acquired in the course of his/her work except when authorized, unless legally obligated to do so." Answer (D) is incorrect because the integrity standard requires the financial manager/management accountant to "refuse any gift, favor, or hospitality that would influence or would appear to influence his/her actions."

14. The IMA Code of Ethics includes a competence standard, which requires the financial manager/management accountant to

A. Report information, whether favorable or unfavorable.

B. Develop his/her professional proficiency on a continual basis.

C. Discuss ethical conflicts and possible courses of action with an unbiased counselor.

D. Discuss, with subordinates, their responsibilities regarding the disclosure of information about the firm.

The correct answer is (B). *(Publisher)*

REQUIRED: The action required of the financial manager/management accountant by the competence standard.

DISCUSSION: One of the responsibilities of the financial manager/management accountant under the competence standard is to "maintain an appropriate level of professional competence by ongoing development of his/her knowledge and skills."

Answer (A) is incorrect because the integrity standard requires the financial manager/management accountant to "communicate unfavorable as well as favorable information and professional judgments or opinions." Answer (C) is incorrect because one of the suggestions from the "Resolution of Ethical Conflict" paragraph is to "clarify relevant ethical issues by confidential discussion with an objective advisor (e.g., IMA Ethics Counseling Service) to obtain a better understanding of possible courses of action." Answer (D) is incorrect because the confidentiality standard requires the financial manager/management accountant to "inform subordinates as appropriate regarding the confidentiality of information acquired in the course of their work and monitor their activities to assure the maintenance of that confidentiality."

15. According to Statements on Management Accounting Number 1C (SMA 1C) (revised), *Standards of Ethical Conduct for Practitioners of Management Accounting and Financial Management*, a practitioner has a responsibility to recognize professional limitations. Under which standard of ethical conduct would this responsibility be included?

A. Competency.

B. Confidentiality.

C. Integrity.

D. Objectivity.

The correct answer is (C). *(CMA, adapted)*

REQUIRED: The standard of ethical conduct related to the responsibility to recognize professional limitations.

DISCUSSION: One of the responsibilities of the financial manager/management accountant under the integrity standard is to "recognize and communicate professional limitations or other constraints that would preclude responsible judgment or successful performance of an activity."

Answer (A) is incorrect because the competence standard pertains to the financial manager/management accountant's responsibility to maintain his/her professional skills and knowledge. It also pertains to the performance of activities in a professional manner. Answer (B) is incorrect because the confidentiality standard concerns the financial manager/management accountant's responsibility not to disclose or use the firm's confidential information. Answer (D) is incorrect because objectivity is the fourth part of the IMA Code of Ethics. It requires that information be communicated "fairly and objectively," and that all information that could reasonably influence users be fully disclosed.

16. At Key Enterprises, the controller is responsible for directing the budgeting process. In this role, the controller has significant influence with executive management as individual department budgets are modified and approved. For the current year, the controller was instrumental in the approval of a particular line manager's budget without modification, even though significant reductions were made to the budgets submitted by other line managers. As a token of appreciation, the line manager in question has given the controller a gift certificate for a popular local restaurant. In considering whether or not to accept the certificate, the controller should refer to which section of Statements on Management Accounting Number 1C (SMA 1C) (revised), *Standards of Ethical Conduct for Practitioners of Management Accounting and Financial Management*?

A. Competency.

B. Confidentiality.

C. Integrity.

D. Objectivity.

The correct answer is (C). *(CMA, adapted)*

REQUIRED: The ethical standard relevant to the controller's acceptance of a gift from a line manager.

DISCUSSION: The integrity standard requires the financial manager/management accountant to "refuse any gift, favor, or hospitality that would influence or would appear to influence his/her actions."

Answer (A) is incorrect because the competence standard pertains to the financial manager/management accountant's responsibility to maintain his/her professional skills and knowledge. It also pertains to the performance of activities in a professional manner. Answer (B) is incorrect because the confidentiality standard concerns the financial manager/management accountant's responsibility not to disclose or use the firm's confidential information. Answer (D) is incorrect because objectivity is the fourth part of the IMA Code of Ethics. It requires that information be communicated "fairly and objectively," and that all information that could reasonably influence users be fully disclosed.

17. In accordance with Statements on Management Accounting Number 1C (SMA 1C) (revised), *Standards of Ethical Conduct for Practitioners of Management Accounting and Financial Management*, a management accountant who fails to perform professional duties in accordance with relevant standards is acting contrary to which one of the following standards?

A. Competency.

B. Confidentiality.

C. Integrity.

D. Objectivity.

The correct answer is (A). *(CMA, adapted)*

REQUIRED: The ethical standard violated by a management accountant who fails to perform professional duties in accordance with relevant standards.

DISCUSSION: One of the responsibilities of the financial manager/management accountant under the competence standard is to "maintain an appropriate level of professional competence by ongoing development of his/her knowledge and skills." (S)he must also "perform professional duties in accordance with relevant laws, regulations, and technical standards." The third requirement under this standard is to "prepare complete and clear reports and recommendations after appropriate analyses of relevant and reliable information."

Answer (B) is incorrect because the confidentiality standard concerns the financial manager/management accountant's responsibility not to disclose or use the firm's confidential information. Answer (C) is incorrect because the integrity standard pertains to conflicts of interest, refusal of gifts, professional limitations, professional communications, avoidance of acts discreditable to the profession, and refraining from activities that prejudice the ability to carry out duties ethically. Answer (D) is incorrect because objectivity is the fourth part of the IMA Code of Ethics. It requires that information be communicated "fairly and objectively," and that all information that could reasonably influence users be fully disclosed.

APPENDIX B: TAXES AS TESTED ON THE CMA/CFM EXAMS

6 pages of outline
9 multiple-choice questions

A. Taxation
B. Fundamentals of Corporate Taxation

Taxes are tested in Parts 1, 2, and 4. The intended emphasis is on a user's point of view rather than a preparer's point of view.

Part 1 - The effect of tax provisions on financing and capital structure decisions, such as deductibility of payments for use of capital and after-tax cost of capital (i.e., debt vs. equity issues), is discussed in Study Unit 6, Capital Structure Finance, and Study Unit 7, Risk.

Part 2CMA - Accounting for deferred income taxes is a separate subunit in Study Unit 5, Liabilities.

Part 2CFM - Accounting for deferred income taxes is a subunit in Study Unit 2, Special Topics in Financial Statements.

The income tax code provisions that impact investment decisions are in Study Units 3 through 7 and cover advanced topics in corporate financial management.

- Deductibility of payments for use of capital
- After-tax cost of capital
- Tax shields from property transactions
- Transaction timing for favorable tax consequences

International tax considerations and their effect on international regulations on business are in Study Unit 8, Risk Management.

The tax implications of multinational corporations are in Study Unit 9, External Financial Environment.

Part 4 - The impact of income taxes on operational decisions, including operating income subject to income taxes, gains and losses subject to income taxes, and tax credits apply to Study Unit 1, Decision Analysis.

The impact of income taxes on investment decisions, including tax shields from sunk costs, transaction timing for favorable tax consequences, and tax elections apply to Study Unit 3, Capital Budgeting.

Important background for the above two study units appears in this appendix.

This appendix provides background and overview of taxes as tested on the CMA/CFM exams. Additional detail required in each part is provided as set forth above.

Obviously taxes are a major expense of doing business, and each business attempts to minimize taxes. Thus, financial managers and management accountants must be knowledgeable about taxes.

A. Taxation

1. Two Principles of Taxation

a. Benefits received. Individuals should pay a tax based on the benefits received from the services (e.g., paying for the use of a public park or swimming pool).

b. Ability to pay. Consumers should pay taxes based on their ability to pay them (e.g., taxes on income and wealth).

2. Three Classifications of Taxes Reflecting Ability-to-Pay Principles

a. **Progressive**. With a higher income, individuals pay a higher percentage of their income in taxes (e.g., income tax).

b. **Proportional**. At all levels of income, the percentage paid in taxes is constant (e.g., sales tax).

c. **Regressive**. As income increases, the percentage paid in taxes decreases (e.g., payroll or excise taxes).

1) EXAMPLE: An excise tax is regressive because its burden falls disproportionately on lower-income persons. As personal income increases, the percentage of income paid declines since an excise tax is a flat amount per quantity of the good or service purchased.

3. Taxes also may be classified as either direct or indirect.

a. **Direct taxes** are imposed upon the taxpayer and paid directly to the government, e.g., the personal income tax.

b. **Indirect taxes** are levied against others and thus only indirectly on the individual taxpayer, e.g., sales taxes and Social Security taxes paid by employers.

4. **Incidence of Taxation** -- the parties who actually bear a particular tax. For example, the person who actually bears the burden of an indirect tax may not be the same one who pays the tax to the government.

a. The incidence of taxation becomes important when a government wants to change the tax structure. Because taxation is a form of fiscal policy, the government needs to know who will actually bear the incidence of taxation, not just who will remit the tax.

b. EXAMPLE: Taxes such as the corporate income tax, the corporate property tax, and the excise tax are often shifted to the consumer in the form of higher prices.

c. EXAMPLE: Taxes such as windfall profits taxes are not shifted to the consumer via higher prices. This type of one-time-only tax levied on part of the output produced does not increase the equilibrium price of the taxed good.

5. In recent years, some authorities have supported a **value-added tax**, a tax based on consumption.

a. Many major industrial nations have already adopted a value-added tax.

b. The tax is levied on the value added to goods by each business unit in the production and distribution chain.

1) The amount of value added is measured by the difference between a firm's sales and its purchases.

2) Each firm in the chain collects the tax on its sales, takes a credit for taxes paid on purchases, and remits the difference to the government.

3) The consumer ultimately bears the incidence of the tax through higher prices.

c. A value-added tax encourages consumer saving because taxes are paid on consumption only, not on savings.

1) Because the value-added tax is based on consumption, people in the lower income groups would spend a greater proportion of their income on taxes.

2) The value-added tax is thus regressive.

d. Only those businesses that make a profit have to pay income taxes. Under the value-added tax, however, all businesses have to pay taxes, regardless of income.

6. **Taxes** as a business expense (federal, state, local, and foreign) are an important consideration because they are frequently 25% to 50% of all costs.

a. They include income, use, excise, property, legal document, payroll, and others.

b. Thus, governmental services (national defense, fire, police, etc.) are an important and costly factor of production.

c. Tax planning is very important in investment and financing decisions.

1) Investment tax credits have at times provided direct reduction of taxes when assets were purchased for use in the business.

a) The net effect is to decrease the cost of the asset.

b) The amount of the credit and limitations on the tax credit on used equipment affect investment decisions.

c) Investment tax credit is currently available for solar and geothermal property (business energy credit), for rehabilitation of historic structures, and for certain reforestation property.

2) Accelerated depreciation is permitted on many types of business assets.

a) Accordingly, in the early periods of an asset's life, depreciation is higher, taxable income is lower, and the rate of return on investment is higher.

3) Corporate capital gains are taxed at regular rates, and the capital gains of individuals are taxed at a maximum rate of 28%.

4) Special loss carryforward and carryback rules permit businesses to deduct net operating losses incurred in one period against income earned in other periods.

5) A dividends-received deduction makes tax free 70% to 100% of dividends received by one company from investments in the stock of another company.

a) This deduction prevents or reduces double taxation.

b) It also encourages one company to invest in the stock of another company.

6) Interest is a tax-deductible expense of the debtor company.

a) But dividends on common or preferred stock are not deductible by the issuer.

d. Federal tax policy is fiscal policy that affects the overall economy, which in turn affects production and the finished-goods markets in which the company deals.

e. Government monetary policy determines the availability and cost of capital, which affects financing (and in turn, investing) decisions.

1) Monetary policy also affects overall economic activity.

7. Stop and review! You have completed the outline for this subunit. Study multiple-choice questions 1 through 3 on page 491.

B. Fundamentals of Corporate Taxation

1. A C corporation is subject to tax liability imposed on its income (S corporations are taxed as partnerships).

2. **Gross income** means all income from whatever source derived (unless excluded by statute).

a. Income is considered realized when certain transactions occur.

1) Mere increases in value (appreciation) do not create income.

a) EXAMPLE: Land owned by a corporation increases in value from $5,000 to $20,000 per acre. There is no income until the land is sold or exchanged.

2) Transactions are normally in the form of a sale, an exchange, or the rendering of services.

3) Taxation of realized income may be excluded or deferred, for example, upon exchange of like-kind property.

4) The term "recognized" is used when income is realized and also taxed.

5) Nonresident aliens (including foreign corporations) are, generally, subject to federal income tax on U.S.-source income.

3. **Deductions** are those expenses and other statutorily prescribed items that are subtracted from gross income to determine taxable income.

a. Deductions should be distinguished from **exclusions**. Exclusions are never included in gross income (e.g., interest on tax-exempt bonds).

4. **Taxable income** is gross income minus deductions.

a. Taxable income is analogous to net income.
b. The tax rates are applied to taxable income to determine the tax liability.

5. **Credits** are subtracted from the tax liability.

a. Credits directly reduce taxes, while deductions reduce taxable income upon which the taxes are computed.

6. **Book Income vs. Taxable Income**

a. CMA/CFM candidates (Parts 2) are required to understand the difference between book income and taxable income. Problems may begin with book income, list numerous transactions, and require the adjustments necessary to arrive at taxable income.

b. The following adjustments are necessary to adjust book income to taxable income:
   1) Add to book income
      a) Federal income tax
      b) Excess of capital losses over capital gains
      c) Taxable income not reported on books
      d) Expenses reported on books but not deducted on tax return (e.g., charitable contributions in excess of limit)
   2) Subtract from book income
      a) Income reported on books but not included on tax return (e.g., interest income from tax-exempt municipal bonds)
      b) Deductions on tax return but not reported on books (e.g., dividends-received deduction)

c. These adjustments are the fundamental differences between net income for financial accounting purposes (book income) and taxable income. The discussion of income and deductions that follows will concentrate on these differences and assume that candidates can already compute book (i.e., accrual accounting) income.

d. According to generally accepted accounting principles (SFAS 109), accounting for income taxes (interperiod tax allocation) is based on the asset and liability method.

7. **Temporary Differences**

a. Depreciation expense arises from using different methods for tax and book purposes.

b. To account for bad debt expense, the direct write-off method is used for tax purposes, and the allowance method (estimating expenses) is used for book purposes.

c. For tax purposes, warranty expense is deductible only when paid, even if reserves based on estimates are used for book purposes.

d. Charitable contributions exceeding 10% of corporate taxable income before charitable contributions and special deductions are deductible during the 5 succeeding tax years.

e. Capital losses in excess of capital gains are not deductible in the current year. Instead, a net capital loss must be carried back 3 years (as a short-term capital loss) and applied towards any capital gains. Any loss remaining can be carried forward for 5 years. Capital losses can be used only to offset capital gains (i.e., ordinary income is unaffected).

f. Prepaid rent income is included in taxable income when received. Prepaid rent expense is deductible in computing taxable income for the period to which it is attributable.

g. The cost of certain intangibles (e.g., goodwill) acquired in connection with the conduct of a trade or business or income-producing activity is amortized over a 15-year period, beginning with the month in which the intangible is acquired.

h. Amortization of organizational costs and business start-up costs can be elected for a period of not less than 60 months for tax purposes.

8. **Permanent Differences**
   a. Life insurance premiums paid on key persons are not deductible if the corporation is the beneficiary. Proceeds from the policy are not taxed.
   b. Seventy percent of dividends received from taxable domestic corporations are deductible by a distributee corporation that owns less than 20% of the stock of the distributing corporation. The percentage deductible is 80 if the distributee owns 20% to 80% of the distributing corporation. A 100% dividend-received deduction is permitted for dividends received among members of an affiliated group of corporations (80% ownership).
   c. Federal income tax expense is not deductible in computing taxable income.
   d. Tax-exempt interest is included in book income. Expense attributable to earning it is not deductible for tax purposes.
   e. Business gifts exceeding $25 are generally not deductible for income tax purposes.
   f. Compensation in excess of $1 million paid to the chief executive officer and certain other employees is not deductible in computing taxable income. Premiums, tax-free benefits, and compensation based on performance goals are excluded from the $1 million limit.
9. **Nonrecognition Transactions**. Certain types of transactions result in deferral or nonrecognition of gains. Examples are like-kind exchanges, involuntary conversions, and tax-free reorganizations.
   a. **Like-kind exchanges**. Sec. 1031 defers recognizing gain or loss to the extent that property productively used in a trade or business or held for the production of income (investment) is exchanged for property of like-kind.
   b. **Involuntary conversions**. A taxpayer may elect to defer recognition of gain, but not losses, if property is involuntarily converted (e.g., by fire, loss, or government condemnation for public use) into money or property that is not similar or related in use. Nonrecognition of gain is contingent on the involuntarily converted property being reinvested in qualified replacement property.
   c. **Tax-free reorganization**. A nontaxable reorganization of one or more corporations is considered a mere change in form of investment rather than a disposition of assets. For this reason, a general rule of nonrecognition of gain or loss applies to qualifying reorganizations. However, gain is recognized to the extent of receipt of cash or other nonqualifying payment.
10. **Taxation on Multinational Corporations**
    a. Multinational corporations frequently derive income from several countries. The government of each country in which a corporation does business may enact statutes imposing one or more types of tax on the corporation.
    b. To avoid double taxation, most countries have adopted treaties to coordinate or synchronize the effects of their taxing statutes.
11. Stop and review! You have completed the outline for this subunit. Study multiple-choice questions 4 through 9 beginning on page 492.

MULTIPLE-CHOICE QUESTIONS

A. Taxation

1. A regressive tax is a tax in which

A. Individuals with higher incomes pay a higher percentage of their income in tax.

B. The burden for payment falls disproportionately on lower-income persons.

C. The individual pays a constant percentage in taxes, regardless of income level.

D. Individuals with lower incomes pay a lower percentage of their income in tax.

The correct answer is (B). *(Publisher)*

REQUIRED: The statement that describes a regressive tax.

DISCUSSION: With a regressive tax, the percentage paid in taxes decreases as income increases. For example, excise taxes and payroll taxes are both regressive taxes. An excise tax is regressive because its burden falls disproportionally on lower-income persons. As personal income increases, the percentage of income paid declines because an excise tax is a flat amount per quality of the good or service purchased.

Answers (A) and (D) are incorrect because a progressive tax is a tax in which individuals with higher (lower) incomes pay a higher (lower) percentage of their income in tax. For example, income taxes are progressive. Answer (C) is incorrect because a proportional tax is a tax in which the individual pays a constant percentage in taxes, regardless of income level. A sales tax is a proportional tax.

2. Two examples of indirect taxes are

A. Taxes on business and rental property and personal income taxes.

B. Sales taxes and Social Security taxes paid by employees.

C. Sales taxes and Social Security taxes paid by employers.

D. Social Security taxes paid by employees and personal income taxes.

The correct answer is (C). *(CMA, adapted)*

REQUIRED: The two forms of indirect taxes.

DISCUSSION: Indirect taxes are those levied against someone other than individual taxpayers and thus only indirectly affect the individual. Sales taxes are levied against businesses and are then passed along to the individual purchaser. Social Security taxes are levied against both the employer and the employee. Those levied against the employee are direct taxes; those levied against the employer are indirect.

Answers (A), (B), and (D) are incorrect because personal income taxes and Social Security taxes levied against the employee are direct taxes.

3. When a fixed plant asset with a 5-year estimated useful life is sold during the second year, how would the use of an accelerated depreciation method instead of the straight-line method affect the gain or loss on the sale of the fixed plant asset?

	Gain	Loss
A.	Increase	Increase
B.	Increase	Decrease
C.	Decrease	Increase
D.	Decrease	Decrease

The correct answer is (B). *(CMA, adapted)*

REQUIRED: The effect of using an accelerated depreciation method instead of straight-line.

DISCUSSION: An accelerated method reduces the book value of the asset more rapidly in the early years of the useful life than does the straight-line method. Hence, the effect of an early sale is to increase the gain or decrease the loss that would have been recognized under the straight-line method.

Answers (A), (C), and (D) are incorrect because the effect is to increase gains and decrease losses.

B. Fundamentals of Corporate Taxation

Questions 4 and 5 are based on the following information. The Hando Communications Corporation (HCC) has just finished its first year of operations. For the year, HCC had $80,000 of income. HCC also earned $11,000 of interest on a tax-exempt bond, a $10,000 depreciation deduction, and an $8,000 tax credit. Assume that HCC has a 30% tax rate.

4. What is HCC's net tax liability?

A. $17,700

B. $15,300

C. $9,700

D. $2,000

The correct answer is (C). *(Publisher)*

REQUIRED: The net tax liability.

DISCUSSION: The first step in calculating HCC's net tax liability is to subtract the exclusion for tax-exempt interest from income, for a gross income amount of $69,000 ($80,000 – $11,000). Next, the deprecation deduction is subtracted from gross income, for a taxable income of $59,000 ($69,000 – $10,000). Then, the taxable income is multiplied by the tax rate, for a gross tax liability of $17,700 ($59,000 x 30%). Finally, net tax liability is computed by subtracting the tax credits from the gross tax liability. Therefore, HCC's net tax liability is $9,700 ($17,700 – $8,000).

Answer (A) is incorrect because $17,700 is the gross tax liability. Answer (B) is incorrect because $15,300 is the net tax liability found when incorrectly treating the tax credit as a direct reduction in taxable income. Answer (D) is incorrect because $2,000 is the net tax liability found when incorrectly treating the exclusion as a credit.

5. Which item reduces HCC's gross tax liability by the largest amount?

A. Gross income.

B. The tax-exempt interest exclusion.

C. The depreciation deduction.

D. The tax credit.

The correct answer is (D). *(Publisher)*

REQUIRED: The item that decreases HCC's gross tax liability by the largest amount.

DISCUSSION: Credits directly reduce taxes, whereas exclusions and deductions reduce income prior to the computation of the gross tax liability. Thus, the credit reduces the gross tax liability on a dollar-for-dollar basis, or $8,000. An exclusion or deduction reduces gross tax liability by the amount of the exclusion or deduction multiplied by the tax rate. Accordingly, the exclusion will reduce HCC's gross tax liability by $3,300 ($11,000 x 30%), and the deduction will reduce HCC's gross tax liability by $3,000 ($10,000 x 30%). Gross income does not reduce the gross tax liability; rather, it increases the gross tax liability by $24,000 ($80,000 x 30%).

Answers (A), (B), and (C) are incorrect because an exclusion or deduction reduces gross tax liability by the amount of the exclusion or deduction multiplied by the tax rate. Therefore, the exclusion will reduce HCC's gross tax liability by $3,300 ($11,000 x .30), and the deduction will reduce HCC's gross tax liability by $3,000 ($10,000 x .30).

6. None of the following items are deductible in calculating taxable income except

A. Estimated liabilities for product warranties expected to be incurred in the future.

B. Dividends on common stock declared but not payable until next year.

C. Bonus accrued but not paid by the end of the year to a cash-basis 90% shareholder.

D. Vacation pay accrued on an employee-by-employee basis.

The correct answer is (D). *(CMA, adapted)*

REQUIRED: The item that is deductible in the calculation of taxable income.

DISCUSSION: Sec. 162(a) states that a deduction is allowed for the ordinary and necessary expenses incurred during the year in any trade or business. A corporation may therefore deduct a reasonable amount for compensation. Accrued vacation pay is a form of compensation that results in an allowable deduction for federal income tax purposes.

Answer (A) is incorrect because warranty expenses are not deductible until paid. Answer (B) is incorrect because dividends on common stock are never deductible by a corporation; they are distributions of after-tax income. Answer (C) is incorrect because amounts accrued by an accrual-basis taxpayer to be paid to a related cash-basis taxpayer in a subsequent period are not deductible until the latter taxpayer includes the items in income. This rule effectively puts related taxpayers on the cash basis.

7. All of the following are adjustments/preference items to corporate taxable income in calculating alternative minimum taxable income except

A. All of the gain on an installment sale of real property in excess of $150,000.

B. Mining exploration and development costs.

C. A charitable contribution of appreciated property.

D. Sales commission earned in the current year but paid in the following year.

The correct answer is (D). *(CMA, adapted)*

REQUIRED: The item that is not an adjustment or preference item in calculating the alternative minimum tax (AMT).

DISCUSSION: Taxable income is adjusted to arrive at alternative minimum taxable income. Some of the common adjustments include gains or losses from long-term contracts, gains on installment sales of real property, mining exploration and development costs, charitable contributions of appreciated property, accelerated depreciation, the accumulated current earnings adjustment, and tax-exempt interest on private activity bonds issued after August 7, 1986. A sales commission accrued in the current year but paid in the following year is not an example of an AMT adjustment.

Answer (A) is incorrect because the gain on an installment sale of real property in excess of $150,000 is an adjustment to taxable income for purposes of computing alternative minimum taxable income. Answer (B) is incorrect because mining exploration and development costs are adjustments to taxable income for purposes of computing alternative minimum taxable income. Answer (C) is incorrect because a charitable contribution of appreciated property is an adjustment to taxable income for purposes of computing alternative minimum taxable income.

8. Which one of the following factors might cause a firm to increase the debt in its financial structure?

A. An increase in the corporate income tax rate.

B. Increased economic uncertainty.

C. An increase in the federal funds rate.

D. An increase in the price-earnings ratio.

The correct answer is (A). *(CMA, adapted)*

REQUIRED: The factor that might encourage a firm to increase the debt in its financial structure.

DISCUSSION: An increase in the corporate income tax rate might encourage a company to borrow because interest on debt is tax deductible, whereas dividends are not. Accordingly, an increase in the tax rate means that the after-tax cost of debt capital will decrease. Given equal interest rates, a firm with a high tax rate will have a lower after-tax cost of debt capital than a firm with a low tax rate.

Answer (B) is incorrect because increased uncertainty encourages equity financing. Dividends do not have to be paid in bad years, but interest on debt is a fixed charge. Answer (C) is incorrect because an increase in interest rates discourages debt financing. Answer (D) is incorrect because an increase in the price-earnings ratio means that the return to shareholders (equity investors) is declining; therefore, equity capital is a more attractive financing alternative.

9. The deferral or nonrecognition of gains is not allowed for tax purposes when the transaction is a(n)

A. Reorganization that is a change in the form of investment.

B. Exchange of property that is used in a business for like-kind property.

C. Reorganization that is considered a disposition of assets.

D. Involuntary conversion of property into qualified replacement property.

The correct answer is (C). *(Publisher)*

REQUIRED: The statement that does not allow for the deferral or nonrecognition of gain.

DISCUSSION: Like-kind exchanges, involuntary conversions, and tax-free reorganizations are examples of transactions that result in the deferral or nonrecognition of gain. A reorganization is nontaxable when it is considered a mere change in investment, not a disposition of assets.

Answer (A) is incorrect because a reorganization that is a mere change in the form of investment is nontaxable. Answer (B) is incorrect because a like-kind exchange allows for the deferral of gain. Answer (D) is incorrect because an involuntary conversion allows for the deferral of gain.

APPENDIX C: IMA MEMBERSHIP, ICMA APPLICATION, AND EXAMINATION FORMS

A. IMA Membership Application
B. Application for Admission to the ICMA
C. Examination Registration Form

You must apply and become an IMA member in order to participate in the IMA Certification programs. The cost is $140 per year for Regular or International membership; $47 for the first year and $93 for the second year for Associate membership (for those within 2 years of completing full-time studies and who reside in the U.S. or Canada); $70 per year for Academic membership (full-time faculty in the U.S. and Canada); and $28 per year for Student membership (must carry at least 6 hours per semester and reside in the U.S. or Canada). The IMA offers three member interest groups at $75 per year: the Controllers Council, the Cost Management Group, and the Small-Business Council. Everyone except students and associates must pay a $15 IMA registration fee. See pages 495 and 496, which can be photocopied and used to apply for IMA membership, or call the IMA at (800) 638-4427 ext. 510 and ask for a CMA/CFM "kit." You may also e-mail the IMA at info@imanet.org to request an information kit.

The application for admission to the ICMA is on pages 497 and 498. This form is required for participation in the IMA Certification Programs. Completion of the registration form on page 499 is required in order to take any and all of the five examination parts.

> Photocopy the following 5 pages and fill them out and mail them today! It will take you less than 10 minutes!

IMA MEMBERSHIP APPLICATION

BATCH NUMBER: ____________ ❑ INITIAL APPLICATION ❑ REINSTATEMENT

PERSONAL INFORMATION

❑ Mr. ❑ Ms. ❑ Miss ❑ Mrs. ❑ Dr. ❑ Male ❑ Female | Social Security Number | Date of Birth / / Month/Day/Year | Send IMA mail to ❑ Home ❑ Business

Last Name/Family Name/Surname | First Name | Middle Initial | Suffix

Home Mailing Address

City | State/Province/Country | Zip Code/Postal Code

COMPANY INFORMATION

Company Name | SIC Code (See Reverse Side)

Business Mailing Address | Job Title Code (See Reverse Side)

City | State/Province/Country | Zip Code/Postal Code | Responsibility Code (See Reverse Side)

Telephone Preference ❑ Business ❑ Home (Include Area/Country/City Codes) | Business Telephone Number with Extension | Home Telephone Number

E-Mail Address | Fax Number: (Include Area/Country/City Codes)

EDUCATIONAL QUALIFICATIONS

College or University	Degree	Major	Date Received/Expected
Undergraduate			
Graduate			

Professional Designations Earned
❑ CPA
❑ CFA
❑ CIA
❑ Other: ________

❑ If you are applying for the CMA or CFM program, complete side two and pay the $50 credentialing fee.

❑ Check here to receive information about the CMA and CFM programs.

CHAPTER AFFILIATION

Chapter Affiliation (your choice of chapter/student chapter - separate listing) | Chapter Number | ❑ Member-At-Large (check here if no chapter affiliation desired) ❑ International Member-At-Large

If you have ever been convicted of a felony check here. ❑ Explain in an accompanying letter.

PAYMENT INFORMATION - FILL IN AS APPROPRIATE. ALL PAYMENTS MUST BE IN US DOLLARS

❑ REGULAR MEMBERSHIP: (You must reside in the U.S. or Canada) ❑ International Member-At-Large	1 Year–$140.00	$
❑ ACADEMIC: (You must be a full-time faculty member and reside in the United States or Canada)	$70.00	$
❑ ASSOCIATE: (You must apply within 2 years of completing full-time studies and reside in the United States or Canada) ❑ 1st Year After Graduation	$47.00	$
❑ 2nd Year After Graduation	$93.00	$
❑ STUDENT: (You must have 6 or more hours per semester and reside in the United States or Canada) Expected Graduation Date ______ YEAR	$28.00	$
MEMBER INTEREST GROUPS: (IMA Membership Required) - 1 Year $75.00 ea. ❑ Controllers Council ❑ Cost Management Group ❑ Small-Business Council No. of MIGs ____	x$75.00	$
OPTIONAL SERVICES: (IMA Membership Required) ❑ Research Publications Service for 1 year (US members)	$85.00	$
❑ Research Publications Service for 1 year (International members)	$120.00	$
CERTIFICATION: (Optional) ❑ U.S. CPA Waiver Fee	**$80.00**	**$**
❑ Credentialing Fee (required of ICMA program applicants only; U.S. college students are exempt)	**$50.00**	**$**
REGISTRATION FEE: Applies to Regular, Academic & International Members *ONLY*. Students and associates are exempt.		$ 15.00
TOTAL DUE		$

❑ Check Enclosed (Make check payable in U.S currency to the Institute of Management Accountants, Inc.)

❑ Charge my credit card: ❑ VISA ❑ MasterCard ❑ American Express ❑ Discover Credit Card Number: ____________

Expiration Date: ___/___ MM/YY

I affirm that the statements on this application are correct and agree to abide by the Standards of Ethical Conduct

Signature of Applicant: ____________ Date: ________ ID Number from Mailing Label ________

PLEASE READ BOTH SIDES **NOTE: PAYMENT IN FULL MUST ACCOMPANY APPLICATIONS - FEES SUBJECT TO CHANGE**

IMA™

IMA • 10 Paragon Drive • Montvale, New Jersey 07645-1760 • www.imanet.org
(201) 573-9000 • (800) 638-4427 • Fax (201) 573-0559

CERTIFICATION PROGRAMS

If you are applying for admission to the ICMA, please complete the following.

Check the programs you wish to enter: ❑ CMA ❑ CFM

ADDITIONAL EDUCATIONAL INFORMATION

Name on transcript (if different from front of application)

Candidates with U.S. CPA License:	State	Year	License Number

Check the appropriate box(es) and make arrangements for supporting documents to be forwarded to the ICMA.

❑ **College Graduate** - Submit official transcript showing university degree conferred and official university seal or arrange for university to send proof of degree directly to the ICMA. If you have more than one degree, submit only one transcript. Candidates with foreign degrees must have their degree evaluated by an independent evaluation agency.

❑ **GMAT or GRE scores** - Provide copy of scores to ICMA.

❑ **U.S. CPA Exam** - Arrange to have proof of U.S. CPA examination completion sent directly from your State Board of Accountancy to the ICMA.

❑ **U.S. CPA Waiver for Part 2** - Arrange to have proof of U.S. CPA examination completion sent directly from your State Board of Accountancy to the ICMA. Enclose the waiver fee with this application or use space on reverse side to charge this fee to your credit card.

❑ **Applying as a Student** - Upon graduation, be sure to arrange for an official copy of your transcript to be sent to the ICMA.

❑ **Applying as Faculty** - In addition to confirming your educational qualification, please provide a letter on school stationery affirming full-time teaching status.

❑ **Later** - You can sit for the exam without submitting your educational credentials, but you will not be certified until your credentials are verified.

STANDARD INDUSTRY CLASSIFICATIONS (SIC)

AGRICULTURE, FORESTRY, FISHERIES
01 AGRICULTURAL PRODUCTION
07 AGRICULTURAL SVCS/HUNTING/TRAPPING
08 FORESTRY
09 FISHERIES

MINING
10 METAL MINING
11 ANTHRACITE MINING
12 BITUMINOUS COAL/LIGNITE MINING
13 CRUDE OIL/LIGNITE MINING
14 MINING/QUARRY NONMETALLICS

CONTRACT CONSTRUCTION
15 BLDG. CONSTRUCTION - GENERAL CONTRACTORS
16 CONSTRUCTION - OTHER
17 CONSTRUCTION - SPECIAL TRADE CONTRACTORS

MANUFACTURING
19 ORDINANCE/ACCESSORIES
20 FOOD/KINDRED PRODUCTS
21 TOBACCO MANUFACTURERS
22 TEXTILE MILL PRODUCTS
23 APPAREL/FINISHED FABRICS
24 LUMBER/WOOD PRODUCTS
25 FURNITURE/FIXTURES
26 PAPER/ALLIED PRODUCTS
27 PRINTING/PUBLISHING
28 CHEMICALS/ALLIED PRODUCTS
29 OIL REFINING/RELATED INDUSTRIES
30 RUBBER/MISC. PLASTICS PRODUCTS
31 LEATHER PRODUCTS
32 STONE, CLAY, GLASS/CONCRETE PRODUCTS
33 PRIMARY METAL INDUSTRIES
34 FABRICATED METAL PRODUCTS
35 MACHINERY, NONELECTRICAL
36 ELECTRICAL MACHINERY
37 TRANSPORTATION
38 PROFESSIONAL, SCIENTIFIC, CONTROL INSTRUMENTS
39 MISC. MANUFACTURING INDUSTRIES

TRANSPORTATION, COMMUNICATION & UTILITY SERVICES
40 RAILROAD TRANSPORTATION
41 LOCAL AND SUBURBAN TRANSPORTATION
42 MOTOR FREIGHT/WAREHOUSING
44 WATER TRANSPORTATION
46 PIPELINE TRANSPORTATION
47 TRANSPORTATION SERVICES
48 COMMUNICATION
49 ELECTRIC, GAS/SANITARY SERVICES

WHOLESALE & RETAIL TRADE
50 WHOLESALE TRADE
52 BUILDING/HARDWARE/FARM EQUIP DEALERS
53 RETAIL TRADE - GENERAL
54 FOOD STORES
55 AUTO DEALERS/SERVICE STATIONS
56 APPAREL/ACCESSORY STORES
57 FURNITURE/FURNISHINGS/STORES
58 EATING/DRINKING PLACES
59 MISC. RETAIL STORES

FINANCE, INSURANCE & REAL ESTATE
60 BANKING
61 CREDIT AGENCIES NOT BANKS
62 SECURITY/COMMODITY BROKERS, AND SERVICES
63 INSURANCE CARRIERS
64 INSURANCE AGENTS, BROKERS
65 REAL ESTATE
66 COMBINATIONS OF REAL ESTATE, INSURANCE, LOANS, LAW OFFICES
67 HOLDING, INVESTMENT COMPANIES

SERVICES
70 HOTELS/ROOMING HOUSES/CAMPS, ETC.
72 PERSONAL SERVICES
73 MISC. BUSINESS SERVICES
75 AUTO REPAIR, AUTO SERVICES/GARAGES
76 MOTION PICTURES
79 AMUSEMENT/RECREATION SERVICES
80 MEDICAL/HEALTH SERVICES
81 LEGAL SERVICES
82 EDUCATIONAL SERVICES
84 MUSEUM/ART GALLERIES/GARDENS
86 NONPROFIT MEMBERSHIP ORGANIZATIONS
88 PRIVATE HOUSEHOLDS
89 PUBLIC ACCOUNTING

GOVERNMENT
91 FEDERAL GOVERNMENT
92 STATE GOVERNMENT
93 LOCAL GOVERNMENT
94 INTERNATIONAL GOVERNMENT

JOB TITLE

01 OWNER
03 CHAIRMAN OF THE BOARD
05 CHIEF EXECUTIVE OFFICER
06 CHIEF FINANCIAL OFFICER
07 PRESIDENT
09 GROUP PRESIDENT
11 CORPORATE SECRETARY
13 CORPORATE TREASURER
15 EXECUTIVE VICE PRESIDENT
17 SENIOR VICE PRESIDENT
19 VICE PRESIDENT
21 ASSISTANT VICE PRESIDENT
23 GROUP VICE PRESIDENT
25 DIVISIONAL VICE PRESIDENT
27 CORPORATE CONTROLLER
29 ASST. CORPORATE CONTROLLER
31 DIVISIONAL CONTROLLER
33 PLANT CONTROLLER
35 DIRECTOR
37 GENERAL MANAGER
39 MANAGER
41 GENERAL SUPERVISOR
43 SUPERVISOR
45 CHIEF ACCOUNTANT
47 ACCOUNTANT
49 ECONOMIST
51 ANALYST
53 SYSTEMS ANALYST
55 PROGRAMMER
57 ADMINISTRATOR
59 AUDITOR
61 BOOKKEEPER
63 ACCOUNTING CLERK
65 DEAN
67 PROFESSOR
69 ASSOCIATE PROFESSOR
71 ASSISTANT PROFESSOR
73 INSTRUCTOR
75 CONSULTANT
77 PRINCIPAL
79 PARTNER
99 OTHER

STRATEGIC FINANCE MAGAZINE

SUBSCRIPTION RATES PER YEAR:
MEMBERS: $45
(INCLUDED IN DUES, NONDEDUCTIBLE)
STUDENT MEMBERS: $24
(INCLUDED IN DUES NONDEDUCTIBLE)
NON-MEMBER: $140
NONPROFIT LIBRARY: $70

MANAGEMENT ACCOUNTING QUARTERLY

SUBSCRIPTION RATES PER YEAR:
MEMBERS: $10
(INCLUDED IN DUES, NONDEDUCTIBLE)
NON-MEMBER: $60

RESPONSIBILITY AREA

01 GENERAL MANAGEMENT
05 CORPORATE MANAGEMENT
10 PUBLIC ACCOUNTING
15 GENERAL ACCOUNTING
20 PERSONNEL ACCOUNTING
25 COST ACCOUNTING
30 GOVERNMENTAL ACCOUNTING
35 FINANCE
40 RISK MANAGEMENT
45 BUDGET AND PLANNING
50 TAXATION
55 INTERNAL AUDITING
60 EDUCATION
65 INFORMATION SYSTEMS
70 STUDENT
75 RETIRED
80 OTHER

DEMOGRAPHIC SURVEY (OPTIONAL)

1. Check all that apply:
   ❑ African American/Black ❑ Asian or Pacific Islander ❑ European/Caucasian ❑ Latino/Latina/Hispanic ❑ American Indian/Native American
   ❑ Middle Eastern ❑ Mixed Ethnic Identity ❑ Other (Please Specify): ______ ❑ Physically Challenged
2. Who will pay your IMA Dues? ❑ You ❑ Your Company
3. Why did you become a member of the IMA? ❑ Certification ❑ Networking ❑ Education ❑ Other (Please Specify): ______

9/00

APPLICATION FOR ADMISSION TO THE ICMA

Institute of Certified Management Accountants
10 Paragon Drive • Montvale, New Jersey 07645-1759
(201) 573-9000 • 1 (800) 638-4427 • FAX: (201) 573-8438
Endorsed by the Institute of Management Accountants

PLEASE CHECK THE PROGRAMS YOU WISH TO ENTER

☐ CMA PROGRAM ☐ CFM PROGRAM

PERSONAL INFORMATION

TYPE OR PRINT CLEARLY

☐ Mr. ☐ Ms. ☐ Miss ☐ Mrs. ☐ Dr. ☐ Male ☐ Female

Social Security Number ☐☐☐-☐☐-☐☐☐☐

Date of Birth ☐☐-☐☐-☐☐

☐ *I would like my mail sent to my home address*

Last Name (Family Name) | First Name | Middle Name | Suffix

Home Mailing Address

City | State | Zip Code (9 digit)

Home Telephone Number (include area code)
( )

☐ *I would like my mail sent to my business address*

Firm Name

Business Mailing Address

City | State | Zip Code (9 digit)

Business Telephone Number (include area code) | Extension
( )

You must be a member of the Institute of Management Accountants (IMA) to qualify for acceptance into the ICMA (IMA application page 15). Members of the Financial Management Association (FMA) may take the examination but must become IMA members prior to certification

☐ IMA Member No. ________ ☐ FMA Member No. ________ ☐ IMA Membership application submitted.

EDUCATIONAL QUALIFICATIONS

A. College or University	Degree	Date Received/Expected
Undergraduate		
Graduate		

Name on transcript (if different than above)

B. Candidates with CPA License: State	Year	License Number

Check the appropriate box(es) and make arrangements for supporting documents to be forwarded to the ICMA. Verification must be received for examination authorization.

☐ **College Graduate.** Submit official transcript showing university degree conferred and official university seal or arrange for university to send proof of degree directly to the ICMA. If you have more than one degree, submit only one transcript. Candidates with foreign degrees must have their degree evaluated by an independent agency. Contact the ICMA for details.

☐ **GMAT or GRE scores.** Provide copy of scores to ICMA.

☐ **CPA.** Arrange to have proof of license sent directly from your State Board of Accountancy to the ICMA.

☐ **CPA Waiver for Part 2.** Arrange to have proof of CPA examination completion sent directly from your State Board of Accountancy to the ICMA Enclose the waiver fee with this application or use space on reverse side to charge this fee to your credit card.

☐ **Applying as Student.** Be sure to provide, in the Character Reference Section on the reverse side of this form, the name of a professor who can verify student status. Upon graduation, be sure to arrange for an official copy of your transcript to be sent to the ICMA.

☐ **Applying as Faculty.** In addition to confirming your educational qualification, please provide a letter on school stationery affirming full-time teaching status.

PLEASE COMPLETE BOTH SIDES

CHARACTER REFERENCES

The names, addresses and telephone numbers of two character references must be supplied. One, your current employer, or current professor if you are a student; the other, a person neither employed by your firm nor a member of your family. The ICMA may contact the references as appropriate.

Name - Employer or Professor -(Circle one)	Name - Personal
Title:	Address:
Address:	Address:
City: State: Zip Code:	City: State: Zip Code:
Phone number:	Phone number:

Have you ever been convicted of a felony? ☐ Yes ☐ No If yes, please explain in an accompanying letter.

EXPERIENCE REQUIREMENT

Appropriate experience is required before the certification is awarded. The experience listed below will be used by the ICMA to identify candidates whose experience may not meet the requirements. For students and others who do not have accounting experience, but who expect to be employed in the accounting field, please check the following space: ☐ Not currently employed in the required field but expect to be in the future.

DATES (MONTH AND YEAR)	EMPLOYER	JOB TITLE	DUTIES & RESPONSIBILITIES
START DATE: END DATE:			
START DATE: END DATE:			

I agree to comply with the Standards of Ethical Conduct. I declare and affirm that the statements made in the foregoing application, including accompanying statements and transcripts, are true, complete, and correct. I authorize the investigation of all statements contained in this application.

I hereby attest that I will not divulge the content of the examination, nor will I remove any examination materials, notes, or other unauthorized materials from the examination room. I understand that failure to comply with this attestation may result in invalidation of my grades and disqualification from future examinations. For those already certified by the Institute of Certified Management Accountants, failure to comply with the statement will be considered a violation of the Standards of Ethical Conduct for Practitioners of Management Accounting and Financial Management and could result in revocation of the certification.

Signature of Applicant*: X ______________________ Date: ______________

*Original signature required; do not fax this form. ID Number from mailing label: ______________

PAYMENT INFORMATION

☐ I am enclosing a check payable to the Institute of Certified Management Accountants ☐ $50. Credentialing Fee (required)**

☐ Charge my: ☐ VISA ☐ MasterCard ☐ American Express ☐ Discover Card ☐ CPA Waiver Fee $80.

Card Number: ☐☐☐☐☐☐☐☐☐☐☐☐☐☐☐☐ Expiration Date: ☐☐-☐☐

Fees are not refundable

Signature of Applicant: X ______________________ Date: ______________

FEES SUBJECT TO CHANGE ** Not required for students.

NOTE: A SEPARATE EXAMINATION REGISTRATION FORM IS REQUIRED.

OFFICE USE ONLY	BATCH NUMBER	PAYMENT BY CHECK # ☐ PERSONAL ☐ COMPANY	AMOUNT

Institute of Certified Management Accountants
10 Paragon Drive • Montvale, New Jersey 07645-1759
(201) 573-9000 • 1 (800) 638-4427 • FAX: (201) 573-8438
Endorsed by the Institute of Management Accountants

EXAMINATION REGISTRATION FORM

PERSONAL INFORMATION

TYPE OR PRINT CLEARLY

☐ Mr. ☐ Ms. ☐ Miss ☐ Mrs. ☐ Dr. ☐ CMA ☐ CFM ☐ Certification Candidate

Social Security Number ☐☐☐-☐☐-☐☐☐☐

Last Name (Family Name) First Name Middle Name Suffix

Preferred Mailing Address ☐ Home ☐ Business

City State Zip Code (9 digit)

Daytime Telephone Number (include area code)

Please Specify ☐ Home ☐ Business

The separate Application for Admission to the ICMA and an application to the IMA must accompany this Examination Registration Form unless they have been previously submitted.

PLACE A CHECK MARK IN THE BLANK SPACES BELOW FOR THE PART(S) YOU WISH TO TAKE AT THIS TIME

☐ PART 1 Economics Finance, and Management

☐ PART 2CMA Financial Accounting and Reporting

☐ PART 2CFM Corporate Financial Management

☐ PART 3 Management Reporting, Analysis, and Behavioral Issues

☐ PART 4 Decision Analysis and Information Systems

TOTAL PARTS ______

X $ 80.00 Domestic Fee............... $ ______

X $120.00 International Fee......... $ ______

Less Student/Faculty Discount...... $ ______
(if eligible)

AMOUNT DUE .... $ ______

It should be noted that examination fees are not refundable (see page 9).

CONFIDENTIALITY STATEMENT & PAYMENT INFORMATION

I hereby attest that I will not divulge the content of this examination, nor will I remove any examination materials, notes, or other unauthorized materials from the examination room. I understand that failure to comply with this attestation may result in invalidation of my grades and disqualification from future examinations. For those already certified by the Institute of Certified Management Accountants, failure to comply with the statement will be considered a violation of the Standards of Ethical Conduct for Practitioners of Management Accounting and Financial Management and could result in revocation of the certification.

Signature: X ______ ID Number from mailing label: ______

☐ I am enclosing a check payable to the Institute of Certified Management Accountants

☐ Charge my: ☐ VISA ☐ MasterCard ☐ American Express ☐ Discover Card

Card Number: ☐☐☐☐☐☐☐☐☐☐☐☐☐☐☐☐ Expiration Date: ☐☐-☐☐

Signature: X ______ Date: ______

FEES SUBJECT TO CHANGE

APPENDIX D
ICMA CONTENT SPECIFICATION OUTLINES

Authors' Note: This is reference material only. The ICMA's CSOs have been carefully analyzed and are incorporated in our Study Units 1 through 10 to provide more systematic and rational coverage of topics within each part of the exam.

We believe we provide comprehensive coverage of the subject matter tested on the CMA/CFM exams. If, after you take the exam, you find topics, concepts, etc., tested that are not covered or are inadequately covered, please call, fax, or e-mail (irvin@gleim.com). We do not want any information about CMA/CFM questions, only information/feedback about our books/software.

The content specification outlines represent the body of knowledge that will be covered on Part 2CMA.

Candidates are responsible for being informed on the most recent developments in the areas covered in the outline. This includes understanding of public pronouncements issued by accounting organizations as well as being up-to-date on recent developments reported in current accounting and business periodicals.

The content specification outlines serve several purposes. These purposes include

- Establishing the foundation from which each examination will be developed
- Providing consistent coverage on each examination
- Communicating to interested parties more detail as to the content of each examination part
- Aiding candidates in their preparation for each examination
- Providing information to those who offer courses designed to assist candidates in preparing for the examinations

Important additional information about the content specification outlines and the examinations is listed below.

1. The percentage range given for each major topic within each examination part represents the relative weight range given to that topic in an examination part. A candidate will be required to answer questions that equal the minimum relative weight but do not exceed the maximum relative weight for a major topic.
2. Each examination will sample from the subject areas contained within each major topic area to meet the relative weight specifications. No relative weights have been assigned to the subject areas within each major topic. No inference should be made from the order in which the subject areas are listed or from the number of subject areas as to the relative weight or importance of any of the subjects.
3. Each major topic within each examination part has been assigned a coverage level designating the depth and breadth of topic coverage, ranging from an introductory knowledge of a subject area (Level A) to a thorough understanding of and ability to apply the essentials of a subject area (Level C). Detailed explanations of the coverage levels and the skills expected of candidates are presented on the next page.
4. The topics for each of the examination parts have been selected to minimize the overlapping of subject areas among the examination parts. The topics within an examination part and the subject areas within topics may be combined in individual questions.
5. Questions containing ethical issues can appear on any part of the examination. The ethical issues will be addressed within the context of a specific subject area. For determining the relative weight distribution of an examination, the questions containing ethical issues will be counted in the major topic area in which the ethical issues are raised.
6. Federal income taxation issues will be divided into two categories and be contained in questions that relate to the two categories.
   a. Accounting for income taxes. The financial reporting requirements for income taxes, including the proper treatment of deferred income taxes, will be contained in questions in Part 2CMA, Financial Accounting and Reporting, and Part 2CFM, Corporate Financial Management.
   b. Tax implications for decisions. The tax code provisions that impact decisions will be contained in: (1) questions that require decision analysis regarding debt versus equity issues in Part 1, Economics, Finance, and Management; (2) questions in Part 2CFM, Corporate Financial Management; and (3) the decision analysis questions in Part 4, Decision Analysis and Information Systems.
7. Candidates for the CMA and CFM designations are expected to have a minimum level of business knowledge that transcends all examination parts. This minimum level would include knowledge of basic financial statements, time value of money concepts, and elementary statistics.

In order to more clearly define the topical knowledge required by a candidate, varying levels of coverage for the treatment of major topics of the content specification outlines have been identified and defined. The cognitive skills that a successful candidate should possess and that should be tested on the examination can be defined as follows:

Knowledge: Ability to remember previously learned material such as specific facts, criteria, techniques, principles, and procedures (i.e., identify, define, list).

Comprehension: Ability to grasp and interpret the meaning of material (i.e., classify, explain, distinguish between).

Application: Ability to use learned material in new and concrete situations (i.e., demonstrate, predict, solve, modify, relate).

Analysis: Ability to break down material into its component parts so that its organizational structure can be understood; ability to recognize causal relationships, discriminate between behaviors, and identify elements that are relevant to the validation of a judgment (i.e., differentiate, estimate, order).

Synthesis: Ability to put parts together to form a new whole or proposed set of operations; ability to relate ideas and formulate hypotheses (i.e., combine, formulate, revise).

Evaluation: Ability to judge the value of material for a given purpose on the basis of consistency, logical accuracy, and comparison to standards; ability to appraise judgments involved in the selection of a course of action (i.e., criticize, justify, conclude).

The three levels of coverage can be defined as follows:

Level A: Requiring an appreciation of the broad nature and fundamentals, the ability to recognize the existence of special features and problems in various business transactions, and the ability to apply this knowledge in new and concrete situations, i.e., requiring the skill levels of knowledge and comprehension.

Level B: Requiring a sound understanding of the broad aspects of practices and procedures and awareness of the problems relating to more detailed aspects, the ability to apply such board knowledge in new and concrete situations, the ability to analyze the components of the material and their relationships, and the ability to reformulate the components into a new whole, i.e., requiring the skill levels of knowledge, comprehension, application, and analysis.

Level C: Requiring a sound understanding of principles, practices, and procedures, the ability to analyze material so that its organizational structure can be understood, the proficiency to apply such knowledge to situations likely to be encountered, the ability to deal with all aspects of the situation without extensive recourse to technical research and assistance, and the ability to judge the value of material for a given purpose, i.e., requiring all six skill levels.

The levels of coverage as they apply to each of the major topics of the Content Specification Outlines are shown on the following pages with each topic listing. The levels represent the manner in which topic areas are to be treated and represent ceilings, i.e., a topic area designated as Level C may contain requirements at the "A," "B," or "C" level but a topic designated as Level B will not contain requirements at the "C" level.

Your authors have organized and presented study outlines and multiple-choice questions in anticipation of the ICMA's questions to appear on the exam. We expect to have 95+% of the questions on your exam explained in the study outlines and/or illustrated in our questions. After you take your exam, please send us your evaluation of this book and our *CMA/CFM Review Test Prep* software. We want to know the topics, concepts, etc., that need to be expanded or added to our CMA/CFM books and software. Remember to check our e-mail updates. See page iv for details.

CONTENT SPECIFICATION
Part 2CMA - Financial Accounting and Reporting

A. ***Development of Accounting Standards (10% - 15%) (Level A)***

1. *Objectives of external financial reporting*
2. *External financial statements: users and their needs*
    a. *Users of financial statements*
    b. *Needs of external users*
3. *Development of accounting standards*
    a. *Due process of developing U.S. financial accounting standards by the FASB*
    b. *User groups that influence accounting standards*
    c. *Influence of the SEC on standard setting*
    d. *Organizational structure for setting U.S. financial accounting standards*
    e. *International Accounting Standards (IASC)*
4. *The annual report*
    a. *Management's responsibilities for financial statements*
    b. *Independent auditor's report*
    c. *Other areas included in the annual report*
5. *The SEC and its reporting requirements*
    a. *Acts establishing SEC and its powers*
    b. *SEC accounting standards and policies*
    c. *Reporting requirements*
    d. *Disclosure requirements*

B. ***Advanced Topics on the Preparation of Financial Statements (50% - 70%) (Level C)***

1. *Principal financial statements and their purposes*
    a. *Statement of Financial Position (Balance Sheet)*
    b. *Statement of Earnings (Income Statement)*
    c. *Statement of Cash Flow*
    d. *Statement of Shareholders' Equity*
2. *Conceptual framework underlying financial accounting*
    a. *Basic objectives*
    b. *Qualitative characteristics of accounting information*
    c. *Elements of financial statements*
    d. *Recognition and measurement concepts*
3. *Limitations of financial statement information*
    a. *Historical cost*
    b. *Entity segmentation*

4. *Public reporting standards*
    a. *Pronouncements issued by the Financial Accounting Statements Board (FASB)*
    b. *Opinions of the Accounting Principles Board (APB)*
    c. *Accounting Research Bulletins of the Committee on Accounting Procedure (CAP)*
    d. *Reporting issues for multinational companies*
    e. *Disclosures that can be made either in the body of the statements or in the notes*
5. *Asset recognition, measurement, valuation, and presentation*
    a. *Cash and cash equivalents*
    b. *Marketable securities*
    c. *Accounts receivable*
    d. *Inventories*
    e. *Investments (current and long-term)*
    f. *Property, plant, and equipment*
    g. *Leases and leasehold improvements*
    h. *Intangible assets*
    i. *Restricted use and other assets*
6. *Liability recognition, measurement, valuation, and presentation*
    a. *Current liabilities and accruals*
    b. *Contingent liabilities and commitments*
    c. *Deferred revenues*
    d. *Long-term liabilities*
    e. *Bonds payable*
    f. *Leases*
    g. *Pensions and other post retirement benefits*
    h. *Deferred income taxes*
7. *Equity account recognition, measurement, valuation, and presentation*
    a. *Preferred stock*
    b. *Common stock*
    c. *Paid in capital*
    d. *Retained earnings*
    e. *Treasury stock*
    f. *Stock options, warrants, and rights*
8. *Revenue and expenses*
    a. *Recognition*
    b. *Measurement*
    c. *Gains and losses*
9. *Other income considerations*
    a. *Discontinued operations*
    b. *Extraordinary items*
    c. *Accounting changes*
    d. *Earnings per share*
    e. *Early extinguishment of debt/debt restructuring*
    f. *Foreign currency translation*
10. *Other financial accounting and reporting issues*
    a. *Business combinations*
    b. *Consolidated and combined financial statements*
    c. *Segment reporting*

C. ***Interpretation and Analysis of Financial Statements (10% - 15%) (Level C)***

1. *Ratio analysis*
   a. *Liquidity ratios*
   b. *Activity ratios*
   c. *Profitability ratios*
   d. *Coverage ratios*
2. *Limitations of ratio analysis*
3. *Comparative analysis*
   a. *Percentage (common-size) analysis*
   b. *Historical analysis*
   c. *Industry trends*

D. ***External Auditing (10% - 15%) (Level A)***

1. *Types of services offered by external auditors relating to financial reporting*
   a. *Attestation*
   b. *Audit*
   c. *Review*
   d. *Compilation*
   e. *Prospective financial statements*
2. *Definition of auditor and management responsibilities*
   a. *Responsibilities and functions of external auditors*
   b. *Relationship between external auditors and management through the audit committee*
   c. *Relationship between external auditors and internal auditors*
3. *Elements of external auditing*
   a. *Professional standards*
   b. *Pre-engagement and engagement activities*
   c. *Understanding the client's business and industry*
   d. *Evidence required*
   e. *Analytical procedures*
   f. *Audit risk and materiality*
   g. *Errors, irregularities, and illegal acts*
   h. *Testing and reporting internal control risk*
   i. *Representation letter*
   j. *Management letter*
4. *Audit reports*
   a. *Standard unqualified audit report*
   b. *Modifications of the standard unqualified audit report*
   c. *Special reports requiring varying levels of assurance*

The topics and subject areas above may include ethical considerations in financial accounting and reporting.

Statement on Management Accounting No. 1C, "Standards of Ethical Conduct for Practitioners of Management Accounting and Financial Management"

-- *Competence*

-- *Confidentiality*

-- *Integrity*

-- *Objectivity*

Fraudulent reporting

External auditor's responsibility for detecting fraud

APPENDIX E
ICMA SUGGESTED READING LIST

The ICMA suggested reading list that follows is reproduced to give you an overview of the scope of each part. You will not have the time to study these texts. Our *CMA/CFM Review* books and *CMA/CFM Test Prep* software will be all you need. For all five parts, candidates are expected to stay up-to-date by reading articles from journals, newspapers, and professional publications.

CMA/CFM PART 1 -- ECONOMICS, FINANCE, AND MANAGEMENT

Economics

Lipsey, Richard G., and Courant, Paul, *Economics*, 12th edition, Harper Collins College Publishers, New York, NY, 1998.

McConnell, Campbell R., and Brue, Stanley L., *Economics: Principles, Problems, and Policies*, 14th edition, Irwin/McGraw-Hill, New York, NY, 1999.

International Business Environment

Salvatore, Dominick, *International Economics*, 7th edition, Prentice-Hall, Inc., Upper Saddle River, NJ, 2001.

Madura, Jeff, *International Financial Management*, 6th edition, South Western Publishing Co., Boston, MA, 2000.

Zuckerman, Amy, *International Standards, Desk Reference*, 1st edition, Amacom, New York, NY, 1997.

Root, Franklin R., *International Trade and Investment*, 7th edition, South-Western Publishing Co., Cincinnati, OH, 1993.

Government and Business

Post, James E., Frederick, William C., Lawrence, Anne T., and Weber, James, *Business and Society: Corporate Strategy, Public Policy, Ethics*, 9th edition, McGraw-Hill Inc., New York, NY, 1998.

Weidenbaum, Murray L., *Business and Government in the Global Marketplace*, 6th edition, Prentice-Hall Inc., Upper Saddle River, NJ, 1999.

Greer, Douglas F., *Business, Government, and Society*, 3rd edition, Prentice-Hall, Inc., Upper Saddle River, NJ, 1993.

Business Finance

Ross, Stephen A., Westerfield, Randolph W., and Jaffe, Jeffrey F., *Corporate Finance*, 5th edition, Richard D. Irwin Inc., Chicago, IL, 1999.

Brigham, Eugene F., and Houston, Joel F., *Fundamentals of Financial Management*, 9th edition, Harcourt Brace College Publishers, Orlando, FL, 2000.

Van Horne, James C., and Wachowicz, John M., Jr., *Fundamentals of Financial Management*, 11th edition, Prentice-Hall, Inc., Upper Saddle River, NJ, 2001.

Brealey, Richard A., and Myers, Stewart C., *Principles of Corporate Finance*, 6th edition, McGraw-Hill, Inc., New York, NY, 2000.

Organization and Management Theory and Communication

Mathis, Robert L., and Jackson, John H., *Human Resource Management*, 9th edition, Thomson Learning, St. Paul, MN, 2000.

Tosi, Henry L., Rizzo, John R., and Carroll, Stephen J., *Managing Organizational Behavior*, 4th edition, Blackwell Publishers, Ltd., Cambridge, MA, 2000.

Moorhead, Gregory, and Griffin, Ricky W., *Organizational Behavior*, 6th edition, Houghton Mifflin Company, Boston, MA, 2000.

PART 2CMA -- FINANCIAL ACCOUNTING AND REPORTING

Financial Statements and Reporting Requirements

Nikolai, Loren A., and Bazley, John D., *Intermediate Accounting*, 8th edition, South-Western Publishing Company, Boston, MA, 1999.

Kieso, Donald E., and Weygandt, Jerry J., *Intermediate Accounting*, 10th edition, John Wiley & Sons, Inc., New York, NY, 2000.

Larsen, E. John, *Modern Advanced Accounting*, 8th edition, McGraw-Hill Book Co., New York, NY, 1999.

Afterman, Allan B., *SEC Regulation of Public Companies*, 1st edition, Prentice Hall Inc., Upper Saddle River, NJ, 1995.

Analysis of Accounts and Statements

Gibson, Charles H., *Financial Statement Analysis*, 8th edition, South-Western Publishing Co., Cincinnati, Ohio, 1999.

Bernstein, Leopold A., and Wild, John J., *Financial Statement Analysis, Theory, Application, and Interpretation*, 7th edition, McGraw-Hill Book Co., New York, NY, 2000.

White, Gerald I., Sondhi, Ashwinpaul C., and Fried, Dov, *The Analysis and Use of Financial Statements*, 2nd edition, John Wiley & Sons, New York, NY, 1998.

External Auditing

Arens, Alvin A., and Loebbecke, James K., *Auditing: An Integrated Approach*, 8th edition, Prentice-Hall Inc., Upper Saddle River, NJ, 2000.

Boynton, William C., and Kell, Walter G., *Modern Auditing*, 7th edition, John Wiley & Sons, New York, NY, 2000.

PART 2CFM -- CORPORATE FINANCIAL MANAGEMENT

Financial Management

Ross, Stephen A., Westerfield, Randolph W., and Jaffe, Jeffrey F., *Corporate Finance*, 5th edition, Richard D. Irwin, Inc., Chicago, IL, 1999.

Brigham, Eugene F., and Houston, Joel F., *Fundamentals of Financial Management*, 9th edition, Harcourt Brace College Publishers, Orlando, FL, 2000.

Van Horne, James C. and Wachowicz, John M., Jr., *Fundamentals of Financial Management*, 11th edition, Prentice-Hall, Inc., Upper Saddle River, NJ, 2001.

Brealey, Richard A., and Myers, Stewart C., *Principles of Corporate Finance*, 6th edition, McGraw-Hill, Inc., New York, NY, 2000.

Financial Environment

Weidenbaum, Murray L., *Business and Government in the Global Marketplace*, 6th edition, Prentice-Hall Inc., Upper Saddle River, NJ, 1999.

Post, James E., Frederick, William C., Lawrence, Anne T., and Weber, James, *Business and Society: Corporate Strategy, Public Policy, Ethics*, 9th edition, McGraw-Hill Inc., New York, NY, 1998.

Greer, Douglas F., *Business, Government, and Society*, 3rd edition, Macmillan Publishing, New York, NY, 1993.

Lipsey, Richard G., and Courant, Paul, *Economics*, 12th edition, Harper Collins College Publishers, New York, NY, 1998.

McConnell, Campbell R., and Brue, Stanley L., *Economics: Principles, Problems and Policies*, 14th edition, McGraw-Hill Book Co., New York, NY, 1999.

Madura, Jeff, *International Financial Management*, 6th edition, South Western Publishing Co., Boston, MA, 2000.

Geisst, Charles R., *Investment Banking in the Financial System*, 1st edition, Prentice-Hall Inc., Upper Saddle River, NJ, 1995.

Boynton, William C., and Kell, Walter G., *Modern Auditing*, 7th edition, John Wiley & Sons, New York, NY, 2000.

Rose, Peter S., *Money and Capital Markets, Financial Institutions and Instruments in a Global Market*, 7th edition, Richard D. Irwin Inc., Chicago, IL, 2000.

Williams, C. Arthur, Smith, Michael L., and Young, Peter C., *Risk Management and Insurance*, 8th edition, McGraw-Hill Inc., New York, NY, 1998.

Analysis of Financial Statements

Gibson, Charles H., *Financial Statement Analysis*, 8th edition, South-Western Publishing Co., Cincinnati, OH, 1999.

Bernstein, Leopold A., and Wild, John J., *Financial Statement Analysis, Theory, Application, and Interpretation*, 7th edition, McGraw-Hill Book Co., New York, NY, 2000.

White, Gerald I., Sondhi, Ashwinpaul C., and Fried, Dov, *The Analysis and Use of Financial Statements*, 2nd edition, John Wiley & Sons, New York, NY, 1998.

Financial Statements and Accounting Standards

Kieso, Donald E., and Weygandt, Jerry J., *Intermediate Accounting*, 10th edition, John Wiley & Sons, Inc., New York, NY, 2000.

Nikolai, Loren A., and Bazley, John D., *Intermediate Accounting*, 8th edition, South-Western Publishing Company, Boston, MA, 2000.

Larsen, E. John, *Modern Advanced Accounting*, 8th edition, McGraw-Hill, Inc., New York, NY, 1999.

Afterman, Allan B., *SEC Regulation of Public Companies*, 1st edition, Prentice Hall Inc., Upper Saddle River, NJ, 1995.

CMA/CFM PART 3 -- MANAGEMENT REPORTING, ANALYSIS, AND BEHAVIORAL ISSUES

Management Reporting and Analysis

Welsch, Glenn A., Hilton, Ronald W., and Gordon, Paul N., *Budgeting: Profit Planning and Control*, 5th edition, Prentice-Hall, Inc., Upper Saddle River, NJ, 1998.

Carter, William K., and Usry, Milton F., *Cost Accounting*, 12th edition, Dame Publications Inc., Houston, TX, 1999.

Horngren, Charles, Foster, George, and Datar, Srikant M., *Cost Accounting: A Managerial Emphasis,* 10th edition, Prentice-Hall, Inc., Upper Saddle River, NJ, 2000.

Blocher, Edward J., Chen, Kung H., and Lin, Thomas W., *Cost Management: A Strategic Emphasis*, Irwin/McGraw Hill, New York, NY, 1999.

CMA/CFM PART 4 -- DECISION ANALYSIS AND INFORMATION SYSTEMS

Decision Analysis and Quantitative Methods

Anderson, David R., Sweeney, Dennis J., and Williams, Thomas A., *An Introduction to Management Science-Quantitative Approaches to Decision Making*, 9th edition, West Publishing Company, St. Paul, MN, 2000.

Carter, William K., and Usry, Milton F., *Cost Accounting*, 12th edition, Dame Publications Inc., Houston, TX, 1999.

Horngren, Charles, Foster, George, and Datar, Srikant, *Cost Accounting: A Managerial Emphasis,* 10th edition, Prentice-Hall, Inc., Upper Saddle River, NJ, 2000.

Blocher, Edward J., Chen, Kung H., and Lin, Thomas W., *Cost Management: A Strategic Emphasis*, Irwin/McGraw Hill, New York, NY, 1999.

Information Systems

Romney, Marshall B., and Steinbart, Paul J., *Accounting Information Systems*, 8th edition, Addison-Wesley Publishing Company, Reading, MA, 1999.

Moscove, Stephen A., Simkin, Mark G., and Bagranoff, Nancy A., *Core Concepts of Accounting Information Systems*, 7th edition, John Wiley & Sons, Inc., New York, NY, 2000.

O'Brien, James A., *Introduction to Information Systems*, 10th edition, Irwin/McGraw Hill Publishers, Barr Ridge, IL, 2000.

Internal Auditing

Sawyer, Lawrence B., and Dittenhofer, Mortimer A., *Internal Auditing*, 4th edition, Institute of Internal Auditors, Altamonte Springs, FL, 1996.

Ratliff, Richard L., Wallace, Wanda A., Summers, Glenn E., McFarland, William G., and Loebbecke, James K., *Internal Auditing Principles and Techniques*, 2nd edition, The Institute of Internal Auditors, Altamonte Springs, FL, 1996.

Index

Gleim Publications, Inc. **P.O. Box 12848** **Gainesville, FL 32604**	TOLL FREE: LOCAL: FAX: INTERNET: E-MAIL:	(800) 87-GLEIM/(800) 874-5346 (352) 375-0772 (888) 375-6940 (toll free) http://www.gleim.com sales@gleim.com	Customer service is available: 8:00 a.m. - 7:00 p.m., Mon. - Fri. 9:00 a.m. - 2:00 p.m., Saturday Please have your credit card ready or save time by ordering online!

CPA REVIEW	Books	Software	Book/Software Package	Audiotapes	Book/Software/ Audio Package	
Auditing	☐ @ $29.95	☐ @ $39.95	☐ @ $62.95	☐ @ $79.95	☐ @ $125.00	$______
Business Law	☐ @ $29.95	☐ @ $39.95	☐ @ $62.95	☐ @ $79.95	☐ @ $125.00	______
TAX-MAN-GOV	☐ @ $29.95	☐ @ $39.95	☐ @ $62.95	☐ @ $79.95	☐ @ $125.00	______
Financial	☐ @ $29.95	☐ @ $39.95	☐ @ $62.95	☐ @ $79.95	☐ @ $125.00	______
A System for Success	☐ FREE with any Gleim *CPA Review* Book					

Save 16% on the Complete Gleim CPA System (add $18 S&H below) .... $500.00 ______
[5 books, 4 cassette albums (41 tapes), 4 CPA Test Prep disks, bonus calculator and versatile book bag]

CIA REVIEW	Books	Software	Book/Software Package	
Part I Internal Audit Process	☐ @ $24.95	☐ @ $39.95	☐ @ $57.95	$______
Part II Internal Audit Skills	☐ @ $24.95	☐ @ $39.95	☐ @ $57.95	______
Part III Mgmt. Ctl. & Info. Tech.	☐ @ $24.95	☐ @ $39.95	☐ @ $57.95	______
Part IV The Audit Environment	☐ @ $24.95	☐ @ $39.95	☐ @ $57.95	______

CPE credit also available (online only). Please visit www.gleim.com/Accounting/cpe/cia

CMA/CFM REVIEW	Books	Software	Book/Software Package	Audiotapes	Book/Software/ Audio Package	
Part 1 Eco., Fin., & Mgmt.	☐ @ $24.95	☐ @ $44.95	☐ @ $62.95	☐ @ $64.95	☐ @ $114.95	$______
Part 2CMA Fin. Acc. & Rep.	☐ @ $24.95	☐ @ $44.95	☐ @ $62.95	☐ @ $64.95	☐ @ $114.95	______
Part 2CFM Corp. Fin. Mgmt.	☐ @ $24.95	☐ @ $44.95	☐ @ $62.95	☐ @ $64.95	☐ @ $114.95	______
Part 3 Mgmt. Rep./Behav. Iss.	☐ @ $24.95	☐ @ $44.95	☐ @ $62.95	☐ @ $64.95	☐ @ $114.95	______
Part 4 Dec. Anal. & Info. Sys.	☐ @ $24.95	☐ @ $44.95	☐ @ $62.95	☐ @ $64.95	☐ @ $114.95	______

CPE credit also available @ $50 per part. Purchase of corresponding book is required.

EA REVIEW	Books	Software	Book/Software Package	
Part 1 Individuals	☐ @ $24.95	☐ @ $39.95	☐ @ $57.95	$______
Part 2 Sole Prop. & Prtnrshps.	☐ @ $24.95	☐ @ $39.95	☐ @ $57.95	______
Part 3 Corp./Fid./Est. & Gift Tax	☐ @ $24.95	☐ @ $39.95	☐ @ $57.95	______
Part 4 IRS Adm/Other Topics	☐ @ $24.95	☐ @ $39.95	☐ @ $57.95	______

"THE GLEIM SERIES" EXAM QUESTION AND EXPLANATION BOOKS, SOFTWARE, & CPE

	Books	Software	Book/Software Package	Book & CPE	
Auditing & Systems	☐ @ $19.95	☐ @ $20.00	☐ @ $29.95	☐ $125.00	$______
Business Law/Legal Studies	☐ @ $19.95	☐ @ $20.00	☐ @ $29.95	☐ $125.00	______
Federal Tax	☐ @ $19.95	☐ @ $20.00	☐ @ $29.95	☐ $125.00	______
Financial Accounting	☐ @ $19.95	☐ @ $20.00	☐ @ $29.95	☐ $125.00	______
Cost/Managerial Accounting	☐ @ $19.95	☐ @ $20.00	☐ @ $29.95	☐ $125.00	______

Shipping (nonrefundable): **First item = $5; each additional item = $1** $______

Add applicable sales tax for shipments within Florida. ______

Fax or write for prices/instructions for shipments outside the 48 contiguous states. **TOTAL** $______

1. We process and ship orders daily, within one business day over 98.8% of the time. Call by noon for same-day service!
2. Please PHOTOCOPY this order form for others.
3. No CODs. Orders from individuals must be prepaid. Library and company orders may be purchased on account.
4. Gleim Publications, Inc. guarantees the immediate refund of all resalable texts and unopened software and audiotapes if returned within 30 days. Applies only to items purchased direct from Gleim Publications, Inc. Our shipping charge is nonrefundable.
5. Components of specially priced package deals are nonreturnable.

NAME (please print) ______________________________

ADDRESS ______________________________ Apt. ________
(street address required for UPS)

____

CITY ______________________ STATE ________ ZIP ____________

_____ MC/VISA/DISC _____ Check/M.O. Daytime Telephone (_____)____________

Credit Card No. __________ - __________ - __________ - __________

Exp. ___/___ Signature ______________________________
Mo. / Yr.

Printed 02/01. Prices subject to change without notice.

Please forward suggestions, corrections, and comments concerning typographical errors, etc., to **Irvin N. Gleim • c/o Gleim Publications, Inc. • P.O. Box 12848 • University Station • Gainesville, Florida • 32604**. Please include your name and address so we can properly thank you for your interest.

1. ____________________

2. ____________________

3. ____________________

4. ____________________

5. ____________________

6. ____________________

7. ____________________

8. ____________________

9. ____________________

10. ____________________

11. ____________________

12. ____________________

13. ____________________

14. ______________________________

15. ______________________________

16. ______________________________

17. ______________________________

18. ______________________________

19. ______________________________

20. ______________________________

21. ______________________________

22. ______________________________

Remember for superior service:	Mail, e-mail, or fax questions about our books or software. Telephone questions about orders, prices, shipments, or payments.

Name: ______________________________

Company: ______________________________

Address: ______________________________

City/State/Zip: ______________________________

Phone: (   ) __________ FAX: (   ) __________ E-mail: __________